The End of Slavery
in Africa

The End of Slavery in Africa

WITHDRAWI

Edited by
Suzanne Miers and Richard Roberts

THE UNIVERSITY OF WISCONSIN PRESS

The University of Wisconsin Press
114 North Murray Street
Madison, Wisconsin 53715

The University of Wisconsin Press, Ltd.
1 Gower Street
London WC1E 6HA, England

5   4   3   2   1

Printed in the United States of America

Library of Congress Cataloging-in-Publication Data
The end of slavery in Africa.
   Includes bibliographies and index.
   1. Slavery—Africa—History—19th century.
2. Slavery—Africa—History—20th century.   I. Miers,
Suzanne.   II. Roberts, Richard L., 1949–
HT1323.E53   1988   306′.362′096   88-40192
ISBN 0-299-11550-X
ISBN 0-299-11554-2 (pbk.)

To Marion Johnson (1914–1988)

and Michael Crowder (1934–1988)

Contents

   The main issues, 3.   Origins of the modern concept of abolition, 8.
   Forms of abolition before the partition of Africa, 10.   The British "Caribbean model," 10.   The British "Indian model," 12.   French and Portuguese forms of abolition, 13.   The antislavery movement and the partition of Africa, 15.   The role of the colonial states in ending slavery, 17.
   Colonial conquest and changes in the political economy, 18.   Colonial
   antislavery policies: slave-raiding and -trading, 19.   Colonial antislavery
   policies: the suppression of slavery, 21.   International pressure to end
   slavery, 24.   The impact of changes in regional and international markets, 25.   The transition from slavery to freedom: a historiographic debate, 27.   The ambiguities of freedom: slaves and owners in the aftermath of slavery, 33.   Women slaves and freedom, 38.   Slave children
   and freedom, 40.   Slave-owners and freedom, 41.   The persistence of
   unfree labor: forced labor and pawning, 42.   Conclusion, 47.   The
   end of slavery in comparative perspective and as an international issue, 54.

   British policy towards slavery before 1874, 73.   Categories of slaves

Contents   xi

Maps

Contributors

Lee V. Cassanelli
    Department of History, University of Pennsylvania, Philadelphia, Pennsylvania
Dennis D. Cordell
    Department of History, Southern Methodist University, Dallas, Texas
Michael Crowder (deceased)
    Department of History, Amherst University, Amherst, Massachusetts, and Institute
    of Commonwealth Studies, London, England
Raymond Dumett
    Department of History, Purdue University, West Lafayette, Indiana
Thomas J. Herlehy
    USAID, Banjul, The Gambia
Linda M. Heywood
    Department of History, Howard University, Washington, D.C.
J. S. Hogendorn
    Department of Economics, Colby College, Waterville, Maine
Allen Isaacman
    Department of History, University of Minnesota, Minneapolis, Minnesota
Marion Johnson (deceased)
    Centre of West Africa Studies, University of Birmingham, Birmingham, England
Martin A. Klein
    Department of History, University of Toronto, Toronto, Canada
Igor Kopytoff
    Department of Anthropology, University of Pennsylvania, Philadelphia, Pennsylvania
Paul E. Lovejoy
    Department of History, York University, Toronto, Ontario, Canada
James McCann
    African Studies Center, Boston University, Boston, Massachusetts
E. Ann McDougall
    Department of History, University of Alberta, Edmonton, Alberta, Canada
Suzanne Miers
    Department of History, Ohio University, Athens, Ohio
Rodger F. Morton
    Department of History, University of Botswana, Gaborone, Botswana
David Northrup
    Department of History, Boston College, Chestnut Hill, Massachusetts

Don Ohadike
Department of History, University of Jos, Jos, Nigeria
Richard Roberts
Department of History, Stanford University, Stanford, California
Anton Rosenthal
Department of History, University of Minnesota, Minneapolis, Minnesota
Michael Twaddle
Institute of Commonwealth Studies, London, England

Preface

The idea for this book was born in the early 1970s while I was writing the conclusion of *Britain and the Ending of the Slave Trade* (Longman 1975). I realized, as I attempted to analyze European suppression policies, that there was a need for a collection of case studies on the end of slavery in Africa. This realization was re-inforced by the debate surrounding *Slavery in Africa* (Wisconsin 1977, edited with Igor Kopytoff), and by the key question, posed in an unpublished paper, by Patrick Manning: how was it that slavery and the slave trade in Africa, which had featured so large in the rhetoric of the colonial powers during the partition of the continent, apparently faded out without repercussions significant enough to be given much place in the histories of colonial rule. That such a widespread and deeply rooted institution should vanish so quietly seemed unlikely, but, at the time, apart from a few suggestive but limited case studies, little research had been devoted to the question.

The problem was to find contributors with sufficient information on the colonial period, and to obtain both a broad geographical spread and coverage of a range of African societies. The process was long and arduous, and authors were recruited over the five years between 1980 and 1985. Richard Roberts was an early recruit who became an invaluable co-editor. Together, we rethought the volume and directed our authors to consider the linkages between colonial policy and rhetoric on the one hand, and what actually took place on the other, and to differentiate between the effects of emancipation on different categories of slaves, particularly female slaves. For many contributors this required further research and often their sources did not yield all the information we would have liked. We owe a debt of gratitude to all of our contributors, but particularly to those who finished the initial drafts of their chapters as early as 1982, and endured patiently the long wait that ensued before the book came to fruition. Equally, we are grateful to those contributors who were recruited very late and hence had to fit the work in between busy teaching schedules and other commitments.

Sadly, two of our contributors died while this book was in press. We

are dedicating the volume to them. It is a small tribute to Marion Johnson's innovative thinking, fine scholarship, and indomitable spirit and to
Michael Crowder's brilliant and far-ranging work and enduring contribution to African history. Both were dedicated and delightful colleagues
who will be sadly missed.

We wish to thank Gervase Clarence-Smith, Frederick Cooper, Philip
Curtin, Stanley Engerman, George Frederickson, Jim Lance, Joseph
Miller, Claire Robertson, Michael Salman, and Marcia Wright, who were
kind enough to comment on drafts of the introduction. We are particularly indebted to Robin Whitaker, who undertook the formidable task
of trying to mold our footnotes into a coherent format, and the delicate
task of pointing out lacunae in the text. We appreciate, too, the gener-
osity of Donna Maier, B. Marie Perinbam, Roger Sawyer, Ibrahim Sundiata and Peter Weil, who allowed us to use their unpublished papers
and manuscripts.

This work is timely since it presents African case studies to comple-
ment the growing literature on the end of slavery in the Americas. We
hope that it will stimulate similar research on areas in which little work
has been done, notably East Asia, South East Asia, South Asia, and the
Middle East. We also trust that it will challenge Africanists just as *Slavery
in Africa* did, and spur them to further investigate the range of social
and economic issues that studies of the end of slavery can provide.

SUZANNE MIERS

Note on Orthography

Historians of Africa have yet to agree on standard usage for identifying the many and varied ethnicities and polities within their field. Actual names as well as the spelling of those names have changed and continue to change as a consequence of decolonization, contemporary political choices (as in Burkina Faso, Zimbabwe, and the République du Benin), and as a result of linguistic advances. With the exception of those which used Arabic and Amharic scripts, most African societies in the precolonial period were preliterate. The earliest written form of indigenous names, therefore, comes to us through these scripts or through European languages. Recent advances in linguistic study have considerably enhanced our understanding of African languages and have yielded an orthography more in tune with them. Changes in nomenclature, however, enter specialized and popular usage unevenly.

Several contributors in this volume deal with histories which bridge both the precolonial and colonial eras, thus posing certain orthographic difficulties: they had to confront the colonial legacy, including its nomenclature, as a historically specific experience with beginning and ending points.

In this volume we have chosen to use Anglicized colonial orthography when examining historical developments which occurred during that time (for example, the French Soudan, Bechuanaland Protectorate, and Ashanti). When dealing with historical developments which preceded colonial rule — or, as in the case of the empire of Ethiopia, which remained effectively outside colonial overrule — we use Anglicized nomenclature reflecting indigenous orthography, recent linguistic conventions, or generally accepted terms to describe precolonial geographical entities for which there may not have been widely accepted indigenous terms (for example, the Western Sudan, Asante, and South-Central Africa). In this we follow A. J. A. Ajayi and Michael Crowder, *Historical Atlas of Africa* (Cambridge: Cambridge University Press, 1985), and J. D. Fage, *An Atlas of African History* (New York: Africana Publishing Company, 1978). The following list indicates the nomenclature used in this anthology:

Precolonial name or geographic term	*Colonial name*	*Postcolonial name*
Angola	Angola	Angola
southern Africa	Bechuanaland	Botswana
Guinea	French Guinea	Guinea
Western Sudan	Haut-Sénégal–Niger / French Soudan	Mali
South-Central Africa	Mozambique	Mozambique
Central Sudan	Northern Nigeria	Nigeria
Igboland	Southern Nigeria	Nigeria
Asante	Ashanti	Ghana
Gold Coast	Gold Coast	
North-Central Africa	Ubangi-Shari	Chad / Central African Republic
Mauritania	Mauritania	Mauritania
East Africa	British East Africa / Kenya	Kenya
Central Africa / Zaire	Congo Free State / Belgian Congo	Zaire
northeastern Africa	Somalia / Italian Somaliland	Somalia
Ethiopia	Ethiopia	Ethiopia

This may be somewhat cumbersome for the uninitiated reader, but it reflects the historical realities of the African experience which we are committed to preserving.

In regard to discussions of slaveholding, the terms *owner* and *master* are used interchangeably. We do not intend a distinction in gender with the term *master*, because both males and females owned slaves.

I

INTRODUCTION

1 *Richard Roberts and Suzanne Miers*

The End of Slavery in Africa

The Main Issues

Slavery in Africa sometimes ended suddenly, causing widespread disruption, and sometimes petered out with apparently minimal repercussions. Some scholars, therefore, see its demise as precipitating a crisis, while others view it as a "nonevent." But whether it involved the dramatic mass departure of the labor force, the gradual loss of small numbers of individuals, or the redefinition of the terms of dependency by ex-slaves who remained with their former owners, the end of slavery always brought the nature of the economic, political, and social structure sharply into focus. It often pitted slaves against owners and sometimes pitted both against the colonial state in a struggle to control labor — a struggle which took place in the context of a changing political economy and was part of deeper transformations set in train by colonial rule. Thus the chapters which follow throw light on much more than just the transition from slave to "free" labor.

Slavery in Africa was a complex system of labor use, of the exercise of rights in persons, and of exploitation and coercion, tempered by negotiation and accommodation.[1] Its form varied over time and place. Slaves

1. For recent research and discussions of definitions and of different types of slaves and

3

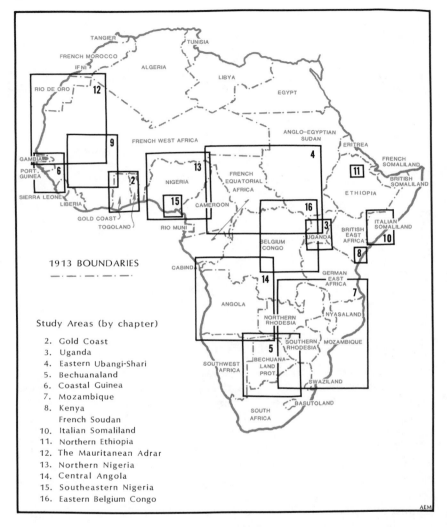

Map 1. Africa in 1913

servitude in Africa see particularly Meillassoux 1975a, 1986; Kopytoff and Miers 1977; Kopytoff 1979; Cooper 1979; Watson 1980: 2ff.; Patterson 1982; Finley 1980: 67ff.; Klein and Lovejoy 1979; Lovejoy 1983; Robertson and Klein 1983; Davis 1984; Law 1985; Willis 1985.

might be menial field workers, downtrodden servants, cherished concubines, surrogate kin, trusted trading agents, high officials, army commanders, ostracized social groups dedicated to a deity, or a ready pool of candidates for human sacrifice. Owners might be corporate kin groups or individuals of either sex. A minority of individual owners and a majority of first-generation slaves were women, valued for their productive as well as their reproductive capacities, since women did much of the agricultural work in sub-Saharan Africa.[2] Most slaves had families, and some accumulated possessions, even slaves, of their own.[3] Slavery might involve merely small numbers of slaves, living in or near their owners' households, whose daily lives were virtually indistinguishable from those of the free, or it could be a sophisticated system of labor organization in which slaves and owners were divided by social, economic, political, and legal barriers and sometimes lived in separate settlements. Different forms of slavery could coexist in the same society. Moreover, slavery was but one type of dependency or exploitation practiced alongside others in a continuum which included clientage and pawnship. A pawn was a person pledged as collateral for debt (see Lovejoy 1983: 5; for further discussion on pawns, see pages 26, 45–47).

African societies usually framed the social and economic relations of slavery in paternalistic terms: slaves were considered adoptive junior kin, albeit perpetual minors, but at the same time they were dependents from whom a surplus could be extracted. They were also valuable capital assets, sometimes the main ones owned by Africans. They were often valued as political supporters, their loyalty being assured by their total dependence. This paternalistic view of slavery, even when it masked purely economic considerations on the part of their owners, was often shared by the slaves (see, for instance, Baldus 1977: 443–56). In many societies, owners sought to control their slaves by using force, imposing supernatural sanctions, and allowing slaves to change masters (Meillassoux 1975b: 231–32; Klein 1977: 346–50). Where states were relatively strong and masters formed a cohesive group, the coercive elements of slavery were often better developed. In almost all societies, however, the power of masters was limited because escape was possible.

Although members of both large- and small-scale societies acquired

2. On women slaves see Robertson and Klein 1983. On women and work see, for example, Boserup 1970; Oppong 1983. Women often owned slaves or, if they did not own them, they often used and controlled slave labor (Robertson and Klein 1983: 13). The majority of owners, however, were men or kin groups controlled by men.

3. Meillassoux (1983), however, argues that the fertility and even the marriage rate among women slaves were low. On slaves owning slaves see Roberts 1981a: 186–89; Weil 1984: 105–106; Meillassoux 1986: 121, 256.

them, expanding states were often the greatest suppliers and users of slaves. The political formation played a part in the development and maintenance of slave systems and determined their form. As the political economy changed, so slavery, never a static institution, also changed, becoming sometimes harsher and sometimes more "benign" (see, for example, Weil 1984: 107–14; Hogendorn and Lovejoy, Ch. 13). Thus, slaves were bound up in a complex, ever-shifting web of social relations, fashioned by political and economic conditions.

The end of slavery put the whole relationship to the test. The response of newly freed slaves frequently revealed the dichotomy between ideology and harsh reality. Some liberated slaves expressed pent-up animosity through mass departure.[4] Others, however, remained with their owners but redefined their terms of service, while some left only to return to live much as before (see, for example, Romero 1986: 509; Cooper 1980: 69ff.). The end of slavery thus provides an opportunity to examine the reality of slavery in Africa as it existed at a discrete point in time — in most cases in the late nineteenth and early twentieth centuries.

Reconstructing this reality poses some problems. The evidence for the nineteenth century, when slavery was at its height, often comes filtered through the eyes of antislavery or colonial enthusiasts, many of them missionaries or explorers. Most twentieth-century evidence is drawn from the reports of colonial administrators or anthropologists, who saw slavery only in its decline, and from court records, which reflect only those conflicts which could not be privately resolved. Furthermore, scholars doing research in recent years have talked mostly with owners or their descendants, who often idealized the institution. Evidence from slaves is hard to come by, because many persons of slave descent are still unwilling to admit their origins. Certainly, the actions of the newly freed indicate how they felt about slavery, but this evidence has to be carefully weighed in the light of the range of options actually open to them.

Just as slavery covered many different situations, so emancipation inevitably meant different things to different people (Kopytoff and Miers 1977: 26–27, 73–76; Kopytoff, Ch. 17). To some slaves it meant closer integration into the owner's kin group, although complete equality was rarely achieved. To others it meant severing all ties with their owners to the point of actual physical departure. To still others it meant continued dependence but on different terms — terms which were in some cases subtly redefined and in others hammered out as ex-slaves strove, sometimes fiercely, for better conditions and more autonomy while former

4. Dumett and Johnson, Ch. 2; Hogendorn and Lovejoy, Ch. 13; Klein, Ch. 6; Roberts, Ch. 9; McSheffrey 1983.

owners tried to preserve their social and economic power. The studies presented here enable us to examine the many variables which determined the reactions of both slaves and owners to legal emancipation, and to consider the various meanings of "freedom" in colonial Africa.

On the eve of the colonial conquests of the late nineteenth century, slavery was taking root in new areas and in some cases was beginning to change qualitatively (see, *inter alia*, Lovejoy 1983: Ch. 6; Weil 1984: 72–114). The end of the transatlantic trade and the decline in the export of slaves to the Muslim world made slaves more cheaply available in Africa just when the demand for African agricultural, hunting, and foraging exports increased the need for labor. This need was often met by the acquisition of slaves. Slavery was such a significant part of the organization of production in some societies that certain scholars have identified them as "slave societies" (Lovejoy 1983: 8–10).[5] The demand for slaves was also generated by such internal factors as the expansion of local markets and the rise of new states over much of the continent. Those struggling for power wanted dependents and loyal followers — a demand frequently filled by slaving. Once areas were conquered, the new elite might put their captives to work as farmers, herdsmen, and craftsmen, often producing for the market. Slave women also produced progeny to swell the numbers of dependents and increase the size of owning groups. States acquired slaves through warfare, and ruling groups were often the main users of slaves, but some kin groups and individuals in small-scale societies, as well as marauding bands of armed traders, acquired sizable numbers of slaves.

Colonial conquest and the establishment of colonial states created the conditions which led to the dramatic decline, if not always the end, of slavery. The colonial rulers undermined it by radically changing the political economy and by antislavery legislation. The eradication of slavery, however, was not a consistently pursued priority for any of the colonial powers. In fact it was a severe test of their expressed ideologies. Although all of them subscribed to antislavery ideology, they usually found it against their immediate interests to emancipate the slaves. The chapters that follow illustrate the different expedients administrators and missionaries adopted as they walked a tightrope, balancing metropolitan ideology and demands against African realities and both against their efforts to gain

5. For slave societies see Finley 1968: 310–11. Recent scholars have described such societies as having had a "slave mode of production." In a slave mode of production slaves were the main producers in vital sectors of the economy, and because they did not reproduce themselves in sufficient quantity a constant flow of new slaves was needed to maintain the social and economic base (Lovejoy 1983: 269–73). For a critique of this view and a reappraisal see Cooper 1979.

control of labor themselves. The study of the end of slavery, therefore, brings us a step closer to an understanding of the realities as well as the mythology of colonial rule.

The chapters in this volume also contribute to our understanding of slavery and abolition as worldwide phenomena. Some common patterns emerge both in the way slavery ended and in the forms of labor control which succeeded it. If, however, this book answers some questions about the end of slavery, it also raises many more, showing where there are gaps in our knowledge and highlighting debates on evidence, interpretation, and methodology, which can be resolved only by further research.

Origins of the Modern Concept of Abolition

Abolition — the declaration by the government that slavery was no longer legal — was not an indigenous African concept. Emancipation was possible in some societies, but it was selective manumission at the discretion of the owners, and it reinforced rather than undermined slavery by manifesting their power over their slaves. Slaves could gain freedom in various ways. Some were allowed to ransom themselves, perhaps with another slave; others were freed by their masters after years of faithful service. Sometimes the descendants of slaves were simply assimilated over several generations until they were in fact indistinguishable from the freeborn — a process described as intergenerational mobility (Kopytoff and Miers 1977: 18–40). This was fastest in societies which allowed unions between slave and free.[6] In many societies total equality with the free was simply not possible. Thus freed slaves in some Muslim societies became hereditary, autonomous clients (see examples in McDougall, Ch. 12; Cassanelli, Ch. 10), and in many non-Muslim societies slave origins were remembered when it came to questions of marriage, inheritance, and rituals (Meillassoux 1986: 307–9). In societies where selective emancipation was theoretically possible, nothing could give an ex-slave the same status as the person who was born into a local kin group (see, for instance, Ohadike, Ch. 15; Heywood, Ch. 14).

Second-generation slaves in many African societies were not normally sold and were thus in theory somewhat more secure than first-generation or "trade" slaves. But in times of crisis, when even some of the free were sold, slaves would probably have been the first to go. Most African slave-owning groups did not have the power to keep large numbers of slaves

---

6. Such unions were usually between a free man and a slave concubine. Their off-spring, although often considered free, were likely to be discriminated against when it came to questions of property, religion, and political rights.

in permanent and complete subordination, which helps account for this intergenerational difference in treatment (Cooper 1979: 118–19). Neither manumission nor intergenerational mobility, however, ended slavery, since newly acquired slaves maintained slave relations of production and dependency.

Full-scale abolition was a western European idea born of the conflicts generated in the eighteenth century by the expansion of capitalism and the profound ideological changes which accompanied it. Abolitionist movements emerged in several countries, but the first successful sustained movement among the European powers that were to partition Africa took root in Britain, where it drew its inspiration from new philosophical, economic, and religious ideas.[7] Slavery came to be regarded by philosophers as incompatible with the rights of man, by economists as incompatible with the needs of the emerging capitalist economy, and by religious activists as a sin.[8] As slavery came to be increasingly seen as morally unacceptable and retrogressive, so its converse, the capitalist, free wage-labor system, came to be considered both morally right and an essential component of human progress.[9] The long campaign against the slave trade and slavery, regarded by the British public as a humanitarian crusade, thus gave capitalism one of its main underpinnings — a fact which cannot be overemphasized. The first great success in this campaign came in 1807, when the slave trade was outlawed to British subjects on grounds of high moral principle as well as national economic interest (Anstey 1975: 403ff.; Drescher 1982; Temperley 1985: 86–107).[10]

Thereafter, Britain embarked on a long struggle to persuade other commercial and maritime nations to outlaw the traffic and prevent this lucrative trade from passing into the hands of rivals and providing them with a source of labor she had denied to her own colonies.[11]

7. Among the colonial powers, Denmark, which had colonies in the Caribbean and forts in Africa until the latter were sold to the British in 1850, passed a law outlawing the traffic in 1792 but with effect only from 1803. This was to allow for planters in the Danish West Indies to stock up slaves and for the development of plantations on the Guinea coast. In any event the law was not enforced in Africa (Nørregård 1966: 172–76).

8. For a discussion of the inconsistencies in abolitionist views see Eltis 1982: 196ff.

9. Eltis 1982; Temperley 1977: 106ff.; Davis 1984: Ch. 6; Davis 1987; Haskell 1985. At the other end of the spectrum, the near autonomy of the subsistence farmer was seen as barbarous and incapable of generating progress and prosperity.

10. The extent to which the abolitionist success was determined by humanitarian feelings, by national interest, or by the new ideology of the expanding capitalist system has been the subject of much academic debate, which need not detain us here. For completely opposing views see Coupland 1964 and Williams 1944. For more sophisticated discussions see Davis 1966; Anstey 1975; Craton 1974; Drescher 1977; Bolt and Drescher 1980; Eltis and Walvin 1981; Temperley 1981, 1985; Engerman and Eltis 1980.

11. The abolitionist arguments proved mistaken. Slavery was compatible with capital-

Forms of Abolition before the Partition of Africa

The British "Caribbean Model"

In Britain a long political struggle resulted in the outlawing of slavery in 1833 in Canada, in the British Caribbean, Indian Ocean, and South African colonies, but not in India and other eastern possessions. Slaveholding by actual British subjects also became illegal everywhere except in the eastern dependencies. The blow was softened in the colonies by the payment of compensation to slave-owners and by a transitional period during which ex-slaves remained with them as apprentices.[12] Laws were also passed maintaining former owners' rights to land and preventing former slaves from gaining political power or combining to express grievances. Moreover, penalties for vagrancy and nonfulfilment of contracts, eviction laws, and regressive tax policies were enacted to discourage ex-slaves from leaving their former owners (see, for example, Craton 1974: 293ff.; Foner 1983: 39–73; Packwood 1975: 185).

Despite these efforts, freed slaves often avoided selling their labor power. Where possible they became artisans, smallholders, and subsistence farmers, and women and children withdrew from the work force. Production declined in many areas and planters resorted to other forms of coerced labor. Indians, Chinese, and for awhile African recaptives were imported as indentured labor.[13] These were ostensibly free people who had voluntarily signed contracts and were to be repatriated at the end of their term of service.[14] But this system, often denounced as a new form of slavery, provided employers with a cheap, coercible, and disciplined labor force.

Most British abolitionists had not set out to break up the plantations or the hierarchical organization of the colonies and were unprepared for the labor crisis and fall in production which followed the end of slavery in some Caribbean colonies (Engerman 1982: 195–205; Engerman 1985: 225–36; Green 1985: 183–96; Eltis 1982: 201–2). They had expected freed slaves to respond more positively to market forces and sell their labor power

---

ism and slave labor continued to yield large quantities of low-cost commodities outside the British empire after the British abolished slavery and the slave trade in their territories (Genovese 1965; Fogel and Engerman 1974; Scott 1985).

12. The apprenticeship system was not mandatory and was not applied, for instance, in Antigua or Bermuda (Craton 1974: 281; Packwood 1975: 183–84; Green 1976: 264–67). Where there was an oversupply of labor and the laws for the control of freed slaves were considered adequate, slaves became completely free immediately.

13. Recaptives were slaves released from slave ships, in most cases by the British navy and taken to Freetown, the Seychelles, and sometimes handed over to missionaries on the East African coast and elsewhere.

14. Green 1976: 276ff.; Tinker 1974: Ch. 3, 1984; Rodney 1981: 32–35; Schuler 1980: 11–29; Cumpston 1953: 78–83.

and agricultural output.[15] The withdrawal of many from the work force combined with quickening racism, supported by contemporary pseudo-scientific theories, and led to the beliefs that Africans were lazy, child-like, and incapable of responding to market incentives and that they had to be led out of barbarism by Europeans (Curtin 1964: 363ff.). Enthusiasm for complete abolition waned in Britain in the face of the responses to freedom of both former slaves and owners.

In the British Cape Colony in South Africa the reactions of slave-owners, who were mainly Afrikaners, also provided a salutary lesson. They had bitterly opposed the emancipation act, and it became one of the grievances which led many of them to leave the colony in the Great Trek, although slave labor was soon replaced by African squatters, tenants, and cheap black labor.[16]

In the tiny British West African colonies, forts, and settlements,[17] which maintained a precarious existence only by adapting to African conditions, administrators convinced their superiors in London that any attempt to interfere with African slaveholding would lead to widespread resistance and drive away the trade upon which they depended for revenue (Newbury 1965, 1: 294–98; Dumett and Johnson, Ch. 2; McSheffrey 1983: 352– 53). Originally, therefore, the laws were enforced only against Europeans, who were made to free their slaves without compensation. But the legal advisors to the British Crown ruled that laws must apply to everyone in the colonies, which were considered actual British soil. To minimize their impact, however, the colonies were henceforth kept as small as possible, and surrounding areas were designated as merely under British "protection." In a protectorate "native customs" could be allowed to continue, except for the more brutal ones, and full British administration did not have to be implemented. Therefore, by the mid-nineteenth century, slavery, although outlawed in theory in Britain's West African colonies, was often "winked at" in practice even decades after abolition (Miers 1975: 157–60). In protectorates, on the other hand, it was not even under attack.

Slaves often made a mockery of these legal niceties when runaways

15. The decline was also attributable to the ending of the preferential market in Britain for West Indian sugar by 1854 (see, *inter alia*, Craton 1974: 306ff.).

16. G. W. Eybers, Ed., *Select constitutional documents illustrating South African history 1795–1910* (New York, 1918), p. 143, 1969 edition, letter from Piet Retief. Feeling was particularly bitter because the compensation for slaves freed was not only low but had to be claimed in London. This was easier for British Caribbean owners than for South African owners, who had to use agents who charged for their services (Davenport 1977: 33ff.; Wilson and Thompson 1969: 297ff.).

17. These consisted of a small colony in Sierra Leone, a fort on the Gambia, and small settlements on the Gold Coast which finally became colonies only in 1843.

from protectorates and neighboring areas took refuge in British West African possessions. This posed a dilemma for administrators. To harbor such fugitives would have risked alienating their owners — some of whom ruled powerful states such as Asante — and driving away trade, if merchants, afraid of losing their slave porters or agents, were to have taken their custom elsewhere. But returning them might have provoked a storm of protest among British humanitarians. Officials, therefore, resorted to pragmatic policies, sometimes liberating fugitives, particularly in cases of extreme cruelty, and sometimes returning them, especially if they belonged to Britain's African allies (see, for example, Dumett and Johnson, Ch. 2).

The British "Indian Model"

The abolition act of 1833 had specifically omitted India, Ceylon, and St. Helena, and it was not applied in the Far Eastern dependencies. In India, the East India Company government, which knew little of the real condition of slaves in its vast territories and in some areas was heavily dependent on the owning class for its administrators, resisted emancipation until the British government, spurred on by the humanitarians, forced it to act in 1843 (Temperley 1972: 93ff.; Hjejle 1966: 96–98; Chattopadhyay 1977: 170ff.). The company found an ingenious solution. Slave-dealing was forbidden and slavery was simply declared to have no legal status in British India.[18] Most slaves, however, were not informed of their freedom, let alone encouraged to leave their owners, but if they did so, they could not be recovered through legal action or by force. No compensation was paid to owners and no consistent attempt was made to provide slaves who left with land or alternative employment. Without legal sanction or new recruits it was believed that slavery would simply die out. Not until 1862 did it become an offence to own slaves.

This Indian model of abolition was designed to end slavery gradually so that slaves would not be suddenly deprived of their livelihood and masters would have time to protect their interests by offering slaves better terms. Meanwhile neither public order nor the economy was jeopardized. In practice, however, many destitute slaves, facing eviction, were forced to borrow from their masters and fell into hereditary debt bondage.[19]

18. The law applied only to areas under direct British rule and not to Indian states under British protection.

19. Hjejle's (1966) study emphasizes that slavery in India was by no means uniform and that the impact of the act of 1843 varied considerably in different localities. She also stresses how little the British actually knew about either slavery or the working of the act. It should be noted that debt bondage remains a problem in India today, but its victims include persons of free as well as slave descent.

If this model did little for the slaves, for the British it offered a cheap and easy solution. It quickly came to be accepted and justified as the least disruptive method of ending slavery among non-European peoples in the expanding British empire. Since the form of slavery practiced in India was believed to be free of the cruelties of Western slavery (Temperley 1972: 93ff.; Hjejle 1966: 93–96; Chattopadhyay 1977: 221–54) — hence "benevolent"— and since little was known about the working of the law at the grass-roots level, this form of emancipation was acceptable to the humanitarians, and it became the model for abolition in British Africa, where slavery was also considered "benign."

Thus in 1874, when the British annexed the Gold Coast, their first sizable protectorate in West Africa, the Colonial Office, acting reluctantly under humanitarian pressure, applied this model. They were assured by Sir Bartle Frere, former governor of Bombay, that in India it had caused "no disturbance of labour relations — where the slaves were content they went on serving . . . there was no excitement and no occasion for compensation" (Dumett 1981: 209).[20] The governor of the Gold Coast issued an ordinance forbidding any court, British or African, to recognize slavery and declaring that all children born after a certain date would be free. Some rulers protested, but there was little open resistance and trade was not affected (Dumett 1981: 210; Dumett and Johnson, Ch. 2; McSheffrey 1983).[21] In the years that followed, British officials were to become firmly convinced that this was the ideal form of emancipation (Cooper 1980: 41; Lugard 1893: 1: 182–83).

French and Portuguese Forms of Abolition

By the time of the partition of Africa all the Western powers had outlawed the slave trade, and all but Brazil, which followed suit in 1888, had abolished slavery. They were driven by a whole range of motives, in which humanitarianism was only one strand. Only the policies of France and Portugal — the major colonial powers in Africa before partition, besides Britain — need concern us here. In neither country did the antislavery movement command the widespread public support it had in Britain. The strong religious fervor that fuelled the British movement

20. Sir Bartle Frere was just back from his famous journey to Zanzibar, as a result of which the sultan was forced to outlaw both the sale of slaves on Zanzibar and Pemba and all export of slaves from his territories. While there, Frere worked closely with Sir John Kirk, whom Frederick Lugard (see pages 23, 26, fn. 27) considered to be the greatest authority on slavery in Africa (Lugard 1893, 1: 182). The views of Lugard were much influenced by Kirk and probably Frere.

21. McSheffrey, (1983: 358ff.), however, believes many slaves did desert their owners. For further discussion see pages 30–31.

was lacking. Both countries were predominantly Roman Catholic, and the pope did not condemn even the slave trade until 1839 (Maxwell 1975: 73–74).

French philosophers had been amongst those who laid the groundwork for the intellectual and moral attack on slavery, and France was the first country to outlaw it throughout its territories in 1794, during the French Revolution. However, this was not in response to any public pressure but because the slaves had rebelled in Martinique and St. Domingue (Seeber 1971: 162–72; Davis 1975: 137–48; Daget 1980: 67). In fact, slavery and the slave trade were reinstated under Napoleon in 1802 to restore order and rebuild the colonial empire. Thus, the first French experiment with emancipation had been short lived or, as in Mauritius, had provoked a planter rebellion and never been enforced (Nwulia 1981: 35). By the time of the restoration of the monarchy in 1815, abolition was associated with the revolution and with the British victors in the recent wars which had robbed France of much of her empire. Most French abolitionists belonged to the small Protestant minority and were isolated into tiny intellectual circles without support from the Catholic masses (Drescher 1980: 44; Daget 1971: 42–58; Daget 1980: 64–77).

France, under British pressure, outlawed the slave trade in 1818. Although she posted an antislavery squadron off the West African coast and signed various short-lived treaties with Britain, she took only sporadic action against the traffic (Daget 1971: 15–58; Bouche 1968: 56; Miers 1975: 15–23). When the revolution of 1848 swept radicals into power, they again abolished slavery in French colonies. Since at that time the French regarded all French possessions as actual French soil, the slaves of French citizens and residents of St. Louis and Gorée, in modern Senegal, were actually freed. But when neighboring peoples refused to come and trade, administrators tried to minimize the effects of the laws. Like the British, they dealt selectively with fugitive slaves, in practice freeing those of their enemies and returning those of their allies. In the 1870s and 1880s they even disannexed some of their conquered territories, turning them into protectorates to avoid having to free the slaves of their African inhabitants (Klein 1986; Barry 1985: 276ff.; Renault 1972: 11–14). Moreover, they allowed slave children to continue to be imported into their colonies and turned a blind eye when Frenchmen outside the colonies held slaves (Klein 1986). In the French Caribbean and Indian Ocean colonies, French planters faced, like their British counterparts, a labor shortage after emancipation, and resorted to importing African slaves from west-central Africa and Mozambique under the guise of "free contract labor," or *libres engagés* (Renault 1976: 60–93). This barely concealed slave traffic from Mozambique to the Indian Ocean islands was still active in the 1880s.

The abolition movement in Portugal was even weaker than in France, being limited to a small group of liberals without popular or Church support. The export of slaves from Portuguese territories was outlawed in 1836, but the decree was ignored. The export traffic continued openly into the 1840s and then illicitly, supplying Brazil until 1853 and Cuba to the late 1860s. After this slaves were still exported, but under the guise of contract labor, to the Portuguese islands of São Tomé and Príncipe in the Gulf of Guinea, as well as to the French Indian Ocean islands.[22] In 1854 a reformist government began to dismantle slavery, believing this was necessary for the economic regeneration of the moribund Portuguese colonies. Owners were not compensated, and slaves were simply declared to be their unpaid apprentices. Complete freedom was scheduled for 1878, and this was confirmed by the abolition law of 1875. Portugal, however, could not enforce this legislation except in coastal towns. But even there slaves continued to be imported, bought, and sold under the guise of contract labor. Former slaves were illegally forced to prolong their contracts and subjected to strict vagrancy laws (Heywood, Ch. 14; Clarence-Smith 1979: 35ff.; Clarence-Smith 1985: 23ff.). On the *prazos* of the Zambezi, which resembled African polities more than colonial states (Isaacman 1972: 156–63), the laws were meaningless. Not only did Portuguese settlers continue to acquire slaves, but officials connived at the contract-labor traffic (Isaacman and Rosenthal, Ch. 7; Duffy 1967: 178ff.). Although the Portuguese had theoretically outlawed slavery in their territories in 1878, in practice both the slave trade and slavery continued on a large scale.

The Antislavery Movement and the Partition of Africa

By the late 1860s Britain had persuaded all the major European and American maritime and commercial powers, except France, to sign treaties outlawing the slave trade and establishing mutual rights to search each others' shipping (Miers 1975: Ch. 1). Britain also had treaties against the traffic with a number of coastal African and Asian polities (ibid.: 2). These distinguished between "domestic" (non-European) slavery, which was not under attack, and the export slave trade, which Britain wished to stamp out. The closure of the markets had virtually ended the export of slaves across the Atlantic, but it continued on a small scale under the guise of contract labor to the French Antilles and Indian Ocean islands, as well as to the Portuguese offshore islands. The traffic to the Muslim

---

22. Duffy 1967: Ch. 6–7; Renault 1976: 60ff.; Vail and White 1980: 14ff.; Heywood, Ch. 14; Isaacman and Rosenthal, Ch. 7.

world, particularly from northeastern and East Africa, also continued as did slaving in Africa itself.

Attention was forcefully drawn to the slave trade in eastern Africa in the 1860s by the British missionary explorer David Livingstone, who revitalized the ideological foundations of emancipation by advocating the salvation and regeneration of Africa through the promotion of legitimate commerce, Christianity, and (European) civilization. His revelations of an active and devastating slave traffic in eastern Africa, supplying Portuguese and French colonies and the Muslim world, led Britain to sign new treaties with Zanzibar, Egypt, and the Ottoman Empire which reduced the export slave traffic to the Muslim world to a small smuggling traffic by the 1880s (ibid., 75–116). Livingstone's appeals also led to increased missionary penetration of eastern Africa. Missions, both Roman Catholic and Protestant, had originally come to the African coast to work with recaptives. Now several Protestant mission societies established missions in the interior. Hard on their heels came the Catholic White Fathers founded by Cardinal Lavigerie. Their work was hampered by wars and raids, the hostility of slavers, and the dilemma posed by fugitive slaves, since harboring them alienated their owners and returning them was against missionary principles (Hanna 1956: Ch. 1; Oliver 1952: 14, Chs. 2–3; Renault 1971, 1: 155ff.). The problems of the White Fathers moved Lavigerie to launch in 1888, with papal blessing, a Roman Catholic antislavery "crusade" (Renault 1971, 2: 73ff.). Preaching fiery sermons, he called on Europe to send out young Christians to fight the scourge and to found antislavery societies to support them. He appealed to all denominations, but he brought firmly into the antislavery movement the Catholics of France, Portugal, and Spain, the latter of which acquired several small and widely dispersed African colonies in the course of the nineteenth century,[23] and the Catholics of the new participants in the scramble for Africa — Italy, Germany, and Belgium, whose king, Leopold II, was building a personal empire in the Congo.

This late nineteenth-century antislavery commitment by both Catholics and Protestants provided the colonial powers with a moral justification for the conquest of Africa, which they used to rally public support. The clearest expression of this was the Brussels Conference of 1889–1890, which resulted in the first far-reaching international agreement against the African slave trade on land and sea — the Brussels Act of 1890. This bound the signatories, who included all the colonial powers, to suppress

23. Spain had abolished slavery in its Rio Muni possession in 1859, long before abolishing it in Puerto Rico or Cuba, in order to induce slaves to flee to Fernando Po from Príncipe and to please the British (Sundiata, forthcoming; Clarence-Smith, pers. comm.).

slave-raiding and -trading, and to succor and repatriate fugitive and freed slaves. Although the colonial powers were, henceforth, committed to action against slaving, they were not bound to end slavery. Their experiences in the Caribbean and elsewhere had made even the British aware of the dangers of wholesale emancipation and wary of any definite commitment to end African slavery (Miers 1975: 206ff.). The Brussels Act also cloaked the entire conquest of Africa in a humanitarian guise by presenting European rule and capitalist enterprise, including the employment of freed slaves, as antislavery measures. Thus, the ideology of the anti-slavery movement became part and parcel of the European mission to civilize Africa. Henceforth the colonial powers could not tolerate open slave-raiding or -trading or allow slave-owners to recapture fugitives without risking protests from fellow signatories of the act or an outcry from the European public, alerted to the slavery issue by the cardinal's crusade and the Brussels Conference.

But this ideological and legal commitment to ending the slave trade and, eventually, slavery was in practice usually subordinated to the pragmatic agenda of colonial administrators, who, even if they wished to take decisive action, found their hands tied by the very real weakness of the colonial state.

The Role of the Colonial States in Ending Slavery

The chapters in this collection reveal the ambivalence of colonial administrators towards slavery, especially during the formative phases of colonial rule, when they were understaffed and underfunded and needed alliances with indigenous elites, whose social and political power and wealth were often tied to the possession of slaves. Slaves were frequently the largest capital investment Africans had, and some administrators were reluctant to interfere with African customs they hardly understood and with forms of property they felt bound to respect in principle. They feared that wholesale abolition would provoke resistance, disrupt the economy, and saddle the colonial government with destitute slaves for whom they would have to provide. Not surprisingly, therefore, they often disregarded metropolitan directives. Sometimes they justified this by arguing that determined action would cause political and economic disruption; in other cases they reported that slavery was not a significant problem or even that it did not exist in their territories (see, for example, Miers and Crowder, Ch. 5).

Nevertheless, colonial rule eventually led to the end of slavery in most of Africa. This was the result of, first, the structural changes in the political economy which affected slave-capture and -holding; second, of the antislavery policies of colonial governments; and third, of changes in regional and international commodity markets, and in local economic and demographic conditions, which affected the demand for labor and determined the options open to freed slaves. All these factors are closely interwoven, and each reinforced the other so that it is not possible to discuss them separately.

Colonial Conquest and Changes in the Political Economy

Colonial conquest and pacification ended the wars which had generated the majority of African slaves. Slaves could still be obtained by kidnapping, judicial sanction, and voluntary enslavement, but their numbers were much reduced. The decline of warfare — and enslavement through capture — precipitated a radical readjustment. For rulers and elites, whose wealth and power had largely depended on the capture and use of slaves as labor, as a form of capital accumulation, as articles of patronage to reward faithful officials and soldiers, and as goods for payment of tribute or for trade, this sometimes amounted to a crisis. It also caused a crisis of authority for some chiefs and lineage heads by undermining their ability to accumulate followers and dependents; and it undercut the activities of those merchants and freebooters who had both traded heavily in slaves and had also used them as agents, porters, and laborers.

Although a number of African states survived conquest and were reconstituted under various forms of "indirect rule," and those elements of the elite who were willing to submit were able to remain intact, colonial rule undercut some of the major reasons for maintaining slaves. Political power now depended, not on large armies, loyal officials, and numbers of dependents, but on the support of the colonial government. While a ruler with many followers might carry more influence with the colonial administration, and an individual with many slaves could still exert considerable power locally, in the new political economy slaves were no longer a direct source of formal political power or prestige. Moreover, they could no longer be used, as in the past, to fight or as tribute payments.

People, however, continued to be in high demand as labor and as dependents. Opportunities for the commercial use of labor expanded during the colonial period, particularly as conquest gave rise to new groups of nonproducers including colonial soldiers and the residents of expanding commercial centers, who turned to local markets for goods and services. The degree to which owners managed to continue to benefit from the labor of their former slaves or to replace them with other dependents or even with free workers depended, as will be shown, on a whole range of changes in the political economy. In many cases owners were able to avert a crisis caused by the drastic reduction in the supply of slaves, because the long delay between conquest and the end of slavery enabled them to find other means of maintaining their wealth and power. The cause of this delay was that colonial states were fragile entities caught between, on one hand, metropolitan pressures to become self-supporting and produce goods for export as soon as possible, and, on the other, the need to conciliate and control the various social groups under their rule. In this dilemma they tackled separately each component of slavery: its reproduction by raids or birth; the sale of slaves; the use of slaves for bridewealth payments, for tribute, gifts, or other transfers; and finally, the possession of slaves. The aim of many colonial administrators was to cause minimal social, political, and economic disruption.

Colonial Antislavery Policies: Slave-Raiding and -Trading
In the last decade of the nineteenth and first decade of the twentieth centuries, the European colonial states, the Amharic Empire of Ethiopia, and the Americo-Liberian state pursued military conquest and pacification. The European powers often justified their military expeditions in terms of ending slave-raiding. This was in fact their first antislavery objective, because raids created disorders and population dislocation, which ran counter to their long-term plans for economic development. But even raiding had to be tolerated until the colonial powers were strong enough to defeat the raiders, and there were unadministered areas which it continued unabated for years.[24] Early colonial efforts were sometimes limited to directing raids away from administered territories. Thus in 1904 the French agreement with Dar al-Kuti merely bound the ruler not to raid to the southeast. Only in 1908 was he forbidden to raid "without French approval" (Cordell, Ch. 4). Slave raids in the Ethiopian borderlands continued into the 1930s, conducted by government officials and explained as "tax collecting" (Garretson 1986: 205–6; Hickey 1984: Ch. 2; Miers, forthcoming).

Far from ending the demand for slave labor, some colonial states became for awhile primary recruiters. Slaves were "freed" and then conscripted into both the Belgian and French forces and the Portuguese police (Echenberg 1986: 312ff.; Roberts, Ch. 9; Northrup, Ch. 16; Isaacman and Rosenthal, Ch. 7). Colonial armies relied heavily on African allies, who were often allowed to keep captives, particularly women (Bouche 1968; see, for example, 80ff.; Twaddle, Ch. 3). Similarly, Ethiopian soldiers acquired large numbers of slaves during their conquests (see,

---

24. See, *inter alia*, Cordell, Ch. 4; Heywood, Ch. 14; Hogendorn and Lovejoy, Ch. 13; McDougall, Ch. 12; Isaacman and Rosenthal, Ch. 7; Dumett and Johnson, Ch. 2; Clarence-Smith 1979: 64, 69; Maier 1985.

inter alia, McCann, Ch. 11). Colonial rule created a growing demand for labor for porterage, for building infrastructure, and for producing food for the burgeoning administrative centers. In some areas officials bought or freed slaves to work or farm for the administration.[25] Catholic missions also initially bought slaves to form a nucleus of converts and to use as labor (Cordell, Ch. 4; Northrup, Ch. 16; Klein 1986; Renault 1971, 1: 172ff.). Sometimes colonial administrators simply demanded labor from local chiefs, who supplied it by reducing their neighbors to slaves or by buying slaves (Northrup, Ch. 16; Heywood, Ch. 14). Cooperative African chiefs sometimes arrested slave caravans in the expectation that they would be allowed to keep the captives they "freed" (Klein 1986). In sum, the ever-growing demand for labor engendered by the economic development accompanying colonial rule was often met by the slave trade as long as there remained sources of supply.[26]

Despite the colonial antislavery rhetoric, officials moved very gradually against the slave traffic for fear of provoking owners denied a primary form of accumulating power and wealth and of disrupting the fragile peace and the gradually expanding production and commerce. All the colonial powers eventually passed laws against slave-dealing, but it was often years before they enforced them. Thus, the French did not mention slave-trading in their treaties with the slaving state of Dar al-Kuti until 1908 (Cordell, Ch. 4), and they did not interfere with the operations of the "grands nomades" of Mauritania even in the 1930s (McDougall, Ch. 12). In most treaties the Portuguese did not forbid the traffic with the Ovimbundu, who were conquered between 1900 and 1910, but who continued to deal in slaves to supply labor for the Portuguese sector of the economy for many years (Heywood, Ch. 14). The Germans passed laws against slave-trading but took no action in northern Togoland until after 1900 (Maier 1985), and in remote areas of Tanganyika slave markets still existed in 1903 (Iliffe 1979: 131). In Cameroon, the Germans outlawed trading in 1895 but did not enforce the laws until after 1901 (Austen 1977: 326–27). The British began really vigorous prosecutions in the Gold Coast only in 1911 (Dumett and Johnson, Ch. 2). Slave-dealing, particularly in women, was rife in the Uele District of the Belgian Congo in 1910 (Northrup, Ch. 16). The Italians outlawed it in Somaliland only in 1903–1904 (Cassanelli, Ch. 10). Sometimes officials interpreted the laws selectively to allow some forms of trafficking but not others. Thus

25. Cassanelli, Ch. 10; Cordell, Ch. 4; Isaacman and Rosenthal, Ch. 7; Klein, Ch. 6; Northrup, Ch. 16; Roberts, Ch. 9; Bouche 1968: Ch. 9.

26. Clarence-Smith 1979: 69; Klein 1977: 338–52; Brooks 1975: 53–54; Swindell 1980: 100–101; Heywood, Ch. 14; Northrup, Ch. 16; Roberts, Ch. 9.

in the Mauritanian Adrar up to 1918, the French tolerated internal slave-dealing but not the export of slaves (McDougall, Ch. 12).

By the First World War, however, open raiding and large-scale dealing had ceased in colonial Africa, and it tapered off in Ethiopia in the 1920s. In Liberia, where indigenous peoples were enslaved by Americo-Liberian colonists and exported to the Spanish island of Fernando Po under the guise of contract labor, the traffic caused a scandal as late as 1930 (Sundiata 1980: 11–32; Sundiata, forthcoming). Cases mainly involving the kidnapping of small children, transfers disguised as adoption or early marriage, persisted but on an ever-decreasing scale right through and even after the colonial period (Ohadike, Ch. 15; Miers 1975: 296ff.; Klein and Roberts 1987). A small export traffic to the Middle East continued even after the Second World War. The victims were kidnapped, tricked by offers of good jobs, or imported under the guise of pilgrims to Mecca (Greenidge 1958: 52; Miers 1975: 295–96; Miers, research notes).

Colonial Antislavery Policies: The Suppression of Slavery

The colonial states were also slow to tackle slavery itself, and then action was often dictated by local events or by metropolitan or international pressure. Administrators defended inaction by arguing that African slavery was "benign" and that if attacked only at the level of reproduction — by ending new enslavement — it would die "a natural death" without injustice to the owners, whose property and customs would be respected, or to the slaves, who were mainly happy with their lot and who, if suddenly released, would have no means of support and might become a burden on the administration or turn to crime and prostitution. Officials may also have had less incentive to attack slavery because a high proportion of slaves were women (see pages 38–40, 52 for a discussion of women slaves and emancipation). In addition, they were anxious to recruit male rather than female labor for the colonial economy, and they were unwilling to undermine male control over women in general (Robertson 1983: 229–30; Lovett 1986), even to the point of actually reimposing such control in areas where it had been broken down during the social and political changes immediately preceding colonial rule (for example, see Wright 1983: 248).

Because of their efforts to soft-pedal and avoid emancipation, the colonial rulers allowed the initiative to pass to the slaves in some cases and provoked the very change in the relations of production that officials most feared — mass departures.

The most dramatic instances of this occurred in parts of French West Africa, when, after a decade of ambiguous policies, the French issued a judicial code in 1903 which did not recognize the legal status of slavery and in 1905 outlawed new enslavement and slave-trading (in effect following the British Indian model of abolition). When slaves in the French Soudan and Guinea realized that owners could no longer force them to stay, thousands either refused to work or simply left (Klein, Ch. 6; Roberts, Ch. 9). This doubtless contributed to the extreme caution of the French elsewhere. Thus in Ubangi-Shari, when they finally conquered the local rulers, they ignored the laws and often returned runaways in the hope of sustaining the little existing economic activity and preventing further emigration from their already depopulated territory (Cordell, Ch. 4). Similarly, in parts of Mauritania, where the French had specifically promised to respect the "customs, values, property and religion" of the nomads as a condition of their submission, the laws were not enforced (McDougall, Ch. 12).

Like the French in the Soudan, the Italians on the Benadir coast also lost the initiative to the slaves. The Benadir Company acquired rights to the Somali coast from the sultan of Zanzibar in 1892, and was ostensibly bound to apply the decrees outlawing the slave trade and slavery which the British had forced on the sultan in the 1870s (Cassanelli, Ch. 10; Miers 1975: 93). In the coastal towns, which were all it controlled, the company bought the freedom of some slaves but discouraged them from leaving their masters, made them pay their masters for board and lodging, and returned runaways. As late as 1903, the governor claimed to know nothing of the sultan's decrees. Only because public attention was focussed by crusading journalists on Italian complicity with slave dealers did the government outlaw the slave trade in 1903–1904 and declare free all slaves born after 1890. The result was a stream of departures to areas beyond Italian control. By the time these were conquered in 1908, many slaves had found refuge in Muslim settlements or autonomous villages, thereby evading Italian efforts to force them into the capitalist sector (Cassanelli 1987; Cassanelli, Ch. 10).

The range of abolition policies was perhaps nowhere greater than in British territories. Although British officials applied the Indian model of abolition most consistently, actual policies varied greatly. In Kenya alone there were three variants. In the islands of Zanzibar and Pemba, where owners were Arab-Swahili Muslims and most slaves worked on clove plantations, the legal status of slavery was abolished in 1897. But owners retained their rights to land and were paid compensation. To prevent ex-slaves from withdrawing their labor and endangering the economy, the abolition decree made them liable to tax, corvée labor, and draconian vagrancy laws. Those who wished to leave had to go to court, where they were pressured into remaining on the plantations as contract labor (Cooper 1980: 72ff.). A decade later when abolition was attempted in the strip of the Kenya coast leased from the sultan of Zanzibar, slavery was in full decline. The Zanzibar experience had shown that ex-slaves would not freely sell their labor, and officials decided that the coastal plantation economy was not likely to revive. The British recognized the owners' titles to land, but they were paid minimal compensation for the loss of their slaves, and freed slaves were not pressured into accepting contracts. To avoid interference in domestic affairs, concubines were excluded from the abolition decrees both on the islands and on the coast. Not until 1909 were all slaves, including concubines, declared free throughout the sultan's dominions (Cooper 1980: 39ff., 173ff.). In Kenya beyond the coastal strip, where owners were not Muslim, where societies were small in scale, and where there was no important commodity production for export, the legal status of slavery was abolished without compensation.

Similar variations in policy emerged in Nigeria. In the north, Frederick Lugard became the first British governor in 1901 and established a system of indirect rule through traditional authorities.[27] He ended the legal status of slavery, prohibited new enslavement, and declared free all children born after 1 April 1901. Since he believed that slaves did not appreciate freedom unless they worked for it, he directed the emancipation process in the Muslim states through an existing Islamic institution known as *murgu,* by which owners allowed slaves to work on their own in return for regular payment of an agreed sum. Under Lugard, slaves could enter into murgu arrangements to buy their redemption (Hogendorn and Lovejoy, Ch. 13). Because Lugard made it difficult for slaves who simply left their owners without permission to get land or jobs elsewhere, murgu arrangements engineered an orderly transition out of slavery and placed part of the cost of manumission squarely on the shoulders of the slaves (Hogendorn and Lovejoy, Ch. 13; Lennihan 1982: 116–24).

On the other side of the coin, Lugard's successors followed tax policies which encouraged owners to break up large slaveholdings whose output was taxed, in favor of tax-free murgu and tenancy payments. This, together with favorable land tenure policies, led to the emergence of smallholders, among them ex-slaves, producing for local and export markets. This process was encouraged by the need to pay their own taxes in cash and by the commodity-production boom generated by the ar-

27. Lugard's views on slavery are discussed in Lugard 1893, 1: 168–212. He had gained experience in East and Central Africa. He had not only fought slave-traders in the Nyasa region but had served in Buganda. He had also negotiated the freedom of the slaves who had taken refuge in British missions on the Kenya coast including the one at Rabai; and he had been involved in arranging for slaves in the fugitive slave settlements at Fuladoyo and Makongeni to redeem themselves. He later served on two of the League of Nations slavery committees.

rival of the railway in 1912 (Hogendorn 1978: 92–113). The British, however, were not fully able to enforce their gradualist policies, because many slaves in Northern Nigeria took the initiative themselves and simply fled (M. Smith 1981: 67–68). Their numbers included concubines, whom the British regarded as similar to wives, but who indicated their own feelings by leaving (Hogendorn and Lovejoy, Ch. 13).

In Southern Nigeria British officials moved faster than in the north. In 1901 they proclaimed all slaves free and all transactions in people illegal. But then their courage failed, and to conciliate owners and avoid dislocating trade, they forbade the now "freed" slaves from leaving the "canoe houses," which were the basic economic and social units in the Niger Delta area.[28] They also allowed owners to procure children as apprentices, and imposed vagrancy laws to discourage ex-slaves from running away. The system remained in force until the eve of the First World War, when the flogging of a boy who left his "house" without permission, caused an outcry among humanitarians in Britain (Ohadike, Ch. 15; Miers 1975: 301–2).

International Pressure to End Slavery

The chapters that follow make it clear that criticism by the European press, the educated public, and national and international organizations affected the timing of abolition. Thus, the British in the Gold Coast and East Africa were pressured by the humanitarian lobby to end the legal status of slavery (Cooper 1980: 34–46; Dumett 1981: 204–10; Dumett and Johnson, Ch. 2). The French ended it in West Africa under metropolitan pressure (Klein 1986). Denunciation in the Portuguese press and British protests caused the new Portuguese Republic to outlaw slavery for the second time in 1910 (Heywood, Ch. 14). Similar revelations led the Italians to outlaw it in Somaliland in 1903–1904, and the scandals attendant on the demise of King Leopold's regime moved the Belgians to outlaw it in the Congo in 1910 (Northrup, Ch. 16).

During the First World War the Brussels Act of 1890 lapsed and in 1919 it was abrogated. But in the 1920s, slaving on the Ethiopian borders and a revival of the export traffic across the Red Sea to Arabia caused a storm in Britain which led to the appointment of the Temporary Slavery Commission by the League of Nations. This resulted in the Slavery Convention of 1926, which bound signatories to "progressively" suppress slavery itself in all its forms. Slavery was loosely defined as the condition of a person over whom "all or any of the rights of ownership" were exer-

28. Not only was the legislation contradictory but it was also extended to areas where there were no "houses" (Ohadike, Ch. 15; Anene 1966: 305–8).

cised (Miers 1986). The convention also condemned forced labor practiced by the colonial powers (see pages 42–45).

The league inquiries and the convention had some impact. For instance, they caused the British Colonial Office to insist in 1927 that the legal status of slavery be abolished in Sierra Leone, where, until the previous year, administrators had helped recover runaway slaves (Grace 1975: 234ff.); and they led to a belated announcement that Basarwa in the Bangwato Reserve were free to leave their masters, although the legal status of slavery was not ended in Bechuanaland until 1936 (Miers and Crowder, Ch. 5). Fear of league inquiries also resulted in more stringent measures against the slave trade in Ethiopia (McCann, Ch. 11; Miers, forthcoming). Conversely, the Italians, hoping to win international support and approval, abolished slavery when they conquered Ethiopia in 1936. In Liberia a league inquiry led to the suppression of the contract-labor traffic to Spanish Fernando Po (Sundiata 1980: 51–79; Sundiata, forthcoming). International attention generated by these league inquiries and the establishment of a permanent league antislavery committee in the 1930s, thus led to legal changes and caused colonial governments to examine their policies. Greater awareness of international antislavery pressure, however, often did little to better the material condition of freed slaves (Miers 1986).

The Impact of Changes in Regional and
International Markets

Legal abolition ended state support for slavery but it was only one factor in the complex process of emancipation. Changes in the material and social well-being of ex-slaves, while they took place in the context of colonialism and were sometimes the result of conscious steps taken by administrators, were usually determined by economic factors. Thus, changes in regional and world markets affected the demand for labor quite apart from colonial policies. For instance, Igbo slaveholdings became less viable because of a drop in palm-oil prices caused by the world depressions in the late nineteenth century (Ohadike, Ch. 15). The depressions of the early 1920s and the 1930s had similar effects on some areas. There were also times of accelerated production like those stimulated by the rubber and peanut booms of the early colonial period, and there were serious dislocations of the economy during both world wars. Temporary disruptions were also caused by natural calamities such as the drought in Central Africa in the late nineteenth and early twentieth centuries (Heywood, Ch. 14; Dias 1981; Miller 1982: 17–22) and the epizootic which hit livestock from Ethiopia to Bechuanaland in the late nineteenth century (see, *inter alia*, Miers and Crowder, Ch. 5). There were also areas where indigenous production was dislocated by colonial policies, as for example on the Kenya and Benadir coasts and parts of Nyasaland (Cooper 1980: Ch. 5; Cassanelli, Ch. 10; Lovett 1986).

In many areas, however, colonial pacification brought an expansion in commodity production for local and export markets. This increased the demand for agricultural labor and for miners. It stimulated service industries, providing an ever-growing need for porters, canoemen, camel drivers, and trading agents (Coquery-Vidrovitch and Lovejoy 1985: 12ff.), as well as for construction workers to build urban, administrative, and mining centers and the roads and railways linking them to the coast.

These economic changes affected slavery in several important ways. In the early years of colonial rule, the demand for ever more labor was often filled by the enslavement of new peoples. Some were captured, some kidnapped, some purchased, and some, as the result of famine caused by droughts or epizootics, were driven to become the slaves or pawns of those who could feed them. This early economic expansion also provided new incentives to owners to invest in slaves even as the supply declined. When the Benguela railway reached the Angolan highlands, the Ovimbundu began growing cash crops for which they acquired numbers of slaves (Heywood, Ch. 14). As the supply of new slaves declined, however, owners often tried to exploit more fully the slaves they had. In the French Soudan, anxious to supply the colonial commodity market in Bamako, they increased the length of the working day and lowered slave rations (Roberts, Ch. 9). Similar steps were taken by Somali owners (Cassanelli, Ch. 10). Such actions soured relations, provoked resistance, and finally led to massive slave departures. On the other hand, the great demand for labor and the expansion of regional economies, made their departure easier by providing opportunities for former slaves to establish themselves on their own (see pages 33–38). Dynamic regional economies, however, were unevenly distributed over Africa, and these opportunities for freed slaves depended on their proximity to areas of growth.

Changes in the economy also influenced colonial policies because administrators worried about upsetting the delicate balance of control and coercion just when local commodity production was beginning to increase. All of them wanted a disciplined, hard-working labor force to produce goods for export and to be available for public works on demand, as well as a small number of urban wage laborers with varying degrees of skill. But there were great differences of opinion as to how to achieve it. Thus, in Nigeria, while Lugard wanted to keep ex-slaves working on their ex-owners' plantations, his successor, Girouard, wanted large slaveholdings to be broken up and ex-slaves and other farmers to become smallholders producing for the market on their own (Hogendorn and Lovejoy, Ch. 13; Lennihan 1982: 121–32). The French governor, William Ponty, began by opposing swift emancipation in the Soudan because he considered slavery the backbone of the economy, but by 1908 he had decided that freeing slaves was economically desirable in order to create a mobile labor force for development along capitalist lines (Klein 1983; Roberts, Ch. 9). A similar but much slower evolution of colonial policy took place in Sierra Leone. There most earlier governors feared the disruptive effects of abolition and believed that the prosperity of the country depended on retaining slavery, but after the First World War emancipation came increasingly to be considered necessary for the economic advancement of the protectorate (Grace 1975: 220ff.). The Portuguese allowed slavery to continue unchecked for many years because it supported the capitalist sector, but eventually replaced it with forms of forced labor (see pages 42–47).

In general it may be said that in the early days of colonial rule it suited the colonial states to maintain slavery. Few of them were, in any case, powerful enough to take determined steps to eradicate it. But, when their power was consolidated and their fears of provoking the owners and disrupting the economy waned, some administrations took conscious steps to hasten its demise. Others merely looked on while slaves freed themselves. In areas where colonial power remained weak, as in the remoter parts of Mauritania, officials turned a blind eye and allowed slavery to continue. Thus the gap which often existed between the legal status of slaves and their actual material and social position reflects the complexities of the social, political, and economic changes taking place in colonial Africa.

The Transition from Slavery to Freedom: A Historiographic Debate

Scholars disagree as to whether the transition from slavery to freedom caused widespread disruption or whether it had little impact on major African social and economic institutions. Before this question can begin to be resolved, the impact of the end of slavery must be considered on several levels. First, there is its impact on the performance of the economy as a whole — the main concern of the colonial administrations. Second, there is its impact on African social structures. And finally, there is its impact on individual slaves and owners. Another subject of disagreement concerns the freed slaves' perceptions of freedom. Did it mean complete personal autonomy or the establishment of new and more acceptable relations of dependence in new communities? Did it mean a return to a freed slave's original society? Alternatively did it mean closer integration into the society and culture of the owner?

There is also disagreement on the validity of much of the evidence from colonial sources. Colonial administrators described slavery in Africa as "benign," because they usually carried with them concepts of slavery framed by Western intellectual and historical experience (Kopytoff, Ch. 17). They seem to have suffered from a form of cognitive dissonance, born of ignorance of the actual experience of slaves, and to have been guilty of illogical thinking. Many also carried with them patriarchal assumptions about African societies which allowed them to ignore women. Thus, while they argued, on the one hand, that slavery was benign and slaves were contented, on the other, they feared that abolition would result in slaves simply downing tools and refusing to work — perhaps at all and certainly not for their owners (see, for example, Twaddle, Ch. 3). Many officials, therefore, painted alarming pictures for nervous governments of newly freed slaves disrupting the fragile economy and turning to financially strapped colonial administrations for support, or taking to crime. As has been shown, they often took precautions, which in many cases succeeded, to prevent any sudden departure and to protect the interests of owners. But their fears of the dire results of abolition contrast sharply in most cases with their subsequent reports showing that there was little dislocation of the economy and that slavery was dying a "natural" death, lingering on because most slaves were content to remain with their owners. The nondisruptive consequences of abolition reinforced the administrators' views that African slavery was indeed benign — a view that had justified their gradualist policies in the first place.

Until recently scholars tended to accept this official view of African slavery as a mild form of domestic servitude, different in kind from that of the New World, and to agree that the end of slavery caused little social or economic disruption. M. G. Smith, in an article comparing Jamaican with Hausa slavery, has drawn what appeared to be the logical conclusion that a mild form of slavery would lead to a smooth end of slavery. He assumed that Hausa slavery was a mechanism for the assimilation of outsiders and could be abolished without "severe dislocation or structural alteration." The fact that by far the greater number of slaves remained with their owners after their legal emancipation supported his belief that Hausa slaves were "relatively content with their lot" (Smith 1965: 149). A. G. Hopkins, dealing with Yorubaland, has also concluded that the transition from slave to free labor was relatively smooth, but not because it was benign so much as because the majority of former slaves not only stayed where they were, but they also continued to work in agriculture, even if they no longer worked for their owners. This was possible because rights to land suitable for growing food and export crops were relatively easy to acquire. There was thus no change in occupation and hence little social or economic disruption (Hopkins 1966: 142–44; Hopkins 1973: 228). John Grace, dealing with abolition in Sierra Leone, agrees that there was little disruption there. Most slaves "sat down with their former masters as clients or cousins" and continued to work without pay in return for the use of land to support their families. The reasons he gives, however, are not that they were content but that they had little choice, since the powers of the traditional authorities made it hard for them to leave and they were bound by economic and family ties to their owners (Grace 1975: 251–52).

Kopytoff and Miers (1977: 73–75) point out that slavery in Africa actually ranged from relatively "benign" systems to harsh chattel slavery, but suggest that, because slavery was only one of a number of dependent relationships in Africa and the economic use of slaves was only one aspect of slavery, its official abolition would not in itself have changed the social organization or ongoing life of slave-using communities. They expect further research to show that there had been a pattern not of "wholesale flight" or of "the mass breakup of relationships" between slaves and owners, but rather of "their complex readjustment." They predict that this research will show that only the most marginal slaves had left and that these will prove to have been mostly first-generation slaves able to return to their areas of origin or those who could join religious communities or find wage labor. Most slaves probably stayed where they were, since they had nowhere else to go and were sufficiently integrated into society to regard freedom as full incorporation into the host society. Where slaves were so little integrated as to form an emergent stratum, Miers and Kopytoff think they probably tried to readjust their relationships in the direction of greater autonomy—to become clients, retainers, servants, or quasi relatives. Alternatively, they may have formed their own independent communities in the midst of their former owners or joined new social groupings such as Muslim brotherhoods or Christian missions.

Kopytoff and Miers (ibid.: 73) recognize, like Hopkins (1973: 228–29), that such desertions ruined some owners with large holdings. The repercussions for individuals, therefore, were sometimes extremely disruptive — both for slaves who had to find a new niche and for owners suddenly deprived not only of their labor force but also of the dependents, who had given them status, power, and wealth. But for society as a whole, unless a large proportion of slaves left — and this would have to have been in the hundreds of thousands in areas such as the French Soudan and

Northern Nigeria—abolition did not cause major disruption. Africans simply adjusted to the situation and continued to "enlarge their households and kin groups, to increase the circle of relatives, to acquire more wives and children, more clients and dependents, adjusting their numbers as in the past to current circumstances" (ibid.: 76). They also point out that complete assimilation was unlikely. Slave descent would be remembered and ex-slaves would form a recognized social stratum long after abolition, and this in itself would make informants wary of giving other than romanticized accounts of slavery (ibid.: 75).

Francophone scholars, however, have posited a less harmonious transition from slavery to freedom (Guéye 1965: 543–51; Pasquier 1967; Boutillier 1968: 532–33; Bouche 1968: 169–72). Recently, a number of scholars, particularly those influenced by Marxist theory, have challenged the concept of a relatively smooth transition. Some of these so-called revisionists have drawn attention to the "dramatic moments" when slaves showed their discontent by leaving en masse (Roberts and Klein 1980: 384–94; McSheffrey 1983: 354–64).[29] Others have focussed on the "quiet and continuous struggle" between ex-slaves and former masters (Cooper 1980: 4). Gerald McSheffrey, using the example of the Gold Coast, contends that those who see African slavery as relatively benign and abolition as having had little repercussion have been "taken in" by the official mythology in the colonial records, both as to the character of slavery and the impact of abolition. However, scholars using these official documents but working on areas where there were large numbers of newly acquired slaves, many of them used in production for the market, have also concluded that slaves deserted in considerable numbers and that, therefore, earlier assumptions that most slaves stayed where they were and that slavery was benign were wrong. Paul Lovejoy, for instance, believes that tens (perhaps hundreds) of thousands left their owners in Northern Nigeria and that, far from wanting full admittance into the owners' kin groups, they wanted autonomy to control their own lives, work, and family relationships (Lovejoy 1983: 247; Hogendorn and Lovejoy, Ch. 13). In other words they wanted freedom in the Western sense of maximum personal autonomy. Similarly, Martin Klein and Richard Roberts show that large numbers of slaves deserted in Guinea and the French Soudan (Klein, Ch. 6; Roberts, Ch. 9). Klein, however, believes that in French West Africa as a whole, although about 500,000 slaves left, the majority actually remained with or near their former owners (Klein 1986).

Wholesale flight, however, was only one tactic used by ex-slaves to

29. For a critique of revisionist views see Dumett and Johnson, Ch. 2.

gain control over their lives and labor, and even when they stayed with their former owners the end of slavery could have far-reaching social consequences. Thus Pollet and Winter argue that among the Soninke of the French Soudan the end of slavery led to a radical transformation of society by weakening the hierarchical principle of the family itself. This led to important changes in the structure and organization of the household, inheritance patterns, and strategies for social reproduction (Pollet and Winter 1972: 371, 394). Martin Chanock has shown that in parts of Central Africa the greatest impact of abolition was upon marriage. Slave marriages had given husbands, or their lineages, complete control over both the women and their progeny and had thus provided a source of dependents, particularly valuable in matrilineal societies, where kin groups could normally expand only at the rate their own women could produce children. Such marriages had also cemented the political power of expanding patrilineal ruling groups over their matrilineal subjects. The elimination of slavery, thus had far-reaching social and legal, as well as economic, ramifications. It caused confusion in male-female relations, threw property rights in children in doubt, and affected the judicial system by ending the transfer of people as compensation for crime (Chanock 1985: Ch. 9). The fact that most slaves at this period were women, most of whom had children they were presumably reluctant to abandon, demands that the impact of abolition should be argued in terms of its structural impact on lineages and families and their respective ideologies.

All the chapters in this volume address the impact of the end of slavery as far as their data permit. Our contributors include supporters of the traditional view that there was a smooth transition from slavery to freedom (the ambiguities of which will be discussed in the following section) and revisionists who hold that it resulted in a radical restructuring not only of relations of production, but of family structure, kinship relations, and strategies for the accumulation of wealth. The result of their research is to emphasize the difficulties of trying to generalize about an institution which varied greatly and the demise of which had a different impact everywhere.

Thus, Dumett and Johnson (Ch. 2) dealing directly with this historiographical debate in relation to the British territories which today form Ghana, accept McSheffrey's revisionist view that historians have relied too much on colonial records and too little on other, often very revealing, sources, particularly missionary reports. But, they show that these, too, have to be approached with the same skepticism, since missionaries and other nonofficial observers also had axes to grind. They demonstrate that in this one heterogeneous territory slavery took a number of forms; treatment and use varied and, therefore, abolition had a range of consequences.

They agree that there was a massive slave exodus in certain areas, but they believe the majority of slaves either stayed with their owners or established themselves nearby. They admit that some chiefs lost wealth, power, and prestige when many of their slaves left, but contend that chiefly power on the whole remained unbroken. In their view, therefore, the end of slavery in the Gold Coast was, as the traditionalists have painted it, one of the "quieter social revolutions of the late nineteenth and early twentieth centuries."

Kopytoff (Ch. 17) also takes issue with those who see abolition as precipitating political, economic, or social crises, since only a minority of slaves overall actually left their owners. For the majority, he believes, there was simply a reshuffling of the systems of dependency to eliminate the chattel slave and absorb ex-slaves into other types of dependency. He believes the end of slavery was a moment of disequilibrium, but one which left the principles of social structure intact. Thus, even ex-slaves who moved away established new ties of dependency and did not become autonomous individuals in the Western sense. On the other hand Hogendorn and Lovejoy (Ch. 13), Klein (Ch. 6), and Roberts (Ch. 9), who all deal with areas of mass desertion, believe as Ohadike (Ch. 15) does that the legal abolition of slavery produced crises or — if the disruption was not immediate — caused considerable changes over the course of the following decades. Deep disagreements thus remain even among our contributors.

Part of the problem is that few of the protagonists in this debate have actually defined what they mean by "crisis," "disruption," or "quiet social revolution." All agree that in some areas there were mass departures; all agree that in others most slaves stayed; all also agree that those who stayed renegotiated the terms of their dependence. What is less clear in the present state of research is whether the result of these negotiations changed relations to such an extent as to constitute a social revolution by introducing what were in effect fundamentally different relations of production, social reproduction, and dependence. The focus of the debate and future research must now be more carefully defined to describe and assess "disruption." A slave leaving an owner even to farm in a neighboring village, obviously had some impact on the owner's fortunes and economic and social strategies. A former slave who became rich, might, as McDougall (Ch. 12) argues, turn the world "topsy turvy," particularly as slaves were never merely units of labor, but integral elements in complex struggles for power, authority, and control (Cooper 1977: 111–25; Cooper 1979: 106–25). The inability to acquire slave wives and concubines had important repercussions for the expansion of lineages. The freeing of concubines may have caused shifts of influence within lineages affecting their children's inheritance rights as well as the rights of free-born wives. The outlawing of the transfer of people as compensation for crime introduced serious changes in the judicial system.

In fact, the end of slavery demanded a new set of strategies by new sets of actors in what may be seen in colonial Africa as part of a wider process of change in the relations of production and social reproduction contributing over time to class formation and class struggle. These processes will now be explored.

The Ambiguities of Freedom: Slaves and Owners in the Aftermath of Slavery

The transition from slave to free status, whether apparently smooth or patently disruptive, was always a complex and continuing process of negotiation, struggle, and adjustment. Notwithstanding the efforts of governments to control the process, the result was a patchwork quilt of different and changing labor and social arrangements, sometimes determined more by the initiatives of the slaves than by the actions of the administration or the owners. Thus, in the French Soudan and Guinea when slaves began leaving in 1905, officials tried to steer them into sharecropping arrangements in order to maintain production while respecting the "freedom" of the ex-slaves and the property rights of former owners (Roberts, Ch. 9; Klein, Ch. 6). However, their efforts were largely unsuccessful. Sharecropping, for instance, was feasible only where natural resources were scarce in relation to labor, or where access to such resources could be controlled. Thus it was possible in Zanzibar because the British upheld the former owners' rights over the clove trees, in Masina because the owners kept control over prime land, and in the southern Sahara because they controlled date palms. In such cases, slaves had little alternative but to accept forms of sharecropping. Elsewhere former slaves had more choice.

Freed slaves had three broad options. They could leave their former owners and move away; they could remain near them but sever ties to the extent that this was possible or desirable; or they could remain in their owners' households or villages but on different terms. None of these options gave them "freedom" in the sense of complete personal autonomy. Those who left had to find a niche in a new social group or reintegrate themselves into their former societies, while those who stayed had to redefine their relationships.

Most slaves had agricultural skills, but those who left faced a crucial period between departure and the first harvest in their new abode. They often had a long walk out of the area and then a lean time during which they might have to survive by hunting, foraging, scavenging, on charity, or by wage labor. Exactly how they survived is still a matter of conjecture (Klein 1986). To leave also often meant leaving behind family and friends, and in the early days it entailed the risk of reenslavement. Just these difficulties were probably sufficient to keep many from leaving.

One might assume that departure was simplest for those who remembered their homelands and who could return and be reintegrated into their own kin groups. In some cases this was so, but new research is casting doubts upon the extent to which they were actually welcomed by their kin, suddenly forced to share resources with long-gone relatives or persons they had sold for various reasons (Meillassoux 1986: 306–7; Hogendorn, research notes). Their return was also often actively discouraged by colonial administrators, either for fear of encouraging further flight, as in Northern Nigeria (Hogendorn and Lovejoy, Ch. 13), or for fear that returnees would not recognize the fragile authority of the colonial chiefs as in the French Soudan (Roberts, Ch. 9). Nevertheless many thousands left, often even before abolition, during the disorders of the conquest period, or when it became apparent that they could do so without fear of reenslavement.[30]

For those who moved away from their former owners but did not return to their homelands, the crucial variable was whether they could get access to land and other vital resources. The most fortunate found that new transport facilities and a boom in commodity markets allowed them to prosper as independent smallholders—to become a "reconstituted peasantry" (Mintz 1979: 219–26; Marshall 1985: 214–21). Thus, many of the former slaves of the Tubakayes of Guinea left their owners in 1908 and went to neighboring districts where chiefs offered them protection, land, and possibly seed (Klein, Ch. 6). Similarly ex-slaves, freed by murgu arrangements, successfully established themselves as autonomous farmers producing peanuts or cotton for export or food for an expanding local market in Northern Nigeria (Hogendorn and Lovejoy, Ch. 13). In the eastern sahel districts of the French Soudan some migrated to the Niger River and produced rice for a growing domestic market (Roberts, Ch. 9).

Some slaves and later ex-slaves sought protection in the expanding range of religious communities, which dotted the African landscape. Numbers of fugitive slaves on the Kenya coast, for instance, took refuge at the Church Missionary Society station at Rabai in the last decades of the nineteenth century and created a new community—the WaMisheni—who successfully inserted themselves into the regional economy (Herlehy and

30. Roberts, Ch. 9; Klein, Ch. 6; Hogendorn and Lovejoy, Ch. 13; Cooper 1980: 46–91; Chanock 1985: Ch. 9; Lovejoy 1986.

Morton, Ch. 8). Both Roman Catholic and other Protestant missions received fugitive and later freed slaves, and some Catholic missions systematically bought slaves to form the nucleus of their Christian communities (Klein 1986; Renault 1971, 1: 155ff.; Northrup, Ch. 16). Muslim brotherhoods also offered protection and access to land. In Italian Somaliland the dramatic expansion of the three Islamic brotherhoods in the first two decades of the twentieth century led to the creation of nearly a hundred agricultural villages which absorbed ex-slaves and fashioned them into new communities, differentiated less on the basis of former status and ethnic affiliations than on the degree of religious learning and commitment (Cassanelli, Ch. 10). The Mourides of Senegal probably owed a large measure of their economic success to former slaves, who joined them and established themselves as peanut farmers in Senegal (Cruise O'Brien 1971: 34–35, 58–59; Klein 1986).

Another option for ex-slaves leaving their owners was to join maroon (fugitive-slave) villages. Many ex-slaves of the Somali, for instance, joined maroon villages in the Juba Valley or on the lower Shabelle (Cassanelli, Ch. 10). Freed slaves also took refuge around the posts of the Congo Free State and in the French *villages de liberté*. Most tried not to stay long in these settlements under the wing of the colonial administration, where they were subject to extensive corvée labor, as indeed were those who went to villages of client cultivators attached to pastoral Somali lineages, from whom the Italians demanded labor (Bouche 1968: 118–20; Klein 1986; Roberts, Ch. 9; Cassanelli, Ch. 10).

A minority of ex-slaves found wage labor in the growing towns. But they often lived precariously, performing the most menial services and sometimes driven to crime or prostitution (Cassanelli, Ch. 10; Dumett and Johnson, Ch. 2; McDougall, Ch. 12). An exception were those educated at the many Christian missions which established themselves in Africa. They often became an elite group of clerical wage earners working for the administration, the missions, or capitalist businesses (for examples, see Herlehy and Morton, Ch. 8; Dumett and Johnson, Ch. 2). Rural wage labor also offered limited opportunities. But while wage labor was a major factor in enabling slaves in some areas, like Igboland, to depart (Ohadike, Ch. 15), it was hardly an option in remote Lasta (McCann, Ch. 11); and few ex-slaves found wage employment in, for example, Mauritania (McDougall, Ch. 12), the Belgian Congo (Northrup, Ch. 16), the French Soudan (Roberts, Ch. 9), or even in the more commercially oriented Gold Coast (Dumett and Johnson, Ch. 2). Similarly, only those slaves of the Bangwato who lived east of the railway and thus near European-owned farms were able to take this route to independence in the 1930s (Miers and Crowder, Ch. 5).

Ex-slaves who were artisans, such as weavers and blacksmiths, were often welcomed into established or new communities (Klein 1986; Roberts, Ch. 9). Others were able to break into occupations hitherto performed only by endogamous castes or monopolized by slave-owning ethnic groups (Barth 1969: 17–28). Thus, in the French Soudan, former slaves of the Maraka began to produce indigo-dyed cloth and those of the FulBe acquired cattle (Roberts 1987: Ch. 5).

The colonial military and police also recruited heavily among slaves and former slaves (Northrup, Ch. 16; Dumett and Johnson, Ch. 2; Echenberg 1986; 312–20; McSheffrey 1983). This was especially true of the Chikunda in Mozambique, who had been slave soldiers and officials at the core of Portuguese power on the estates (prazos) along the Zambezi. In the late nineteenth century, many had become mercenaries of warlords beyond Portuguese control, but when they were eventually conquered by the Portuguese, they were absorbed into the Portuguese forces and administration (Isaacman and Rosenthal, Ch. 7).

The second general option for freed slaves was to sever ties more or less with their former owners, but to remain in the region or even in the same villages where they had been slaves. This was the response of many slaves in, for example, Yorubaland, where land was easy to acquire (Hopkins 1973: 228), and in Guinea, where the former slaves of the Tubakayes simply stated that they were now working for themselves and did not even bother to move (Klein, Ch. 6). In the relatively fluid situation of the early colonial period, chiefs and district officers often welcomed newcomers, who enlarged their tax base. Many slaves simply moved a few miles to a new location but remained in the same area (Roberts, Ch. 9), and some retained social ties with their former owners. Since such movements may have escaped the notice of colonial administrators or missionaries, our contributors shed all too little light on them.

The last option was for ex-slaves to remain as part of their former owners' households, kin groups, or communities, and to use their new legal mobility to renegotiate their terms of dependency. Many did this with varying degrees of success.[31] This option was most likely to be chosen in situations where the choices for ex-slaves were most limited. In Lasta, for instance, a kin-based land tenure system, combined with the lack of opportunity to enter the urban wage-labor force or to get the oxen needed for farming, kept many ex-slaves tied to their owners' households

31. See, for instance, Hogendorn and Lovejoy, Ch. 13; Dumett and Johnson, Ch. 2; McDougall, Ch. 12; Roberts, Ch. 9; Klein, Ch. 6; Miers and Crowder, Ch. 5; Clark 1983: 62–82; Grace 1975: 249–53; Romero 1986: 501ff.

(McCann, Ch. 11). In Bechuanaland, the invasion of Batswana with their herds into the Basarwa's hunting grounds and water sources, and the Basarwa's own inability to get cattle, seed, and tools, forced many "freed" Basarwa herders to remain on the cattleposts of their former owners (Miers and Crowder, Ch. 5). In Sierra Leone, where the traditional authorities retained economic and social power, as late as 1956 many former slaves had to perform unpaid labor from time to time in return for the use of land and even of their houses (Grace 1975: 252–53).

Some categories of slaves such as household and court slaves, who had achieved relatively high worldly status, and second-generation, fully acculturated slaves remained because they were relatively content with their situation, or the alternatives were no better. They may have seen freedom as greater acceptance into the society or kin group (Kopytoff and Miers 1977: 73). One might expect this to be particularly true if slaveholdings were small and slaves were treated like dependent or junior kin and if abolition did not rupture their social bonds with their former owners. Women slaves for whom departure was likely to mean the loss of their children were also unlikely to leave. There are also recorded cases of slave parents who remained with their former owners but accumulated the means to buy the freedom of their children (McDougall, pers. comm.). In some cases slaves did not consider themselves free unless they had ransomed themselves: only this could confer freedom in their own eyes and those of their owners (Wright 1983: 260, 264; for references to many examples see Miers 1975: 304).

Colonial records certainly contain numerous examples of slaves who expressed no desire to leave their former owners (see, for example, Ohadike, Ch. 15). Further case studies are required, however, to establish a pattern for such cases. Continued dependence may have offered the officially freed a web of security, and in some cases social standing, in return for very minor tasks such as cooking at festivals and acknowledging their dependent status (Clark 1983: 78–79; Romero 1986: 510; Klein, Ch. 6). Moreover, owners, realizing that their slaves could now leave, probably treated them better than in the past. Some freed slaves, however, continued to internalize their dependency in the same ways as before emancipation and to perform even the most arduous and menial tasks for their former owners (Baldus 1977: 443–56; Meillassoux 1986: 307–9; Roberts, Ch. 9).

Estimating the proportion of slaves who took each of the three general options described above is fraught with difficulty. Statistical collection during the early colonial period was haphazard, officials often guessed at numbers, and colonial policies tended to push slaves into moving secretly to avoid administrators' attempts to control their movements as well as to escape taxation.[32] We cannot simply subtract the numbers estimated to have moved from the numbers estimated to have stayed and assume that the latter all remained with their former owners. Negative evidence is not sufficient to prove the size of this pool, and researchers must hold their sources, archival and oral alike, in healthy skepticism. In all cases, the end of slavery ushered in a new phase in the organization of labor and of social and political power. Former slaves responded differently to the opportunities and strains of emancipation. Their responses reflected their experiences as slaves, the economic opportunities of the colonial period, and the political and economic constraints on their geographic and social mobility.

The extent to which those slaves who left their owners exchanged one form of dependency for another remains to be extensively explored. Some of our contributors raise this issue. Herlehy and Morton argue that the ex-slaves of Rabai maintained their independence from the missionaries, unlike those in their mission communities, as well as from neighboring Mijikenda (Strayer 1978: 14–29; Ranger 1975: 9–10; Morton 1976: 283–313). The extent to which Muslim brotherhoods controlled their followers is the subject of debate (Klein 1986), and little is known of the workings of the Somali Sufi brotherhoods (tariqāt) (Cassanelli, Ch. 10). Former slaves who joined villages of client cultivators became little esteemed members of Somali corporate lineages; while those who joined independent villages founded by fugitive or ex-slaves found themselves in a subordinate position in communities strictly controlled by the earliest settlers (ibid.). Although the ending of slavery often had some "levelling effect" on former slaves and masters, it did not end all vestiges of the servile condition. Former slaves were often the first to be sent to perform forced labor for the colonial administration (Ohadike, Ch. 15). Those who returned to their kin groups presumably tried to reestablish their former relationships, but little is yet known about how their return contributed to the complex readjustment of kin ties and relations of dependence which took place during the colonial period.

Women Slaves and Freedom

It is particularly important to distinguish between the experiences of male and female slaves when dealing with the end of slavery. Women slaves faced the same difficulties as men on the road to emancipation, but their options were usually more limited because all women were in general

---

32. In Sierra Leone, for instance, no one could leave his chiefdom without paying a fee to the paramount chief (Grace 1975: 250).

subordinated to men, and slave women suffered under the double disability of being both female and slave (Wright 1975, 1983: 247; Robertson and Klein 1983: 5–12). On their own they could rarely achieve economic security. There is evidence that most slaves who left did so in family groups or as couples (see, for example, Wright 1983: 257), and that flight was more difficult for single women than for single men. Many may have stayed because their owners represented the best security they could expect at the time (see, for example, Robertson 1983: 230). Although many did leave (Romero 1986: 502ff.; Northrup, Ch. 16; Hogendorn and Lovejoy, Ch. 13), there are reported instances in which masters were less willing to let women go than men (McDougall, Ch. 12; Grace 1977: 423; Robertson 1983: 223–25; B. Marie Perinbam, pers. comm.). Colonial administrators often discouraged their departure for fear of upsetting domestic arrangements and because they tended to view women slaves, particularly concubines, as being similar to wives, who belonged with their husbands (Hogendorn and Lovejoy, Ch. 13; Robertson 1983: 230). Concubines, although always slaves, were not initially covered by the laws ending the legal status of slavery in either Northern Nigeria or the territories of the sultan of Zanzibar.[33] Muslim officials also opposed the departure of female slaves on moral grounds, arguing that they might become prostitutes (Romero 1986: 505).[34] Colonial officials were also less interested in emancipating women, since, unlike men, they were not usually directly recruited into the colonial labor force.

A woman might seek freedom through marriage to a free man (Ohadike, Ch. 15; Twaddle, Ch. 3; McDougall, Ch. 12; Klein 1986), but her owner, even if he or she agreed and accepted bridewealth, might retain rights to the woman's children. If a slave had been a concubine, her former master would certainly retain the rights over their children. In patrilineal African societies even free women who left their husbands usually had to give up rights to their children. There is also evidence that in some societies, particularly matrilineal ones, the loss of control over slave wives and their progeny was the most important result of abolition (Chanock 1985: Ch. 9). Women ex-slaves also sometimes found that their former owners competed with their husbands for their labor power, even in cases where bridewealth had been paid (Wright 1983: 265).

33. However, on the Kenya coast concubines could leave if they could show that they had been ill-treated (Romero 1986: 500). Similarly, in the Gold Coast, laws were passed allowing wives to leave their husbands for mistreatment (Robertson 1984: 239).

34. The argument that women might take to prostitution if allowed to leave was also used by colonial administrators opposing the freeing of female slaves and, it is to be noted, by Africans seeking to prevent free women from going into the wage-labor force (see Lovett 1986: 55).

More research is needed to assess the impact of abolition on women slaves and the extent to which those who remained with their former owners were able to renegotiate their terms of dependency. Hogendorn and Lovejoy (Ch. 13) suggest that the increased incidence of purdah in Northern Nigeria may have equalized the position of concubines vis-à-vis free women and reduced their desire to escape. However, although this certainly changed their daily lives, it did not affect their status under Muslim law, which gave free women important rights denied to slave women, particularly in questions of inheritance, property, and marriage. On the other side of the coin, the children of concubines were usually considered free, which would mitigate against their departure.

The fact that the majority of slaves were women (see Robertson and Klein 1983) and that women faced particular difficulties in securing emancipation and in finding security after they had been legally freed may be the reason that so many slaves stayed with their former owners. Moreover, transactions in females were easier to hide than dealings in males, and slavery and slave-dealing often continued for many years under the guise of marriage, or a man might ransom a woman slave through the courts simply to acquire her as a concubine (Klein and Roberts 1987; Hogendorn and Lovejoy, Ch. 13). Colonial courts were also used by owners and their heirs to get bridewealth or compensation for their former slaves (Wright 1983: 264–66).

Slave Children and Freedom
Further research is also needed into the effects of emancipation on children. In cases where colonial laws declared that all slaves born after a certain date were free, some children were liberated before their parents. Our contributors throw little light on the practical effects of such laws. But there is evidence that some owners, while allowing adult males to depart, tried to retain the children, as well as the women (McDougall, Ch. 12; Grace 1977: 423; Perinbem, pers. comm.). In Central Africa the loss of control over the children of slave women was often crucial to the power and wealth of a lineage, and claims to such children proliferated in courts of law (Chanock 1985: Ch. 9). It also seems clear that as adult slaves became more difficult to obtain, as well as to retain against their will, so new enslavement was in many areas limited to children, who were more easily kidnapped, controlled, and acculturated (for examples, see Ohadike, Ch. 15; Miers 1975: 296–97). Thus in the 1920s, little girls obtained in Adamawa by dealers were kept for a year or more, during which time they were well treated and were taught Hausa, before being smuggled into Kano. A similar traffic between western Ethiopia and southern Sudan, mainly in girls, was suppressed by the British only in the late

1920s (Miers 1975: 296–97). The enslavement of children on a small scale continued right through the colonial period. As late as 1966 the case of a child kidnapped in Algeria by her father's former owner and taken to Mauritania to tend his herds, so that his own children could attend school, was reported to the United Nations Economic and Social Questions Commission (Miers interview: Jacob Oleol, 20 October 1984, Geneva). Child slaves could also be passed off as adopted children or as wards and, in the case of girls, as young brides (Grace 1975: 206–8; Robertson 1983: 230; Klein and Roberts 1987; Miers, research notes).

Slave-Owners and Freedom

Most contributors have concentrated on the experiences of former slaves. Yet the end of slavery was also a period of crisis or adjustment for their owners. For most owners, with the possible exception of those with large herds or many kin, slaves were their most significant capital asset. In virtually all the cases presented in this volume, slaveholding both reflected and engendered social change and struggles for political and economic power. Among the Igbo it led to social stratification (Ohadike, Ch. 15). Among the Bangwato of Bechuanaland, control over Basarwa slave herders helped expand the cattle-post economy and played a part in leading to the rise of aristocratic status among those who controlled cattle, water sources, and Basarwa (Miers and Crowder, Ch. 5). In the highlands of Angola, slave-owning led to social differentiation among the Ovimbundu and enabled them to contribute to the boom in commodity production in the early twentieth century (Heywood, Ch. 14). Among the Maraka of the Western Sudan and Tubakayes of Guinea, slavery had led to a profound transformation of the organization of work and to the ideological degradation of manual work (Klein, Ch. 6; Roberts 1981a: 190–91).

The degree to which the end of slavery brought about comparable changes depended on the role and importance of slaves and the ability of owners to maintain their privileges. Some were able to use the colonial courts to secure compensation for the loss of their slaves (Wright 1983: 264–65). Owners whose slaves left, however, often had to make radical readjustments. Thus in Guinea and the French Soudan many former owners were obliged to work in the fields themselves, sullying their hands for the first time in generations. French administrators welcomed this addition to the productive labor force of men who had formerly been engaged in war, politics, and trade, and women who had enjoyed aristocratic leisure. In many cases the end of slavery led to increased exploitation of family labor: wives, children, and junior kin became the new "captive" labor of household heads (Roberts, Ch. 9).

One of the features of slavery in some societies was that slaves of one gender could be made to do work normally exclusively performed by the other gender. Free women, therefore, had been among the prime bene-factors of slave labor. Once their slaves left, they were often forced to work in the fields. In Buganda, where the end of slavery coincided with the conversion of many people to Christianity and the introduction of monogamy, Christian women were particularly hard hit by the simul-taneous loss of slave labor and the labor of junior wives and concubines (Twaddle, Ch. 3). Interestingly, in some communities established by freed slaves, the women continued, at least for awhile, to perform men's work just as they had done in bondage (Roberts, Ch. 9). Much further research is needed before we can assess the various ways in which the end of slav-ery altered conditions of family labor, marriage patterns, and family and household composition for both former owners and former slaves, and before we can make distinctions between the effects on male and female owners and slaves.

Not all owners parted with their slaves unwillingly. For instance, in the kingdom of Wuli in Senegambia, slaveholders responded to overseas commodity demand in the nineteenth century by acquiring more slaves and having them grow peanuts instead of food. This was possible while the kingdom was strong and able to appropriate food from its neighbors as tribute or booty, but when it began to disintegrate on the eve of colo-nial conquest, the cost of feeding slaves rose. Owners then turned to cheaper and more flexible arrangements with migrant ("strange") farm-ers, many of whom doubtless were newly freed slaves who had left their owners in other areas (Weil 1984: 110–11). Colonial taxation policy fur-ther weakened the logic of slaveholding (as it had in Northern Nigeria), and by the 1930s owners in Wuli were dismissing their remaining slaves.

The colonial period thus opened new opportunities for the ex-slaves and posed new challenges for former owners. The end of slavery, however, rarely gave either of them full freedom to define new labor relationships, for the colonial states did not hesitate to recruit labor directly for their own needs and, sometimes directly and sometimes indirectly, for the capi-talist sector of the economy, which they promoted and nurtured.

The Persistence of Unfree Labor: Forced Labor and Pawning

Three factors combined to prevent the emergence of a completely free labor market. First, the colonial states took steps to produce a nonmarket supply of cheap labor with which to build a viable colonial enterprise. This entailed mobilizing labor to build infrastructure and for the colo-nial capitalist sector. Cheap labor was especially needed during the for-mative period, when armies of porters and builders were required to supply the colonial forces and construct the roads and railways linking coast and interior. During these early years all the colonial powers used slaves and former slaves in some capacity. In Ubangi-Shari, fugitive slaves were conscripted and were able to use part of their wages to redeem themselves (Cordell, Ch. 4). In the Soudan, the French settled fugitive slaves at strategic points along the railway (Roberts, Ch. 9). In Angola, slaves and ex-slaves helped build the Benguela railway (Heywood, Ch. 14). In the Congo Free State, "liberated" slaves were settled in villages to farm for the administration or were recruited into the army (Northrup, Ch. 16). In Mozambique, Nigeria, and French West Africa, they were also an important element in colonial armies (Isaacman and Rosenthal, Ch. 7; Hogendorn and Lovejoy, Ch. 13; Echenberg 1975: 171–72; 1986). But as the colonial rulers secured their preliminary objectives—conquest, pacification, and the construction of initial infrastructure—so this pool of labor evaporated as many former slaves renegotiated ties with their former owners, reestablished themselves as peasants, joined religious and other communities, or became petty traders, subsistence farmers, or urban laborers.

Faced with a decline in easily coercible labor and unwilling to raise wage levels, the colonial rulers turned to what in Northern Nigeria was called political labor (Mason 1978: 56–57). This was not supplied by the market but by administrators, who ordered the chiefs to send the required number of workers. These forced laborers were sometimes minimally paid or not paid at all. Such labor was initially used for private as well as public purposes—to supply European-owned farms or plantations and other capitalist-sector ventures (see, for example, Clayton and Savage 1974: Chs. 2, 4; Clarence-Smith 1979: 32–34; Perrings 1979: Chs. 1, 5; Freund 1981: 137–51). In the worst cases, those conscripted had to supply their own food and were forced to work far from home (see, *inter alia*, Ohadike, Ch. 15; Twaddle, Ch. 3; Heywood, Ch. 14; Northrup, Ch. 16).

In some areas those called upon to supply forced labor were able to shield themselves temporarily by sending slaves. Thus the Ovimbundu, themselves engaged in profitable peasant agriculture, continued to acquire slaves in the first two decades of this century to meet Portuguese demands for labor for the European sector in Angola, as well as for São Tomé and Príncipe (Heywood, Ch. 14). In the Mauritanian Adrar, colonial needs were met by the enterprise of a client of slave descent, who also acquired and used slaves himself (McDougall, Ch. 12). However, as the supplies of slaves dried up with the decline of slave-raiding and -trading, and as slaves asserted their new rights to resist exploitation, so the free were drawn more and more into the colonial efforts to build up a disciplined and available labor pool.

The second factor preventing the emergence of a free wage-labor force was that most Africans had access to land or livestock even if only as dependents. As long as they had other means of support, many were unwilling to sell their labor power for the wages offered in the capitalist sector, which had to compete in a world market already considerably specialized. Colonial administrations, faced with the parsimony of metropolitan governments, were equally unable to pay attractive wages. Hence, as time went by, they used a number of devices, besides outright crude forced labor, to provide cheap labor for both the private and public sectors (Roberts 1981b: 318–21).

These devices included raising taxes beyond the amount Africans could earn from cash-crop production; keeping down the price paid for African agricultural produce, as in Angola (Heywood, Ch. 14), forbidding Africans to grow the more lucrative cash crops, as in Kenya, or allowing them to sell crops only to concession companies at whatever price the companies set, as in parts of the Belgian Congo, French Equatorial Africa, and Mozambique; making taxes payable in cash which could be earned only in the capitalist sector; and forcing — or at least pressuring — Africans into work contracts, as, for example, the British did in Zanzibar (Cooper 1980: 84–92), the French in Guinea (Fall 1986), the Portuguese in Angola (Heywood, Ch. 14), and the Italians in Somaliland (Cassanelli, Ch. 10). In some colonies, particularly those with European settlers, the colonial powers resorted to large-scale alienation of African land to the point that numbers of Africans had to seek paid jobs in the local rural or urban sectors to go farther afield as migrant labor. They also limited African access to higher-paid jobs and restricted their personal and occupational mobility by pass laws, as in South Africa and other settler colonies. Moreover, they sheltered European agriculture from African competition by such means as building roads and railways into areas of European farming, as in Kenya and Southern Rhodesia, and restricting African access to markets as in Angola and South Africa.

The need for cheap labor in the public and capitalist sectors of the economy conflicted with the colonial desire to increase African agricultural production. Thus, when the French built the Congo-Ocean railway in the 1920s, much man power was siphoned away from the peasant economy (Coquery-Vidrovitch 1985: 360–61). Compulsory rubber and copal collection in King Leopold's Congo (see, *inter alia*, Northrup, Ch. 16) led to a crisis in the colonial state's ability to balance the capitalist demand for wage labor and the concessionaires' demand for peasant production. Because neither the public nor the private sector paid attractive prices for labor or crops, some colonial administrations and concession companies imposed production quotas for cash and food crops on each village (see, *inter alia*, Vail and White 1980; Northrup, Ch. 16). These exactions led many Africans to complain that under colonial rule the free were worse off than slaves had been in precolonial times (Twaddle, Ch. 3; Heywood, Ch. 14; Ohadike, Ch. 15) or that they were now all slaves of the colonial chiefs (Northrup, Ch. 16).

Forced labor in its many forms reflected the weakness of the labor market, the peculiar conditions of colonial capitalism, and the fact that Africans had alternative sources of support to wage labor (Van Zwanenberg 1975: 104–6; Roberts 1981b: 318–19; Iliffe 1983). The issue of forced labor was raised at the League of Nations Temporary Slavery Commission of 1924–1925, and the resulting Slavery Convention of 1926 forbade its use except for paid work on local public works (Miers 1986). In 1930 the International Labor Organization negotiated a convention forbidding forced labor, except for limited public purposes, as well as the forced cultivation of export crops. It also condemned the other devices to generate cheap wage labor.

However, even when adequate laws were passed, they were often ignored. Thus, the British resorted to forced labor during the Second World War, when African mining and agricultural products were in great demand (see, *inter alia*, Freund 1981: 136ff.). The Belgian Congo, which did not ratify the convention until 1944, gave up crude forced labor in the late 1920s, but forced crop growing, justified as "educational," continued into the 1950s (Northrup, Ch. 16). The French continued to pressure Africans into accepting labor contracts (Fall 1986; Touré 1984), and in spite of a further convention against forced labor in 1957, they tried to impose compulsory cotton growing in parts of Ubangi-Shari as late as 1958 (Cordell, Ch. 4). The most persistent use of forced labor was in the Portuguese colonies, where Africans were forced to work for months at a time for little or no wages, either for the government or the private capitalist sector by a combination of tax and labor laws. By the 1940s Portuguese policies had impoverished the Ovimbundu and driven freeborn and ex-slave alike increasingly into the labor force (Heywood, Ch. 14). The Portuguese ended forced labor and crop growing only in the 1960s after Ghana complained to the International Labor Organization that Portugal was contravening the 1957 convention.

The third factor inhibiting the development of a wage-labor force was that Africans, forbidden to acquire slaves, resorted to pawning. This was a precolonial method of raising credit. A pawn, unlike a slave, remained a member of his or her lineage of birth, and hence was neither kinless nor the property of the creditor. He or she was held by the creditor for an indefinite period in return for a loan. Pawns lived in the creditors' households' and in some cases the work they performed was considered interest on the debts. The pawn was redeemed when the debt was paid. The institution worked in many different ways in different areas and changed over time.[35] Pawns were usually better treated than slaves, particularly if the creditor took them in order to get the political support of their kinsmen (Oroge 1985: 76–86). Female pawns often ended by marrying into the creditors' households' and the brideprice went towards cancellation of the debts. In general pawns were distinct from slaves, since they had kin to protect them. Their servitude was theoretically temporary, but if the debt was not repaid it could become hereditary or they might be sold into slavery.

Pawning was widely used in times of disaster and saved the lives of many people. For instance, children were extensively pawned by their parents during the Yoruba wars of the nineteenth century in order to transfer them temporarily to the safety of the households of the rich and powerful (ibid.: 76–79). Pawning was also used to raise the means to pay bridewealth, fines, or compensation for crime, and by the ambitious to acquire trade goods or, in some societies, to raise their social status by taking titles.

The system was obviously open to abuse. For example, among the Ovimbundu in the 1940s, the institutions of pawnship and slavery merged into one. A desperate family, in a bad year, might pawn a child either to a rich Mbundu or a Portuguese merchant in order to pay colonial taxes, and then, unable to repay the debt, would have to pawn more children in a vicious circle of indebtedness from which it was often impossible to escape (Heywood, Ch. 14). Among the Igbo, children were widely pawned to raise the money for poll tax as late as the 1930s (Ohadike, Ch. 15). As slave-dealing declined, pawning enabled wealthy men to increase the number of their dependents and to acquire extrafamilial labor (Oroge 1985: 96). As the spread of commercial capitalism encouraged more lavish spending and with it greater indebtedness, the supply of pawns increased (Dumett and Johnson, Ch. 2), particularly in West Africa during the Great Depression of the 1930s (Klein and Roberts 1987).

Pawning was a problem for colonial administrations because it lay in the vague middle ground between slavery, which they were committed to end, and African institutions, with which they preferred not to interfere. Pawning was also hard to detect because, in the case of girls, it could be disguised as marriage. Thus in times of famine people might give their daughters to neighboring peoples for very low bridewealth and then try to redeem them later. The British, dealing with cases in the Mandara

35. Miers 1975: 140ff.; and examples in Miers and Kopytoff 1977: particularly Holsoe: 289; Miller: 222ff.; Douglas 1964: 301–12; A. N. Klein 1981: Ch. 6; Oroge 1985.

Mountains, where such brides changed hands frequently, regarded these transfers as tantamount to slaving, but the parties to the transactions maintained they were betrothals in accordance with their customs (Miers 1975: 298). Similar cases occurred elsewhere (Morton 1972: 412–13; Uchendu 1977: 126; Grace 1977: 422). Humanitarians, antislavery societies, and the growing French women's movement attacked pawning and forced marriages, and pressured colonial administrators to deal with these issues. Some responded by establishing rates of interest and counting the work of the pawn towards the extinction of both the debt and the interest (Klein and Roberts 1987). Most officials, however, did little about it.

All too little is known about pawning, but the studies that exist show that it reemerged in force, for instance, in the French territories during the Great Depression (Klein and Roberts 1987), continued in the Gold Coast into the 1930s (Dumett and Johnson, Ch. 2), and supported the colonial economy in Angola in the 1940s (Heywood, Ch. 14). In Southern Nigeria, where the British outlawed successively the pawning of children, the marrying of girls under 13, and finally in 1938 all pledging of labor as interest on loans, prosecutions for pawning continued as late as 1949, and there were still "faint echoes" of it in 1975 (Ohadike, Ch. 15; Oroge 1985: 99). It is clear that pawning provided former owners and other creditors — including former slaves and Portuguese businessmen (Heywood, Ch. 14) — with opportunities to assert or reassert their control directly over certain forms of labor, particularly that of women and children.

Some of our contributors mention the greater availability of wage labor by the middle decades of this century. Thus Dumett and Johnson (Ch. 2) point to the increased use of migrant labor from the north in the Gold Coast, replacing both slaves and pawns in the indigenous economy, and Twaddle (Ch. 3) mentions the arrival of migrants from Ruanda-Urundi in Buganda during the 1920s to produce cash crops for Ganda employers. Nevertheless, a sizable labor force totally divorced from the means of production had not emerged in sub-Saharan Africa by the time the colonial period ended. The long persistence of forced labor for the capitalist sector and of unfree labor in the indigenous economy reflects the fact that capitalist penetration had neither divorced producers from the means of production nor marginalized their subsistence production sufficiently to generate a sizable proletariat.

Conclusion

The end of slavery in Africa provides a lens through which to examine the social experiences of the early colonial period in ways that studies

48   I. INTRODUCTION

of resistance, collaboration, colonial policy, and labor history have so far
been unable to do.

The end of slavery and the establishment of new economic and social
systems clearly emerge as long and complex processes, which up to now
have been little understood because of the relative paucity of information. We have tried to remedy this by providing case studies specifically
focussed on this subject, by pointing out major areas of academic disagreement, by suggesting new lines of approach, and by demarcating important areas for further research.

Our case studies show that all the colonial states were forced by metropolitan and international pressures to subscribe to antislavery ideology,
which was part of the ideological justification for the European conquest
of Africa and, indeed, of capitalism itself. Antislavery ideology had been
popularized at a time when little was known about African (or indeed
any non-Western) slavery, and was based on the premise that slavery was
everywhere the highly oppressive system practiced by Europeans in the
New World and in certain other colonies.[36] As the colonial rulers came
to know more about African slavery during the nineteenth century, their
image of it came to be based on another misconception—that it was a
mild form of servitude.[37] Even abolitionists in Britain, the most active
exponents of antislavery ideology, generally accepted the proposition
that African slavery was usually benign, and they were initially willing
to see the attack on slavery concentrated on the elimination of its cruelest
features—the enslavement, buying and selling of slaves, and, in a few
societies, their use as human sacrifice. Slavery itself could be tolerated
until such time as it could be eliminated without causing political resistance and social and economic dislocation, or until it withered away
through natural attrition as new enslavement ended.

This view of a benign African slavery was used to justify the very
gradual approach to emancipation in colonial Africa. Gradualism was
dictated by the military weakness of the colonial states, fearful of provoking the resistance of elites, of causing a decline in agricultural production, and of upsetting African social structures; for slavery was
embedded in webs of personal dependency and property relationships
about which the colonial administrators knew little. They soon realized
that their aim—the economic exploitation of Africa—did not require mass
liberation of slaves. Some believed that abolition would lead to a decline

36. American slavery took many forms, but what matters is the image in the public
mind of the time.
37. We know that African slavery ranged from mild to harsh, but what matters is what
officials and the public believed.

in production and even cause hardship to the slaves, as it had in parts of the Caribbean.[38] The result, as we have seen, was a pragmatic approach to the problem by colonial administrations, juggling intermittent metropolitan and international demands to end slavery against their own desire not to cause social upheavals, which they could not control. The government of Ethiopia performed a similar balancing act between the need to conciliate international opinion and the necessity to retain the support of local elites.

Although all the European colonial states tackled slavery slowly, their policies varied widely even in different territories of the same colonial power. Individual administrators also interpreted, bent, and even disregarded their own laws as they deemed necessary. Moreover, colonial policies changed over time, as administrators came to understand the African scene better or pursued short-term goals of their own (see, for example, Miers and Crowder, Ch. 5). Thus, although all the colonial states, as well as Ethiopia and Liberia, eventually passed laws against slavery, former slaves could not assert their "freedom" unless the laws were combined with economic policies and changes.

Therefore, while we may say that Britain applied the Indian model rather than the Caribbean model for abolition in the Gold Coast, this merely tells us that slavery ceased to exist as a legal status. To know what this meant to the slave, we have to know how the antislavery policies were enforced, how they were combined with land tenure policies (which determined whether and on what terms ex-slaves had access to land), whether the taxation system discriminated against large slaveholdings, and whether colonial policies eventually eliminated the material differences between slaves and freeborn by forcing them all into the wage-labor economy. Vitally important to the reconstruction of the postemancipation era was how the legal system worked. It mattered little if slavery was not recognized by British courts, if claims over slaves were dealt with in Muslim courts or "native courts," if officials returned fugitives to their masters in their executive rather than judicial capacity, if they determined the price for the ransoming of slaves, or if chiefs were given powers to control personal mobility, which could be used to prevent slaves from leaving.[39]

It was in the protection of freed slaves that the colonial states, as well as Ethiopia, failed most obviously. At the outset they usually protected

38. This view was endorsed by African owners (see, for example, Miers and Crowder, Ch. 5).

39. Miers 1975: 302–3; Chanock 1985: Ch. 9; Wright 1983: 261ff.; Grace 1975: 250; Hogendorn and Lovejoy, Ch. 13; Miers and Crowder, Ch. 5.

the rights of owners over those of slaves, and in some areas, notably parts of Mauritania, slavery continued throughout the colonial period. This was particularly true in the case of women, because their work was not only highly labor intensive but increasingly vital to the domestic economy as more and more men went into the wage-labor force (McDougall, pers. comm.; Robertson 1983: 223). But colonial policies were only one factor in the end of slavery.

The historiographical debate as to whether or not the transition from slavery to freedom was highly disruptive or was one of the "quieter social revolutions" is not resolved in this volume, but our case studies bring us a step nearer to an understanding of the issues involved and suggest possible approaches for future research. Our contributors show that, in some areas, many thousands of slaves left their owners, sometimes suddenly and sometimes over a period of time. They also make clear that, at the level of economic performance and the maintenance of public order, the predictions of administrators that abolition would lead to massive economic and social disruption and political resistance were not realized. They show that in some cases slave-owners found other labor, or they and their families performed the work previously done by slaves. In other cases freed slaves, who broke all ties with their former owners, simply established themselves as autonomous farmers, often in neighboring areas, and continued to produce as before, but on their own account.

Attempts to quantify the proportion of former slaves who left are hampered by lack of precise census data. Demographic research now in progress will doubtless throw more light on this. But we would suggest that a fruitful line of inquiry to help us understand the full ramifications of the end of slavery would be to focus on the new arrangements made by those who stayed. Some of our contributors see these readjustments as part of ongoing struggles, often localized and subtle, which completely changed the relationships between slaves and owners. From this they deduce that, whether ex-slaves stayed or left, the transition was not smooth and led to the emergence of completely different relations of production and dependency (see, for example, Roberts, Ch. 9). Others see the transition as relatively smooth, other than in exceptional cases, and believe that emancipation did not undermine the dominant position of the slaveholding elites (see, for instance, Dumett and Johnson, Ch. 2).

This leads us to a consideration of the meaning of freedom to Africans. Here too there is no consensus. Kopytoff (Ch. 17) argues that freedom in the Western sense — the severance of all ties of dependence — was meaningless in many sub-Saharan African societies. Instead freedom was to remain a dependent but on one's own terms, to establish new relations of dependency elsewhere, or, in the best of worlds, to establish a new group with dependents of one's own. For Kopytoff the end of slavery was a moment of disequilibrium when the most marginal slaves departed, causing some complex readjustments but not undermining the principles of community organization and reproduction. His interpretation of the evidence of emancipation in Africa reaffirms his view that Africans considered the security of dependency necessary and desirable, and that the safest course for ex-slaves was simply to remain with their former owners and renegotiate terms. These new terms might have merely bound ex-slaves to salute their former owners in public or to cook for them at festivals (Klein 1986; Clark 1983: 78–79), but it kept them within the protective network of the owning group. Other contributors, however, including Roberts (Ch. 9), Klein (Ch. 6), Hogendorn and Lovejoy (Ch. 13), believe that many former slaves sought freedom by completely separating themselves from their former masters.

Our efforts to explore the consequences of the end of slavery have been bedevilled by lack of data, compounded by the faulty perceptions of administrators, who only slowly penetrated below the surface of African societies as they began to deal with disputes about control over people often arising out of claims to slaves (see, for example, McDougall, Ch. 12; Chanock 1985: Ch. 9; Robertson 1983). A further difficulty is that scholars working on widely different societies have a tendency to argue from the particular to the general. But many colonial possessions, like Nigeria and the Northern Territories of the Gold Coast, were composed of heterogeneous and complex societies, where the end of slavery took many different forms. We suggest that the main lesson of this volume is that we need to treat all evidence with skepticism, and resist the temptation to try to generalize from the few examples we now have.

In order to reach the next stage in this ongoing debate we must qualify and refine the terms we use to understand the complex phenomena of social, economic, political, and ideological readjustment. We must recognize the wide range of variables which determined the reactions and responses of both slaves and owners.

At present we know all too little about the new terms of dependency negotiated by ex-slaves who remained in the households or communities of their former owners and how these arrangements changed over time. We need to know more about the sharecropping and tenancy arrangements, as well as how ex-slaves fitted into changing power structures, how emancipation changed strategies for social reproduction and how it influenced ritual life. We need to know, especially where large numbers of slaves left their masters, how they survived and established themselves in new areas. We need to know how the fate of freed women differed from that of freed men.[40] We need to find out the extent to which, for those ex-slaves who remained, full assimilation was easier for women. In some societies ex-slave women could lose the stigma of slavery by marriage to freeborn men (Ohadike, Ch. 15); in others they also felt the need to repay their purchase price (Wright 1983); in still others such marriages were not possible. During the colonial period the labor burden on many women increased as more men were drawn into wage labor, and we need to know whether or not the burden was greatest on women of slave descent and how perceptions of and about women changed. Among the Tonga in Nyasaland, for instance, Margot Lovett found that freeborn women began to consider themselves to be the equivalent of slaves, because the departure of men as migrant wage labor not only increased their work load but changed male attitudes towards their wives, whom they came to regard, like slaves, as economic investments (Lovett 1986).

Among the questions for further research is the degree to which emancipation led to a levelling process and its impact on class formation. Thus in Lasta, former slaves became part of a growing rural proletariat composed also of the freeborn poor (McCann, Ch. 11). Similarly among the Ovimbundu, Portuguese policies impoverished ex-owners and ex-slaves (Heywood, Ch. 14), and the distinction between them also narrowed among the Igbo (Ohadike, Ch. 15), the Maraka (Roberts, Ch. 9), and the Tubakayes (Klein, Ch. 6). From the Lagos hinterland to the Somali coast, we have examples of former owners ruined by the loss of their slaves. In other cases, particularly where indirect rule was practiced, owners such as the Hausa-Fulani elites, the nobles of Mauritania, the chiefs of the Gold Coast and Sierra Leone, and the Tswana rulers retained their political influence and social and economic dominance. Moreover, where servile groups were ethnically identifiable, like the Basarwa or Bakgalagadi in Bechuanaland, upward mobility was difficult. In many societies marriages between persons of free and slave descent are rare.

Slave origin does not necessarily imply economic or political deprivation in Africa today. Some descendants of Igbo slaves are now more affluent than the children of the freeborn (Ohadike, Ch. 15). They prospered, like the descendants of those slaves and ex-slaves who went to Christian missions in Kenya, because they had early access to Western education and skilled employment. Similarly, the Chikunda, who joined the Portu-

40. Some of our contributors see the end of slavery as having had a levelling effect on women by decreasing the disabilities of female slaves (Ohadike, Ch. 15; Hogendorn and Lovejoy, Ch. 13). Others believe that they suffered more than freeborn women, because slave men were the ones driven into wage labor first (McDougall, pers. comm.).

guese forces and administration, prospered under colonial rule (Isaacman and Rosenthal, Ch. 7). The most striking success story in this volume is that of Hammody, a Mauritanian client, who became not simply
the owner of slaves, but a creditor of nobles (McDougall, Ch. 12). In parts
of Africa today slave origins are no barrier to the holding of high office,
although elsewhere the hint of such descent is enough to ruin the chances
of a candidate. Slave origins are still particularly important in matters
of inheritance, marriage, control over children, and in issues of ritual
and qualifications for religious office.

We need to know about the impact of emancipation on household formation and marriage strategies, and how the loss of slaves as property
affected the general change in concepts of property and rights to property which accompanied colonial rule. One of the great problems is that
slavery declined in the aftermath of military conquest and during the
period of colonial rule, which brought changes in the political economy
and in the structure of the economy. Conquest and colonial rule also
brought the ideological challenges of Western ideas of the rights and
place of the individual in society and of Christianity. The difficulty is
to isolate the results of the end of slavery from the more general results
of European rule. Thus we must ask whether the wider readjustments
and renegotiations which took place at this time did not affect entire
households, kin groups, and communities — slave and free. Did sons and
daughters, wives, concubines, adopted relatives, and all other dependents also seek to redefine the nature of their participation in these social
units? Did the end of slavery and the implantation of colonialism lead,
as Pollet and Winter found among the Soninke, to the breakdown of
household relations, encourage household fission, and bring about new
relationships of work and reproduction? Or did such changes take place
as the result of the new economic opportunities presented to junior kinsmen by the economic expansion of colonial rule independently of the
end of slavery? We need to consider how far the spread of Christianity
and capitalist ideologies of private property and individual freedom not
only led to increasing commercialization of land and labor, but also affected the way marriage partners and lineage members perceived their
roles towards each other and changed their conception of property and
rights to dispose of it.[41] We need to consider how far the emancipation
of slaves was merely the tip of complex social processes set in train by
colonial rule itself.

We also need to sort out the results of the end of slavery from the de-

---

41. Hay 1982; Chanock 1985: Ch. 9; Mann 1982, 1985: Ch. 6; Hopkins 1980; Lance
1985.

velopment of the other forms of labor, some of which coexisted with slavery before the colonial period but greatly increased in scope under colonialism. Wage labor and slave labor coexisted for many years, and slaves were often the first wage laborers. Indentured labor was often simply a disguised form of slave labor, and migrant labor over the long run often became a form of indentured labor. Wage labor, instead of freeing the worker, often created new dependencies and was often more exploitative than slavery. Although our contributors have begun to provide information on this, more research is surely needed.

To put the end of slavery into its complete context, fuller use of certain types of historical sources should prove particularly valuable. Our contributors show the importance of well-used records such as mission archives, tax records, and, of course, oral sources. Among a variety of relatively untapped sources, one of the most revealing has been court records. These may provide the most detail on the actual social experience and conflict, since they capture real-life events, but they deal mainly with cases too intractable to be solved without recourse to the courts. The hundreds of thousands of private negotiations between parties which were settled without litigation went unrecorded. Court records are, nevertheless, extraordinarily revealing as to the issues which concerned Africans, and they also show how colonial officials reacted to the thousands of cases which reached them, and often tested to the limit their power to comprehend African attitudes (see, for example, Chanock 1985: Ch. 9; Wright 1983).[42]

The End of Slavery in Comparative Perspective and as an International Issue

A comparison between the end of slavery in Africa and in other areas of the world is beyond the scope of this volume, but it is an important subject for future research. Abolition in Africa was part of the same worldwide set of changes in the organization of production that emanated from the spread of the world capitalist economy. In all slaveholding societies, emancipation brought complex changes in the economic and social order and in the dominant ideologies of power and control. In relatively few areas did the end of slavery initiate abrupt changes in production. In most cases, however, it led to changes in how land and labor were controlled (Bolland 1981). From the standpoint of former

42. Legal records have been used in Africa for studies of property transactions (Cooper 1980), for women's history (Hay and Wright 1982; Mann 1982; Wright 1983; Robertson 1983), and for studies of law and the political and economic history of colonialism (Chanock 1985; Christelow 1985a), but they have only rarely been effectively used for the study of changing labor relationships.

slaves, the "progression toward freedom was circuitous and uneven" (Mintz 1985: 273).

At present we know a great deal more about slavery, including slave cultures, fertility, and demography, and about the form and results of abolition in the United States, in Brazil, and in parts of the Caribbean than we do about other areas of the world, including Asia and the Middle East; and we still have many unanswered questions about Africa. Some comparisons, however, may be drawn at this point between slavery and emancipation in Africa and in the Americas in order to point out areas for future research.

In both regions slavery took a number of forms in the sense that individual slaves were used in many different tasks and some were more privileged and held positions of greater responsibility than others. Although slaves in the Americas worked in a whole series of nonplantation contexts, ranging from independent artisans to factory workers, the most important use for slaves was as plantation labor. In contrast, plantation slavery was relatively rare on the African mainland. It was more common on the offshore islands,[43] but the proportion of slaves working on plantations was overall comparatively small.[44] The reasons for this — among them epidemiological, demographic, and agronomic — have still to be explored.

African slaveholdings were in general also smaller, and the differentiation in terms of life style between slaves and owners was usually slighter than in the New World, in spite of the fact that many American slaves lived and worked side by side with their owners and some African slaves lived in villages apart from the free. Discipline was usually less rigorous, and social mobility, at least between generations, was also higher. Manumission was more frequent in Africa, where few societies had the power to keep large numbers of people in permanent subordination. Furthermore, in Africa a few slaves held positions of power and influence. In both Africa and the Americas slaves were valued for their productive capacity and as prestige items. However, in the Americas, slaves were not valued as the kin group resource they were in Africa, nor for direct use as currency, or for payment of tribute or judicial compensation. Nor were large numbers of dependents central to political power.

Both in Africa and the Americas masters were forced to free their slaves by government action. In the case of the United States and Cuba, emancipation was the result of bitter civil war. In Haiti it followed a slave sei-

---

43. These include Zanzibar, Pemba, São Tomé, Príncipe, and Fernando Po.
44. For examples, see Cooper 1977: 1–20; Lovejoy 1979, 1983: 8ff.; Roberts 1980: 173–76; Sundiata, forthcoming; Duffy 1969.

zure of power. In some cases, such as Brazil, it was the result of international pressures and a growing conviction that slavery was an anachronism in the modern world (Conrad 1972: 70ff.). In most of Africa it
was the result of colonial conquest. Everywhere, present evidence shows
that owners initially resisted emancipation and sought to retain the social and political power necessary to keep control over their ex-slaves. There
are, however, instances where they were willing to let slaves go in response
to changing economic conditions.

The degree to which freed slaves had viable alternatives to remaining
with their former owners or working for other members of the owning
elites is an area for comparative research. In the Americas most postemancipation conflicts centered around planters' efforts to maintain the
viability of the plantation as a unit of production. In cases such as Bar-
bados and the smaller sugar islands, the plantation survived because freed
slaves had no alternatives, whereas in British Guyana and certain other
Caribbean islands, they soon found other forms of livelihood and plantations had to import indentured labor. Planters in the southern United
States tried to resuscitate the plantation as a system of production following the Civil War, but former slaves struggled fiercely for autonomy.
Few, however, could get access to land of their own, and eventually they
were forced into sharecropping and tenancy arrangements. In the process, however, they made planters abandon the gang labor of the plantations (Woodman 1977; Ransom and Sutch 1977: 67–73, 87–99; Wiener
1978: 3–73; Foner 1983: 84–93). In the African plantations, slave-owners
also tried to keep control over the labor of their former slaves, but not
necessarily to maintain the plantation as a production unit. As long as
their property rights were protected, as in Zanzibar, former masters used
squatters and tenants to satisfy their demand for labor. Where there were
no plantations, former owners offered many inducements, including integrating former slaves more fully into webs of kinship and dependency
in order to keep them from leaving.

Whether or not former slaves stayed with their owners was usually
determined by their ability to find alternative livelihoods and equal security. Access to land (or to cattle for herders) was a crucial factor, and
this was determined not simply by the ratio of useable land to labor, but
also by the willingness of freed slaves to respect existing property rights
and by the ability of the former owners and the state to uphold them.
In a few instances these rights were not maintained. Thus in Haiti, former slaves turned the plantations into smallholdings. In the rice country
of coastal South Carolina, some freed slaves took over plantations and
others seized the land, at least temporarily (Foner 1983). Former-slave
squatters seized abandoned plantations and Crown land in Jamaica. In

Zanzibar, ex-slaves became squatters on the clove plantations (Cooper 1980: 121ff.). In northeastern Brazil, on the other hand, owners began freeing slaves before formal abolition, secure in the knowledge that they could not acquire land and had little alternative to becoming paid agricultural labor (Martins and Filho 1984). In general freed slaves seem to have preferred working their own land or self-employment, which allowed them to control their own work rhythms, to wage labor or tenancy arrangements.

Control over access to economic resources was thus obviously central to the postemancipation labor systems in both the New World and Africa. Almost everywhere in the Americas, the property rights of former masters and their political dominance were successfully upheld. The exceptions were Haiti, where ex-slaves gained and retained political power, and the southern United States during the brief period of Radical Reconstruction, when former slaves were able to vote and hold political office and formed an important part of local militias. Former owners and other whites, however, waged fierce struggles to regain control over the state in order to shape the freed into obedient workers. They ultimately prevailed throughout most of the South, and once in power, they eroded the freed slaves' political and economic power through contract and vagrancy laws, voter qualifications, and restrictions on their economic activities. In the Americas most former slaves remained in the lower classes, as tenants, sharecroppers, or subsistence farmers, or as low-paid wage labor, although some managed to establish themselves as craftsmen and prosperous smallholders. Their access to education and their social mobility varied considerably with their location, but was generally limited everywhere.

In most of Africa the picture was somewhat different. Except in settler colonies, land was relatively plentiful, and the power of former owners and even of the colonial state, which often tried to protect their interests, was rarely sufficient to prevent freed slaves from simply moving to areas where land was available and where they were welcomed. Some chose or were forced to become squatters, sharecroppers, or tenants; others joined religious communities. In areas of scarce economic resources, such as the Mauritanian desert and the scrub lands of Bechuanaland, some remained under the domination of their former owners right through the colonial period. But many ex-slaves, mostly male, became autonomous producers, successfully joining or forming new communities or remaining with or near their former owners, suffering social and, sometimes, economic discrimination. In British settler colonies and parts of the Portuguese colonies, where massive alienation of land and regressive tax policies drove large numbers of Africans into wage labor, former slaves were sometimes the first to go, but the freeborn were also eventually affected. Thus, because of the peculiar circumstances of colonial rule, the end of slavery perhaps had a greater levelling effect in Africa than in the New World. Certainly slave origins, although remembered and still important in the domestic sphere and sometimes in religious and political matters, have only in some areas been a barrier to gaining elite status in modern Africa. Often this is because freed slaves were the first to acquire Western education and become skilled labor. In this connection one of the subjects ripe for comparative study is the role of Christian churches and missions in working among freed slaves.

An area which has been barely explored is the relationship of the forms of abolition, the timing of abolition, and the experiences of former slaves to changes in the international economy. In the British Caribbean, abolition took place in the era of British industrial hegemony. In the United States it occurred in a period of economic crisis, following the midcentury decline in world prices, and at a time when the United States and other European nations were beginning to challenge British industrial dominance. Postemancipation adjustments to the end of slavery were certainly influenced by the world economy. In discussing the nature of economic adjustments to the end of slavery, Klein and Engerman note that where the demand for plantation crops remained constant or increased there was a corresponding effort to maintain the plantation system or to maintain the production of export crops in the face of emancipation by shifting to other forms of labor, including sharecropping, indentured labor, and the import of free immigrant labor. Thus changes in the world supply and demand for plantation crops such as sugar cane, coffee, and cotton had an impact on the labor strategies of postemancipation societies in the United States, the Caribbean, Brazil, and Cuba (Klein and Engerman 1985: 259–68).

Africa was conquered at a time of growing concern over current and future supplies of raw materials for Western industries, and administrators frequently expressed fears that emancipation would disrupt production. Clearly abolition needs to be seen in the context of the international economy, and the processes of social change in postemancipation Africa need to be examined critically and carefully with this in mind (Cooper 1981: 26–48).

Another area which requires examination is the changing international ideological climate — the development of what might be called an international public opinion — which increasingly condemned slavery as a form of labor organization. The condemning of slavery by the League of Nations, the negotiation of the Slavery Convention of 1926, and the formation of the International Labor Organization and its attempts to extend protection to colonial labor manifested in the Forced Labor Convention of 1930 and subsequent treaties, and the passing of the slavery question, along with the issues of forced labor, child labor, migrant labor, and related questions, to the United Nations are evidence of a new international interest in labor exploitation. Why these occurred when they did needs to be clarified.

It is clear that much research remains to be done before we can attempt a general discussion of the reasons for and effects of the abolition of slavery as a global phenomenon. This volume aims to add some comparative material which will enhance our understanding of this whole issue. If students of African emancipation have anything to teach students of emancipation elsewhere, it is to be aware of the full range of contexts in which slaves were used and how these influenced the experience of emancipation. They should also be aware of the range of strategies — political, legal, economic and social — employed by both former owners and former slaves to protect their interests. The chapters which follow explore in more detail many of the topics and issues we have raised in relation to Africa in this introduction.

REFERENCES

Anene, J. 1966. *Southern Nigeria in transition, 1885–1906: theory and practice in a colonial protectorate.* Cambridge: Cambridge University Press.

Anstey, R. 1975. *The Atlantic slave trade and British abolition, 1760–1810.* Atlantic Highlands, N.J.: Humanities Press.

Austen R. 1977. Slavery among coastal middlemen: the Duala of Cameroon. In *Slavery in Africa*, ed. S. Miers and I. Kopytoff, 305–33. Madison: University of Wisconsin Press.

Baldus, B. 1977. Responses to dependence in a servile group: an exploration. In *Slavery in Africa*, ed. S. Miers and I. Kopytoff, 435–58. Madison: University of Wisconsin Press.

Barry, B. 1985. *Le Royaume de Waalo: le Sénégal avant la conquête.* Paris: Editions Karthala.

Barth, F. 1969. Introduction. In *Ethnic groups and boundaries*, ed. F. Barth, 9–38. Boston: Little, Brown.

Bolland, N. 1981. Systems of domination after slavery: the control of land and labor in the British West Indies after 1838. *Comparative Studies in Society and History* 22(4): 591–619.

Bolland, N. 1984. Reply to William A. Green's "The Perils of Comparative History." *Comparative Studies in Society and History* 26(1): 120–25.

Bolt, C., and S. Drescher, eds. 1980. *Anti-slavery, religion, and reform: essays in memory of Roger Anstey.* Folkestone: Dawson.

Boserup, E. 1970. *Women's roles in economic development*. London: Allen and Unwin.

Bouche, D. 1968. *Les villages de liberté en Afrique noire française*. Paris: Mouton.

Boutillier, J-L. 1968. Les Captives en A.O.F. (1903–1905). *Bulletin de l'IFAN*, ser. B 30(2): 513–35.

Brooks, G. 1975. Peanuts and colonialism: consequences of the commercialization of peanuts in West Africa. *Journal of African History* 16(1): 29–54.

Cassanelli, L. 1987. Social construction on the Somali frontier: Bantu former slave communities in the nineteenth century. In *The African frontier: the reproduction of traditional African societies*, ed. I. Kopytoff, 214–38. Bloomington: Indiana University Press.

Chanock, M. 1985. *Law, custom and social order: the colonial experience in Malawi and Zambia*. Cambridge: Cambridge University Press.

Chattopadhyay, A. K. 1977. *Slavery in the Bengal presidency, 1772–1843*. London: Golden Eagle.

Christelow, A. 1985a. *Muslim courts and the French colonial state in Algeria*. Princeton: Princeton University Press.

Christelow, A. 1985b. Slavery in Kano, 1913–1914: evidence from the judicial records. *African Economic History* 14: 57–74.

Clarence-Smith, G. 1979. *Slaves, peasants, and capitalists in southern Angola, 1840–1926*. Cambridge: Cambridge University Press.

Clarence-Smith, G. 1985. *The third Portuguese Empire, 1825–1975: a study in economic imperialism*. Manchester: Manchester University Press.

Clark, A. 1983. The Maccube of Bondu (Senegambia). M.A. thesis, Ohio University, Athens, Ohio.

Clayton, A., and D. Savage. 1974. *Government and labour in Kenya, 1895–1963*. London: Frank Cass.

Conrad, R. 1972. *The destruction of Brazilian slavery, 1850–1885*. Berkeley and Los Angeles: University of California Press.

Cooper, F. 1977. *Plantation slavery on the East Coast of Africa*. New Haven: Yale University Press.

Cooper, F. 1979. The problem of slavery in African studies. *Journal of African History* 20(1): 103–25.

Cooper, F. 1980. *From slaves to squatters: plantation labor and agriculture in Zanzibar and coastal Kenya, 1890–1925*. New Haven: Yale University Press.

Cooper, F. 1981. Africa and the world economy. *African Studies Review* 24(2-3): 1–86.

Coquery-Vidrovitch, C. 1985. The colonial economy of the former French, Belgian and Portuguese zones, 1914–35. In *General history of Africa: Africa under colonial domination, 1880–1935*, ed. A. Adu Boahen, 351–81. Berkeley and Los Angeles: UNESCO and University of California Press.

Coquery-Vidrovitch, C., and P. Lovejoy. 1985. The workers of trade in precolonial Africa. In *The workers of African trade*, ed. C. Coquery-Vidrovitch and P. Lovejoy, 9–24. Beverly Hills: Sage.

Coupland, R. 1964. *The British antislavery movement*. 2d ed. London: Frank Cass.

Craton, M. 1974. *Sinews of empire: a short history of British slavery*. Garden City, N.Y.: Anchor Books.

Cruise O'Brien, D. 1971. *The Mourides of Senegal: the political and economic organization of an Islamic brotherhood*. Oxford: Clarendon.

Cumpston, I. M. 1953. *Indians overseas in British territories, 1834–54*. London: Oxford University Press.

Curtin, P. 1964. *The image of Africa: British ideas and action, 1780–1850*. Madison: University of Wisconsin Press.

Daget, S. 1971. L'abolition de la traite des noirs en France de 1814 à 1831. *Cahiers d'études africaines* 11(1): 14–58.

Daget, S. 1980. A model of the French abolitionist movement and its variations. In *Anti-slavery, religion and reform: essays in memory of Roger Anstey*, ed. C. Bolt and S. Drescher, 64–79. Folkstone: W. Dawson.

Davenport, J. R. H. 1977. *South Africa: a modern history*. Toronto: University of Toronto Press.

Davis, D. B. 1966. *The problem of slavery in Western culture*. Ithaca: Cornell University Press.

Davis, D. B. 1975. *The problem of slavery in the age of revolution: 1770–1823*. Ithaca: Cornell University Press.

Davis, D. B. 1984. *Slavery and human progress*. New York: Oxford.

Davis, D. B. 1987. Reflection on abolitionism and ideological hegemony. *American Historical Review* 92: 797–812.

Dias, J. 1981. Famine and disease in the history of Angola, c. 1830–1930. *Journal of African History* 22(3): 349–78.

Douglas, M. 1964. Matriliny and pawnship in Central Africa. *Africa* 34: 301–13.

Drescher, S. 1977. *Econocide: British slavery in the era of abolition*. Pittsburg: University of Pittsburg Press.

Drescher, S. 1980. Two variants of anti-slavery: religious organization and social mobilization in Britain and France, 1780–1870. In *Anti-slavery, religion and reform: essays in memory of Roger Anstey*, ed. C. Bolt and S. Drescher, 43–63. Folkstone: W. Dawson.

Drescher, S. 1982. Public opinion and the destruction of British colonial slavery. In *Slavery and British society, 1776–1846*, ed. J. Walvin, 22–48. London: Macmillan.

Duffy, J. 1967. *A question of slavery: labour policies in Portuguese Africa and the British protest*. Oxford: Oxford University Press.

Dumett, R. 1981. Pressure groups, bureaucracy, and the decision-making process: the case of slave abolition and colonial expansion in the Gold Coast, 1874. *Journal of Imperial and Commonwealth History* 9(2): 193–215.

Echenberg, M. 1975. Paying the blood tax: military conscription in French West Africa, 1914–1929. *Canadian Journal of African Studies* 9(2): 171–92.

Echenberg, M. 1986. Slaves into soldiers: social origins of the African Tirailleurs. In *Africans in bondage*, ed. P. Lovejoy, 311–33. Madison: African Studies Program.

Eltis, D. 1982. Abolitionist perception of society after slavery. In *Slavery and British society, 1776–1846*, ed. J. Walvin, 195–213. London: Macmillan.

Eltis, D., and J. Walvin, eds. 1981. *The abolition of the Atlantic slave trade: origins and effects in Europe, Africa, and the Americas.* Madison: University of Wisconsin Press.

Engerman, S. 1982. Economic adjustments to emancipation in the United States and British West Indies. *Journal of Interdisciplinary History* 13(2): 191–220.

Engerman, S. 1985. Economic change and contract labour in the British Caribbean: the end of slavery and the adjustment to emancipation. In *Abolition and its aftermath: the historical context*, ed. D. Richardson, 225–44. London: Frank Cass.

Engerman, S., and D. Eltis. 1980. Economic aspects of the abolition debate. In *Anti-slavery, religion and reform: essays in memory of Roger Anstey*, eds. C. Bolt and S. Drescher, 272–93. Folkstone: W. Dawson.

Eybers, G. W., ed. 1918. *Select constitutional documents illustrating South African history, 1795–1910.* London: G. Routledge.

Fall, B. 1986. Economie de plantation et main d'oeuvre forcée en Guinée Française 1920–46. Paper presented at the Ninth International Economic History Congress, Bern.

Finley, M. I. 1968. Slavery. *International encyclopaedia of the social sciences* 14:307–13.

Finley, M. I. 1980. *Ancient slavery and modern ideology.* London: Chatto and Windus.

Fogel, R., and S. Engerman. 1974. *Time on the cross: the economics of American Negro slavery.* Boston: Little, Brown.

Foner, E. 1983. *Nothing but freedom: emancipation and its legacy.* Baton Rouge: Louisiana State University Press.

Freund, B. 1981. *Capital and labour in the Nigerian tin mines.* London: Longmans.

Garretson, P. 1986. Vicious cycle: ivory, slaves, and arms on the new Maji frontier. *The southern marches of imperial Ethiopia: essays in history and social anthropology*, ed. D. Donham and W. James, 196–218. Cambridge: Cambridge University Press.

Genovese, E. 1965. *The political economy of slavery: studies in the economy and society of the slave South.* New York: Vintage.

Grace, J. 1975. *Domestic slavery in West Africa.* New York: Barnes and Noble.

Grace, J. 1977. Slavery and emancipation among the Mende in Sierra Leone, 1896–1928. In *Slavery in Africa*, ed. S. Miers and I. Kopytoff, 415–34. Madison: University of Wisconsin Press.

Green, W. 1976. *British slave emancipation: the sugar colonies and the great experiment, 1830–66.* Oxford: Oxford University Press.

Green, W. 1985. Was British emancipation a success? The abolitionist perspectives. In *Abolition and its aftermath: the historical context, 1790–1916*, ed. D. Richardson, 185–202. London: Frank Cass.

Greenidge, C. W. W. 1958. *Slavery.* London: Allen and Unwin.

Guéye, M'Baye. 1965. L'affaire Chautemps (avril 1904) et la supression de l'esclavage: de case du Sénégal. *Bulletin de l'IFAN*, ser. B 27(3–4): 543–59.

Hanna, A. J. 1956. *The beginnings of Nyasaland and northeastern Rhodesia, 1859–95.* Oxford: Clarendon Press.

Haskell, T. L. 1985. Capitalism and the origins of humanitarian sensibility. Parts 1 and 2. *American Historical Review* 90: 339–61, 457–566.

Hay, M. J. 1982. Women as owners, occupants, and managers of property in colonial western Kenya. In *African women and the law: historical perspectives*, ed. M. J. Hay and M. Wright, 110–23. Boston: Boston University Press.

Hay, M. J., and M. Wright, eds. 1982. *African women and the law: historical perspectives*. Boston: Boston University.

Hickey, D. 1984. Ethiopia and Great Britain: frontiers and slavery, 1916–36. Ph.D. dissertation, Northwestern University, Evanston, Illinois.

Hill, P. 1976. From slavery to freedom: the case of farm-slavery in Nigerian Hausaland. *Comparative Studies in Society and History* 18(3): 395–426.

Hitchcock, R. K. 1978. *Kalahari cattle posts: a regional study of hunters-gatherers, pastoralists, and agriculturalists in the western Sandveld region, Central District, Botswana*. 2 vols. Gaborone: Ministry of Local Government and Lands.

Hjejle, B. 1966. Slavery and agricultural bondage in South India in the nineteenth century. *The Scandinavian Economic History Review* 14(2): 71–126.

Hogendorn, J. 1978. *Nigerian groundnut exports: origins and early developments*. Zaria: Ahmadu Bello University Press.

Holsoe, S. 1977. Slavery and economic response among the Vai (Liberia and Sierra Leone). In *Slavery in Africa*, ed. S. Miers and I. Kopytoff, 287–303. Madison: University of Wisconsin Press.

Hopkins, A. 1966. The Lagos strike of 1897: an exploration in Nigerian labour history. *Past and Present* 35: 133–55.

Hopkins, A. 1973. *An economic history of West Africa*. London: Longmans.

Hopkins, A. 1980. Property rights and empire building: Britain's annexation of Lagos, 1861. *Journal of Economic History* 40(4): 777–98.

Igbafe, P. 1975. Slavery and emancipation in Benin, 1897–1945. *Journal of African History* 16(3): 409–29.

Iliffe, J. 1979. *A modern history of Tanganyika*. Cambridge: Cambridge University Press.

Iliffe, J. 1983. *The emergence of African capitalism*. Minneapolis: University of Minnesota Press.

Isaacman, A. 1972. *Mozambique: the Africanization of a European institution: the Zambezi prazos, 1750–1902*. Madison: University of Wisconsin Press.

Klein, A. N. 1981. Inequality in Asante: A study of the forms and meaning of slavery and social servitude in pre- and early colonial Akan-Asante society and culture. Ph.D. dissertation, University of Michigan, Ann Arbor.

Klein, H., and S. Engerman. 1985. The transition from slave to free labor: notes on a comparative economic model. In *Between slavery and free labor: the Spanish speaking Caribbean in the nineteenth century*, ed. M. Fraginals, F. M. Pons, and S. Engerman, 255–69. Baltimore: Johns Hopkins University Press.

Klein, M. 1977. Servitude among the Wolof and Sereer of Senegambia. In *Slavery in Africa*, ed. S. Miers and I. Kopytoff, 335–66. Madison: University of Wisconsin Press.

Klein, M. 1983. Slavery, forced labour and French colonial rule in Guinea. Paper presented at the American Historical Association meeting, San Francisco.

Klein, M. 1986. Slavery and emancipation in French West Africa. Paper presented
    to the History, Culture and Science Program, Woodrow Wilson International
    Center for Scholars, Washington, D.C.
Klein, M., and P. Lovejoy. 1979. Slavery in West Africa. In *The uncommon mar-
    ket: essays in the economic history of the Atlantic slave trade*, ed. H. Gemery
    and J. Hogendorn, 181–212. New York: Academic Press.
Klein, M., and R. Roberts. 1987. Pawning in the depression in French West Af-
    rica. *African Economic History* 16: 23–37.
Kopytoff, I. 1979. Commentary one. *Historical Reflections* 6(2): 62–77.
Kopytoff, I., and S. Miers. 1977. Introduction: African "slavery" as an institution
    of marginality. In *Slavery in Africa*, ed. S. Miers and I. Kopytoff, 3–81. Madi-
    son: University of Wisconsin Press.
Lance, J. 1985. Customary law, colonial law, and African litigants. Unpublished
    paper, available at the Hoover Institution Library, Stanford University.
Law, R. 1985. Human sacrifice in precolonial West Africa. *African Affairs* 334:
    53–88.
Lennihan, L. 1982. Rights in men and rights in land: slavery, wage labor, and
    smallholder agriculture in Northern Nigeria. *Slavery and Abolition* 3(2): 111–
    39.
Lovejoy, P. 1979. The characteristics of plantations in the nineteenth century So-
    koto Caliphate (Islamic West Africa). *American Historical Review* 84(5): 1267–
    292.
Lovejoy, P. 1983. *Transformations in slavery: a history of slavery in Africa*. Cam-
    bridge: Cambridge University Press.
Lovejoy, P. 1986. Fugitive slaves: resistance to slavery in the Sokoto Caliphate.
    In *In resistance: studies in Afro-American, African, and Caribbean history*,
    ed. G. Okihiro, 71–95. Amherst: University of Massachusetts Press.
Lovett, M. L. 1986. From wives to slaves: changing perceptions of Tonga women
    within the context of twentieth century male labor migration from Nyasa-
    land, 1903–1953. Unpublished paper presented at the 20th Annual Meeting
    of the African Studies Association, Madison, Wisconsin.
Lugard, F. 1893. *The rise of an East African empire*, 2 vols. London: Frank Cass;
    reprinted 1968.
McSheffrey, G. 1983. Slavery, indentured servitude, legitimate trade and the im-
    pact of abolition in the Gold Coast, 1874–1901: a reappraisal. *Journal of Afri-
    can History* 24(3): 349–68.
Maier, D. 1985. Slave labor/wage labor in German Togoland, 1885–1914. Paper
    presented at the African Studies Association Meeting, Los Angeles.
Mann, K. 1982. Women's rights in law and practice: marriage and dispute settle-
    ment in colonial Lagos. In *African women and the law: historical perspec-
    tives*, ed. M. J. Hay and M. Wright, 151–71. Boston: Boston University Press.
Mann, K. 1985. *Marrying well: marriage, status and social change among the
    educated elite in colonial Lagos*. Cambridge: Cambridge University Press.
Marshall, W. K. 1985. Apprenticeships and labour relations in the four Wind-
    ward Islands. In *Abolition and its aftermath: the historical context*, ed. D.
    Richardson, 203–24. London: Frank Cass.

Martins, R., and A. M. Filho. 1984. "Slavery in a nonexport economy": a reply. *Hispanic American Historical Review* 64(1): 135–46.

Mason, M. 1978. Working on the railway: forced labor in Northern Nigeria, 1907–1912. In *African Labor History*, ed. P. Gutkind, R. Cohen, and J. Copans, 56–79. Beverly Hills: Sage.

Maxwell, J. F. 1975. *Slavery and the Catholic church: the history of Catholic teaching concerning the moral legitimacy of the institution of slavery.* Chichester: The Antislavery Society for the Protection of Human Rights.

Meillassoux, C., ed. 1975a. *Esclavage en Afrique précoloniale.* Paris: Maspero.

Meillassoux, C. 1975b. Etat et condition des esclaves à Gumbu (Mali) au xixᵉ siècle. In *Esclavage en Afrique précoloniale*, ed. C. Meillassoux, 221–52. Paris: Maspero.

Meillassoux, C. 1983. Female slavery. In *Women and slavery in Africa*, ed. C. Robertson and M. Klein, 49–66. Madison: University of Wisconsin Press.

Meillassoux, C. 1986. *Anthropologie de l'esclavage: le ventre de fer et d'argent.* Paris: Presse Universitaire de France.

Miers, S. 1975. *Britain and the ending of the slave trade.* London: Longmans.

Miers, S. 1986. Britain, the League of Nations and the suppression of slavery. Unpublished paper presented at the Ninth International Economic History Congress, Bern.

Miers, S. Forthcoming. Britain and the suppression of slavery in Ethiopia. In *Proceedings of the Eighth International Conference on Ethiopian Studies.* Addis Ababa: Addis Ababa University Press.

Miers, S., and I. Kopytoff, eds. 1977. *Slavery in Africa: historical and anthropological perspectives.* Madison: University of Wisconsin Press.

Miller, J. 1977. Imbangala lineage slavery (Angola). In *Slavery in Africa*, ed. S. Miers and I. Kopytoff, 205–37. Madison: University of Wisconsin Press.

Miller, J. 1982. The significance of drought, disease and famine in the agriculturally marginal zones of west Central Africa. *Journal of African History* 23(1): 17–61.

Mintz, S. 1979. Slavery and the rise of peasantries. *Historical Reflections/Réflexions historiques* 6(1): 213–53.

Mintz, S. 1985. Epilogue: divided aftermaths of freedom. In *Between slavery and free labor: the Spanish speaking Caribbean in the nineteenth century*, ed. M. Fraginals, F. M. Pons, and S. Engerman, 270–78. Baltimore: Johns Hopkins University Press.

Morton, R. 1972. The Shungwaya myth of Miji Kenda origins: a problem of late nineteenth century Kenya coastal history. *The International Journal of African Historical Studies* 5(3): 397–423.

Morton, R. 1976. Slaves, fugitives, and freedmen on the Kenya coast, 1873–1907. Ph.D. dissertation, Syracuse University.

Nelson, S. 1986. Colonialism, capitalism, and work in the Congo Basin: a history of social change in the Tshuapa region, 1880s to 1940. Ph.D. dissertation, Stanford University.

Newbury, C. W. 1965. *British policy towards West Africa: select documents, 1786–1874.* 2 vols. Oxford: Clarendon Press.

66   I. INTRODUCTION

Nørregård, G. 1966. *Danish settlements in West Africa, 1658–1850.* Boston: Boston University Press.
Nwulia, M. D. E. 1981. *The history of slavery in Mauritius and the Seychelles, 1810–1875.* Rutherford, N.J.: Fairleigh Dickenson University Press.
Oliver, R. 1952. *The missionary factor in East Africa.* London: Longmans.
Oppong, C. 1983. *Female and male in West Africa.* London: Allen and Unwin.
Oroge, E. A. 1985. Iwofa: an historical survey of the Yoruba institution of indenture. *African Economic History* 14: 75–106.
Packwood, C. O. 1975. *Chained on the rock: slavery in Bermuda.* New York: Eliseo Torres and Sons.
Pasquier, R. 1967. A propos de l'emancipation des esclaves en Sénégal en 1848. *Revue française d'Histoire d'Outre Mer* 54(1): 188–208.
Patterson, O. 1982. *Slavery and social death: a comparative study.* Cambridge: Harvard University Press.
Perrings, C. 1979. *Black mineworkers in Central Africa.* London: Heinemann.
Pollet, E., and G. Winter. 1972. *Société soninké (Dyahunu, Mali).* Bruxulles: Editions de l'Institut de Sociologie.
Ranger, T. O. 1975. *Dance and society in eastern Africa, 1890–1935.* London: William Hunt.
Ransom, R., and R. Sutch. 1977. *One kind of freedom: the economic consequences of emancipation.* New York: Cambridge University Press.
Renault, F. 1971. *Lavigerie, l'esclavage africain et l'Europe, 1868–92.* 2 vols. Paris: Editions de Boccard.
Renault, F. 1972. *L'abolition de l'esclavage au Sénégal: l'attitude de l'administration française, 1848–1905.* Paris: Société française d'Histoire d'Outre Mer.
Renault, F. 1976. *Libération des esclaves et nouvelle servitude.* Abidjan: Nouvelles Editions africaines.
Roberts, R. 1980. Long distance trade and production: Sinsani in the nineteenth century. *Journal of African History* 21(2): 169–88.
Roberts, R. 1981a. Ideology, slavery, and social formation: the evolution of Maraka slavery in the Middle Niger Valley. In *The ideology of slavery in Africa,* ed. P. Lovejoy, 171–99. Beverly Hills: Sage.
Roberts, R. 1981b. The peculiarities of African labour and working class history. *Labour/Le Travailleur* 8/9: 317–33.
Roberts, R. 1987. *Warriors, slaves, and merchants: the state and the economy in the Middle Niger Valley, c. 1712–1914.* Stanford: Stanford University Press.
Roberts, R., and M. Klein. 1980. The Banamba slave exodus and the decline of slavery in the Western Sudan. *Journal of African History* 21(3): 375–94.
Robertson, C. 1983. Post proclamation slavery in Accra: a female affair? In *Women and slavery in Africa,* ed. C. Robertson and M. Klein, 220–45. Madison: University of Wisconsin Press.
Robertson, C. 1984. *Sharing the same bowl: a socioeconomic history of women and class in Accra, Ghana.* Bloomington: Indiana University Press.
Robertson, C., and M. Klein, eds. 1983. *Women and slavery in Africa.* Madison: University of Wisconsin Press.

Rodney, W. 1981. *A history of the Guyanese working people, 1881–1905.* Baltimore: Johns Hopkins University Press.

Romero, P. 1986. Where have all the slaves gone: emancipation and postemancipation in Lamu, Kenya. *Journal of African History* 27(3): 497–512.

Schuler, M. 1980. *"Alas, alas, Kongo:" a social history of indentured African immigration into Jamaica, 1841–1865.* Baltimore: Johns Hopkins University Press.

Scott, R. 1985. *Slave emancipation in Cuba: the transition to free labor, 1860–1899.* Princeton: Princeton University Press.

Seeber, E. 1971. *Antislavery opinion in France during the second half of the eighteenth century.* New York: B. Franklin.

Smith, J. E. 1976. *Slavery in Bermuda.* New York: Vantage Press.

Smith, M. 1981. *Baba of Karo.* New Haven: Yale University.

Smith, M. G. 1965. Slavery and emancipation in two societies. In *Plural societies in the British West Indies,* ed. M. G. Smith, 116–61. Berkeley and Los Angeles: University of California Press.

Strayer, R. W. 1978. *The making of missionary communities in East Africa: Anglicans and Africans in colonial Kenya, 1875–1935.* London: Heineman.

Sundiata, I. K. 1980. *Black scandal: America and the Liberian labor crisis, 1929–1936.* Philadelphia: Institute for the Study of Human Issues.

Sundiata, I. K. In prep. The black planters: African environment and ecology in the Bight of Biafra in the era of abolition, 1827–1930.

Swindell, K. 1980. Serawollies, Tilibunkas and strange farmers: the development of migrant groundnut farming along the Gambia River. *Journal of African History* 21(1): 93–104.

Tamuno, T. N. 1972. *The evolution of the Nigerian state: the southern phase, 1898–1914* New York: Humanities Press.

Temperley, H. 1972. *British antislavery, 1833–1870.* London: Longmans.

Temperley, H. 1977. Capitalism, slavery, and ideology. *Past and Present* 75(1): 94–118.

Temperley, H. 1981. The ideology of antislavery. In *The abolition of the Atlantic slave trade: origins and effects in Europe, Africa, and the Americas,* ed. D. Eltis and J. Walvin, 21–35. Madison: University of Wisconsin Press.

Temperley, H. 1985. Abolition and national interest. In *Out of slavery,* ed. J. Hayward, 86–109. London: Frank Cass.

Tinker, H. 1974. *A new system of slavery: the export of Indian labour overseas, 1830–1920.* London: Oxford University Press.

Tinker, H. 1984. Into servitude: Indian labour in the sugar industry, 1833–1970. In *International labor migration: historical perspectives,* ed. S. Marks and P. Richardson, 76–89. London: Maurice Temple Smith.

Touré, O. 1984. Le refus du travail forcé du Sénégal oriental. *Cahiers d'études africaines* 24(1): 25–38.

Uchendu, V. 1977. Slaves and slavery in Igboland, Nigeria. In *Slavery in Africa,* ed. S. Miers and I. Kopytoff, 121–32. Madison: University of Wisconsin Press.

Vail, L., and L. White. 1980. *Capitalism and colonialism in Mozambique: a study of Quelimane District.* London: Heineman.

Van Zwanenberg, R. 1975. *Colonial capitalism and labour in Kenya, 1919–39.* Nairobi: East Africa Publishing.

Watson, J., ed. 1980. *Asian and African systems of slavery.* Berkeley and Los Angeles: University of California Press.

Weil, P. 1984. Slavery, groundnuts and capitalism in the Wuli Kingdom of Senegambia, 1820–1930. *Research in Economic Anthropology* 6: 77–119.

Wiener, J. 1978. *The social origins of the New South: Alabama, 1860–1885.* Baton Rouge: Louisiana State University Press.

Williams, E. 1944. *Capitalism and slavery.* New York: Russell and Russell.

Willis, J. R., ed. 1985. *Slaves and slavery in Muslim Africa: Islam and the ideology of enslavement.* London: Frank Cass.

Wilson, M., and L. Thompson. 1969. *Oxford history of South Africa,* Vol. 1. Oxford: Oxford University Press.

Woodman, H. 1977. Sequel to slavery: the new history views the postbellum South. *Journal of Southern History* 41(4): 523–54.

Wright, M. 1975. Women in peril: a commentary on the life stories of captives in nineteenth century east Central Africa. *African Social Research* 20: 800–819.

Wright, M. 1983. Bwanika: consciousness and protest among slave women in Central Africa. In *Women and slavery in Africa,* ed. C. Robertson and M. Klein, 246–67. Madison: University of Wisconsin Press.

II

A HISTORIOGRAPHICAL DEBATE

2 Raymond Dumett and Marion Johnson

Britain and the Suppression of Slavery in the Gold Coast Colony, Ashanti, and the Northern Territories

Historians who have written about the demise of internal slavery in colonial Africa can be divided roughly into two schools: those who with A. G. Hopkins have argued that the "transition from slave to free was achieved without widespread economic and social dislocation" (Hopkins 1973: 226–31) and a newer group, influenced by Marxist theory, who contend that the imposition of colonial antislavery laws often had a harsh and disruptive impact on traditional economic and social structures (Klein and Lovejoy 1979; Cooper 1979). While the views of this latter school are neither uniform nor immutable,[1] they have gained considerable favor in the last decade. Recently the revisionists have turned their attention to the ending of slavery in the lands that compose modern Ghana. One such scholar has argued that earlier historians failed to understand the

We would like to thank Edward Reynolds, Bruce Haight, Gareth Austin, Tom McCaskie, and Martin Klein for comments on earlier drafts of this chapter.

1. In his 1983 book Lovejoy tends to revise his earlier analyses of the conventional, or "liberal," school of interpretation by showing that the variations between areas of Africa where the emancipation of slaves took a disruptive turn and those places where it declined relatively peacefully depended in large part on whether the precolonial system of production was organized around a gang slave–plantation system or whether the use of slaves in production occurred mainly in small groups organized on a lineage basis (pp. 256–60).

71

Map 2. The Gold Coast Colony, Ashanti, and the Northern Territories

fundamental nature and pervasiveness of slavery in the Akan productive system and that in assessing the effects of emancipation laws they relied too heavily on the official view, presented in government documents, to the exclusion of evidence from other sources, particularly missionary documents (McSheffrey 1983: 349–68; and following McSheffrey, Lovejoy 1983:

253; for a less revisionist conclusion, see Austin 1984). We would concur with some of this criticism with respect to methodology, adding only that all available data should be sifted and collated and that missionary sources should be examined with the same careful scrutiny as other records.

We also agree with the revisionists that in some instances colonial anti-slavery laws had a harsh and disruptive impact on the lives of slaves and slaveholders and on the underlying socioeconomic system. But these findings cannot be extended to blanket the entire continent. Even in so small a country as Ghana the process by which the internal slave trade and slavery itself faded out varied greatly from region to region and from district to district. The impact of abolition should in the future be evaluated in detail, ideally in every area of the country, or at least in major states, before definitive conclusions can be drawn. This chapter seeks to start the process by examining the impact of British antislavery policy over time in a fairly wide range of territories and ethnic groups and by utilizing government documents plus missionary and other non-official sources to which the revisionists have rightly drawn attention. In this we shall attempt to show subtle distinctions in both the method and impact of British antislavery policy in the three major zones of the Gold Coast Colony, Ashanti, and the Northern Territories. The crucial periods are, for the Gold Coast Colony, the first two decades after the issue of the antislavery ordinances in 1874–1875 and, for Ashanti and the Northern Territories, the decades after British occupation. Thereafter, too many other factors intruded to make possible any assessment either of policy or its effects. This chapter does not pretend to be exhaustive, but we hope that it may provide a somewhat fuller picture than preceding studies.

British Policy towards Slavery before 1874

For the first half of the nineteenth century the coastline of what is today Ghana existed under various forms of subservience to British, Dutch, and Danish commercial and jurisdictional control. Known simply as the Gold Coast Settlements, the British forts (which occupy the main attention here) were from 1807 to 1823 and again from 1828 to 1843 administered informally by councils of merchants. In 1843 the British government took over full responsibility for administration; but it was not until 1850 that the Gold Coast was detached from Sierra Leone to form a separate Crown colony (for details see Kimble 1963: 168–70, 192–95).

The Atlantic slave trade, outlawed by Parliament in 1807, had declined fairly rapidly in waters off the British Gold Coast forts at least by the 1830s (Curtin 1969: 221, 240, 247, 258); but slaves continued to be smuggled from the more remote parts of the eastern coastline (the Adangme and Ewe country), which remained largely unpatrolled by the British until its cession from Denmark in 1850.[2] Strict rules limiting "sovereignty" to the immediate surroundings of the coastal forts, as opposed to the "protected territories" of the interior, also curtailed British interference with the inland slave trade and with African internal slavery. The British Slave Trade Abolition Acts of 1842 and 1843 (6 & 7 Vict., c. 98) had outlawed the furtherance of the slave trade within Her Majesty's dominions and had authorized prosecution of British offenders wherever they might reside; but the laws did not allow the interdiction of internal slavetrading or prosecution of slaveholding by foreigners (including Africans) outside the areas of British sovereignty.[3]

In the absence of formal legal sanctions, some administrators used indirect methods to modify, though not to abolish, African traditional slavery. One of the earliest was Governor Charles Macarthy's effort to persuade the leading British mulatto merchant, James Bannerman, to turn his slaves into indentured servants in order to set an example for his colleagues. Bannerman had imagined that Macarthy was "speaking from authority," but he later felt he had been tricked into signing away his property.[4] The most vigorous informal efforts to curb the worst abuses of domestic slavery occurred during the administration of George Maclean, who served successively as president of the Council of Merchants and as judicial assessor from 1831 to 1847 (Metcalfe 1962: 1–70 and passim). During the 1830s and 1840s British coastal magistrates gradually acquired a limited jurisdiction over Africans of nearby interior districts by means of custom and usage and by signed agreements with kings and chiefs such as the famous Bond of 1844. However, neither the Bond nor other formal agreements with chiefs had mentioned British judicial rights over slavery; and it was only gradually through careful diplomacy and a reputation for fairness that the judicial assessor's persuasive powers were accepted in cases involving domestic servitude.[5] The main legal

2. Along part of the coastline still farther east (and outside the British sphere) slaves continued to be exported overseas even after 1850. See, for example, PRO, Governor Winniett, 30 May 1850. Richard Burton reported slave baracoons at Ada, at the Volta mouth in the 1860s. See also article in *The African Times*, 22 November 1862: 5.

3. By the 1844 Order-in-Council, the British Foreign Jurisdiction Act was interpreted as being applicable to states and chieftaincies in the Gold Coast. However, the ordinance specifically stated that submission by chiefs to such jurisdiction had to be voluntary (Johnston 1973: 61–62).

4. PRO, Bannerman 1826, reads, "Thus without the slightest compensation I voluntarily emancipated these people, being of course under the impression that his Excellency was acting from authority." (Thanks to Margaret Renehan for this citation.)

5. Testimony from both African and European sources makes it clear that most Africans brought cases before Maclean and his magistrates on a purely voluntary basis because

loophole for allowing Maclean's intervention was cases pertaining to property rights. As one official later put it, "Slaves being among the chief property of natives," it simply happened that a large number of disputes which
came before the assessor's court involved slavery (PRO CO, Fairfield 1874).
If a slave bringing a grievance could prove cruelty, the assessor's courts
would either liberate him or find another master.[6] Maclean mounted no
broad frontal attack; magistrates were warned that they could not use
the English law to abolish the institution of slavery. Both Maclean's supporters and detractors conceded that his policies were ambiguous: many
of his judgments amounted to a tacit recognition of slavery.

Following Maclean's death Gold Coast officials retreated somewhat
from his activist stance. But Maclean's standard of concern about harsh
practices had become entrenched enough for the colonial courts to take
occasional action when cases of extreme cruelty were brought before them.
Viewed against the outcries of abolitionists in England against Gold Coast
slavery, the dilemma facing administrators is apparent. Slavery was so
deeply interwoven into the fabric of Akan and Ga-Adangme culture that
officials were wary about proceeding against it, whether by executive decree or legislation, owing to the risk of widespread sociopolitical upheaval.

Categories of Slaves and Pawns

The many forms of servile labor in the traditional sociocultural systems
of Ghana[7] cannot be described in detail here. The word *slave* covers a
variety of categories of servitude, some of which had distinctive local
names. The commonest term in Twi, *akoa* (pl. *nkoa*), is generally translated as "subject" and implies subordination rather than servitude.[8] *Ɔdonko*

---

they expected a sympathetic hearing and a fair judgment (PP, Hackett testimony, Questions 6521–6546, in Minutes of Evidence, 1865, [C. 170], 264).

6. Maclean adhered to no rigid pattern with respect to slavery. On many occasions
he harbored fugitive slaves or paid for their freedom; but in other instances he returned
slaves to their masters, thus bringing down on his head the wrath of abolitionists in London.

7. The major ethnolinguistic group of the Gold Coast Colony and Ashanti (today
southern Ghana) is that of the Akan people, who compose about 60 percent of the total
population. The two other major groups are the Ga-Adangme and Ewe peoples of the eastern region. The term used for slave in the Adangme region (east of Accra and west of the
Volta River) was *nyongwe*. The term for an ordinary ("free") member of the indigenous
society was *tabon* (interview by R. E. Dumett with the *mantse* and elders of Prampram,
20 December 1971, Prampram, Ghana). The term used for a male slave in the Ewe region
east of the Volta was *klu* (Sandra Greene, pers. comm.). Little detailed work on slavery
and abolition has been undertaken for these regions.

8. According to an authoritative study by the African civil servant J. C. de Graft Johnson, akoa in the 1920s and *afunaba* ("client, subordinate") were the commonest general
terms applied to *all* forms of servitude (GNA [Tamale], de Graft Johnson 1927).

76   II. A HISTORIOGRAPHICAL DEBATE

(pl. *nnonko*), "foreigner, northerner," was generally applied to first-generation slaves recognizable by tribal marks, speech, and so forth. *Akyere* (pl. *nkyere*) were slaves, often condemned criminals, intended for sacrifice at funerals or religious ceremonies; but any slave could be sacrificed on his master's death. *Awowa* (pl. *nnwowa*), "pawns," were in the strictest sense not slaves at all but sureties for debts, working to pay off the interest on the loan.[9]

The term *akoa* was so broad in meaning and so loosely applied as to seem all-encompassing. According to one leading African authority nearly everyone in Akan society was someone else's akoa (GNA [Tamale], de Graft Johnson 1927). A number of nineteenth-century writers may have based their conclusions concerning the pervasiveness of "slavery" on the *akoa-awura* (subject-master) relationship; some said it embraced from three-fourths to nine-tenths of the population.[10] People living in the Akan region in the last century were certainly aware of the difference between a person who was someone else's akoa and an ɔdonko, or other slave. But it is very difficult to discover the differences in labor requirements for a dependent in the two categories.

Colonial officials were certainly ignorant of the nuances of Akan "slavery." Moreover, the treatment of servile labor varied greatly with custom and usage in particular areas; and the master-subject relationship governed not only labor and production but also a broad spectrum of social affiliations. Some observers contended that conditions of slavery were harsher in the interior kingdom of Ashanti and several other centralized states (Akyem, Nzema, etc.) than in the coastal and intermediate central districts, which had been exposed to the ameliorative influences just described.[11] However, the harshness of the master-slave relationship de-

9. There is disagreement among contemporary sources as to how pawning worked in practice. According to Francis Swanzy in 1842, pawning was not tantamount to slavery, since a pawn might work off his bondage by earning wages or by going off into the bush to dig for gold. However, Swanzy was writing about his experiences in the western Ahanta country, and this flexibility does not seem to have pertained elsewhere (PP, Swanzy, in Report of the Select Committee, 1842, [551], X, 60–61). A more critical view that "pawning [was] undoubtedly a species of slavery" is found in PRO, Phillips 1893.

10. Statement by Andrew Swanzy of 15 May 1865, Question 4820; see also statement of R. Pine, 1 June 1865, Question 7592 (PP, Minutes of Evidence, 1865, [170], 200, 295). Another factor which must be considered here is the probable increase in the holding of slaves internally after the abolition of the Atlantic slave trade (Wilks 1975: 262–67.)

11. One close observer of the coastal scene said that the authoritarian element was so weak there that slaves obeyed their masters only when it suited them. How far this applied elsewhere is uncertain (PRO, Governor Winniett, 22 May 1850). See also statements by F. Swanzy, 22 and 29 April 1842 (PP, Report of the Select Committee, 1842, [551], X, 32, 53, 60). For a contrasting view on a more authoritarian type of slavery in the Kete-Krachi state, see Maier 1983: 30–36.

pended greatly on the attitudes and personal idiosyncracies of individual family heads, kings, and chiefs. Some of the most oppressive forms of slavery could be found among some African and Eur-African merchants of the coastal towns (see p. 90).

There is insufficient space in this chapter to analyze all of the methods — economic, social, and political — by which Akan slaves could be categorized. Conditions of servitude varied greatly, both with the type of slavery involved and with the status of the master. Some of the principal economic relationships are the following:

1. slaves included in the households of small-scale farmers (here slave status was largely forgotten after a period of years, except when questions of inheritance and marriage arose);
2. "plantation" slaves, settled in hamlets to grow cash crops by their masters and food for their own maintenance (and sometimes to sell in markets or to passersby);
3. slaves of Europeanized or Muslim merchants, unlikely to be absorbed into the master's family;
4. recently purchased or captured slaves, unassimilated into the host society, saddled with onerous and distasteful tasks — included among these were the slave porters in the caravan trade (arguably the most exploited group of all and the category that produced many of the runaways);
5. royal and "court" slaves in centralized state systems — some were engaged in agricultural work for the support of the chief, but every chief or "big man" needed a retinue of subordinates to follow him as he made his regular rounds of the community. And these "social prestige" and "welfare" features are remembered as the most pervasive and binding functional elements in Akan traditional slavery.[12] Although detailed observations on the daily work routines of slaves are rare, there is evidence to suggest that many household slaves and perhaps some state slaves did not have to labor very hard.[13]

Very gradually a transformation of this older system took place over time largely outside the scope of governmental edict and judicial decision. With certain exceptions — which we shall discuss — most slaves did not seem anxious to give up this paternalistic system of subordination.

12. Personal communication with Professor A. M. Opoku (State University of New York at Brockport) and Dr. J. H. Kwabena Nketia (University of Pittsburgh) at the international conference "Asante and Its Neighbors," American Museum of Natural History, New York City, October 1984.

13. BMS, Ramseyer's comments 1893. This conclusion has been confirmed by numerous other observers.

Many knew no other home than that of their masters, or could not return to their place of origin because of distance or continual slave-raiding. The fact that there were so few money-earning jobs available for ex-slaves, even in the coastal towns, was one reason for the slow spread of the emancipation idea before, and even after, the mid-1870s. A fundamental method by which slavery in the Akan region was gradually phased out was that of the time-honored method of assimilation or incorporation of slaves into the host family or lineage. According to Wilks and other authorities this generallly took place over the course of a generation or two (see Wilks 1975: 36; Rattray 1929: 35; Poku 1969: 35). Subsequently exogenous forces such as Western acculturation and economic change also became an important part of the process.

From midcentury through the 1880s the Basel Mission Society played a significant subordinate role in the protection of fugitive slaves and in the amelioration of slavery, especially in the eastern zone of the Gold Coast and lands bordering Ashanti. But, like the government, the mission operated in cycles and adhered to no uniform or systematic policy. Since the 1830s individual missionaries or the mission itself had occasionally freed African slaves in order to convert them to Christianity or turn them into skilled craftsmen or commercial farmers. The Reverend Elias Schrenk testified that his mission had been prompted to take a more decisive antislavery stance in the Gold Coast as a result of the terrible experience of President Lincoln and the United States which had led to the Civil War (PP, Schrenk, 4 May 1865, in Minutes of Evidence, [170], 142). In the 1860s, they laid it down that slaveholding was incompatible with membership in their Christian congregations, and thereafter arranged for the emancipation of more than 200 slaves so held. Such freedmen were then bonded over to their former masters on a wage-payment basis so that they could earn their own purchase price (PP, Schrenk letter, 20 March 1875, in Papers relating to West Africa, [c. 1343]). Many of the church elders were uneasy about this move, however. It did not lead to widespread emancipation; and the precise status of the recently indentured servants to their ex-masters' households was sometimes difficult and undefined. Some Basel Mission employees, even ministers, were holding slaves as late as the 1890s.

Enactment of and Immediate Reactions to the Antislavery Legislation in the Gold Coast Colony, 1874

The one unavoidable conclusion that emerges from policy minutes and British government documents on slave emancipation is that there was no compelling pressure from the European commercial interests most actively involved on the west coast for any kind of radical interference with Gold Coast domestic slavery. Longtime west coast traders, such as the F. and A. Swanzy firm, Alexander Millers, and, apparently, their wholesale suppliers in London and Liverpool, and even politicians in Westminster in the 1870s saw no reason to upset the status quo. The one British-based interest group which maintained relatively consistent pressure over the years and favored outright abolition both of the inland slave trade and of slavery as an institution was the evangelical humanitarian lobby, led by the Aborigines Protection Society and a number of its allies in Parliament. They were backed by a small group of West African professional men, led by Dr. James Africanus Horton and Ferdinand Fitzgerald, who also favored abolition (for details see Dumett 1981: 203).

From 1850 to 1873 the Gold Coast Colony still occupied only a narrow strip of inland territory surrounding the British coastal forts. But the next year, following annexation of the last Dutch forts and the conclusion of the 1873–1874 Ashanti War, the British government acquired "formal" administrative control over the "protected" states of the interior up to (but not including) Ashanti.

Except for new forces and facts brought to light during the Ashanti War and the resultant "annexation" orders in council, "domestic slavery" would probably have remained a dormant issue in official discussions (ibid.: 200–207). In the first instance, the imperial government's aim was simply to ensure the protection of the coastal settlements and their surrounding hinterlands from further Ashanti invasions. But it soon dawned on members of the Colonial Office hierarchy that extension of the government's legislative authority over the newly annexed "protectorate" would have to include the controversial topics of the inland slave trade and domestic slavery (PRO, Holland 1874). Matters were brought to a head by lurid reports from the Aborigines Protection Society and in the popular press about continued slave-dealing within close proximity to the British coastal forts. Following pressure by the Liberal Opposition in Parliament,[14] the Earl of Carnarvon, secretary of state in Disraeli's Conservative government, reluctantly authorized passage of both anti-slave-dealing and emancipation ordinances for the Gold Coast in 1874 (PP, Draft Proclamation 1874, in Correspondence, 1875, [c. 1139], 97).

Throughout the 1870s the imperial government's overriding aim was at all costs to prevent any serious social disturbance resulting from a sudden mass exodus of slaves. Strongly influenced by the precedents of slave emancipation laws in British India, Carnarvon intended that the new Gold Coast laws would do no more than abolish the "legal status" of

14. United Kingdom 1874. Also quoted in Dumett 1981: 207, 215 fn. 61.

80   II. A HISTORIOGRAPHICAL DEBATE

slavery. There would be no attempt to free slaves *en bloc*, although any slaves who sought freedom would be assured the protection of the British colonial courts.[15]

The two new ordinances — Ordinance No. 1 of 1874 ("To Provide for the Abolition of Slave Dealing") and Ordinance No. 2 of 1874 ("To Provide for the Emancipation of Persons Holden in Slavery") were gazetted in March 1875.[16] Colonial Office fears that the speed with which Governor George Strahan had rushed through the ordinances might spark violent resistance (PRO, Hemming 1875) were partly allayed after the governor reported amicable meetings with little open bickering from chiefs about the new anti-slave-dealing law. The slave emancipation ordinance was a different matter: some 40 kings and chiefs of the "Fanti country" denounced Strahan for having exceeded his authority, complaining that he had misrepresented the real meaning of the new law in his preliminary announcements. Though few instances of open resistance were reported, it is possible, as Kimble (1963: 303) states, that the two edicts came as a "severe shock" to at least some kings and chiefs who believed that they might lose power over their cadres of servants as a result of such legislation.

In the aftermath the imperial government took much more seriously the rumor that the two ordinances (particularly the slave emancipation law) would lead to the diversion and stoppage of trade from the interior to the coast. According to this suggestion, slave porters bearing produce from Ashanti and other interior states, upon hearing about the new laws, escaped their trading parties in order to gain the rumored refuge of the British forts. Such news seemed to confirm the worst misgivings of the antiabolitionists in the Colonial Office. "If there should really be a falling off in the exports of palm oil, the revenue of the Colony will suffer, and with it our plans for improvement and development."[17] In fact, fears of oil-trade decline or diversion as a consequence of slave emancipation proved exaggerated. While some palm-oil carriers escaped to the anonymity of the coast towns (as they had done long before the ordinances), palm oil and kernel exports remained fairly steady, 1875–1880, with a generally rising trend over the early 1880s (see Table 2.1).

The dips which did occur in 1875 appear to be traceable in part to

15. Information on abolition of slavery in India was brought to Carnarvon's attention by Sir Henry Bartle Frere (PRO, Carnarvon Papers, Bartle Frere 1874; quoted in Dumett 1981: 209, 215).
16. Enclosures in Strahan to Carnarvon, 20 September 1874; Carnarvon to Strahan, 28 October 1874 (PP, Correspondence, 1875, [C. 1139], 18–19, 22).
17. Reference to diversion of Ashanti trade in PRO, Wray 1877; PP, Lonsdale, in Report on Mission to Ashanti and Gyaman, 1883, [C. 3687], 127.

Table 2.1. Export Trade of the Gold Coast (values in £ Sterling[a])

Year	Gold Dust		Palm Oil		Palm Kernels	
	Ounces	Value	Gallons	Value	Tons	Value
1875	11,801	42,484	2,686,528	222,594	4,677	47,253
1876	17,280	62,308	3,865,007	306,000	7,655	67,645
1877	10,611	38,199	3,458,700	260,087	7,828	62,624
1878	11,147	40,129	3,889,917	295,246	5,251	48,707
1879	15,479	55,724	3,746,981	280,725	6,217	53,114
1880	9,125	32,865	3,420,279	307,114	9,511	101,606
1881	12,567	45,241	3,107,737	230,572	6,289	47,508

Sources: Gold Coast *Blue Books* for the years shown.
[a]£1.0.0 = U.S. $4.86.

factors other than loss of carriers due to slave emancipation, among which were intermittent interior warfare and fluctuating export-produce prices.

There were also quite unsubstantiated charges that the ordinances had interrupted and diminished gold production in the interior, which might, if true, lend some support to the controversial notion of a "slave mode of production" in traditional gold mining (for examination of this issue, see Dumett 1979). According to information supplied by the explorer Richard Burton and the colonial administrator Hesketh Bell (not the two most reliable of authorities), most of the colony's gold exports came from such interior states as Wassa and Ashanti and most of the gold production in these states was by slave labor. The colonial government's ill-advised emancipation of slaves, these critics averred, meant that no African workers in the gold-producing regions of the interior were any longer willing to mine for gold.[18] The statistical record, however, shows that there was no appreciable fall-off in gold dust exports between 1875 and 1879. Since European mechanized gold mines had not yet come into production, this indicates that indigenous gold mining proceeded as normal. Traditional gold extraction in Wassa was primarily by free family labor, together with family slaves. There is no evidence that such slaves left their adopted families in large numbers. Indeed, there was a wholesale rush of African traditional miners (using household slaves) into the Wassa gold fields in 1877 just three years after the issue of the ordinances. The dip

18. Both Burton and Bell were extremely unhistorical in their analysis, basing their suppositions concerning decline in the use of slaves in interior production not on the 1874 ordinances, but on the British Anti-Slave Trade Act of 1807 (designed to combat the Atlantic slave trade), which had little negative impact on internal slaveholding by African states and, in fact, probably boosted it (Burton and Cameron 1883, 2: 353; H. J. Bell 1898: 37).

in traditional gold exports in 1880 is mainly traceable to warfare between a weakened Ashanti Kingdom and its separatist state of Adansi (PRO, Gouldsbury 1875). George Ekem Ferguson made it clear that the abandonment of African mines in Akyem by 1890 was the result of the rubber boom, which offered higher profits. Again, we must point out that Ashanti, the main gold-producing state, remained independent of British rule until 1896; there are no reports of any decline of traditional gold mining (with or without slave labor) before 1900.

The Attack on the Overland Slave Trade

From the outset the colonial state viewed the destruction of the overland slave trade as its top priority (see section "Suppressing the Slave Trade and Slavery in the Northern Territories," below). If the inflow of new slaves, mainly from the savanna areas of the north, could be cut off, slavery itself might die out gradually. District magistrates claimed to have acted decisively between 1875 and 1895 in breaking up the public sale of slaves whenever they heard of it and in prosecuting offenders in the colonial courts.[19] By the late 1880s, a travelling commissioner could state unequivocally, "There are now no slave markets within the Protectorate, nor any raids staged for slaves on villages within the sphere of British jurisdiction" (PRO, Phillips 1893). This was not true, however, for distant perimeters of the coastline and the frontier areas of the north: in Nzema, adjacent to the French Ivory Coast, slaves were still brought down from the northwest by way of the flourishing market of Bonduku in Gyaman; and at Keta on the Anlo (Ewe) coast to the east, nnonko were brought from the great slave market at Salaga in the far north, through Kete-Krachi on the Volta, and through German territory where German officials tolerated the trade until at least 1900 (Maier 1985: 5–7; Johnson 1986a).

Though large-scale and open sale of adult slaves within the protectorate was largely suppressed,[20] the smuggling of small numbers of slaves — particularly women and adolescents — continued at Elmina, Winneba, Accra, and other coastal towns until well into the twentieth century (Robertson 1983: 220–45). On the western coast in the Achowa and Dixcove districts, local commissioners were unusually candid about the continuing traffic in new domestic slaves; demand was "brisk" but it was hard to punish cases or even to discover prices, as the trade was carried on

19. The Gold Coast colonial secretary reported that some 60 infractions of the law were prosecuted from June 1888 to June 1889 (PRO, Hodgson 1890).
20. Even *The African Times*, heavily critical of Gold Coast colonial administration, conceded this much about the colonial government's antislavery policy. See the article "Slavery in a British Colony," 1 October 1890: 149.

"clandestinely" (PRO, district commissioner at Dixcove 1898). After the ordinances, the main pattern seems to have been the smuggling of young boys and girls from the northern savanna regions into the coastal towns, both on the west and on the east. A considerable slave trade continued down the river Volta, with Kete-Krachi and Kpandu as the main entrepôts all during the 1880s and 1890s (BMS, D. Asante 1882; BMS, Hall 1887). Other slaves were brought into the Krobo states from Kpong or the Volta. The district commissioner at Elmina, wrote: "As far as I can gather, there is and always has been a demand for slave children on the coast. The difficulty is to catch the delinquents."[21]

Outlying sections of even the best-policed towns, such as Cape Coast and Accra, continued to be touched by the trade. Slave-dealers could easily evade patrols or create exchange points up-country. In the early 1890s new problems of slave inflows into the western and central coastal districts stemmed from the slave-raiding and slave-trading operations of the Manding warrior Samori Touré far to the northwest at Gyaman in the hinterland of the French Ivory Coast.[22] The Cape Coast district commissioner reported that people who wanted slave children often travelled to the Gyaman market of Bonduku, where a surplus of slaves existed. Once purchased, such youthful slaves were treated as the "adopted children" of their host families. Because these purchases were difficult to detect, most officials gave up trying to prosecute cases involving boys and girls and concentrated on those involving the sale of adult slaves. Between September 1896 and December 1897 the Cape Coast district commissioner reported that he had found only 15 cases concerning youthful slaves, all of which were promptly prosecuted (PRO, district commissioner at Cape Coast 1898).

Statistics show that Keta, east of the Volta in the Ewe region, and Cape Coast continued to be the two major coastal districts where predictable numbers of slave-dealers (usually about 10–15 in each place) were convicted each year. Overall, slave-dealing convictions averaged about 29 per year for the Gold Coast Colony and Protectorate from 1903 through 1911.[23] But it is almost certain that the number of slaves actually sold

21. PRO, district commissioner at Elmina, 1898. For comments on child slaves who continued to be shipped and sold down the Volta, see BMS, Ramseyer 1885; and BMS, Hall 1897; also Johnson 1986a.

22. In 1892, after Samori's capital at Bisandugu in the Western Sudan was sacked by French forces, he began a systematic retreat to the south and west, harrying the land and people as he proceeded. By 1895 his Sofa army was encamped outside Bonduku in Gyaman. His forces also conducted raids into the British sphere of influence in western Gonja (Muhammad 1977).

23. *Gold Coast Police Department Report for 1901:* 16; *Gold Coast Native Affairs De-*

both in the coastal towns and in the inland "protected states" greatly exceeded these figures. When the colonial government set its mind to crack down hard on the illicit traffic, far greater numbers of slave-traders — 151 in 1911 and 181 in 1912 — were taken to court and convictions were obtained.[24] How many new slaves continued to be absorbed into the coastal towns and into expanding cocoa-farming states such as Krobo and Akuapem during the early twentieth century will probably never be known.[25] Estimates of the Krobo population by the well-informed Basel Mission for 1881 and Gold Coast returns for 1891 and 1901 suggest a growth rate of about 2.75–3.5 percent per annum. This is far above any probable rate of natural increase at this period and suggests the continued absorption of northern slaves, for which there is other evidence.[26] Most district commissioners learned how to look the other way on both the slave-dealing and domestic-slavery problems, except when prodded by an unusually vigorous supervisor. For as one incisive report noted, the highly variable numbers of slave-trade arrests each year were "wholly a function of effective policing duties" (*Gold Coast Judicial Department Report for 1909:* 16).

Slaveholding and Slave Emancipation

It is far more difficult to generalize about the impact of the "slave emancipation ordinance." There was no consistency in the vigor with which district and travelling commissioners implemented this ordinance. Seldom have the contradictions in colonial administration — the divorce between law and practice, variations in court actions between one district and another, the way in which periods of dedicated effort by some officers were followed by laxity — been more obvious than on this question.

---

partment Report for 1905, 8; *Gold Coast Annual Reports for 1906:* 63; and *for 1908:* 36; *Ashanti Annual Report for 1911:* 8.

24. These figures included about 100 arrests for each of these two years in Ashanti (*Gold Coast Police Department Report for 1914:* 9). In most instances slave-dealing cases were tried in the so-called inferior courts, and convictions were by summary judgment.

25. Few slaves left their masters in Krobo as a result of the ordinance, and presumably some new slaves continued to be brought into Krobo by Ada and other traders via the river Volta from the north (R. E. Dumett, interviews, Ada, Ghana, 1971–1972). Edward Reynolds (pers. comm., December 1983) has commented on the continued use of slaves and younger laborers of slave parentage in the cocoa-growing revolution in Akuapem, 1895–1920. Reynolds' new data on this important question will be explored in detail in a book entitled *Chiefs, Farmers and Preachers: Tradition and Modernization in Akuapem* (forthcoming).

26. See Johnson 1977, which shows that these figures agree with later estimates and returns. (See also Christaller 1881, plus *Gold Coast Census,* 1891; 1901; 1911.) The importation of slaves into Krobo was no new thing, and similar population growth rates appear to have been obtained earlier in the century.

The ordinance stated that slaveholding was illegal.[27] But officials were forbidden from interfering with existing master-servant relations, except under the following circumstances: if a slave requested legal assistance from a magistrate or district commissioner, or if a slave lodged a complaint against his master for forcible constraint or cruelty. These provisions reflect continuity rather than drastic change from the time of Maclean. Despite repeated criticism by the humanitarian lobby in London that the colonial government had failed to make this ordinance widely known, there is evidence that news of the government's new stance had spread fairly quickly through printed circulars, announcements at palavers by travelling officials, and, more important, by ordinary "bush telegraph" (word of mouth) among the people.

The most formidable roadblock against wholesale emancipation of slaves was the reluctance of slaves themselves to come forward even when they had a just case against their masters. Given the strong dependency/welfare element inherent in Akan traditional servitude, plus powerful group pressures with the threat of ostracism or worse if a slave testified against his master, it was remarkable that any slaves whatsoever brought cases forward in the colonial courts. People also hesitated to inform against their neighbors.

The natives are so terribly afraid of each other, and of what their countrymen would do to them, if they assisted the government with evidence of wrong-doing . . . that it is impossible to get them to come forward to give information. (PRO, Griffith 1892)

Equally important was the indifference and outright opposition of many officials towards an activist interpretation of the slave emancipation ordinance. Too many other pressing administrative tasks held higher priority—roads and public works, town sanitation, law and order (arrests for ordinary crimes), and cordial relations with chiefs—for district magistrates to interfere with such a fundamental feature of indigenous social relationships. Cases were publicized where certain officials, in direct contravention of their legal mandate, not only failed to provide certificates of freedom for slaves who should have had them but even took steps to see that such slaves were returned to their owners. One of the worst offenders was Governor William Brandford Griffith during the first half of the 1890s.[28] From a welter of confused evidence on judicial and

27. Ordinance No. 2 of 1874: "To Provide for the Emancipation of Persons Holden in Slavery"; and Ordinance No. 1 of 1875: "To Amend the Gold Coast Emancipation Ordinance of 1874" (Griffith 1887: 26–28).

28. Many of these cases, which raised an outcry among abolitionists arose in the diffi-

administrative actions, the impression gained is that of a government which hoped by mere expressions of disapproval to reduce the harsher aspects of indigenous slavery gradually—but which preferred the status quo and looked paternalistically on slaves remaining close to former masters as the most effective means of social control.

Yet to focus on official attitudes and the role of the colonial government alone in the emancipation process would be to tell only part of the story. Many of the changes resulting from the manumission law took place outside the purview of colonial authorities; some derived from the efforts of missionaries and received scant attention in British official documents. Clearly the emancipation ordinance had some impact in the Gold Coast Colony and Protectorate. We must now examine the evidence to determine whether, as some of the revisionists have argued, the new laws also brought radical change and social disruption.

Akyem Abuakwa and the McSheffrey Hypothesis

In his interesting article "Slavery, Indentured Servitude, Legitimate Trade and the Impact of Abolition in the Gold Coast: 1874–1901," Gerald McSheffrey (1983) contends that indigenous slavery in the Akan region was not the relatively mild institution observed in many ethnographic accounts of the colonial period, but was more often a harshly authoritarian form of social stratification and exploitative labor, and that the 1874–1875 emancipation ordinance led to wholesale desertion by slaves. Yet he himself relies somewhat uncritically on a narrow group of sources for his overview on the nature of Akan slavery—especially Brodie Cruikshank—whose interpretation has been questioned (see Cruikshank 1853, 1: 188–89, 241–44, 313, 331, and critical comment by K. A. Busia, 23). We have suggested that Akan slavery embraced a great variety of relationships and work requirements which have to be investigated in detail before we can generalize with confidence.

To measure the effects of emancipation, McSheffrey concentrates on a major state in eastern Ghana, Akyem Abuakwa, and relies mainly on the selected testimony of those few Basel missionaries who served there.

---

cult area where district courts had to decide what to do with child slaves who were too young to know the meaning of emancipation. In May 1890 four men and one woman were charged with possession of seven girl slaves before the Accra district commissioner's court. Before the district commissioner could proceed with the trial, the governor intervened and ordered the children returned to these very slave purchasers. Under Griffith's governorship (1886–1895) any administrator who took an interventionist stance in slavery cases (particularly with respect to the property rights of slave-owners) ran the risk of being overruled. (For a detailed recounting of these and other instances see PRO, Aborigines Protection Society 1890; and PRO, secretary of state for colonies 1890; also printed in *The African Times*, 1 October 1890: 149).

Extrapolating from scattered references in the Basel reports, he creates the impression that a vast wave of slaves escaped their masters, and he estimates that the total number of pawns and slaves from Akyem Abuakwa who eventually secured their freedom may have reached 10,000 or more. He then extends the notion of an "exodus" of emancipated slaves (based on the Akyem Abuakwa records) to other parts of the eastern Gold Coast, such as Akuapem, Krobo, and the area surrounding Accra as well (Mc-Sheffrey 1983: 356 fn. 33, 359).

A close scrutiny of the evidence, however, shows that political circumstances in Akyem Abuakwa were exceptional. That this state was one of the most centralized and authoritarian in the Akan region at this time means that its servile labor system and its history after issuance of the antislavery ordinances can hardly be taken as characteristic of the entire Gold Coast Protectorate or even of the eastern region.

Role of the Basel Mission in Akyem

But the added element which complicates any effort to base a hypothesis on the decline of slavery throughout the country, or even in the eastern region, on the Akyem reports lies in the fact that the Basel missionaries there, led by David Asante, had a vested interest in the outcome and were, in fact, the prime instigators of the emancipation movement in the capital at Kyebi. Relations between the missionaries and Ata, the king (or *ɔkyenhene*) of Akyem Abuakwa, were decidedly uncordial even before the ordinances, partly because the king had forbidden Christian proselytization of his slaves, and partly because of the cruelties which the king was said to have practiced (including human sacrifice). David Asante and King Ata were totally at odds on these and other issues. When Asante became the prime promoter of the emancipation ordinance in Akyem Abuakwa it further strained relations between the king and the mission.[29] King Ata felt humiliated when an estimated 100–200 of his royal slaves threw off his authority on the basis of the ordinances; and it was quite natural that he blamed this undermining of his power at Kyebi on the work of the Reverend Asante and the mission. One missionary tells vividly of attempting to form a Christian community from former royal slaves who, unsupported by the king, had had to fend for themselves by ravaging the countryside, at the expense of the townspeople, "like a robber band"— a less pleasant picture of royal slaves[30] than that remembered elsewhere in the Akan region.

However, King Ata and the conditions in Kyebi were an extreme ex-

29. Report by D. Asante, *Der Evangelische Heidenbote*, 1875: 66; BMS, D. Asante 1877.
30. For a full discussion of the upheaval surrounding the freeing of the royal slaves,

ample. Indeed, these same mission documents show that most chiefs and elders in the greater Akyem Abuakwa state survived without any flights of slaves whatever. It is important to restate that David Asante was hardly an unbiased observer of events,[31] and we would argue that the Kyebi case was in fact untypical. Furthermore, for his reconstruction of the long-term results of slave emancipation in Akyem Abuakwa, McSheffrey tends to concentrate on the Basel correspondence for the rather brief period 1875–1878; he gives less than full attention to other Basel Mission reports for the 1880s and for areas outside Kyebi that do not corroborate or extend the rather cataclysmic picture given by David Asante and his immediate colleagues.

Estimates of Numbers of Freed Slaves
It is impossible to estimate the total numbers of slaves emancipated as a direct result of the ordinance. Only a tiny number of runaways took advantage of the colonial courts. Clearly, few illiterate slaves from the far interior would have had the confidence (or the linguistic ability) to take such legal action — and this particularly applied to adolescent or child slaves. The regulation that commissioners in each district were to maintain an official "register of emancipated slave children" and then help such young people by apprenticing them out to local farmers, merchants, or missionaries does not seem to have been effectively enforced. There were other instances where prosperous slaves, often themselves slave-owners, did bring cases against their masters,[32] but this was not common.

The greater number of slaves who claimed their freedom did so without the direct intervention of the courts and largely outside the colonial system. In a few cases of recently enslaved persons, the timely intervention of family members helped them to return to their traditional homelands; but the majority of slaves who chose emancipation at all decided

see report by Buck on Kyebi, "A Congregation of Freed Slaves," *Der Evangelische Heidenbote*, 1881: 27.

31. Because of the turmoil of Kyebi, caused in part by the zealousness of David Asante, the Basel Mission was forced against its wishes to remove him from Akyem in 1878. In 1880 the colonial government sentenced the king to five years imprisonment on charges which included disregard of the slave emancipation ordinance and complicity in human sacrifice as well as arson. Details on the reasons for the removal of David Asante from Kyebi can be found in Basel Mission Correspondence, 1878 (BMS, Gold Coast Mission Executive Committee 1878). The final stage in the history of King Ata and the anti-Christian persecutions which occurred in Akyem after his return in 1878 are reported in *Der Evangelische Heidenbote*, 1880: 74; and for 1888: 2, 9 and 17. Also PRO, Governor Ussher 1880.

32. Such slaves would have had considerable confidence in the proceedings of the colonial courts, because they could bring a charge against their masters almost as an equals (BMS, Dieterle 1875).

to remain as tenant (and often dependent) cultivators on or near the farmlands of their former owners (PP, Chalmers' report 1875, in Papers relating to West Africa, [c. 1343], 70–71). The new arrangements by which these scattered "freed" slaves were able to fend for themselves are interesting and worthy of further study. They include at least two categories: slaves who moved some miles from their former villages and cleared new farms for themselves in unoccupied virgin wilderness; and slaves who received plots of land from (and often adjacent to) their former masters and who in return supplied the latter with a portion of their produce in a kind of share-cropping arrangement (BMS, Binder 1875; BMS, Zimmerman 1875). Still, the total number of inland farm slaves who actually fled the paternalism of their masters for the unknown factor of "freedom" as a direct result of the 1874 ordinance was relatively small: one reads of a mere 13 who left out of a village of 1,000 and 19 out of a village of 700.[33] Everything rested on individual choice and on such criteria as the degree of oppression that had existed under a particular slaveholder, the extent to which information about emancipation was circulated, and, most important, the chance for refuge and for material support once the step towards independence had been taken. Yet another point deserves comment in this connection: More than one missionary observed that it was mainly the troublesome slaves and slaves known for their "misdeeds" who left their masters (see, for example, BMS, Rösler 1893).

Slave Villages of Refuge

An especially interesting feature of this phase in Ghanaian history was the emergence of small "krooms," or hamlets, made up of ex-slaves and their families which grew up in the plains and foothills north of Accra. By the early 1890s the Basel agent Schoff estimated that there were about 1,000 ex-slaves living in such hamlets as Apankwa and Abokobi, scattered around the Accra plain, and another 2,000 in Accra itself (BMS, Schopf, 23 May and 8 September 1893). What is most interesting, however, is that most of the ex-slaves in these villages were originally from the northern region (Grunshis, Dagombas, etc.), and appear to have escaped from captivity in Ashanti (not yet subject to British administration and the antislavery laws) by way of the Fanti states. They were traditional "runaways," many of whom had fled to the south before the emancipation ordinance of 1874 (ibid.; BMS, Mohr 1893). This could, of course, show the long-term effects of the mere colonial pres-

---

33. When questioned if many up-country slaves truly understood what was meant by "freedom," one observer said "No" (BMS, Dieterle 1875; Zimmerman 1875).

ence on the coast, which had existed since at least the time of Maclean. It offers some comment on the complex and variable nature of Akan and Ga-Adangme traditional slavery that one of the most oppressive forms of servitude (in terms of labor requirements) was said to exist, not within the local market and subsistence economies of the rural areas, but among certain merchants and chiefs in the commercial-capitalist enclaves of the port towns and coastal districts. Here there was apparently little of the semiequality that pertained in most ordinary rural households, where family heads, family members, and slaves usually ate the same food and performed most of the same tasks in the field. Slaves were expected to man the surfboats which loaded and unloaded awaiting offshore vessels, to head-load goods to and from the interior, to grow and supply food, and to maintain premises. In fact, one commentator went so far as to compare this unusual form of coastal-town servitude as the closest thing to American plantation slavery.

Admittedly the situation of the slave is different with the educated slave-owners, the merchants of the coast, mulattos and the great princes among the twis. Such people do not work and eat with their slaves, and in general stand further away from them. Among such people slavery has more or less lost the character of mild house-slavery, and often seems similar to American slavery. . . . (BMS, Zimmerman 1875)

In the past, government administrators had kept silent about such practices. After all, the African "merchant princes" included some of the staunchest supporters of the colonial regime; and a number of these coastal chiefs and bourgeois traders had in the past rented out cadres of their house slaves and pawns to European firms and even to the government for loading stores or works projects. These "big men" now complained that they could no longer get their ex-slaves to work or deliver such levies because the men knew they no longer had to work without pay. At the Ada port and farther up the Volta River, slaves left the premises of African merchants and chiefs in small numbers of ones, twos, or threes.[34] While this shows that the slave emancipation ordinance could have had a sharp effect in certain sectors where slavery had taken on an oppressive form, the numbers of slaves and slave-owners so affected in the coastal areas were too few to have led to severe deprivation or dislocation.[35]

Such instances of dissonance, while interesting, do not detract from

34. For Accra see PP, Report by Sir David P. Chalmers 1878, [C. 2148], 2–3. For Ada see BMS, Binder 1875.
35. King Tackie of Accra informed the governor of the temporary "hardship" of such slaves leaving their masters without cause (PRO, Carnarvon Papers, Strahan 1875).

our general conclusions (for the Gold Coast and Ashanti) concerning the scattered nature of social disruption traceable to emancipation and the broader continuities between the pre- and postemancipation ordinance periods. Not only did most slaves who chose "freedom" do so quietly and remain close to their districts of adoption, but in Akyem, as elsewhere, most slaves did not choose "freedom" at all (BMS, Rottman 1875; BMS, Eisenschmid 1878). Even in Akyem Abuakwa—where the biggest movement took place—the majority of slaves who secured emancipation remained on the land under their old masters; we have seen that the royal slaves who fled suddenly numbered only 100–200.[36] In Akyem Kotoko, sister state of Akyem Abuakwa, there appears to have been no movement at all by slaves towards freedom. Thus, one Basel missionary wrote: "Here there is still much house slavery. No one is there helping slaves to go to law or to escape" (BMS, Mohr 1882). Throughout the Ga and Adangme areas of eastern Ghana (with the exception of major port towns like Accra and Ada, just discussed), the greater proportion of slaves, having been treated like members of their masters' households (and perhaps entitled to a portion of the master's property when he died), also tended to remain with them. Speaking of the interior Adangme state of Krobo, one member of the Basel brotherhood, Schoenfeld, reported that with "only one or two exceptions, no slaves had left their masters in Krobo." Similarly in the remote Akan state of Kwahu, and all along the river Volta, slaves stayed with their owners (BMS, Schoenfeld 1875; BMS, Müller 1884). In the important farming state of Akuapem, which lay nearer to Accra and where one would have expected emancipation to be very popular, the missionary Widman estimated that about 200 all told had left their masters (BMS, Widman 1875). Thus, the guesswork of McSheffrey, repeated by others, on approximately 10,000 slaves leaving their masters in Akyem Abuakwa alone creates a misleading picture which cannot be sustained.[37] It is unlikely that even the total number of emancipated slaves in the whole of the eastern Gold Coast Colony and Protectorate reached that figure. The fact was that throughout most of the hinterland slaves left their host families only sporadically—one, two, or three at a time. For better or for worse the vast majority of slaves chose to remain connected with their masters' households.

36. McSheffrey (1983) takes the higher part of this estimate. Some of the Basel missionaries said it was 100 (BMS, Asante, Mohr, and Werner 1875).

37. Lovejoy (1983: 283) compounds McSheffrey's error when he says, "Whole villages of slaves deserted, especially in Abuakwa, which may have lost as many as 10,000 slaves in the later *1870's*" (emphasis added). McSheffrey had said that it was "probable" that this number was reached *"eventually"* (emphasis added) and referred to no dates (McSheffrey 1983: 356 fn. 33).

Alternatives for Former Slaves:
Emancipation and Wage Labor

Can the impact of the emancipation ordinance be regarded as a stage
in the advancing tide of capitalism in Ghana introduced under the um-
brella of a "free labor" system which masked new forms of coercion and
control by the colonial state? This is an intriguing revisionist model which
can provide the historian with neat niches for encapsulation of data into
stages — precolonial "slaves," colonial "forced labor," and capitalist "wage
slaves"— and it appears to have rather strong applicability to other parts
of colonial Africa. At the pure policy level there is also some basis for
this coercive hypothesis in contemporary Gold Coast discussions on the
need for a new Master and Servant law that would induce ex-slaves and
others to honor contracts for long-term employment with European
firms.[38] But there was no strong pull of ex-slaves towards such jobs in the
colony in the years immediately following the emancipation ordinance,
nor were the Gold Coast master and servant laws (in contrast to British
East Africa and South Africa) stringently enforced in the way that would
please expatriate capitalists or foster long-term contracts. A major
methodological problem is the lack of any detailed evidence on the possible slave origins of those who worked under the new wage-labor system
of the colonial government (military porters and railway workers) or for
the gold mines. Still, we must bear in mind that wage laborers working
for Europeans constituted an extremely small segment (perhaps 5 percent) of the total adult male work force in the Gold Coast even as late
as 1900.

From the standpoint of substantive trends it is clear that the great majority of Gold Coast ex-slaves chose to remain as subsistence farmers close
to their former masters. It was only a minority who sought free wage
labor. Some who passed through the hands of the Basel Mission were trained as skilled artisans; but many of these remained in the employ of the
Mission Trading Society. Others sought their fortunes farther afield, in
Cameroon, in King Leopold's Congo, and the island of Fernando Po.

Considerable numbers of ex-slaves who lacked vocational training
joined the ranks of the Gold Coast Constabulary, where literacy was not
required.[39] Still others found work as porters, boatmen, or warehouse-

38. As in other aspects of the government's slavery replacement policy, enforcement
of the master and servant laws was sporadic. For a summary of Gold Coast master and
servant legislation see Pouncy 1981.

39. For information on ex-slaves in the colonial constabulary see BMS, Binder 1875.
There were never enough recruits in the colony. Expeditions were sent to Salaga to obtain
recruits against "head-money" (Johnson 1986).

men, or sought casual work as messengers, domestic servants, or general odd-job men. Probably the majority of freed slaves joined the ranks of part-time petty traders, already numerous in the towns. But there was a thin line between many of these pursuits and unemployment: steady jobs were few and far between during the depressed years of the 1880s. David Chalmers and others who had hoped that emancipation might be a step on the road to labor mobilization and "development" expressed disappointment that many ex-slaves seemed to withdraw from the labor market altogether.[40] (Chalmers would not have regarded petty trading as "employment.") But Chalmers was inclined to be hypercritical, and we must also keep in mind the depressed state of the economy in 1880–1885. The government commissioner at Ada reported that a number of ex-slaves had gone to Accra in search of employment — some, he said, had obtained work with mercantile firms, more had joined the police; but many more had joined the large, growing, floating population of "idlers and drifters," some of whom were led into petty crime. Bands of vagabonds and robbers were reported to be molesting travellers and traders along the coast road from Accra to the Volta, and these were reported to be made up of ex-slaves.[41] Insofar as the story lends itself to any kind of "class analysis," a case could be made on the basis of data from the coastal towns, that the inability of local labor markets to absorb many ex-slaves during the period 1875–1895 led to the emergence of an embryonic *lumpenproletariat*, rather than a genuine working class. To what extent the growth of these marginal groups was a consequence of the ordinance must remain unknown. Predatory gangs of runaway slaves were no new thing, and those who deplored Strahan's initiative were inclined to blame everything on it.

The Gold Coast government — like most European governments of the period — regarded the provision of employment for those who came to the towns as none of its concern. That ex-slaves included some rogues was inevitable — some, indeed, had been enslaved by their African rulers for criminal offences in the first place. But it was clearly unrealistic to blame every breakdown of law and order or diminution of chiefs' power on the ordinance, as if such things had not occurred before 1874. "Eman-

40. Not even the promise of higher wages, Chalmers argued, had been sufficient to induce ex-slaves to work more than a few days a week. However, three days per week was often the maximum that a slave had to work for a master under some forms of Akan slavery. In addition, of course, the slave would work on his own farm (PP, Report by Sir David P. Chalmers 1878, [C. 2148], 2–3.

41. BMS, Binder 1875. However, one observer argued that these "vagabond" ex-slaves were not indigenous Akan people, but ex-slave porters used by General Wolseley's military expedition of 1873–1874, drawn from "foreign countries."

cipation" became the colonial government's scapegoat for its own failure to perform the elementary duties of a government in many districts. That said, it is the more remarkable that the ordinance produced so little trouble that the Basel Mission and the district commissioners had to search hard for disruptive consequences to report.

Impact of the Ordinances on Pawnholding

The antislavery ordinances of 1874–1875 apparently had no diminishing effect whatsoever on the transfer of individuals from one household to another as security for debts. On the contrary, the laws appear to have sparked a trend in the opposite direction, as well-to-do merchants, heads of farming families, and kings and chiefs turned to pawnage as a way of continuing to add domestic servants and dependents to their households as a substitute for "slavery." This was a common trend in the 1880s and 1890s according to both missionaries and educated Africans on the coast.[42] A variation on this criticism was that those family heads who could afford it were still taking as pawns numbers of young girls whom they wanted as sexual partners in order to bear progeny and to increase the size of their families and retinues.[43] This upsurge of pawning was also bound up with the spread of commercial capitalism. With the increased availability of money and imported consumer goods, many families tended to spend more lavishly than before — both on material goods for their own comfort or for gifts and entertainments associated with traditional ceremonial occasions. As just one example, the Basel missionaries reported that the problem of overindulgence in alcoholic beverages was one cause of indebtedness and that pawning had intruded even into the African Christian community at Begoro in Akyem.[44] With the great value placed on land and leases beginning in the late 1870s, as a result of mechanized gold mining, and expanding later in the era of cocoa farming, there was a spate of legal disputes, which together with spiralling debts for lawyer's fees and court costs added still further to the pawning tendency.[45]

42. For comments on the increase of pawning reported by Basel missionaries, see BMS, Müller 1888.

43. For comments on the so-called sale of young girls by their parents, see article in the *Gold Coast Chronicle*, 17 December 1892: 2–3. Corroborated in PRO, quarterly district report for Akuse, March 1896. (We must allow, of course, for the possibility of biased observation in these reports, since some officials could have been confusing the sale of young girls as concubines with traditional "bride price.")

44. See BMS, Martin 1896; BMS, D. Asante, report for second quarter, 1877. Rates of interest on loans ran 50–100 percent and sometimes higher.

45. Edward Reynolds (pers. comm., December 1983) believes that land disputes and

DUMETT & JOHNSON: *The Gold Coast*   95

Calling attention to the fact that in Akuapem "thousands of boys and girls" were now living in that form of bondage, Adolph Mohr concluded that "slavery . . . [had] in fact changed into the holding of pawns."[46]

Pawning had been prohibited under the original terms of the slave-dealing ordinance, and by 1892 the colonial government felt strongly enough about the problem to make it a felony under the Gold Coast Criminal Code. Even so, little was done under the law to prosecute alleged perpetrators of pawning. It was difficult even for the most ethnocentric officials to conceive of pawning as a "criminal offense." Still, humanitarian critics complained that the government could have done much more to curtail pawning by putting a ceiling on the rates of interest that could be charged on loans (at that time 50 percent or higher), or by making it mandatory that time spent by pawns working for their creditors should be applied to paying off the original debt and interest. Others argued that the government could have provided some inducement for creditors to cancel their original debts.

So far as can be determined, pawning continued in its various forms until at least the 1930s (GNA [Tamale], de Graft Johnson 1927). It is possible to argue, furthermore, that the term *pawn* served as a convenient intermediate stage in the context of Akan culture between the gradual phasing out of "slavery" and the nearly full assimilation of slaves into the kinship group with whom they resided. According to Rattray (1929: 48) slaves in Ashanti had to pass through a kind of "fictional phase" midway between slavery and freedom before acceptance as near equal members of the family household (reported in A. N. Klein 1980, 2: 408).

Ashanti

The centralized kingdom of Ashanti was occupied by British colonial troops in 1896 and then annexed as a separate colony (yet subordinated to the Gold Coast) after the Yaa Asantewa War in 1900–1901. British administration was placed under the control first of a "resident" and after 1901 under the "chief commissioner of Ashanti" (Ordinance No. 1 of 1902; in Griffith 1903, 2: 1263–66). Because of the unusual administrative relationship, many of the slave emancipation problems which had been encountered in the Gold Coast Colony gave rise in Ashanti to correspondence between the chief commissioner and the governor at Accra in which the intentions, attitudes, and fears of the officials were made explicit.

---

lawyers' fees were a prime reason for increase of family indebtedness in the eastern cocoa-growing region in the early twentieth century.
46. PRO CO, Mohr 1879; BMS, Müller 1895.

Even though the impact of colonial rule in Ashanti did not come until a generation later than in the colony, paid jobs were still almost non-existent there in the 1900s, so that emancipation problems were fairly similar. It is therefore useful to look in some detail at administrative problems surrounding the emancipation of slaves and pawns in Ashanti. A section of Gareth Austin's Ph.D. thesis (1984) relates to this subject.

Though some captives had escaped from Ashanti during the troubled years of defeat and civil war in the last quarter of the nineteenth century,[47] there were still great numbers of household and farm slaves at the time of the first British occupation in 1896, as well as the more noticeable slaves belonging to the major chiefs. Many free Ashanti households would include at least a few slaves at various stages of assimilation.[48]

Slavery in Ashanti was basically similar to slavery in other Akan states, though certain aspects were more significant than in the colony.[49] Human sacrifice, which had largely died out or had been suppressed in the colony, was still practiced in Ashanti, though it was reported to have diminished. Probably it did not survive the British conquest on a large scale, though the fear of it did.[50] The centralized powers not only of the *asantahene* but also of the Ashanti chiefs (*ɔmanhene*) meant that "court slaves" were more numerous and more important than anywhere in the colony, except perhaps Akyem Abuakwa. They loom large in the correspondence.[51]

The Dilemma of Colonial Rule

One of the immediate concerns of the colonial government in Ashanti was to put a stop to slave-trading, and in this they were largely success-

47. One of these was Rosie, who had been nurse to the infant daughter of the Ramseyers during their imprisonment in the course of the 1869 war.

48. Ashanti, like the coastal Akan states, had an elaborate procedure for the gradual assimilation of slaves into the ordinary clan and kinship structure over the course of a generation or more. Because the infusion of new slaves was a continuing process, with the most recent acquisitions filling the lowest strata, subjugation and oppression were maintained despite the opportunity for upward mobility (Tom McCaskie, pers. comm., 1986).

49. For analysis of the structure and ideology of slavery in Ashanti see A. N. Klein 1980, 1: 168–74, 248–52, and passim. For some contemporary accounts of Ashanti slavery see PRO CO, Ewart 1888–1889; GNA (Tamale), Armitage 1903.

50. See, as a single example, the case of Amma Tanowa, who escaped to the Basel Mission in Abetifi after her sisters had been beheaded ("A girl-slave's fear of death," *Der Evangelische Heidenbote*, 1887: 67–70). Ivor Wilks tends to deemphasize human sacrifice in Ashanti religion and as an instrument of state power, viewing it as mainly "capital punishment" reserved for criminals (see Wilks 1975: 592–95 and passim.) For a different view see McCaskie 1986. Ramseyer noted the decline of human sacrifice by 1882 (BMS, Ramseyer 1882).

51. Most of the correspondence cited in this section is included in GNA (Kumasi), "Slaves and Pawns." We are grateful to Gareth Austin for allowing us to use his xeroxes of this file.

ful, as even the critical Basel missionary Ramseyer conceded (GNA [Kumasi], Ramseyer 1904 and 1905). It should also be borne in mind that the weakening of the Ashanti Union, following the British invasion of 1874, had reduced the capacity of Kumasi to levy an annual tribute in slaves on many of the former subject states of greater Ashanti (BMS, Perregaux 1894).

On slaveholding, the situation facing the chief commissioner of Ashanti at the beginning of British rule was not unlike that facing the governors of the Gold Coast Colony in 1874 — the need to reconcile the maintenance of law and order (to prevent further rebellions) with the legal requirement and humanitarian urge to end slavery. But the problem in Ashanti was much more acute, and the commissioners were understandably more concerned with the rather precarious maintenance of colonial rule than with what they saw as legalistic arguments or abstract principles on human rights. They had to govern an unwilling, conquered territory with totally inadequate resources and very little in the way of force; and they needed the support of the chiefs. When the commissioner for the southern provinces reported in 1906 that he feared the antislavery ordinances could not be implemented without the use of force, he was saying that they could not be implemented at that time.

Slave-trading and human sacrifice, but not slavery, had been excluded from those "customs of the country" that, according to the 1896 Anglo-Ashanti treaties, would be respected or tolerated by the colonial authorities. Repeated assurances had been given to the Ashanti chiefs in 1896 that stool property (which included slaves) would not be interfered with. Chief Commissioner Fuller and Acting Chief Commissioner Armitage felt themselves bound by these undertakings, though the view of the Accra government would be that they had been abrogated by the Yaa Asantewa rising of 1900.[52] The commissioners believed that the prestige and authority of the chiefs rested on their court slaves — which may have been partly true, since many of the chiefs now depended for their appointment on British approval, and often had no other traditional legitimacy than that conferred by court ritual (the "true" chiefs being in many cases in exile with the king in the Seychelles). The chiefs were certainly economically dependent on their slaves, and became even more so between 1901 and 1914.[53]

Chief Commissioner Fuller was evidently prepared, over the slavery

52. GNA (Kumasi), Fuller 1907. See also treaties cited in Austin 1984. GNA (Kumasi) Bryan 1907.

53. See GNA (Kumasi), commissioner of southern districts 1906, in "Slaves and Pawns" file and enclosed in letter from "King, chiefs and headmen of Adansi," which includes the following: ". . . All our drums, blowing horns, swords, elephants tails, basket carrying,

question, to let sleeping dogs lie; and in some cases to countenance its revival.[54] British authorities were aroused by the Basel missionary Ramseyer, who was more concerned with the rights of escaped slaves, especially those who escaped to his mission, than with the prestige of chiefs. He complained that slavery was being protected in Ashanti and masters were being allowed to hunt for escaped slaves (GNA [Kumasi], Ramseyer 1904 and 1905). Armitage wrote a memorandum on slavery in reply.

Fuller succeeded in postponing the issue until 1907, though not without considerable exchange of correspondence with Accra. In that year he issued rules about slavery and pawning in Ashanti, making it clear that no positive action regarding slavery was expected of political officers (GNA [Kumasi], chief commissioner 1907). This was too much for Accra. The governor, though he recognized that action was constrained by the situation in Ashanti, pointed out that the Gold Coast ordinances had been applied to Ashanti in 1902. Undoubtedly influenced by the still-potent antislavery lobby at Westminster, the governor stated that he could not approve administrative instructions which recognized the continued existence of slavery anywhere in His Majesty's dominions (GNA [Kumasi], acting colonial secretary 1907).

The wrangle continued, complicated by the absence on leave of both the governor and the chief commissioner. Acting Chief Commissioner Armitage issued revised instructions early in 1908, with the approval of Acting Governor Bryan, but not of Governor Rodger, who had just returned from leave (GNA [Kumasi], Armitage 1908). Eventually the newly returned governor cut the Gordian knot by writing his own instructions and "requesting" the chief commissioner to issue them. These instructions made it clear that involuntary slavery (and pawning) were illegal and that no assistance was to be given in the recovery of fugitive domestic slaves. But the governor's instructions stated that "if a person chooses to work for another in return for his keep, without further wage, there is nothing criminal in the transaction, provided that such work be voluntary, and that their relations be clearly understood by both parties concerned." The instructions, as finally issued by the chief commissioner, omitted the last two provisos (GNA [Kumasi], colonial secretary 1908).

In the course of the correspondence, the commissioners had explicitly stated that there were no unwilling slaves in Ashanti — they had only to move into the colony to "sever all connection with their masters." (If there were no unwilling slaves, the acting governor inquired, why the admin-

and farming works are done by these [slaves] as we have no money like Europeans to hire men to do necessaries for us. . . ." The letter contains much more to the same effect.

54. There was an initial (and largely ineffective) rule that Ashantis could retain possession of all slaves held before the British campaign of 1896 but not those acquired afterwards (PRO CO, Stewart 1901).

istrative instructions?) Armitage, in his revised instructions, had laid it down that, if a slave claimed his freedom, it must be conceded, but he must move away from the place where he had been a slave—to spare the feelings of the former master, who would be "humiliated" by the presence of his former slave as a freeman. This provision was not included in the governor's final instructions (GNA [Kumasi], Armitage 1908; GNA [Kumasi], chief commissioner 1908). It would have made impossible the Gold Coast Colony practice of the ex-slave continuing to farm the land he had previously cultivated as a slave.

Behind the scenes the Basel brethren in Ashanti tried to prepare a few runaway slaves for a new life through Christian education as members of the mission station. A "slave home" was established. But progress was slow owing to the inability of Basel teachers to speak any of the northern (non-Twi) languages and their need to speak to the ex-slaves through interpreters (BMS, Ramseyer 1897 and 1898).

Pawns in Ashanti

In the course of the long wrangle over slaves and pawns in Ashanti, references to "court slaves" and the prestige they conferred gradually disappeared from the discussion. The commissioners believed that if slave-dealing were suppressed, slavery itself would wither away, as slaves ran away, died, or became assimilated into their host families. Pawns, on the other hand, gave rise to increasing concern. In Ashanti, as elsewhere, pawning was seen as the only practical security for loans (apart from underwriting by a man of wealth). The commissioners, by about 1908, were hoping that the practice would soon be replaced by promissory notes. The Basel Mission, on the other hand, saw every new pawn as an addition to the "dependent population," and regarded pawning as tantamount to slavery. The same word was used in Twi for both pawn and slave in the early twentieth century.

Pawning, like slavery, had been illegal in Ashanti since 1902, but nothing had been done to suppress it. The commissioners were very reluctant to take action, since they held that pawning was, for Ashanti, a perfectly normal, legal, and well-understood process. Under pressure from Accra, it was proposed by Fuller to give a year's warning that pawning would not be recognized after a given date. But, like the instructions about slavery, this would imply the previous legality of the practice. So pawning, like slavery, was actively made illegal in Ashanti by the governor's final instructions. It was no longer possible to produce a pawn in court as proof of a debt. (This had long been true in the colony, but pawning continued there nonetheless.) The governor's instructions conceded that the law about pawning was "not intended to apply to voluntary contracts."

After the circulation of the new instructions in 1908, attempts were made to enforce the law against pawning, and a number of cases were brought against chiefs and others, mainly in 1909 and 1910 (Austin 1984). There was also a spurt in activity against slave-dealing in 1911–1912.[55] Thereafter, either enthusiasm for suppression waned or pawning and slave-dealing largely died out, though there were several big token slave cases in the 1920s.

The Demise of Slavery and Pawning in Ashanti
Chief Commissioner Fuller in *A Vanished Dynasty: Ashanti* (1921), wrote, "A few years sufficed to suppress both institutions [slavery and pawning] for ever" (cited in Austin 1984: 508). As with the title of his book, Fuller was premature. Some cases reached the courts, and as late as 1931 the district commissioner at Bekwai wrote, "I am aware that by old native custom there are many people still bound to others through ties said to be slavery. . . ."[56] Some ex-slaves flourished, establishing their own cocoa farms. Numerous slaves remained with their old masters — as early as 1899 there had been newspaper reports of slaves refusing to leave their masters (A. N. Klein 1980: 181) — and many helped to create the cocoa farms which were to revolutionize relations of production in Ashanti. With increasing money incomes, wage labor in cocoa farming increased (though not as a result of government policy).

Survivors of this period were to recall "a breath of freedom blowing everywhere" and slaves refusing to work for their former masters.[57] New sources of labor became available in the form of migrant laborers from the north, in place of the old northern slaves. *ɔdonko*, formerly used for slaves of northern origin, became the term for northern laborers. Some Ashanti chiefs made a distinction between "our ɔdonko" (slaves) and "their ɔdonko" (laborers); this distinction vanished only in the 1950s, owing to the widespread use of wage labor (Tom McCaskie, pers. comm.).

Suppressing the Slave Trade and Slavery
in the Northern Territories

Space prevents coverage of the history and ethnography of northern Ghana prior to British rule, but there is no doubt that slave-raiding and

---

55. Slave-dealing cases averaged about 12 per year in the colonial court in Ashanti, 1902–1910, but rose to well over 100 each year in 1911 and 1912 (*Gold Coast Judicial Department Reports* for the years shown).

56. NAGK Bki, DAO File 39, item 112: district commissioner to Esumejahene, 9 December 1931 (cited in Austin 1984: 510).

57. Austin (1984: 509), citing his own fieldwork; and Poku 1969: 35. Also *The African Times*, 1 February 1899, cited in Klein 1980, 1: 181, 297.

the slave trade played central parts in the traditional economies of many of the northern peoples prior to annexation in 1901–1902. In addition slaves were the primary food producers in a number of states and districts. During the nineteenth century the major centralized kingdoms in the region were those of Wa in the northwest, Gonja in the west-central area, Mamprusi with its capital at Gambaga in the northeast, and Dagomba (Dagbon) with its capital at Yendi in the east. (For details on the major ethnic groups and states of the northern region see Northcott 1899; Rattray 1932; Tait 1961; Goody 1967; Staniland 1975).

None of the centralized states of the north was as powerful as Ashanti — even in its late nineteenth-century decline: Gonja and Dagomba had, indeed, been tributary to Ashanti before 1874. The Zaberima, a group of mounted freebooters originally dependent on Dagomba, had formed a "state" in the northwest and adjacent areas of what was to become Upper Volta.[58] All were cavalry states practicing organized slave-raiding. Their victims were the Dagarti, the Isala, the Tumu, the Konkomba — commonly referred to as "Grunshi," a blanket name for the stateless societies on both sides of what is now the Ghana–Burkina Faso frontier.

True, slave tributes to Ashanti had ceased after 1874, but these northern slaving states combined sent far larger numbers through the market of Salaga each year in the 1880s than had ever reached Ashanti as tribute. (One estimate was 15,000 a year, in contrast with 1,000 each as tribute from Gonja and Dagomba to Kumasi.)[59] In addition, as noted earlier, western Gonja was invaded and raided by Samori's forces.

Much of the area, including the great slave market at Salaga, had been turned into a neutral zone in the 1880s by a treaty between Britain and Germany. One German official believed that any interference with the slave trade would lead to a widespread rising like that of al-Mahdi in the Sudan, and suggested that the British had avoided formal empire there for fear of having to deal with the question of the slave trade (GCA, Wolf 1889). By the later 1890s, however, in order to forestall similar German moves, a more imperialist Britain had despatched forces to occupy what remained of Salaga and then went on to occupy what was to become the Northern Territories of the Gold Coast.

58. Holden (1965: 64–65) notes constructive aspects of the Zaberima system such as bringing order to divided segmentary societies and restoring it to centralized states that had been frequently at war with one another. On the other hand the studies by Anafu (1973) and Iliasu (1975: 1–5) show that the Mamprusi and Dagomba states, if not others, maintained their territorial and administrative integrity and that the Zaberimas simply infiltrated and collaborated with them.

59. PRO CO, Ferguson 1894. For the larger estimate see Johnson 1986b.

British Administration in the North

The first concern of the British in the Northern Territories was necessarily the suppression of slave-raiding and the breaking up of the great slave markets. Upon this depended the hope of administrators farther south that it would be impossible for the slave system to reproduce itself if the supply were eliminated. So the British set out quite deliberately to "disrupt" the social disorder of the Northern Territories. No general rising took place. Dagomba had been cut in half by the new Anglo-German frontier, and Gonja was already in civil turmoil, while the Zaberima were also much divided. The defeat of the Zaberima by the British and of Samori by the French, while undermining those robber states, laid the foundations of the new order in the north. The campaigns which followed were concerned with the reestablishment of law and order and the suppression of minor raiding and slave-dealing.

Major H. P. Northcott, military commandant and later chief commissioner of the Northern Territories, laid down his strategies for strangling the slave traffic at its source. Clauses calling for the prevention of the slave trade were written into practically all of Britain's treaties with the various northern states and chiefdoms. For several years the chief commissioner ruled the Northern Territories as the proconsul of a military frontier province. The main thrust of Northcott's anti-slave-trade campaign came in the form of expeditions by the West African Frontier Force against known slave markets and roving bands of brigands. Using broad powers of summary jurisdiction, he meted out harsh punishments for slave-raiding, slave-dealing, and plundering of trade caravans. Shortly after the new government was established, he reported that two bands of robbers had been broken up, and "80 cases of slave dealing, looting and raiding of women and children had been dealt with" (*Northern Territories Annual Report for 1901*). Although cases involving violations of the anti-slave-dealing law continued to be prosecuted before district and provincial commissioners' courts, one suspects that it was the mere presence of patrolling officers in key districts rather than arrests and convictions that inhibited would-be slave traffickers. From most accounts it would appear that a sense of personal safety was, in fact, brought to many of the areas where it had not existed for a long time. At Bawku in the extreme northeast, the district officer reported, "A large number of natives from outlying areas now attend the market, who before our advent rarely, if ever, visited it for fear of being captured and sold as slaves" (*Northern Territories Annual Report for 1909: 8*). On the other hand, the main aim of British officials in the north was to develop and maintain the free flow of general trade whether by land or down the river Volta. Administrators would not, therefore, have jeopardized that trade by intervening in every small case involving slave-trading or use of slaves as porters by major African merchants, even if they had had the staff to do so.

Evidence for a Revisionist Interpretation

Some of the strongest evidence for support of a revisionist "disruptive impact" line of argument with respect to slavery suppression in Ghana can be found in the north. While conventional opinion concludes that the British assault on slave-raiding and the overland slave trade benefitted the many men, women, and children who might otherwise have been enslaved, it is important to note a number of locally disturbing effects of the so-called *Pax Britannica*. We have long known that some of the "Hausa" soldiers recruited for the Gold Coast Constabulary and later for the West African Frontier Force—the very groups assigned to keep order in the Northern Territories—were recruited from the ranks of Zaberima warriors, who had been active slave-raiders. In addition many northern "ex-slaves" continued to be recruited as carriers for the government transport service that supplied the military campaigns. Once employed by the British, many of these so-called Hausas exceeded their authority by "liberating" at random household slaves in many of the northern villages (David Killingray, pers. comm., 8 June 1984; Haight 1981, 1: 85). Under these circumstances it was not surprising that Hausa troopers on British "pacification" expeditions often had a poor reputation among the local people. They were known to have plundered the houses and farms through which they passed and carried off some of the women for their own use.[60]

In two recent doctoral dissertations Glenna Case (1979) and Bruce Haight (1981) argue that British suppression of the overland slave trade was initially injurious to the traditional socioeconomic systems of the Wasipe and Bole divisions of Gonja. Case argues that both slave-dealing and slavery as an institution were central to the functioning of Wasipe's traditional economy. Case and Haight differ somewhat in their view of the centrality of slave labor to food crop production for their two respective districts. Haight points out that "traditionally" slaves produced little surplus of agricultural products for sale or distribution in Bole division; most families lived by their own subsistence farming. Although the two writers agree that Gonja chiefs lost greatly in wealth, power, and prestige as a consequence of the effective prohibition of slave-raiding by British armed patrols (Case 1979, 1: 381–85), Haight is less certain than

---

60. One ex-soldier said he "understood from the white man that the followers might catch women for wives from Zoko but that there was to be no selling of them afterwards" (GNA [Tamale], Legal Records Book; reference supplied by Roger Thomas).

Case that Britain's anti-slave-trade policy overturned the entire economic equilibrium of his region (Haight 1981, 1: 87–88; Haight 1984: 8–9). For one thing, Haight points out that western Gonja had endured its main losses of slaves and economic destruction as a result of the Samorian invasions of the middle 1890s. To say that kings and chiefs of Gonja were shorn of wealth and power as a result of British rule does not prove that their entire populations suffered or that the entire economy was altered for the worse. On the contrary, it is quite likely that the victims of slave-raiding, the common people—whether among the local and nearby Gonja populations or among neighboring and distant tribes—benefitted from the long-term peace and stability and growth of trade under the new system. In his own critical study of the British impact, Haight makes a clear-cut distinction between abolition of the Gonja slave trade and slave-raiding (a demise which, he concludes, probably improved the lives of a majority of people) and later aspects of modernization under colonial rule—such as the coming of motor lorries in the 1920s—which reduced the importance of local production and trade and helped to turn Gonja into an economic backwater (Haight 1984: 13–14).

Slave-trading from the north did not altogether cease; some slaves continued to be brought down the Volta from the Northern Territories through Togoland to the Gold Coast during the early 1900s and perhaps even later. This was a small and furtive trade, however, mainly in children, tragic enough for its victims, but not like the terrible mass trading (15,000 a year was one estimate for the late 1880s) of the days when the great Salaga slave market stood undisturbed by the Germans or British (Johnson 1986). Britain's anti-slave-trade campaign had its most radical impact in the northern savanna region, because this was the primary source of the traffic. The reduction in numbers of slaves exported during the first years of the twentieth century was clearly traceable to the destruction of slave markets and to British punitive attacks on slave-raiding, which led to the suffocation of slave supplies.

So far as the active suppression of slavery (as distinct from the suppression of raiding and open sale) in the Northern Territories was concerned, the effects of British administration were much less severe. Here the story of the Salaga area in the first decade of the present century is instructive. Abolition of slavery had been written into the treaty with the sultan at the time of the British reoccupation, but at the same time the governor had warned the civil commandant not to let his Hausa troops interfere with the people's slaves, as nothing was more likely to cause "trouble" (PRO CO, commissioner in chief of the Northern Territories 1897). In a policy very similar to that invoked in Ashanti in this same period, the British made little effort to assist even unwilling slaves to leave their masters. In the Salaga District, the district commissioner actually prevented unwilling "Grunshi" slaves from leaving.[61] A few years later, however, the slaves took the matter into their own hands and left en masse — the only instance of a mass exodus known to us, unless the Akyem Abuakwa case qualifies. Salaga, just recovering from the disasters of the 1890s, thereupon went into a new decline, from which it never recovered (Johnson 1986). In the Wasipe division of Gonja, however, most household slaves remained with their masters; and, over time, masters simply stopped referring to them as slaves (Case 1979; 1: 382). On the whole, then, we see a rather restrained policy with regard to slave emancipation. Whereas in the Gold Coast Colony slaves had been free to leave their masters, though not necessarily encouraged to do so (except, perhaps, by some missionaries), and in Ashanti "unwilling" slaves were to be freed if they left the district, in the north the British authorities denied slaves even these rights.

Conclusion

In making up the account of British antislavery policy in the Gold Coast, Ashanti, and Northern Territories, a distinction must be made between the forceful suppression of the inland slave trade and the government's gradualist, noncoercive policy with respect to slaveholding and pawning. Based on a variety of sources, it is clear that colonial administrators were effective in a relatively short period of time in destroying major open slave markets and in putting an end to slave-raiding. This represented strong intervention and a decisive change which began in 1874 and became effective in the slaving areas of the Northern Territories after 1898. The colonial state was less successful in putting an immediate end to the surreptitious smuggling of small numbers of slaves — particularly women and children — from the northern region into the societies of the south.

It is with the "holding" of slaves and pawns that the continuities between pre- and postordinance periods are most apparent. This can be seen in the extreme reluctance of the colonial governments to promote actively, or even encourage, the freeing of old or established slaves and pawns, especially in Ashanti and the Northern Territories. With one or two rare exceptions there were no mass movements of slaves who sought sudden freedom; instead only small groups exercised their new rights to leave their host families in the aftermath of the ordinance. While the

61. GNA (Tamale), district commissioner 1904. (Thanks to Roger Thomas for this reference.)

government's emancipation policy created a climate of opinion that was more conducive to the exercise of this option, few of these newly self-emancipated slaves sought or received the direct protection of the colonial courts.

The short-term effects of colonial laws and executive instructions on slaveholding were, therefore, meliorative and eroding rather than abolitionist in effect. The outlawing of human sacrifices helped to eliminate one of the harshest features of Akan and Ga-Adangme slavery; however, this process had been ongoing even without colonial intervention in most Akan states. Again, the major recourse open to individual slaves subjected to cruel treatment had always been to run away, and use of this route to freedom accelerated after implementation of the antislavery laws. But the total numbers of slaves who obtained freedom in this way in the immediate aftermath of the ordinances can never be known, and we must set against these "guesstimates" the smuggling of new slaves and pawns for another three decades after 1874. Since runaway slaves now had some legal protection, it was possible to argue (as the colonial government did) that no "unwilling" slaves remained. Very similar policies were followed in Ashanti during the first decade of colonial rule, though runaways had to cross into the colony to be safe. In the Northern Territories we have noted that some officials even attempted to prevent slaves from running away.

This chapter has presented new evidence to show that an expansion of the traditional institution of pawnholding served as a buffer in enabling African families and chiefdoms to weather the transition from slave to "free" fairly comfortably without great loss of labor or social prestige. It is also possible that pawning in Ashanti, as in parts of the colony, became little more than another term for enslavement (as the missionaries claimed).

Over the long run, the government's antislavery policy when combined with the influence of various Church mission groups did have considerable impact in changing traditional attitudes and practices with regard to servile labor.[62] But these effects worked in conjunction with a variety of other exogenous and impersonal forces and trends — improvements in transportation and communications, education, growth of cash-crop agriculture, expansion of trade, and Westernization.

The decline of slave-raiding and slave-trading worked, along with these

62. One elderly Ghanaian stated that he believed that over time Christian churches and schools generally had exerted a greater influence against the holding of slaves than British colonial officials. This would have included a much wider influence than the Basel Mission alone (interview: Opanin Kwaku Adu, 27 July 1969).

other trends, to undermine the powers of many northern chiefs. It is probable that the powers of some chiefs in the southern forest region were
also reduced with the decline of slaveholding. However, this can be exaggerated, for even in Akyem Abuakwa the emancipation of slaves did not
break the power of the chiefs, as witness later examples of chief-inspired
local resistance against colonial rule in that state right up to the cocoa
holdup of 1937–1938.

There is no strong evidence for arguing as a central thesis that the colonial government ordered emancipation for the prime purpose of achieving capitalist development. There had been, of course, occasional comments by imperial statesmen and editorials by coastal African lawyers
and journalists that slavery was part of "a primitive stage" which was
incompatible with modern industrial development. And it is true that
the Basel Mission tried in its small way to use its congregation of freed
slaves to promote commercial agriculture and skilled trades. But the
statements in contemporary speeches about the key importance of slavery abolition were often rationalizations for imperialist controls for other
reasons. The weight of evidence shows that the main mercantile and
mining firms on the coast, as well as many officials, were either indiffer-
ent to or opposed to interference with African traditional slavery on
straight economic grounds. Neither is there much support in the Gold
Coast evidence for the neo-Marxist argument that slave relations of production were deliberately preserved so that they might supply the modern capitalist sector with cheap labor.[63]

A well-informed African official in the 1920s could find no direct
causal connection or linear development between emancipation and the
movement of up-country people into wage employment (GNA [Tamale],
de Graft Johnson 1927). Preliminary investigation suggests the possibility of some very thin links between the traditional use of coerced labor
in the economic systems of some northern states and the *areas* selected
for recruitment of the first northern wage labor for the European-owned
gold mines and the African-owned cocoa farms of the forest zone.[64] How-

63. Many of the economic issues raised by this study are discussed in relation to Ashanti
in Austin 1984. He considers and rejects a Marxist interpretation of the emancipation policy of the Ashanti commissioners. He notes that "rather than saying that slavery and pawning must be eliminated to facilitate the growth of capitalist wage labour and promissory
notes," officials argued "that slavery and pawning should not be abolished *until* they could
be replaced by more modern instruments of appropriation" (Austin 1984: 486). Austin also
rejects Meillassoux's neo-Marxist interpretation that traditional modes of production were
preserved so that they might supply the modern capitalist sector with cheap labor. "There
is no evidence that any of the advocates of a gradualist approach to abolition ever considered this kind of calculation, even unconsciously" (ibid.: 488).
64. The evidence so far is mainly circumstantial. Edward Reynolds (pers. comm., 1983)

ever, the major factors which maintained the north as a vast labor-supply zone were not an alleged connection between traditional slave labor and modern capitalist wage labor but the continuities that derived from the basic ecological differences and varying resource endowments of the two regions.

By the beginning of the Second World War, slavery in the Gold Coast was largely a thing of the past, though rare allegations of slave-dealing and slave usage continued to reach the governor's desk down to the 1940s (see, for example, GNA [Tamale], Kwashie 1936; GNA [Tamale], Armory 1941). The primary external force for change in the transition from "slave" to "free"— particularly in Ashanti and the Northern Territories — was the spread of the capitalist exchange economy in which the main generating elements were the rapidly expanding cocoa-growing industry of Ashanti and the southeast, and to a lesser extent the railway, mining, and trading enclaves of Accra, Cape Coast, and the southwest.

Although there were certain exceptions, notably in Akyem Abuakwa and in the north, the ending of slavery in the Gold Coast (despite traces and relics here and there) must be one of the quieter social revolutions of the late nineteenth and early twentieth centuries. We have stressed throughout this chapter that some of the most powerful— but not the only— mechanisms for transforming slavery lay within the traditional Akan and Ga-Adangme cultures. The main pathway for change, in the south at least, continued to be the assimilation of slaves into the host kinship group, and intermarriage remained one of the principal means of assimilation.[65] Still, if one takes as a definition of social revolution, not mass migration or a wholesale breakdown of law and order, but major (if gradual) changes in the structure of society and the position of the ruling class, then there certainly was a social revolution in progress, 1874–1930. But numerous causal factors were at work, of which the disappearance of slavery was only one.

The fact that the word for "slave" is no longer so acceptable in open discourse has undoubtedly served as a cutting edge for the erosion of slavery itself over time. It is true that unmannerly people sometimes taunt

---

argues that many of the ordinary laborers who worked on the early cocoa farms were members of ɔdonko families who had been brought south earlier. Some of the first northern workers brought to the gold mines of Wassa under a government-sponsored scheme of forced conscription were members of the same small-scale societies earlier subject to slave-raiding, as were many of the "free" recruits. But it is difficult to say whether the first northern mine laborers included slaves (Thomas 1973).

65. Recent oral interviews suggest that early twentieth-century slaves, particularly those brought into host communities as children or as wives for the purchasers, were assimilated more rapidly than the full generation cited as a requirement in older written sources (interviews in Ghana by R. E. Dumett, 1971–1972, 1987).

members of their communities with mention of slave origins, and so long as they confine this within the household little can be done about it. But such behavior is contrary to indigenous morality, and for a long time such offenders could be fined in a chief's court. It is still rare to find anyone, particularly in the south, who will admit to being of slave origin.[66] The stigma, if nothing else, remains; and it appears that in some areas of Ghana descendants of slaves are still expected to undertake the harder and more menial work of the household.

GLOSSARY

Unless otherwise indicated the words here are from the Twi language of the Akan people of the Gold Coast.

afunaba	client or subordinate.
akoa (pl. *nkoa*)	a subject.
akyere (pl. *nkyere*)	a slave intended for human sacrifice.
asantahene	the king (or paramount ruler) of the Ashanti Union and Empire.
awowa (pl. *nnwowa*)	pawn or person given over to a creditor as sureties for debt.
awura	master.
klu	a male slave in the Ewe region, east of the river Volta (Ewe language).
krooms	small villages or hamlets.
mantse	the king (or paramount ruler) in the Adangme region of the eastern Gold Coast/Ghana (Adangme language).
nyongwe	a slave in the Adangme region of the Gold Coast/Ghana, east of Accra and west of the Volta River (Adangme language).
ɔdonko (pl. *nnonko*)	foreigner, northerner, slave.
ɔkyenhene	the king (or paramount ruler) of Akyem Abuakwa State.
ɔmanhene	stool holders or chiefs of substates in the political systems of the Akan people.

66. In interviews, one finds an occasional admission that a deceased relative had been a slave. A Wa informant related that he had been told by his grandfather that his wife, the informant's grandmother, had originally been purchased (R. E. Dumett, interview with Ismail bin Yahya, of Wa, northern region, Ghana, at Lafayette, Indiana, U.S.A., May 1984). In Konongo, Dwaben, Asante the Queen Mother (mother of the present Konongohene) states that she had originally been purchased as a slave while a young girl early in this century (interview by R. E. Dumett with Nana Efua Tenkroman, 25 May 1987, Konongo, Asante, Ghana).

REFERENCES

Oral sources

All interviews were conducted by R. E. Dumett.

Interviews with informants in Ghana, 1969, 1971–1972, and 1987.
Ismail bin Yahya, of Wa, northern region, Ghana, interview in Lafayette, Indiana, May 1984.
The mantse and elders of Prampram, interview in Prampram, Ghana, on 20 December 1971.
Nana Efua Tenkroman, interview in Konongo, Asante, Ghana, on 25 May 1987.
Opanin Kwahu Adu, interview in Mampong-Akrofoso, Ashanti, on 27 July 1969.

Archival sources

BMS: Basel Mission Society Archives, Basel, Switzerland.

All sources listed below indicate page references to the translation in abstract form by Paul Jenkins of the Basel Mission Society Archives and are referred to in the notes simply as "Abstract." We are grateful to Paul Jenkins for making his translations and abstract available to us.

Abetifi Station Correspondence
    Asante, D., report on journey to the north, 11 April 1882; Abstract, 172.
    Hall, report on journey to the north, 25 February 1887; Abstract, 226.
    Mohr, A., to Basel, 15 May 1882; Abstract, 168, 170–72.
    Müller, J., to Basel, 5 May 1884; Abstract, 194.
    Ramseyer, F., to Basel, October 1882; Abstract, 162.
    Ramseyer, F., to Basel, March 1885; Abstract 203.
Akyem Station Correspondence
    Asante, D., report for second quarter of 1877, 9 July 1877; Abstract, 593.
    Eisenschmid to Basel, 28 February 1878; Abstract, 607.
    Gold Coast Mission Executive Committee to Basel, 29 January 1878; Abstract 607.
Gold Coast Slave Emancipation Commission
    Asante, D., A. Mohr, and P. Werner to Basel, 26 June 1875; Abstract, 585(a).
    Binder, J., to J. A. Mader, 3 July 1875; Abstract, 585(c)–586.
    Dieterle, N., to Basel, 22 June 1875; Abstract, 583–84.
    Eisenschmid to Basel, 25 June 1875; Abstract, 585.
    Rottman, H., to Basel, 30 June 1875; Abstract, 585(b)–585(c).
    Schöenfeld to Mader, 8 July 1875; Abstract, 586.
    Widman, subscript on reports to Basel, 20 August 1875; Abstract, 588.
    Zimmerman, G., to Basel, 26 July 1875; Abstract, 586–87.
Kumasi Station Correspondence
    Ramseyer, F., to Basel, 26 July 1897; Abstract, 365.
    Ramseyer, report for the year 1897, 11 February 1898; Abstract, 362.

Miscellaneous Documents concerning Slave Trade and Slave Emancipation
Martin to Basel, 18 November 1896; Abstract, 359.
Mohr, comment on the project, 7 May 1893; Abstract, 306.
Müller to Basel, 28 May 1888 (Anum Station correspondence); Abstract, 248.
Müller, report for 1890 (Anum Station); 18 February 1891; Abstract, 266f.
Müller to Basel, 17 September 1895; Abstract, 341–42.
Perregaux, E., report for the first quarter of 1894, 10 May 1894; Abstract, 319–20.
Ramseyer, comment on ex-slave resettlement project, 5 May 1893; Abstract, 306.
Rösler, comment, 28 May 1893; Abstract, 307–8.
Schopf, quarterly report, 8 September 1893; Abstract, 308.
Schopf, subscript, 23 May 1893; Abstract, 306.
GCA: German Colonial Archives, Potsdam, German Democratic Republic. Wolf. Akte 4086 (1889).
GNA (Kumasi): Ghana National Archives, Kumasi, Ghana. "Slaves and Pawns." File No. D234.

All correspondence listed below for the GNA at Kumasi can be found in the file entitled "Slaves and Pawns" under the reference M.P. 1905 and 1907 — apparently the years when the files were opened and which correspond to Accra file numbers.

Acting colonial secretary to chief commissioner, Ashanti, 20 November 1907, M.P. 64/1905.
Armitage to acting colonial secretary, 28 February 1908, M.P. 41/1907.
Bryan, confidential letter to Armitage in reply to Fuller's letter [Fuller having gone on leave], 13 December 1907.
Chief commissioner, Ashanti, instructions issued, 1 November 1907.
Colonial secretary to chief commissioner, 17 June 1908, M.P. 64/1905; also enclosed in Confidential M.P. 41/1907, June 1908.
Commissioner of southern districts, letter, 11 December 1906.
Fuller to Acting Governor Bryan, 2 December 1907.
Ramseyer to governor, 31 October 1904.
Ramseyer to governor, 1 November 1905.
GNA (Tamale): Ghana National Archives, Northern Branch, Tamale, Ghana.
Armitage, C. H., memo to acting colonial secretary on slavery and pawning, 20 May 1903. File M.P. 41/1951.
Armory, C. G. R., assistant district commissioner (Bawku), letter to acting chief commissioner (Tamale), 25 September 1941. No. 352/6/1930, SFT.
de Graft Johnson, J. C., "Memorandum on the Vestiges of Slavery in the Gold Coast," 17 October 1927. Encl. in H. Walker-Leigh, chief commander of the Northern Territories, to colonial secretary (Accra), 12 January 1928. Confidential No. 16/35/1928. RAT 1/23, File on Domestic Slavery.
District commissioner, monthly report, January 1904. Admin. 56/4/111.
Kwashie, Dan A., (very private) letter to colonial secretary (Accra), 26 May

1936. Encl. in inspector general of the police (Accra), 12 June 1936. RAT 23/1.

Legal Records Book, chief commissioner's court. Admin. 56/4/1.

PRO: Public Record Office, London.

Aborigines Protection Society, letter to secretary of state for colonies (Lord Knutsford), 20 August 1890. C.O. 96/214.

Bannerman, letter, 24 February 1826. C.O. 267/78 under "B."

Carnarvon Papers. P.R.O. 30/6/41.

Bartel Frere, Sir Henry, to Carnarvon, 25 June 1874.

Governor Strahan to Carnarvon, 22 January 1875.

District commissioner at Cape Coast, report. Encl. in Hodgson (52) to Colonial Office, 29 January 1898. C.O. 96/311.

District commissioner at Dixcove, report. Encl. in Hodgson (52) to Colonial Office, 29 January 1898. C.O. 96/311.

District commissioner at Elmina, report. Encl. in Hodgson (52) to Colonial Office, 29 January 1898. C.O. 96/311.

Gouldsbury, V. S., report on mission to Akyem. Encl. in Strahan (22) to Carnarvon, 13 November 1875. C.O. 96/116.

Governor Ussher (160) to Colonial Office, 25 May 1880. C.O. 96/131.

Governor Winniet to Earl Grey, 22 May 1850. C.O. 96/18.

Governor Winniet to Earl Grey (Separate), 30 May 1850. C.O. 96/18.

Griffith (278) to Ripon, 12 October 1892. C.O. 96/226.

Hemming, minute, 1 April 1875, on Strahan to Carnarvon, 6 March 1875. C.O. 96/112.

Hodgson (49) to Colonial Office, 17 February 1890. C.O. 96/208.

Holland, Henry, memorandum to Earl Carnarvon. Encl. in Law Offices to Carnarvon, 24 June 1874. C.O. 96/113.

Phillips, S., report to colonial secretary, 18 December 1893. Encl. 2 in Hodgson (Confidential) to 60, 1 February 1894. C.O. 96/243.

Quarterly district report for Akuse, March 1896. Encl. in Hodgson (280), 13 July 1896. C.O. 96/275.

Secretary of state for colonies, reply to Griffith, 27 August 1890. C.O. 96/214.

Wray, J. C., to Sir Michael Hicks Beach, 11 March 1877. C.O. 96/129.

PRO CO: Colonial Office Confidential Prints, Public Record Office, London.

Commissioner in chief of the Northern Territories to Inspector Aplin, 1 September 1897. C.O. African (W) Confidential Print 538, pp. 150, 152.

Ewart, J. H., report, "Ashanti" (1888–1889). Encl. in Ewart to Colonial Office, 24 October 1889. C.O. African (W) Confidential Print 354, No. 61, pp. 116–22.

Fairfield, E., "Domestic Slavery. The Jurisdiction of the Judicial Assessor and the Legal Character and Limitations of British Power upon the Gold Coast," 19 March 1874. Confidential Print No. 47, pp. 10–12.

Ferguson, George E., report, 18 August 1894. Encl. in Griffith (19) to Ripon, 28 September 1894. C.O. African (W) Confidential Print 479, No. 19, pp. 21–30.

Mohr, Rev. A., to Governor Ussher, 15 October 1879. Encl. 9 in Ussher to Hicks Beach, 21 January 1880. C.O. African (W) Confidential Print 379, No. 4, p. 99.

Stewart, Donald, British resident, Kumasi, to Governor Nathan, 9 September 1901. Encl. in Nathan to Colonial Office, 28 September 1901. C.O. African (W) Confidential Print 649, No. 90, pp. 79–82.

Other sources

African Times, The (London). Various issues.

Anafu, M. 1973. The impact of colonial rule on Tallensi political institutions, 1898–1967. *Transactions of the Historical Society of Ghana* 14: 17–37.

Austin, G. 1984. The growth of cocoa-farming in south Ashanti, 1896–1914. Ph.D. thesis, University of Birmingham.

Bell, H. J. 1898. *The history, trade, resources and present condition of the Gold Coast settlement.* Liverpool: Liverpool Chamber of Commerce.

Bowdich, T. 1819. *Mission from Cape Coast Castle to Ashantee.* London: John Murray; reprint, London: Frank Cass, 1966.

Burton, R. and Cameron, V. L. 1883. *To the Gold Coast for gold,* Vol. 2. London: Chatto and Windus.

Case, G. 1979. *Wasipe under the Ngbanya: policy, economy and society in Northern Ghana,* 2 vols. Ph.D. dissertation, Northwestern University, Evanston, Illinois.

Christaller, J. G. 1881. *Dictionary of the Asante and Fante language.* Basel: Basel Evangelical Mission Society. Rev. ed., 1933 (omits the geographical index).

Clark, R. 1860. *Remarks on the topography and diseases of the Gold Coast.* London: privately printed.

Cooper, F. 1979. The problem of slavery in African Studies. *Journal of African History* 20(1): 103–25.

Cruickshank, B. 1853. *Eighteen years on the Gold Coast,* 2 vols. London: Hurst and Blackett.

Curtin, P. D. 1969. *The Atlantic slave trade: a census.* Madison: University of Wisconsin Press.

Dumett, R. E. 1979. Precolonial gold mining and the state in the Akan Region: with a critique of the Terray hypothesis." In *Research in economic anthropology,* Vol. 2, ed. G. Dalton, 37–68. Greenwich, Conn.: JAI Press.

Dumett, R. E. 1981. Pressure groups, bureaucracy and the decision making process: the case of slave abolition and colonial expansion in the Gold Coast. *Journal of Imperial and Commonwealth History* 9 (2): 193–215.

Evangelische Heidenbote, Der. 1875–1895. Basel, Switzerland.

Gold Coast Chronicle (Accra).

Gold Coast, Government of. *Annual Colonial Reports; Gold Coast Annual Reports; Ashanti Annual Reports* and *Northern Territories Annual Reports;* yearly *Departmental Reports; Gold Coast Census Reports of 1891; 1901; and 1911.* London: H. M. Stationery Office.

114   II. A HISTORIOGRAPHICAL DEBATE

Goody, J. 1967. The over-kingdom of Gonja. In *West African kingdoms in the nineteenth century*, ed. D. Forde and P. M. Kaberry, 179–205. Oxford: Oxford University Press.

Griffith, W. B. 1887. *Ordinances of the settlements on the Gold Coast and of the Gold Coast Colony in force April 1887*. London: Stevens and Sons.

Griffith, W. B., Jr. 1903. *Ordinances of the Gold Coast Colony . . . in force 31 March 1903*, 2 vols. London: Stevens and Sons.

Haight, B. 1981. Bole and Gonja, contributions to the history of Northern Ghana." 3 vols. Ph.D. dissertation, Northwestern University, Evanston, Illinois.

Haight, B. 1984. The ebb and flow of subordinate labor in Gonja: 1844–1937. Paper presented at the African Studies Association Annual Meeting, 25 October, Los Angeles.

Hayford, J. E. C. 1903. *Gold Coast native institution*. London: Sweet and Maxwell; reprint, London: Frank Cass, 1970.

Holden, J. J. 1965. The Zaberima conquest of North-West Ghana. *Transactions of the Historical Society of Ghana*, Part I, 3: 60–86.

Hopkins, A. G. 1973. *An economic history of West Africa*. London: Longman Group.

Iliasu, A. A. 1975. The establishment of British administration in Mamprugu (Mamprusi), 1898–1937. *Transactions of the Historical Society of Ghana* 16: 1–28.

Johnson, M. 1965. *The Salaga papers*, Vol. 1. Legon, Ghana: Institute of African Studies.

Johnson, M. 1977. Census map and guesstimate. In *African Historical Demography*, Centre of African Studies, University of Edinburgh, 272–94.

Johnson, M. 1986. The slaves of Salaga. *Journal of African History* 27: 341–62.

Johnston, W. R. 1973. *Sovereignty and protection*. Durham, N.C.: Duke University Press.

Kimble, D. 1963. *A political history of Ghana*. London: Clarendon.

Klein, A. N. 1980. Inequality in Asante — a study of the forms and meanings of slavery and social servitude in pre- and early colonial Akan society and culture. 2 vols. Ph.D. dissertation, University of Michigan.

Klein, M., and Lovejoy, P. 1979. Slavery in West Africa. In *The Uncommon Market: Essays in the Economic History of the Atlantic Slave Trade*, ed. H. A. Gemery and J. S. Hogendorn, 181–212. New York: Academic Press.

Lovejoy, P. 1983. *Transformations in slavery: a history of slavery in Africa*. Cambridge: Cambridge University Press.

McCaskie, T. 1986. The body and the blood: death and corporeality in Ashante thought. *Past and Present*.

McSheffrey, G. 1983. Slavery, indentured servitude, legitimate trade and the impact of abolition in the Gold Coast: 1874–1901. *Journal of African History* 24 (3): 349–68.

Maier, D. J. E. 1983. *Priests and power*. Bloomington, Ind.: Indiana University Press.

Maier, D. J. E. 1985. Arbeit macht frei: slave labor/wage labor in German Togoland, 1885–1914. Paper presented at the Annual Meeting of the African Studies Association, 24 November, New Orleans.

Metcalfe, G. E. 1962. *Maclean of the Gold Coast*. London: Oxford University Press.

Muhammad, A. 1977. The Samorian occupation of Bonduku: an indigenous view. *International Journal of African Historical Studies* 10(2): 242–57.

Northcott, H. P. 1899. *The Northern Territories of the Gold Coast*. London: Intelligence Division, War Office.

PP: *Parliamentary Papers*, Great Britain.
  Correspondence relating to the Abolition of Slavery on the Gold Coast. *Accounts and Papers* (1875), [C. 1159], LII.
  Correspondence relating to the Affairs of the Gold Coast. *Accounts and Papers* (1875), [C. 1140], LII.
  Correspondence relating to the Queen's Jurisdiction on the Gold Coast and the Abolition of Slavery within the Protectorate. *Accounts and Papers* (1875), [C. 1139], LII.
  Despatches on the subject of Domestic Slavery and the Introduction of Slaves by Ashante into the British Protectorate. *Accounts and Papers* (1874), [C. 1007], XLVI.
  Minutes of Evidence taken before the Select Committee on Africa (Western Coast). *Accounts and Papers*, (1865), [170], XXXVII.
  Papers relating to Her Majesty's Possessions in West Africa. *Accounts and Papers* (1875), Part 2 — Gold Coast, [C. 1343], 63–642, LII.
  Report by Sir David P. Chalmers on the Effect of the Steps which have been taken by the Colonial Government in reference to the Abolition of Slavery within the Protectorate, 27 June 1878; encl. in Lees to Hicks Beach, 3 July 1875. *Accounts and Papers* (1878), [C. 2148], LV.
  Report of the Select Committee on the West Coast of Africa. *Reports of Committees* (1842), [551], X.
  Report for the Select Committee on the West Coast of Africa. *Reports of Committees* (1842), [551-II], Part II, Appendix and Index, XII.
  Report on Mission to Ashanti and Gyaman (April-July 1881), Encl. in R. La T. Lonsdale to C.O., 14 April 1883. *Accounts and Papers* (1883), [C. 3687], XLVIII.

Poku, K. 1969. Traditional roles and people of slave origin in modern Ashanti — a few impressions. *Ghana Journal of Sociology* 8(1): 34–38.

Pouncy, H. 1981. Colonial racial attitudes and colonial labor laws in British West Africa. Ph.D. dissertation, Massachusetts Institute of Technology.

Rattray, R. S. 1929. *Ashanti law and constitution*. London: Oxford University Press.

Rattray, R. S. 1932. *Tribes of the Ashanti hinterland*. Vol. 2. Oxford: Clarendon Press; reprint, 1969.

Reynolds, E. Forthcoming. *Chiefs, farmers and preachers: tradition and modernization in Akuapem*.

Roberts, R., and M. Klein. 1980. The Banama slave exodus of 1905 and the decline of slavery in the Western Sudan. *Journal of African History* 21: 375–94.

Robertson, C. 1983. Post-proclamation slavery in Accra: a female affair." In *Women and Slavery in Africa*, ed. C. Robertson, and M. A. Klein, 220–45. Madison: University of Wisconsin Press.

Staniland, M. 1975. *The lions of Dagbon: political change in Northern Ghana.* Cambridge: Cambridge University Press.

Tait, D. 1961. *The Konkomba of Northern Ghana.* London.

Thomas, R. G. 1973. Forced labour in British West Africa: the case of the Northern Territories of the Gold Coast 1906–1927. *Journal of African History* 14(1): 79–103.

United Kingdom. 1874. *Hansard Parliamentary debates*, 3d ser., Vol. 220, cols. 607, 637–39.

Wilks, I. 1975. *Ashanti in the nineteenth century.* Cambridge: Cambridge University Press.

III
THE POLITICS OF ANTISLAVERY

3 *Michael Twaddle*

The Ending of Slavery in Buganda

Buganda was one of the most powerful kingdoms in nineteenth-century Africa. Its kings (or *kabakas*) enjoyed unusual powers, and its plundering expeditions devastated a broad swath of what is nowadays northeastern Zaire, northwestern Tanzania, and eastern Uganda. Indeed, during the nineteenth century both royal power and plundering expeditions peaked as the age-old search for women, slaves, and cattle combined with a newer search for ivory wanted by traders from the coast (Tosh 1970: 115; Cohen 1977: 199–200; Marissal 1978: passim). These coastal traders contributed to Buganda's still-rising power by supplying firearms at ever lower prices as European armies sold off old weapons and continuously reequipped themselves with newer firearms.

Such was the resultant spiral of violence in the East African interior that the Buganda Kingdom nearly fell apart in the course of a war of succession which began in 1888, shortly before the Imperial British East Africa Company (IBEAC) sent Captain Lugard to establish colonial rule there. In fact colonial rule not only saved the kingdom of Buganda from

A British Academy grant enabled me to revisit Uganda in 1981 and also to consult archives in Rome in that year. Debts to colleagues and students at London University and Makerere are even more considerable. Thanks also to the archivists of the CMS, Mill Hill Mission, Rhodes House Library, Uganda Government, Makerere, and White Fathers, for facilitating access to records in their care.

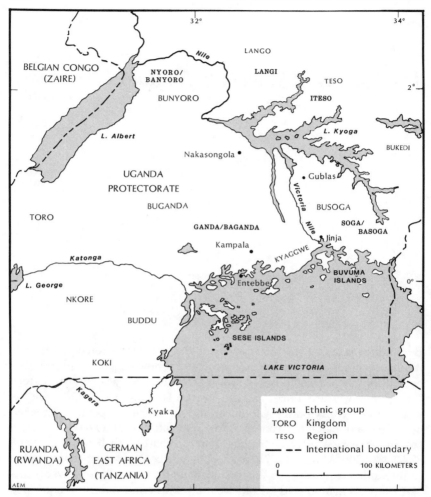

Map 3. Uganda

probable dismemberment, but the treaty concluded between the British
and leading Baganda chiefs in 1900 gave it a substantial degree of internal self-government and a distinctive form of quasi-freehold land tenure, which quickly made Buganda the envy of other East African peoples
under British colonial "protection" (Low 1960; Twaddle 1969). This treaty,
popularly known in Buganda as the Uganda Agreement, was crucial in
transforming Buganda into the modernizing autocracy described by schol-

ars associated with the Makerere Institute of Social Research (Richards 1960; Apter 1961; Fallers 1964; Richards, Sturrock, and Fortt 1973). The agreement of 1900 also put a seal upon a very violent set of developments, as a result of which indigenous slavery in Buganda had been effectively curtailed within a span of less than 20 years.

Precisely how this curtailment took place is the concern of this chapter. Much of the story of the British colonial takeover of Buganda is now well-known (Marcia Wright 1985: 565–81; Lonsdale 1985: 723–46, 762). But the parts that the ending of slavery played in the British takeover are not presently widely understood. This itself is an intricate story in which European missionaries, publicly committed at home to the outright abolition of slavery, often proved as reluctant as collaborating chiefs to emancipate slaves wholesale, and in which British colonial officials were concerned principally about retaining "definite advantages" of slavery "in the prevention of idleness, and the enforcing of respect for rank" (Lugard 1893: 171), while simultaneously stopping the forcible acquisition of slaves through raiding or external trade (ibid.: 212; Miers 1975: 236–91). The process was riddled with contradictions and sabotaged at vital points, as we shall see, by individual runaway slaves. Above all, British colonial officials and their local allies had to fight off armed resistance by Ganda chiefs and freemen anxious to maintain the centrality of slave-procurement in the general framework of labor relations within Buganda.

Precolonial Ganda Slavery

Whether they had become slaves by capture, through purchase, or by birth, in appearance, language, and custom there was often little to distinguish Ganda chattel slaves from their owners, except that they were basically aliens. This was because of the overriding importance of kinship in Buganda and the exclusion of chattel slaves from membership in the 40 or so clans which sustained and constrained social life between birth and burial (Twaddle 1983). Indeed, they were not buried at death precisely because they were slaves; instead their corpses were thrown into swamps or to the vultures. Slaves did not receive clan names. When sudden group sacrifices, called *biwendo*, took place, slaves were not redeemed from death as free persons might have been by their clan relatives. They also suffered facial mutilation and bodily torture more frequently; hence the widely quoted saying in precolonial times: Muddu awulira: y'awangaaza amatu ("A slave who is obedient gives long life to his ears") (Walser 1982: 254).

Slaves seem to have been of several types. There were administrative slaves owned by Ganda chiefs and richer peasants. Then, as in many neighboring societies, there were the farm slaves who cultivated the gardens of freemen and cooked for the ever-growing army of warriors upon whom Ganda kings depended for the expansion and consolidation of their kingdom. Slaves also served as laborers and porters for Ganda chiefs, bringing them food when they were in residence at the royal capital and working on roads and other public projects. Slaves made the chiefs who owned them attractive patrons for free cultivators, who were thus freed, at least partly, from such chores; and those chiefs with the largest slaveholdings automatically attracted the largest numbers of free followers. Other slaves worked for temples and spirit cults, the greatest of which had mediums whose wealth and lands paralleled those of the most powerful administrative chiefs. But the greatest concentration of slaves in any one place worked at the royal capital as palace functionaries, porters, and cultivators of food for the court. Most palace and farm slaves were women, whereas administrative slaves were mostly men, as were many porters and laborers.

This slave population was undoubtedly ancient, but it reached its greatest size in the century immediately preceding the British colonial takeover, when the kingdom itself was at its biggest. The arrival in Buganda of merchants from Zanzibar and Khartoum bringing cloth and guns during the second and third quarters of the nineteenth century led Ganda chiefs to intensify external predation in order to meet the merchants' demand for slaves as well as their own continuing need for them. Indeed, the first Christian missionaries, who reached Buganda during the 1870s and 1880s, had great difficulty in deciding to what extent the horrors of the slave trade were attributable to indigenous slavery, and to what extent they were the direct consequences of the much more recent external trade with Khartoum and the East African coast.

Slavery was not confined to Buganda but was common throughout the interlacustrine area, amongst the so-called stateless societies occupying so much of what is nowadays Uganda to the north and east of the river Nile, as well as in the kingdoms of Bunyoro, Nkore, Toro, and Koki. All round Buganda, at Kyaka in what is today northwestern Tanzania, along the Kyaggwe lakeshore in southeastern Buganda, and on several islands in Lake Kyoga bordering on the Bunyoro Kingdom and Teso and Lango country in the north, there were markets where slaves could be exchanged for cattle, hoes, barkcloth, and other goods (Uzoigwe 1972: 445–47; Kenny 1979: 104–5; Cohen 1977: 134–35). Slaves could thus be bought as well as acquired by plundering expeditions.

Other servile statuses associated with pawnship during times of famine or family misfortune, and ones associated with judicial condemna-

tion falling "between slavery and freedom," as M. I. Finley (1964) has described them, were all common among both Bantu-speaking and Nilotic-
speaking peoples. In fact slaves were classifiable by degrees of servility
as well as by occupation. Eridadi Mulira, for example, tells us that in
preprotectorate times in Buganda

Peasants were rewarded for valour in battle by the present of slaves by the lord
or chief for whom they had fought. They could be given slaves by relatives who
had been promoted to the rank of chiefs, and they could inherit slaves from their
fathers. There were the *abanyage* (those pillaged or stolen in war) as well as the
abagule (those bought). All these came into the category of *abenvumu* or true
slaves, that is to say people not free in any sense. In a superior position were the
young Ganda given by their maternal uncles into slavery [or pawnship], usually
in lieu of debts. . . . Besides such slaves both chiefs and king were served by sons
of well to do men who wanted to please them and attract favour for themselves
or their children. These were the *abasige* and formed a big addition to a noble
household. . . . All these different classes of dependents in a household were classed
as *abaddu* (male servants) or *abazana* (female servants) whether they were slave
or free-born. (Richards 1954: 170–71)

Mulira also remarks:

It appears to have been quite common in the past for foreigners as well as Ganda
peasants to apply to a chief or a lord to become his man. The process was known
as *kusenga*, to serve or become a subject-tenant of a chief and the man in question was known as *musenze* or, more simply, the *musajja* (man) of his lord. Such
a man would usually be given a plot of land and thus become the *mukopi* or
customary tenant, but he might remain a personal follower only. (ibid.: 172)

Such clientship was clearly distinguishable from slavery but, as Robert
Ashe of the Church Missionary Society (CMS) remarked, a chief might
well give a wife to a follower of this sort,

sometimes two; but she may be taken away from him and given to his neigh-
bour, for any or no reason.
    The Mukopi is free; but often loses his wife and children, and even his own
liberty, by getting into debt, when he descends to the miserable class of Badu
or slaves. (Ashe 1889: 95–96)

Equally, by hard work, good fortune, or help from clan relatives, formerly free followers could redeem themselves, as too could abenvumu
by agreement with their owners (frequently by getting the replacements
for themselves during plundering expeditions).
    This mixture of servile statuses in Buganda bolstered both royal and

chiefly power in a complicated, intricate, and dynamic manner. When richer Ganda parents sent their children to serve as abasige in the royal and other households, it was "to preserve them from harm, such as slavery, if the father falls into disgrace" (Roscoe 1902), since enslavement of the families of disgraced persons was a frequent punitive sanction employed by nineteenth-century Ganda kings. Thus, slavery served as a form of punishment as well as patronage for the chiefly elite. Moreover, the sheer complexity of servility reinforced a Ganda king's judicial role as numerous disputes over status were brought to him.

In Buganda, as elsewhere in Africa, slavery seems to have been part of a continuum of relations which at one end was part of the realm of kinship and at the other involved using persons as chattels. It was "a combination of elements, which if differently combined — an ingredient added here or subtracted there — might become adoption, marriage, parentage, obligations to kinsmen, clientship, and so forth" (Kopytoff and Miers 1977: 66). But, continuum or no continuum, there was nonetheless an immense social distance in the old kingdom between the palace servants, who were slaves only in a weak sense of the word (*baddu* if they were men or boys; *bazana* if women or girls), and those who were chattel slaves in a very real sense (abenvumu, "true slaves").

Christianity and Slavery

Publicly both the CMS, which arrived in Buganda in 1877, and the White Fathers, who came two years later, were vigorously opposed to both slavery and the slave trade. Privately, it was a rather different matter. Simply to get followers and converts initially, both the CMS and the White Fathers purchased slaves in Buganda. The CMS mostly used them as personal retainers, whereas the White Fathers bought them to start an orphanage and also used them as house servants. These were the first Christian converts. Christianity was thus initially a slaves' religion in Buganda — because slaves "redeemed" by missionaries were regarded by local people as falling into the category of "those bought," or abagule. However, Christianity in both its Anglican and Roman Catholic formulations also attracted a small but devoted following of free persons from the royal court, especially amongst the palace pages and craftsmen.

Some of the first Ganda Christians slaughtered by Kabaka Mwanga II, shortly after he had taken over from Mutesa I, therefore were slaves. Their bravery under ordeal was by any standard most remarkable, and has given rise to a literature of its own (Thoonen 1941; Faupel 1962; Ddiba 1969; see Rowe 1964). But what subsequently strikes Christians as spiritual fortitude appeared to Mwanga II at the time as insolence (*ekyejo*) at best or, more dangerously in view of what Swahili-speaking merchants from the East African coast were currently telling him about European colonial annexations there and the clearly close ties between the converts and *European* missionaries locally, potential political subversiveness. Missionaries of both denominations indeed despaired for a while of Christianity ever making much headway in Buganda. The White Fathers actually withdrew completely from the country for several years during the mid-1880s, and the CMS nearly departed on several occasions. On the CMS side only Alexander Mackay stayed, hoping that British imperial rule and the consequent suppression of the slave trade would eventually promote true Christianity there (although, somewhat incongruously, he also at one time favored the Ganda king behaving as "a Christian Bismarck" in the wider interlacustrine area).

In September 1888, however, several Christian converts in the king's bodyguard seized control of the Ganda political system in alliance with more powerful Muslim chiefs and, in succeeding years, gained predominant power with the assistance of the incoming British colonial rulers. This "Christian revolution," as it has been called (Wrigley 1959), started as a palace coup to oust Mwanga II from power but quickly turned into something much more bitter and protracted when Muslim Ganda chiefs overthrew their Christian allies, installed a new kabaka, Kalema, and then proclaimed Buganda an Islamic state. In the ensuing civil war, Christian and other non-Muslim Ganda cooperated to oust Kalema. In the process, tensions between Catholics and Protestants increased, and within a very short period the Christians had not only further subdivided into rival politico-religious parties but were capturing and selling one another into slavery in neighboring countries. Muslim Ganda under Kalema behaved in a similar fashion. Such was the situation in December 1890, when Frederick Lugard marched into southern Buganda as an early representative of the IBEAC.

European missionaries of both denominations had exhibited a certain ambivalence towards indigenous slavery before any of their converts acquired significant political power, regarding it as a lesser evil than polygyny. Their ambivalence increased when a number of early converts to Christianity were given leading positions in plundering expeditions against neighboring countries and became as a result themselves the owners and sellers of substantial numbers of slaves. But then, after the successful Christian counterrevolution of 1888–1889 against Kalema and his Muslim supporters, Christian chiefs developed even larger slave followings and yet another problem arose: intra-Christian competition for slaves. Because of the bifurcation of Ganda Christianity into rival Anglican and Roman Catholic politico-religious parties, and because Ganda chiefs determined the religious allegiance of most of their followers whether slave or free, most Protestant missionaries hesitated to recommend the immediate emancipation of their slaves. The Catholics were even more dilatory because the Catholic party in Buganda was considerably larger than the Protestant one, and many more slaves would therefore have had to be emancipated. Both groups of missionaries wrote to the new IBEAC authorities on behalf of their converts. Robert Walker, for instance, wrote to Lugard arguing that Protestant chiefs should get their fair share of Sese slaves ("that an advantage like that of owning canoes & sailors should be denied to the Protestants when they have fought for it and won it is unjust") (RHL, Lugard Papers, Walker to Lugard, 16 February 1892), and as a result, for a time the Protestant Baganda chiefs got their "fair share" of slaves from the Sese Islands in Lake Victoria.

A further complication for European missionaries concerned the question of polygyny. Though many Ganda slaves were men and boys, most were women and girls, and many wives in nineteenth-century Buganda were acquired initially as slaves. Father Waliggo (1976: 277) may be correct in stating that, in peripheral areas of the old kingdom such as Buddu, abenvumu formed only a small minority amongst local housewives. But it is difficult to account for the reported "excess of females over males, being about 3½ to 1" in the more central areas of Buganda except by the "constant influx of women into the country as prisoners of war" (Felkin 1885–1886: 744) and the prevailing system of polygynous marriage in which many wives would have been slaves. Another authority considers that "the increase in Buganda's population, which was estimated at somewhat over a million in the 1870s, was largely the result of the assimilation of captive women and their offspring" (Rowe 1975: 66). Assimilation was accomplished principally by the convention whereby the *children* of slave mothers were regarded as free so long as their fathers were not also slaves (RHL, Roscoe MS, 1906), and by the downward social mobility suffered even by the children of free women in a society characterized by widespread chiefly polygyny. As somebody who was a youth at this time in Buganda said with evident feeling, "The women were very numerous here in Buganda but it was very difficult to get one" (Oded 1974: 346).

For Christian missionaries brought up in Europe to regard monogamy as the will of God (Goody 1983: passim), polygyny was a further factor in their early pessimism about the prospects for Christianity in precolonial Buganda. But for British administrators like Frederick Lugard and his immediate successors during the 1890s, the prevalence of polygyny and slave marriage provided them with a very convenient excuse for considering much of the domestic slavery in Buganda to be "native marriage" and cracking down only on the wider slave trade, though to start with they did very little about this either.

Lugard

Frederick Lugard, a man of great color and courage, arrived in Buganda in December 1890, when the two Christian politico-religious parties were uneasily cohabiting the southern portion of the old kingdom under the nominal kabakaship of the restored Mwanga II. They were united only by the threat that the Muslim Ganda in the north, under Kalema and later Nuhu Mbogo, might displace them at any time. Lugard hastily concluded a treaty with Mwanga which, *inter alia*, outlawed slave-trading, but he had no power to enforce it until he could strengthen the IBEAC position (Perham 1956: 232). Basically he did this by acting as arbiter between the Catholic and Protestant factions, by recruiting mercenaries from the remnants of Emin Pasha's troops left behind in the southern Sudan by the collapse of the Turko-Egyptian Empire, and by reintegrating the Muslims into a single reunited Ganda kingdom (Rowe 1969; Michael Wright 1971). But then the IBEAC decided to withdraw from Buganda, and there was a period of further uncertainty before a formal British protectorate was declared in 1893–1894.

Lugard took no steps against slavery itself. And neither Christian political party exhibited any enthusiasm for a premature or one-sided ending of slavery. Lugard noted in his diary on 17 March 1892:

they [the Protestant Baganda chiefs] said: our missionaries long ago told us that slavery was contrary to our religion; now you come and say the same thing. We were willing to free *all* domestic and other slaves throughout Uganda [meaning Buganda], but the Catholics would not agree. The priests have many slaves whom they buy and teach (this is fact). It would have been futile for us to free our slaves while all the others did not, and would probably have caused a quarrel, so we put it off. At the present we do not think it advisable to proclaim the freedom of slaves. (RHL, Lugard Diaries)

Lugard replied that it was not English custom to "overturn at once the customs and traditions and institutions of a country to which we have freshly come," and therefore he had not, "so far, objected to domestic slavery in Uganda." Only Swahili slaves, subjects of the sultan of Zanzibar, would have to be freed immediately because Zanzibar was now a British protectorate. But even here he was prepared to sacrifice individuals in order to please his supporters. Thus, later in the same diary entry, Lugard recorded his ruling regarding a man who they [the Protestant Ganda chiefs] said was really a Munyoro [from the neighboring kingdom of Bunyoro], and had become an Arab's slave, and so spoke Swahili. I said, has he ever been to the coast? They said *no* he had not. Then I said, he certainly cannot be a subject of the Sultan of Zanzibar since he has never been in his dominions and he does not come under the rule. They were much pleased.

Besides the essential weakness of local IBEAC power and the reluctance of Ganda chiefs to give up one of their principal material assets, Lugard also feared overhasty emancipation might multiply problems for British colonial administrators, for domestic slavery had "definite advantages in the prevention of idleness, and the enforcing of respect for rank, which alone enables the government of a semi-savage country to be carried on." He feared overhasty abolition might well cause social chaos (Lugard 1893, 1: 171–73). He also argued that domestic slavery was much more benign in Buganda than it had been in the British West Indies (ibid.: 176–79). This was inconsistent, because "benign" slavery was hardly likely to be very effective in reinforcing "respect for rank."

To the horror of the missionaries Lugard suggested that the CMS should run settlements, like that of the Livingstonia mission in what is now Malawi, for the few Swahili-speaking slaves freed in Buganda and those that he had forced his Sudanese mercenaries to liberate (RHL, Lugard Diaries, 2 June 1892). Lugard's proposals were turned down by Robert Ashe and Robert Walker, who preferred Ganda methods of emancipation.

They said that in the case of some slaves handed over to Mackay by Stanley [presumably several years before, during the Emin Pasha Relief Expedition], they distributed the girls among well-known and trusted Protestants, who had adopted them into their households, and the results had been singularly successful. They had lived a very happy life, and had many of them comfortably married, and their religious instruction had been well looked after. (ibid.)

Ashe and Walker also told Lugard that their basic idea was "to establish a [mission] station at the headquarters of each chief" (ibid.: 31 May 1892), thereby consolidating the spiritual benefits of the recent Christian counterrevolution in Buganda within the existing chiefly structures of patronage rather than setting up further largely separate compounds of their own. This indeed was to be a major recruitment strategy by both Catholics and Protestants in Buganda (Waliggo 1976; Hansen 1984).

The abolition of slavery, however, very quickly became a more immediate issue for Protestant chiefs and CMS missionaries as a result of a runaway slave's taking refuge in a Protestant chief's enclosure and the chief's refusal to return the slave to his Muslim owner.

The Protestant Declaration Abolishing Slavery

In 1893 when the British government sent Sir Gerald Portal to Buganda to determine its future (and, inevitably, with it also the future of the immediately adjacent areas which were to form the Uganda Protectorate), the Protestant chiefs declared publicly that they would abolish slavery among their followers. As the smallest of the three politico-religious parties in Buganda and the closest to British officials like Lugard and Portal, they had the least to lose from slave emancipation. They were also least likely to attract and retain runaway slaves of the Muslims, whom Lugard had persuaded to return to Buganda and acknowledge Mwanga II as king, because under existing Ganda law runaway slaves had to be returned to their owners if the latter were living within Buganda.

The matter was brought to a head by decisive action by one particular runaway slave. Bishop Tucker (1908, 1: 261–64) subsequently related:

A demand for the surrender of a runaway slave belonging to a Mohammedan, who had taken refuge with a Christian chief, named Batolomayo, brought the question to an issue. Batolomayo refused to give up the slave. What was to be done? The matter was referred to me. My first question to them was, "What is the law of the land? Does it recognise slavery?" The answer was "Yes!" Then I said: "You have no option. You must give him up. You must obey the laws. But," I added, "if you think the law a bad one I should advise you to get it altered." They went away, but a few days later they came back with a request that I would tell them what my views were upon the question of slavery generally. . . . It was not difficult . . . to point out how utterly inconsistent with the gospel of love was the subjection by force of one man to another, and the buying and selling of our fellow creatures. . . . They went away once more, and on March 31 [1893] there was signed and brought to me the following declaration embodying their determination to abolish slavery absolutely. . . .

"All we the Protestant chiefs desire to adopt these good customs of freedom. We hereby agree to untie and to free completely all our slaves. Here are our names as chiefs. . . ." [Tucker's translation from Swahili]

This document, which is still in my possession, I prize as one of my most precious treasures. Its signature is, to my mind, one of the greatest triumphs to which Christianity can point either in primitive, medieval or modern times.

Sir Gerald Portal, to whom the declaration was taken by Bishop Tucker, was less confident about its long-term positive character, while the White Fathers were frankly hostile.

April 8th. A paper given to me by forty Protestant chiefs, saying they had declared to follow "coast custom" and free all slaves. This seems suspicious, also rather too radical, as throwing thousands of people free at once. It would make it impossible at first to get any work done by any one, and it is perhaps only a pretext to avoid work on roads, etc, by pleading as excuse no slaves. Mgr Hirth is against the measure. (Portal 1894: 227)

Quite why the Catholic bishop was so opposed to slave emancipation is not made clear in surviving archives, but it was to be several years before Catholic chiefs in Buganda would openly adopt a similar policy to the Protestants.

Just a few months after the Protestant chiefs' declaration abolishing slavery, a fresh batch of slaves running away from Muslim chiefs again raised the question of slave emancipation more generally in Buganda. Sir Gerald Portal had by now departed for the East African coast, and the Ganda Muslims had again revolted. After the suppression of their rebellion, many Ganda Muslims fled westward, taking their slaves with them. When the Muslims lost a decisive battle, Christian Ganda chiefs seized a considerable number of female captives and other booty. A number of women slaves also came over to the Ganda Christian side of their own accord. Somewhat extraordinarily, the British officer in charge of operations, Major Owen, expressly ordered the Ganda commander "to take good care of them, as they might be restored to their Mohamedan husbands in the event of the latter's surrender" (MUL, Miti and Rock MS: 430). The Christian chiefs, however,

met and discussed what was to be done with the Mohamedan womenfolk then under their charge; should they be restored to their husbands or should they be left under the charge of the Christian army?

As not all the Mohamedan women in question had been secured as captives, a great many of them having left their Mohamedan masters and joined the Christians entirely of their own accord, *which class of women was then a free one* [emphasis added] — it was decided that, as also many of those women had simply been forced to live in conjugal relations with their former Mohamedan husbands as slaves or female prisoners of war, they should be given a choice of each lady selecting any one of the three religious parties and of attaching herself to it without coercion or restriction whatsoever.

On August 30, 1893, therefore, after each party had presented the number of women that its members had previously held as captives, each of the one thousand such women that there were made her choice and joined either the Protestant or the Catholic or even the Mohamedan group according as each lady chose to do. (ibid.: 432–33)

Apparently Major Owen was not pleased at this show of independent-minded behavior by Christian Ganda chiefs (ibid.: 434), but such behavior was characteristic of them throughout the 1890s. As the decade wore on, however, British military officers became much stricter in stopping their Christian Ganda allies from acquiring substantial further supplies of slaves either through plunder or by trade.

British Curtailment of Further Substantial Slave-Procurement

The first occasion on which Christian Ganda chiefs were expressly told by British officials not to seize men or women as slaves was on the Buvuma expedition of January 1893 (MUL, Miti and Rock MS: 407). Nevertheless, hundreds of Bavuma captives were smuggled into Buganda, seven female captives and six male prisoners of war seized by James Miti alone. Because of British opposition, however, slave-taking by Ganda Christian chiefs became more surreptitious. Nonetheless, it continued. During the Bunyoro campaign of 1893–1894, for example, Colonel Colvile (1895: 134–35) reported holding

a parade of the ladies who had been captured or come in to us during the course of the operations. There were about one hundred and fifty of them in all, of whom forty were Wanyoro, and the remainder Waganda, whom Kabarega's raiding parties had at various times seized as slaves. I dealt with the latter first, asking each in turn whether she wished to stay with the Wanyoro, or return to her own people. Only two chose to stay, so, putting them aside, I started on the delicate task of deciding who was to take care of the remainder. The younger and stronger ones seemed to have a quite remarkable number of uncles, cousins and brothers in camp, who all declared that they were the only fit and proper persons to take charge of them until they were handed over to their husbands or fathers.

These Colvile allowed to be selected by the supposedly Ganda women in turn, but the 40 Banyoro ones he returned to Bunyoro. In subsequent hostilities against Bunyoro, Apolo Kagwa tried to trick Major Cunningham, the British officer in charge, into allowing him to return Banyoro captives to Buganda, along with Ganda women earlier enslaved by the Banyoro, through the simple expedient of dressing them all up "in sheets of cloth after the manner of Baganda women so that their nationality might not be identified at the time of their being led away to Buganda" (MUL, Miti and Rock MS: 485). Cunningham, however, got to learn of this trick, and the Banyoro captives had to be returned to Bunyoro; Apolo Kagwa himself got off with a warning, while the Ganda slaves whom they had managed to free "attached [themselves] to one or other of his men as her relation" (ibid.) as Kagwa marched his men back into Buganda.

Further misdemeanors of this kind were not treated so lightly. Trevor Ternan, for example, proved much tougher in meting out punishments

to his Ganda allies for taking women captives during operations against
Bunyoro as well as for other forms of plunder of which he disapproved:
"It appears that the Waganda took 8 women. I gave the man 50 [lashes]
in presence of the Wanyoro; he is to get 50 more tomorrow and to remain
two years in the chain-gang." This is a typical entry in his private diary
for 1895 (RHL, Ternan Diaries, 5 June). Ternan also took much tougher
action against Baganda chiefs as well as against their followers, actually
putting in the guardroom the Ganda commander accompanying him,
Yona Waswa, the country chief of Singo, whom Mwanga II had formally
invested beforehand at the Ganda royal capital and whom he considered
guilty of covering up slave-taking by subordinates. When operations
against Bunyoro concluded, Waswa was not released from detention (as
Ternan's predecessors most probably would have done) but was sent back
to Kampala under armed escort a few weeks later. When Mwanga II
subsequently raised the standard of revolt against the British authorities
in July 1897, Yona Waswa's followers were amongst his most fervent supporters (Michael Wright 1971: 166–67). Ternan realized that there was
a basic contradiction in British punishment of slave-taking by Ganda warriors and chiefs whilst non-Ganda remained free to raid for slaves in
Buganda itself (e.g., his diary entry for 25 December 1895: "The Waked-
di took off 30 ladies and killed 6 men"). But all he could think of as a
practicable remedy was strengthening the number of Ganda warriors
manning the various frontier posts (e.g., the same entry in his diary continues: "I sent in a note to Berkeley giving him this information—and
advising that the garrisons of Waganda who are holding the posts along
the lakes as far as Mrooli should be strengthened"). It would be only after
the successful suppression of Mwanga's rebellion in May 1899 that one
particular Christian Ganda chief would be given carte blanche to conquer Bukedi country once and for all (Twaddle 1967).

In the meantime the problem of slaves acquired by purchase for use
in Buganda also needed to be dealt with as speedily as practicable. Here
the basic problem was that all round Buganda slaves were still being
bought and sold:

Wasoga from mostly all parts of Usoga send slaves for sale at Gublas. There are
I understand two markets where slaves are disposed of. They are sold to Wakedi
and Wanyoro for foes. The price of females varies from 30 to 60 hoes a head.
On my return I brought 3 women who were sold by Wasoga to Wanyoro. They
state that there are many Wasoga women and children still in Unyoro.

So reported William Grant, the British subcommissioner in Busoga (EA,
Grant 1895). Furthermore, the tribute paid to the Kabaka of Buganda

by the Soga states — and of which British officials initially took a half share after the imposition of their protectorate upon Buganda in 1893–1894 — necessarily implicated the British as well as the Ganda in this particular aspect of the slave trade in the wider Uganda region. In December 1895 the British protectorate commissioner at Entebbe proposed that the Busoga tribute should henceforth be paid in a lump sum to the Ganda king instead of Mwanga's men being allowed to go there personally to collect it, and that the British government anyway should give up its claim to half shares (FOCP: Berkeley 1895). Then in January 1896 William Grant again wrote to Entebbe, reporting that Ganda chiefs now said that "they *could* purchase ivory (without bartering women) providing a market were established at Gublas with a responsible person or persons in charge" (EA, Grant 1896). It was through actions such as these that slavery by purchase was progressively attacked by British administrators throughout the Uganda Protectorate, as the area of settled administration outside Buganda gradually increased and slave-procurement by more violent means was increasingly curtailed too.

Contradictions amongst Christian Chiefs

Why did Christian chiefs so meekly accept British restrictions on further slave-procurement, and indeed fight on the British side when it became one of the issues in Mwanga II's rebellion against the protectorate authorities in 1897?

Clearly, the declaration against slavery made by the Protestant chiefs to the Protestant bishop in 1893 was important; but it had probably been composed by the Protestant party partly for tactical reasons at a moment when Muslim women were more likely to become Protestant followers and be considered free persons than remain Muslim and be considered runaway slaves, who would have had to be returned to their former owners, and when Protestant chiefs in Buganda were under attack in Europe for allegedly enslaving Catholic chiefs' followers during 1892. Furthermore, as we have already noted with respect to military operations against the neighboring kingdom of Bunyoro in 1893–1895, in certain respects the Protestant chiefs' earlier declaration against slavery proved decidedly more symbolic than real. To be sure, there *were* considerable numbers of Ganda women in Bunyoro whom Christian Ganda warriors could very legitimately claim to be liberating from Kabarega's sway; and willingness not to seize female captives in Bunyoro as chattel slaves (abenvumu) did not prevent them from being seized by either the Catholic or the Protestant party in order to be distributed to its male adherents *as wives*. This was a very important loophole in Ganda custom, and it enabled Protestant chiefs who had solemnly signed the 1893 declaration abolishing slavery to carry on seizing female prisoners of war during further plundering expeditions against Bunyoro with a clear Christian conscience—whenever they could, that is.

Of course, British military superiority in the technology of war was clearly important in ensuring a certain degree of continuing support for British curtailment of slave-procurement regardless of personal feelings; the British *did* have several maxim guns. There were also limited political options for Ganda Christian leaders like Apolo Kagwa and Stanislas Mugwanya (head of the Catholic party) apart from supporting the protectorate authorities. Kagwa may not have liked the fact that his men were being deprived of their Banyoro captives by Major Cunningham, but he clearly acquiesced in their deprivation because, politically speaking, he had nowhere else to go. Plunder in the form of cattle and other commodities *did* also continue to flow into the possession of both Kagwa's and Mugwanya's followers; indeed the British authorities appear on more than one occasion to have assisted their Ganda allies in obtaining *more* cattle than might have been customary during plundering expeditions hitherto, in order to compensate for their opposition to slave-taking. Sizable swathes of Bunyoro too, subsequently to be known as the lost counties, were added to the kingdom of Buganda during the 1890s, and this meant more jobs for Ganda Christian chiefs. All these were positive factors, as far as the two Christian politico-religious parties were concerned, when Mwanga II raised his standard of revolt against the British protectorate authorities.

To a considerable extent, too, the continued competition between the two Christian politico-religious parties in Buganda further mystified matters. The White Fathers' diaries are full of references to Catholic converts being harassed by minor Protestant chiefs, especially during 1895 and 1896, which must have diverted much political attention from other concerns. In August 1896, however, intrachief tension within the Protestant party erupted when two runaway slaves took refuge in the enclosure of the Reverend Henry Wright Duta Kitakule.

The fullest account of this conflict is provided by the Rubaga Diary of the White Fathers, who evidently recorded its principal details with relish. The Musoga owner of the two runaway adolescent slaves had appealed to Apolo Kagwa to persuade Kitakule to return the slaves, but Kitakule, an old political rival of Kagwa within the Protestant party, refused and appealed over Kagwa's head to the British protectorate official at Kampala Fort:

M. Wilson objected to the Protestant Katikiro: "Did you not write in Europe that everybody in Buganda was now free? Did you not put your signature at the bottom of the letter saying this in England? In Europe people admire your civilisation, and now you want to move backwards again?

And the Katikiro replied: "The country will die if our slaves may thus desert us without reason."

M. Wilson: "You still have some slaves therefore?"

[The Katikiro:] "Yes, we do have, and many." (WF, Rubaga Diary, 4 August 1896; my translation)

Upon which, the Rubaga diarist comments upon the evident hypocrisy of the Protestants and reports that George Wilson seemed somewhat confused and moved on quickly to other business.

It is at this point in the Rubaga Diary that the White Fathers' attitudes towards British protectorate policy on slavery become clear. Besides feeling generally that the 1893 declaration totally abolishing slavery in Buganda had been premature and likely to cause considerable social unrest, they had two other basic reservations. One concerned the local *expansion* of slavery as an institution, which resulted from the British employment of Sudanese mercenaries in the country and was evidenced by the facial incisions enforced upon Ganda women enslaved by these Sudanese ("les horribles cicatrices," "les tatouages de date récente" [WF, Rubaga Diary, 10 April and 23 October 1894]). Protectorate administrators might have repeated that, with Sudanese mercenaries as with Ganda chiefs, British policy was not to recognize slavery as a legal status; they also said:

Colonel Colvile, by the simple declaration that the status of slavery [was] not acknowledged in Uganda, abolished slavery and all its evils. Of course one knows that every Soudanese household has a number of slaves and should any of these complain of ill-treatment or express a desire to leave their master or mistress, practical effect is given to the Colonel's now historic declaration. On the other hand, there is no uncalled for interference with any man's household. (Ansorge 1899: 111)

But to the White Fathers such declarations as these were just humbug.

There are also a number of tart references in the White Fathers' archives to the British protectorate authorities talking so much about the suppression of slavery in Buganda at the very same time that extremely heavy amounts of forced labor were being imposed upon the Ganda populace. However, as these massive *corvées* were demonstrably organized for the benefit of the Ganda king as well as the British commissioner—one of them involving excavation of a new royal lake as much as two kilometers long and one kilometer wide (WF, Rubaga Diary, 28 and 29 August 1895) — the resultant resentment was doubtless directed as much against Mwanga II as against George Wilson. It was not until Mwanga had been so affronted at British curtailment of the size of his palace establishment that he raised the standard of revolt against the British in Buddu, and a substantial realignment of popular resentment against the protectorate authorities became possible.

Mwanga's Revolt

Undoubtedly this revolt had more than one cause, not least amongst them the steady but relentless diminution in power of the Ganda king, as British protectorate officials progressively tightened their control upon his kingdom. In particular, the displacement of slave-procurement from its central position within the earlier framework of labor relationships, in which a ready supply of slaves through fresh and continuous external raiding made for a much more open set of alternative futures for freemen in Buganda (as well as a fairly rapid means whereby slaves could redeem themselves, if they were men, by capturing further slaves), seems to have caused considerable social strains during the closing years of the nineteenth century. This caused even Protestant chiefs such as Apolo Kagwa, supposedly committed on paper to renouncing slavery completely, to make every effort to retain as many of their existing slaves as they could. Admittedly, during Colonel Colvile's time (1893–1894) British officials may have behaved with greater harshness and less self-discipline than under George Wilson's subsequent regime, as one CMS missionary remarked (CMS, Walker Papers, Walker to Stockdale, 8 August 1897). In December 1893 it was still possible for Kabaka Mwanga to joke with his chiefs that the British prohibition on slave-taking did not mean "that there was any positive prohibition against them picking up any young Banyoro beauties they might chance to come across and keeping them with them in their own tents and eventually disposing of them as they pleased" (MUL, Miti and Rock MS: 446). But by July 1897 even the diminished authority which Mwanga had enjoyed immediately after his restoration by the Christian Ganda chiefs in October 1889 was a mere memory when George Wilson and Apolo Kagwa displaced him from most of his remaining duties. By this time it was abundantly clear that British protectorate officials *did* mean what they said about the suppression of Ganda slave-taking. It was also abundantly clear that the British protectorate authorities were now also extremely unpopular throughout Buganda.

That grievance against British rule was now widespread amongst several social strata is made clear by that most informative of CMS missionary observers of Buganda, Robert Walker:

There is a very strong anti-European feeling in the country. There is a regular saying "we won't make bricks for the Europeans," which means we won't be their slaves. One of their grievances is that the Katikiro [Apolo Kagwa] and a few other chiefs, supported by the Government, will not allow men to hold women as slaves. Another is that men are forced to carry loads for the Government, though they are well paid for it. . . . When good laws are made for the real benefit of the country there is a general outcry that the Katikiro is eating [i.e., ruling] the country [and people] work for the removal of European activity.

Nonetheless, Walker thought that there was no way in which Mwanga II could hope to live as his father Mutesa I had done, killing and mutilating people for reasons which were unacceptable under the new order (CMS, Walker Papers, Walker to family, 14 July 1897). But the fact remained that the legitimacy associated with the old kingship vanished once Mwanga raised his standard of revolt in Buddu, and in the short term there was very little to support British administration apart from brute force. Not until a lot more administrative effort and missionary education had been deployed in Uganda would an alternative set of values be developed to make the new order ideologically secure, in a Gramscian sense, though Trevor Ternan's swift action in arranging for the baby prince, Daudi Chwa, to be placed upon the Ganda throne within a few weeks of Mwanga's flight from the capital certainly helped ideologically in a small way.

Two years later the old order had been effectively defeated by sheer force of British arms, despite a serious additional mutiny which occurred in September 1897 amongst the Sudanese soldiery; Sikh soldiers reinforced George Wilson's maxim gun and Kagwa's and Mugwanya's "friendlies." Effectively deprived of its main means of reproduction through external raiding or purchase of slaves from neighboring societies, or even as a result of punitive enslavement through internal judicial review, and with the outlawing of the former sanctions of death and mutilation under the new order enshrined in the Uganda Agreement of 1900 (Low 1960), the status of slavery and associated servile statuses in Buganda slid remorselessly into the immediately adjacent and more general social category of people called *bakopi* ("peasants"). Apart from a few hiccups, this seemingly reversed the earlier process whereby bakopi had moved in the opposite direction, descending into the "miserable class of Badu or slaves," as Ashe (1889: 96) put it, whenever afflicted by debt or other misfortune. The social chaos that Lugard had feared might result from a premature and wholesale abolition of slavery had been avoided, albeit at some political cost. The increased activity by British protectorate officials against slave-raiding and -trading during the 1890s was clearly a factor in the widespread support accorded to Mwanga's rebellion in 1897. That rebellion was defeated within two years, but it was not exactly clear what survivals of slavery would persist into the twentieth century, nor what "new systems of slavery" (to appropriate the title of Hugh Tinker's [1974] magisterial study of the postslavery era in the British Caribbean and elsewhere) might emerge under the new order.

The New Order

Slavery continued to be an important social institution for some time after the signing of the Uganda Agreement of 1900, which confirmed the Christian Ganda chiefs formally in power and established the pattern of quasi-freehold *mailo* estates, upon which a cash-cropping tenantry, growing cotton as the principal money-earner, was firmly established by the First World War (Wrigley 1959). Slavery seems to have become increasingly a social affair during these years and, as Frederick Cooper (1979: 111) has remarked more generally, the "emphasis on the integrative nature of slavery" in many anthropological accounts compiled during the era of European colonial rule "may largely reflect the fact that with the removal of its coercive and exploitative dimensions — and above all its means of reproduction — the social dimension is all that is left."

Not that this was exactly unimportant. During the 1900s the redemption of slaves for specific sums became a regular business of the Buganda Lukiko (or chiefly council), as these entries in the Nsambya Diary of the Mill Hill Mission (which joined the White Fathers as a second Catholic missionary society in Buganda in 1895) indicate:

Petero reports . . . A slave woman of the mother of Karema [Kalema] was discovered by her relatives who claim her freedom. The woman is allowed to return to them. They will pay the mother of Karema 2,000 shells. . . . A woman of one of the King's ladies wishes to marry. She is given her freedom. Her lover has to pay the usual sum of 10,000 shells. (7 November 1902)

Petero reports . . . A woman from Kisubi was given her freedom from her master. The latter, it was decided, would receive 6000 shells from the woman's future husband. The man objected to this, demanding 30,000. The Lukiko, fearing that he may revenge himself . . . has ordered him to find surety for good behavior. (10 November 1902)

Besides slave redemption and marriage, the Buganda Lukiko was also involved when slaves were mistreated or murdered:

Petero reports . . . The Omyuka of Kikebezi was ordered to give 20 hds of cloth and a shirt to a slave whom he had beaten and to give the slave his freedom.

Petero reports . . . A man from Bugerere is accused of having killed his slave boy. Witnesses have been summoned.

Thus the Nsambya Diary for 17 and 27 January 1902. Or take an entry in it for 15 September of the same year:

Petero reports . . . Sabalangira [the head of the princes clan of Buganda] . . . has his right to that position questioned. Some say that originally he was only a slave. Case postponed until Mbogo [the leading Muslim chief and a senior member of the princes clan himself] is able to come.

During the 1920s, when Apolo Kagwa's long career as *katikiro* (or chief minister) of Buganda was nearing its close and there was a widespread whispering campaign against him in the new vernacular newspapers as well as in the still-lively oral culture of the country, one of the charges made against him was that he too was originally a slave and therefore disqualified from holding office — a charge that Kagwa rebutted through a libel action in one of the new protectorate law courts. This particular smear campaign appears to have started during the 1900s when Kagwa's membership of the Grasshopper clan of Buganda had been questioned on the ground that he was really a Musoga not a Muganda by birth. Christine Obbo (1979: 232), who reports both cases, also says she was told in Buganda fairly recently "that the worst insult one Ganda can hurl against another is to insinuate that he is not true Ganda."

But this is very small beer compared with the continuing subjection of women in Buganda after the imposition of British protectorate rule. Admittedly, there is a basic problem with most earlier discussions of this subject, because the numerical preponderance of women amongst Ganda slaves before the British protectorate period has usually been taken as evidence of the mildness of Ganda slavery in general rather than of its harshness towards women in particular. Here, as elsewhere (Twaddle 1983), we have assumed differently. Besides the few women (such as "the mother of Karema") who owned slaves themselves and the ones working at religious shrines, those at the royal capital labored in daily fear of death and mutilation (Speke 1863). Agricultural work in precolonial Buganda too was predominantly the concern of women (Rowe 1975: 66), and we should not necessarily assume that the work of farm slaves was lighter than plantation employment on the East African coast. Murder and mutilation were now outlawed, but the agricultural workload under the new order seems actually to have increased in intensity. Indeed, Father Waliggo

(1976: 283) implies that the Ganda single women coming forward to become nuns during the early years of the twentieth century had little to tempt them into marriage, because in the new Christian monogamous family the work burden on the wife was so great "that many Christian wives began to regard themselves as 'prisoners' (basibe) of their husbands." Legally the new order had some startling defects regarding the general treatment of women too, as the Nsambya Diary (MHM) for 3 June 1901 illustrates:

There was a murder case before the lukiko today. Two women from Bulemezi took a man into their house. Whilst the man was with them, their master appeared on the scene. The stranger ran, and was followed by the master of the house and some other men. In the struggle which ensued, the stranger was killed.

Decision: 12 months for each of the women.

This was oppressive treatment for the women, in addition to the death penalty meted out to the man, but it was not oppression that can properly be called slavery.

Under the new Christian dispensation in Buganda, slavery admittedly still occupied a somewhat ambiguous situation. We have already seen that in the early 1900s it was mistreatment of slaves and the details of individual cases of marriage and redemption that occupied the attention of the Buganda Lukiko rather than the continuance of domestic slavery itself, and this fitted in with the stress upon New Testament Christianity by both CMS and Catholic missionaries. It was the mistreatment and murder of people still subject to slavery, rather than any thoroughgoing desire to abolish slavery itself completely, that prompted action. As regards marriage, however, where there was considerable missionary disapproval of polygyny, slaves sometimes benefitted at the expense of free wives when a Christian man came to decide which of his various consorts should become his ring wife. Thus, Sesilia Nsingisira was chosen by Chief Nsingisira as his ring wife despite the fact that she had formerly been his slave (Ddiba 1969, 3: 223–49) — indeed, perhaps partly because she had been his slave, since former slaves "tended to be more obedient than the Baganda wives, and as foreigners were more ready than local ones to fulfil every demand the [Christian] religion imposed" (Waliggo 1976: 213). Sesilia Nsingisira was able to fulfill the demands of the new religion and her husband's relatives to the satisfaction of both much more easily because she did not have brothers and uncles of her own in Buganda to whom she owed rival allegiance. It is notable that the spirituality of a Sesilia Nsingisira was to be eulogized by subsequent Roman Catholic writers in Buganda as an integral part of a newly Christianized, much changed, but demonstrably still-continuing Buganda Kingdom. It would have been a very different kind of eulogy had freed slaves lived in special "villages of freedom" in Buganda, as Lugard had suggested that they should and which existed at various places bordering the East African coast as well as in West Africa.

After the suppression of Mwanga's rebellion there was a certain reflux of liberated slaves from Buganda to other parts of the Uganda Protectorate (and some comparable movement in the reverse direction too). But we know very little about these diasporas. We know about only the odd individual — like Hassan Kamihanda, who was captured by Ganda Muslims in Toro, taken to Buganda, and returned to western Uganda only when "Our King Kasagama went to Buganda and pleaded that since slavery had ended all Batoro should be sent home," presumably sometime during the early 1900s (King, Kasozi, and Oded 1973: 43–47), or Nuwa Kasang'ano, who became a chief in eastern Uganda in 1903 ("He was taken to Buganda as a slave: baptized & has been able to return to his people," the CMS missionary William Crabtree noted in his diary [RHL] on 4 April of that year). Other case histories of former slaves must await further research in Uganda, when it may also be possible to say something sensible about the ending of slavery and urbanization. At present we can say virtually nothing about this, apart from pointing it out as an important area for future research.

What we can say, however, is that when British protectorate officials thrust their enormously burdensome labor obligations onto a peasantry no longer able to acquire new slaves through warfare or trade, there was inevitable resentment ending, as we have seen, in actual rebellion in 1897, led by chiefs also angry at the curtailment of substantial slaveholdings. Burdensome as the mid-1890s were for many Ganda experiencing the first pangs of British protection, these years were as nothing compared with the period between Mwanga's rebellion and the First World War, when British labor demands upon the Ganda peasantry probably exceeded anything suffered before. Dr. Atanda (1969: 136) quotes a report on bakopi grievances in 1903, which states:

They say they have to work for a month or produce Rs 3 every year for Government; then they have to cultivate a patch of ground for Government, and at all times they are called on to make roads, schools, churches, etc and they really don't know what is going to happen next. There is free talk amongst the people that they are going to be taken presently to the Nile.

Things began to get better for the Ganda peasantry only after the First World War, when cotton really became profitable for them and the system of forced labor known as *kasanvu* was abolished.

"New Systems of Slavery"

It would be a mistake to attribute to the British too much foresight and long-term planning for the development of a cash-cropping peasantry alongside a property-owning aristocracy. Frederick Cooper (1981: 305) states that "the transformation of relations of production was . . . at stake as British policy makers . . . pondered the kind of agricultural organization and class structure . . . they should foster" in Zanzibar, Buganda, and Northern Nigeria. "The British," he says, "thought they could transform the ruling class . . . into a landowning class, although such policies involved a rather fanciful conception of what such a class was capable of doing." In fact, the British had no such clear-cut plans with regard to Buganda, as evidenced by the way British officials kept open the option of establishing a class of white settlers and even considered the possibility that Buganda might become a labor reserve for the South African mines. Thus, in October 1902, when a group of Rand recruiters reached Buganda "looking for native labour (100,000 men) to go and work the mines in the Transvaal" (MHM, Nsambya Diary, 24 October 1902), it was Ganda, not British, resistance which killed the plan. "The Baganda will not consent to go there," remarked Apolo Kagwa, the Ganda chief minister, when the matter was raised in the Buganda Lukiko, and a request was made for 10 leading persons from Buganda to go down and see things for themselves in South Africa instead (ibid.: 27 October 1902). But, as things turned out, "not a single man could be induced to go" (Stock 1916: 41); the CMS and other humanitarian bodies in London also lobbied British parliamentarians vigorously against the proposal. Quite apart from sheer distance, doubtless Ganda chiefs like Apolo Kagwa objected to their people migrating to the South African mines, because this would have prematurely subverted the quasi-feudal system that they were busily establishing, with missionary and official help, to replace the earlier slave-dominated order.

The alternative possibility of white settlement on the Kenyan model must similarly be taken seriously. Until the world economic depression of 1921 finally knocked them out of the running in the Ugandan political economy (Taylor 1978: 16; Youé 1978: 174), white planters were always pestering British protectorate administrators for labor, and the kasanvu system was in fact introduced by Governor Hesketh Bell (1906–1909) partly for their benefit. This rendered all men liable to one month's labor each year, and in return they would be paid "according to current rates fixed by the government." Officially, Hansen (1984: 178) points out:

the new system was justified as furthering the progress of the country; but it had important side effects, as, by exempting men in permanent employment [persons farming their own land were not considered such], it made it easier for private employers, especially the European planters, to recruit labour. It enabled them to keep wages fixed at a low level; in addition, conscripted labourers were sometimes handed over to the planters by colonial officials.

By the end of the First World War even Ganda chiefs were protesting vigorously about it.

Andereya Luwandaga, one of the two Ganda generals who had captured the rebellious Mwanga in 1899 and had subsequently become a county chief at Nakasongola, wrote in some desperation to the British protectorate authorities in 1917:

The people who are called out for Kasanvu labour cry out in agony saying "where is the English freedom, which we have heard [about] so often" and saying that the present slavery is much worse than the slavery of the old times when the people were sold and bought. . . . It has caused great poverty in the country among the peasants for when a man is called upon to do kasanvu labour, where he only receives Rs 3/- or Rs 4/-, on his return [home] he finds most of his property has suffered on account of his absence and the loss thus occasioned far exceeds the money he can obtain working away in kasanvu. How is wealth to be obtained in this way?

A man so employed cannot possibly learn anything or think anything useful which [brings] progress or glory to his country. It makes people grow up in a bad way owing to the anxiety caused by the coming slavery, and as soon as they grow up they naturally run away from their homes to avoid it.

We call out men to work for the Government but most of them appear to be given away to planters and traders; whereas in our Agreement [of 1900] we only undertook to supply labour to the Government and not to Planters or Traders who seek their own wealth: If these Planters and Traders require any labour they should either beat a drum on the road or offer higher wages in order to obtain it. . . . In the old days before kasanvu labour was introduced, there were many safaris to be carried on the heads and houses were built and all this was always done without any difficulty, yet in those days there were no such things as steamers on the Lake, motor cars or hamali carts on the roads. Yet now that we have all these things to help us our people are much more pressed and cry out in agony. (RHL, Coryndon Papers, Luwandaga to Cooper, 13 July 1917)

So unpopular by now were the Christian chiefs brought to power by the "Christian revolution" of 1888–1889 and confirmed in position by the Uganda Agreement of 1900 that Joseph Kasirye (1963: 84) tells us some nasty songs were sung about them. One may be translated thus:

Those overmighty men make us cry!
You behave heartrendingly.
But, when the rain pours down,
That will be Mugwanya's downfall!

Here it should be pointed out that Mugwanya is the name not only of
one of the leading Christian Ganda chiefs of the time, Stanislas Mugwanya, but also the word commonly used for the latrines Ganda were
required to dig in accordance with early colonial health regulations; the
mugwanya inevitably became unpleasantly slippery during the rainy
season, and the wish of Ganda peasant songsters now clearly was that
Mugwanya and his fellow chiefly organizers of oppression would come
to a similarly slippery end.

In fact, relief from the kasanvu system came in 1922 as a by-product
of British parliamentary concern with forced labor in the neighboring
Kenya Colony and the resultant decision that in future all forced-labor
demands would have to be independently vetted in London. Opposition
to Ganda chiefs now rallied around the symbols of clanship in the shape
of the Butaka Federation formed by newly educated and kinship-stressing
political activists; and the British protectorate authorities responded to
this agitation by "persuading" the Buganda Lukiko to pass the Busulu
and Nvujo Law of 1927, whereby peasant cultivators of land in Buganda
were guaranteed security of tenure and their rents to Ganda landlords
frozen at what became progressively nominal levels. Thenceforward,
politics in colonial Buganda became increasingly a matter of "peasants
versus chiefs," though at the very end of the British protectorate period
during the 1950s and early 1960s, the question of Buganda's possible independence as a separate entity once again became a live issue.

It was in this setting that pioneering studies of both colonial and precolonial Buganda were undertaken by scholars associated with the Institute of Social Research at Makerere. As portrayed in *The King's Men*
(Fallers 1964), in many ways their intellectual flagship, before the British
protectorate Buganda was sociologically a royal despotism characterized
by substantial internal mobility as well as maximum mobilization for external predation — a brigand state in which relations between slaves and
masters were subsumed within more important ties between peasants and
chiefs and, most important of all, between the Ganda king and everybody else (Waller 1971). It is understandable why the power of the Ganda
king should have been stressed so strongly during the Kabaka crisis of
1953–1955. But a consequence of undue stress upon the development of
the Buganda Kingdom as a royal despotism without significant social
distinctions within the peasantry was an undervaluing of the role of precolonial slavery. Chiefs were divided into intricate orders of clan and administrative chiefs, which successive kings were assumed to have en-
deavored to play off one against another — instead of mediating between
them within a much more complex context involving slavery as well as
intermediate statuses "between slavery and freedom," to quote the title

of M. I. Finley's (1964) famous article on ancient Greece. Peasants, on the other hand, were the "undistinguished ordinary people who were *not* something else," and the lives of slaves were assumed to have been "not very different from the lives of ordinary peasants, except that they were affected by lack of kinsmen". (Perlman 1970: 137–41).

However, lack of kinsmen was no minor matter. Slaves *do* appear to have differed crucially from free cultivators regarding life chances in pre-protectorate Buganda, and the ending of slavery was the source of considerable trouble and strife for British colonial officials, even when they insisted upon banning only the external raiding and left indigenous structures as untouched as possible. During the twentieth century, as preprotectorate slaves died out, their children were assimilated into surviving Ganda clans rather than accommodated in special villages of freedom or proletarianized as migrant workers to white farms or mining complexes. Instead, especially after the ending of the kasanvu system of forced labor in the 1920s, there was an increasing tendency for migrant workers to move *into* Buganda, particularly from the two neighboring Belgian-ruled territories of Ruanda-Urundi, in order to work on Ganda cotton and coffee farms (Richards 1954). The resultant rural class structure reported by Christopher Wrigley in the 1950s of

large farmers	2 percent
well-to-do peasants	19 percent
middling peasants	27 percent
poor peasants	32 percent
landless laborers	20 percent

has been characterized by Peter Worsley (1967: 220) as "the statistics of latent revolution." The consequences of these statistics are still being worked out today. But that is another story.

GLOSSARY

abenvumu (sing. *nvuma* if female, otherwise *omunvumu*)	chattel slaves.
baddu (sing. *muddu*)	male slaves or servants—the weakest word for slaves.
bagule (sing. *mugule*)	slaves by purchase.
bakopi (sing. *mukopi*)	peasants.
banyage (sing. *munyage*)	slaves by seizure or plunder.
basajja (sing. *musajja*)	lit., "man"; by extension, follower of a chief.

basenze (sing. *musenze*)	tenants.
basibe (sing. *musibe*)	prisoners.
basige (sing. *musige*)	children sent as servants to king or chief.
bazana (sing. *muzana*)	female slaves or servants — in weakness, equivalent to baddu.
biwendo (sing. *kiwendo*)	sudden group sacrifices.
ekyejo	insolence.
kabaka	king; capitalized when signifying a particular king.
kasanvu	name for early colonial forced-labor system, literally "the seven thousand."
katikiro	chief minister; capitalized when signifying a particular chief minister.
lukiko	council; capitalized when signifying the principal one in Buganda.
mailo	quasi-freehold land tenure introduced in 1900, from the English "mile."
mugwanya	lavatory trench.

REFERENCES

Archival sources

CMS: Church Missionary Society Archives, London.
  Walker, R. Papers. 1887–1906. CMS/ACC/88.
EA: Entebbe Archives, Entebbe (located in the basement of the president's office, next door to Tanzanian military headquarters in 1981).
  Grant to Entebbe, 17 June 1895. A/4/1.
  Grant to Entebbe, 8 January 1896. A/4/4.
FOCP: Foreign Office Confidential Prints, Institute of Commonwealth Studies Library, London.
  The Institute of Commonwealth Studies has copies of Foreign Office Confidential Prints reproducing British FO correspondence in printed form, for internal FO use at that time.
  Berkeley to Salisbury, 8 December 1895.
MUL: Makerere University Library, Makerere, Uganda.
  Miti, J., and G. Rock MS, "History of Buganda," n.d. (translation and amplification of Luganda originals; another version at the School of Oriental and African Studies, London University; Luganda originals at Makarere only).
MHM: Mill Hill Mission Archives, London.
  Nsambya Diary. 1895–1899. (Mill Hill Fathers' journal, recording principal events and correspondence).
RHL: Rhodes House Library, Oxford.
  Coryndon, Robert. Papers. 1917–1925. Ms. Afr. S. 633.

Crabtree, W. Diary. 1892–1903. Mss Afr. S. 1417(1). (Copy also in author's possession.)

Lugard, F. Papers (including his diaries, 1890–1892). Mss. Brit. Emp. S. 30–99. (original papers, 1890–?; printed version of diaries published in Perham and Bull 1959).

Roscoe, J. MS notebook. 1906. Ms. Afr. S. 17.

Ternan, T. Diaries. 1894–1897. 4 vols. Mss. Afr. T. 128–131.

WF: White Fathers headquarters, Rome.

Rubaga Diary. 1897–? (White Fathers' journal, recording principal events and correspondence).

Other sources

Ansorge, W. J. 1899. *Under the African sun.* London: Heinemann.

Apter, D. E. 1961. *The political kingdom in Uganda.* Princeton: Princeton University Press.

Ashe, R. P. 1889. *Two kings of Uganda.* London: Sampson Low.

Atanda, J. A. 1969. The Bakopi in the kingdom of Buganda. *Uganda Journal* 34: 151–62.

Cohen, D. W. 1977. *Womunafu's Bunafu: a study of authority in a nineteenth century African community.* Princeton: Princeton University Press.

Colvile, H. 1895. *Land of the Nile springs.* London: Edward Arnold.

Cooper, F. 1979. The problem of slavery in African studies. *Journal of African History* 20: 103–25.

Cooper, F. 1981. Peasants, capitalists and historians: a review article. *Journal of Southern African Studies* 7: 284–314.

Ddiba, F. 1969. *Eddini mu Uganda,* 3 vols. Masaka, Uganda: St. Liberatum Press.

Fallers, L. A., ed. 1964. *The king's men: leadership and status in Buganda on the eve of independence.* London: Oxford University Press.

Faupel, J. F. 1962. *African holocaust: the story of the Uganda martyrs.* London: Chapman.

Felkin, R. W. 1885–1886. Notes on the Waganda tribe of Central Africa. *Proceedings of the Royal Society of Edinburgh* 13: 699–770.

Finley, M. I. 1964. Between slavery and freedom. *Comparative Studies in Society and History* 6: 233–49.

Goody, J. 1983. *The development of the family and marriage in Europe.* Cambridge: Cambridge University Press.

Hansen, H. B. 1984. *Mission, church and state in a colonial setting: Uganda 1890–1925.* London: Heinemann Educational.

Kasirye, J. S. 1963. *Obulamu bwa Stanislas Mugwanya.* Dublin: Fallon.

Kenny, M. G. 1979. Pre-colonial trade in eastern Lake Victoria. *Azania* 14: 97–107.

King, N. Q., A. Kasozi, and A. Oded. 1973. *Islam and the confluence of religions in Uganda, 1840–1966.* Tallahassee, Fla.: American Academy of Religion.

Kopytoff, I., and S. Miers. 1977. African "slavery" as an institution of marginality. In *Slavery in Africa: historical and anthropological perspectives*, ed. S. Miers and I. Kopytoff, 3–81. Madison: University of Wisconsin Press.

Lonsdale, J. 1985. The European scramble and conquest in African history. In *Cambridge history of Africa*, Vol. 6, ed. R. Oliver and G. N. Sanderson. Cambridge: Cambridge University Press.

Low, D. A. 1960. The making and implementation of the Uganda Agreement of 1900. In *Buganda and British overrule*, by D. A. Low and R. C. Pratt, 3–159. London: Oxford University Press.

Lugard, F. D. 1893. *The rise of our East African Empire*, 2 vols. Edinburgh: Blackwood and Sons.

Marissal, J. 1978. Le commerce zanzibarite dans l'Afrique des grands lacs au xixe siècle. *Revue française d'histoire d'Outre-Mer* 65: 212–35.

Miers, S. 1975. *Britain and the ending of the slave trade*. London: Longmans.

Obbo, C. 1979. Village strangers in Buganda society. In *Strangers in African societies*, ed. W. A. Shack and E. P. Skinner, 227–41. Berkeley: University of California Press.

Oded, A. 1974. *Islam in Uganda: Islamization through a centralized state in pre-colonial Africa*. New York: Wiley and Sons.

Perham, M. 1956. *Lugard: the years of adventure*. London: Collins.

Perham, M., and M. Bull, eds. 1959. *The diaries of Lord Lugard*, 4 vols. Evanston, Ill.: Northwestern University Press.

Perlman, M. L. 1970. The traditional system of stratification. . . . In *Social stratification in Africa*, ed. A. Tuden and L. Plotnicov, 125–61. New York: Free Press.

Portal, G. 1894. *The British mission to Uganda in 1893*. London: Edward Arnold.

Richards, A. I. 1954. *Economic development and tribal change*. Cambridge: Heffers.

Richards, A. I., Ed. 1960. *East African chiefs*. London: Faber and Faber.

Richards, A. I., F. Sturrock, and J. M. Fortt. *Subsistence to commercial farming in present-day Buganda*. Cambridge: Cambridge University Press.

Roscoe, J. 1902. Apolo Kagwa, katikiro and regent of Uganda. *Church Missionary Gleaner* 1 July 1901: 108.

Roscoe, J. 1911. *The Baganda*. London: Macmillan.

Rowe, J. 1969. *Lugard at Kampala*. Kampala, Uganda: Longmans.

Rowe, J. 1975. The pattern of political administration in precolonial Buganda. In *African themes*, ed. I. Abu-Lughod, 65–76. Evanston, Ill.: Northwestern University Program of African Studies.

Speke, J. H. 1863. *Journal of the discovery of the source of the Nile*. Edinburgh and London: Blackwood and Sons.

Stock, E. 1916. *History of the Church Missionary Society*, Vol. 4. London: CMS.

Taylor, T. F. 1978. The struggle for economic control of Uganda, 1919–1922: formulation of an economic policy. *International Journal of African Historical Studies* 11: 1–31.

Thoonen, J. P. 1941. *Black martyrs*. London: Sheed and Ward.

Tinker, H. 1974. *A new system of slavery: the export of Indian labour overseas, 1830–1920*. London: Oxford University Press.

Tosh, J. 1970. The northern interlacustrine region. In *Pre-colonial African trade*, ed. R. Gray and D. Birmingham, 103–18. London: Oxford University Press.

Tucker, A. R. 1908. *Eighteen years in Uganda and East Africa*, 2 vols. London: Edward Arnold.

Twaddle, M. 1967. Politics in Bukedi, 1900–1939: an historical study of administrative change among the segmentary peoples of eastern Uganda under the impact of British colonial rule. Ph.D. thesis, London University.

Twaddle, M. 1969. The *Bakungu* chiefs of Buganda under British colonial rule, 1900–1930. *Journal of African History* 10: 309–22.

Twaddle, M. 1972. The Muslim revolution in Buganda. *African Affairs* 71: 54–72.

Twaddle, M. 1983. Slaves and peasants in Buganda. Paper presented at the Canadian Association of African Studies conference at Laval University, Quebec, 15–19 May 1983.

Uzoigwe, G. N. 1972. Precolonial markets in Bunyoro-Kitara. *Comparative Studies in Society and History* 14: 422–55.

Waliggo, J. M. 1976. The Catholic church in the Buddu Province of Buganda. Ph.D. thesis, Cambridge University.

Waller, R. 1971. The traditional economy of Buganda. M.A. research essay, Centre of African Studies, London University.

Walser, F. 1982. *Luganda proverbs*. Berlin: Reimer.

Worsley, P. 1967. *The third world*. London: Weidenfeld and Nicolson.

Wrigley, C. C. 1959. The Christian revolution in Buganda. *Comparative Studies in Society and History* 2: 33–48.

Wright, M[ichael]. 1971. *Buganda in the heroic age*. Nairobi: Oxford University Press.

Wright, Marcia. 1985. East Africa, 1870–1905. In *Cambridge history of Africa*, Vol. 6, ed. R. Oliver and G. N. Sanderson. Cambridge: Cambridge University Press.

Youé, C. P. 1978. Peasants, planters and cotton capitalists: the "dual economy" in colonial Uganda. *Canadian Journal of African Studies* 12: 163–84.

4 *Dennis D. Cordell*

The Delicate Balance of Force and Flight: The End of Slavery in Eastern Ubangi-Shari

Despite colonial rhetoric proclaiming liberation of the slaves as a justification for occupation, the French were not particularly preoccupied with ending slavery in eastern Ubangi-Shari (part of today's Central African Republic) in the late nineteenth and early twentieth centuries. French actions were dictated not by concerns for slaves or for their emancipation, but rather by local economic and demographic imperatives.

By the late nineteenth century slave-raiding and the slave trade had depopulated the region. Demographic statistics do not exist for the period, but Pierre Prins and other French visitors around the turn of the century were struck by the number of ruined villages and the vast deserted zones through which they travelled (Prins 1925).

Although the French in eastern Ubangi-Shari in the 1890s were primarily concerned with finding porters and foodstuffs for their expeditions to the upper Nile, even at this early date, officials voiced a second concern: how to "develop" such a sparsely populated zone. In this case, "de-

I would like to express appreciation to the Social Science Research Council, whose doctoral and faculty grants programs partly supported research for this article in 1973–1975 and 1985; to the National Endowment of the Humanities, whose Travel to Collections Program provided funds for travel to archives in Paris and Aix-en-Provence; and to Dedman College, Southern Methodist University, which generously allowed me a semester's leave for work on this and other projects.

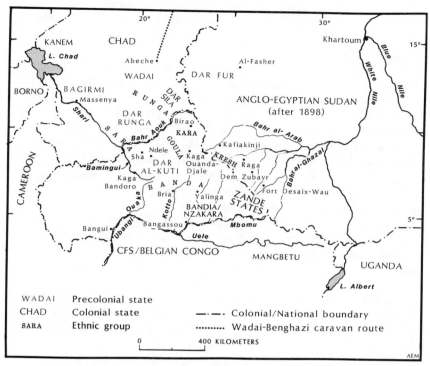

Map 4. North-Central Africa

velopment" meant economic reorientation. By the 1890s eastern Ubangi-Shari had become a periphery of the Muslim economy with links to the Nile Valley to the east and the sahel and Sahara to the north (Cordell 1983; Collins 1971). The French arrived determined to sever these ties and integrate the region into the expanding capitalist economy of the Atlantic zone to the south and southwest: "[It] is necessary to envisage the commercial future of this immense territory where pagan peoples and already civilized Muslims on the route to progress are impatient to receive European products necessary for their welfare and livelihood" (ANF-SOM [Paris], Liotard 1896).

But following confrontation with the British at Fashoda in 1898, the French withdrew from the Nile Valley. Eastern Ubangi-Shari became a cul-de-sac far from major French administrative and economic centers. Development options were limited. Moreover, it had long borders with the Anglo-Egyptian Sudan in the east (so named after 1898), and the Congo Free State (or Belgian Congo after 1908) in the south. The remote-

ness and openness of the region made it difficult for the French to apply
force to achieve their objectives without provoking the flight of the small
population that remained.

The elimination of slavery was not central to coping with economic
development or depopulation. Ending slave-raiding and the slave trade,
however, was crucial. Both threatened the viability of the colonial political economy by removing the people who collected rubber, ivory, and
other products which helped finance early French occupation as well as
the concessionary companies established to exploit the territory after 1898
(Coquery-Vidrovitch 1972). Later, Africans paid the head taxes which
furnished a large part of colonial revenues, and supplied the labor for
public and private work projects. It was hoped, too, that they would eventually become buyers of European imports.

The slave trade also hindered economic reorientation. Slaves were the
major export from eastern Ubangi-Shari to the Muslim sphere, supporting commerce in other products such as beads, cloth, and odorific plants
that would not otherwise be viable. By the 1920s, however, French policies aimed at combatting slave-raiding and the slave trade in eastern
Ubangi-Shari brought the end of slavery itself. The pages that follow trace
these developments both in the region as a whole, and in detail in Dar
al-Kuti, one of the region's major slave-raiding and slave-trading states.

Eastern Ubangi-Shari, 1860s–1890s: Slave-Raiding, the Slave Trade, and Depopulation

The integration of eastern Ubangi-Shari into the Muslim economy of the
sahel and the Nile Basin was largely the work of Muslim traders who
ventured into the region between the 1820s and the 1850s in search of
ivory and a few slaves. Their numbers were small and their means of
violence limited; consequently, they tended to become part of local communities, while retaining commercial links with Muslim societies. Around
the middle of the century, however, three factors combined to shift the
regional balance of power towards the Muslims. First, there was an increased demand for slaves in the Muslim world in general and in the Nile
Valley in particular. Second, the dissemination of Western military technology — most notably advanced firearms — in North Africa and the Middle East altered Muslim armies and warfare in the sahel. Hence, a claim-
ant to the throne of Dar Fur wrote to the European traveller S. Perron
in Cairo: "When I return to Dar Fur, you must come visit the land. I
will inaugurate there the modes of warfare that I have seen here; I will
introduce another method of administration. I have seen Egypt and Muhammad 'Ali" (Perron 1845: 156 n. 1, and notes at end).

Although the actual transformations were not as great as these ambitions, by the later decades of the century even nominally Muslim states on the fringes of the Muslim world, such as Wadai and Dar Fur, had access to weapons that altered the balance of power between themselves and their non-Muslim neighbors (Cordell 1985a: 17–18), probably making raiding less dangerous and more profitable than earlier. These innovations, along with the rising demand for captives, translated into increased raiding among non-Muslim peoples of eastern Ubangi-Shari.

But the third and perhaps most important factor in the shift of power to Muslims was the arrival of independent merchants from the Nile region in the southern and southwestern Sudan in the 1850s. Known as the Khartoumers, their activities increased the scale and frequency of slave-raiding and slave-trading, causing depopulation and the radical restructuring of local economies. They inaugurated what has come to be called the *zariba* (Arabic: "armed camp") system (Santandrea 1964: 18–19). Arriving in large numbers and better armed than their non-Muslim neighbors, Khartoumer merchants generally made alliances with local peoples who allowed them to settle in exchange for military aid and imported goods. The armed merchants and their hosts often raided surrounding populations, bringing captives back to their camps. There, some were settled and some were selected for export. Although a few settled slaves became part of the merchants' raiding forces, most grew crops to supply food for the zariba. In the 1870s Georg Schweinfurth (1874, 2: 410–32) found such armed camps every 20 miles along the major trade routes, separated by vast depopulated regions whose inhabitants had either been killed, had fled in the face of attack, or had been captured and sold or resettled.

With the closure of the Nile to the slave trade in the 1860s, a result of measures taken by Egypt under pressure from the British, the zariba system began shifting westward to Ubangi-Shari. Later, violence associated with the Mahdist regime (1881–1898) blockaded commerce on the Nile. Relocated west of the divide separating the Nile and Ubangi-Zaire river basins, slave-raiders and slave-traders had access to the Wadai-Benghazi caravan route, one of the last trans-Saharan itineraries free from European intervention, for the remainder of the century (Cordell 1977a).

The Khartoumers consolidated the changes introduced by the increased demand for slaves and the dissemination of Western firearms, resulting in the violent restructuring of local political economies in eastern Ubangi-Shari. In many societies a slave mode of production became dominant (Jewsiewicki 1981: 103). Up until this time, local societies had for the most part been small-scale. Most production occurred within work groups based on the household; kinship ideology predominated. Peoples such as the Sara, Banda, and Kresh lived in dispersed villages, practicing shifting agriculture; gathering and hunting remained important (Cordell 1983). Only in the south along the Mbomu and Uele rivers, which converge to form the Ubangi, were there centralized political formations. In the west the Bandia/Nzakara Kingdom, a product of the Bandia conquest of the Nzakara peoples, straddled the ecological frontier between forest and savanna along the Mbomu around modern Bangassou (Dampierre 1967). To the east were a series of small states whose rulers were Zande from the southwestern Sudan (see Evans-Pritchard 1971). And to the south lay the Mangbetu Kingdom of northeastern Zaire (Keim 1979). Although indigenous slavery had existed in all of these states, increased ties with the zariba system in the late nineteenth century led to the export of captives to the Muslim world (Prins 1925: 124). In short, their rulers were co-opted by the expanding Muslim economy.

By the 1890s three decades of slave-raiding had not only resulted in the depopulation of much of the region but had also dramatically altered the distribution of those people who remained (Schweinfurth 1874, 2: 437–42; Prins 1925: 168–69). Some survivors of raids had scattered into isolated regions where they attracted little attention.

Seeking shelter from likely invasions, and hoping not to attract attention, local peoples avoided forming large settlements. Small "familial" villages, composed solely of a head of household, his wives, children, and slaves, were scattered across the countryside, hidden in inaccessible places near sources of water. People often reached these settlements by following streambeds, thus leaving no traces of their passage. (Daigre 1950: 48)

Other groups gathered into large, walled villages (Lotar 1937: 75; Prins 1925: 122–23, 133–34, 158) — adopting if possible the weapons of their foes to defend themselves. Still others had become avid slave-raiders, using the tactics of Muslim raiders for their own aggrandizement.

Santandrea (1981: 87) summarizes the careers of three such Kresh leaders whose strategies paralleled those of other raider/traders in eastern Ubangi-Shari in the late nineteenth century:

Saʻid, . . . Mbele, . . . and Mereke . . . were originally choice "alumni" of Zubeir's [sic] training school of leaders. Placed at the head of tribal groups, with a well balanced degree of personal independence and control from higher authority, they commanded larger or smaller numbers of troops, fairly well equipped with firearms. After Zubeir's . . . fall, they took the best advantage of the new favourable situation, first asserting their own authority over their peoples, then gradually enlarging their power over neighbouring natives by means of their army. By dint of tireless efforts, backed by experience and fortune, they succeeded in organising small "kingdoms" in that now "no man's land."

With the rise of a slave mode of production, wealth and power in eastern Ubangi-Shari translated into control over and trade in people (Cordell 1985b). Land was ample and, for the most part, deserted. Ivory was in demand for long-distance commerce, but the region functioned mainly as a labor reservoir for the larger Muslim economy. Over time, however, people became a rarer and rarer commodity; they were difficult to find and difficult to retain. These local dilemmas became those of the French as their expeditions marched into the region in the 1890s, eager to link their Central African territories to their sphere of influence on the Red Sea Coast.

The Limits of Power: The French in Eastern Ubangi-Shari, 1890s–1910

The continuation of slave-raiding and the slave trade threatened the success of the colonial venture in eastern Ubangi-Shari and the Sudan. The French dealt with the menace in several contradictory ways. First, they adopted the strategy of the raider/traders, establishing posts and concentrating people around them. In the 1890s, for example, in hopes of carving out a sphere of influence in the southwestern Sudan, they founded posts at Fort Desaix and Dem Zubayr just east of the Nile-Ubangi divide. These centers attracted local peoples who fled from the zaribas of raider/traders to place themselves under French protection. Near the end of the decade when the French withdrew from the Nile Basin, they tried to persuade their protégés to relocate around new posts farther west (Huot 1902: 398).

Another strategy involved alliances with local leaders, such as the Kresh leader Mbele (Cordell 1977b, 1986). Liotard, the local commandant in 1896, recommended support for the Bandia/Nzakara and Zande sultanates. This policy, too, had dual objectives. The first was to hold onto people by protecting them from Muslim slave-raiding from the southwestern Sudan, and from Mahdist bands in particular. The second aim was to bring the region into the French commercial sphere, laying the basis for "development." Although the formal division of Ubangi-Shari into private concessions controlled by individual companies did not come until 1898, the French envied the financial "success" of a similar scheme initiated in the Congo Free State in the late 1880s (Coquery-Vidrovitch 1972: 26; M'Bokolo 1985: 187–90). In this context it is not surprising that Liotard went on to suggest that many local rulers in the border region had already severed commercial ties with the Sudan and would welcome trade with French companies (ANF-SOM [Paris], Liotard 1896). After the inauguration of the concessionary system, the companies themselves lobbied intensively for help from the administration in stopping trade between eastern Ubangi-Shari and the Sudan (ANF-SOM [Paris], Groden 1902). These basic policies were echoed elsewhere in North-Central Africa. Several years later Emile Gentil (1902: 268–69) counselled similar alliances for similar economic reasons with the Muslim states of Dar al-Kuti in northern Ubangi-Shari, and with Bagirmi and Kanem in Chad.

These objectives created contradictions. On the one hand, because they possessed neither the clout nor the personnel to control and administer the region, the French had to maintain good relations with local leaders, who were very often the raider/traders whose activities threatened the demographic and economic viability of their colonial enterprise! Initially the French hoped to wean them of their unsavory habits and set them on the "route to progress" (ANF-SOM [Paris], 1896, Gabon/Congo IV/14c). Administrators, therefore, did not address the issue of slavery.

On the other hand, French labor needs in eastern Ubangi-Shari and elsewhere in the colony led them to acquire slaves themselves, either through attacks on Muslim slave caravans or through purchase. French official Possel's instructions to a subordinate in the Ubangi River region in 1890 succinctly describe the policy:

As you need them, get yourself men by liberating slaves. The price of liberation will be deducted from the salary you deem appropriate, but must not in any case exceed fifty iron bars per man per month. You must make a special effort to make [the freed slaves] understand you: that they are free men from the date of their redemption, but still owe reimbursement of what we paid for them. (ANF-SOM [Aix], Possel 1890)

In the first decades of the colonial era, Christian missions in eastern Ubangi-Shari adopted similar practices. They wanted converts to be sure, but freed slaves also provided labor for chronically understaffed outposts. Tisserant, a French missionary posted to the central Ubangi River region around 1910, noted that earlier in the century the mission La Sainte Famille des Banziris with its "model farm" included many former slaves (Tisserant 1955: 10–11).

But this practice, too, had its contradictions. While the juridical status of former slaves was certainly different, and they would presumably be free to leave once they had compensated their liberators, local raider/traders and local peoples perceived the "villages de liberté," populated with former slaves, to be just the opposite: European equivalents of the zaribas. In the case of the mission La Sainte Famille, Tisserant noted that the freed slaves, who made up a large part of the population, were not accepted by other peoples in the region. Graver still was the perception of the missionaries as "child thieves." Missionaries ultimately concluded that slave purchases actually retarded evangelization, and by the time Tisserant arrived at the mission, the policy had been abandoned (ibid.). Although evidence regarding perceptions of administrative posts in the region is not available, it is probably safe to conclude that surrounding populations viewed them in a similar light.

During these initial decades of colonial penetration, the French lacked both the power and the resolve to convince their local protégés to curtail raiding and trading. Additional constraints included fears that such policies would undermine the authority of local leaders leading to anarchy. Hence colonial administrators faced a dilemma. If they forced the issue too far, local raider/traders could pull up stakes and shift their zaribas back to the east — into the vast and remote areas that lay between the French and British spheres of influence. Or they could simply relocate in neighboring foreign colonies. The difficulties of achieving this delicate balance between force and flight in this part of Africa may perhaps be best appreciated by examining them in a specific context, in this case by looking at French dealings with the Muslim sultanate of Dar al-Kuti.

Dar al-Kuti, the French, and Slavery, 1890s–1911

In the last decade of the century, Dar al-Kuti was the most important slave-raiding and slave-trading center in northern Ubangi-Shari. Located on the Islamic frontier, it had become an important outpost for northern Muslim traders by the 1830s. The region prospered through the middle decades of the century, mainly by exporting ivory and small numbers of slaves (Cordell 1985a: 37–40). Beginning in the 1870s, however, the level of trade and violence in Dar al-Kuti rose as the westward shift of slave-raiders and slave-traders from the Nile Basin increased the level of raiding. At first these incursions were sporadic; a lieutenant of al-Zubayr of Dar Fur devastated the region in the mid-1870s, for example, but returned to the Sudan (Julien 1925: 106–7, 113, 124–25). But the permanent westward migration of another raider, Rabih Fadl-Allah, transformed the political economy of the region.

Rabih fled the Nile Basin in 1876 following the arrest of his patron, al-Zubayr, by Egyptian authorities. He spent the dry season of 1876–1877 raiding in the northern border regions of the Bandia/Nzakara and Zande states. Conflict with clients of Bangassou, ruler of the Bandia/Nzakara, eventually led Rabih to migrate northward, to the area of Dar al-Kuti (Dampierre 1983: 26–28; Cordell 1985a: 53–59).

Through the 1880s Rabih and Kobur, the local ruler of Dar al-Kuti, coexisted uneasily. In 1890, Rabih replaced him with Muhammad al-Sanusi, a more pliant member of the ruling class (Julien 1925: 106, 111–13, 115, 125–27, 134–35, 141), whose later power and wealth earned him the title "sultan" among peoples of the area. Al-Sanusi spent much of the 1890s maneuvering between Rabih and Wadai, to which Dar al-Kuti had paid tribute since midcentury (Cordell 1985a: 61–62, 64–65). In 1891 the ambush of the first French expedition to reach the area provided him with numerous flintlocks and a large number of rapid-fire arms. These weapons enabled al-Sanusi to expand his own slave-raiding, French arms thus ironically contributing to the growth of the state, which became the fiercest threat to the viability of their colonial enterprise in eastern Ubangi-Shari (Dybowski 1893: 68–74, 76; Nebout 1892: 217–47; Kalck 1968; ANF-SOM [Paris], "Mission Crampel," ca. 1896).

Following Rabih's departure for Bagirmi and Borno in 1893, Wadaian revenge against al-Sanusi took the form of a devastating attack on his settlement at Sha in 1894. The sultan sought refuge in rock outcroppings to the southeast, inaccessible to Wadaian cavalry (Julien 1925: 134–37, 142; Grech 1924: 21, 23; Cordell 1985a: 65–66). Between 1894 and 1896 al-Sanusi shifted his camp from one fortified point to another, both to be in proximity to populations to raid and to protect himself from attack. Finally he settled at Ndele in 1896, where he built a permanent, fortified capital on the plateau that dominated the site. He made peace with Wadai and over the next few years eliminated rival raiders; by the late 1890s, Dar al-Kuti had become the major slave-raiding and slave-trading state in the region (Cordell 1985a: 66–68, 173).

Ndele, the sultan's capital, became a major center peopled by resettled slaves and refugees from throughout eastern Ubangi-Shari. Slaves fell into several categories, greatly differentiated according to wealth and power. As in the zaribas of the southwestern Sudan (Schweinfurth 1874, 2: 420–25), there was an elite group of slave soldiers, many of whom had been taken captive as young boys or adolescents. The vast majority, however, were agricultural laborers who either worked in large gangs, or, more often, in kin-based groups forcibly relocated in Ndele (Cordell 1985a: 82–86, 90, 92–93, 103–12, 115–17, 122–29).

The age-sex composition of the slave-labor force is not known. Evidence on slave-raiding, however, suggests that villages which surrendered peaceably to raiders were often relocated en masse around al-Sanusi's capital, whereas resistance often resulted in the massacre of most adult males. Presumably then, the Ndele labor force included women, girls,

and boys forcibly taken from their homes, along with "peaceably" relocated villages that included adult males. In any case, raiding and resettlement depopulated the surrounding territory; by the turn of the
century Ndele had become one of the major towns of North Central Africa, with a population estimated at 20,000–30,000.[1]

Aware of the important central place that Ndele occupied in the regional economy, the French wanted to incorporate the city and the surrounding territories of Dar al-Kuti into their zone of influence and re-
orient commerce southward. Although they aimed to end the slave trade,
they only aspired to limit raiding, because they wished neither to remove
the sultan, who maintained order in the region, nor to threaten him to
the point that he would flee with his people. Indeed there was ample
precedent for flight: not only had al-Sanusi fled from Sha in the wake
of the Wadaian attack in 1894, but he had also threatened to abandon
Ndele on two later occasions: in 1899 when he felt trapped by Rabih,
Wadai, and the French, and in 1900 when the French and Wadai again
pressured him (Julien 1927: 110–12, 114–17; 1928: 61–63; 1929: 45–46;
Chevalier 1907: 139–41).

Between 1897 and 1911 the French concentrated on developing "legitimate" commerce, expanding imports of cloth, beads, salt, tea, sugar,
and soap in exchange for exports that consisted mainly of ivory, rubber,
wax, and other gathered products (Chevalier 1907: 153–54; Julien 1929:
74; Julien 1904: 39). They also sought to control slave-raiding and to stop
the slave trade. Treaties in 1897, 1903, and 1908 between the French and
al-Sanusi reflect these aims, as well as the shifting balance of power between them.

The 1897 agreement demonstrated the weakness of the French in northern Ubangi-Shari due to their continued preoccupation with the Nile
region at that time. Al-Sanusi pledged not to trade with any other Europeans. This was not difficult, since only French commercial houses had
representatives in the region. He also promised not to interfere with French
expeditions sent north against Rabih. The agreement did not mention
slave-trading or slavery. In fact, the French supplied carbines and per-
cussion caps, which actually permitted al-Sanusi to expand these activities
(AAV, dossier 1, 1897).

By 1903, the date of the next treaty, the French position had improved.
Although Wadai remained a threat, the Fashoda crisis of 1898 had ended
French initiatives in the east, and they had begun to shift primary atten-
tion to the Chad Basin. This agreement reinforced the commercial clauses

---

1. Julien 1929: 49; Prins 1900: 193–96; Chevalier 1903: 360; Courtet 1904: 485 n.; Cordell 1985a: 82–86, 103–12; 115–17, 139–43.

of the earlier accord giving priority to French trading houses. Al-Sanusi undertook to pay the French government an annual tribute in rubber, ivory, coffee, grain, and livestock, and to provide courier service and porters for French expeditions heading north. Again there was no mention of slave-raiding or slave-trading, and again the French agreed to furnish arms, ammunition, and military advisors, which allowed extension of these activities (AAV, dossier 1, 1903).

It was only in an informal agreement in 1904 and in a third and final treaty signed in 1908 that the French explicitly sought to resolve these contradictions. The first accord bound al-Sanusi not to raid in the Kotto and Ouaka river regions to the southeast, where French commercial companies had established trading posts around which they were concentrating freed slaves (Tisserant 1955: 17; Dampierre 1967: 502–4). The 1908 treaty went further, forbidding all trade in slaves and requiring French approval for all raids and military expeditions. In a second proviso, the sultan promised to impose a head tax and pay one-third of the revenue to the colonial administration. Thirdly, he agreed to adopt some French administrative procedures, take a census, and furnish supplies to an expanded French garrison. Finally, he said he would cut all commercial ties with the Muslim sphere. The French would no longer provide arms or training in their use (AAV, dossier 1, 1908). Since Rabih had been killed in battle by the French in 1900, and by 1907 Wadai was much weakened by internal unrest, the Europeans were clearly in a position to place greater pressure on Dar al-Kuti than had been possible earlier.

None of these agreements touched on slavery itself. It was apparent to the French that slave labor was essential for the maintenance of Dar al-Kuti, and that al-Sanusi would never agree to emancipation. Only Chevalier, a French visitor to the area in 1902–1903, suggested freeing the slaves, and the idea was immediately rejected by al-Hajj Tukur, one of the sultan's most influential advisors:

What would you have us do without slaves? Where would you want the sultan to obtain the porters necessary for your travels? Who would cultivate the fields? Look at our arms (and he showed me the thin arms of a Fulbe). Do you think they are strong enough to turn over the earth? Where would you have us find the cattle that your government requests if we had no slaves to give to the northern Arabs in exchange for their herds? (Chevalier 1907: 160–61)

Far from pressuring the sultan to free the slaves, in 1904 French officials in Kaga Bandoro, a French post just west of the sultanate, actually returned slaves who fled Ndele. The practice stopped in 1906 only when it came to the attention of the French parliament during a broader investigation of the activities of concessionary companies in the colony (Kalck 1970, 3: 189).

Following the 1908 treaty, relations with al-Sanusi deteriorated, but the French, fearing chaos, did not remove him even though he ignored many of the provisions of the agreement and continued sporadic raiding. Eventually two rival power centers emerged in Ndele — the sultan with his followers on the plateau at the heart of the settlement, and the French with their clients on a high hill at the southwestern entrance to the city. Neither was strong enough to impose its will on the other (Cordell 1985a: 73–74).

Only in 1910 when rumors of al-Sanusi's imminent flight were rife did the French take action. Early in that year, al-Sanusi besieged Kaga Ouanda-Djale, a fortified rock outcropping to the east, beyond the effective control of either the French or the British. Apart from being free of European control, Ouanda-Djale also lay on the trade routes to the northeast, and would thus allow continued export of slaves. During the year, tensions increased. The sultan began sending his wives and large stores of food to the east (ANF-SOM [Aix], rapport annuel 1911). In late 1910 Ouanda-Djale fell, opening the way for an escape.

The French concocted a ruse to take al-Sanusi and his son prisoner. Modat, the French resident in Ndele, announced that a mission would be leaving for the southeast — for the French post of Bria. According to custom, al-Sanusi greeted such expeditions as they departed Ndele. When the party arrived at the sultan's compound on 11 January 1911, the French called for al-Sanusi, who appeared with his son. The commander pulled a pistol; in the ensuing melee the sultan and his son were killed. Pandemonium broke out and fighting lasted two days, when al-Sanusi's remaining forces fled to Ouanda-Djale, where they held out for the next year.[2]

The day after the assassinations, Modat proclaimed the liberation of the slaves. In addition, he removed the sultan's sons, other Muslim officials, and 650 women and many children of non-Muslim origin from the compounds of al-Sanusi; many non-Muslim parents came forward to claim their offspring.[3] In most respects, however, emancipation was a mere formality, because most captives had liberated themselves with the outbreak of violence. Some sought refuge in the environs of the city, and in the wake of the collapse of the agricultural system resorted to gathering, hunt-

2. Interviews: Yadjouma Pascal, 15 and 18 May; Ngrekoudou Ouih Fran; Anonymous 1911; Carbou 1912, 2: 176–85; ANF-SOM (Aix), rapport annuel 1911.

3. Interviews: Yadjouma Pascal, 15 and 18 May and 30 June; Modat 1912: 288; Kalck 1970, 3: 223.

ing, and fishing to escape starvation. By the next year, small settlements surrounded by fields had appeared throughout the region. Other former slaves not from the Ndele area set out for distant homelands. For the next several years colonial reports from Kémo-Gribingui, the *circonscription* in central Ubangi-Shari, mention the arrival of people from Dar al-Kuti; however, they do not describe their activities in any detail.[4]

As for the Muslims, many Runga slaveholders as well as Runga farmers fled to Dar Runga to take shelter with kinspeople. Other Muslims settled in the "no man's land" between Dar al-Kuti and the Sudan, where they continued to raid for slaves.[5] By early 1912, al-Sanusi's former capital had almost become a ghost town; only 350 houses were inhabited (ANF-SOM [Aix], rapport politique, 31 July 1912). Thus, when faced with the flight of the inhabitants of the largest settlement in northern Ubangi-Shari, the French finally resorted to force. But the removal of the sultan indeed led to the disorder they feared.

Dar al-Kuti, 1911–1920: The End of Slavery, the Persistence of Raiding, and the Return to Subsistence Agriculture

French failure to focus on slavery between 1897 and 1911 was underscored by the absence of a plan for resettling freed slaves after the fall of Ndele. After al-Sanusi's death Modat simply told people to go back to their villages — many of which no longer existed — and prepare to plant their fields when the rains began (interviews: Yadjouma Pascal, 18 May; Khrouma Sale). The policy was unrealistic and led to famine; by early 1912, the new French commandant in Dar al-Kuti was complaining that people had been lax in their labors, and blamed them for the shortfall in food supplies (ANF-SOM [Aix], rapport, 1er trimestre, 1912).

Following the defeat in Ndele, some members of al-Sanusi's family and his closest lieutenants fled to Ouanda-Djale, where Kamun, a son, proclaimed himself sultan. From this site on caravan routes to Dar Fur, the Bahr al-Ghazal, and eastern Chad, it is likely that he hoped to re-create his father's slave-raiding/slave-trading operation (Kalck 1970, 3: 213–16; ANF-SOM [Aix], rapport, 3e trimestre, 1917). For the next two years, the zariba at Ouanda-Djale threatened French control over Ndele. They finally laid siege and conquered it in December 1912 (Cornet n.d.: 9).

Yet this action did not end the threat. As many of the victims of their

---

4. For example, see ANF-SOM (Aix), rapport politique 1912; and ANF-SOM (Aix), résumé 1912.

5. Interviews: Yadjouma Pascal, 18 May; Yacoub Mahamat Dillang, 20 and 25 May; Adoum Oumar; Yacoub Soudour Tekai; ANF-SOM (Aix), rapport mensuel 1914.

violence had done before them, Kamun and other sons fled to the Sudan whence they threatened French hegemony in eastern Ubangi-Shari for the rest of the decade. But the refugees in the Sudan were not limited to members of the ruling family; important numbers of ordinary Banda from Ndele joined them (Santandrea 1957: 154). Administrative reports of 1916, 1917, and 1918 note that rumors of the return of Kamun and other slave-raiders were constant, and preoccupied former slave populations. Such fears undermined French efforts to get them to venture out of their villages to collect rubber — one of the "legitimate" goods desired by the concessionary companies and the colonial administration (ANF-SOM [Aix], rapports annuels for 1916, 1917, and 1918).

Throughout the first half of the colonial period, the refugee communities in the Sudan posed a threat to the demographic stability of eastern Ubangi-Shari. Settlements were numerous along the road between Dem Zubayr and Raga, a short distance from the border. People initially fled Ndele because they feared further French violence in the wake of the assassinations of al-Sanusi and his son. With time these fears subsided, but people remained in the Sudan to avoid the policies of forced collection of rubber and wax for head taxes and forced labor imposed by the colonial administration (Santandrea 1957, 1981: 21 n. 2; Kalck 1974: 186–88; Cordell 1987). During the same period, other refugees from Ubangi-Shari joined them.

Hoping that the return of al-Sanusi's family would stem flight to the Sudan, the French finally succeeded in getting the sultan's son Abdul Kadir to return to Ndele in the late 1920s. They reconstituted the sultanate, which had been dismembered in the 1910s, and allowed him to preside over it. In 1934 they even constructed a mosque near the sultan's residence — to show that they were not hostile to Muslims. Nonetheless, as late as 1937 French administrative reports note that the presence of others of al-Sanusi's sons in the Sudan along with a large number of the sultan's former subjects served to attract people from Dar al-Kuti who were dissatisfied with French policies (ANF-SOM [Aix], rapport semestriel 1938).

As elsewhere, the end of the slave trade and the freeing of slaves altered relations of production in Dar al-Kuti. However, the evidence suggests that people by and large reverted to earlier social relations of production and survived through subsistence agriculture. During the initial decade of colonial rule, they collected ivory, wax, and rubber for payment to the colonial state as head taxes in kind; the administration then sold these goods to commercial companies for the world market, using the proceeds to finance the colony. Integration into the capitalist economy was hence limited at best; to most people, the provision of wax, ivory, and rubber probably more closely resembled tribute payments to al-Sanusi than a new kind of economic activity. No one in Dar al-Kuti made a living by supplying labor or cash crops to the colonial economy.

By the 1920s there is some evidence that the collection of these items had expanded, although the extent of the change and its impact are unclear. In 1922, for example, the administration or private agents purchased five-and-a-half tons of ivory in Ndele (Cordell 1985a: 237 n. 56). But the supply of ivory, at least that which was sold in the market, gave out shortly thereafter, for a 1932 report identifies wax (14 tons in 1931 and 22 in 1932) as the sole export (ANF-SOM [Aix], rapport annuel 1932). Wax continued to grow in importance; collection exceeded 50 tons annually for every year but one between 1940 and 1948 (ANF-SOM [Aix], rapport politique 1948). As for rubber, production dropped off in the 1920s and 1930s, resumed in the 1940s when supplies from Southeast Asia were cut off during the Second World War, and ceased with the end of hostilities (ibid.).

Imports of European goods were supplied by foreign merchants. A 1923 report notes the presence of seven French and Levantine merchants in the city; and oral accounts note the appearances of Portuguese traders in the 1930s.[6] Most of them imported small quantities of cloth and other manufactured goods from Bangui, the colonial capital on the Ubangi River to the south, which was joined to Ndele about this time by a dry-season dirt road. These merchants remained important in the city until the 1950s; by 1974 only one remained.

It is difficult to assess the degree to which these activities—the continued collection of products of the land and their exchange for European goods—transformed life in Ndele in the middle decades of the colonial era. People hunted and gathered ivory, rubber, and wax during the dry season, when their labor was not needed for agricultural production. As for the transformation of consumer patterns, the bulk of these goods was collected to pay head taxes; only the excess was exchanged for imports. Further research is needed to determine how these transactions changed the lives of ordinary people; the evidence at hand suggests that they never became the primary means of earning a living.

Ironically, then, gathering and hunting were the major activities that linked the Dar al-Kuti region to the world economy as late as the 1940s and 1950s. The reasons behind the failure to introduce cash crops are by now familiar: fear of flight prevented the French from imposing cotton cultivation in the 1920s as they had in the western and southern parts of Ubangi-Shari (Guibbert 1949). Only in 1958 did the administra-

6. Interviews: Abakar Tidjani, 23 and 28 May; Maarabbi Hasan; ANF-SOM (Aix), rapport mensuel 1923.

tor Petitjean introduce forced cultivation of the crop (Petitjean 1958: 19–29). In the mid-1970s the Commune du moyen-exercice du Dar-el-Kouti remained a remote, very sparsely populated outpost (Pantobe 1984), only tenuously linked with the Muslim economy to the north and the capitalist economy to the south and southwest. Nor was this fate limited to Dar al-Kuti; it was shared by all of eastern Ubangi-Shari.

Ending Raiding, Trading, and Slavery in Eastern Ubangi-Shari, 1910–1920

The ambiguity of French policy on slaves and their liberation was not limited to Dar al-Kuti. A handwritten comment on a report written from the Ubangi River region in 1913, presumably by the lieutenant governor of the colony, illustrates the dilemma caused by slave-raiding, the slave trade, and slavery in eastern Ubangi-Shari as a whole:

One does not reform the morals of a people or a race through violence. One can and should oppose the crimes of the [slave] trade and barbarity. [But] it is not only the Arabs who maintain the slave trade. We cannot at the present time think of liberating all the captives, much less speak of it. The chiefs, the people, those who are sold as well as those who sell are implicated.[7]

In eastern Ubangi-Shari the French adopted a broader policy to contain the population following the flight of many of al-Sanusi's supporters to the Sudan. Early in 1912 they began to set up a defense perimeter around the entire southeastern part of the colony in an effort to prevent the remnants of al-Sanusi's forces at Ouanda-Djale and elsewhere from raiding in the Bas-Mbomou region (ANF-SOM [Aix], rapport, 1er trimestre, 1912). Following the conquest of Ouanda-Djale, they established a post there, thus extending the defense line farther north.

Despite these efforts, however, the slave trade continued. The French presence was not sufficient to control the immense territories within the perimeter delineated by their posts, much less the vast region between these centers and the zone of real British control in the Sudan. The annual report of the colony in 1913 suggests the dimensions of the problem:

[The slave trade continued with small parties of] "Arab" traders. They know how to conquer the inhabitant, trading their goods [such as cloth, leather items, iron tools, and salt] and their arms for his rubber and ivory, [and thereby] procuring the human merchandise that can still be disposed of in the markets of Dar Fur and the Bahr al-Ghazal. Their commerce has the tacit protection of the local people [who are] their clients or their accomplices. (ANF-SOM [Aix], rapport d'ensemble 1913: 24–25)

7. ANF-SOM (Aix), résumé 1913. Presumably those who were sold were "implicated" because they would have sold others had they had the chance.

The report continues on to cite slave-raiding as one of the two major threats to the colony (along with sleeping sickness, which was rampant in the southwest) (ibid.: 124).

The colonial regime extended the campaign of "pacification" into the following year. Schmoll, the commandant at Ndele, imposed French authority on the Kara and Goula to the northeast. He also met with British authorities to formulate a joint policy on the suppression of the slave trade and arms smuggling (ibid.: 26–27). In addition, the French combined several administrative districts afflicted by continued slave-raiding and -trading to mount a more coordinated attack on the problem (ANF-SOM [Aix], rapport annuel 1914).

Numerous administrative reports give examples of the continuation of the trade. Cornet, for example, patrolling in the northeast between Dar Sila (in southern Chad) and Kafiakinji (in the Anglo-Egyptian Sudan), came across an escaped slave, a boy from Wadai who told him that 10 Hausa merchants had purchased about 40 women and children, whom they were taking to Kafiakinji to sell. The Frenchman caught up with the slave caravan. Two traders escaped, but the patrol captured 11 Bornoans, Hausa, and Fulani, along with 39 captives purchased in Wadai for varying quantities of guinea blue cloth according to the age and sex of the captives (Cornet n.d.: 32). Other French officials reported similar incidents (ANF-SOM [Aix], Estebe 1913; ANF-SOM [Aix], Teulière 1913).

Despite these initiatives, the problem of depopulation and continued channelling of commerce towards Muslim zones persisted. The annual report of 1915 notes that government-appointed chiefs had no authority and that people continued to trade slaves for ivory, powder, and guns (ANF-SOM [Aix], rapport annuel 1915). At the same time the Ndele region suffered from periodic incursions of "bandits," often refugees from the Sudan who returned to raid (ANF-SOM [Aix], résumé 1915). Similar problems plagued the district around Yalinga the following year (Collection Cabaille, Monographie, n.d.: 31), and in 1917 the French set up a post at Birao in the far northeast in an effort to stop the continuing traffic between regions south of Wadai and Dar Fur and the Sudan (ANF-SOM [Aix], rapport, 3e trimestre, 1917).

Conclusion

Eastern Ubangi-Shari and Dar al-Kuti are important pieces of the puzzle depicting the end of slavery in Africa. Some elements of this transformation resemble those observed elsewhere. For example, the French concentrated their efforts on stopping slave-raiding rather than on abolishing slavery itself. And like the British, they, too, tended to return the slaves of their allies and free those of their foes. The responses of former slaves to their emancipation likewise echoed reactions in other regions. Many first-generation slaves—who probably constituted the vast majority of captives in the region—returned to their homelands, where the depopulation occasioned by several decades of upheaval had left vast expanses of land available for cultivation. As was the case in other parts of the continent, ample access to land and the limited ability of the colonial state to impose its authority seem to have precluded the emergence of a "free" market for wage labor.

Despite these parallels, however, the ending of slavery and the ways peoples in eastern Ubangi-Shari responded to it represent an extreme. For example, in the Senegal Valley and the southern Ivory Coast, Africans—some of whom were former slaves who migrated from the interior—began producing cash crops for the international economy. And in Kenya or South Africa, white settlement and stringent vagrancy laws forced substantial numbers of former slaves into wage labor on European farms. In eastern Ubangi-Shari, however, former slaves made their livelihood by returning to earlier patterns of production in subsistence agriculture. And rather than stimulating the rise of capitalist social relations of production, colonial demands for head taxes in the form of ivory, rubber, wax, and honey ironically encouraged people to abandon agricultural production for gathering and hunting.

Although force eventually undermined local political economies based on slavery and severed economic ties with the neighboring colony, eastern Ubangi-Shari remained nonetheless peripheral to the colonial economy. Refugees never returned in large numbers, and the region, like Dar al-Kuti within it, has never recovered demographically or economically from the traumas of slave-raiding, the slave trade, and colonial conquest.

REFERENCES

Oral sources

The people of Dar al-Kuti supplied much of the information about the recent history of northern Ubangi-Shari. Microfilm copies of interviews conducted in Dar al-Kuti in 1974 have been deposited with the Archives of Traditional Music, Indiana University, and the Memorial Library, University of Wisconsin–Madison. More detailed information will be found in the bibliography of Cordell 1985a.

Abakar Tidjani, age 55 in 1974, Runga-Nduka, 23 May, OA6.2; 28 May, OA7.2/8.1.

Adoum Oumar, about age 50, Runga, 24 September, OA22.1.
Khrouma Sale, about age 80, Runga Bagrim, 19 June, OA13.1.
Maarabbi Hasan, about age 55, Runga-Nduka, 28 May, OA7.2/8.1.
Ngrekoudou Ouih Fran, about age 80, Banda Toulou, 7 July, OA17.2/18.1.
Yacoub Mahamat Dillang, age 80, Runga, 20 May, OA5.1; 25 May, OA7.1.
Yacoub Soudour Tekai, about age 80, Runga Bua, 12 October, OA24.1.
Yadjouma Pascal, age 76, Banda Mbagga, 15 May, notes (in English) on the Ndele
    ruins from a tour of the site with Yadjouma Pascal, OA3.1; 18 May, OA4.1;
    30 June, OA15.2/16.1.

Archival sources

AAV: Archives nationales de France, Ministère d'État chargé de la Défense na-
    tionale, Service historique de l'Armée, Château de Vincennes.

All documents listed are located in Section Outre-Mer, Série O³, Afrique
équatoriale française, Généralites, Oubangui-Chari.

    Dossier 1, 1897. Carton 1.
    Dossier 1, 1903. Carton 1.
    Dossier 1, 1908. Carton 1.

ANF-SOM (Aix): Archives nationales de France, section d'outre-mer, Aix-en-
    Provence.

All documents listed are located in A.E.F., Série D, S/série 4(3)D, Oubangui-
Chari, 1889–1940s.

    Estebe, Rapport d'ensemble, October 1913. 4(3)D19.
    Possel to Voisin, 1890. 4(3)D1.
    Rapport annuel, 1911. 4(3)D18.
    Rapport annuel, 1914. 4(3)D21.
    Rapport annuel, 1916. 4(3)D23.
    Rapport annuel, 1917. 4(3)D24.
    Rapport annuel, 1918. 4(3)D25.
    Rapport annuel. 1932. 4(3)D42.
    Rapport d'ensemble, 1913. 4(3)D20.
    Rapport mensuel, Dar-el-Kouti, July 1914. 4(3)D21.
    Rapport mensuel, June 1923, Dar-Kouti occidental. 4(3)D45.
    Rapport politique, 31 July 1912. 4(3)D19.
    Rapport politique, 1er trimestre, 1912. 4(3)D19.
    Rapport politique, année 1948. District autonome de Ndele. 4(3)D59.
    Rapport semestriel, Ndele, 10 February 1938. 4(3)D49.
    Rapport, 3e trimestre, 1917. 4(3)D24.
    Résumé, Bas-Mbomou, April 1913. 4(3)D20.
    Résumé, des rapports mensuels, October 1912. 4(3)D19.
    Résumé, des rapports mensuels, December 1915. 4(3)D22.

Teulière, "A/s de la traite des esclaves," 13 March 1913, Bangassou. 4(3)D20.
ANF-SOM (Paris): Archives nationales de France, section d'outre-mer, Paris.
Groden au M. le Ministre des colonies, Libreville, 25 November 1902. Gabon-Congo VI/19.
Liotard, 20 January 1896. Cabon/Congo IV/14c.
"Mission Crampel," ca. 1896. Gabon/Congo III/13b.
1896. Gabon/Congo IV/14c.
Collection Cabaille, Bangui (in Cabaille's house).
Monographie de Yalinga, n.d. Unpublished manuscript.

Other sources

Anonymous. 1911. Les derniers événements des territoires du Tchad. *Afrique française* 21 (2): 53–56.

Bruel, G. 1918. *L'Afrique équatoriale française.* Paris: Larose.

Carbou, H. 1912. *La région du Tchad et du Ouadai,* 2 vols. Paris: Leroux.

Chevalier, A. 1903. Mission scientifique au Chari et au lac Tchad. *La Géographie* 7: 354–61.

Chevalier, A. 1907. *Mission Chari-lac Tchad, 1902–1904: L'Afrique centrale française, récit du voyage de la mission.* Paris: Challamel.

Collins, R. O. 1971. Sudanese factors in the history of the Congo and central West Africa in the nineteenth century. In *Sudan in Africa,* ed. Yusuf Fadl Hasan, 156–67. Khartoum: Khartoum University Press.

Coquery-Vidrovitch, C. 1972. *Le Congo au temps des grandes compagnies concessionaires 1898–1930.* Paris and The Hague: Mouton.

Cordell, D. D. 1977a. Eastern Libya, Wadai, and the Sanusiya: a Tariqa and a trade route. *Journal of African History* 18 (1): 21–36.

Cordell, D. D. 1977b. Secondary empire and slave-raiding beyond the Islamic frontier in northern Equatorial Africa: the cases of Bandas Hakim and Sa'id Baldas. Paper presented at the annual meeting of the American Historical Association, December, Dallas.

Cordell, D. D. 1983. The savanna belt of North Central Africa. In *History of Central Africa,* Vol. 1, ed. David Birmingham and Phyllis Martin, 30–74. London and New York: Longman.

Cordell, D. D. 1985a. *Dar al-Kuti and the last years of the trans-Saharan slave trade.* Madison: University of Wisconsin Press.

Cordell, D. D. 1985b. Modes of production, articulation, and history. *Canadian Journal of African Studies – Revue canadienne des études africaines* 19 (2): 58–63.

Cordell, D. D. 1986. Warlords and enslavement: a sample of slave-raiders from eastern Ubangi-Shari, 1870–1920. In *Africans in bondage: essays presented to Philip D. Curtin on the occasion of the 25th anniversary of the African Studies Program,* ed. P. Lovejoy, 335–65. Madison: African Studies Program.

Cordell, D. D. 1987. Extracting people from precapitalist production: French

170   III. POLITICS OF ANTISLAVERY

Equatorial Africa from the 1890s to the 1930s. In *African population and capitalism: historical perspectives*, ed. D. D. Cordell and J. W. Gregory, 137–52. Boulder: Westview.

Cordell, D. D., and J. W. Gregory, eds. 1987. *African population and capitalism: historical perspectives*. Boulder: Westview.

Cornet. n.d. [ca. 1916]. *Au coeur de l'Afrique centrale*. N.p.

Courtet, H. 1904. Mission scientifique Chari-lac Tchad: le pays Snoussi. *Revue des troupes coloniales* 3: 483–86.

Daigre, P. 1950. *Oubangui-Chari: souvenirs et témoignages, 1890–1910*. Issoudun: Dillen.

Dampierre, E. de. 1967. *Un ancien royaume Bandia du Haut-Oubangui*. Paris: Plon.

Dampierre, E. de. 1983. *Des ennemis, des Arabes, des histoires. . . .* Paris: Société d'ethnographie. (Recherches oubanguiennes, 8).

Dybowski, J. 1893. *La route du Tchad du Loango au Chari*. Paris: Firmin Didot.

Evans-Pritchard, E. E. 1971. *The Azande: history and political institutions*. London: Oxford University Press.

Gentil, E. 1902. *La chute de l'empire de Rabah*. Paris: Hachette.

Grech. 1924. Essai sur le Dar Kouti au temps de Snoussi. *Bulletin de la société des recherches congolaises* 4: 19–54.

Guibbert, J. 1949. Le coton en Oubangui-Chari. Mémoire, Centre des hautes études sur l'Afrique et l'Asie modernes, Paris.

Huot. 1902. Les peuplades de l'Oubangui et du Bahr-El-Ghazal, *Revue scientifique de la France et de l'étranger* 17 (13): 394–400.

Jewsiewicki, B. 1981. Lineage mode of production: social inequalities in equatorial Central Africa. In *Modes of production in Africa: the precolonial era*, ed. D. Crummey and C. C. Stewart, 92–113. Beverley Hills: Sage.

Julien, E. 1904. La situation économique du Dar-el-Kouti. *Afrique française: renseignements coloniaux* 14 (1): 38–40.

Julien, E. 1925, 1927, 1928, 1929. Mohammed-es-Senoussi et ses états. *Bulletin de la société des recherches congolaises* 7: 104–77; 8: 55–122; 9: 49–96; 10: 45–88.

Kalck, P. 1968. Paul Crampel, le centrafricain. *L'Afrique littéraire et artistique* 2: 60–63.

Kalck, P. 1970. Histoire de la République centrafricaine des origines à nos jours, 4 vols. Doctorat d'état thesis, Université de Paris (Sorbonne).

Kalck, P. 1974. *Histoire de la République centrafricaine des origines préhistoriques à nos jours*. Paris: Berger-Levrault.

Keim, C. A. 1979. Precolonial Mangbetu rule: political and economic factors in nineteenth-century Mangbetu history (Northeastern Zaire). Ph.D. dissertation, Indiana University, Bloomington.

Lotar, (R. P.) L. 1937. *La grande chronique du Bomu*. Brussels: Institut royal du Congo belge. (Mémoires, Section sciences morales et politiques, Vol. 9: 3.)

M'Bokolo, E. 1985. *L'Afrique au XXᵉ siècle: le continent convoité*. Paris: Editions du Seuil.

Modat. 1912. Une tournée en pays Fertyt. *Afrique française renseignements coloniaux* 22 (5): 177–98; (7): 270–89.

Nebout, A. 1892. La Mission Crampel. *Bulletin de la société normande de géographie* 14: 217–47.

Pantobe, D. 1984. Population. In *Atlas de la Republique centrafricaine*, 26–31. Paris: Les éditions Jeune Afrique.

Perron, S. 1845. Notes et éclaircissements. In *Voyage au Darfour*, by Mohammed ibn-Omar el-Tounsy (Muhammad ibn Umar al-Tunisi), at end. Paris: Duprat.

Petitjean, J. 1958. Situation des anciens états senoussistes au milieu du xxe siècle. Mémoire d'entrée, Centre des hautes études sur l'Afrique et l'Asie modernes, Paris, No. 2864.

Prins, P. 1900. Voyage au Dar Rounga: resultats scientifiques. *La Géographie* 1 (3): 193–96.

Prins, P. 1907. L'Islam et les musulmans dans les sultanats du Haut-Oubangui. *Afrique française: renseignements coloniaux* 17 (6): 136–42.

Prins, P. 1925. Observations géographiques et physiques en pays Zande, Banda, Wassa, Adja, et Kreich. *Bulletin de la société des recherches congolaises* 6: 117–70.

Santandrea, S. 1957. Sanusi, ruler of Dar Banda and Dar Kuti in the history of the Bahr el-Ghazal. *Sudan Notes and Records* 38: 151–55.

Santandrea, S. 1964. *A tribal history of the western Bahr el-Ghazal.* Bologna: Centro librario dei Missionari Comboniani.

Santandrea, S. 1981. *Ethno-geography of the Bahr el Ghazal (Sudan).* Bologna: Editrice Missionaria Italiana.

Schweinfurth, G. 1874. *The heart of Africa: three years' travels and adventures in the unexplored regions of Central Africa, 1868–1871*, 2 vols., trans. Ellen Frewer. New York: Harper and Brothers.

Tisserant, C. 1955. *Ce que j'ai connu de l'esclavage en Oubangui-Chari.* Paris: Plon.

El-Tounsy, M. i-O. (Muhammad ibn Umar al-Tunisi). 1845. *Voyage au Darfour*, trans. S. Perron. Paris: Duprat.

5 Suzanne Miers and Michael Crowder

The Politics of Slavery in Bechuanaland: Power Struggles and the Plight of the Basarwa in the Bamangwato Reserve, 1926–1940

"The Masarwa are slaves. They can be killed. It is no crime, they are like cattle. They have no liberty. If they run away their masters can bring them back and do what they like in the way of punishment. They are never paid. If the Masarwa live in the veld, and I want any to work for me, I go out and take any I want" (BNA, Simon Ratshosa evidence 1926: 316).

In 1926, some 40 years after the establishment of British rule over the Bechuanaland Protectorate, these allegations that slavery still existed, particularly in the Bamangwato Reserve,[1] made headlines in both the South African and the British press. For more than a decade thereafter the servile status of the Basarwa[2] embroiled the administration of the protectorate, the regent of the Bangwato and his aristocratic supporters and opponents, as well as the London Missionary Society, in acrimonious debate. This chapter will consider the extent to which some Basarwa were

1. Bamangwato Reserve was the British name for the area reserved for the Bamangwato, or Mangwato. Today they are called Bangwato (sing. Mongwato; adj. Ngwato). They are a branch of the Batswana peoples (sing. Motswana; adj. Tswana). Their language is Setswana. In this chapter peoples will be called by their present names but place-names will follow colonial usage.

2. Basarwa (sing. Mosarwa; adj. Sarwa) is today the official name for people who were called Masarwa in colonial times and were referred to in the literature as San and in older

172

Map 5. Bechuanaland Protectorate

really "slaves" of the Bangwato and explain why it took so long to give them even the semblance of "freedom."

It will show that what began as a relationship between Bangwato pastoralists and traders and their Basarwa hunting partners and pastoral clients changed into a servile relationship wherein the Basarwa served first the Ngwato state and later became the private property of Ngwato pastoralists. It will discuss the reasons for the failure of the British, in spite of their ideological commitment to end slavery, to take action until forced to do so when a power struggle between Ngwato aristocrats brought the question dramatically to international attention in 1926. Finally it

174   III. POLITICS OF ANTISLAVERY

will argue that the steps subsequently taken to allow the Basarwa to
dispose of their own labor merely gave them the option of taking low-
paid wage employment or left them to become increasingly dependent
upon their erstwhile masters and, in the long run, brought little improvement in either their material condition or their social standing.

The Origins of Basarwa "Slavery"

The form of servitude at issue in 1926 was known as *bolata*, and those
subject to it were called *malata* (singular *lelata*) by the Bangwato.[3] This
institution, which already existed, expanded rapidly as the result of the
political, economic, and ecological changes in the decades immediately
preceding the imposition of British rule.

When the British took over the Bechuanaland Protectorate in the 1880s,
much of the country was under the control of strong, centralized, and
highly stratified Tswana kingdoms, the largest being that of the Bangwato.
In each of them political, economic, and ritual control was in the hands
of a king (*kgosi*). Most people lived in towns or villages divided into
wards—administrative and judicial units under headmen, who tried
cases in public in the *kgotla* (pl. *dikgotla*)[4] and decided how rights to
land were to be allotted. Around November people moved out of their
towns or villages to farm surrounding fields. Since they were cattle keepers, beyond their farms were their grazing lands and beyond these their
hunting grounds.

In Tswana society wealth was counted in cattle, and status depended
upon birth. The elite comprised the extended royal family and rich commoners. Then came ordinary commoners. Below these were non-Tswana
groups who had been conquered or absorbed as the kingdoms expanded,
particularly in the second half of the nineteenth century. They were incorporated as "subject tribes,"[5] each of which had a different status in
the social and political hierarchy and was largely endogamous. The degree of incorporation varied with each group's ethnic identity, its cul-

works as Bushmen. None of these terms is satisfactory. Basarwa is a generic name for a
multitude of different hunting and gathering groups who are both ethnically and linguistically diverse. While many were hunters and gatherers in the late nineteenth century, some
were pastoralists, and contrary to colonial belief, their remote ancestors may also have
been pastoralists (Wilmsen and Denbow 1986).
   3. Similar institutions called by other names existed in other areas of Bechuanaland
(e.g., *botlhanka* in Ngamiland).
   4. The kgotla was the public forum where justice was dispensed, administrative decisions made, and public meetings held.
   5. The British also called them subordinate or subservient tribes, whereas the Batswana
were dominant tribes. *Tribe* will be used here as it was in colonial times.

tural distance from the Batswana, its strength and cohesion, its physical distance from the capital, its ability to resist domination by moving into remote areas, and its ability to retain access to water and land. Some had their own wards and headmen and hence a voice in politics and in the allocation of land; some became clients, herding Ngwato cattle as well as their own, others lost their land, stock, and all political rights.[6] These were the servile groups at the very bottom of the social hierarchy.

In the Ngwato Kingdom, the principal servile "ethnic" group was the Basarwa.[7] Before the extension of the Ngwato Kingdom into the eastern Kalahari in the early nineteenth century, most Basarwa had been hunters and gatherers, operating in clearly defined "territories." Some, however, were cattle keepers (Wilmsen 1984: 3–4), and others had already been reduced to servile status by the Bakgalagadi — immigrants who had preceded the Batswana. Initially the Bangwato came into Sarwa country to hunt, and the Basarwa helped them as trackers and guides in return for meat and sold them hunting products for tools, grain, pottery, and tobacco. With the arrival of white traders in the 1840s there was a dramatic expansion of this hunting economy to meet the rising demand in the Western world for skins, furs, ostrich feathers, and ivory (Parsons 1977: 117ff.). The scale escalated with the introduction of guns and horses for hunting and ox-wagons for transport. The Bangwato soon began to profit from this southern African hunting economy. At first, they merely supplied the Basarwa with hunting dogs and guns in return for a share of their hunting products. But the relationship changed to one of Basarwa dependence as the Bangwato invested the proceeds of their trade in cattle and began to dig wells and establish cattle posts[8] in what had been hunting country. The process was stimulated as the export and domestic trade in cattle and small stock expanded and the hunting economy declined in the 1870s and 1880s (Parsons 1977: 122ff.). The Ngwato king now claimed political control over these hunting grounds, appointing first overseers and then, at the end of the nineteenth century, district governors in each newly occupied area, with the right to exact tribute from the inhabitants in hunting goods and labor (Hitchcock 1978, 1: 101ff.).

Initially many Basarwa were attracted to these cattle posts as sources of water, milk, and, occasionally, meat, but as game was hunted out to supply the hunting economy and vegetation was eroded by increasing

6. Tlou 1977 and Wilmsen 1982 throw much light on this process in Ngamiland.

7. Other servile groups were Bakgalagadi and Batswapong. It should be noted that not all Basarwa were servile; some groups actively and successfully resisted domination (Wylie 1984: 143), and some Bakgalagadi owned Basarwa.

8. Following Wilmsen 1982: 29, we are using *cattle post* to mean a water point where the cattle of an absentee owner are kept.

numbers of cattle and people, they came to depend more heavily on the cattle posts, relying on hunting and gathering only seasonally. Others were initially drawn into the cattle-post economy when the pastoralists left cattle with them to look after, thus reducing their foraging time.[9] In both cases the result was increasing dependence of the Basarwa on the Bangwato cattle owners. Many became malata, losing their independence and property rights, forced to work for and pay tribute to Ngwato "masters" (Hitchcock 1978, 1: 101ff.). The power of individual Bangwato masters over them increased after King Khama III proclaimed an end to all state ownership of cattle and hunting products in 1875. Henceforth all royal headmen, commoner family heads, and even clients could establish rights of private ownership over cattle. Malata also now became private property (Parsons 1973: 33; Parsons 1977: 119). Khama himself became the owner of many hundreds as he built up his herds and extended his cattle posts into remote Basarwa hunting grounds (Parsons 1973: 34–35). The masters were probably always relatively few in number; estimates in the 1930s varied from 10 percent (BNA, Tagart 1931, Motsete evidence) to 2 percent of all Bangwato (BNA, Joyce, 3 October 1936), but they had the greatest power. The rinderpest epizootic of 1896–1897, which killed some three-quarters of the antelope along with the cattle in southern Africa (Wilmsen 1984: 4), exacerbated the dependence of Basarwa on the pastoralists. Whereas the cattlemen soon restocked their posts (Wilmsen 1982: 14) and benefitted from the new economic opportunities resulting from the British wars of conquest in Rhodesia and the South African War (Parsons 1977: 125ff.), whole Sarwa families were forced to attach themselves to cattle posts as malata as their hunting and gathering economy became less viable (Hitchcock 1978, 1: 101ff.; 1979: 2ff.).

Malata could not leave their masters (beng ba bone: sing. mong wa bone), whose heirs inherited them, often dividing up families on the death of an owner. They usually married other malata. Sometimes the women were used as concubines by their masters. Both labor and hunting goods could be exacted from malata, who were not paid except in kind. On the cattle posts, they were usually paid only with milk, and occasionally meat and the odd blanket. They met their other needs by foraging (Wilmsen 1982: 13). Malata who worked in the household were given food and clothing. All were subject to arbitrary punishment by their masters, and on the rare occasions when they were able to complain of ill-treatment

---

9. Wilmsen (1982: 13), writing on Ngamiland, shows the process by which the Batswana superimposed themselves on foraging groups, turning their water sources into cattle posts and the foragers into part-time herders, thus they were divorced at times from their means of production. The Batswana then took away some of the Basarwa children and turned these into a servile labor force completely divorced from the means of production.

in the kgotla, the best they could hope for was transfer to another master. They belonged to their masters' wards, had no control over land and no absolute rights to property. Originally malata children could be sold, though this was stopped by Khama III (BNA, Tagart 1931, Tshekedi evidence: 21). However, they could still be transferred as gifts or by inheritance from one master to another and could be moved about by their owners at will. Thus, the children of malata on the cattle posts, who still hunted seasonally, could be seized for work in the household, in the fields, or on other cattle posts — wherever and whenever owners required them. Moreover, new malata could be taken by force from those Basarwa and other subject groups who still foraged in remote areas.

Malata thus formed a fully controlled, and partly transferable, hereditary labor force, performing the most menial tasks in return for the barest necessities of life, and in hard times even these sometimes were not forthcoming. Their treatment depended on the wealth and compassion of their masters, who considered them their property. From this miserable situation the average malata had little hope of escape. Thus, at the very time when the British were taking over the Bechuanaland Protectorate, this form of servitude was not only well entrenched but was spreading into new areas. In fact, most Basarwa in the Ngwato Kingdom were now malata. The system lay at the very roots of the highly successful Tswana pastoral economy, allowing the masters to build up large herds while freeing them from pastoral, agricultural, and domestic chores and enabling them to engage in politics, herd management, trade, and wage labor.

The British and Bolata

By the time the Bechuanaland Protectorate was established, the British had long considered themselves the leaders of the international antislavery movement. The cause was popular,[10] and the suppression of slavery was generally regarded as an integral part of Britain's imperial mission to "civilize" subject peoples. It was a linchpin of an ideological package which included the imposition of the *Pax Britannica*, the rule of law, the development of a market-oriented monetarized economy based on capitalist relations of production, all underpinned by Christianity — a package used to justify the conquest and then the reorganization of the political, economic, social, and spiritual order of colonial peoples. Slavery

10. Although, as Frederick Cooper (1980: 34) has pointed out, it was not a major concern of the British working classes, it was popular with the vocal middle classes and with church-goers of all classes.

was considered both morally wrong and economically unsound: the ideal was a mobile wage-labor force in which the worker was theoretically free to choose his occupation and terms of service. Successive British governments believed the public expected them to take the lead in the suppression of slavery, and there existed a society — the Antislavery Society[11] — dedicated to keeping them up to the mark. However, British colonial administrations, faced with practical difficulties, adopted pragmatic policies under which the slave trade was attacked but slavery among Africans was often allowed to continue. This was justified because African slavery was considered relatively "benign" and certain to die a natural death once the slave trade — its main source of supply and greatest cruelty — was ended.

In the Ngwato Kingdom missionaries preceded colonial rule and denounced bolata, claiming it was slavery and incompatible with Christianity (Chirenje 1977: 261). Khama III had been converted to Christianity in 1860 and was well aware of the British attitude towards slavery at the time when the protectorate was established. In the early years of colonial rule he exhorted his followers to treat their malata well, even urging them to give their malata the occasional animal as a reward for good herding. He pointed out that this would not only give them less incentive to steal stock, it would also enable masters to exact an animal in compensation if they did steal or lose one (LMS Report 1935: 7). He declared that malata were not to be transferred from one master to another, that they must be allowed to leave their owners, and should not be forced to give their masters hunting or other products (Hitchcock 1978, 1: 103). He allowed malata to bring cases to the kgotla and sometimes punished masters who ill-treated them (BNA, Tagart 1931, Ratshosa evidence). However, neither the missionaries nor the royal exhortations seem to have had much impact. The enlightened Khama III himself sometimes prevaricated when called upon by British officials to punish masters who forcibly removed their malata from European employ and flogged them for desertion. While professing sympathy, he simply said he could not find the offenders (BNA, Tagart 1931, Cuzen evidence). Rulers clearly had to tread warily when it came to interfering with the interests of their supporters, and the hunting products exacted from the malata were particularly profitable for their owners (BNA, Tagart 1931, Ratshosa evidence).

Furthermore, from the late nineteenth century, forces were at work

11. Originally the British and Foreign Anti-Slavery Society, this amalgamated with the Aborigines Protection Society in 1909 and became the Anti-Slavery and Aborigines Protection Society. It will be called here the Antislavery Society.

which increased the importance of the elite's having a readily available cheap labor supply. Traditionally cattle herding was done by boys, normally the sons of the cattle-owners, while their daughters performed domestic and agricultural chores. Now the sons and daughters of wealthy Bangwato went to Western schools and their places were taken by malata (Parsons 1973: 243), whose work also increasingly freed Ngwato men for wage labor in the burgeoning southern African capitalist economy, especially in the gold mines of the Transvaal.[12] In the early days some masters sent their malata out to work in this European-dominated economy (Parsons 1973: 140) — presumably in order to pocket the lion's share of their wages, a practice formally forbidden by Khama. This, however, could work against the interests of masters because some malata never returned (BNA, Joyce, 28 February 1936), and others used their earnings to buy stock for themselves (BNA, acting resident commissioner 1936). Moreover, Basarwa, who had neither permanent huts or money, were exempted from the hut tax levied on all African adult men after 1899, but if they earned wages they became and remained liable for tax. If they then returned, their masters either had to pay taxes for them or give them the means to pay themselves (ibid.). Masters, therefore, had every incentive to prevent their malata from taking wage employment; and they had the power to do so, for, under the colonial system, no Mongwato could leave the Bamangwato Reserve without permission from the chief, and malata also needed permission from their masters.

The question is why the British administration turned a blind eye to all this. At the heart of the problem lay doubt over the future of the protectorate. It was the veritable stepchild of a far-flung empire. Annexed mainly for strategic reasons, but also under pressure from missionaries anxious to protect the Batswana from the domination of the Afrikaners, and later also from Cecil Rhodes's British South Africa Company, it was unclear for many years whether it would remain a separate entity under British rule.[13] From the start the primary British concern was that it should not become a drain on the imperial treasury. A mere handful of British magistrates and policemen was scattered around the country to keep the peace, collect taxes, and keep out of trouble. The head of the administration, although called the *resident* commissioner, actually lived across the border at Mafeking in South Africa. The Tswana kingdoms were designated "native reserves" under their kings, now called chiefs, who were

12. Wilmsen 1982: 14. For a brief outline of the policies which drove the people of Bechuanaland into the South African wage-labor force in increasing numbers, see Parson 1984: 21ff.

13. The South Africa Act of 1909 provided for the protectorate's incorporation under certain conditions.

to govern in accordance with "native law and custom"—the meaning of
which the British did not even try to determine until the early 1930s.[14]
Under this loose—and cheap—form of indirect rule, power remained in
the hands of the Batswana elite; the rest of the population being designated "subordinate tribes" with little voice in government. The British
resident magistrates, stationed in the capitals of the reserves, could rarely
afford to travel around their territories and made only occasional tours
and sorties to trouble spots. The total forces of the protectorate were too
small to risk alienating the Tswana elite. Although British policy towards
servitude was part and parcel of the general policy of not disturbing the
status quo, in the first decade of the twentieth century subordinate officials sometimes took action against it, fearing that they would be cen-
sured for not doing so. However, their superiors in Mafeking, mindful
of the weakness of their forces, not only gave them no encouragement
but actually denied that slavery existed in Bechuanaland (Miers 1983).
     Thus in 1906 the resident commissioner wrote to the high commis-
sioner:[15]

One point which . . . will undoubtedly be criticised sooner or later is the relation that exists between the dominant tribes of the Batawana and Bamangwato
and subservient people. . . . I wish to put it on record that the position of these
people is not slavery in any sense. . . . As far as I can learn the essential elements
of slavery are all wanting and the conditions are not such as to need interference.
(BNA, Williams 1906)

Significantly, neither he nor the high commissioner, who endorsed his
view, defined these "essential elements of slavery." Six years later when
the resident magistrate in the Batawana Reserve, who considered some
of the "subservient peoples" to be definitely slaves, put forward a plan
to liberate them, the resident commissioner asked him "for goodness sake
not to draw attention to slavery"; the last thing the administration wanted
was any questions in the British Parliament as to whether steps were being taken to abolish slavery in the protectorate (Miers 1983).
     Two events, however, eventually brought the question to the fore: the
League of Nations' inquiry into slavery launched in 1923, and the unwelcome publicity given to allegations of slavery in an otherwise obscure trial
in 1926.

     14. By the 1930s when I. Schapera began his many studies there had already been time
for the elite to change "customary" law to their advantage. For a complete list of Schapera's
works see the bibliography in I. K. Shapera, *The Tswana* (London: International African
Institute, 1976).
     15. The high commissioner was the senior British official in South Africa. Until 1925
he reported to the Colonial Office in London and after that to the Dominions Office.

When the league asked for information for its Temporary Slavery Commission, the resident commissioner of the day, J. Ellenberger—who had long been an official in the protectorate, and spoke Setswana—stated unequivocally, "Slavery is not known to exist in the Bechuanaland Protectorate" (BNA, resident commissioner 1924). He subsequently quoted Williams' despatch of 1906, adding that the "subservient people" were simply subject to a "modified form of hereditary service," recognized by native law and custom legalized by Order-in-Council and a proclamation in 1891, and that there had never been any need for proclamations against either slavery or the slave trade.

The League of Nations Slavery Convention of 1926, however, defined a slave as someone "over whom all or any of the rights attaching to ownership are exercised." By this definition malata were indisputably slaves. Faced with this, Ellenberger grudgingly admitted that these "hereditary servants" were domestic or praedial slaves or serfs, whose masters regarded them as "personal property" and would "brook no interference" with them; but they did not sell them and most were content with their lot because they would not want to "work strenuously to earn a living." As proof, he fell back on the specious argument that Basarwa outside the reserves on Crown lands, rarely went to "the mines or to civilization" (BNA, resident commissioner 1926).

Officials at the Colonial Office in London now knew for the first time that the condition of the "servile peoples" was a form of slavery. However, mindful of Britain's image, they decided that she must sign the Slavery Convention as it stood, in spite of the misgivings of the high commissioner, particularly as it merely bound them to suppress slavery "progressively and as soon as possible" (PRO DO, minutes, July 1926). But the whole matter was now brought dramatically to public attention by press reports of the trial of the brothers Simon and Obeditswe Rathshosa for attempting to assassinate the newly installed regent of the Bangwato, Tshekedi Khama.

The Ratshosa Affair

During this trial Simon Ratshosa declared that slavery was rampant in the reserve and malata were ill-treated. These allegations were so irrelevant that the British magistrate presiding over the case protested that the administration was "being attacked under the cover of a criminal trial" (BNA, Simon Ratshosa evidence 1926: 336–37). The real target, however, was the new young regent, who was caught in a power struggle between aristocrats. On the one side were the Ratshosas, members of the royal family (see Crowder 1985a: 195, 197–98), who had been the most powerful faction in the state during the last years of Khama III and the short reign of his son, Sekgoma II (1923–1925); on the other was a faction led by Phetu Mphoeng, nephew of Khama III and cousin of Tshekedi, whose exile the Ratshosas had engineered in 1924. He was allowed back, bent on revenge, just before Sekgoma's death. Both factions vied for Tshekedi's favor—a struggle won by Phetu, as the strong-willed young regent realized the Ratshosas would try to dominate him. Even Sekgoma, chafing under their overbearing ways, had, shortly before his death, demanded the return of three Basarwa girls he had given to his daughter Oratile, the wife of Simon Ratshosa. She gave them up with great reluctance, and, immediately after her father's death, reclaimed them. The ensuing quarrel caused the downfall of the Ratshosas (Crowder 1985a).

Egged on by Phetu and others, Tshekedi dismissed Johnnie Ratshosa from his post as secretary of the tribe and commanded Oratile to return the Basarwa girls. When she refused, he had them removed and called the Ratshosa brothers to a meeting with the resident magistrate to discuss the dispute. When they disobeyed, Tshekedi had them brought to his kgotla and sentenced to be flogged. In the ensuing melee, Simon and Obeditswe escaped and returned with guns to kill Tshekedi, whom they only wounded.

The issue of the ownership of the girls was germane to the case, but Simon Ratshosa ensured that the whole question of servitude among the Basarwa dominated the trial, to the embarrassment of Tshekedi and the administration.

The Reaction of the British Administration

The British government, aware of the real position for the first time as a result of the correspondence over the Slavery Convention and now faced with this unwelcome publicity, responded, as Simon had anticipated, by demanding a complete investigation of hereditary service in Bechuanaland.[16]

The high commissioner, too, was spurred into action. On a routine tour, he came to the Ngwato capital, Serowe, on 3 August, and, to the surprise of Tshekedi (BNA, Tshekedi, 30 August 1930), made a statement in the kgotla which became famous as the Athlone Declaration:

It has been said that the Masarwa are slaves of the Mangwato. The Government does not regard them as slaves, but realises that they are a backward people who serve the Mangwato in return for the food and shelter they receive. I understand

16. BNA, high commissioner, 29 July 1926; PRO DO, minutes, correspondence, press cuttings, June 1926. A letter to the editor of the *Diamond Fields Advertiser* (February 1926) charged that slavery was also rife in the Batawana Reserve in Ngamiland.

that for the most part they are contented and that they do not wish to change. But the Government will not allow any tribe to demand compulsory service from another and wants to encourage the Masarwa to support themselves. Any Masarwa who wish to leave their masters and live independently of them should understand that they are at liberty to do so and that if the Mangwato attempt to retain them against their will, the Government will not allow it. It is the duty of the Chiefs and Headmen to help these people to stand on their feet. (BNA, high commissioner, 13 August 1926)

On the face of it, this declaration, made to the masters and not to the malata, might appear naive in the extreme. It called upon the very people who benefitted from the services of the malata to help them become independent. To help the Basarwa build up their own herds, to give them land and tools to dig wells and produce their own food, and to enable them to market their own hunting products would simply reduce the revenues of the masters and add to the competition for scarce resources. As it was the Basarwa were given just enough to ensure their survival, and only those malata surplus to the needs of their masters were allowed to leave.[17]

The declaration was prompted by the resident commissioner, Ellenberger, who warned that anything more "drastic" would cause a "commotion" (BNA, resident commissioner 1926). It must be remembered that the existing political economy of the reserves suited the administration as much as it suited the owners of malata. It required minimal British supervision and expenditure, since it left political and economic power and responsibility in the hands of the Ngwato elite, who were thus effectively co-opted by the administration. The fact that their prosperity largely depended on a servile labor force which had grown in importance and numbers with the expansion of the cattle-post economy (Parsons 1973, 1977; Hitchcock 1978, 1979) could be accepted as part and parcel of "native law and custom," into which the British had not inquired too closely. It suited them to believe that all the people in the reserves were content and largely self-sufficient, their needs, including education and social services, being met from their own "subsistence" economy. The taxes they paid went some way towards the costs of the skeletal British administration. Any real interference with the system might require increased expenditure or provoke resistance costly to suppress. Athlone's declaration was an attempt to put the administration in the clear over the malata problem while passing the buck of solving it to the chief and masters, who would take the blame for any further scandals and, if they did help their Basarwa to "stand on their own feet," would bear the loss of profit and privilege.

17. There was a surplus by 1926 (PRO DO, resident commissioner 1926).

There the matter might have rested but for continued pressure from the Ratshosas and their allies, from the Dominions Office in London, and finally from Tshekedi himself. Simon Ratshosa was now in prison. His house and property had been burnt down by Phetu on Tshekedi's instructions as punishment for treason. Tshekedi had also freed the Ratshosas' malata, thus using his right to release them as a political weapon against his enemies. Simon Ratshosa, with no more to lose, accused close supporters of Tshekedi of ill-treating malata, and painted the Ratshosas as champions of Basarwa freedom, although he had been heavily fined for killing a Mosarwa (BNA, Edirilwe Seretse affidavit 1926) and been punished by Khama III for flogging another (BNA, resident magistrate, Serowe, 1926). He claimed that the Ratshosas would have set the Basarwa free, hence the bitter opposition to them among the elite.

Bolata was thus a convenient weapon in the feud among Bangwato aristocrats. Simon calculated that, if it were kept in the public eye, the administration could hardly allow it to continue, but they could effectively abolish it only with the cooperation of the young and inexperienced regent, who had not only inherited many Basarwa himself, but who would alienate his headmen if he cooperated with the British to eliminate an important source of their wealth.

Meanwhile in London, the secretary of state for the colonies, remote from the scene, highly sensitive to parliamentary criticism, and fearful of further League of Nations interest, asked Athlone how he proposed to ensure that Basarwa could really leave their masters. Thus pressed, Ellenberger reluctantly had the Athlone Declaration read in all dikgotla in the protectorate and directed the resident magistrates to "encourage" people to give equal rights to the subject tribes (BNA, resident commissioner 1927; BNA, circular minute 1928). Needless to say, neither the resident magistrates nor the chiefs took any direct action.[18] Simon Ratshosa's charges of individual crimes against Basarwa were investigated, however, but could not be proved; and in response to the Colonial Office's orders, resident magistrates began to furnish annual reports on "hereditary servants" (see PRO DO, documents in 9/3; and BNA, documents in S 43/7).

The Politics of Inquiry

The initiative now passed to Tshekedi, who mobilized the rulers of the Bangwaketse and Bakwena and saw the high commissioner in Cape Town in November 1927. There, among other things, he raised the Basarwa ques-

18. A recommendation that the declaration be distributed on leaflets in Setswana was ignored (BNA, Tagart 1931, Cuzen evidence).

tion. Athlone replied that he wished the Basarwa to be free to leave their masters if they gave due notice and to be treated like other Bangwato (BNA, minutes 1927). Tshekedi was so incensed that when he went to London to see the secretary of state, Lord Passfield, to protest against the introduction of mining in the reserve, he asked him to send people "to see for themselves how the Masarwa are treated," adding "if it should appear that they are not properly treated we shall be glad to be advised so that we may treat them properly." Passfield ignored this request for an inquiry (BNA, interviews 1930).

While Tshekedi was in London, Colonel Charles Rey became resident commissioner. He decided that the protectorate was in a "shocking" state of neglect and that Tshekedi was "a swollen headed young devil, standing out for his *personal* privileges, ignoring the interests of his tribe, illusing them, mal-administering justice, using forced labour to an extent that practically amounts to slavery, and impeding the administration in every way." Rey determined to bring "the little brute into line" on his return from England (BNM, Rey Diaries, 17–21 February 1930) and to "go all out with both hands to reform, develope, discipline and organise" his little "kingdom" (ibid.: 20 October–17 November 1929). He was an authoritarian man with one great merit—a burning desire to improve African living standards. He believed that this required "modern" government and economic development along capitalist lines. His farreaching plans included limiting the powers of the chiefs, eradicating all forms of involuntary servitude, encouraging wage labor, and promoting the European-dominated capitalist sector of the economy, including mining operations in the reserve.

To Tshekedi, Rey's reforms were an attack not just on his powers as a chief, but on the very independence of his people, who, he feared, would become a depressed, impoverished work force like the Africans in South Africa. This was a model to be avoided at all costs and one which had already been partly transferred to the protectorate, in that its people were being increasingly forced into wage labor by the taxation system, by laws limiting their trading activities, and by South African restrictions on the import of cattle from Bechuanaland (Parson 1984: 21ff.). Tshekedi therefore doggedly resisted Rey's proposals (Crowder 1985b). The subsequent history of the Basarwa question must be seen against the background of political conflict, on a wide range of issues, between these two strong men, each convinced of the righteousness of his cause, each anxious to improve African living standards, but with diametrically different views as to how it should be done.

The inevitable clash over the Basarwa soon occurred. In Tshekedi's absence, two Bangwato tried to recover malata who had escaped from their masters and were working for Europeans outside the reserve. When these Bangwato were arrested, it transpired that they had gone with the knowledge of Tshekedi's cousin, the acting chief in Tshekedi's absence, and without the permission of the resident magistrate in Serowe. Rey called on Tshekedi to punish all concerned. He refused on the grounds that Athlone had said that Basarwa should not leave their masters without due notice and that, like all his subjects, they had no right to leave the reserve without his permission. Furthermore he refused to admit, in the absence of an impartial inquiry, that the treatment of the Basarwa warranted government interference or that the Athlone Declaration had sufficient legal force to punish those who disregarded it (BNA, Tshekedi, Serowe, 30 August 1930) — a view shared by the Crown prosecutor (BNA, Crown prosecutor 1930; BNA, government secretary 1930). In fact the British magistrate dismissed the Ngwato pursuers with a warning. Rey, however, eventually forced Tshekedi to punish them.

But these very same culprits then abducted a Mosarwa woman and her children from the Tati District. This time they were tried for "man stealing" and sentenced to fines or three months in prison (BNA, resident commissioner, 4 February 1931). Tshekedi attempted in vain to get the case delayed until he could raise it with the new high commissioner, Sir Herbert Stanley (BNA, Tshekedi, 26 December 1930). In the midst of this struggle, he was faced with a new antagonist, William Ballinger, trade unionist turned journalist, who was convinced by Tshekedi's opponents in the reserve that the Basarwa were slaves (UW, Ballinger Papers, Ballinger to Margaret Hodgson, 2 September 1930) and who now published some highly critical articles on the powers of Batswana chiefs, particularly Tshekedi, endearing himself to Rey in the process.

To compound Tshekedi's problems a horrendous case now came to light. Some Bangwato seized three Basarwa from a cattle post outside the reserve, claiming they had the authority of the chief, and beat them so severely that one of them, who had over 300 wounds on his body, died (BNA, resident magistrate, Francistown, 1931, and further correspondence in file). Rey decided to act:

I have made up my mind that we cannot stand this enslavement of the Masarwa by the Bamangwato any more, and I have proposed a cocked hat official enquiry into the whole question. This will raise Hail Columbia and make the Colonial Office wild — as the policy hitherto has been hush-hush. But there is bound to be a row about the Masarwa sooner or later, and then I shall be blamed for having allowed it to go on. So I've decided to make the row myself and a drastic despatch has gone home — great fun another hairy battle. (BNM, Rey Diaries, 4–7 February 1931)

Rey suggested Ballinger should be a member of the commission of inquiry. Both Rey and Tshekedi now wanted, for very different reasons, "a searching and impartial inquiry" into the condition of the Basarwa. Significantly, Rey limited it to the Bamangwato Reserve—although he was well aware that servitude was widespread in the protectorate. Inquiries elsewhere, he explained, would create needless "unrest and disturbance" (BNA, resident commissioner, 3 February 1931). There is no doubt that one of his motives for focussing only on the Bangwato was his desire to cut Tshekedi, the most forceful and able of the protectorate chiefs, down to size. But his diaries reveal that he had a deep sympathy for the plight of the Basarwa, although he thought them "a decadent and dying race" for whose preservation money and energy should not be expended (Gadibolae 1984: preamble).

The high commissioner decided a one-man commission would be quick, cheap, and would ensure unanimous recommendations.[19] He chose E. S. B. Tagart, former secretary for Native Affairs in Northern Rhodesia, who was assisted by a Setswana-speaking protectorate police officer.

It was a relief to Rey that the inquiry had been set in motion before the trial of the murderers of the Mosarwa brought a blaze of publicity ("Man Skinned Alive" read the headline in *The Star* on 30 April 1931) and revelations that Basarwa were frequently flogged, were inherited, and that the accused had never heard of the Athlone Declaration. Moreover, Rey was incensed when, owing to a technicality, the murder charge could not be sustained and the accused could be sentenced to only 15 years hard labor and 10 lashes for "culpable homicide," whereas Africans convicted of killing a European had shortly before been condemned to death (BNM, Rey Diaries, 30 April 1931; BNA, Blaststove 1931). Foreseeing embarrassing questions in Britain as to the relative value of European and African life, Rey hoped the forthcoming inquiry would enable him "to give the Bamangwato hell" (BNM, Rey Diaries, 30 April 1931). Tshekedi, on the other hand, was confident that it would prove that Basarwa were in general well treated and were not slaves.

The Tagart Commission

Tagart was less than two months in the protectorate, interviewing officials, prominent Bangwato, including Tshekedi and the Ratshosas, and some white residents. He spent only three weeks touring cattle posts by

19. BNA, resident commissioner, 3 February 1931; BNA, Rey 1931. The high commissioner, however, feared that Ballinger would seek publicity for himself. Rey also suggested including D. T. Jabavu, a black South African proposed by Tshekedi.

ox-wagon to talk to groups of Basarwa. Tshekedi's opponents claimed that drastic reform was needed, but Tagart, perceiving that "they were using the Masarwa question as a stalking horse with their eyes on more important game," discounted their evidence. Similarly he realized that the European unofficial witnesses—who depended on the goodwill of Tshekedi for the success of their trading, mission work, or other activities in the reserve—were also biased (BNA, Tagart 1931: 13).

Tagart's report confirmed that there were Basarwa groups who roamed freely in remote areas, but many others were tied to masters, for whom they worked without pay as herdsmen, servants, agricultural laborers, and hunters. He considered them serfs rather than slaves, since their services were limited by custom and they changed hands only by inheritance within the owning family or—rarely—by order of the chief. However, their children were liable to be forcibly taken from them to work on cattle posts or in homes. Moreover, malata could not leave their masters without consent—and this was usually refused. Their rights to property, while recognized in theory, were limited in practice by lack of opportunity to acquire any. In fact they could do so only at the discretion of their masters, who regarded the "acquisition of any considerable quantity of property with jealous eyes" and were quick to seize any pretext to deprive Basarwa of their possessions.

On the other hand, Tagart did not think they suffered any great material hardship. On the cattle posts their work was limited to little more than the watering of cattle which roamed free and required little supervision. Their life was "primitive, easy, carefree and unprogressive." He considered them backward—even to speaking "a barbarous language"! He did not, however, accept Tshekedi's argument that if emancipated they would either revert to the "miserable nomadic existence" from which the Bangwato had "rescued" them or take to stock theft. The Basarwa almost unanimously declared that they wanted to be free of their masters, but they were divided as to whether or not they could survive without a share of the cattle they herded, since they depended on the milk. They also said that they would need land and tools, including ploughs. Evidence was contradictory as to whether they could seek work outside the reserve. Some said their masters would not allow it; others had been to the mines and returned without hindrance. Significantly the best cared for and the most content were Tshekedi's own malata. On balance, Tagart believed that the position of the Basarwa was inconsistent with Britain's imperial mission, even if they were not greatly oppressed, and he recommended measures to give them the same rights, political, economic, and social, as other members of the reserve.

These measures included a census of all Basarwa and their masters, to be taken by a European officer who would also help them find paid employment, but only in accordance with terms to be laid down in a proclamation to protect African labor. Tagart also recommended that Basarwa should pay hut tax unless they could show that they were unable to do so, that the chief or the government should make farmland available to them, that those who wished to settle in villages should be assisted by an agricultural demonstrator, and that a proclamation should be issued affirming that slavery was illegal.

Rey was disappointed that Tagart had not condemned bolata as outright slavery (BNA, resident commissioner, 9 February 1931). He was pleased enough with the recommendations (ibid.), however, he considered it politic to delay implementing them until after his unpopular reforms curtailing the administrative and judicial powers of the chiefs had been promulgated. He even witheld the report from Tshekedi until May 1933. Tshekedi was furious when he read it (BNA, Tshekedi and Rey 1935). Bitterly he pointed out that in South Africa the whites had hunted and shot out the Basarwa like game—whereas the Bangwato had *looked after* them. As for their political rights, most Africans in South Africa had none. Most alarming was his contention that bolata was not an economic institution, as 3 men could do the work of the 30 or so malata on most cattle posts (BNA, resident magistrate, Serowe, 1934, and enclosure). If masters had to pay them, they would have to sell the milk upon which the Basarwa largely depended. They would evict whole families; and where would they go? The Bangwato, he said, would now leave the Basarwa to the government; Tagart's proposals were impractical and masters would resent a census which would make public the numbers of malata they owned (BNA, Tshekedi and high commissioner 1935).

"Missionary Slaves": The London Missionary Society Inquiry

Until late in 1934 the London Missionary Society, which had been given a monopoly of evangelization in the Bamangwato Reserve by Khama III, had kept out of the fray. They were helping Tshekedi with several other battles with the administration, and this was a ticklish subject on which they preferred not to commit themselves. They were now, however, forced to do so by Ballinger, the self-styled champion of African causes, who published a sensational article in the *News Chronicle* (1934)—the voice of the British liberal nonconformist conscience—claiming that English missionaries, supported by subscriptions from Britain, owned cattle tended by slaves. Eventually he was forced to retract this, but the London Missionary Society, anxious to protect their fund-raising activities at home, decided to hold their own investigation (CWM, Cocker Brown 1935).

Tshekedi was the star witness, and no evidence was taken from his enemies, let alone from any malata. Predictably their report, published in 1935, denied that malata were slaves or even serfs, objected to the census with its inclusion of masters' names, and expressed Tshekedi's doubts about any attempts to force their emancipation, since they lacked alternative means of livelihood. As Rev. Albert Jennings explained: "There is no barbed wire fence round the territories of the the tribes of the Protectorate, and the Bushman, if he so desired, could at any time take his bow and arrow and go straight to Central Africa," but owing to the scarcity of game "today there is practically only one means of support for both Bamangwato and Masarwa, and that is cattle. . . . The Bushmen have clung to the cattle posts of the Bechuana for self-preservation" (LMS Report 1935: 24). The missionaries did make the positive proposal, however, that they should begin the conversion and education of the Basarwa.

The Masarwa Census

The government, aware of the interest of both the League of Nations Advisory Committee of Experts on Slavery, established in 1934, and of the Antislavery Society (BNA, Harris 1935), now began to put the Tagart recommendations into effect. Two proclamations were issued in 1936: one affirming that slavery was illegal (Proclamation No. 15 of 1936), the other requiring that all "native labourers" be paid "in cash or kind" and stating that they could work where and for whom they wished, but the employment could not be terminated without one month's notice on either side (Proclamation No. 14 of 1936). Moreover, the services of dependents or relatives of employees could not be called upon without their express consent or that of their guardians if they were minors. This legislation raised some thorny legal and practical questions, among them the fear that European employers might seize the opportunity to pay their African employees less or to pay them in kind (BNA, high commissioner 1935, and documents in S 359/12/1). For this reason the law applied only to Africans employed by other Africans. Tshekedi unsuccessfully protested against both proclamations. The first he thought unnecessary because "we all know that in the British Empire slavery has long been unlawful," while the second introduced legislation based on color distinction — an invidious precedent (BNA, Tshekedi, 27 July 1935).

The second proclamation left the extent of the remuneration unspecified, because officials simply could not decide on what constituted an adequate wage or how they could enforce payment. It was so vague that the legal advisor to the resident commissioner pointed out that the tiniest sum, paid monthly, would meet the requirement (BNA, Fforde 1935).

On the other hand the needs of the different categories of workers varied considerably. Whereas milk might be adequate payment for a small herd boy, an adult would clearly require more (BNA, government secretary, Serowe, 1935). It was decided to await reports from the "Masarwa officer," J. W. Joyce, who had been appointed in 1935 to take a census of the Basarwa and investigate their condition, before attempting to lay down any minimum-wage scale or even to put the proclamation into force, for fear that masters, faced with the need to pay them, might indeed evict the majority of their malata, and the administration would then be forced to support them.[20]

Joyce began work in 1935, and in spite of obstruction from the Bangwato, he tracked down 9,505 Basarwa, and thought there were another 1,000 or so out of reach or too scattered to justify the expense of searching for them (BNA, Joyce, 3 October 1936). He found wide variations in their condition (see BNA, Joyce reports, 1935–1936). Those east of the railway along the Shashi and Macloutsie (now Motloutse) rivers had virtually emancipated themselves. With little or no interference from their masters, they were herding or doing farm work for Europeans in the Tati District, Southern Rhodesia, and the Transvaal, and some were going to the South African mines. They ploughed their own lands, owned cattle, often paid taxes, wore European clothes, appeared generally prosperous, and were "rapidly becoming civilized." If masters tried to ill-treat them, they simply left. North of Serowe some worked, sometimes with the permission of their masters, for Bapedi and Bakalanga both as herdsmen and on the land. Remuneration here was in kind—food, milk, sometimes a blanket—and on the cattle posts they could earn a cow in three to five years.

In more inaccessible areas where outside work was not available, notably west and southwest of Serowe, however, the Basarwa were tied to their masters and were the most exploited (BNA, Joyce, 3 October 1936). Although complaints were few and none of them wished to be resettled in new areas by the government, it was clear that abuses were still taking place. Joyce uncovered a few cases of children forcibly removed from their parents (BNA, Joyce report, 30 June 1936), and he was told that if a woman had children by a lelata and then was widowed and remarried, she had to look after the children until they were about nine, when the owner of the first husband would take them (BNA, Joyce final report 1936: 33). He found little evidence that Basarwa on more remote cattle posts received any remuneration. Milk was all that was regularly given them,

20. In case evictions did take place, a small sum was set aside (BNA, resident commissioner 1935).

and that was available only for half the year. He found, however, that when there was a drought malata on the cattle posts were sometimes better off than free Basarwa foragers.

Masters still inflicted arbitrary punishment—usually for the loss of an animal. Since the malata rarely had any property with which to pay a fine or compensation and it was impractical to take them the long distances to the nearest magistrate or chief's court, masters normally flogged offenders on the spot. However, they were beginning to say that they should not "touch" Basarwa, who now "belonged" to the government (BNA, district commissioner 1936), but they complained that, since the British had punished cases of abuse of malata, stock theft was on the rise, as the Basarwa now thought they could steal with impunity.[21]

Joyce's reports revealed that the property rights of those Basarwa fortunate enough to have any property were being respected, and many owned cattle and small stock (BNA, Joyce report, 1 April 1936). The main way in which they had been able to improve their position had been by earning wages. Where opportunities for this existed, their lives had improved. Moreover, he believed that the Basarwa population had increased in recent years, although drought and disease had reduced cattle holdings by about a third (BNA, Joyce report, 30 April 1936), causing considerable underemployment on the cattle posts in the reserve, where several families were doing the work of two or three boys (BNA, Joyce report, 28 February 1936); and where boreholes had been sunk, the need for labor was further reduced. Owners were, therefore, more willing to let some malata go, and many of the young men were actually being driven into the wage-labor force. Conversely, those who remained on the cattle posts were more than ever dependent upon their masters.

The surprise was that only 100 or so Bangwato actually "owned" Basarwa. The largest owner was Tshekedi, whom some 1,300 malata claimed as their master. Joyce thought many of these were afraid to identify their real owners, and Nettelton, the resident magistrate in Serowe, believed that not more than a quarter of them gave Tshekedi any real service (BNA, Joyce report, 30 June 1936; BNA, resident magistrate, Serowe, 1937). Nettelton considered that, by his quiet perseverance, Joyce had inflicted a defeat on the Bangwato, who now realized that "the Masarwa question is one which the Administration is determined to pursue" (BNA, resident magistrate, Serowe, 1937).

---

21. BNA, Joyce report, 29 October 1935. Stock theft was of concern to both the British and the Bangwato. In 1929 half the prisoners in Serowe jail were Basarwa convicted of stock theft (Wylie 1984: 57–58).

Compromise and Cooperation

In 1937 Rey left Bechuanaland after seven combative years. The new resident commissioner, Charles Arden-Clarke, soon gained Tshekedi's cooperation by friendly persuasion, and together they agreed on a program to implement Tagart's recommendations (BNA, note of meeting 1937). To Tshekedi's satisfaction, the aim was (as it had always been) to integrate the Basarwa into the Ngwato community on exactly the same terms and with the same rights and obligations as everyone else. Those who could pay taxes were to do so; the rest were exempted until such time as they could pay. To some Basarwa this was a very important point: paying their own taxes was the hallmark of a truly free man.[22] As a result of Joyce's work most Basarwa now knew that they could leave their former masters, and they were encouraged to seek paid labor. Moreover, the proclamation requiring remuneration and giving notice was put into force in 1938, although significantly no minimum scale of payment was laid down. It was now up to employer and employee to make their own arrangements. Tshekedi impressed upon the ex-masters that they must bring erring Basarwa to court and not inflict arbitrary punishment on them; Joyce told the Basarwa that they could bring grievances, including nonpayment for their services, to the dikgotla (BNA, Joyce 1938). The chief and the administration agreed to cooperate against stock theft, and Tshekedi promised wholehearted cooperation with British attempts to turn the Basarwa into a settled peasantry.

With this in view an agricultural demonstrator was appointed to encourage farming, improve crop yields, and introduce new crops. He was given seed to distribute and minimal sums to supply tools and donkeys for ploughing. He found many groups uninterested, but around Lotlhakane (now Letlhakane) the response was good. This became a center, and the people even produced a small agricultural show for the high commissioner in 1939. The demonstrator was withdrawn to Serowe in 1940 when it was deemed that he had served his purpose and should work in a bigger community (BNA, Forsyth Thompson 1940).

Both the government and the London Missionary Society started schools for Basarwa. One at Lotlhakane, in an area where Tshekedi had cattle posts, was well attended once parents were assured they would not have to pay fees and that attendance was voluntary. A cattle post teacher began work in the Macloutsie area, and some Basarwa children began to attend ordinary schools in the reserve (BNA, Joyce 1938). The London Missionary Society sent an evangelist to work on some 40 cattle posts north

---

22. Rey recorded that a Mosarwa in the Kalahari District said, "If I pay my hut-tax that shows I am a man, not a dog" (BNM, Rey Diaries, 2 May 1930).

of Serowe. By December 1938 the missionary in charge of their efforts felt sufficiently confident to inform the Antislavery Society that "the lot of the Masarwa is generally on the upward trend" (NAZ, Burns Papers, Burns to Harris, 24 December 1938).

Conclusion

But was it? Certainly the British believed they had broken the back of the problem and that in time the economic and social position of the Basarwa would improve as more of them entered the wage-labor force and acquired stock of their own or took to farming.

However, their progress towards becoming independent food producers was hampered by ecological conditions and their own cultural traditions. Those lucky enough to be given the odd cow, Joyce noted, were likely to eat it when food was scarce rather than keep it for breeding. Similarly the demonstrator at Lotlhakane battled the tendency of his new farmers to eat seed grain in bad times, and to abandon their fields and return to the veldt when hunting was good (BNA, England 1939). Moreover, Basarwa who wished to accumulate stock or grow crops faced social pressure to share food and possessions, which discouraged their efforts. Thus, their cultural traditions, compounded by the natural hazards of disease and drought, militated against any long-term improvement in the economic situation of many Basarwa groups. Joyce noted, however, that those who had been away and accumulated wages were more careful to build up their stock. Wage labor in the capitalist sector was thus considered a positive step towards the transformation of those who returned into settled farmers, since it enabled them to acquire the necessary tools and stock and induced a change of outlook. Numbers were recruited for the mines in 1938. This was doubly welcome to the financially strapped administration, because they paid taxes.

As long as former malata were free to dispose of their labor in the best market and the law protected them against forcible removal of their children and arbitrary punishment, the British believed that market forces would work themselves out to the mutual benefit of the administration and the Basarwa. They also thought that incorporation of Basarwa into the Bangwato would assure their advancement.

But this was not the way things worked out. Although Basarwa were now free in theory to leave their masters, had to be paid, could keep their products and accumulate property, and had recourse to the courts, in practice they were not assured of either a regular or a minimum wage or a share of the cattle they herded, and they found it difficult to get a hearing in the dikgotla (Hitchcock 1978, 1: 122). Nothing was done on any scale to improve their productivity. Most still did not own ploughs, oxen, or wells. The small wages they could earn even in the white sector of the economy were rarely enough to ensure them savings on a sufficient scale to build up real economic independence over time, particularly in the face of recurrent droughts and cattle disease. Few had access to Western education, which would have improved their earning power; some could not speak Setswana (ibid.: 118). Most crucial of all, they did not have wards under headmen of their own, which would have given them a political voice and access to land and water. Most, in fact, remained where they were with little change in their actual condition (ibid.: 104, 317ff.), perhaps partly because they were unwilling to leave the masters, who provided what little security they had.[23]

Despite the expenditure of time and effort, and the considerable publicity given to the question in the 1930s, the great majority of the Basarwa in the reserve were worse off when the colonial period came to an end three decades later. There is even evidence that at the very time of these British inquiries of the 1920s and 1930s, Ngwato cattle owners were using cases brought to the dikgotla and other legal means to deprive Basarwa of stock systematically and to dispossess those who still had any control over land and, most crucial, over sources of water (Wilmsen 1984: 6). In fact, the expansion of the Ngwato cattle-post economy, which had begun the deterioration in their condition in the nineteenth century, depressed them further in the course of the twentieth century (Hitchcock 1978: Wilmsen 1984). Their incorporation into the Bangwato, instead of raising their status, turned many of them into a landless, cattle-less proletariat. It should be noted that this process of proletarianization was also taking place among the poorer strata of Ngwato—and indeed of all Tswana society (Parson 1984), but the Basarwa suffered the additional disability of being socially despised.

In the final analysis, their plight had not really been the major concern of any of the protagonists in the long debate, each of whom had ulterior motives or faced serious dilemmas. The Ratshosas and their allies, far from being true champions of Basarwa freedom, had used the issue to avenge themselves against Tshekedi and his supporters. The missionaries had taken up the question only when cornered by Ballinger, and since they could not afford to alienate Tshekedi or their British supporters, their report was designed to protect their interests. Their subsequent work among the Basarwa was hardly on an impressive scale. Tshekedi could not attack an institution which was fundamental to the prosperity of his

---

23. Massey 1981: 252. Massey suggests that as one reason why some Basarwa in the Khubidu area took low-paid jobs near home rather than higher-paid ones in South Africa.

chief supporters and provided him with virtually free labor, but neither could he be thought to countenance slavery. He, therefore, fought a delaying action against the government, while denying that malata were either slaves or were oppressed.

What of the administration? The early resident commissioners, fearing the resistance of the Tswana elite, simply turned a blind eye to an institution which they knew would not be acceptable to the British public. It is doubtful if any action beyond the Athlone Declaration would have been taken, even after the revelations of 1926, had it not been for the appointment of Rey as resident commissioner — a man who saw the whole issue as a God-given opportunity to attack Tshekedi and reform the whole protectorate government, and who was spurred on by the fear that cases of ill-treatment of Basarwa would attract widespread media attention and reflect upon his administration. He, therefore, had every incentive to take up the question. The British government, with whom the ultimate responsibility lay, was for many years unclear about the facts, but, once alerted, it was primarily concerned with its image as the leader of the antislavery crusade, and it took just sufficient action to appease critics in Parliament, in the Antislavery Society, and in the League of Nations. But it was the government's penny-pinching policy that had led the local administration to cover up the facts in the first place. Moreover, the government was never willing to provide the Basarwa with the resources necessary to make them truly economically independent or to remove them from Ngwato political control. As for the League of Nations, its various slavery committees were dominated by the colonial powers, who saw to it that all they could do was write reports which were vetted by colonial governments before they were published (Miers 1981).

Whether or not malata could fairly be called slaves is largely a matter of semantics. The fact is that they were in involuntary servitude with severe restrictions on their liberties compared with the Bangwato. But then, as Tshekedi pointed out, under the colonial dispensation all Africans were subject peoples. The Basarwa were simply on the lowest rung of the hierarchy and had a different set of fleas on their backs to bite them.

GLOSSARY

Bamangwato (sing. Mangwato)   colonial name for Bangwato.

Bangwato (sing. Mongwato; adj. Ngwato or Bangwato)   people of the Ngwato state.

Basarwa (sing. Mosarwa;   people formerly called Masarwa (Bushmen) and
   adj. Sarwa)   sometimes called San.
Bechuana   colonial name for Botswana or Tswana people.
Bechuanaland   colonial name for Botswana.
beng be bone (sing.   masters of *malata*.
   mong wa bone)
bolata   institution of servitude described in this chapter.
botlhanka   Tswana name for institution of servitude similar
                              to *bolata* in Ngamiland.
chief   colonial designation for Tswana kings.
kgosi   king.
kgotla (plur. *dikgotla*)   public assembly where meetings were held, de-
                              cisions were made in consultation among the
                              king, his headmen, adult male royal relations,
                              and adult male members of the tribe, and
                              where justice was dispensed.
lelata   see *malata*.
malata (sing. *lelata*)   serf or slave as described in this chapter.
Masarwa   see Basarwa.
Setswana   language of the Tswana people.
tribe   colonial designation for the various ethnic group-
                              ings in Botswana. This appellation is freely
                              used today by the Batswana people.

REFERENCES

Archival sources

BNA: Botswana National Archives, Gaborone.

Edited versions of the Tagart and Joyce reports and the Rey Diaries have
been published (see Tagart 1933; Joyce 1938; and Rey 1987, under OTHER
SOURCES), but the references in this chapter are to the unpublished versions,
listed below.

Acting resident commissioner to high commissioner, 7 August 1936. S 43/7.
Blaststove, telegram no. 81 to high commissioner, 1 May 1931. S 204/5.
Circular minute to magistrates, 7 July 1928. S 43/7.
Crown prosecutor to government secretary, 17 April 1930. S 96/8.
District commissioner, Serowe, to acting resident commissioner, March
    1936. S 360/8/1.
Edirilwe Seretse affidavit, oath before the resident magistrate, 17 Novem-
    ber 1926. Encl. in letter from resident magistrate, Serowe, to govern-
    ment secretary, 18 November 1926. DCS 5/2.
England to government secretary, 26 January 1939. S 360/2.
Fforde minute, 7 August 1935. S 359/12/1.

198   III. POLITICS OF ANTISLAVERY

Forsyth Thompson to England, 22 July 1940. S 360/2.
Government Secretary to resident commissioner, 22 April 1930. S 96/8.
Government Secretary to resident magistrate, Serowe, 4 November 1935. S 360/4.
Harris to Thomas, 5 April 1935. S 360/7.
High commissioner, telegram to resident commissioner, 29 July 1926. S 43/7.
High commissioner to secretary of state for the colonies and dominions, 13 August 1926. S 43/7.
High commissioner to Dominions Office, 12 November 1935. S 360/4.
Interviews, Tshekedi and Lord Passfield, 27 March and 1 April 1930. S 63/9.
Joyce reports, 1935–1936, original unexpurgated reports. S 360/1.
Joyce final report, 1936, original unedited version of report dated 28 December 1936. S 360/8/2.
Joyce to resident magistrate, Serowe, 28 February 1936. S. 360/1.
Joyce to district commissioner, Serowe, 3 October 1936. S 359/12/2.
Joyce to resident magistrate, Serowe, 12 August 1938. S 359/12/2.
Minutes, 23 November 1927. S 6/1.
Note of meeting, 10 October 1937. S 359/12/2.
Ratshosa, Simon, evidence, June 1926, evidence of Simon Ratshosa in Rex versus S. and O. Ratshosa, in the Court of the Additional Magistrate for the Ngwato District of the Bechuanaland Protectorate. DCS 8/6.
Resident commissioner, telegram no. 67 to high commissioner, 14 May 1924. S 43/7.
Resident commissioner to high commissioner, conference on 21 April 1926. S 43/7.
Resident commissioner to high commissioner, 24 February 1927. S 43/7.
Resident commissioner to high commissioner, 3 February 1931. S 204/4.
Resident commissioner to high commissioner, 4 February 1931. S 175/9.
Resident commissioner to high commissioner, conference on 9 February 1931. S 204/10.
Resident commissioner to high commissioner, 12 December 1935. S 360/1.
Resident magistrate, Serowe, to government secretary, 18 November 1926. DCS 5/2.
Resident magistrate, Francistown, to resident magistrate, Serowe, 26 January 1931, N. 22. S 194/9.
Resident magistrate, Serowe, to high commissioner, 26 January 1934. S 359/14.
Resident magistrate, Serowe, to acting resident commissioner, 7 October 1937. S 360/8/1.
Rey minute, 28 April 1931. S 204/4.
Tagart unpublished report, 1931, original unexpurgated report with appendices in S 204/8 and S 204/11.
    Cuzen evidence. S 204/8.
    Motsete evidence. S 204/8.
    Simon Ratshosa evidence. S 204/8.
    Tshekedi evidence. S 204/8.

Tshekedi to resident magistrate, Serowe, 30 August 1930. S 96/8.
Tshekedi to resident magistrate, Serowe, 26 December 1930. S 175/9.
Tshekedi to resident magistrate, Serowe, 27 July 1935. C/3/630 R1-1, Vol. 1.
Tshekedi and high commissioner, minute of interview, 6 March 1935.
S 360/6.
Tshekedi and Rey, minute of interview, 19 February 1935. 360/6.
Williams to high commissioner, 10 July 1906. S 32/7.
BNM: Botswana National Museum, Gaborone.
Rey, Lieutenant-Colonel Charles. Diaries, 1929–1937.
CWM: Council for World Mission Archives, London Missionary Society, School
of Oriental and African Studies, London.
Cocker Brown to Burns, 17 January 1935. LMS Africa Odds 25.
NAZ: National Archives of Zimbabwe, Harare.
Burns, J. H. L. Papers. 5/2/3.
PRO DO: Public Record Office, Dominions Office, London.
Minutes, July 1926. 9/2 D6951.
Minutes, correspondence, press cuttings, June 1926. 9/1 D5350.
Resident commissioner to high commissioner, 7 August 1926, conference
no. 333. Encl. in high commissioner to colonial secretary, 13 August
1926. 9/2.
UW: University of the Witwatersrand.
The Ballinger Papers. A3.1.14.

Other sources

Chirenje, J. M. 1977. *A history of northern Botswana 1850–1910.* Madison, N.J.:
Fairleigh Dickinson University Press.
Cooper, F. 1980. *From slaves to squatters: plantation labor and agriculture in
Zanzibar and coastal Kenya, 1890–1925.* New Haven and London: Yale University Press.
Crowder, M. 1985a. The succession crisis over the illness and death of Kgosi
Sekgoma II of the Bangwato, 1925: Western versus traditional medicine. Paper
presented to the African Studies Association, New Orleans.
Crowder, M. 1985b. Tshekedi Khama and opposition to the British administration of the Bechuanaland Protectorate 1926–1936. *Journal of African History*
26: 193–214.
Diamond Fields Advertiser (Kimberley). February, 1926.
Gadibolae, M. N. 1984. Serfdom (bolata) in the Nata area 1926–1960. B.A. research essay, University of Botswana.
Hitchcock, R. K. 1978. *Kalahari cattle posts: a regional study of hunter-gatherers,
pastoralists, and agriculturalists in the western Sandveld region, Central District, Botswana.* 2 vols. Ministry of Government and Lands: Gaborone.
Hitchcock, R. 1979. Socio-economic change among the Basarwa in Botswana:
an ethnohistoric perspective. Paper presented at the University of Botswana
and Swaziland, 20 March 1979.
Joyce, J. W. 1938. Report on the Masarwa in the Bamangwato Reserve Bechuana-

land Protectorate. *Slavery: Report of the Advisory Committee of Experts,* League of Nations C112. M.98. 1938.VI. annex 6 C.C.E.E. 189, pp. 57–76.

LMS Report. 1935. *The Masarwa (Bushmen): report of an inquiry by the South Africa District Committee of the London Missionary Society.* Alice, South Africa: Lovedale Press.

Massey, D. 1981. Labor migration and rural development in Botswana. Ph.D. dissertation, Boston University.

Miers, S. 1981. Britain and the suppression of slavery 1919–39. Paper presented at the School of Oriental and African Studies, London.

Miers, S. 1983. Botlhanka/Bolata under colonial rule: a preliminary report. Paper presented at the University of Botswana.

News Chronicle (London). 5 November 1934.

Parson, J. 1984. *Botswana: liberal democracy and the labor reserve in southern Africa.* Boulder and London: Westview Press.

Parsons, Q. N. [Neil]. 1973. Khama III, the Bamangwato and the British with special reference to 1895–1923. Ph.D. dissertation, Edinburgh University.

Parsons, N. 1977. The economic history of Khama's country in Botswana, 1844–1930. In *The roots of rural poverty in central and southern Africa,* ed. R. Palmer and N. Parsons, Ch. 5. London: Heinemann.

Rey, Sir Charles. 1987. *Monarch of all I survey: Bechuanaland diaries 1929–1937,* ed. N. Parsons and M. Crowder. Gaborone: The Botswana Society, and London: James Currey.

Star, The (Johannesburg). 30 April 1931.

Tagart, E. S. B. 1933. *Report on the conditions existing among the Masarwa in the Bamangwato Reserve of the Bechuanaland Protectorate and certain matters appertaining to the natives living therein.* Pretoria: Government Printer.

Tlou, T. 1977. Servility and political control: Botlhanka among the BaTawana in northwestern Botswana, ca. 1750–1906. In *Slavery in Africa: historical and anthropological perspectives,* ed. S. Miers and I. Kopytoff, 367–90. Madison: University of Wisconsin Press.

Wilmsen, E. N. 1982. *Remote area dwellers in Botswana: an assessment of their current status.* Boston University, African Studies Center Working Paper No. 65.

Wilmsen, E. 1984. The impact of land tenure policies on the future of the San. Paper presented at Boston University.

Wilmsen, E. N., and J. R. Denbow. 1986. The advent and course of pastoralism in the Kalahari. *Science* 234 (19 December): 1509–50.

Wylie, D. 1984. The center cannot hold: the decline of the Ngwato Chieftainship 1925–50. Ph.D. dissertation, Yale University.

IV

THE DIVERSITY OF SLAVE INITIATIVES AND EX-SLAVE EXPERIENCES

6 *Martin A. Klein*

Slave Resistance and Slave Emancipation in Coastal Guinea

In 1908, a large number of slaves in the Rio Nunez region on the coast of Guinea refused to continue working for their masters. Those involved were slaves who had been brought down to the coast to produce peanuts for export. The revolt was a product of tensions within the system of slavery, resulting largely from slave initiative and helping to alter the relations of production definitively on the Guinea coast.

The Rio Nunez was for four centuries a base for slave-trading operations. Much of this trade was controlled by two groups from outside the region who were able to gain control, probably because of the relatively uncentralized nature of indigenous societies. The first group consisted of the mulatto descendants of Eureopean and American slavers who had developed bases along the coast and controlled the export of slaves. The second was composed of Muslim traders from the interior, who provided most of the slaves. Both groups were oriented towards external markets and both were economically efficient. When the Atlantic slave trade went into decline in the middle of the nineteenth century, these two groups redirected slaves into commodity production. Like other rivers on the

I am grateful to Richard Roberts, Paul Lovejoy, and George Brooks for comments on an earlier version of this chapter. The research on which it is based was done on a grant from the Social Sciences and Humanities Research Council of Canada.

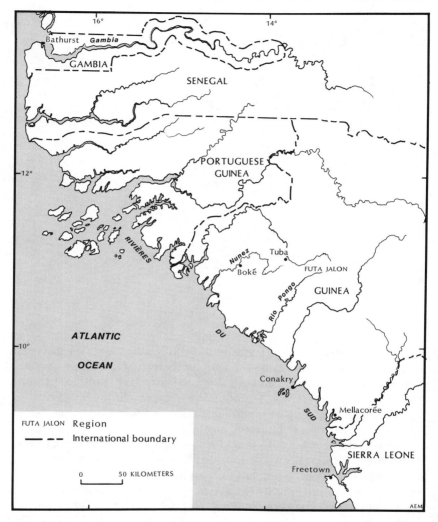

Map 6. Coastal Guinea

deeply indented Guinea coast, the Rio Nunez became a center of plantation agriculture.[1] Of the two groups, it was the Muslims who were the
most oriented to commodity production and who created the harsher,
more rational, and more exploitative system. The Eurafrican traders had

1. For a survey of Guinean history, see Arcin 1911. On the mulatto traders, see Brooks

larger slaveholdings, but they clung longer to the slave trade and seem
to have made a less successful adaptation to commodity production (Goerg
1985). It was primarily against the Muslims that this revolt was directed.[2]

The attack on slavery in the Rio Nunez and elsewhere along the Guinea
coast came largely from the slaves, but they were given the opportunity
by measures forced on the colonial regime by metropolitan public opinion. Though governors varied in their attitudes, the very cautious men
who made policy were generally reluctant to deprive valued allies of their
slaves and were nervous about possible unrest. In this, the colonial administration in Guinea was even more hesitant than that in Senegal and
the Soudan. There, action was sometimes slow in coming, but at a certain point it was quite decisive (Klein and Roberts 1980; Renault 1971),
whereas in Guinea antislavery policies had to be forced on the administration by higher authority, and were enforced reluctantly, if at all. The
hesitation of the regime made the events that took place in the Rio Nunez
in 1908 and 1909 all the more striking.

Trade and Politics

Guinea was an area where the French had long had important interests
(Schnapper 1961; Arcin 1911; Goerg 1980, 1986). The decline of the Atlantic slave trade took place at a time when African traders based at Gorée
and Freetown were rapidly developing a coastal trade in commodities.
During the 1840s, they found in the peanut a product that could absorb
the increasing surplus of slave labor (Brooks 1975). By 1850, trading posts
had been established on a number of the coastal rivers and were dealing
with both coastal planters and caravans from the interior. By the end
of the 1860s the export of peanuts had risen to over 4,000 tons a year in
the Rio Nunez and to over 2,000 in the Rio Pongo. In addition, there
was a lively trade in coffee, kola, rice, hides, and palm kernels (Arcin
1911). About 30 French or Senegalese traders operated from posts on the
rivers. The Rio Nunez was the more important river, both for peanut
production and for trade from the Futa Jalon (Goerg 1985). Competition
between traders often involved the giving of credit and advances of seed

---

1970, 1983; and Mouser 1983. There is no similar treatment of the Tubakayes (see below),
but for a good general discussion of the trade system, see Goerg 1980, 1981. In general,
there is little available on coastal politics and social structure after the decline of the Atlantic trade. On colonial rule, see Suret-Canale 1960, 1971.

2. During a stay in Guinea in 1980, I was discouraged from doing fieldwork. The archival material on which this chapter is based seemed particularly interesting, but there
is a need for a fuller social history of this area and for research on the aftermath of
emancipation.

(Rivière 1971; Brooks 1970: 198–206). The flag followed trade. In 1866, the French set up a military post on the Rio Nunez under a treaty with a local chief. In 1882 a treaty with Great Britain established the border between Guinea and Sierra Leone.

A large reservoir of slave labor, heavy rainfall, and easy transport made the Guinea coast an ideal area for the commodity trade, though the land was not ideal for peanut production. Despite heavy soils, which made cultivation difficult, and the extended rainy season, which often endangered the harvest, peanut production in the area expanded because of the existence of labor and the willingness of the French commercial houses to buy the crop. Soon after the beginning of the peanut trade, planters from the Jaxanke town of Tuba began to move slaves down to the coast to produce peanuts. Tuba was a major clerical center, and like many clerical centers, it was deeply involved in both trade and the exploitation of slave labor.[3] These planters, called Tubakayes, which means "people of Tuba," may have been involved in the slave trade and seem to have combined trade and agriculture. They were strict Muslims, had large slaveholdings numbering up to 250 slaves, and were market oriented (ANG, monographie, Rio Nunez, 1912). The French saw the Tubakayes as allies in the commercial development of the coast and, in an 1884 treaty with the Nalou chief in Rio Nunez, placed them under French protection: "The Tubakayes, who are a cause of prosperity in the Rio Nunez, depend only on the French government and can neither be troubled, nor requisitioned nor punished by the Nalou chiefs" (Goerg 1980: 471).

Ironically, the 1884 treaty was signed at a time when peanut production was becoming insignificant. The rubber boom began in the 1870s. In the early 1880s, rubber prices rose as peanut prices declined, and labor was redirected. This period also saw the establishment of larger and better financed commercial houses, of which the most important was the

3. There are differing views of the Jaxanke. Philip Curtin (1971) sees them primarily as a commercial group. Lamine Sanneh (1976, 1979) stresses their clerical vocation and argues that slave labor provided the economic support they needed for their clerical activities. It is probable that both are correct. There is no contradiction between the three activities. It is clear that Islam was basic to the image the Jaxanke had of themselves, but in the context of this study, what is important is that they were hard men with a good eye for opportunity in both agriculture and trade. Archival sources differ on when the Tubakayes arrived, but it was probably in the 1850s or 1860s. They were certainly there before 1868. In that year, the local commandant referred to "numerous migrations of Toubakayes who have come to establish themselves" (ANS, correspondance, 4 October 1868). They provided about 80,000 bushels of peanuts (ibid., 22 December 1868). From that time forth, the various commandants regularly commented on the Tubakayes, their industry, and their productivity. See also Goerg 1981: 84–87; Suret-Canale 1970b. On the process of emancipation in Tuba, see Marty 1921: 119, 134–35.

Compagnie française de l'Afrique occidentale (CFAO). The Rio Nunez continued to produce peanuts and towards the end of the century, when most of the vines in the coastal area had been destroyed and the rubber zone had moved inland, peanut exports became important once again (Goerg 1980, 1986; Suret-Canale 1960). The Tubakayes were still the major producers.

In spite of the importance of Guinean exports, the French were much more interested in the imagined wealth of the Soudan and directed greater resources to that land-locked and poor area. When the colony of Rivières du Sud was set up in 1889, it consisted of a series of trading posts along the coast, none of which controlled any hinterland. Budgets were limited and military forces remained small. In 1896, the first force to move into the Futa Jalon contained only 150 soldiers (McGowan 1981). More than anything else, it was the shortage of money and the limited military force available that shaped the French approach to slavery. The administration was aware of the vast numbers of slaves — probably between a third and a half of the population — and their importance to the economy (Klein 1987; ANS, enquête 1904). The absence of beasts of burden and of major river transport routes meant that Guinea's highly developed trade systems depended on slave porters. Slaves also made up the bulk of the forced-labor levies called out by the French to build the Conakry-Niger Railroad between 1901 and 1914. The French relied on local elites to produce this labor and were afraid of provoking them to resist. Not surprisingly, therefore, they found excuses for not acting on the slavery question. To justify their inaction on slavery, administrators wrote frequently of their respect for property and the obligation not to interfere with African ways. In 1902 the governor insisted to his superiors in Paris that the French had a solemn obligation to respect local customs. Freeing the slaves, he wrote, would be "a real injustice unless reasonable indemnities were given to the masters" (ANF-SOM, lieutenant gouverneur 1902). Policy at this time was to sign treaties with various African rulers making new enslavement and the sale of slaves illegal (ANG, arrêté 1902; ANG, administrateur, 13 October 1902). While this probably put a damper on the trade, it did not completely stop it and did little to ameliorate the condition of slaves. There was still, for example, a regular trade in slaves between the Rio Nunez and the Futa Jalon, where slaves could be exchanged for cattle (ANG, journal de poste 1902).

In 1903 a new law code was proclaimed for the whole of French West Africa which denied slavery the recognition of the courts (Renault 1971). Instructions accompanying the law code simply stated that masters could not go to French courts to reclaim slaves. In spite of this, as late as 1905, local French authorities still returned runaway slaves to their masters and slavery was recognized in inheritance cases (ANG, administrateur, 3 November 1902). In December 1905, a comprehensive law abolished all forms of the slave trade and the alienation of the liberty of any person. This did not abolish slavery, though it was often interpreted as having done so (*Journal officiel de la Guinée* 1906). Within months, however, slaves in many parts of West Africa began acting in such a way that the French had either to put the authority of the state behind the slave masters or let slave-based labor systems collapse.

Slavery on the Guinea Coast

The best sources on slavery in the first years of the century are the questionnaires filled out by French administrators in 1904 (ANS, enquête 1904). The Rio Nunez questionnaire is not a very good one, in part because the administrator had been on the job for only seven months, but administrators in the other maritime *cercles*, Rio Pongo and Mellacorée, produced better reports. Putting the three reports together, we get a good picture of coastal slavery. Slaves were estimated at only about 10 percent of the population in the Rio Nunez, but it is not clear whether the slaves of the Tubakayes and the mulatto families were counted. In the Rio Pongo, by contrast, slaves were estimated at almost two-thirds of the population and in Mellacorée at one-third. The higher figures are much more likely to be accurate. There is no reason to think the numbers in the Rio Nunez were lower than the other rivers. In fact, the Rio Nunez was probably the most important center of slave-based production (Goerg 1985). The slave trade had been suppressed, though some clandestine slave trade was still being conducted, especially near the borders with Sierra Leone and Portuguese Guinea, where it was difficult to control.

The slaves can be divided either between those who were acquired and those born in the master's household, or between those who lived in the master's compound and those who lived in separate slave villages. The first distinction was more important juridically because those born in the household could not be sold. But for the purpose of this chapter, the patterns of residence are more important. Slaves who lived with their masters included both many of the newly enslaved and many trusted retainers and concubines. They were fed and clothed by the master and were totally at his disposition. These were probably the best off and the worst off. Slaves who lived separately worked under slave chiefs five days a week and spent two days on their own plots. As in many other areas, slaves probably worked from early morning until early afternoon prayer (about 2 P.M.). The condition of the slaves and their treatment differed radically, however, as the administrator in Mellacorée reported:

The relations between master and captive vary greatly and depend on the character and resources of the master, the number and quality of his slaves. The rights of the captives are determined by custom, but masters forget these rights as often as slaves forget their obligations. In fact, we can say that slaves have no guarantees. A captive always remains a captive and is always wrong when he makes a complaint; free men consider captives beneath them, they barely deign to hear them, they recognize with difficulty their rights, and they receive their complaints with even more difficulty. (ANS, enquête 1904)

The slaves could have their complaints heard only when they acted together. Thus, their only chance of influencing the conditions of their exploitation was collective action, which was made possible by the pattern of settlement. Sometimes, as described by the administrator from Mellacorée, slaves went out on strike, refusing to work and retreating into the bush until the masters were willing to discuss their grievances. Eventually, the masters would negotiate and the slaves would return to work (ANS, enquête 1904, Mellacorée). In the slave villages, the larger numbers and the relative autonomy made possible the development of leadership and the articulation of grievances. The most important grievances were probably over the amount of food they received, the days they worked for their masters, and the amount of time left them to work their own plots.

Slave Emancipation

In 1904 the administrator in the Rio Nunez listed four circumstances under which slaves could be freed. Some were freed when illegal caravans were stopped. Some were freed because they were not being fed or clothed properly, and some because they were being mistreated, that is to say, beaten or held in chains. Finally, some were ransomed by free relatives living elsewhere. Obviously, in the first three cases, the wrong committed had to be brought to the attention of the administrator. For the others, the only option was self-purchase. The price was 150 francs (U.S. $30 in 1904 values) for a male and 200 ($40) for a female. Furthermore, once a slave was freed, he or she still had to work to ransom spouses and children. Not surprisingly, in 1904 few slaves were being freed. In the 12 months before submitting the report, Rio Nunez had issued 16 certificates of liberty, 4 of them voluntary manumissions of trusted retainers by elderly masters (ANS, enquête 1904, Rio Nunez). In Mellacorée, however, the administrator reported an increase in demands for liberation: "They say they are tired of working for their master, that they have worked long enough for others, and that the liberty they seek is so that they can work for themselves and reap the fruits of their own labor" (ANS, enquête 1904). It is thus clear that some administrators were aware of tensions in the slave villages. Slave flight was not massive, but it was constant. French and British efforts to deal with slavery must have awakened hopes of a better day in slave villages. Certainly, slave-owners saw in those efforts a threat to their authority and several times warned French administrators that their actions could lead to increased flight or conflict over labor obligations (ANG, administrateur, 13 October 1902; ANG, administrateur, 3 November 1902). In the spring of 1906, at almost the same time as slaves began to move away in massive numbers from Banamba in the Soudan, the system was clearly beginning to unravel in the Rio Nunez (Klein and Roberts 1980). Throughout 1906, there were constant demands for liberation, some slaves claiming mistreatment, some wanting to purchase their freedom. The names listed in the archives were mostly Muslims and the certificates contained this sentence: "This native has paid in front of me the sum demanded by custom to obtain this document" (ANG, correspondance, Boké, 1906). The major difference between the Guinea coast and Haut-Sénégal–Niger (the Soudan) in 1906 was that in Guinea slaves still had to buy their freedom. Nevertheless, almost 50 did so during the course of the year. They were persons of all ages and generally sought their freedom one or two at a time (ibid.). Throughout 1907, as pressure from slaves increased, administrators (three within a year) began to worry about a series of problems. One asked how he could justify self-purchase, which recognized that the slave was property although slavery had no legal status. Transactions in persons were, in fact, clearly illegal, but the administrator dealt with the problem by simply ceasing to demand the statement about payment (ANG, correspondance, Boké, 25 February 1907). He also began to receive more and more requests for liberation. In February, he wrote that he had freed 26 in six weeks (ANG, correspondance, Boké, 28 February 1907). In March he had a request for 44 liberations in a case involving the inheritance of a Landoman chief (ANG, correspondance, Boké, 22 March 1907). In April the administrator was worried about a very different problem in a case involving 50 slaves of another chief. The chiefs were unhappy, he wrote, because they could no longer buy slaves. The administrator asked the lieutenant governor if it was necessary to demand compensation for the master, although he himself already seemed to think that it was. If slaves were freed without compensation, he wrote, there would be great resentment among the masters (ANG, correspondance, Boké, 6 April 1907). There were over 200 requests for liberation in the first half of 1907. In January 1908, a third concern surfaced when a new administrator wrote of his increasing unhappiness about "slaves who, feeling themselves free, refuse all labor to their masters, or rather, to their former masters. These people do not even work for themselves, and it is with greatest reluctance that I daily deliver them certificates of identity" (ANG, correspondance, Boké, rapport politique, 1908). Disgruntled though he was, he continued to administer the policy. Some 436 slaves were freed between 28 January 1907 and 25 June 1908 (ANG, 2 D 37, 1908).

The Slaves Stop Work in the Rio Nunez

Early in 1908, William Ponty became governor general of French West Africa. In the Soudan, Ponty had been the governor who authorized the Banamba exodus (Klein and Roberts 1980). Though hesitant at the time, he had become convinced that the freeing of the slaves was not only politically necessary but economically desirable in that it created a mobile labor reserve for French West Africa.[4] If he had any doubts, they were resolved by pressures from Paris. In April 1908, he wrote Poulet, the acting lieutenant governor of Guinea that the minister of colonies wanted domestic slavery definitively suppressed. He made clear in the letter his dissatisfaction with Guinea's slow progress, and he insisted that the colony move more vigorously. Poulet responded by prohibiting the further issue of certificates of liberty, the logic behind this being that they were redundant because the administration no longer recognized slavery (ANG, circulaires 1901–1912). The slaves were free under law and the colonial state no longer stood behind slavery. Two months later, Poulet visited the Rio Nunez and gave instructions to end the payments for liberation. The news of the change in policy spread rapidly and the administrator was deluged by slaves "coming in mass to the Post to claim their liberty, to say that they were tired of working for their masters and wanted only to work for themselves" (ANG, pièces, rapport politique, 8 March 1909). At first, they came in groups of 50 or 60, almost all of them the slaves of Tubakayes. And then, towards the end of August, they stopped work. Happening in the middle of the growing season, this threatened not only the Tubakayes, but also the French commercial houses, and in particular the CFAO, which had made advances of rice and peanut seed to the masters. Lands had been seeded. If they were not worked, weeds would destroy the crop and the investment would be lost. The commercial houses telegraphed Conakry, and then, on the advice of his superiors, the administrator convened several meetings of slaves and masters in Tubakaye

4. ANG, correspondance 1908. Ponty used one of his first speeches as governor general, the opening of the Conseil de Gouvernement in December 1908, to boast of the success of his liberation policies and to encourage similar policies elsewhere. When Camille Guy was sent to Guinea as lieutenant gouverneur in 1911, it was with even more explicit instructions on the slavery issue. See Ponty's instructions (ANS, Ponty 1911).

villages. Pushed by the administration, former slaves and former masters accepted a compromise. The slaves would remain through the harvest, but on three conditions. First, they would be free after the harvest. Second, the masters would reconstitute families, making a particular effort to restore children, who had been dispersed under various pretexts, to their parents. Third, the masters promised good treatment and adequate food. One group, working for a particularly harsh master, insisted that the master and his family work alongside them, which they consented to do. For the slaves, it was crucial that they had from the administrator an explicit statement that they were free and had a right to live and work where they wished. The administrator also clearly wanted them to stay where they were, which meant conceding them the right to use the land they worked.

The agricultural season on the Guinea coast is a long one. The rains last six months, the harvest is not finished until March, and in May the lands are already being prepared for a new season. This gave the administration some time for reflection. Treillard, the administrator, made an inquiry about villages that had been freed. He looked at three. At Rafrasse, 236 slaves of Marie Curtis, a member of an old mulatto family, insisted on their freedom when their aged mistress died. They remained in their villages when it was granted (ANG, journal de poste 1908; ANG, pièces, rapport politique, 8 March 1909). At Kibola, the masters contested the liberation of 115 slaves and tried to seize part of their harvest. The conflict ended with the slaves leaving to seek lands and presumably protection from a Baga chief. In the third case, the slaves simply dispersed. Of 84, only 4 remained with the master (ANG, pièces, rapport politique, 8 March 1909). Treillard believed that the process of emancipation in the Rio Nunez was being eased both by the availability of land and by the desire of chiefs to increase the number of their subjects. He argued that slaves were most likely to remain in their villages when their liberation was not seriously contested. Finally, he suggested that administrators help the freedmen find land and accept the probability of a short period of reduced production.

By the spring of 1909, there was a new administrator. Unlike Treillard, he feared the effects of liberation for two major reasons: first, that slaves would leave and in the absence of labor the area would decline, and second, that they would simply stop working and everyone would starve. The Tubakayes exacerbated the administrator's fears with constant complaints and threats to return to Tuba. In April, when slaves from three Tubakaye villages came in to claim their freedom, three conditions were imposed on them by the administrator: first, that they remain in their villages until instructed otherwise; second, that they work to meet their own needs, as if they were planning to do otherwise; and third, that they pay the head tax (ANG, pièces, administrateur, 13 April 1909). The head tax had previously been paid by the slaves' masters. Throughout the whole emancipation process, local administrators were constantly afraid that slaves would either leave their districts or simply stop working. Ponty's letter to Poulet in 1908 had suggested the possibility of sharecropping contracts as an alternative. This was an increasingly popular idea for local administrators who feared the effects of an exodus, but it was not welcomed by the freedmen (Klein 1983).

Increasing violence took place as the Tubakayes tried to use force to keep freedmen under their control. In late April, there was a fight at the village of Baralandé when some Tubakayes tried to force former slaves to work. Finally, the administrator called a meeting of about 300 slaves and 20 Tubakayes. The administrator's account implies that the 300 were adult males, which would mean that between 1,000 and 1,500 slaves were involved in the protest, including women and children, with perhaps some nearby groups waiting for the outcome. The administrator gave a speech in which he insisted that the Tubakayes had to obey the law and the slaves had to work to meet their own needs. He suggested that sharecropping contracts might take care of everyone's needs. None of the freedmen responded to this idea. There was still plenty of land in the Rio Nunez and the slaves knew it. After the administrator's speech, an old slave stood up. He thanked the administrator on behalf of his fellows and expressed their appreciation of the lieutenant governor's decisions. They had, he asserted, decided to work only for themselves:

They were determined to work not only to guarantee their own subsistence and the well-being of their families, but also to increase their own wealth because thenceforth they would be sure of benefitting from the fruits of their own labour. None of them would agree to remain one day longer in the service of their masters. (ANG, pièces, rapport politique, May 1909)

They agreed to stay in their villages, to work hard, and to pay taxes. The administration had essentially been called on its promises of the previous year, and the slaves had in essence been given the land they already worked.

The Tubakayes recognized their defeat and left the meeting in silence. The freedmen gathered their wives and children and proceeded to the marketplace, where they held a boisterous celebration. When the administrator submitted his report several weeks later, he indicated that both groups were visibly at work on their lands. For many of the Tubakayes, and for their women and children, it was the first time they had ever actually worked the land. A month later, the administrator wrote that not even 1 percent of their slaves had remained with the Tubakayes — and not a single sharecropping contract had been registered (ibid.). A passing remark also suggests another problem that had not been fully discussed in previous reports. With the situation settled, the administrator wrote in June 1909, he expected no more visits from women seeking children held in servitude. Clearly, one of the crucial issues in Boké, as in many parts of the Soudan, had been former slaves' control of their offspring (ANG, pièces, rapport politique, June 1909).

The Rio Pongo and Mellacorée

In the Rio Pongo and Mellacorée, the period after 1908 also saw significant slave movement, though there was no single confrontation like that which took place in the Rio Nunez. One administrator in Mellacorée even stopped giving certificates of identity in 1908 because he did not approve of the use to which ex-slaves put their liberty (ANS, administrateur 1908). Presumably, they were not working hard enough, though in most areas, former slaves were quite productive. Many slaves were also freed because their masters were hostile to French rule.[5] This had been policy throughout the period of conquest and remained important as the French tried during Ponty's governorship to trim the power of the most important chiefs. More important than such political acts, however, was the steady stream of departures. In Mellacorée, it was happening as early as February 1908:

> The natives complain often of the flight of their servants, but it is incontestable that this sort of desertion would be more rare if masters treated their people with more kindness, if they secured for them more well-being and if they did not consider them beasts of burden. (ANG, rapport politique, April 1908)

By April 1908, the administrator felt that the disappearance of slavery was imminent (ibid.). In the Rio Pongo, the administrator reluctantly began freeing slaves in 1909 without demanding any payment:

> Despite the discretion with which I greet the claims of numerous servants who have been coming for a while to demand their liberty, and in conformity with policies set by higher authority which is legitimately concerned not to spread trouble in the land by mass liberations, I have been forced during the month

5. On the case of Ibrahima el Koundetou, all of whose slaves were freed in 1907, see ANG, Pièces périodiques 1907. On Almamy Theory from the Rio Pongo, see ANG, pièces périodiques 1908.

of July to tell about 20 natives, who have come one by one to ask for their freedom, that they have the right to work for themselves. (ANG, rapports politiques et commerciaux, 1909)

Many of them came from the estates of old slaving families like the Turpins and the Curtises. In some cases, the first freed slaves returned to the slave villages to encourage others to go. The administrator tried to suppress such agitation, but he probably lacked the personnel to do so effectively. The same administrator promised an amelioration of working conditions to some Turpin slaves, but this did not prevent their leaving (ibid.). In April 1910, the administrator wrote that several hundred had freed themselves in the previous year, but that there were still several thousand living under control of their masters in the Rio Pongo (ANG, rapports périodiques 1909–1911).

In Mellacorée, the proximity of the Sierra Leone border tended to undercut the control of the slave masters (ANG, rapports, lettres 1908). Despite the ease of escape, Mellacorée saw a particularly intense effort by a local administrator to impose sharecropping contracts. The contract he first proposed had to be rewritten by higher authority because he simply put into the contract the existing obligations of the slaves (ANG, correspondance, lieutenant gouverneur, 28 June 1912). Nevertheless, by 1912 there were over 500 people under contract (ANG, monographie, Forécariah 1912). It is not likely that the contracts lasted long or had any significant effect on social relationships. Perhaps more important in the long run was the tendency of former slaves to move out of villages to homesteads on the lands they farmed. This was a change that undermined an already weak local authority (ANG, rapport politique 1912).

Conclusion

Events in the Rio Nunez did not take place in isolation. Elsewhere in Africa, large numbers of ex-slaves were returning to previous homes, establishing new communities, or changing relationships with former masters. Events in the Rio Nunez probably speeded up the process on the coast. In a sense, conflicts like that in the Rio Nunez were inevitable. Local political interests and conservative values influenced local administrators to tolerate slavery, but senior figures in the colonial administration were aware both that slavery could compromise the colonial enterprise in the eyes of the French public and that economic growth demanded mobility of labor.

Moreover, it was the slaves who saw the breakdown of the old system and forced the issue. The crisis came first to those societies that were harshest and most exploitative. These systems depended increasingly on coercion as the desire for profit pushed slave owners to intensify systems of production by increasing hours of work and supervision, cutting back on feeding, and reducing time available for the slaves' own work. This happened in the Americas and it happened in Africa among groups like the Maraka and Jaxanke, who were involved in the production of commodities for market. The struggle of the slaves here, as elsewhere in the world, was a struggle both for control of their own labor and control of their family life. The masters could have maintained some control over labor only if they could have controlled the land. The slaves in the Rio Nunez benefitted from both the availability of free land and the fact that the administrator wanted them to stay in the cercle. Thus, they ended up keeping the lands they were already working. This was not true everywhere. In other areas, the shortage of land meant a much more intense struggle over a longer period of time. Another important factor throughout Guinea as in the Soudan was that in the harsher systems, slaves tended to live in separate villages. Here they developed their own leadership and established a de facto social autonomy. They were more likely to act than the slaves who lived within the masters' compound.

That leaves us with one other question: what were the effects of the liberation of slaves on the Guinea coast? In the absence of fieldwork and of good sociohistorical work on the coast in the twentieth century, any generalizations must be limited. The Guinea coast was in decline when the Rio Nunez rising took place, not because of social conflict but because the colonial policy of forcing trade into the new capital of Conakry hurt the commerce of the older coastal ports (Goerg 1980). It is interesting that peanut production increased sharply in the years just before the First World War (Suret-Canale 1960). This was probably a result of increased work by the freedmen. Nevertheless, peanut exports disappeared after the war when the Guinea coast turned increasingly to the production of bananas. We do not know much about the organization of work among the freed communities or about the relations of production. We do not know whether links were maintained between the freed slaves and their former masters. There is clearly no evidence of any subsequent exploitation of the labor of the former slaves. Most of the labor for the banana plantations came from areas in the interior (Fall 1986). I would guess that links between the former slaves and the Tubakayes were minimal, largely because the hostility ran so deep. Writing just after the war, Paul Marty suggested that those Jaxanke who remained in Boké ran Koranic schools. In some areas, clerical elites like the Jaxanke were able to use Islam to develop more subtle forms of hegemony, but Marty's brief remark raises questions rather than giving answers (Marty 1921: 146). The interwar period saw the emergence of a new group, the colonial chiefs, many of whom exploited their position in the colonial state to develop plantations (Suret-Canale 1966). They probably depended less on traditional forms of servility than on labor dues from the whole of the peasantry. It is clear that the first Tubakaye response to emancipation was the use of family labor. It is also clear that many remained in the area, but we do not know if they maintained any further relationship with their former slaves. In one crucial way, the Guinea coast differs from other parts of Guinea. While slavery seems to have virtually disappeared along the coast, slave questions remained important elsewhere. Suret-Canale (1966) argues that slave labor was still being systematically exploited in the Futa Jalon up to 1956. On the Guinea coast, the issue seems to have died, presumably because it was resolved to the satisfaction of the slaves themselves.

REFERENCES

Archival sources

ANG: Archives nationales de la Guinée, Conakry.
Administrateur, Boké, au lieutenant gouverneur, 3 November 1902. 2 D 32.
Administrateur, Rio Pongo, au lieutenant gouverneur, 13 October 1902. 2 D 13.
Arrêté de Gouverneur Tautain, 22 October 1902. 1 A 16.
Circulaires, lieutenant gouverneur, Guinea, 1901–1912. 2 A 4.
Circulaires, lieutenant gouverneur, Guinea, 1911–1914. 2 A 12.
Correspondance, Boké, 1906–1908. 2 D 33.
   Rapport politique, January 1908.
Correspondance, Boké, 1907–1909. 2 D 34.
   Administrateur au procureur, 25 February 1907.
   Administrateur au lieutenant gouverneur, 28 February 1907.
   Administrateur au lieutenant gouverneur, 22 March 1907.
   Administrateur au lieutenant gouverneur, 6 April 1907.
Correspondance, gouverneur-général, 1908. 11 B 48.
Correspondance, lieutenant gouverneur, 1912. Lieutenant gouverneur au Mellacorée, 28 June 1912. 2 B 65.
Correspondances et monographie, Rio Pongo, 1876–1908. 1 D 43.
Journal de poste, Boké, 1908. 2 D 36.
Journal de poste, Timbo, 1902–1905. 1 D 47.
Monographie, Forécariah, 1912. 1 D 14.
Monographie, Rio Nunez, by J. Figarol, 1912. 1 D 42.
Pièces périodiques, Boké, 1909. 2 D 37.
   Administrateur au lieutenant gouverneur, 13 April 1909.

Rapport politique, 8 March 1909.

Rapport politique, May 1909.

Rapport politique, June 1909.

Pièces périodiques, Mellacorée, 1907. 2 D 94.

Pièces périodiques, Rio Pongo, 1908. 2 D 15.

Rapport politique, Rio Pongo, September 1912. 2 D 19.

Rapports, lettres, affaires diverses, Mellacorée, 1908. 2 D 95.

Rapport politique, February 1908.

Rapport politique, April 1908.

Rapports périodiques divers, Rio Pongo, 1909–1911. 2 D 242.

Rapports politiques et commerciaux, etc., Rio Pongo, 1909. 2 D 239.

ANF-SOM: Archives nationales de la France, Section Outre-Mer, Paris.

Lieutenant gouverneur, Guinea, au ministre de colonies, 24 September 1902. Guinée XIV 3.

ANS: Archives nationales du Sénégal, Dakar.

Administrateur, Mellacorée, au lieutenant gouverneur, 3 January 1908. 2 G 7/12.

Correspondance, Boké, 1868. 7 G 7.

Enquête sur l'esclavage, 1904, Guinea. K 20.

Ponty au Lieutenant Gouverneur C. Guy, 26 September 1911. 7 G 63.

Other sources

Arcin, A. 1911. *Histoire de la Guinée française.* Paris: Challamel.

Brooks, G. 1970. *Yankee traders, old coasters, and African middlemen: a history of American legitimate trade with West Africa in the nineteenth century.* Boston: Boston University Press.

Brooks, G. 1975. Peanuts and colonialism. Consequences of the commercialization of peanuts in West Africa 1830–70. *Journal of African History* 16: 29–54.

Brooks, G. 1983. A Nhara of the Guinea-Bissau region: Mae Aurelia Correia. In *Women and Slavery in Africa,* ed. C. Robertson and M. Klein, 295–319. Madison: University of Wisconsin Press.

Curtin, P. 1971. Pre-colonial trading networks and traders: the Diakhanké. In *The development of indigenous trade and markets in West Africa,* ed. Claude Meillassoux, 228–39. London: Oxford.

Fall, B. 1986. Economie de plantation et main-d'oeuvre forcée en Guinee française, 1920–1946. Paper presented to Ninth International Economic History Congress, Berne, Switzerland, August.

Goerg, O. 1980. La destruction d'un reseau d'échange précolonial: l'exemple de la Guinée. *Journal of African History* 21: 467–84.

Goerg, O. 1981. Echanges, reseaux, marchés. L'impact colonial en Guinée, XIXe–1913. Unpublished thesis, Université de Paris–VII.

Goerg, O. 1985. Deux modalités d'adaptation à l'abolition de la traite atlantique: le Rio Nunez et le Rio Pongo (actuelle Guinée). Paper presented to Colloque international sur la Traite des Noirs, Nantes, July.

Goerg, O. 1986. Commerce et colonisation en Guinée 1850–1913. Paris: Harmattan.

Journal officiel de la Guinée. 1906. Circular of 24 January 1906 proclaiming law on slavery of 12 December 1905.

Klein, M. 1983. From slave to sharecropper: an effort at controlled social change in the French Soudan. *Itinerario* 8: 102–15.

Klein, M. A. 1987. The demography of slavery in the Western Soudan during the late 19th century. In *African population and capitalism: historical perspectives*, ed. J. Gregory and D. Cordell, 50–61. Boulder: Westview.

Klein, M., and P. Lovejoy. 1979. Slavery in West Africa. In *The uncommon market: essays in the economic history of the Atlantic slave trade*, ed. H. A. Gemery and J. S. Hogendorn, 181–212. New York: Academic Press.

Klein, M., and R. Roberts. 1980. The Banamba slave exodus of 1905 and the decline of slavery in the Western Sudan. *Journal of African History* 21: 375–94.

Lovejoy, P. E., ed. 1981. *The ideology of slavery in Africa.* Beverly Hills: Sage.

Marty, P. 1921. *L'Islam en Guinée.* Paris: Leroux.

McGowan, W. 1981. Fula resistance to French expansion into Futa Jallon. *Journal of African History* 22: 245–62.

Mouser, B. 1983. Women slavers of Guinea-Conakry. In *Women and Slavery in Africa*, ed. C. Robertson and M. Klein, 320–39. Madison: University of Wisconsin Press.

Rivière, C. 1971. Les bénéficiaires du commerce dans la Guinée précoloniale et coloniale. *Bulletin de l'Institut fondamentale d'Afrique noire* 33: 257–84.

Renault, F. 1971. L'abolition de l'esclavage au Sénégal: l'attitude de l'administration française (1848–1905). *Revue français de l'Histoire d'outre-mer* 59: 5–81.

Roberts, R. 1987. *Warriors, slaves, and merchants: the state and the economy of the Middle Niger Valley, c. 1700–1914.* Stanford: Stanford University Press.

Sanneh, L. 1976. Slavery, Islam and the Jakhanke people of West Africa. *Africa* 46.

Sanneh, L. 1979. *The Jakhanke.* London: International African Institute.

Schnapper, B. 1961. *La politique et le commerce français dans le Golfe de Guinée de 1838 à 1871.* Paris: Mouton.

Suret-Canale, J. 1960. L'économie de traite en Afrique noire sous Domination française (1900–1914). *Recherches africaines* 2: 3–39.

Suret-Canale, J. 1966. La fin de la chefferie en Guinée. *Journal of African History* 7: 459–93. Translated into English in *Perspectives on the African past*, ed. M. Klein and G. W. Johnson, Boston: Little, Brown, 1972.

Suret-Canale, J. 1970a. *La République de Guinée.* Paris: Editions Sociales.

Suret-Canale, J. 1970b. Touba in Guinea—holy place of Islam. In *African Perspectives*, ed. C. Allen and R. W. Johnson, 53–81. Cambridge: Cambridge University Press.

Suret-Canale, J. 1971. *French colonialism in tropical Africa 1900–1945.* Translated from the French. New York: Pica.

7 *Allen Isaacman and Anton Rosenthal*

Slaves, Soldiers, and Police: Power and Dependency among the Chikunda of Mozambique, ca. 1825–1920

The Zambezi Valley of Mozambique was the site of extensive social turbulence for over three centuries as it witnessed the uneven imposition of colonial rule, the relentless penetration of merchant capital through the ivory trade, and the establishment of various forms of slave relations. In this whirlwind of rapidly acquired fortunes, famines, war, and mass migrations, relations of power emerged and distintegrated virtually overnight. At the center of these changes were the Chikunda, an ambiguous group of slaves who shifted their social status with the prevailing winds but were able to carve out their essential economic niche repeatedly as armed laborers, from which they had been born centuries ago. It was the very ambiguity in their slave position, so unlike chattel slavery, which provided them with the flexibility to weather the changes of the early colonial era.

Their history offers an occasion to examine the fluctuating nature of power, freedom, and dependency in the unstable world of the Zambezi.

Research for this project was funded through a grant from the Graduate School of the University of Minnesota and the National Endowment of the Humanities. The authors would like to thank Kings Phiri for access to oral interviews, Joseph Gutsa and John Peter Tembo, who collected some of the oral data, and Barbara Isaacman, Paul Lovejoy, Russ Menard, George Roberts, and Stuart Schwartz for their criticism of an earlier draft of this chapter.

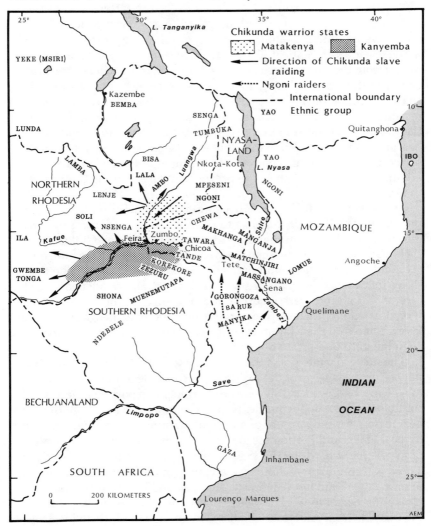

Map 7. South-Central Africa

As slaves who performed military functions they enjoyed power, mobility, and autonomy. In this respect their situation was similar to that of slave-soldiers in other parts of the world who enjoyed considerable power and yet remained slaves.[1]

1. Although we have treated the Chikunda primarily as military slaves, two qualifica-

Drawn from a variety of ethnic groups outside the region, the Chikunda were fashioned into an elite corps of slaves by Portuguese settlers in the seventeenth century. These settlers had ventured hundreds of miles inland from the Indian Ocean coast to lay claim to Crown estates (*prazos*) on the southern bank of the Zambezi River (Isaacman 1972a; Newitt 1973). In the absence of an effective colonial army, the estate-owners (*prazeiros*) recruited their own slave armies, whose primary function was to protect the prazos from invasion and to extract tribute and labor from the free peasantry (*colonos*). While the Chikunda themselves did not farm, they served the prazeiros as members of hunting and trading caravans, thus adding to the production of the prazos while performing their military function.

As the world of the Zambezi became engulfed in the social turbulence precipitated by the early nineteenth-century slave trade and as the prazos disintegrated under internal and external pressures, the Chikunda shed their slave status and pursued a variety of strategies to maximize their economic opportunities and ensure their physical security. The former slaves followed three paths of survival: some attained independence before abolition and were incorporated into surrounding societies; some served as clients for newly emerging merchants-turned-warlords; and lastly, some sold their labor as police and mercenaries to the expanding colonial state and estate-owners.

The survival strategies of the Chikunda were tied to the rapidly changing political economy of the region. By the middle of the nineteenth century, ivory had replaced slaves as the principal export commodity. This shift created new opportunities for freedmen who remained in the Zambezi region, forming groups of autonomous hunters or selling their labor to local chiefs and Portuguese and Afro-Asian merchants. The depletion of the elephant herds by the 1880s, however, left them with few options. Those working for merchants were transformed from elephant hunters to slave raiders and formed the nucleus of emerging warlord armies. Other Chikunda began to work as police and militia in the service of the Portuguese. Their military skills and fierce reputation made them ideal agents for the colonial state, which was anxious to impose its hegemony in the face of British threats to annex the region.

This chapter traces the social and economic development of the Chi-

---

tions are necessary. First, they performed other tasks as well, most notably hunting and portering. Some also worked as gunsmiths, ironworkers, and blacksmiths. Second, because of the highly decentralized and fluid context in which they lived, they did not develop into the self-generating professional regiments of soldiers occupying high status and power which characterized the classic form of military slaves found in the Islamic world. For discussion of military slaves see Paterson 1982: 299–334; Pipes 1981; Buckley 1979.

kunda and their transformation in the course of the nineteenth century from slaves to freedmen. We argue that their somewhat contradictory position as military slaves shaped a process of emancipation which was quite distinct from those in other parts of Africa. On the one hand, the estate-holders could ill afford to free the Chikunda without jeopardizing their own power and class position. On the other, the well-armed Chikunda had the means to escape slavery, and many did so in the decades preceding the formal abolition decree of 1878. In particular, we examine the changing nature of their labor organization and the ambiguities and complexities in their relationships of subordination to a variety of "masters." We contend that the formal juridical distinction between slaves and freedmen masks the structural similarities in the actual working conditions of the Chikunda slaves on the prazos and their various descendants, who as merchants, hunters, warriors, and police transformed Zambezia in the nineteenth and early twentieth centuries. Thus, their shifting legal status is less significant than the critical but changing role they played in the region's political economy for over three centuries.

Chikunda on the Prazos in the Early Nineteenth Century

From their inception, the Chikunda constituted the key element in the success of the prazos and in the establishment of a Portuguese economic presence in the Mozambican hinterland. As a condition of the land grant, the Portuguese Crown imposed obligations on the prazeiros which were more properly state functions and which the prazeiros in turn entrusted to their Chikunda slaves. Among these were the collection of tribute, which the peasants were required to pay in agricultural produce, cloth, gold, and ivory; the administration of justice; the preservation of peace within the prazos; and the maintenance of defense against external enemies.[2] Since the Portuguese themselves were ill-equipped to exert a military presence in the interior in times of national emergency, the Chikunda served as state militia. Throughout the eighteenth and the first half of the nineteenth century, the number of Portuguese soldiers stationed in the Zambezi usually ranged from 100 to 300. According to state officials, this was less than one-third of the minimum required to provide even a modicum of defense and stability. Most of these Portuguese soldiers were poorly armed, poorly organized, and poorly trained. Many were ex-convicts, debtors, and vagrants anxious to improve their lot, and willing to abuse their power to do so (see, for example, AHU, Carrazedo 1836).

2. Isaacman 1972b. See also, AHU, Lacerda e Almeida, n.d.; AHU, Carrazedo 1836; BPA, Alves Barbosa, analyse, 1821.

By contrast, the Chikunda were a well-organized military force, quite able to carry out the directives of the prazeiros and to protect the estates from external enemies. Totalling 20,000–30,000 at the beginning of the nineteenth century, the Chikunda numbered from a few dozen to several hundred on a single prazo.[3] While the prazos extended for hundreds of miles along the Zambezi, from the coast to Tete, the Chikunda shared a common military organization throughout the region. On every prazo they were divided into a number of permanent regiments, known as *butaka*, with fixed residences separate from those of the colonos. Each butaka was headed by a slave chief, known as the *mukazambo*, whom the estate-holder selected for his demonstrated loyalty, military prowess, and ability to command the respect and obedience of his Chikunda subordinates. In return the mukazambo received wives, cloth, imported trade goods, choice land, and guns — a portion of which he redistributed to his subordinates. Many slave chiefs were even permitted to acquire captives of their own, thus creating the paradoxical situation of slaves owning slaves. Next in this military hierarchy were lieutenants, or *chuanga*, who provided intelligence for the slave chiefs and who were primarily responsible for tax collection. These were in turn followed by *sachikunda*, who directed *nsakas*, groups of 10–12 male slaves and their families (Isaacman 1972b: 452–55; Newitt 1973: 187–99).

Because the Chikunda lived in separate villages, strategically scattered throughout the vast expanse of the prazos, the slaves remained physically isolated from the indigenous population. Over time they developed their own social identity, network of kinship relations, and new cultural forms. The Chikunda forged a distinct set of rituals, dances, and religious ceremonies surrounding hunting and warfare. These involved the propitiation of ancestor spirits (*muzimu*) and lion spirits (*mhondoro*). But above all else, it was their role as the military arm of the prazeiros which set the Chikunda off from the peasants. They were deployed throughout the estates to punish disobedient colonos, crush periodic revolts, and prevent peasant flight. In the course of preserving the social dominance of the prazeiros, they also raided the colonos for food, slaves, and women.[4]

Besides fulfilling this police function, the Chikunda also engaged in a range of economic activities which contributed to the profitability of the prazos and eventually enabled them to serve as the point men of Por-

3. ANTT, Pinto de Miranda, "Memória," 1760; Truão 1889. These figures included the small number of slaves who performed domestic and agricultural labor for the estate-holders and probably the families of the Chikunda.

4. Coutinho 1904: 191–92; Weise 1983: 56–57; interviews, 1974: Tiyago Matega; Maliko Mpuka et al.; Lacerda e Almeida 1938: 63; interviews, 1968: Luís Gonzaga Cebola; Andisseni Tesoura.

tuguese merchant capital. Sometimes numbering into the hundreds, caravans of slave warriors, porters, and hunters ranged from the Lunda kingdom of Kazembe in the north to the Shona kingdoms of Manyika and the Muenemutapa in the south. As Indian and American markets for ivory expanded in the nineteenth century, Chikunda hunters and porters became increasingly important in the Portuguese mercantile sphere. Whether armed with half-moon scimitars or European guns, their daring and skill in stalking their prey made the Chikunda the most successful elephant hunters in South-Central Africa. These warrior-hunters were highly celebrated in song, and they created their own esprit de corps and identity which further set them apart from agricultural peoples (interview: Maliko Mpuka et al., 1974).

Despite this degree of mobility and power, the Chikunda, like other slaves, were seen as commodities who served the class interests of their owners. Most were purchased in the interior or at slave auctions in the towns of Tete or Sena. Others were captured in warfare and raiding. Some became slaves "voluntarily," seeking an escape from famine, war, or social ostracism. This change in status was accomplished through the ritual of breaking the *mitete*, the symbolic act of destroying an object of limited value which belonged to the prazeiro. This ritual prohibited the new master from selling his slave.

Whatever their origin, their juridical status was never in doubt. "The Chikunda are our slaves," wrote one Zambezi inhabitant in the middle of the eighteenth century (ANTT, Pinto de Miranda, "Memória," 1760). A contemporary acknowledged that the "respect and power of the estate-holders rests . . . on their slaves under the direction of a slave chief known as the [mukazambo] and a second in command called the [sachikunda]" (AHU, Jesús 1752). Their legal position and internal organization remained unchanged 80 years later (Gamitto 1960, 1: 36).

As slaves the Chikunda were unable to choose their occupation or employer, to dispose of their property, or to protect themselves or their families from physical abuse by their masters. Commenting on the notorious excesses of many prazeiros, one eighteenth-century traveller noted, "Few are those who act within the judicious limitations of propriety" (Lacerda e Almeida 1938: 105). The Chikunda were thus both objects of domination and the means by which the prazeiros dominated the peasantry. Their position was permanent and hereditary, since their owners could not afford to manumit them without undermining their own power.

On the other hand, the Chikunda enjoyed a powerful position and under certain conditions could effectively negotiate their status with the prazeiro. Their bargaining power was enhanced when the prazeiro's position was threatened by peasant uprisings or external attacks or when the estate passed from one owner to another.

An heir often had great difficulty establishing control over the slaves he inherited but even more difficult was the task of a senhor, newly granted a prazo and with slaves of his own, who found the territory in the possession of the slaves of his predecessor. . . . Either he would have to come to terms with their leaders or reduce them by other means. (Newitt 1973: 192–93)

Led by their slave chiefs, the Chikunda periodically engaged in open rebellion against prazeiros who either abused their position or abdicated their authority (Isaacman 1972b: 457–58). One eighteenth-century estateholder complained, "A prazeiro cannot give a single negro of the slave regiments away without the others all mutinying" (AHU, Jesús 1752). Equally important, their military might enabled them to liberate themselves.

The Chikunda also enjoyed a fair degree of physical mobility which could be converted into political and economic freedom. Chikunda raiding parties and caravans were somewhat autonomous and on occasion disappeared into the interior with the prazeiro's goods.[5] Similarly, porters deserted caravans and returned to their home villages if labor conditions were too demanding (ibid.). Competition between prazeiros enabled those Chikunda who were more tied to the prazo itself to attach themselves to less abusive owners (AHU, Diniz 1790). In other cases the Chikunda extricated themselves from the prazo system altogether by seeking sanctuary among neighboring chiefs or by running off into the interior and forming *musitu*, roughly equivalent to the Brazilian *quilombos*, or self-sufficient, fugitive slave communities.[6]

Other slaves on the prazos enjoyed neither the potential power of the Chikunda nor their mobility. Although the documentation is fragmentary, most prazeiros employed a retinue of household slaves to meet their domestic needs (Gamitto 1859: 397–400). Some also used captives to cultivate their fields. The state's failure to transform the prazos into plantations and the predominance of peasant agriculture suggest that the number of field hands was extremely limited. In addition to slaves belong-

5. ANTT, Aboime 1779; AHU, Ribeiro do Castro 1799; AHU, Ferrão, 20 December 1828.
    6. In the 1750s slave flight had become such a serious problem that rival estate-holders joined together to mount major campaigns against both the Manganja and Chewa chieftaincies, who were suspected of harboring runaways. Despite these punitive raids, flight continued, and in 1803 the Portuguese government sent a formal delegation to Lundu, the senior Manganja chief, demanding that his subjects return the runaways (AHU, Pereira 1756; Newitt 1973: 202).

ing to the prazeiros, an indeterminant number of land chiefs (*amambo;* sing. *mambo*), village headmen (*afumu;* sing. *mfumu*), and prosperous peasants owned slaves (*akaporo;* sing. *kaporo*), who worked in their gardens and performed a variety of household tasks. Over time, they and their descendants were often incorporated into their owners' kinship groups. For the akaporo, unlike the Chikunda, the prospect of manumission, if not power, was thus real (Isaacman and Isaacman 1977).

In the first half of the nineteenth century, the world of the prazos was torn apart. Three factors combined to intensify Chikunda flight and rebellion and thereby dismantled the support structure of the prazos by the 1840s.

First, there was a dramatic increase in the export of slaves from Mozambique to Brazil and subsequently to Cuba and the French islands of the Indian Ocean. Whereas fewer than 1,500 captives were exported from the Zambezi in 1806, by 1820 their number had increased fivefold (Isaacman 1972a: 88). During the next two decades approximately 15,000 slaves per year were exported from Quelimane (Gamitto 1859: 369–72, 397–400; Vail and White 1980a: 22). Unable to acquire sufficient numbers of captives in the interior, short-sighted prazeiros resorted first to selling peasants living on their estates and then to exporting Chikunda slaves. In the process they violated the custom of mitete, lost the source of their own power, and precipitated large-scale Chikunda insurrections and flight. By 1830 a senior Portuguese official concluded that slave revolts and famine had left ". . . their district in the most deplorable state of misery" (AHU, Mendes de Vasconcellos e Cirne 1830). His words were echoed by David Livingstone (1858: 630–31), who surveyed the area in the 1850s: "When the slave trade began, it seemed to many of the merchants a more speedy mode of becoming rich, to sell off the slaves, . . . and they continued to export them until they had neither hands nor labor to fight for them. It was just the story of the goose and the golden egg." The second factor in the demise of the prazos was a series of droughts and locust infestations. This led to a further decline in agricultural production and left the vulnerable Chikunda, who were dependent on peasant produce, to fend for themselves (AHU, Ferrão, 28 October 1828). The final calamity was the invasion of the Barue and Ngoni between 1826 and 1840 (Isaacman 1972a: 119–20), whose armies destabilized the entire region, leading to the near total collapse of the prazo system.[7]

7. In the Sena-Tete region there were only about 20 prazos still functioning in the middle of the century. Most were a pale copy of their predecessors. Prazo Cheringoma, for example, estimated to have 6,000 slaves in 1750, had only 50 in 1856 (ANTT, Pinto de Miranda, "Memória," 1760; Ministério da Marinha e Ultramar 1897: 38).

The Portuguese administration unsuccessfully attempted to reverse this decay and to stimulate free peasant production through legislation aimed at restraining the slave trade and restructuring the prazo system. As early as 1825, Governor General Botelho had publicly condemned the slave trade and warned that it would destroy Mozambique's economy (Botelho 1835). A decade later, the reformist Portuguese prime minister Sa da Bandeira promulgated a decree abolishing the slave trade in the Portuguese territories. He predicted that the successful implementation of the law would foster "a love of agricultural and industrial labor, creating among individuals the necessities of a civilised life which will bring them to acquire through their own labor the means to satisfy their own new necessities" (quoted in Newitt 1981: 21). In an effort to remedy past abuses the governor general of Mozambique declared in 1847 "the immediate and unconditional emancipation of all peasants illegally enslaved by the estateowners."[8] In the 1850s, a series of decrees was enacted with the goal of abolishing slavery in all Portuguese territories. The decree of 14 December 1854 created the status of *liberto,* a "freedman" with the obligation to continue working without pay for a specified period. In 1858, it was proclaimed that slavery would be abolished in 20 years. At about the same time Lisbon outlawed the French *engagé* system, which siphoned off thousands of Mozambican conscripts each year for work on the sugar plantations of Reunion under the guise of free contract labor. Legal abolition of slavery finally took place in 1878.

In the Zambezi Valley, these decrees had little impact. With the cooperation of high government officials, slave-trading at the Quelimane markets and coastal baracoons boomed. One British naval commander in charge of an anti-slave-trade patrol in the Mozambique Channel noted with disgust that "it appears, that any number of slaves may be obtained and shipped from Quelimane itself within a few hours notice, and that the Governor had been in the habit of receiving fixed bribes from the slave dealers, whose launches are always ready to start the moment a ship makes her private signal" (Barnard 1848: 37). On the eve of the 1858 abolition pronouncement, more than 6,200 slaves were sent as engagés to work on the sugar plantations of Reunion (Gamitto 1859: 398). Moreover, the recurring Ngoni attacks had reduced the Portuguese inland presence to a handful of prazos and two small garrisons, which were so weak that they actually paid tribute to Ngoni chiefs to avoid annihilation and could not enforce colonial decrees.

Within this unstable environment, the Chikunda ex-slaves had taken advantage of the changing political and economic landscape to free them-

8. AHU, Fortunato de Valle 1847. See also AHU, Teixeira 1847.

selves long before the process of legal abolition had even begun. Some formed autonomous hunting communities. Others regrouped in the interior and ultimately spearheaded the enslavement of other peoples during the decades on either side of official abolition, making a mockery of Portugal's proclaimed control of the Mozambican interior. In effect, the Chikunda acted and would continue to act without reference to the decrees promulgated in Lisbon.

Freedom before Abolition, ca. 1850–1877

The rapid disintegration of the prazos left many Chikunda without masters, but also without access to food, a ready supply of arms, or a secure base of operations. Within this whirlwind, they followed several paths to survival, some leading to cultural disappearance and some to fame and wealth.

First, unattached individuals attempted to return to the societies of their birth. For most, this was a difficult venture. Many had been acquired hundreds of miles away by caravans or had been raised on the prazos as Chikunda, losing their former ethnic ties. An 1856 list of 659 ex-slaves indicates that they came from such distant peoples as the Bisa, Nsenga, Yao, and Lomue (AHM, registo dos libertos 1856). Even for those individuals enslaved near to their villages, returning home alone was dangerous, and there was no certainty that they would find their families, since many had fled to avoid famines and enslavement.[9]

Other Chikunda, unable to return to their natal societies, nevertheless elected to leave the area of the prazos altogether. Individuals, families, and small bands sought sanctuary among the indigenous chieftaincies located along the margins of the Zambezi River and its hinterland. Like many runaway slaves before them, these Chikunda found it expedient to seek refuge among the Manganja, Chewa, Tawara, Nsenga, Gwembe Tonga, and Korekore, who made up the wider Zambezi community. Individuals were often absorbed by these groups, but autonomous bands of 5–10 men, probably the remnants of Chikunda butaka, retained their corporate identity. They established temporary hunting camps and entered into trading relationships with their hosts (interview: Luís Francisco Kaitano, 1972).

9. In addition, groups of ex-slaves opted to join the forces of disorder and formed marauding bands which plundered peasants living on the old prazo lands. Not much is known of these bandits, some of whom were reenslaved by the conquest states of Massangano, Makhanga (Makanga), and Matchinjiri (Massingire), whose history falls outside the scope of this chapter. For a discussion of these states see Isaacman 1972a: 124–54; and Newitt 1973: 234–95.

The remainder of the Chikunda stayed in the area near the Portuguese communities at Tete and Sena, selling their services as gold miners, coal diggers, ironsmiths, masons, firewood hawkers, porters, canoemen, and, above all, hunters and soldiers to Tete merchants eager to open up new areas of trade in the interior. As the prazeiros had pushed back the frontiers of trade and settlement, mestizo merchant families of African, Portuguese, and Goan descent had established themselves at these garrison towns. Now they sought the services of experienced Chikunda soldiers and hunters in their quest for slaves, territory, and ivory.

By the middle of the nineteenth century, ivory had replaced slaves as the principal export and source of profits for Zambezi traders. Whereas ivory exported from the Zambezi amounted to only 5 percent of total trade value in 1821, about 50,000 pounds (ca. U.S. $120,000), by 1865 the volume of exports had jumped to over 161,000 pounds (ca. U.S. $775,000) (AHM, relatório do governo 1866). One colonial official noted, "Ivory is the most important export commodity in the colony" (AHU, Tavares de Almeida 1863). For the merchants of Tete it was the only commodity. In 1867, over 95 percent of the total value of exports was derived from the sale of ivory (Sousa e Silva 1927: 55). Under the pressure of American and Indian demand, the price of ivory on the international market skyrocketed.

Whatever path the ex-slaves pursued, ivory became the key element in the survival of a distinct Chikunda identity, which extended throughout the Zambezi. It provided the economic basis of a unique but temporary autonomy in the history of Chikunda relations with the merchant and landholding community of the interior. This window of freedom between the eras of slavery and state-sanctioned forced labor gave many Chikunda the opportunity to forge their own destiny.

With ivory at the center of a developing Chikunda economy, great prestige was accorded to all those connected with the caravans. Hunters and the warriors who protected the expeditions were celebrated in songs and stories, and even today village elders trace their ancestry to these men rather than to peasants.

> I have shot the elephant
> There it is on the bank of the river
> I have shot it, there follow the vultures
> I have shot the man, there he is
> I have shot him
> There he is on the bank of the river
> I have broken the world
> There follow the vultures
>   (interview: Tiyago Matega, 1974)

Hunting and military prowess were also surrounded by ritual, including ceremonial dances and the preparation of special medicines to ensure success; these rituals became a cornerstone of Chikunda religious practices (Livingstone and Livingstone 1865: 57; Weise 1983: 56; Coutinho 1904: 191–92).

Chikunda hunters had two options in the postprazo period. They could work for the merchant families of Tete and Sena. They could hunt independently, entering into exchange agreements with local chiefs. While the latter path often brought them prestige in a large community, the former held out the possibility of wealth and greater freedom.

Initially, free Chikunda bands relocated in the Chewa and Manganja areas immediately adjacent to the prazos. These areas had traditionally been zones of sanctuary and important hunting regions. These Chikunda brought gifts of ivory and old guns which they had stolen from their former masters (Phiri 1975: 61). The Chewa and Manganja chiefs were quick to appreciate the value of the skills which these refugees could bring to their villages, and they therefore made concerted efforts to incorporate them into their societies or to make political, military, and economic alliances with them. As expert hunters of elephant and buffalo the Chikunda provided ivory and meat, which the local peoples and their chiefs much appreciated during chronic periods of famine.[10] In addition, the Chikunda made use of their prazo experience as warriors. They instructed the Chewa in the manufacture of guns and ammunition, which they made from worn-out iron hoes (interview: Sambane Mwale et al., 1973). More important, the Chikunda served as an effective shield against Yao and Ngoni incursions (interview: Leonese Chikuse Mwake and Kafandiye Chipwata Nkoma, 1974).

Because of the limited numbers of Chikunda in these bands, the caravans they organized initially tended to be quite small and faced strong competition from other inland traders, particularly the Yao and the Swahili.[11] However, they did receive help from Chewa chiefs, who invested in their caravans and on occasion provided conscript porters.[12] Given such support, it is not surprising that some of these former slaves became quite successful merchants. Some Chikunda entrepreneurs subsequently acquired their own slaves to transport their ivory.[13] One reason behind

10. Interviews: Josiaya Chitseka Phiri et al., 1974: Mabalame Mwale et al., 1974; N. P. Mbewe et al., 1973.

11. Interviews: Zephaniya Mwale and Chatsalira Banda, 1973; N. P. Mbewe et al., 1973; Josiya Chitseka Phiri et al., 1974.

12. Interviews, 1973: Lukiya Chiwanga Phiri; N. P. Mbewe et al.; Zephaniya Mwale and Chatsalira Banda.

13. Interviews: Mkota Nkhoma Zakaliya; N. P. Mbewe et al., 1973; Zephaniya Mwale and Chatsalira Banda.

the success of such independent hunters was their ability to bypass Portuguese and Indian middlemen by bringing the ivory to entrepôts as diverse as Quelimane and Nkota-Kota, thus receiving as much as 25 percent more of the selling price (AHU, Custódio Silva 1860).

The main drawback to this relatively autonomous life was a lack of security. Under conditions of intense competition, the small Chikunda caravans were no match for the better capitalized Yao and Swahili traders, who, together with Ngoni, were liable to attack the Chikunda, seize their ivory, and reenslave them. (Weise 1983: 57) As elephant herds were decimated, these Chikunda bands were forced to move to new areas, build new encampments, and create new agreements with local chiefs and merchants. Their activity extended over a vast area from the Luangwa Valley to the forest regions adjacent to the Zambezi and Kafue rivers, coming into contact with the Tande, Tawara, Gwembe Tonga, Lenje, Soli, Ambo, and Lala chieftaincies, many of whom had previously been outside the circuit of merchant capital. As long as they were willing to acknowledge the local land chiefs' authority, their reputation as skilled hunters, traders, and ironworkers made the Chikunda welcome.[14] Their skills with firearms also enabled them to defend their host communities and to aid local chiefs against internal opponents. In the middle of the nineteenth century, Chikunda musketeers were instrumental in turning back Ndebele raids against the Gwembe Tonga chiefs and helped the Korekore against Zezuru rivals (interview: Luís Francisco Kaitano, 1972; Matthews 1981: 29–32).

While many Chikunda were absorbed into the local society, other bands became the nucleus for large Chikunda villages scattered along the elephant frontier. By the 1870s, such communities ranged from the islands in the middle Zambezi to the northern regions of the Luangwa Valley (Weise 1983: 95; Matthews 1981: 32).

The second option for the liberated slaves was to work for merchant families based in Tete or Sena. The skyrocketing demand for ivory, the depletion of elephant herds in the immediate Sena and Tete environs, and the failure of the merchants to lure Yao and Bisa ivory caravans all enhanced the bargaining position of the Chikunda. Based on a mixture of freedom and mutual obligation which is best described as "clientage," the ex-slaves negotiated a new work relationship with the merchants. They were often referred to as *moleques*, which connotes a servant, rather than as *escravos*, or "slaves." Although many of these traders still owned

14. Matthews 1981: 29–33; interviews, 1974: White Mbuluma; Tiyago Matega. See also Isaacman and Rosenthal 1984: 641–45; Stefaniszyn and de Santana 1960; interview: Luís Francisco Kaitano, 1972; Weise 1983: 95.

slaves, they acknowledged the relative autonomy of these freedmen. "I am not the master of the mentioned Blacks," conceded a leading merchant in 1861.[15]

These Chikunda enjoyed far greater economic and physical mobility than they had had as slaves on the prazos. Their expertise as boatmen and hunters allowed them to secure wages which were appreciably higher than those paid to other free Africans. Laborers in the 1860s earned 16 yards of calico cloth per month; expert hunters commanded several times that amount. In addition merchants paid Chikunda bonuses to ensure prompt delivery of ivory (Weise 1983: 56; interviews, 1968: Alface Pangacha; José António). Moreover, there was plenty of opportunity for the Chikunda to make their own deals. As one merchant bitterly noted: "The hunters have returned and they brought back one ivory tusk. Something is not right here . . . [in light of] the great quantity of gunpowder they used" (Pacheco 1980: 60). Some Chikunda bands deserted in the interior and worked for themselves.

> Kabendeza is one of the many hunters who, having received goods from those who patronize them, settle down in the presence of some chief; forms with his consent a village and later a stockade, gather around themselves more hunters and other people; and finally sell to the Arabs the ivory they get from hunting, without ever giving news of themselves to the person who supplied them with the capital. (Weise 1983: 263)

Most Chikunda, however, remained dependent on their merchant employers, who provided them with food, clothing, and protection, as well as guns, and bought their elephant tusks. In the final analysis they had little legal recourse if the politically connected merchants reenslaved them.

This dependency became even more pronounced as the Chikunda hunters followed Tete merchants to Zumbo in search of elephant herds. The history of an independent Chikunda presence at Zumbo begins around 1860, with the arrival from Tete of a small band of Chikunda elephant hunters, perhaps numbering between 100 and 200, under the leadership of an Afro-Portuguese trader known as Emmanuel José Anselmo de Santana, or Chikwasha.[16] The increased world demand for ivory

---

15. Pacheco 1980, 2: 7. The free status of these hunters and the payment which they received in cloth, guns, and ammunition are recalled in a number of oral traditions as well (interviews, 1968: Zacarias Ferrão; Alface Pangacha; José António). Several Sena and Tete merchants also used slaves to hunt elephants, especially in the transition period before abolition (Livingstone and Livingstone 1865: 51).

16. Interview: Tiyago Matega, 1974; Stefaniszyn and de Santana 1960: 363; Isaacman and Rosenthal 1984: 648–52.

had led to intense competition at Tete, with a consequent depletion of supply. Chikwasha's band was initially welcomed by the Nsenga and their chief, the Mburuma, the owner of the lands around Zumbo, who gave them permission to hunt in the region in exchange for the tusk falling closest to the ground of each elephant they killed. The hunters themselves received some of the profits from this productivity, enabling them and their families to dress differently from and to live appreciably better than the local Zumbo population (interview: Tiyago Matega, 1974). Chikwasha's Chikunda were also welcomed by the Nsenga because of their trading connections and access to highly prized cloth and other imported commodities, the supply of which had been largely cut off since the Ngoni depredations and the destruction of the fair at Zumbo in the 1830s. Chikwasha's Chikunda now assured the Nsenga of a share of hunting products and a regular supply of trade goods. In addition, Chikunda blacksmiths brought to Zumbo by Chikwasha traded high quality hoes and axes to the Nsenga, destroying local industry in the process (interview: Mwandenga and Chief Mwanvi, 1974).

Because of a fortuitous conjunction of political events, Chikwasha was given a plot of land by the Mburuma at Feira, just across the Luangwa River from Zumbo at the confluence of the Zambezi River. This served as a base for the expansion of trading operations and the addition of an agricultural component to the Chikunda economy, because the peasants living there now owed Chikwasha tribute in crops, which he collected through Chikunda chuangas or in labor.[17]

By the time of Chikwasha's death in 1868 several other Afro-Portuguese merchants had permanently relocated in the Zumbo region and had built up a large Chikunda following. Like Chikwasha, their main concern was the ivory trade. They acquired slaves on a relatively small scale from the Nsenga and Chewa and exchanged them for elephant tusks in the Shona areas to the south, where the population had been depleted by Ndebele slave-raiding (Pacheco 1980: 60). As ivory began to diminish in this region over the next decade and as slave-trading evolved into slave-raiding, new types of Chikunda entities emerged — the conquest states. These were led by mestizo merchants-turned-warlords, who commanded hundreds and sometimes thousands of Chikunda warriors. The most powerful of these warlords were Kanyemba and Matakenya, who dominated the region near Zumbo for nearly three decades. During this period their slave raids produced thousands of captives for the Indian Ocean plantation system.

17. Interviews, 1974: Maliko Mpuka et al.; Gwashelo Chimbuya et al.; Moses Mwatigola et al.

Abolition: From Ivory Hunters to Slavers and *Sepais*, 1878–1920

The intensive slaving of Zumbo warlords openly defied Lisbon's 1878 abolition decree, rendering it meaningless in the Mozambican interior. Captives were still covertly exported throughout the Indian Ocean Basin under the guise of engagés to work on the French plantations of Reunion, Comoros, Mayote, and Nossi Be. Others ended up in Madagascar (Vail and White 1980: 86). In the 1880s the governor general of Mozambique admitted that between 2,000 and 4,000 people were exported annually and the internal slave trade was growing (ibid.: 87). Some slaves were also bought to work on the newly organized Portuguese oil seed plantations located around Ibo, Angoche, and Mozambique Island in the northern part of the colony. Others were exchanged for ivory in the Zumbo hinterland or imported for the conquest states of Massangano, Makhanga, and Matchinjiri, which dominated the northern bank of the Zambezi from the Shire to Tete. Contemporaries estimated that together the three states had more than 20,000 slaves.[18]

Moreover, state officials were profoundly ambivalent about abolition. In 1881, under French pressure, Lisbon again permitted the forced recruitment of captives for the engagé system (Vail and White 1980a: 84). In the Zambezi region, colonial authorities, including the governor of Tete, continued to cooperate openly with the Zumbo merchant warlords. This assistance was spurred on by the decline of ivory supplies, which encouraged Kanyemba and Matakenya to convert their Chikunda hunters into mercenaries and slave-raiders (Isaacman and Rosenthal 1984: 650–51).

When he [Kanyemba] makes an attack upon a tribe, he goes through certain forms. He sends a letter down to the Governor of Tete complaining of the injury done to Portuguese traders, and Portuguese subjects by a certain tribe and asks for a permis de guerrao license to make war upon them in order to chastize them for their insolence. As far as I can learn, I do not think he finds much difficulty in getting this license granted. (Selous 1970: 299)

Thus, with state sanction and often with government-supplied weapons, these warlords raided for slaves throughout the Luangwa Valley, exporting many captives and retaining some for their own use as agricultural laborers.[19]

The predatory nature of these slave-raiding states heightened the in-

18. AHU, Silva 1869; AHM, Sousa Nunes de Andrade 1885; AHM, Augusto, n.d.

19. Interviews, 1974: Maliko Mpuka et al.; Moses Mwatigola et al.; Tiyago Matega; Sharpe 1890: 746; Selous 1970: 298.

creasingly antagonistic relationship between the warlords and their Chikunda followers. The tension was due in large measure to the ill-defined status of the ex-slaves, the cruel treatment they received at the hands of Kanyemba and Matakenya, and their ultimately contradictory roles as producers of slaves and as local police. Their ambiguous status was affected by the different ways in which they had become attached to the warlords. At one extreme were the individual ex-slaves and the autonomous Chikunda bands whose members had lived as free hunters after the demise of the prazos. These freedmen initially constituted the core of the emerging conquest states (interviews, 1974: Tiyago Matega; Gwashelo Chimbuya et al.; Kamowa). At the other extreme were those captives incorporated into the ranks of these Chikunda. The many victims of hunger and internal violence who sought sanctuary and were willing to exchange their labor for food and protection fell somewhere between.

Since they had been incorporated into these conquest states as captives, refugees, and even as autonomous bands of hunters, the Chikunda were neither slave nor free, but all except the most powerful and privileged Chikunda chiefs were subject to the brutal behavior of their leaders, who used fear as a powerful mechanism of social control.

Kanyemba castrated men who broke the rules of the country and warriors who never fought well in battle. He cut women's breasts off and sometimes those who offended him had their ears and eyes cut out. . . . Warriors were thrown into the Zambesi River tied to huge stones, at a place called Kibira near the present *boma* of Feira. (interview: Maliko Mpuka et al., 1974)

Furthermore, the long-term interests of the warriors did not always match those of the warlords. As the military arm of the warlords their principal task was to maintain order and to quash dissidents. As raiders they were to produce slaves but were generally prohibited from claiming any of the captives as wives. Since the Chikunda lived in segregated villages and intermarriage with the local population was rare, they could acquire spouses only by either covertly withholding a portion of the slaves they captured in state operations or engaging in unauthorized raids on the subject population. Both placed them at odds with the warlords, who considered the captives to be state bounty and feared that uncontrolled warriors preying upon the local population would only serve to heighten opposition to their rule. Limiting the ability of the Chikunda to acquire slaves, necessary for their own social reproduction, further increased their dissatisfaction. At several critical junctures Chikunda defected en masse or rose up against the warlords.[20]

20. Mesquita e Solla 1907: 348, 438; interview: Gwashelo Chimbuya et al., 1974.

Their options, however, were severely narrowed because of the British efforts to secure the area adjacent to Zumbo, which also threatened Portuguese claims to the Zambezi region. In response to this Lisbon sought to recolonize this region by transforming the prazos into profitable agricultural estates and to subjugate the autonomous states headed by the Afro-Portuguese warlords.

To shore up its frail position the Portuguese colonial state began in earnest to rent out abandoned prazos. By 1875, 25 had been rented in the Sena region, and by 1900, more than 150 had been leased throughout the Zambezi, some to companies and some to individuals (Freire de Andrade 1949: 248–50). But legal possession was not the same as actual possession. The latter required the new prazeiros to establish their authority over peasants residing on the estates, some of which had been abandoned for over 50 years. Force was necessary to regain the land and establish even a modicum of authority.

The new prazeiros turned to the Chikunda ex-slaves living in the Tete-Sena region, many of whom were finding it increasingly difficult to earn a living, since elephant herds as far west as Zumbo had been depleted. "Thousands of native hunters still leave Tete every year with their flintlocks and spears and go very far afield in search of the much coveted animal," noted one British explorer in 1883. "Success in hunting," he continued, "is slight and year by year the results are diminishing" (Kerr 1886: 47). Five years later Carlos Weise, a prominent Tete merchant and estateholder, observed that "there were many examples [traders and hunters] who stood good chances only to lose everything to the last penny" (Weise 1983: 55). As the century closed, ivory exports plummetted, and by 1908 they were less than 500 pounds.[21]

In the changing political economy of the Zambezi these Chikunda hunters had few options. Their contempt for farming made that an unattractive alternative except under the most dire circumstances. Portering was another possibility, but wages were low and working conditions extremely difficult and hazardous (Coutinho 1904: 194). On the other hand, Chikunda military skills and their fierce reputation made them ideal agents for the reestablishment of prazeiro authority.

Many Chikunda hunters were thus converted to sepais,[22] the military

21. Silva 1909: 52. To make matters worse, in 1907 the colonial state imposed an elephant-hunting tax plus a fee for a license (Ribeiro 1909: 501–2).

22. The term *sepais* is a corruption of the English term *sepoys*. It refers to Indian soldiers recruited into the British army. The Portuguese began bringing their own sepais from Goa to Mozambique as early as the eighteenth century. Ultimately, the term was used to refer to African police and soldiers in the service of the Portuguese. "Cypais" is an alternative spelling.

and police power of the new prazos.[23] Initially, individuals and small groups of ex-slaves negotiated informal agreements with the new estate-holders. Traditions in the Sena region recount how two prazeiros, Gambete and Dona Inez, each hired between 50 and 100 Chikunda who had formerly hunted in the Gorongoza forests and the Dlabinyini marshes. They were paid in cloth and alcohol in addition to receiving arms, ammunition, and a promise of land for their families. With this show of force, the two estate-holders were able to convince the indigenous land chiefs and their subjects to recognize their respective suzerainties, in return for protection against the Ngoni and Barue raiders.[24] To the north in the Tete District, prazeiro José de Miguel Lobo had to hire 600 Chikunda hunters as sepais in 1885 to compel chief Boroma to acknowledge the estate-holder's right to his land (AHM, Lobo 1885).

The relationship between the new prazeiros and the Chikunda ex-hunters was initially negotiated on an ad hoc basis, and it was later formalized under the prazos reforms of 1890 and 1892 as well as subsequent legislation. Article 10 of an 1890 decree which established guidelines for transforming the prazos authorized the prazeiro to raise a designated number of sepais to assist in fulfilling his police and judicial functions (Ministério da Marinha e Ultramar 1897: 93). Most estates were authorized to hire between 60 and 250 sepais, a force sufficient to keep order but not large enough to pose a threat to the colonial regime. The actual figure seems to have been roughly proportional to the size of the peasant population living on the estates. Thus, Prazo Macuse with an adult population of 12,500 had 250 sepais, and Prazo Nameduro had 100 sepais to supervise 4,500 peasants. Prazos Tangalane and Cherinngone, with a quarter the number of peasants, were authorized to have only 25 (ibid.: 138–44). Strategically important estates or those where the peasants had a long history of insurgency could raise a larger contingent.[25] The 1890 decree also exempted the sepais from the head tax and from forced-labor requirements. Subsequent legislation guaranteed them a modest wage when they provided specific services for the state.[26]

23. AHM, Lobo 1885; AHM, Costa 1892; Weise 1983: 41; Coutinho 1904: 191–92.

24. Interviews, 1968: Alface Pangacha; Donna Anna Mascalenha; António Vaz; Chale Penga and Tomás Chambe; Tomás Chave and Oliveira Sinto.

25. AHM, Texeira de Souza 1893; AHM, Carreira to Zambézia 1894; AHM, Coutinho, relatório, 1897.

26. Sepais, in the service of the state received 30 reis (ca. U.S. 3¢) in peacetime and 45 when they fought in military campaigns (Botelho 1936, 2: 120). (The conversion of reis and milreis to U.S. currency was based on equivalent rates found in A. H. de Oliveira Marques, *Historia de la Republica Portuguesa* (Lisbon: Iniciativas Editoriais, 1978); M. Halpern Pereira, *Livre cambio e disenvolvimento economico Portugal na segunda metade do século XIX* (Lisbon: Ediçoés cosmos, 1971); I. R. Butts, *The Business Man's Adviser*

In addition to Chikunda hunters, the other significant source of sepais was the Chikunda who had continued to reside on several of the larger prazos. These prazos had survived the years of turmoil with their slave armies intact. After the abolition decree of 1878 their Chikunda regiments were transformed en masse into sepais under their traditional military and religious leaders (Coutinho 1904: 191–94).

Despite Lisbon's desire to transform the prazos into large, modern plantations, the underfinanced companies or individual lessees generally opted to re-create the old tributary relations which had existed on the prazos decades earlier.[27] Thus, within this precapitalist context the sepais of the post-"scramble" era essentially played the same role as had their Chikunda predecessors.

Like their slave counterparts on the old prazos, the sepais were employed to collect taxes, enforce the prazeiros' commercial monopoly, quash peasant opposition, and contain flight. To maximize control of the peasants many prazeiros revived the old slave institution of the chuanga, or village overseers. They appointed their most trusted sepais to perform the task.[28] This system of absentee administration led to serious abuses; one estate-holder lamented:

. . . [The] chuanga has been imposed who previously could not sit in the presence of the chief [because of his slave background] but who now torments his authority by giving orders in the name of his master. The chuanga asks everything of the chief and forcibly takes what is denied him. The chuanga employs all the excesses expected from a person of such low origin. (Weise 1983: 89)

A local official complained to the governor of Tete that throughout the district the chuanga had usurped so much authority "that they have become petty tyrants" (AHM, Fonseca de Mesquita e Solla 1889).

Of all the police functions which the sepais performed, tax collection, which produced the principal source of wealth, was the single most important. Although the 1890 decree specified that the tax was to be paid

---

(London: I. R. Butts, 1856); R. Chalmers, *A History of Currency in the British Colonies* London: Eyre and Spottiswoode, n.d.).

27. To be sure, there were exceptions such as Sena Sugar Estates, the Bororo and Madal copra plantations, and the coastal sisal plantations, but these were few and limited primarily to the Quelimane District. On these plantations sepais served primarily as labor recruiters and to control workers living in the compounds (Vail and White 1980a: 220–23). In the zone stretching from Sena to Zumbo, which is the principal focus of this chapter, the low rainfall and speculative interests of the lessees precluded the growth of a plantation economy.

28. Interviews, 1968: Gaspar Cardoso; Aleixo José; Andisseni Tesoura; Dauce Angolete Gogodo; José António de Abreu; Marco Coutinho; António Vaz.

in currency and labor, most estate-holders were content to extract whatever commodities they could. They often imposed rates that were two or four times the legal amount and ordered the police to beat and arrest those peasants who were either unwilling or unable to pay.[29] The sepais also tracked down colonos who tried to flee (ibid.; AHM, Priau 1898). "The renters of the prazos, without inconvenience or expenses, obtained, through the collection of the mussoco [tax], fabulous profits at a minimum expense," noted one Quelimane state official in 1888. "As a result there is no necessity for them to develop agriculture or industry" (Amorim 1888). His words were echoed over the next three decades by frustrated colonial officials and critics in Portugal.[30]

According to the 1912 revenue figures from the 119 prazos in the Tete District, sepais officially collected approximately 150,000 milreis (ca. U.S. $150,000) in taxes, of which approximately a quarter went to the colonial state (Carrilho 1913: 12). These taxes represented more than double the value of exports from the Tete District, leading the governor of Tete to condemn the prazeiros as nothing but "tax parasites" (ibid.: 7).

Just as the sepais carried out many of the functions of the old Chikunda, so too their living and working conditions bore striking similarity to those of their predecessors. Although legally free, the sepais remained subject to the capricious behavior of their prazeiros, who set the terms of their employment. The prazeiros generally recruited whom they wanted, arbitrarily deciding on the length and conditions of service. Descendants of sepais recall how their relatives were publicly flogged and their salaries and food allowances withheld for failing to carry out their masters' orders (interviews, 1968: Domingo Fernandes; José da Costa Xavier). Such abuses sparked sepai opposition and occasional uprisings.[31] Furthermore, while the sepais were legally free and could, at least theoretically, sell their labor, it is unclear whether those Chikunda who were still slaves in 1878 had any alternative to being conscripted into the prazeiros' police force following abolition (Coutinho 1904: 191–93). The famines and political instability in the region as well as the continued covert trade in slaves also make it probable that a number of sepais were forcibly recruited. Among the sepais who helped Dona Inez and Gambete impose their hegemony over Prazos Chemba and Caya, for example, were ex-colonial soldiers from Angola. Labelled as vagrants, they had been

29. Carrilho 1913: 13; Weise 1983: 52–53; interviews, 1968: Andisseni Tesoura; António Vaz; Gente Renço and Quembo Pangacha.
30. Carrilho 1913: 7–18; Vilhena 1910; 539; Ulrich 1910: 382–89; Alvares 1916.
31. AHM, Carreira to Zambézia 1894; AHM, Costa 1892; AHM, Coutinho, relatório, 1897; Xavier 1889: 29–32.

pressed into the Portuguese army and sent to Tete, from whence they escaped and were subsequently recruited by the estate-holders.[32] In the most flagrant violation of the abolition decree, the prazeiro Gouveia swelled the ranks of his hunter mercenaries with slaves captured in warfare. By the 1880s, he had acquired a sepai force estimated to be more than 10,000 strong.[33]

Their status as wage laborers was equally ambiguous and, at least in the first instance, varied from one estate to another. To recruit mercenaries most estate-owners had to pay some wages, although it was not initially required by the 1890 legislation. On Prazo Anguase, for example, this amounted to 30 reis (ca. U.S. 3¢) a day in 1894; the owner of Bororo paid his police an equivalent amount in cloth.[34] The fact of the matter is that such wages were totally insufficient for the sepais and their families, even allowing for their exemption from taxes. Thirty reis a day bought three-eighths of a liter of rice in 1894 and appreciably less a decade later. By comparison, African carpenters earned as much as 600 reis a day (ca. 60¢), stone masons upwards of 400 (ca. 40¢), and cooks about 300 (ca. 30¢). Even lowly house servants and porters earned double the minimum paid to sepais (Pimenta 1909: 68).

Estate-owners were able to offer such minimal salaries because they gave the sepais license to plunder the peasants. Village elders recall how the chuanga and the sepais took everything of value, from chickens and grain to homespun cloth and women.[35] Contemporary Portuguese accounts confirm that looting was a way of life on the prazos. Writing at the turn of the century, one Portuguese official noted approvingly that being a sepai offered the "opportunity to become a rich and respected man, with many wives and slaves . . ." (Coutinho 1904: 194). Moreover, particularly effective chuanga and sepais were often appointed to replace insurgent local chiefs.[36] In short, the wealth and power of the

32. Interviews, 1968: António Vaz; Alface Pangacha; Joint interview: Chale Penga and Tomás Chambe. For a discussion of the forced recruitment of vagrants in Angola, see Botelho 1936, 2: 71–99; Martins 1936: passim.

33. In the period from 1870 until his death in 1892, Gouveia put together an armed force of several thousand with which he gained control over a number of prazos in the Sena hinterland, drove the Ngoni out of the Zambezi, and, temporarily, established informal control over the Barue (AHU, Paço de Arco 1881; interviews, 1968: João Pomba; Gimo Tito; Newitt 1973: 313–40).

34. AHM, Moura, inspecção, 1894; AHM, Carreira to Zambézia 1894.

35. Interviews, 1968: Gaspar Cardoso; José da Costa Xavier; Marco Coutinho; Gimo Tito; João Pomba; Andisseni Tesoura; Alface Pangacha. See also, Weise 1983: 52–54; Xavier 1889: 33; Carrilho 1913: 18.

36. Interview: Domingo Fernandes, 1968; AHM, Jones da Silveira, relatório, 1943.

sepais, like that of their predecessors, depended upon the appropriation of peasant production. It is little wonder that both were feared and
despised.

One important distinction, however, which existed between the sepais
and their predecessors was their mode of social organization. Unlike the
Chikunda, who lived in segregated villages and created a network of social relations which linked them to other members of their regime, the
sepais were dispersed among the indigenous population, with whom they
intermarried. Their physical and social mobility as well as their desire
to shed their identity as descendants of slaves enabled many to blend into
the local population gradually. At times, sepais of Chikunda descent
merged with Chikunda who were not sepais and other strangers to form
a number of hybrid ethnic groups such as the Nhungue (see Isaacman
1972b: 443–44; Santos 1944).

In addition to their role on the prazos, many sepais also played a critical role as shock troops in the service of the colonial regime. Under the
1892 legislation, the sepais were designated as standing militia under the
ultimate authority of the military commander of the region. They were
to undergo regular military training and could be mobilized in times of
national emergency. In a clause which reflected their ambiguous social
and legal relationship to the estate-holder, the state agreed to reduce the
rent which the prazeiro paid by a fixed sum for each of his sepais killed
in battle (Ministério da Marinha e Ultramar 1897: 118–20).

There were several reasons why the state created a black militia in
the 1890s to establish control over the interior. First, it had a successful
precedent. Dating back to the seventeenth century, Chikunda on loan
to the state had helped the ragged army maintain a minimal colonial
presence in the Zambezi. Second, the sepais were immune to malaria,
which ravaged the European forces. Third, unlike the colonial soldiers,
they were familiar with the local terrain. But most important, Lisbon
was already engaged in military campaigns in the more strategic southern zones, as well as against the Muslim sultanates in the north and also
in Angola and Portuguese Guinea. These wars stretched the military
capacity of the metropole to the breaking point.

This military use of manumitted slaves was not unique. The British
in the West Indies, the Germans in Cameroon, and the French in Senegal
relied to varying degrees on the recruitment of ex-captives into their colonial armies (Pipes 1981: 35–44; Buckley 1979: passim). In Mozambique
the sepais constituted the bulk of Lisbon's army, and they "pacified" the
Zambezi region. In Zambezia, the colonial force which defeated Massangano in 1888, for example, had more than 3,500 sepais and only a

handful of regular troops, and 1,900 sepais with fewer than 100 European soldiers put down the Cambuemba tax revolt in 1897 (Castilho 1891: 61–76; AHM, Coutinho, relatório, 1897). The colonial state relied heavily on the sepais against the powerful kingdom of the Barue, which had defied the Portuguese for 400 years and threatened their tenuous hold on the Zambezi. To the delight of the commander, the sepais "fought valiantly never ceasing to advance in the face of enemy fire" and were instrumental in defeating the Barue (Coutinho 1904: 577). As a reward, they were allowed to plunder enemy villages and carry home a number of women and children.

The division among the Chikunda descendants became most apparent in the wars of subjugation, which often pitted ex-slaves against each other. Unlike the sepais, many of the Chikunda living in the Zumbo interior, either in autonomous bands or under the mestizo warlords, had maintained their ethnic identity and sense of community. As hunters and slavers on the frontier they were unwilling to recognize the legitimacy of Portuguese rule. Despite their fundamentally antagonistic relationship with the warlords and periodic uprisings, most eventually found themselves fighting under the mestizo-slavers in opposition to sepai armies of the expanding colonial state (Isaacman and Rosenthal 1984: 669–70).

Initially, Lisbon had tried to co-opt the most powerful of the mestizo warlords, Kanyemba and Matakenya, by transforming them and their Chikunda into imperial agents serving the metropole. Both were awarded the prestigious title of *capitão môr*, as well as land grants to legitimate their claims to territory which they had already conquered. The colonial government also allowed them to continue to trade in slaves. However, by the time of the "scramble," Lisbon had come to realize that the personal power of the warlords and their Chikunda followers "constituted a source of instability and a roadblock to increased Portuguese prestige in the region" (Mesquita e Solla 1907: 356). War became inevitable, and during the 1890s, a large military force of sepais and regulars, backed by the most sophisticated weapons in the Portuguese arsenal, laid siege to the Zumbo hinterland. Matakenya was the first victim. Squeezed between the Portuguese and the British, he and his Chikunda followers tried to forge an antiimperialist alliance. He drew together loyalist Chikunda forces, plus a small number of Nsenga, Chewa, and Tawara chieftaincies and several other minor warlords, all of whom shared a common commitment to retain their autonomy. With Matakenya's death in 1893 the coalition fell apart and was conquered, and over the next decade Lisbon unleashed its forces against Kanyemba and a number of autonomous

Chikunda communities located between Chicoa and Zumbo (Isaacman 1976: 22–39; Newitt 1973: 295–312).

Many of the defeated Chikunda were disarmed and absorbed into the new prazo system as peasants (AHM, "Usos e costumes indigenas," n.d.; Ribeiro 1907: 297–307). They were subject to the same extortions and abuses at the hands of the prazeiros and their sepais as were the surrounding peasants who were incorporated into the estates. Other Chikunda fled across the border into Northern or Southern Rhodesia, where they regrouped into distinct Chikunda communities, some of which were governed by the heirs of Chikwasha, Matakenya, and Kanyemba. A 1913 Northern Rhodesian census of the Feira District, just opposite Zumbo, indicated that more than 2,500 Chikunda resided there (NAZ, Feira notebook: 245). Some hunted while others worked as canoemen and porters. Most had no alternative but to farm (ibid.: 378).

It is interesting to note that when the Barue rose up against the Portuguese in 1917 a number of Chikunda on both sides of the border joined the insurrection. They were instrumental in driving the Portuguese from Zumbo. Ultimately, they found themselves fighting against the sepais recruited from the Zambezi prazos, who continued to play a critical military role during the first two decades of this century.[37]

Despite the colonial state's dependence on the sepais and the perpetual shortage of European soldiers, the Chikunda-turned-sepais never formed a permanent contingent in the Portuguese army. Unlike the *tirailleurs* of French West Africa, they remained reserves. Two factors contributed to this anomaly. On the one hand, Portuguese colonial officials, operating under notions of biological determinism, believed that the Ngoni rather than the Chikunda possessed the appropriate physical prowess and love of war to be the military arm of the state (Martins 1936: 39; Xavier 1889: 23; Albuquerque 1913: 231–32). "The Landeens [Ngoni]," wrote Governor Albuquerque (1913: 231–32), "have enormous physical capacity which comes from the long hours which they devote to their war dances, and without a doubt of all the blacks they are the ones who exhibit the greatest military instinct." "By comparison," noted one of Albuquerque's contemporaries, "the Negros of the Zambesi lack the warrior quality . . . of the Landins. . . . 250 landins from Inhambane directed by a dozen Europeans . . . could conquer all of the Zambesi" (Xavier 1889: 32). From the point of view of the Chikunda descendants, on the other hand, the low pay and the policy of sending African soldiers to other parts of the colony and even to such remote areas as Macau and

37. ZNA, Powley 1918; ZNA, Molyneux 1917; NAZ, Feira notebook: 210; interview: Jili Mpuka et al., 1973.

Portuguese Guinea were prime deterrents to enlisting as regulars. Those who did serve were usually conscripted.[38]

In the newly formed colonial administration of the 1900s, a relatively small number of sepais did become state police, performing tasks similar to those of their counterparts on the prazos. They supervised tax collection, recruited military conscripts and corvée labor for state projects, and helped to quell peasant insurrections.[39] In 1912 a battalion of Tete sepais was organized to prevent peasants from fleeing to neighboring Southern Rhodesia, where taxes were lower and wages higher (AHT, Sousa Fernandes 1914). Finally, when the state introduced a forced cotton-growing system in 1916, the sepais brutally coerced peasants into participation and precipitated the 1917 rebellion (AHM, Arriscado Nunes 1917; AHM, Ferreira da Costa 1917). A quarter of a century later, more than three-quarters of a million Mozambican peasants had been converted to bound laborers under the cotton regime (see Isaacman, Stephen, et al. 1980; Vail and White 1980b). The legacy of slavery continued.

Conclusion

As slaves who performed important military functions, the Chikunda enjoyed both power and privilege. However, the issue of their manumission placed them in fundamental opposition to the prazeiros. The estate-owners could ill afford to free the slaves or even relax their grip on them without jeopardizing their own power and class position. Yet the estate-holders lacked an alternative power base to control disgruntled Chikunda, who, therefore, could and did use their military might and physical mobility to free themselves from prazeiro domination. This process of self-liberation began well before the disintegration of the prazos in the 1830s. It was virtually complete by the 1858 announcement heralding the end of slavery 20 years hence.

Thus, for most Chikunda the ending of slavery and their subsequent transformation into freed men and women had little to do with legal changes but were inextricably tied both to the shifting balance of power and changing political economy within the region. In the immediate postabolition period the power of the colonial state to implement anti-slavery legislation was limited. It was, after all, a fragile entity whose viability in the interior depended primarily on the merchants-turned-warlords. State officials were not initially in a position to challenge the

38. Accounts of the dissatisfaction of the African conscripts can be found in Carrilho 1913: 35–37; Weise 1907.

39. ZNA, Kugayisa, n.d.; Carrilho 1913: 17–18, 35–36; Isaacman 1976: 75–145.

slave-trading activities of Kanyemba, Matakenya, and lesser-known Zumbo powers. Only when the ending of slavery became linked to the recolonization of the Zambezi and the dream of an agricultural system based on "free" labor did the colonial state make a serious effort to enforce abolition.

The relatively fluid and unstable conditions within Zambezia also meant that when manumission occurred it was not an irreversible process. Freed men and women were reenslaved and peasants turned into captives. The revival of the engagé system, the growth of slave-based plantations, the continued vitality of the internal slave trade, and the tendency of Gouveia and other new prazeiros to recruit sepais forcibly all contributed to this phenomenon. Indeed, as late as 1917 colonial officials reported isolated cases of peasants being enslaved as sepais on Prazos Tanhame and Chipera in the Tete District (AHM, "Usos e costumes indigenas," n.d.).

Finally, the history of the Chikunda offers an occasion to examine the shifting nature of power and dependency in a precapitalist setting. Although slavery is the most extreme form of domination, we have argued that the juridical dichotomy between captives and freedmen masked the many structural similarities in the working conditions and daily lives of the Chikunda slaves and those of their descendants. A narrow legalistic view would preclude a discussion of differentiation between Chikunda at any historical juncture. Yet, the evidence suggests that the Chikunda chiefs, from those who directed the slaves on the prazos to those who commanded the sepais (Coutinho 1904: 191–94), all had greater access to power and wealth than their subordinates. Over time, the shifting balances of power and dependency which the Chikunda experienced formed a continuum. At one extreme, the disintegration of the prazos and the ivory boom offered many a brief opportunity to negotiate a relatively autonomous and privileged existence. Some freedmen ultimately gained influential political position, accumulated a great deal of capital, and even acquired slaves of their own. They did, however, remain dependent on friendly land chiefs for food, hunting rights, and labor. Other Chikunda entered into a client relationship with the inland merchant community. Although legally free, their position was less well defined than that of their unattached counterparts. In a variety of ways, they also remained dependent on the Portuguese merchants who provided them with arms, supplies, and access to imported commodities. And they had little recourse if the latter tried to reenslave them. On the other hand, they could and did use these arms and trade goods to forge autonomous hunting and commercial enterprises. In doing so, they bypassed their former employers. The Chikunda-warlord relationship was of a different order. It was based on violence and a mutual commitment to slave-raiding. To the extent that the warlords abused their authority, they faced the possibility that their Chikunda subjects might defect or even rebel — which they did at several critical junctures. If we consider the structural significance of their roles and their ambiguous relationship to the estate-owners, the positions of warrior slaves and sepais exhibit the highest degree of congruence.

Both were armed contingents responsible for the extraction of taxes and labor from the peasantry and as such were the cornerstone of prazeiro survival. Whether formally "free" or "slave," the Chikunda and their descendants managed to reproduce their critical political and economic roles and retain a degree of autonomy as the regional political economy underwent extensive transformation. In all the paths which they followed, the real issue was power. And power was not a static element reified in formal legal categories, but was negotiable and changing.

GLOSSARY

baracoon	coastal stockade where slaves were held temporarily prior to exportation.
breaking the *mitete*	ritual of enslavement which established mutual obligation between master and slave.
butaka	permanent Chikunda regiments.
chuanga	slave officials who supervised peasant villages.
colonos	free peasants who lived on the prazos.
engagé	conscripted recruits forced to work on the French Indian Ocean island plantations under the guise of free contract labor.
kaporo (pl. *akaporo*)	slaves owned by chiefs, village headmen, and prosperous peasants.
liberto	a "freedman" with obligation to continue working without pay for a specified period.
mambo (pl. *amambo*)	land chiefs.
mfumu (pl. *afumu*)	village headmen.
mhondoro	royal lion spirits.
mukazambo (pl. *mikazambo*)	slave chiefs.
musambadzi	Chikunda who served as trading specialists.
musitu	fugitive slave communities.
muzimu	ancestor spirits.
nsaka	slave groups of 10–12 under the command of a sachikunda.
prazos	legally defined as Crown estates.

prazeiros   estate-holders.
sachikunda   slave officers in charge of 10–12 Chikunda.
sepais   African police.

REFERENCES

Oral sources

Malawi

Josiaya Chitseka Phiri et al., interview on 15 April 1974 in Chimutu.
Leonose Chikuse Mwale and Kafandiye Chipwata Nkoma, interview on 16 April 1974 in Dowa.
Lukiya Chiwanga Phiri, interview on 27 July 1973 in Chulu.
Mabalame Mwale et al., interview on 20 February 1974 in Karonga.
Mkota Nkhoma Zakaliya, interview on 1 August 1973 in Santhe.
N. P. Mbewe et al., interview on 23–24 September 1973 in Mkande.
Sambane Mwale et al., interview on 8 April 1973 in Dowa.
Zephaniya Mwale and Chatsalira Banda, interview on 24 September 1973 in Dzoole.

Mozambique

Aleixo José, interview on 16 July 1968 in Boroma.
Alface Pangacha, interview on 9 September 1968 in Cheringoma.
Andisseni Tesoura, interview on 8 September 1968 in Cheringoma.
António Vaz, interview on 13 September 1968 in Chemba.
Chale Penga and Tomás Chambe, interview on 7 September 1968 in Cheringoma.
Dauce Angolete Gogodo, interview on 8 September 1968 in Cheringoma.
Domingo Fernandes, interview on 18 October 1968 in Makanga.
Donna Anna Mascalenha, interview on 9 September 1968 in Caya.
Gaspar Cardoso, interviews on 15–18 July 1968 in Boroma.
Gente Renço and Quembo Pangacha, interview on 4 September 1968 in Caya.
Gimo Tito, interview on 9 August 1968 in Sena.
João Pomba, interview on 31 August 1968 in Caya.
José António, interview on 7 September 1968 in Cheringoma.
José António Abreu, interview on 16 and 22 July 1968 in Tete.
José da Costa Xavier, interview on 22 July 1968 in Tete.
Luís Gonzaga Cebola, interview on 18 July 1968 in Boroma.
Marco Coutinho, interview on 23 July 1968 in Degue.
Tomás Chave and Oliveira Sinto, interview on 14 August 1968 in Chemba.
Zacarias Ferrão, interview on 4 September 1968 in Caya.

Zambia

Gwashelo Chimbuya et al., interview on 21 July 1974 in Feira.

Jili Mpuka et al., interview on 13 December 1973 in Zavendo.
Kamowa, interview on 22 January 1974 in Kamowa.
Maliko Mpuka et al., interview on 19 July 1974 in Kamowa.
Moses Mwatigola et al., interview on 23 July 1974 in Feira.
Mwandenga and Chief Mwanvi, interview on 26 March 1974 in Kabulungu.
Tiyago Matega, interview on 18 February 1974 in Chausa.
White Mbuluma, interview on 21 March 1974 in Feira.

Zimbabwe

Luís Francisco Kaitano, interview on 22 September 1972 in Guta.

Archival sources

AHM: Arquivo histórico de Moçambique, Maputo.
Arriscado Nunes, João Luíz, Alferes, 7 October 1917. Negócios Indigenas, Cx.132, Processo 55.
Augusto, Frederico, to governador dos Rios de Sena, n.d. Fundo do Século XIX, Quelimane, Governo do Distrito, Cx.5.
Carreira, José Silvestre, to governador da Zambézia, 4 September 1894. Fundo do Século XIX, Quelimane, Governo do Distrito, Cx.45.
Costa, Eustácio da, to governador do distrito de Tete, 6 September 1892. Fundo do Século XIX, Governo do Distrito de Tete, Cx.107.
Coutinho, J. Relatório da Campanha na Zambézia contra o Cambeumba, 20 September 1897. Fundo do Século XIX, Cx.4-175, M.2.
Ferreira da Costa, Silvinho, to governador do territorio da Companhia de Moçambique, 4 December 1917. Negócios Indigenas, Cx.132, Processo 55.
Fonseca de Mesquita e Solla, Augusto da, 7 April 1889. Fundo do Século XIX, Tete, Governo Geral, Cx.38.
Jones da Silveira, Carlos Henriques. Relatório e documentos referentes a inspecção ordinária feita na província de Niassa, la parte, 1943. Secção Reserva, Inspecção dos Servicos Administrativos e dos Negócios Indigenas, Cx.99.
Lobo, José de Miguel, to governador do distrito de Tete, 23 July 1885. Fundo do Século XIX, Governo do Distrito de Tete, Cx.24.
Moura, Gorjão de. Inspecção dos prazos da Coroa, relatório 1894. Fundo do Século XIX, Quelimane, Prazos da Corôa, Cx.5(2).
Priau, José Adolpho, to governador do distrito da Zambézia, 18 May 1898. Fundo do Século XIX, Quelimane, Governo do Distrito, Cx.43(2).
Registo dos libertos do distrito da villa de Tette, 1856. Códice 2-1167, Livro no. 1, fols. 1–59.
Relatório do governo do distrito de Quelimane, 25 January 1866. Códice 1760, fols. 132–33.
Sousa Nunes de Andrade, João de, to Tito Augusto de Araujo Sicard, 5 July 1885. Códice 2-439, Fe 5, fol. 69.
Texeira de Sousa, João António, 15 December 1893. Fundo do Século XIX, Governo Geral, Cx.la.

"Usos e costumes indigenas," n.d., relatório do governador do distrito de Tete, 1917–1918. Administração Civil, Pacote 171, Pasta 900.

AHT: Arquivo histórico de Tete, Tete.

Sousa Fernandes, José Joaquim de,, sargento d'infantária, to commandante do Corpo de Cipaes de Tete, January 1914. Papeis Diversos, Secretária Civil do Distrito de Tete, Ano de 1914, Processo no. 398.

AHU: Arquivo histórico de Ultramarino, Lisbon.

Carrazedo, Izidro Manoel de, 19 March 1836. Códice 1470, fol. 147.

Diniz, Jozé Pedro do, 1 December 1790. Moçambique, Cx.21.

Ferrão, Francisco Henriques, to Sebastião Botelho, 28 October 1828. Moçambique, Maço 3.

Ferrão, Francisco Henrique, 20 December 1828. Códice 1315.

Fortunato de Valle, Domingos, 8 June 1847. Moçambique, Pasta 8.

Jesús, Father Fernando, M.A., 13 April 1752. Moçambique, Cx.3.

Lacerda e Almeida, Francisco José de. Mappa geral da guarnição desta praca e artilhara della Senna, n.d. Cx.34.

Mendes de Vasconcellos e Cirne, Manoel Joaquim, 1830. Códice 1315.

Paço de Arco, Visconde de, to ministro e secretário d'Estado dos Negócios da Marinha e Ultramar, 3 December 1881. Moçambique, Pasta 1, Primeira Repartição.

Perreira, Pedro Jozé, 1 December 1756. Moçambique, Cx.3.

Ribeiro do Castro, Mello, 27 April 1799. Cx.38.

Silva, Custódio José da, to José Maria Pereira Almeida, 15 July 1860. Códice 1462, fol. 42.

Silva, Germano Augusto da, to secretário do governo geral, 10 April 1869. Códice 1453, fol. 89.

Tavares de Almeida, João, to ministro e secretário d'Estado dos Negócios da Marinha e Ultramar, 19 September 1863. Moçambique, Pasta 21.

Texeira, Custodío António, to ministro e secretário dos Negócios da Marinha, 3 April 1847. Moçambique, Pasta 8.

ANTT: Archivo nacional de torre do Tombe, Lisbon.

Aboime, Diogo Guerreis de, 27 August 1779. Ministério do Reino, Maço 604.

Pinto de Miranda, António. "Memória sobre a costa de África," ca. 1760. Ministério do Reino, Maço 604.

BPA: Biblioteca pública de Ajuda, Ajuda.

Alves Barbosa, José Francisco. Analise estatística, 30 December 1821. 51-X-2, No. 3.

NAZ: National Archives of Zambia, Lusaka.

Feira notebook. KSV/4.

ZNA: National Archives of Zimbabwe, Harare.

Kugayisa, statement to S. Marley, n.d. N3/26/2/6/8.

Molyneux, C. F., to district commissioner, Broken Hill, 16 June 1917. A3/18/38/4.

Powley, D. M., native commissioner, to Native Commissioner's Office, 16 March 1918. A3/18/38.

Other sources

Albuquerque, J. M. de. 1913. *Moçambique 1896–98.* Lisbon.

Alvares, P. A. 1916. *O regime dos prazos da corôa da Zambézia.* Lisbon: Tipografico Universal.

Amorim, J. G. de. 1888. Relatório do districto de Quelimane referido ao anno económico de 1887–1888. *Boletim oficial de Moçambique,* 43.

Barnard, R. N. 1848. *Three years cruise in the Mozambique Channel.* London.

Botelho, J. T. 1936. *História militar e política dos Portugueses em Moçambique.* 2 vols. Lisbon: Centro Tipografico Colonial.

Botelho, S. X. 1835. *Memoría estadística sobre os domínios portuguezes na Africa oriental.* Lisbon.

Buckley, R. 1979. *Slaves in red coats.* New Haven: Yale University Press.

Carrilho, J. L. 1913. *Distrito de Tete: relatório do governador 1911–1912.* Lourenço Marques, Moçambique: Imprensa Nacional.

Castilho, A. de. 1891. *Relatório de guerra da Zambézia em 1888.* Lisbon: Imprensa Nacional.

Coutinho, J. de A. 1904. *A campanha de Barue em 1902.* Lisbon: Livraria Ferih.

Coutinho, J. de A. 1941. *Memória de um Velho Marinheiro e Soldado de África.* Lisbon: Livraria Bertrand.

Freire de Andrade, A. A. 1949. *Relatório sobre Moçambique.* Lourenço Marques: Imprensa Nacional.

Gamitto, A. C. P. 1857. Prazos da corôa em Rios de Sena. *Archivo Pittoresco* 1: 60–61, 66–67.

Gamitto, A. C. P. 1859. Escravatura na África oriental. *Archivo Pittoresco* 2: 369–73, 397–400.

Gamitto, A. C. P. 1960. *King Kazembe.* Trans. I. Cunnison. 2 vols. Lisbon.

Isaacman, A. 1972a. *Mozambique: the Africanization of a European institution, the Zambesi prazos, 1750–1902.* Madison: University of Wisconsin Press.

Isaacman, A. 1972b. The origin, formation and early history of the Chikunda of South Central Africa. *Journal of African History* 13: 443–61.

Isaacman, A. 1976. *The tradition of resistance in Mozambique.* Berkeley: University of California Press.

Isaacman, A., and B. Isaacman. 1977. Slavery and social stratification among the Sena of Mozambique. In *Slavery in Africa,* ed. S. Miers and I. Kopytoff, 105–20. Madison: University of Wisconsin Press.

Isaacman, A., and A. Rosenthal. 1984. War, slaves and economy: The late nineteenth-century Chikunda expansion in South-Central Africa. *Cultures et developpement* 16: 639–70.

Isaacman, A., M. Stephen, Y. Adam, M. J. Hanen, E. Macamo, and A. Pililão. 1980. Cotton is the mother of poverty. *International Journal of African Historical Studies* 13: 585–613.

Kerr, M. 1886. *The far interior.* Boston: Houghton Mifflin.

Lacerda e Almeida, F. C. de. 1938. *Travessia de África.* Lisbon: Agencia Geral das Colonias.

Livingstone, C. 1858. *Missionary travels*. New York: Harper.

Livingstone, C., and D. Livingstone. 1865. *Narrative of an expedition to the Zambesi*. New York: Harper.

Martins, A. 1936. *O soldado Africano de Moçambique*. Lisbon: Agencia Geral das Colonias.

Matthews, T. I. 1981. Portuguese, Chikunda and peoples of the Gwembe Valley: the impact of the lower Zambezi complex on southern Zambia. *Journal of African History* 22: 23–42.

Mesquita e Solla, A. de F. 1907. Apontamentos sobre o Zumbo. *Boletim da sociedade de geografia de Lisboa* 25: 247–57, 274–87, 319–27, 340–56, 382–91, 436–56.

Ministério da Marinha e Ultramar. 1897. *Regime dos prazos da corôa: colleção de leis, regulamentos e mais disposições legais promulgados desde 1832 a 1896*. Lisbon: Agencia Geral das Colonias.

Miracle, M. 1962. Aboriginal trade among the Senga and Nsenga of northern Rhodesia. *Ethnology* 1: 212–21.

Montagu, Kerr W. 1886. *The far interior*. London.

Newitt, M. D. D. 1973. *Portuguese settlement on the Zambesi*. New York: Africana Publishing.

Newitt, M. D. D. 1981. *Portugal in Africa*. Harlow, England: Longmans.

Pacheco, A. M. 1980. A voyage from Tete to Zumbo. In *The Shona and the Portuguese*, ed. D. N. Beach and H. de Noronha. Harare, Zimbabwe. Unnumbered, unpublished manuscript.

Paterson, O. 1982. *Slavery and social death*. Cambridge: Harvard University Press.

Phiri, K. 1975. Chewa history in central Malawi and the use of oral traditions, 1600–1920. M.A. thesis, University of Wisconsin, Madison.

Pimenta, F. A. de S. 1909. *Relatório do governador de districto de Tete*. Lourenço Marques: Imprensa Nacional.

Pipes, D. 1981. *Slave soldiers and Islam*. New Haven: Yale University Press.

Ribeiro, S., ed. 1907. *Regimen dos prazos da corôa*. Lourenço Marques.

Ribeiro, S., ed. 1909. *Annuário de Moçambique*. Lourenço Marques.

Santos, J. R. dos, Jr. 1944. *Contribuição para o estudo da Anthropologia de Moçambique: algumas tribos do distrito de Tete*. Lisbon: Tipografia Mendonça.

Selous, F. C. 1970. *A hunter's wanderings in Africa*. Bulawayo, Zimbabwe: Books of Rhodesia.

Sharpe, A. 1890. A journey from Lake Nyasa to the great Luangwa and the upper Zambesi River. *Proceedings of the Royal Geographical Society* 12: 746.

Silva, F. A. de. 1909. *Distrito de Tete: Relatório do governador 1908–1909*. Lourenço Marques.

Sousa e Silva, P. A. de. 1927. *Distrito de Tete*. Lisbon: Livraria Portugalia Editora.

Stefaniszyn, B., and H. J. de Santana. 1960. The rise of the Chikunda "condottieri." *Northern Rhodesia Journal* 4: 361–68.

Truão, A. N. de B. de V. B. 1889. *Estatísticas da capitania dos rios de Sena no anno de 1806*. Lisbon: Imprensa Nacional.

Ulrich, E. 1910. *Economia Colonial*. Coimbra, Portugal: n.p.

Vail, L., and L. White. 1980a. *Capitalism and colonialism in Mozambique.* Minneapolis: University of Minnesota Press.

Vail, L., and L. White. 1980b. Tawani machambero: Forced cotton and rice growing on the Zambesi. *Journal of African History* 19: 239–63.

Vilhena, E. 1910. *Questões coloniaes.* Lisbon: E. Vilhena.

Weise, C. 1907. Zambesia—a labour question em Nossa Casa. *Boletim da Sociedade de Geographia de Lisboa* 25: 241–47.

Weise, C. 1983. *Expedition in East Central Africa, 1888–1891,* ed. H. W. Langworthy. Norman: University of Oklahoma Press.

Xavier, A. C. 1889. *Estudos coloniaes.* Nova Goa, India: Imprensa Nacional.

8 *Thomas J. Herlehy and Rodger F. Morton*

A Coastal Ex-Slave Community in the Regional and Colonial Economy of Kenya: The WaMisheni of Rabai, 1880–1963

The WaMisheni of Rabai (coastal Kenya) originated in the late nineteenth century as a maroon settlement under the protection of a mission, in this case the Church Missionary Society (CMS). The CMS connection, which first helped runaway slaves escape attack and reenslavement, enabled them before and after abolition in 1907 to interact with other freed slaves and neighboring freeborn Africans, to pool a variety of skills and procure land for resettlement, and to gain ready access to wage employment. Throughout this period, however, the WaMisheni acquired only a veneer of Christianity while devising means of becoming economically and socially independent of mission control. Many who attended church and mission schools also integrated with the indigenous Mijikenda surrounding Rabai.[1] Some left the Church altogether and became practicing Muslims. The large majority of WaMisheni used Mijikenda land as

1. Mijikenda is a collective term referring to the nine related groups situated in the Kenya coastal hinterland. According to the vernacular designations, they are the AChonyi, ADigo, ADuruma, AGiriama, ADzihana, AKambe, AKauma, ARabai, and ARihe. ARabai is also written as ARavai (*v* = bilabial *b*), but standard orthography is used here. The prefix "A" (meaning "people of") is preferred in order to distinguish clearly the indigenous inhabitants from the place-name associated with the mission (i.e., Rabai). Mijikenda itself is a Swahili term derived from the vernacular *midzi chenda* ("nine villages") and is rendered in two words (Miji Kenda) by writers of coastal origin.

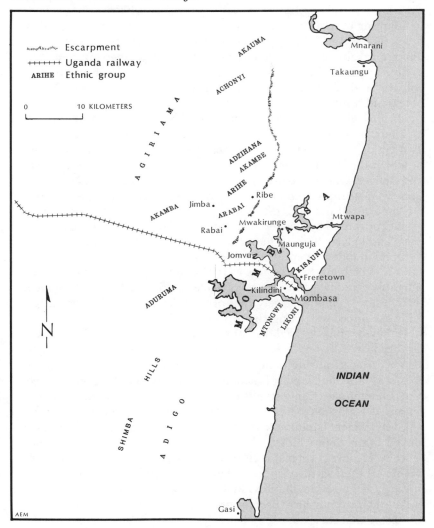

Map 8. The coastal hinterland of Kenya

both resource and residence and entered the traditional regional economy centered around palm tree production; a significant number joined
the skilled wage sector of the new colonial economy by using education
acquired from CMS schools. Thus the WaMisheni of Rabai provide an
example of freed men and women who exercised considerable flexibility

in adapting to their immediate surroundings and the emerging colonial order. For a time, Rabai also represented an extremely heterogeneous and remarkably harmonious community that contained opposing forces in nineteenth- and twentieth-century coastal Kenya: slave and free, pre-colonial and colonial, European and African, Christian and Muslim, black and white.

On first glance, the WaMisheni would appear to be a unique, even an aberrant, case in the postslavery literature pertaining to East Africa. Two major conclusions have been reached about the ex-slave experience in which the WaMisheni clearly do not fit. One is advanced by Strayer and Ranger, who argue in separate works that ex-slaves attached to missions were either economically or psychologically dominated by white missionaries, if not both (Strayer 1978: 14–29; Ranger 1975: 9–10). The second, advanced by Cooper in his study of ex-slave squatters on the Kenya coast and in Zanzibar, is that ex-slaves were unable to acquire land and to function independently of ex-owners, colonial officials, and the structures in which all three groups were "bound up." Though ex-slaves considerably redefined their economic role and limited their dependency, their history remains largely that of a "quiet and continuous struggle" with the forces restricting them (Cooper 1980: 4, 6).

It may be that the WaMisheni represent a third, distinct, response to legalized freedom on the Kenya coast. Their success in withstanding mission control, acquiring land, integrating themselves among indigenous coastal culture, and readily functioning within both the regional and colonial economies certainly stands them in contrast to the prevailing paradigms. It is possible, too, that the WaMisheni simply bring into sharp relief an element common to the coastal ex-slave experience and one overlooked in previous studies. The WaMisheni case underlines the importance to ex-slaves of social factors in plotting the future, just as the persistence of their identity as an ex-slave community reflects a shared sense of the past. The desire of individual ex-slaves to belong to the society that enslaved them may have been as great as the need for personal security and economic survival.

The WaMisheni originated in the 1880s, when the slave population on the Kenya coast had reached its peak. Throughout the nineteenth century, slaves had been imported in steadily increasing numbers, principally from the Zanzibar entrepôt of the East African slave trade.[2] In 1887 the total number of slaves on the Kenya coast, from Gasi to Pate,

2. For the East African slave trade, see Alpers 1975; Beachey 1976; Cooper 1977: 38–46, 114–30; Nicholls 1971; and Coupland 1968: 152–234.

has been estimated to have been slightly more than 40,000, or roughly 25 percent of the total population (Morton 1976: 403–6). They were owned mainly by Arab and Swahili families, and most were used as agricultural laborers on grain plantations located near Gasi, Mombasa, Takaungu, Malindi, Lamu, and Pate (Cooper 1977: 80–113; Morton 1976: 44–88). In coastal towns and ports slaves were also put to work as common laborers, porters, artisans, palm-wine tappers, fishermen, and sailors; and in the homes of their owners, they served as domestic servants or, in the case of young women, as concubines. Wealthy Swahili and Arab families also had slave retainers who provided military, political, and social support for their owners.

From the time slaves arrived on the coast, the more daring ran away and attempted to form free communities in the coastal hinterland. In the 1830s the first were founded at Koromio, near Takaungu, and at Mwazang'ombe, in the Shimba Hills southwest of Mombasa. Neither survived very long. In 1848 slave-owners attacked and destroyed Koromio, and at Mwazang'ombe the refugees turned to the selling of slaves to coastal plantation owners. Other runaway slaves, who joined the mercenary ranks of coastal Arab and Swahili rebels, merely exchanged one form of servility for another. From the 1860s until the 1890s both Mbaruk bin Rashid of Gasi and Sultan Ahmed bin Fumo Luti of Witu employed large numbers of runaway slaves as armed retainers while first challenging the coastal authority of the Busaidi sultan of Zanzibar, then the Imperial British East Africa Company (IBEAC), and finally, the British East Africa Protectorate (EAP). A few runaways did manage, for a short period, to gain a measure of independence from their ex-masters. Fuladoyo and Makongeni, settlements founded during the 1870s in the Malindi hinterland, were the most successful in this respect. For two decades they managed to survive a series of Arab and Swahili attacks. The people of Fuladoyo and Makongeni, however, lived precariously at the best of times, and their settlements gradually disappeared. In the 1890s their inhabitants were scattered by the last coastal raids on their communities and by Mijikenda farmers and traders settling north of the Sabaki (Galana) River (Morton 1976: 183–229; Ylvisaker 1979: 92–93 and passim; Strayer 1978: 37–39).

In the 1870s runaways from the Malindi-Mombasa region found sanctuary on European mission stations, but they received only a temporary welcome. Originally established for the conversion of the Mijikenda, the CMS station at Rabai (1846) and the United Methodist Free Church (UMFC) station at nearby Ribe (1862) failed to attract more than a handful of these and other indigenous peoples to the gospel, and in the early 1870s missionaries began to give refuge to runaway slaves and convert them. In 1878, however, when slave-owners threatened to attack, the CMS and UMFC dispersed the runaways and prevented others from settling on their stations (Bennett 1964). Thereafter both missions adhered officially to an antiharboring policy, though the CMS had already begun to channel its energies into the maintenance of slaves captured by British antislavery patrols sailing on the Indian Ocean. In 1874 the CMS established Freretown, on the mainland opposite Mombasa, specifically for rehabilitating and converting these recaptured slaves, known as *mateka*. And by 1880 the CMS began to resettle these mateka in Rabai, where most became permanent residents.

The mateka at Rabai were soon joined by mission contraband in the form of runaway slaves from the Mombasa-Malindi region. During the 1880s, official mission policy regarding runaways was actively subverted by the African minister placed in charge of Rabai, the Reverend William H. Jones. At the UMFC Ribe mission, two Sierra Leonean ministers, Revs. W. H. During and F. A. Heroe, also opened their doors to runaways.[3] Jones, himself an ex-slave educated in India and familiar with the coast since 1864, governed the mission community for most of the years from 1882 to 1888, while his European supervisors remained in Freretown, preoccupied with other matters (Morton 1976: 230–82). Between 1884 and 1888 Jones, During, and Heroe settled more than 900 runaway slaves on their respective stations and concealed this from their superiors. In 1888, when irate coastal slave-owners threatened to recapture their slaves from Rabai by force of arms, the director of the newly established government of the IBEAC intervened to prevent an attack on the mission stations and to salve the feelings of the Muslim community on whose support the company depended. The IBEAC agreed to pay the owners, who in turn manumitted the runaways at Rabai, Ribe, and two smaller stations. Of the 1,422 runaways thereby redeemed, nearly half were living in Rabai. After 1888, almost all of them remained on and around the mission stations.[4]

In 1888 nearly 1,200 ex-slaves were living in Rabai. Over 900 were former runaways, mainly from the Muslim coast, but they included 238 persons who had been slaves of Mijikenda. The next largest ex-slave element was the mateka, who numbered no more than 200 men, women, and children. In addition to these were several families of India-trained ex-slaves, like Jones, who were known to their contemporaries as Bom-

3. W. H. During was in charge of Ribe from 1880 to 1884, F. A. Heroe from 1888 to 1890 (MMA, During; MMA, Heroe).
4. PRO, Euan-Smith 1888; McDermott 1895: 25–32. The runaway problem was not completely solved until the formal abolition of slavery in 1907.

bay Africans. Each of these three elements contributed important characteristics to the community as a whole. From the 1880s, they gradually coalesced, together with Christianized Mijikenda who resettled on and next to the mission, into a less differentiated group, known to the surrounding Mijikenda as WaMisheni ("people of the mission"). This sizable community stood out conspicuously from the people living around it. In 1888 the Mijikenda people in the immediate area, the ARabai, numbered no more than 5,000 persons, and until the First World War roughly one out of every five persons residing in the area was a WaMisheni.

The strongest force in the creation of this new community was the runaway element. Most of the runaways had been born into slavery or had lived a long time on the coast. Those who settled in Rabai were either practicing Muslims or were familiar with Muslim culture. Many arrived at the mission settlement with spouses or lovers, and children. Many came, too, as artisans possessing the knowledge of building, carpentry, or fishing, or skills such as butchery, blacksmithery, and the making of fish traps, roof mats, drums, and sandals.[5] They popularized the rectangular Swahili-style house, with wattle and mud walls and palm-mat roof, as well as the circular grinding stone (*liwala kidzomba*), and introduced a host of other material objects and their musical culture, which included songs and dances popular among slaves on the coast.[6] The ARabai referred to the runaways as *adzomba* ("uncles" or "nephews," depending on the context), the same name they gave to black, Muslim, coastal residents (Morton interviews, 1973: Debwani Ramadhani; Tsochizi Tsimba).

Before their manumission by the IBEAC in 1888, the adzomba acquired a veneer of Christianity in order to remain at the Rabai mission station. Rev. Jones demanded strict adherence to mission rules in return for the privilege of residence and protection (Morton interview: Gibson Ngome, 1970). The adzomba regularly attended church on Sundays, many used Christian names, married in the Church, placed their children in mission schools, and accepted baptism. Once they had acknowledged Jones's authority they were encouraged to cultivate and settle on land in the unoccupied fertile plain stretching west and northwest from the Rabai mission at Kisulutini. They lived primarily as farmers, craftsmen, fishermen,

---

5. Cooper argues that "escape was most likely to occur among those who were the least acculturated, the least indoctrinated with the idiom of paternalism, and had the fewest stakes [land, a spouse, children] in the plantation, the lowest rank in slave society, and the least knowledge of how to manipulate their masters" (Cooper 1977: 208). Pace Cooper, this simply is not true, especially in the case of ex-slaves living in Rabai, as well as the other runaway slaves on the Kenya coast.

6. Morton interviews, 1973: Chombo Bedena; Selina Sylvanos; and Debwani Ramadhani. See also Harford-Battersby, n.d.: 67–68; and CMS, Streeter 1879.

and petty traders, although men often took jobs as porters or cooks for the CMS mission and, after 1887, for the IBEAC.[7] By the 1890s many had reverted to Islamic and Animist religious observances.

The mateka, who were recent arrivals on the coast, had less to contribute. Apart from the knowledge of the hoe, few brought productive skills. By and large the mateka depended on agriculture to maintain themselves, though by 1890 a number of men had acquired the skill of porterage. Nearly all mateka came to Rabai as adults with at best a modest knowledge of KiSwahili and a keener sense of their ethnic origins than did the other ex-slaves. Mateka pioneers grouped themselves ethnically around the mission station, those from the Lake Nyasa region forming the largest neighborhood. Their special dances and other forms of entertainment, performed regularly on mission ground, reflected the mateka habit of preserving old ways. In the privacy of their homes, first-generation mateka spoke their original languages. The ARabai distrusted the mateka and imputed to them the most diabolical forms of imported witchcraft. Like the adzomba, the mateka adopted Christianity largely for convenience and protection but set themselves apart from other ex-slaves by wearing the "mission dress" of shirt and wrapper. As strangers to the coast, they were far more dependent on the mission and less apt to resettle elsewhere. They dressed and behaved like foreigners. Mateka children, many of them orphans, were particularly susceptible to missionary influence. They commonly adopted names and habits acquired from close association with European missionary teachers and mission culture.[8] In the 1880s and 1890s the children made up the dominant group in the catechism classes and schools and openly imitated European styles of dress. The ARabai applied to these Westernized mateka, and to others who behaved like them, the derisory label *makoroboi* ("call a boy").[9]

The third ex-slave group at Rabai, the Bombay Africans, was both the smallest and, until 1888, the most important.[10] Between November 1873 and January 1876, the CMS transferred 128 Bombay Africans to East Africa to assist Rev. William S. Price, a European, in building Frere-

7. Morton interviews, 1973: Stanley Saburi; Debwani Ramadhani; Gibson Samuel; Mama Mashaka; Nellie Peter Mwamba; Bessie David Maraga; Patience Foster; Solomon Foster; and Francis Khamisi. Also KNA, Hollis 1898; Jackson 1969: 164.

8. Morton interviews, 1973: Mama Mashaka; Ernest William; Abel Stephen Brown; Rawson Gilbert Ngbwede; Nellie Japhet; Bemkoka Morris; and Gideon Sababu.

9. Morton interview: Joseph Tinga, 1973. These included mateka orphans schooled in Freretown who then took up residence in Rabai.

10. Morton 1976: 283–313 and passim; Temu 1971; and Strayer 1978: 14–29. These latter two sources contain many errors, and Strayer examines Bombay African–European missionary relations only within the context of class and race, thereby overlooking the more significant factors arising from the larger Kenyan coastal environment.

town and revitalizing Rabai.[11] The most highly trained and skilled remained at Freretown and the rest, comprising 28 married couples and their children, were sent to Rabai to form a farming community on the old mission grounds (CMS, Price journal, 6 and 21 March 1875). Although many Bombay Africans at Rabai and Freretown soon became disillusioned with their role and abandoned the CMS, a number of families remained on both stations, and the CMS placed much of the operation of the mission in their hands, especially those of Rev. "Fundi" Jones.[12] Because of their link to the mission, the Bombay Africans assumed the leadership of the ex-slave community. Except for the mateka children educated by Rev. John Handford at Freretown, the Bombay Africans also included the only WaMisheni literate in both English and KiSwahili. In appearance, the Bombay Africans were the most European of all the ex-slaves. They preferred wearing British styles of dress, straightening their hair, speaking no African language except KiSwahili, and emulating European attitudes towards the other coastal residents. Many looked down on the ARabai as barbarians and despised coastal Muslims for their ownership of slaves. At times the Bombay Africans themselves were resented by CMS missionaries, who took their European imitations as an insult, rather than a compliment. CMS missionaries labelled these ex-slave *deracines* as Bombays or Nassickees (after the CMS African Asylum in Nasick, India). The ARabai called them Adzungu Airu ("Black Europeans"), a term they also applied to Mijikenda who imitated European ways. Yet, in Rabai, certain Bombays, together with mateka and runaways, established close economic and social links with the ARabai and functioned free of European missionary control.

CMS neglect of Rabai was instrumental to its success. Freretown's beachfront climate was much healthier and control over freed-slave residents more absolute than at Rabai, which for Europeans was fever-ridden and its population too mixed and dispersed for adequate supervision in the short periods of duty served. African converts administered the settlement even to the point of defying European superiors temporarily in residence. The area of mission land, moreover, was much smaller than the area of settlement, and jurisdiction over the Christian community was confined to denying access to church and schools. Thus, accepting Christianity was necessary for those seeking entry, but the WaMisheni were able to ignore the purposes which the CMS intended its Rabai sta-

11. Price 1890; CMS, Price correspondence and reports 1873–1875. See Morton 1976: 407–9 for a complete list of the original Bombay Africans.

12. Morton 1976: 261. *Fundi* is KiSwahili for "craftsman" or "artisan," and often carries the added meaning of "capable" or "talented." In India, Jones had been trained as a blacksmith.

tion to serve. Among the WaMisheni were more practicing Muslims and Animists than Christians. By 1902, less than a kilometer from the mission, a mosque was erected, and not far away was a Muslim cemetery, where many WaMisheni were buried.[13] Religion was closely connected with the economic and social changes occuring at the close of the nineteenth century. Coastal Muslim traders ran a regular market at nearby Batani, and others settled among the ex-slaves and converted them and Mijikenda to Islam (Morton interview: Kijala Jayo, 1973; Herlehy interview: Felix Katimbo). At Somali, several kilometers east of Rabai, Muslim traders and Somali herders ran a flourishing cattle market, supplying Mombasa with beef. The WaMisheni were located, in fact, at the hub of an established regional economy that received new impetus with their settlement.

WaMisheni and the Regional Economy

As early as 1800, long before the WaMisheni arrived, Rabai was a center for local and regional trade. It was situated on a narrow, hilly ridge running parallel to the coast and separating the Swahili-speaking peoples of the coast from the interior. Rabai was important in channelling ivory into Mombasa, and the ARabai were active as porters, traders, and brokers for coastal merchants. Gradually, after the 1820s, the ARabai were overtaken in this respect by other Mijikenda and AKamba traders who settled near Rabai; the ARabai themselves established a vigorous food-importing economy that was unique in nineteenth-century East Africa.

By 1850, if not earlier, the ARabai had become the premier producers of cocunut-palm products within the coastal hinterland. The ARabai occupied the center of a regional network of exchange in which peoples from throughout the coastal hinterland came to purchase *uchi* — "coconut-palm wine."[14] So much effort was devoted to uchi production in the nineteenth century that the ARabai acquired most of their foodstuffs through the palm-wine trade. In 1848 the first missionary to live among the ARabai, Rev. J. L. Krapf, observed that the ARabai met most of their basic needs by using products from the coconut palm tree, and whatever they did not produce themselves they bought by selling uchi (CMS, Krapf journal, 2 May 1848). This arrangement persisted well into the twentieth cen-

13. Morton interview: Sheikh Mwidadi b. Johari, 1970. The cemetery is located one kilometer north of the mosque at Kavirondo.
14. Uchi (*uchi wa mnazi*, ChiRabai; or *tembo la mnazi*, KiSwahili) is the sweet sap procured three times daily from a coconut palm by binding and shaving the tip of the spadix, the fruit-bearing branch of the tree, while the flower buds are still enclosed within their sheaths. A tree being tapped for uchi cannot yield coconuts.

tury, when the ARabai became even more dependent on the uchi trade. The economic importance of palm wine among the ARabai had a significant impact on their cultural lives; virtually every aspect of ARabai civic and religious activity involved the ritual use of uchi. As the uchi trade assumed wide regional importance, palm wine permeated the cultures and economies of the other Mijikenda also (Herlehy 1985: 60–102, 130–47).

The settlement of WaMisheni at Rabai in the 1870s and 1880s reinforced, as well as protected, the ARabai's economic position. WaMisheni arrived at a time when widespread insecurity in the coastal hinterland had forced the ARabai to retreat inside their stockaded villages (*kaya*) and abandon cultivation and tapping temporarily beyond a short distance from the kaya.[15] The ARabai allowed the WaMisheni to settle west of the mission in these recently vacated areas known as Mwele, Jimba, Kaliang'ombe, Mgumopatsa, Kokotoni, and Simakeni. The WaMisheni cultivated extensively and planted coconut, mango, orange, and other fruit trees, as well as cereals and vegetables.[16] The ARabai gained from the growth of the mission population and WaMisheni fields. As it expanded, the cultivated zone increased local food supplies and stimulated trade in palm wine, palm products, and other goods. WaMisheni settlement also created a welcome buffer between the ARabai kaya and the open, previously undefended plain, from which attacks had come in recent years. WaMisheni access to the mission supply of Snider rifles enabled a combined force of WaMisheni and ARabai to drive back Kwavi rustlers in 1882 and to repel Mbaruk bin Rashid's mercenaries in 1882 and 1895.[17] As a result, Rabai became a relatively secure spot in a turbulent region and attracted refugees from the AGiriama, ADigo, and smaller Mijikenda groups, in addition to runaway slaves.[18]

The growing interdependence of WaMisheni and ARabai was reflected in the failure of missionaries to keep mission settlers away from the palm-wine trade. Before the WaMisheni settled in Rabai the CMS had actively opposed the drinking and selling of uchi, but the few ARabai whom mis-

15. Herlehy interviews: Tsama Mkuzi; Ambari Washe; Tsuma Mumba; Nzaka Ngao; and Dagamra Shaha; Morton interviews, 1973: Johnson Henry; Mkamba Benyoka; and Malanga Bedena. Also CMS, Price, 3 July 1875; Wakefield 1872–1887.

16. CMS, Price, 3 July 1875; CMS, Jones 1878; and CMS, Price report 1882. Also, Herlehy interviews: Harry Fanjo; Charo Munga and Komolo Dzomba.

17. Herlehy interviews: Tsuma Mumba; Wesa Mwambawa; and Morton interviews: Gibson Ngome, 1970; Solomon Foster, 1973. For an account of these mercenaries and their attacks, see Morton 1976: 137–48, 277, 360–62; Wakefield 1904: 178.

18. Many of these AGiriama and other immigrants also joined local ARabai patriclans, particularly the Mkavyo (Morton interviews: Nzaka Kunya, 1970, 1973).

sionaries managed to convert and settle on the CMS station in fact made their living as tappers.[19] After ex-slaves began to settle at Rabai, the missionary campaign against palm wine intensified and just as dramatically failed. By 1879 Rev. H. Binns was aware that the new mission residents, particularly the Bombay Africans, had become "especially fond" of uchi (CMS, Binns, 29 November 1879). By this time the CMS had already begun attempts to cripple the palm-wine industry by introducing controls over mission residents and encouraging them and the ARabai to turn to copra production instead of wine tapping. The mission challenge to uchi persisted for decades (Herlehy 1985: 155–92). Yet missionaries were either too briefly in residence or too overworked, unhealthy, or incompetent to prevent ARabai from bringing palm wine onto mission ground or to stop the WaMisheni from leaving the station to procure it. As Binns admitted, "They can easily go out among the coconut trees and either buy or be given it by their friends" (ibid.: 30 December 1879).

Apart from consuming uchi, WaMisheni integrated palm production into their own economic activities. By 1914 WaMisheni owned over 17 percent of all the palm trees in Rabai.[20] Like the ARabai, WaMisheni coconut-palm farmers earned the major share of their farm income from wine selling.[21] WaMisheni hired ARabai to tap their trees and occasionally to harvest copra, which brought lower returns than uchi (Herlehy 1985: 241–54). The major economic difference to emerge between the two communities during the early colonial period was that the Mijikenda of Rabai derived almost all their cash earnings through palm production, whereas nearly all WaMisheni supplemented any farming, fishing, or palm cultivation with wage earnings. Both uchi and copra were minor economic attractions for the WaMisheni, who owned comparatively few trees. The WaMisheni were nevertheless an important part of the palm-dominated economy of Rabai, especially during the early colonial period, when they became the ARabai's major cash customers, even though they consumed but a fraction of what ARabai tappers collected.

19. Herlehy interviews: Figo Dzogofya; Tsuma Mumba; and Tarazo Ndune; CMS, Rebmann 1868; CMS, Price, 27 February 1875.

20. Based on a list of farm owners collected by J. M. Pearson, district commissioner of Rabai (KNA, Coconut Commission Report, 1913–1914), and corroborated by biographical data on WaMisheni collected by Morton in 1973.

21. Parkin (1970: 221) and Spear (1978: 139) argue that ex-slaves harvested coconuts for the copra market, reflecting their cooperation with market-oriented capitalism, whereas the ARabai tended to tap their trees for uchi. Ample evidence shows, however, that enough WaMisheni tapped their trees and enough ARabai harvested nuts for copra, to disprove such a neat dichotomy (Morton interviews: Emmanuel Deimler, 1970, 1973; Joseph Tinga, 1973; Debwani Ramadhani, 1973; Tsochizi Tsimba, 1973; Tuguu Baya, 1973; also KNA, Rabai Sub-District Annual Report, 1913–1914).

Also in support of the uchi industry, the WaMisheni taught the ARabai how to preserve surplus wine in the form of distilled liquor. This very strong, clear, ginlike drink known as *piwa* became popular throughout the palm belt and the entire coast. By the mid-1930s the production and distribution of piwa had become a lucrative business, not only for many ARabai palm owners but for a few WaMisheni as well.[22]

By the late nineteenth century, interaction between WaMisheni and ARabai had already resulted in a marked level of cross-acculturation. The ARabai, who along with other Mijikenda originated in the coastal hinterland as early as the seventeenth century, were organized around loose collections of patriclans and subclans governed through councils of elders.[23] Socially flexible, the Mijikenda absorbed a wide spectrum of persons and families from the coast and hinterland.[24] Through traditional rituals for incorporating strangers, a large number of ex-slaves became members of ARabai patriclans. The ritual most commonly utilized was *kurya tsoga* ("to eat the cut"), which created blood brotherhood between two men, in this case ARabai and ex-slave. The two men cut themselves with a knife, dipped cooked meat in one another's blood, then ate the meat. The ex-slave thereby became a member of the patriclan of his ceremonial partner, acquiring rights and obligations in his adopted clan and community (Herlehy 1984: 299–301). On occasion ex-slaves paid fees to the elders of an ARabai patriclan, entitling them to the privileges and obligations of all other clansmen. Other ex-slaves married into local clans. In all such cases ex-slaves were entitled upon entry to receive the support of their ARabai nominal kin for gaining and holding land, raising capital for feasts or bridewealth, paying for curative medicines sold by local doctors, and acquiring ARabai wives.[25] At Ribe a much smaller runaway slave community was, in this fashion, totally absorbed by the neighboring ARihe and AKambe and disappeared as a distinct UMFC mission group.[26]

22. Prominent piwa brewers included ex-slaves and their descendants (Herlehy 1985: 185, 255–77).
23. Spear 1978: 1–106. The 1897 census shows that the Mijikenda population was close to 70,000 at that time (Morton 1976: 404–5).
24. Many Mijikenda clans and subclans were founded by or incorporated outsiders such as ATaita farmers and traders, AKamba cattle herders and brokers, Waata (Ariangulo or Laa) hunters, and other peoples.
25. Morton interviews: Nzaka Kunya, 1970, 1973; Debwani Ramadhani, 1973; Mboga Kinda, 1973; Malanga Bedena, 1973; Margaret Simeon Ramshaw, 1973; Lucas Mwakampya, 1973; Tuguu Baya, 1973.
26. Two hundred ex-slaves, all runaways, were living on UMFC mission ground at Ribe in 1888. The small, lightly supported UMFC establishment offered few attractions for settlement. Ribe lay off the trade routes leading to Rabai and was rendered almost inacces-

Conversely, at Rabai, a number of ARabai families became part of the WaMisheni community. Historians have assumed that the CMS was unsuccessful in gaining converts among the ARabai and Mijikenda.[27] Yet, from the time the ex-slave community took shape, Mijikenda began to convert. And, by the late nineteenth century, the largest Mijikenda group on mission ground was the ARabai. Even several kaya elders, who functioned as ritual and political leaders in traditional ARabai society, settled on the station.[28] As converts they lived among the WaMisheni and were regarded as part of that community by insiders and outsiders, even though they made no attempt to conceal their origins. They adopted biblical first names, for example, and retained the names of their respective progenitors. Moreover, ARabai and other Mijikenda converts married almost exclusively among themselves.[29]

The WaMisheni community was itself a major attraction for the ARabai living outside the station. They visited often to witness the myriad forms of entertainment and enticements. Church services and evening *ngoma* (dancing to drums) were heavily attended. Apart from their distinctive appearance, the WaMisheni exposed the ARabai to new and often dazzling distractions. Some ex-slaves, such as Brown Baraka and Bemaasai, achieved notoriety as magicians who could transmogrify themselves, set fingers on fire, and travel great distances in seconds. Rev. William Jones, himself a spellbinding orator who packed ARabai into Sunday services on the hottest of days, was regarded by them as a prophet.[30] In times of famine, confrontations between ARabai and WaMisheni could occur, as during the Bom-Bom famine (1894–1895), when Jones came into open conflict with the ARabai (CMS, Ackerman journal, 6 January and 2 February 1895). In general, however, the trend of ARabai-

sible to runaways by a web of creeks separating the hilltop mission from the coastal plains below. ARihe and Oroma (Galla) predominated among the converts, and few runaways became Christians. Most remained Muslims. (Herlehy interviews: esp. Hamadhi bin Tofiki and Tofiki bin Mwidhani. See also KNA, Tisdall, Safari Diary, 1924. For early UMFC history, see Morton 1976: 233–35.)

27. Spear (1978: 139), for example, writes that "their only converts during the first few decades were a few social outcasts, and to this day there are few Mijikenda Christians." Spear seems to build his argument on the inaccurate assessment made by Temu (1972: 7–8, 20–29) and Strayer (1978), the latter of which takes no notice of the Mijikenda factor within coastal mission communities.

28. Herlehy interviews: Figo Dzogofya; Tsuma Mumba; Tarazo Ndune; CMS, Taylor 1885 and 1886.

29. Morton interviews, 1973: Selina Sylvanos; Nellie Peter Mwamba; Bessie David Maraga; James Lawrence Deimler; Mboga Kinda; Herlehy 1985: 177–84, 320–27.

30. Morton interviews: Nzaka Kunya, 1970, 1973; Joseph Tinga, 1973; Chombo Bedena, 1973; Debwani Ramadhani, 1973; Tsochizi Tsimba, 1973; and Bedzuya Dawa, 1973; Morton 1976: 324–26.

WaMisheni relations into the colonial period was towards integration rather than separation owing to the increasing importance of the Rabai station to both communities.

WaMisheni and the Colonial Economy

From the beginning of their settlement at Rabai, the WaMisheni became part of British efforts to penetrate the interior. In the 1880s Rabai became a principal staging center for long-distance caravans sent inland by the CMS, the IBEAC, and eventually the East Africa Protectorate government. Until the railroad reached Nairobi in 1897 caravans generated contract employment for a number of WaMisheni men and filled other pockets that were subsequently lightened at Rabai, where, within earshot of the CMS church, returning porters and other caravan employees bought their pleasures from uchi sellers and prostitutes (Morton 1976: 329–32). By 1895 over 25 shops had been established on mission ground by Hindu merchants invited by the CMS.[31]

Of greater importance to the WaMisheni in the long run, the EAP used Rabai as its first administrative headquarters for the Mijikenda. After 1896 the British recruited numbers of WaMisheni into the local colonial administration and increasingly into junior civil service employment throughout the colony. WaMisheni graduates from the CMS school in Rabai readily left home and accepted salaried positions in Mombasa and up-country as clerks, interpreters, and messengers (Morton 1976: 335; Hollis 1955: 33). The most conspicuous group in this respect were mateka teenage boys who proved their worth in the field of telegraphy. In 1911, the colonial government employed one of them, Edward Brenn, to instruct local schoolboys at the Rabai Post and Telegraph Office (KNA, Gosling, 16 May and 16 June 1911). Many of these apprentices, who included ARabai youths, later manned posts up the rail line all the way to Uganda.

For a time WaMisheni successfully blended their activities in the regional and colonial economies. In local political matters, WaMisheni deferred to the ARabai and did not use Europeans to assert themselves. For the most part, WaMisheni eschewed chieftaincy.[32] And when ARabai opposed colonial economic policies, they received WaMisheni support. In 1914 when the British began their attempts to destroy the palm-wine industry and stimulate copra production in its place, the WaMisheni connived with the ARabai to undercut the ordinances intended to place the

31. KNA, Pearson report 1913; Herlehy interviews: Ambari Washe; Nzaka Ngao.

32. The few who accepted this role lived in Ruruma, several kilometers from the Rabai community. They were Mackenzie Piko (1924–1929), Paul Mwazuma (1929–1945), Samuel Gideon (1945–1951), and Gideon Mkando (1952–1964) (Herlehy, research notes).

uchi trade under state control. As a result, the ordinances failed utterly to regulate tapping and selling in Rabai. In spite of efforts to promote cash cropping, copra prices fluctuated too radically to induce farmers to abandon tapping and turn to harvesting nuts, while the illicit wine trade grew throughout the colonial period (Herlehy 1985: Ch. 5). Wa-Misheni wage earners, who increased the amount of cash circulating in the local uchi market, played a quiet but equally supportive role. The periodic return of WaMisheni from the private and public wage sector also encouraged ARabai to enter mission schools and become teachers, telegraphers, and other salaried employees. In the first two decades of the twentieth century, the movement of ARabai onto the WaMisheni settlement reached its peak.

By the 1920s the WaMisheni community had begun to change in form. The process of merging with the ARabai through clan entry and inter-marriage continued. More ex-slave Christians reverted or converted to Islam, a step that often drew individuals, especially women, permanently into Mombasa and its suburbs.[33] Wage-labor migration, which had begun with porterage in IBEAC days, continued into the twentieth century in a different form, primarily with young educated WaMisheni who entered public service or private business and returned for only a week or so a year. Migrating wage earners increasingly became the dominant element among the WaMisheni and their attitudes and behavior the prevailing ethos. Furthermore, the type of people who remained in Rabai — mainly the dependents of wage earners, unmarried women and the elderly— showed a diminishing interest in the surrounding ARabai and coastal culture, and displayed instead an increasingly strident elitism vis-à-vis their neighbors. This residue of nonassimilated WaMisheni was primarily first- and second-generation mateka and, to a lesser extent, Bombay Africans, who were gradually shifting their residences to Freretown.

Along with the importance of schooling and wage-earning careers, these WaMisheni imparted to their children notions of cultural superiority. Importance was attached to the possession of such symbols as European-style clothing, large and square plastered houses, store-bought household furniture and goods, literacy in English and KiSwahili, and a diet that included rice, meat, and canned foods. Europeanized living among these WaMisheni, particularly the young, was a convenient and conspicuous way of isolating themselves from the larger community with which they and their parents had never been forced to come to terms.

33. CMS, Ackerman journal, 10, 12, and 29 May, 5 and 19 June, and 8 July 1897; KNA, Rabai Sub-District Annual Report 1913–1914; Morton interviews: William George Kombo, 1970; Joseph Binns, 1973. Muslim converts who remained within Mijikenda society had much different motives for converting (see Parkin 1970).

In a sense, mateka identity was not as much an artificial or empty shell
as a symbol of independence that had been present among the mateka
since their resettlement in Freretown and Rabai in the 1870s. Though
mateka were recognizably African, especially in the musical forms of their
popular ngoma and in the spiritual concepts underlying their *uanga* (a
form of witchcraft), mateka culture as a whole appeared alien and imported.[34] In time, the resistance of the contracting mateka core to broader
acculturation resulted in conflict with the expanding ARabai population.

The decline of the Rabai WaMisheni as a community was tied closely
to the territorial expansion of the ARabai themselves. In the 1890s, after
two decades of famine and upheaval, the ARabai began spreading into
thinly settled or unoccupied land.[35] During the early twentieth century
ARábai farmers, herders, and tappers penetrated the coastal plain to the
east and southeast, a process abetted by the inability of Muslim landowners to control labor and maintain production on their plantations
(Cooper 1980: 219; KNA, Hollis map). To the south and southwest the
ARabai expanded at the expense of the ADuruma, resulting in border
disputes. A similar ARabai thrust to the northwest brought them into
conflict with AKamba herders. Many ARabai young men also began to
work as tappers for other Mijikenda and for Swahili palm owners throughout the entire coastal region.[36] Within Rabai, ARabai farmers eased into
the district north of the CMS mission and reclaimed land once used by
the WaMisheni, who, as wage dependency increased, left more and more
of their farms idle, and underutilized, or unsupervised. In 1910 colonial
authorities began to mention WaMisheni-ARabai land disputes arising
from this movement — disputes which, in succeeding years, became more
frequent (KNA, Platts 1910).

In order to preserve their land claims without shedding their community identity, some WaMisheni joined ARabai clans merely as a means
of gaining supporters in land disputes with other ARabai. Others buried
their dead on family land, instead of the community cemetery, as a form

34. The ARabai associated uanga, a form of witchcraft introduced by the mateka to
Rabai, with murder, grave robbing, and cannibalism. ARabai respondents maintain that
the practice of uanga was confined to the ex-slave community and was the major reason
for the decline of the mateka community (i.e., mateka killed one another through witchcraft) (Morton interviews, 1973: Silas Edward; Debwani Ramadhani; Tsochizi Tsimba; Francis Khamisi; James Lawrence Deimler; Selina Maftaha; and Brown Baraka).
35. This process continued well into the twentieth century. Kilifi and Mombasa district annual reports (KNA) are replete with references, especially after 1920. See also Brantley 1981: 33–53; and Cooper 1980: 215–30.
36. KNA, 1898 correspondence; KNA, Kilifi District Annual Reports, 1910–1920; Johnstone 1902: 263–72. In 1980 Herlehy found that 52 of 65 ARabai tappers interviewed (i.e.,
80 percent) had worked on Swahili coastal estates from Tanga (in Tanzania) to Malindi.

of establishing proof of long-term use. Both of these practices, together with WaMisheni reluctance to adopt more than a minimum of ARabai culture, heightened resentment. Small indiscretions, as when WaMisheni cut down coconut palms or used the wood for fires, could lead to acts of retaliation on both sides, often in the form of witchcraft or sorcery.[37]

Within the mission community, the steady takeover by ARabai of positions previously held by ex-slaves also caused conflict. The earliest inroads occurred in the mission church, which, after the 1890s, depended increasingly on ARabai and other Mijikenda for its catechists and pastors.[38] During the First World War, the first and only mateka priest in Rabai was replaced by an ARabai minister, who led the church for the next four decades.[39] Most of the pastors, subordinate clergy, and church workers in other parts of Mijikenda territory were ARabai. In the schools attached to the CMS mission the ARabai also achieved early prominence. By the First World War, WaMisheni schoolchildren were being taught almost entirely by ARabai schoolmasters.[40] Where originally many ARabai in the religious and educational wings of the mission were products of the WaMisheni community, by the 1920s a significant number of teachers were emerging from traditional ARabai families.[41] ARabai converts, pastors, and teachers assumed a leading role in advancing the interests of the ARabai community against the WaMisheni whenever the two groups came into conflict. They were supported by those ex-slaves and their descendants who had joined ARabai clans, even though they had retained their Christian faith and worked as wage earners. WaMisheni resentment towards these ex-WaMisheni was greater than for any other members of the opposing group.

At Rabai, where the WaMisheni adult male population was absent for all but a week or two every year, open confrontation between WaMisheni and ARabai became the province of youth, especially schoolboys. Until after the Second World War, ARabai students were a distinct

37. Morton interviews, 1973: Debwani Ramadhani; James Lawrence Deimler; Herlehy interviews: Figo Dzogofya; Nzaka Kunya; Garero Mwawara.

38. PP, Binns 1898, [C. 9502]. A list of CMS catechists for 1914 is in the Rabai Political Record Book (KNA). Other lists can be found for catechists, pastors, and conference delegates in CMS, 1902–1930 correspondence.

39. Rev. Samuel B. Kuri, ordained at Freretown Divinity School in 1922, took over the Rabai parish the same year and held it until his death in 1953. Kuri was made a canon of the Church in 1934 (Morton and Herlehy interviews, 1973 and 1980, respectively: Harry Fanjo).

40. Herlehy interviews: Tarazo Ndune; Jeremiah and John Tsuma; Dubi Lenga; Morton interviews: former students during First World War era.

41. Herlehy interviews: Tarazo Ndune; Dubi Lenga; Morton interviews: Joseph Tinga, 1973; Julia Paul, 1970.

minority in the classrooms of Rabai.[42] ARabai fathers and elders wanted their sons working on family farms, tapping palm wine, harvesting coconuts, or herding livestock, and their daughters contributing to daily agricultural and household tasks, instead of going to school. Early marriage also removed some youths from the classroom.[43] By the 1930s, however, boys looking for easier and more adventurous employment outside Rabai steadily increased ARabai enrollments in school.[44] As a large and growing minority the ARabai students represented a threat to their WaMisheni classmates. In the close confines of the schoolyard, ARabai and WaMisheni youths played and formed friendships within separate, opposing camps. With their finer clothes and longer educational tradition, WaMisheni lads looked down on the ARabai. Being more numerous and living closer to the school, which was located on mission ground, the WaMisheni found easy opportunities for waylaying and beating up the odd ARabai schoolboy. WaMisheni also monopolized Rabai's major form of entertainment, the monthly ngoma, at which some of the best coastal instrumentalists played into the night for young men and women (Morton interviews, 1973: Stanley Saburi; Gideon Ngale). These dances became a major source of irritation, particularly because the WaMisheni excluded ARabai young men while allowing ARabai young women to attend (Morton interviews 1973: Johnson Henry; James Lawrence Deimler; Gideon Ngale).

In the 1940s, educated ARabai were also beginning to politicize local issues along lines that tended to divide the ARabai from the WaMisheni. After the colonial government had embarked on a wartime registration drive and the WaMisheni classified themselves as "Nyassa," "Makua," or "Mgindo," instead of "Rabai," a group of ARabai men led by Edward Binns publicly challenged WaMisheni rights to land and to the sufferance of their ARabai hosts. Binns called the WaMisheni, Ahendakudza (lit., "newcomers"), a coinage that rapidly displaced other ethnonyms used by ARabai youths and hardened feelings on both sides. At Christmastime 1941, Binns's group organized an ngoma to rival that of the WaMisheni, and a large-scale fight nearly erupted.[45] WaMisheni leaders were convinced that ARabai anger over the dances and the Ahendakudza brou-

42. Herlehy interviews: Harry Fanjo; Jeremiah and John Tsuma; Morton interviews, 1973: Joseph Tinga; Edward Binns.

43. Herlehy interviews: Figo Dzogofya; Tsama Mkuzi; Tsuma Mumba; Bewamba and Muwawa Dena; Morton interview: Befukwe Kagumba, 1973.

44. Herlehy interviews: Dzombe and Tarazo Ndune; Morton interviews, 1973: Gibson Samuel; Daba Karisa.

45. Morton interviews, 1973: Johnson Henry; Debwani Ramadhani; James Lawrence Deimler; Elijah Mwang'ombe.

haha were merely disguises for ARabai land hunger. Since the 1930s the farms of many WaMisheni were being taken over by ARabai cultivators, some of whom, in these politically charged times, crudely pushed aside the previous WaMisheni occupants. What rankled most was that the recent assertiveness of the ARabai was being led by men, such as Binns, who were descended from WaMisheni.[46]

After the Second World War, ARabai ascendancy was assured. The new generation of schoolboys resumed the old feuding, though by the 1950s the ARabai constituted the majority in the primary schools, and most victories in the skirmishes on and off school grounds were theirs (Morton interviews: Emmanuel Deimler, 1970, 1973; Elijah Mwang'ombe, 1973; Frederick Fukwe, 1973). In 1956 WaMisheni scholars formed the exclusive Rabai Society, and ARabai youths countered with the open Rabai Local Social Club. But Harry Fanjo, then chief of Rabai location, ARabai ex-schoolboy leader, and part of Binns's group in the 1940s, quickly dissolved the Rabai Society (Morton interviews, 1973: Harry Fanjo; Emmanuel Deimler). From that time WaMisheni youths had few options but to swallow their pride until old enough to work outside Rabai. ARabai attention has therefore shifted to the elderly WaMisheni, who in place of the schoolboys have become the principal targets of abuse. In 1966 a number of them were victimized during a popular antiwitchcraft campaign led by a young, traditional doctor, Tsuma wa Washe, popularly known as Kajiwe (Parkin 1970). Kajiwe publicly confronted old WaMisheni, mostly women, and accused them of witchcraft, burned their purported tools of trade, and had them flogged.[47] Kajiwe's campaign also challenged the position of some ARabai Christians who were entering business and asserting themselves in local and national politics. Two of these men, strident members of the Kenya African Democratic Union, attempted to stop Kajiwe's antiwitchcraft campaign by assaulting Kajiwe himself. Kajiwe's popularity among tradition-oriented ARabai was the result of growing distrust of ARabai Christian politicians, chiefs, and businessmen, all educated and the most successful having WaMisheni connections. WaMisheni values persisted long after the political and economic eclipse of the WaMisheni community, and they remained a source of conflict within ARabai society into the 1970s.

46. Before he died in 1973, Edward Binns maintained that he was a pure ARabai, a claim supported by his brother and most ARabai interviewed. But many WaMisheni assert otherwise, saying that Binn's father became the blood brother of a member of the ARabai Tiga clan, thereby making his son a member, too.

47. We both heard testimony regarding these events, but because of the sensitive nature of Kajiwe's activities, our sources will remain anonymous. For a recent cameo of Kajiwe, see the *Sunday Standard* (Nairobi), 12 September 1982.

WaMisheni, Ex-Slaves, and East African Coastal History

Rabai provides the only example in East Africa of ex-slaves who, before and after the abolition of slavery, assimilated themselves with indigenous Africans, diversified their economy, and retained some degree of distinctiveness in the process. In part, the WaMisheni community retained its vitality because its members were free to choose their spouses, neighbors, employment, religion, and cultural activities. Though anchored on the CMS mission station, the WaMisheni were neither dependent on nor psychologically dominated by European missionaries, unlike other mission-based freed slaves (see Strayer 1978: 14–29; Ranger 1975: 9–10). The WaMisheni were, in fact, able to reject mission influence, even Christianity itself, without leaving the community. At Rabai, the mission owned too little land to become a coercive power (Herlehy 1985; 150). Independence from mission control was possible, too, because of the location of the WaMisheni settlement. Rabai was the center of an active regional trade in palm products; it sat astride the major commercial route connecting Mombasa with the interior; it contained one of the few mission schools in existence at the opening of the colonial period; and it stood in close proximity to wage opportunities in the colonial sector.

The WaMisheni stimulated the economic growth of Rabai, just as they pulled in surrounding Mijikenda to participate in their community's achievements. Rabai was an open community in which different types of ex-slaves lived together and welcomed a steady flow of freeborn settlers. As Rabai grew into a prosperous agricultural community and center of education and wage employment, additional Mijikenda settled among the WaMisheni to gain access to their resources, skills, and opportunities for economic advancement and material comfort. The predominantly ex-slave composition of Rabai gradually gave way to outside influence, particularly that of ARabai farmers living on and around the mission. In the twentieth century, heterogeneity became the Rabai community's most striking feature.

In contrast, other ex-slave communities on the coast quickly declined, disappeared, or became dependent on missions. Some of the settlers from Fuladoyo and Makongeni relocated themselves north of the Sabaki River at Bura, Pumwani, and Kwa Ali Tete, but by 1915 their communities had greatly dwindled in size.[48] In Ribe, seven kilometers north of Rabai, a small community of Islamized ex-slaves was completely integrated into ARihe society within two generations (Herlehy 1985, and fn. 26 herein). At Freretown, ex-slaves lived in isolation from the surrounding Muslim

48. Morton 1976: 380–88. Cooper (1980: 229) has criticized this interpretation, but Morton's argument is that ex-slave communities, rather than ex-slaves, were dying out.

populations and identified themselves closely with European missionaries, to whose authority they remained subject and on whom they depended for their Western education and the economic security that came with it.[49] In contrast to the Freretown *wahuru* ("free people"), a term often used as the paradigm of the mission ex-slave experience, the more numerous and diversified Rabai WaMisheni had considerably more freedom of movement and played a positive role in the immediate community. In addition, the Rabai mission was situated among the Mijikenda, who exercised greater influence over ex-slaves than did the Church.

The ease with which ex-slaves and ARabai furthered individual and community interests by overlapping themselves socially and economically had its parallel for a time on Arab and Swahili estates in the Takaungu hinterland. In the 1880s many slaves had begun to benefit from a decline in owner supervision and from the eastward colonization of Islamized Mijikenda farmers. Intermingling with these *mahaji* helped in changing the status of slaves to something akin to tenant farmers paying their owners rent for land. In 1895, however, the Anglo-Mazrui War reversed this process by dislocating the peoples of the Takaungu District and destroying crops and trees (Morton 1976: 341–74). When these slaves were eventually freed by the Abolition of Legal Status of Slavery Ordinance of 1907, the great majority returned to or remained on the land they had worked as slaves, without gaining any title or other rights of possession. In theory these ex-slaves could marry into landowning families or swear blood-brotherhood with them, as the WaMisheni were doing among the ARabai. In practice, however, Swahili and Arab landowners regarded ex-slaves as their inferiors and, in contrast to the ARabai, denied them the social means to gain permanent claims on family estates.

As Frederick Cooper stresses, ex-slaves who became squatters on the plantations were potentially the most dynamic element on the coast, but the failure of landowners and colonial officials to recognize their need for security on the land resulted in the absence of improvement and experimentation on old plantation land and in the deterioration of coastal grain production. Some owners, especially around Mombasa, attempted to maintain their estates and keep squatters on the land by switching to tree crops such as coconuts and mangoes. Aside from their labor, however, ex-slaves had little to offer landowners in return for permission to reside as squatters. Only a few freed slaves had the capital resources to purchase land, which during the colonial period became virtually the only means of acquiring it (Cooper 1980: 191–215).

49. Freretown also included Africans converted at up-country mission stations, but they constituted a small minority.

The proximity of Rabai to these estates and to other, less successful ex-slave settlements suggests, however, that the WaMisheni, in spite of living in what appears to have been exceptional circumstances, were not regarded by other ex-slaves as particularly advantaged. Between 1895 and 1899, many coastal slaves fled to Rabai, primarily to take up jobs as porters (Morton 1976: 374–76). But after 1899, few slaves or ex-slaves transferred their residence to Rabai, even though it would have been relatively easy to do so. Coastal ex-slaves largely remained in places where they had been slaves. Movement subsided as the legal slavery period drew to a close and the coercion of labor and service ended.

With abolition, in other words, ex-slaves on the Muslim coast accepted their status as subordinate, but protected, members of society. Though inferior socially, Muslim ex-slaves were roughly on the same plane economically with the large majority of the freeborn. And, in the larger coastal context, the social status of Muslim ex-slaves ranked above that of African non-Muslims in the adjacent hinterland. Even during the days of slavery, Muslim slaves thought themselves superior to the Mijikenda, or WaNyika ("people of the bush"), as KiSwahili-speakers called them (Morton 1976: 102–3; Cooper 1977: 215–17). Arab chauvinism, which pervaded the Muslim coast from the mid-nineteenth century well into the twentieth, was as appealing to slaves and ex-slaves as it was to the dominant freeborn KiSwahili-speaking communities and as it would later become to Africans in the hinterland, including the Mijikenda themselves (Morton 1977).

The WaMisheni of Rabai, therefore, may be understood as part of a general social phenomenon that accompanied the transition from slavery to ex-slavery. In Rabai, economic advancement was possible without cultural integration, and some chose to remain independent of the surrounding freeborn societies. Yet, the fact that many opted for cultural integration demonstrates the stress individual ex-slaves placed on group membership, as does the persistence of a distinct, ex-slave, WaMisheni community. Further studies of ex-slaves on the coast might therefore benefit from moving beyond questions of property and labor relations among ex-slaves, ex-masters, and colonial officials — the point at which Cooper's landmark study ends — to explore the means by which ex-slaves became part of society at large.

Epilogue

As late as 1980, the WaMisheni were still present at Rabai, though as a residue of impoverished old and retired people. Most of the former WaMisheni land in Simakeni, Kokotoni, and elsewhere was then occupied by ARabai farmers. A few WaMisheni still cultivated farms, but most of the economically active were involved in petty commerce or shopkeeping in the WaMisheni section of Rabai Township. The WaMisheni ward had become shabby in appearance. Many houses were decrepit and contained hardly any material objects, though a few WaMisheni did enjoy some of the only indoor plumbing, electricity, and telephone service available in Rabai. Poverty was nevertheless all too common, inflation having devoured the pensions and savings of most retired WaMisheni residents. Only elderly people with devoted children working outside Rabai continued to live at a respectable standard. Within the WaMisheni community, traditions of filial loyalty had largely disappeared. Vanished, too, were the entertainments and cultural activities that once gave the WaMisheni community in Rabai some of its charm. In 1980 the calendar was filled with idleness, relieved by drinking sessions and funeral feasts.

The WaMisheni remnants in Rabai provide but a faint image of a group which, from its emergence in the late 1880s, became a significant element in the history of colonial, and even postindependence, Kenya. In addition to two and three generations of civil servants, railwaymen, teachers, musicians, telegraph operators, soldiers, clerical employees, and churchmen, the WaMisheni of Rabai have produced a prominent journalist, a diplomat, a member of Parliament, as well as numerous politicians and municipal councillors. Such individuals reflect a constant underlying theme in the history of this ex-slave community. Since they began to settle in Rabai in the late nineteenth century, ex-slaves have desired adoption or at least acceptance by the larger community in which they, as mission settlers, as coastal dwellers, and as members of an emerging national society, have been a part.

GLOSSARY

adzomba   lit., "uncles"; used by the Mijikenda with reference to Islamized Africans dwelling on the coast plain (see *mahaji*).

ARabai   the indigenous people living around the Rabai market and mission station; one of the nine Mijikenda groups.

copra   dried coconut meat, which when pressed yields oil.

kaya   stockaded village (among the Mijikenda).

mahaji   Swahili term for Islamized Africans recently settled on the coastal plain (see *adzomba*).

mateka   recaptured slaves, used with reference to ex-slaves placed on mission stations by the British consul in Zanzibar.

Mijikenda   lit., "nine towns"; Swahili term used with reference to the nine related groups settled in the coastal hinterland between Gasi and Malindi.

ngoma	drum(s); also dancing to drums and music.
uchi	wine tapped from the coconut palm (*uchi wa mnazi*).
WaMisheni	lit., "people of the mission," the term applied to ex-slaves settled on or near the Church Missionary Society mission station at Rabai.

REFERENCES

Oral sources

Herlehy interviews.

All interviews took place in 1980. Transcripts of them (collectively titled Coconut Palm Traditions) are located in the African Studies Library, Boston University.

Ambari Washe, kaya elder, Rabai.
Amos C. Ramadhani, pensioner, Rabai.
Athmani Kinda, ex-chief, Ruruma.
Bedzuya Mrenje, kaya elder, Rabai.
Befukwe Kagumba, kaya elder, Rabai.
Bemunga Abdallah, farmer, Ruruma.
Bewamba and Muwawa Dena, farmers, Rabai.
Charo Munga and Komolo Dzomba, farmers, Rabai.
Dagamra Shaha, ex-subchief, Rabai.
Daniel Katana and James Mwachai, farmers, Kambe.
Dubi Lenga, farmer, Kambe.
Dzombe Ndune, farmer, Ribe.
Felix Katimbo, shopkeeper, Rabai.
Figo Dzogofya, kaya elder, Rabai.
Garero Mwawara, farmer, Rabai.
Gideon Mkando, ex-chief, Ruruma.
Hamadhi bin Tofiki, farmer.
Harry Fanjo, ex-chief, Rabai.
Jeremiah and John Tsuma, teachers, Ruruma.
Kailo Mzuka, farmer, Rabai.
Mdigo Katimbo and Mishi Dzua, farmers, Rabai.
Ndegwa Bendegwa, kaya elder, Rabai.
Nzaka Kunya, kaya elder, Rabai.
Nzaka Ngao, kaya elder, Rabai.
Rufus Chimvatsi, farmer, Ribe.
Samson Bajila Baya, farmer, Kambe.
Tarazo Ndune, farmer, Ruruma.
Tofiki bin Mwidhani, farmer, Ribe.
Tsama Mkuzi, kaya elder, Rabai.
Tsuma Mumba, kaya elder, Rabai.
Wesa Mwambawa, kaya elder, Rabai.

Morton interviews.

All interviews took place in 1970 and 1973. Transcripts of them are located at the Bird Library, Syracuse University.

Abel Stephen Brown, pensioner, Rabai, 1973.
Bedzuya Dawa, farmer, Rabai, 1973.
Befukwe Kagumba, kaya elder, Rabai, 1973.
Bemkoka Morris, pensioner, Rabai, 1973.
Bessie David Maraga, housewife, Rabai, 1973.
Brown Baraka, pensioner, Rabai, 1973.
Chombo Bedena, farmer, Rabai, 1973.
Daba Karisa, farmer, Rabai, 1973.
Debwani Ramadhani, pensioner, Rabai, 1973.
Edward Binns, pensioner, Rabai, 1973.
Elijah Mwang'ombe, pensioner, Rabai, 1973.
Emmanuel Deimler, unemployed, Rabai, 1970, 1973.
Ernest William, pensioner, Rabai, 1973.
former students during First World War era.
Francis Khamisi, journalist, Nairobi, 1973.
Frederick Fukwe, civil servant, Rabai, 1973.
Gibson Ngome, pensioner, Rabai, 1970.
Gibson Samuel, pensioner, Rabai, 1973.
Gideon Ngale, farmer, Rabai, 1973.
Gideon Sababu, pensioner, Rabai, 1973.
Harry Fanjo, chief, Rabai, 1973.
James Lawrence Deimler, pensioner, Rabai, 1973.
John Gideon, pensioner, Rabai, 1973.
Johnson Henry, pensioner, farmer, Rabai, 1973.
Joseph Binns, pensioner, Rabai, 1973.
Joseph Tinga, retired teacher, Rabai, 1973.
Julia Paul, housewife, Rabai, 1970.
Justin Fussel Gore, pensioner, Rabai, 1973.
Kijala Jayo, trader, Ruruma, 1973.
Lucas Mwakampya, farmer, Rabai, 1973.
Malanga Bedena, farmer, Rabai, 1973.
Mama Mashaka, housewife, Rabai, 1973.
Margaret Simeon Ramshaw, pensioner, Rabai, 1973.
Marie Deimler Muzo, housewife, Mombasa, 1973.
Mboga Kinda, farmer, Rabai, 1973.
Mkamba Benyoka, farmer, Rabai, 1973.
Mwidadi bin Johari, sheik, Rabai, 1970.
Nellie Japhet, housewife, Rabai, 1973.
Nellie Peter Mwamba, housewife, Rabai, 1973.
Ngao of Hodi Boys, musician, Rabai, 1973.
Nzaka Kunya, kaya elder, Rabai, 1970 and 1973.
Patience Foster, housewife, Rabai, 1973.

Rawson Gilbert Ngbwede, farmer, pensioner, Rabai, 1973.
Selina Maftaha, pensioner, Rabai, 1973.
Selina Sylvanos, housewife, Rabai, 1973.
Silas Edward, pensioner, Rabai, 1973.
Solomon Foster, pensioner, Changamwe, 1973.
Stanley Saburi, pensioner, Rabai, 1973.
Tsochizi Tsimba, farmer, Rabai, 1973.
Tuguu Baya, farmer, Rabai, 1973.
William George Kombo, teacher, Mazeras, 1970.

Archival sources

CMS: Church Missionary Society Archives, London.
  Ackerman, M. Journal, 1895. G3/A5/108.
  Binns, H. K., to Wright, 29 November 1879. CA 5/0/3/13.
  Binns, H. K. Annual letter to CMS, 30 December 1879. CA 5/0/3/19.
  Jones, W. H., to Wright, 10 October 1878. CA 5/0/14/2.
  Krapf, L. Journal 1847–1849. CA 5/0/16/172.
  Price, W. S. Correspondence and reports, 1873–1875. CA 5/0/23.
  Price, W. S., to Hutchinson, 27 February 1875. CA 5/0/23/15.
  Price, W. S., to Hutchinson, 3 July 1875. CA 5/0/23.
  Price, W. S. Journal, 1875. CA 5/0/23.
  Price, W. S. Report, 6 October 1882. G3/A5/1.
  Rebman, J., to CMS, 2 May 1868. CA 5/0/24.
  Streeter, J. W., to Hutchinson, 29 January 1879. CA 5/0/6/19.
  Taylor to CMS, 28 September 1885. G3/A5/139.
  Taylor to CMS, 8 June 1886. G3/A5/203.
  1902–1930 correspondence. G3/A5.
KNA: Kenya National Archives, Nairobi.
  Coast Province collection (CP)
    Coconut Commission Report, 1913–1914. CP MP 113-115.
    Gosling to CMS, 16 May 1911. CP MP 1/16.
    Gosling to Platts, 16 June 1911. CP MP 1/16.
    Hollis to Crauford, 9 October 1898. CP MP 67/15.
    Hollis map. CP MP 67/15.
    Pearson, J. M., Report, December 1913. CP 4/275.
    Platts to district commissioner, Mombasa, 7 December 1910. CP MP 99/198.
    Rabai Political Record Book, 1898–1914. CP MP 2/73.
    Tisdall. Safari Diary, 1924. CP MP 1188.
    1918 Correspondence. CP MP 67/15.
  Kilifi District Annual Reports, 1910–1920.
  Mombasa District Annual Reports.
  Rabai Sub-District Annual Reports, 1913–1914.
MMA: Methodist Missionary Archives, London.
  During, W. H. Correspondence. N/T 46.

Heroe, F. A. Correspondence. N/T 105.
PRO: Public Record Office, London.
Euan-Smith to Salisbury, 20 November 1888, with encls. FO 541/28.

Other sources

Alpers, E. A. 1975. *Ivory and slaves in east Central Africa*. Berkeley: University of California Press.

Beachey, R. W. 1976. *The slave trade of eastern Africa*. London: Rex Collings.

Bennett, N. R. 1964. The Church Missionary Society at Mombasa, 1873–1894. In *Boston University papers in African history*, Vol. 1, ed. J. Butler, 157–94. Boston: Boston University Press.

Brantley, C. 1981. *The Giriama and colonial resistance in Kenya, 1800–1920*. Berkeley: University of California Press.

Cooper, F. 1977. *Plantation slavery on the east coast of Africa*. New Haven: Yale University Press.

Cooper, F. 1980. *From slaves to squatters: plantation labor and agriculture in Zanzibar and coastal Kenya, 1890–1925*. New Haven: Yale University Press.

Coupland, R. 1968. *The exploitation of East Africa, 1856–1890: the slave trade and the scramble*. 2d ed. London: Faber and Faber.

Harford-Battersby, C. F. n.d. *Pilkington of Uganda*. n.p.

Herlehy, T. J. 1984. Ties that bind: palm wine and blood brotherhood at the Kenya coast during the 19th century. *The International Journal of African Historical Studies* 17: 285–308.

Herlehy, T. J. 1985. An economic history of the Kenya coast: the Mijikenda coconut palm economy, 1800–1980. Ph.D. dissertation, Boston University.

Hollis, A. C. 1955. The life of Justin. *Tanganyika Notes and Records* 41.

Jackson, F. 1969. *Early days in East Africa*. 2d ed. London: Dawsons of Pall Mall.

Johnstone, H. B. 1902. Notes on the customs of the tribes occupying Mombasa sub-district, British East Africa. *Journal of the Royal Anthropological Institute* 32: 263–72.

McDermott, P. L. 1895. *British East Africa or IBEA: a history of the formation and work of the Imperial British East Africa Company*. 2d ed. London: Chapman and Hall.

Morton, R. F. 1976. Slaves, fugitives, and freedmen on the Kenya coast, 1873–1907. Ph.D. dissertation, Syracuse University.

Morton, R. F. 1977. New evidence regarding the Shungwaya myth of Miji Kenda origins. *The International Journal of African Historical Studies* 10(4): 628–43.

Nicholls, C. S. 1971. *The Swahili coast: politics, diplomacy and trade on the East African littoral, 1798–1856*. London: George Allen and Unwin.

Parkin, D. J. 1968. Medicines and men of influence. *Man* 3: 424–39.

Parkin, D. J. 1970. Politics of ritual syncretism: Islam among the non-Muslim Giriama of Kenya. *Africa: Journal of the International African Institute* 40: 217–33.

PP: *Parliamentary papers*, Great Britain. Binns to Hardinge, 7 December 1898. (1899), [C. 9502], XVII.

Price, W. S. 1890. *My third campaign in East Africa: a story of missionary life in troubled times.* London: William Hunt.

Ranger, T. O. 1975. *Dance and society in eastern Africa, 1890–1935.* London: Heinemann.

Spear, T. T. 1978. *The Kaya complex: a history of the Mijikenda peoples of the Kenya coast to 1900.* Nairobi: Kenya Literature Bureau.

Strayer, R. W. 1978. *The making of mission communities in East Africa: Anglicans and Africans in colonial Kenya, 1875–1935.* London: Heinemann.

Sunday Standard (Nairobi). 12 September 1982.

Temu, A. J. 1971. The role of the Bombay Africans (liberated Africans) on the Mombasa coast, 1874–1901. In *Hadith 3*, ed. B. A. Ogot, 53–81. Nairobi: East African Publishing House.

Temu, A. J. 1972. *British Protestant missions.* London: Longmans.

Wakefield, E. S. 1872–1887. Letters to the United Methodist Free Church. *UMFC Magazine* 15(1872): 207 and 340; 16(1873): 432; 21(1878): 251; 26(1883): 250–51; 30(1887): 410.

Wakefield, E. S. 1904 *Thomas Wakefield: missionary and geographical pioneer in East Equatorial Africa.* London: Religious Tract Society.

Ylvisaker, M. 1979. *Lamu in the nineteenth century: land, trade, and politics.* Boston: African Studies Center, Boston University.

9 *Richard Roberts*

The End of Slavery in the French Soudan, 1905–1914

Although the end of the legal status of slavery in the Soudan followed French colonial expansion into the area, colonial antislavery policy was only one factor in the transformation of precolonial labor systems. French policies eroded the legal underpinnings of slavery and the slave-supply mechanisms without actually abolishing slavery. French conquest of Samori of Wasulu and Babemba of Kenedugu, the two leading suppliers of slaves for the Western Sudan, led to a dramatic decline in the numbers of new slaves available on the market just when the expansion of commodity markets and demand for agricultural produce led to growing tensions between masters and slaves. This was the context in which the slaves of the French Soudan asserted their own freedom: between 1905 and 1911 slaves throughout the region either walked away from their masters or negotiated a new relationship with them.

The French, however, were unprepared when the slaves first started to leave. They aimed at protecting property and maintaining production while still respecting the liberty of the former slaves. Local administra-

I wish to thank the Social Science Research Council and the National Endowment of the Humanities for opportunities to conduct research in Mali. I am also grateful to and thank Martin Klein, Paul Lovejoy, Fred Cooper, Suzanne Miers, Bill Worger, and the students in my graduate colloquia for their comments on this chapter.

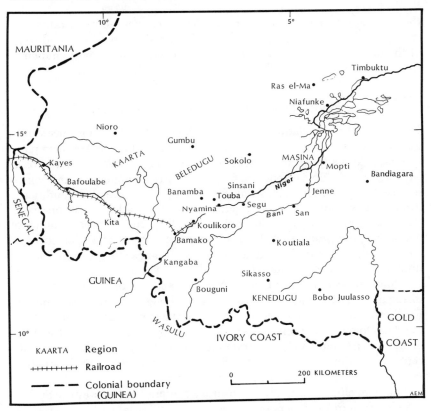

Map 9. French Soudan

tors tried to ease the transition to a new labor system by directing former masters and slaves into sharecropping and tenancy relationships. Unless they considered it to be in their direct interests, however, former slaves refused such arrangements. Those who left their masters not only undermined the precolonial patterns of labor but also eroded ethnic monopolies certain groups had erected over economic resources. Thus, slaves who were trained as weavers, dyers, herders, fishermen, and traders often established themselves as independent craftsmen and entrepreneurs. Not all former slaves, however, left their masters.

This chapter builds on a previous study of the Banamba slave exodus of 1905 (Roberts and Klein 1980) by focussing on the expansion and consequences of the exodus in the French Soudan. The chapter begins with a brief overview of French colonial antislavery policy and then assesses the evidence on the end of slavery in selected *cercles* (administrative districts). By 1914 the vast emigration of former slaves was over and some of the patterns of social and economic adjustment in the postemancipation era are visible.

French Policy and the Abolition of Slavery

In 1848, the French National Assembly abolished slavery in France's colonial possessions. Although abolition was directed at French Antillean plantations, it also applied to France's tiny colony on the West African coast. In Gorée and St. Louis, abolition frightened African merchants and caused some economic dislocation. Louis Faidherbe, who succeeded Baudin and Protet as governor in 1854, summarized the senior administration's position when he argued that Senegal, unlike the Antilles, was a colony of commerce, not production. He also argued that the colony's political and commercial viability depended largely on alliances forged with indigenous elites and merchants, and that slavery was a cornerstone of their commercial system. Since Faidherbe and his successors could not totally disregard French law, they proceeded to bend it to their advantage. Faidherbe, for example, expelled fugitive slaves of friendly chiefs, forcing them to return to their masters, whilst freeing and harboring the slaves of enemies (Renault 1972). Throughout the second half of the nineteenth century, administrators applied antislavery legislation selectively and thus managed to maintain and even expand trade.

Far from eliminating slavery, military conquest of the Western Sudan, which began in 1879, generated new demands for labor. This was often filled by slaves. Recruits were needed for the new companies of the Tirailleurs Sénégalais — the Senegalese Rifles. In Senegal, tirailleurs were often recruited by purchasing slaves directly (Martin Klein, pers. comm.). Fugitive slaves who volunteered were offered pay, uniforms, and occasionally their liberation. However, along the Middle Niger, slaves were recruited who not only remained legally bound to their former masters but paid them a share of their income (Echenberg 1975; Bouche 1968; ANM, rapport politique, Segu, 1898). Porters also were needed to haul goods and military equipment along the supply route. And between 1879 and 1904, manpower was needed to build the railway which was gradually making its way from Kayes to Bamako. Demand for railway labor competed with the demand for porters, and local administrators constantly called on the inhabitants living along the supply route for food, livestock, and labor. Consequently, those who could, fled, thus jeopardizing the annual military campaigns. The French, therefore, settled fugitive slaves and indigent women and children along the route at strategic points in so-called liberty villages (ANM, Grodet 1894; ANM, Charnet 1899).

Inhabitants of these villages constituted a coercible labor pool. District commanders often called upon them to perform unpaid labor locally or sent them to make up for recruitment shortfalls throughout the region. Inhabitants of these villages were considered to be "the slaves of the whites" (Deherme 1908: 366).

While the French were using slaves and freed slaves to man and supply their armies, slaveholdings among the Bambara, the FulBe, and especially the Maraka in the Middle Niger region increased. In 1883 the French established a forward position at Bamako on the Niger, but they did not conquer the Umarian state at Segu until 1890. By 1893, they had crushed the Umarians. Paradoxically, French conquest coincided with the state-building activities of Samori in upper Guinea and Wasulu, of Tieba and later Babemba in Sikasso, and of the efforts by Shehu Amadu to consolidate his power within the Umarian state. Slaves had always been a product of West African patterns of state building, and the French therefore confronted not only strong rivals but a flourishing of the slave trade, which fed the growing demand for labor (Person 1968–1975; Holmes 1978). Slave-owners, particularly the Maraka, responded to the development of colonial commodity markets in Bamako by buying more slaves and by increasing the absolute surplus they extracted from the labor of their slaves through prolonging the working day, decreasing rations, and disregarding customary labor practices (Roberts and Klein 1980; Roberts 1981). Colonial administrators were pleased with the evidence of commercial development, but they were uneasy about slavery. While the administration did not actually support slavery as a foundation to the colonial economy, officials on all levels were prepared to turn a blind eye to it.

Fearing a public outcry in France against the persistence of slavery in their African colonies and concerned with the military's exclusive hold over the Western Sudan, the minister of colonies in 1893 appointed a civilian, Alfred Grodet, as governor of the French Soudan, one of the federated colonies of French West Africa (Schoelcher 1880, 1886; Kanya-Forstner 1969; Klein 1986). Grodet decided to end French acquiescence in the slave trade, and he actually punished French officers for distributing slaves. In 1894, Grodet issued several decrees prohibiting slave markets and slave caravans and empowering chiefs to halt slave caravans and to bring them to the nearest administrative post, where they were fined 20 francs (ca. U.S. $4.00)[1] for each slave brought into French territory.

---

1. By the end of the first decade of the twentieth century, slightly over five French francs exchanged for one United States dollar. Cowrie rates were subject to considerable regional and historical variation. In 1892, a five-French-franc coin was exchanged for 2,500

This hit directly at the profit margins for slave traders and pushed the slave trade underground (ANS-AOF, étude 1894; ANS-AOF, Deherme 1906).

Grodet left the Soudan before his policies could be fully implemented. His successor, Colonel Trentinian, followed a more gradualist course. "The issue of slavery," he wrote several months after Grodet's departure, "require infinite tact and prudence, if one does not wish to turn the land topsy turvy and result in its complete economic ruin" (ANS-AOF, Trentinian 1895; ANM, Trentinian 1895). At least for a brief while, the military sealed the cracks in their efforts to build the colonial state on precolonial economic and political foundations (Roberts 1987).

In spite of French caution, the actions of the colonial state frightened masters. The commandment of Segu assured them that the French had no intention of ending slavery. In 1895 he reported that owners "were happy to learn that if captives are mistreated by their masters, they can find protection with us, but if they evade their masters without motive, they will be returned" (ANM, rapport général, Segu 1895). The slaves, however, realized that conditions were changing. In 1895 when Grodet's decrees were posted in both French and Arabic in the central markets of Bamako, Kangaba, Nyamina, Banamba, and Touba, significantly more slaves ran away than in the previous year (ANM, rapport sur la répression 1895). From 1895, when increased slave flights began, to 1905, when the large-scale slave exodus started, the archival reports are full of references to population movement. A significant percentage of those moving were free people who had fled from the wars of conquest in Wasulu and settled on the left bank of the Niger, and were now, as Samori moved his state eastward, returning to their homelands. Many slaves throughout the Western Sudan fled homeward alongside the free emigrants (ANM, rapport politique et militaire 1895; ANS-AOF, Ponty 1901).

In 1898, the French conquered Babemba's state and captured Samori. This eliminated the largest suppliers of new slaves for the expanding colonial economy. Although enslavement remained widespread well into the first decade of the twentieth century, the numbers of slaves entering the commercial circuits were sharply reduced. This contraction of the labor supply coincided with the expansion of commodity production and increased the strains between masters and slaves. Slaves responded to increased demands by work stoppages, flight, and occasionally by physical violence. They had always used flight as a form of resistance (Lovejoy

---

cowries, but 10 years later, the same coin was exchanged for 5,000 cowries. The United States dollar equivalences cited in this chapter are roughly those of 1910–1914 rates of exchange. For conversions of French francs to U.S. dollars I used F. Pick and R. Sédillot, *All the Monies of the World* (New York: Pick Publishing, 1971), and P. Cowitt, *1985 World Currency Yearbook* (New York: International Currency Analysis, 1985).

1986), but from 1895, when escapes involved greater numbers, they threatened the institutional basis of slavery.

During this period William Ponty became governor of the French Soudan. His appointment ended military rule in the Soudan. At the time of his appointment in 1899, Ponty was convinced that slavery lay at the base of the commercial activity of the colony. He was afraid of moving too rapidly against it, just when trade was reaching levels unmatched before. He also had more concrete tasks before him. He had to ensure that population density along the supply route remained stable while the railway was being built. Labor requisitioned by district officers invariably consisted of slaves sent by their masters (Klein 1983). Moreover, slaves expressed their fears to at least one administrator that if the French were to take measures "on their behalf, that they do not brusquely deprive them of their current means of existence" (ANS-AOF, Brevié 1904).

Ponty, however, was convinced that slavery would have to be ended as soon as it was feasible to do so without disruption. The administration's gradualist position, which in essence followed the Indian model, resonated in district reports. "The principal notables of the cercle," reported the Segu administrator in 1904, "consider that emancipation of slaves should operate naturally and completely [by generational assimilation] . . . without recourse to special measures" (ANM, rapport sur la captivité 1904). Judicial changes and the actions of slaves, however, were to make this belief in a natural elimination of slavery illusory.

In 1903, as part of the general reorganization of the judicial system in French West Africa, Governor-General Merlin sent explicit instructions that slavery was no longer to have any legal status and that no magisterial, military, or native tribunals could recognize litigations involving claims over slaves (ANS-AOF, instructions 1903). This was a fatal blow to slavery: in one judicial move the legality behind returning fugitive slaves to their masters was abolished. No longer could the state support the power of the master over his slaves. The political and legal structures which bound slavery to the economic base of society were thus changed.

In a political economy in which the state no longer participated in the reproduction of precapitalist relations of production, slaves now took action to gain their freedom. In 1905, they began a massive exodus, which spread throughout the French Soudan in ever widening circles over the next six years.

The Process of Emancipation and the Diversity of Freed Slaves' Experiences

In March 1905, large numbers of slaves belonging to the Maraka started to leave their masters. Many returned to their homes in the districts of

Bouguni, Sikasso, Koutiala, Bobo Juulasso, and the territories of the northern Ivory Coast and eastern Guinea. Some stopped along the way. They swelled Bamako's population dramatically between the end of 1904 and the end of 1906, and small towns along the routes or near the river, like Gouni across the Niger from Koulikoro, absorbed fugitives (interview: Koke Jara, 1984).

The Banamba slave exodus was exactly what the French had most dreaded: events were taking a course consonant with their purported objective — to end slavery — but an alternative labor system had not yet been established. By the middle of May the situation turned critical. Armed slaves attempting to leave confronted armed masters determined to retain them. The French no longer hesitated. Governor-General Roume declared that the emigration of slaves was not authorized and should not be halted by "administrative means." Chiefs of neighboring villages were ordered to stop fugitives, and slaves caught leaving without permission were declared vagabonds and arrested. Roume sent Acting Lieutenant Governor Fawtier and a detachment of tirailleurs to Banamba to seek a "reconciliation by reciprocal concessions" (ANM, Roume 1905; ANS-AOF, Fawtier 1905; ANM, rapport politique, Bamako, May 1905). Fawtier held talks with masters and slaves and he convinced the slaves to return to the fields. Fawtier's reconciliation reaffirmed the customary reciprocity of the master-slave relationship, which had characterized slavery during the early nineteenth century (Roberts 1981). In December 1905, fully seven months after the first incidents at Banamba, Governor-General Roume formally decreed an end to the slave trade and the alienation of any person's liberty throughout French West Africa. Since the courts could no longer recognize the status of a slave and therefore the property the master held in his slave, Roume's decree outlawed the remaining components of the reproduction of slave labor.

By early spring 1906, the reconciliation between masters and slaves in Banamba collapsed. The French had intervened in 1905 to protect the agricultural productivity of the region; but when the exodus resumed again in the spring of 1906, the French did nothing to prevent slaves from leaving. Slaves began to leave in April, and by the end of May 3,000 had walked away from their masters in the region of Banamba (ANS-AOF, Ponty 1906). At the end of May 1907, officials assessed the net loss of population to the Banamba District at 11,944 (ANM, rapport politique, Bamako, May 1907). When the dust of their departures finally settled in 1910, an estimated 20,000 slaves had left the larger Banamba region (ANM, rapport politique d'ensemble 1910).

Maraka masters had clearly understood the instrumental role of the state in guaranteeing the form of plantation slavery that had emerged in the Western Sudan, and they had warned the French already in June 1905 that, unless they stopped the slave exodus, what was happening in Banamba would spread throughout the Soudan.[2] Just as masters had predicted, between 1906 and 1911 the events of Banamba were reproduced in hundreds of villages and hamlets all over the colony. Slaves either left their masters or negotiated a new relationship. In each case, slaves were now the ones who determined how and for whom they would work.

In 1907, the exodus spread to the districts of Bamako, Segu, Kayes, Kita, Bafoulabe, Sikasso, and Bouguni. Slaves left most frequently between April and June, just before the beginning of the new agricultural season. Between April and June 1907, the Segu commandant counted 5,331 slaves, out of an estimated slave population of 25,000, who had officially requested permission to leave (ANM, rapport politique, Segu, 1907; ANS-AOF, rapport politique 1907; Klein 1987). By the end of 1908, the exodus from these districts was virtually over. After the initial one or two years of massive departures, only very small numbers of slaves continued to leave (ANS-AOF, rapport politique 1909).

The colonial administration has left us a potentially invaluable source for measuring the numbers of slaves who left their masters, since it was illegal to cross district boundaries without carrying written permits. At the height of the exodus from Segu during late spring and early summer, the commandant issued 5,542 *laissez-passer*, of which 3,416 were for neighboring cercles (ANS-AOF, Ponty, rapport politique, 1907). There are, however, at least three problems in using the laissez-passer to measure the slave exodus and to follow its flow. First, the series are incomplete. Second, anyone leaving the cercle was required to have permission, and therefore it is hard to separate former slaves from traders, travellers, and individuals visiting relatives. In this series, we can assume that at least 211 laissez-passer were issed to individuals other than former slaves. And finally, although colonial officials required all individuals to register their movements, they could not enforce their decree. Thus, there is no easy way of estimating how many slaves simply left without informing the authorities or how many wound up in places other than those identified on the laissez-passer. In any case, the administration's position was now clear: any slave who paid his taxes was free to go wherever he wished (ANM, Ponty 1907; ANF-SOM, governor-general 1908). Some immigrants were faced with a double burden: the cercle of Bouguni required that all settlers also pay tax upon their arrival (ANM, rapport politique, Bouguni, May 1907). To avoid these taxes, many former slaves left without

2. ANS-AOF, Fawtier 1905. On how plantation slavery differed from slave use in less differentiated societies, see Lovejoy 1979; Klein and Lovejoy 1979; Cooper 1977.

informing anyone of their departure or arrival (ANM, rapports politique, Bouguni, June and October 1907).

From the beginning of 1906 to the end of 1908, the French watched the forces of change sweep through the land. Only when change threatened one of the central sectors of the economy, the cattle industry, as it did in 1908, did the administration intervene. The conflict between the pastoral FulBe and their agricultural slaves, called the *rimaibe*, was over access to land and the product of their labor. In December of that year, the administration negotiated an agreement between FulBe masters and their slaves which resembled the former master-slave relationship but reduced the level of exploitation and offered freed slaves some safeguards against dispossession of the land they worked. It thus asserted the rights of the freedmen to use the land without contesting FulBe property rights over the land.[3] The accord reflected Governor-General Roume's vision of an established class of property owners whose land was worked by sharecroppers. In 1905 Roume had written:

The experience [of Banamba] which has been imposed on us by force of circumstances, and was not something we expected, demonstrates that with firm resolve to respect the individual liberty of all natives, one can arrive at a rational decision which conforms to our principles in regard to the delicate question of agricultural workers. These workers would be regulated as well as protected by an equitable division of the product between owners of the land and the cultivators, based on an analogous model of sharecropping as in France between owners and peasants. Contracts are at once respected by the community and guaranteed by the tribunals. (ANS-AOF, Roume 1905)

The conflict between the FulBe and the rimaibe in Masina revolved around two conjoined sets of property relations. The first was the property relationship between the master and the slave, and the second involved ownership and use of the land. Since these two relations were embedded in social relations of dependence and exploitation, the administration's efforts to direct the rimaibe into sharecropping arrangements promised to preserve the status quo. Where the rimaibe were willing to accept the conditions of the 1908 accord, they remained in their villages working land belonging to their previous masters and acknowledged their dependence. But since neither land nor other economic resources in the French Soudan

3. ANM, Gaubert 1908. Martin Klein argues that the conflict was over rice, and indeed rice was the central issue of the rights to the product of labor, but I think that the French were more concerned with maintaining the flow of cattle than with the flow of rice. For similar efforts to maintain production, compare policies in Northern Nigeria (Shenton 1986; Lennihan 1982).

could be effectively monopolized by masters, former slaves simply rejected sharecropping, moved away, and established separate villages (interview: Mamuru Fomba et al., 1981; ANM, rapport politique d'ensemble 1910).[4] Despite the administration's efforts, sharecropping could not and did not in most cases replace slave labor.

In 1908, the slave exodus affected the sahelian districts of Sokolo and Gumbu. Following the pattern of Banamba and Segu, the exodus began in early spring of 1908 and ended with the 1909–1910 harvest. By the end of 1910, departures from the sahel had diminished to a trickle (ANM, rapports politiques, Gumbu, 1910; ANM, rapports politiques, Sokolo, 1910).

Statistics on the slave exodus from Gumbu are the most detailed I have come across. The commandant of the cercle kept a detailed record of former slaves requesting permission to leave the cercle from March 1908 to November 1910, with only a few gaps. Figs 9.1 and 9.2 plot officially requested departures by month and the destinations indicated. As with the Segu data, we have no way of estimating how many slaves left without informing either their former masters or officials, nor do these statistics show how many former slaves moved to other parts of the same cercle. Unlike the neighboring cercles of Sokolo and Nioro, in Gumbu attractive productive land was not easily available.

The flow of departures reflects the agricultural cycle, in that most former slaves chose to leave between the end of the harvest and the beginning of the new planting season, roughly from January through early June. Some slaves might have waited as late as possible into the new season in order to conserve their resources for the lean year ahead. As Fig. 9.1 indicates, the first two years consisted of massive departures, each following roughly the same seasonal variations. Departures for the third year, 1910, constitute only 11 percent of the total recorded departures. In 1911, only 243 former slaves left the cercle. Not included in these statistics are the 2,000 former slaves who "declared their liberty, but who, having been born for the most part in this land, . . . established themselves [independently] near their former masters, or like the rimaibe of Kolom, . . . formed new villages" (ANM, rapport politique, Gumbu, June 1908). Taken together, the former slaves who left the cercle and those who left their masters but remained in the cercle constituted 35 percent of the total slave population of the Gumbu cercle.[5]

---

4. The case was considerably different in areas of white settlement and where coastal plantations had emerged. On Zanzibar, for example, clove trees were privately owned and sharecropping and squatting arrangements emerged (Cooper 1980).

5. Unfortunately, we have no way of determining how many of those who declared their freedom without leaving eventually did leave the cercle, nor do we have the records

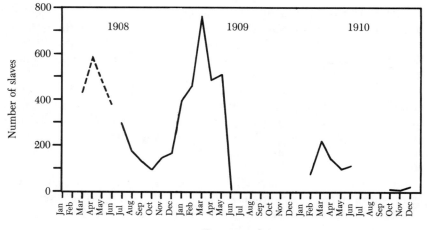

Figure 9.1. Gumbu slave departures, January 1908–December 1910 (a total of 6,279 departures). Note: the dotted line for 1908 is based on estimated monthly departures, because the data are presented as a total for the period January through June. I have estimated that the seasonality of emigration for 1908 reflects the patterns of 1909 and 1910. The peak departures were April, and the total for January–June 1908 equals 76 percent of the same period in 1909.

By far the largest number of former slaves who left the cercle officially returned to the cercles of Bouguni and the Sikasso and to the northern Ivory Coast and eastern Guinea. The slaves going to these areas accounted for 79 percent of the emigrants from Gumbu. These were the areas where Samori, Tieba, and Babemba had been active, and these emigrants were probably first-generation slaves. Of those who went elsewhere, a significant number emigrated to Bamako and to the cercles along the Niger and Bani rivers (Segu, Jenne, and Niafunke), which presumably offered attractive economic opportunities.

Freed slaves occasionally departed individually, but most seem to have travelled in groups. Often several dozen and sometimes as many as several hundred former slaves departed for the same cercle in the same month. The commandant of Gumbu reported that former slaves organized in family units requested that permission to leave be given to the leader they had appointed (ANM, rapport politique, Gumbu, April 1908). How former slaves made their choices about staying or leaving, how they set about preparing to leave, and in what sorts of groups they made their way remain largely unanswered.

---

to indicate the numbers of former slaves who freed themselves but remained in the cercle in subsequent years. The best estimates of slave populations come from Klein 1987.

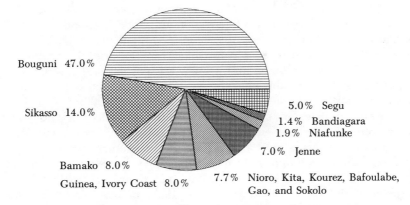

Bouguni 47.0%

Sikasso 14.0%

Bamako 8.0%

Guinea, Ivory Coast 8.0%

5.0% Segu

1.4% Bandiagara
1.9% Niafunke

7.0% Jenne

7.7% Nioro, Kita, Kourez, Bafoulabe, Gao, and Sokolo

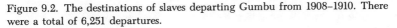

Figure 9.2. The destinations of slaves departing Gumbu from 1908–1910. There were a total of 6,251 departures.

Although local administrators could not keep the freed men and women from leaving, assistant commandant de Laur of Gumbu tried to dissuade them. His arguments do not conceal his concern to minimize the impact of their departure on agricultural production.

With each slave, I hold the following discussion. "The rainy season has started. You are absolutely free to work for yourself, to pawn yourself, or to hire yourself out. In one word, you can make whatever decision you want. The season, however, is not propitious for travelling. The time has come to work, to prepare the fields. The commandant of the cercle has only one goal, to allow the cultivators to work. The season of agriculture is here and we seek to avoid all disruption during this period. Work now, the harvest will come, the best season for travelling will come, and your resources to make such a voyage will be much better." (ANM, rapport politique, Gumbu, June 1909)

De Laur's speech clearly indicated the administration's new tactic: persuade, cajole, negotiate in order to keep the freedmen on the farm, but in no way prevent them from exercising their right to leave when they want to.

Adjustments to the End of Slavery

The end of slavery offered freed men and women three choices, and infinite variation within them. They could return to their homelands, they could declare themselves autonomous without returning home, or they could redefine relations with their masters. When the slaves decided to leave, they left quickly. This was often a difficult decision to make, especially when it meant leaving family and friends. Many went home. In

1907, for example, more than 11,000 immigrants were officially reported as having returned to eight cantons of Bouguni (ANM, rapport politique, Bouguni, November and December 1906; ANM, Saillard 1907).[6] But because the administration sought to collect taxes from each immigrant, the movement of freed men and women was pushed underground and the numbers were probably much larger (interview: Santa Kulubali, 1977; ANM, rapports politiques, Bouguni, May and June 1907).

The return of former slaves was not uniformly welcomed, however. Many were men and women whose families had long dispersed, and while additional labor was almost always needed, their return without clearly defined lines of kinship or patronage threatened the new canton chiefs, many of whom were already compromised by their participation in the colonial administration (ANM, rapport politique, Bouguni, October 1906). "The freed slave," wrote an official in 1906, "is a dissolvent, a fomentor of trouble in the village when he returns" (Deherme 1908: 366). We still know too little about postemancipation migrations and reintegration to assess this generalization, but the arrival of significant numbers of freed men and women may have severely tested kinship ties, especially during the first year or so when those returning were especially needy.

Throughout the French Soudan, some former slaves settled in established villages; others established new villages which were wholly autonomous. Still others, such as the slaves on the Niarela plantation belonging to the Sukule family of Sinsani, decided to remain where they were, but severed all ties with their former masters (interview: Binke Sukule, 1977). In Segu, for example, 20 percent of the slaves requesting formal permission to leave their masters chose to remain in the district (ANS-AOF, Ponty 1907). In Sokolo, 354 slaves settled in the southeastern

6. The following table depicts population changes in the Bouguni Cercle:

Population of Selected Cantons, Bouguni Cercle, ca. 1900 and 1907

	Number of Villages	1900	1907	Change
Zana	7	970	1,350	+ 380
Tiondugu	33	1,481	2,033	+ 552
Niene	28	1,968	4,309	+ 2,341
Gonautiedugu	54	4,603	6,437	+ 1,834
Foubala	24	980	1,846	+ 866
Yorababugu	34	2,663	4,883	+ 2,220
Nonolodiana	17	860	1,159	+ 299
Ziendugu	65	3,663	6,244	+ 2,581
Total	262	17,188	28,261	+ 11,073

Sources: ANM, Saillard 1907; ANM, rapports politiques, Bouguni, November and December 1906.

districts of the cercle, but according to the commandant, "this [was] a temporary settlement with the goal of allowing the liberated people to procure through agriculture some resources before their definitive departure" (ANM, rapport politique, Sokolo, November 1910). In 1907, the Bamako commandant reported that former slave villages had fallen into decay and that new agricultural communities had been founded nearby (ANM, rapport sur la politique 1907). In all cases, however, the first few years were the most difficult. In some of these new villages, freed men and women worked side by side in the fields, as they had during slavery and contrary to a customary gender division of labor. Descendants of freedmen explained why:

At the start of liberation former slaves who installed themselves in a new village had to create a new life. For that end, effort was necessary. During this period the [slaves'] organization was observed. That is to say, that men and women did the same work. But with time, prosperity arrived. Women undertook food preparation and domestic chores. However, each [woman] retained the right to the "field of the night," just as the slaves had the right to their own fields. (interview: Mamuru Fomba et al., 1981)

Female former slaves in the American South and in the Caribbean, in contrast, demonstrated their new freedom by withdrawing from the labor market and staying at home (Wiener 1978: 47; Foner 1983: 19, 44).

Not all freed men and women left their masters. Masters were forced to change work rhythms, increase rations, and modify social relations in an effort to retain their former slaves. In a report on Banamba written in 1914, Rougier noted that a few former slaves stayed with their masters, but those who did were "well treated and [considered] almost members of the family" (ANM, Rougier 1914). Although these inducements sometimes worked, as a general rule, slaves who remembered their origins left, while second-generation slaves probably remained. More women and children remained than adult males (ANM, rapport sur les coutumes 1909). In all cases, the end of slavery demanded that ex-slaves and ex-masters redefine their relations (Meillassoux 1975). Former masters tried to establish new forms of hegemony, and with all former slaves who remained, they established new relationships. According to one of my informants, who was a descendant of slave-owners,

a type of kinship was substituted for [slavery]. But the masters retained a certain superiority. The former slave, however, had the right to work for himself, but he continued to render services to his former master. The former master remained his protector and the head of the family. He presided over marriages, baptisms, and circumcisions of the children of former slaves. He called him his "son" and the former slave called him "father." Former slaves would never agree to their former masters carrying even the smallest load in their presence. Age meant nothing. (interview: Baye Fofana, 1981)

Some freed men voluntarily paid what they termed the *zakkat* to their masters in recognition of the master's ownership of the land they used (interview: Binke Sukule, 1977; ANM, Rougier 1914). Others worked side by side with their masters and became more closely enmeshed within their masters' households.

Even if masters and freedmen now "ate from the same bowl," subtle distinctions remained. Freedmen, for instance, did not marry their former masters' daughters (interviews: Santa Kulubali, 1977; Binke Baba Kuma, 1976; Sidi Yahaya Kone, 1977). In the period after the First World War, some of the distance separating former masters and former slaves disappeared. With the beginning of military conscription in 1914, former slaves who had remained in their masters' households were often recruited into the army in place of their masters' sons. When they returned to their former masters, they used the opportunity to renegotiate once again the conditions of their participation in the households. They bargained for better food rations, working conditions, and marriage options. Army veterans of slave origin apparently also began to marry women of free birth during the postwar period (Kersaint-Gilly 1924; interview: Musa Kouyate, 1977).

The administration expected the end of slavery to portend the decline of the once flourishing agricultural region of Beledugu. Governor Clozel's report for 1908, however, signalled the contrary:

Far from being ruinous for the colony, as certain pessimistic spirits predicted, the liberation of the former servants has created a happy transformation of the conditions of production, which tends at the same time to increase the numbers [of people working] and the return on their labor [as a result of the new manner of working]. . . . [F]ormer masters must participate in agricultural labor in order to meet their needs. [And former servants realize a greater] return [on their labor], as a result of the increase in [their productivity], . . . which comes from their consciousness of their liberty and the personal nature of their efforts. (ANS-AOF, Clozel 1908)

Despite the departure of nearly 12,000 slaves, the administration estimated that the total area of cultivated land in the Banamba region had not declined (ANM, rapport politique, Bamako, 1906).

Not all areas of the French Soudan fared as well as Banamba and the Middle Niger. The sahelian districts, once composed of important and flourishing agricultural and commercial communities, were confronted

Table 9.1. Population of the Sokolo Cercle, 1900 and 1910

Village	1900	1910	Net Loss or Gain
Canton of Akor[a]			
Akor	800	545	− 255
Bandjiguna	700	386	− 314
Boundidadie	515	102	− 413
Guida	642	274	− 368
Dougirel	50	26	− 24
Sabelliat	160	disappeared	− 160
Sarabakou	300	52	− 248
Total	3,167	1,385	− 1,782
Canton of Nampala[a]			
Nampala	550	1,125	+ 575
Amarekole	206	disappeared	− 206
Barkarou	305	327 .	+ 22
Boubounodi	475	448	− 27
Kobaddi	243	234	− 9
Diamelli	380	321	− 59
Foutankole	120	92	− 28
Giumbalankole	208	disappeared	− 208
Goudiou	699	788	+ 89
Linguikole	78	disappeared	− 78
Moussankole	41	disappeared	− 41
N'Dondi grande	416	disappeared	− 416
N'Dondi petite	479	236	− 243
N'Douga	522	162	− 360
Oudiabe	172	245	+ 73
Rangabe	169	151	− 18
Sokobara	160	disappeared	− 160
Tindarabe	303	disappeared	− 303
Torobe	185	115	− 70
Total	5,711	4,244	− 1,467
Canton of Segala[a,b]			
Segala	1,675	613	− 1,062
Boala	91	154	+ 63
Manzona	902	405	− 497
Ortobila	1,150	340	− 810
Sinbila	153	65	− 88
Sirani	600	313	− 287
Tonbakoro	790	396	− 394
Yemougou	132	80	− 52
Total	5,493	2,366	− 3,127
Canton of Monimpe[c]	3,429	5,158	+ 1,729
Canton of Diagana[c]	3,115	5,803	+ 2,688
Canton of Diouna[c]	4,024	7,274	+ 3,250
Total	24,939	26,230	+ 1,291

Source: ANM, Logeau 1913.
[a]Cantons located on the desert edge.
[b]Only selected villages of the canton.
[c]Cantons bordering on the Niger River, no villages recorded, population by canton only.

by a triple catastrophe in the years after 1908. Not only did masters see their slaves depart, but a series of poor agricultural seasons led to an erosion of grain and cattle stocks as inhabitants dug deeply into their reserves to survive. And finally, in the western sahel, household heads saw their young unmarried men migrate to the peanut fields of Senegambia, where they hoped to accumulate the capital necessary to enter trade, to meet the bridewealth costs on their own, or to pay taxes (ANM, rapport politique d'ensemble 1912; ANS-AOF, Clozel 1912). As a result, whole villages in the region were abandoned, and those that remained were much smaller and consequently less able to store surpluses in order to survive the recurrent droughts along the desert edge (ANM, rapport politique d'ensemble 1912; ANM, Logeau 1913). From the eastern sahelian districts of Gumbu, Sokolo, and Niafunke and from the desert district of Ras el-Ma, former slaves moved to the better watered Niger Basin. Figures for the Sokolo Cercle in Table 9.1 illustrate this dramatic shift in population. Although the cercle saw a net population increase of only 1,291 (5.2 percent) between 1900 and 1910, the riverine districts, including the cantons of Monimpe, Diagana, and Diouna, increased by 73 percent. This shift in population left the desert-edge cantons relatively depopulated (a 44 percent decline), and some villages disappeared altogether.

Resettling near the river offered former slaves considerable advantages. They were far from their former masters, and therefore they were physically separated from the legacy of dependence and exploitation. The river also provided access to the expanding grain and commodity markets of the colonial economy. In particular, demand in upper Guinea and Senegambia for rice, which was cultivated along the Niger, provided freed men with an assured market for their surplus (ANM, bulletin agricole 1906).

The end of slavery thus left the sahel in economic and social decline (ANM, rapport politique d'ensemble 1912). But, in contrast it brought relative prosperity to the Middle Niger Valley, which was well located to participate in the expanding colonial commodity markets.[7] The region of Banamba provides an example of the mechanisms used to maintain production. First, former Maraka slave-owners tightened their belts and turned their wives and children into their new labor force. "The Markas [sic]," wrote the Bamako commandant at the end of 1906, "who for a long time have lost the habit of work and constituted unproductive elements, have begun resolutely to take a counter approach, that of re-

---

7. The markets for grain and cotton provided long-term opportunities for freedmen and for former masters to market their surplus production. I have described the Bamako grain market elsewhere (Roberts 1980), but some figures from the Segu cotton market between 1907 and 1918 indicate the possibilities offered:

placing their lost manpower [through their own work], and because of
the lower returns [expected] of these inexperienced workers, [they] have
also lowered their consumption levels" (ANM, rapport général, Bamako,
1906). Where only recently, Maraka women had been secluded in their
homes and the household heads had overseen the labor of their slaves,
"the fields [were] now cultivated by the women and the heads of families"
(ANM, rapport politique d'ensemble 1910). Second, some proprietors
quickly discovered a supply of temporary agricultural workers among
neighboring Bambara villagers (ANM, rapport politique, Bamako 1906;
ANS-AOF, rapport politique 1906). In 1909, the Maraka regularly hired
Bambara agricultural workers and paid them 320 cowries (between U.S.
6¢ and 12¢) per day plus food and lodging (ANM, Robin 1909). Demand
was such that labor contractors and labor gangs emerged. "Daily agricultural wages vary according to the cercles, between 30 and 50 centimes
[between 6¢ and 10¢]; often work contracts are conducted between a pro-
prietor and a large team head, who engages 70–80 workers."[8] And third,

Stocks of Cotton on Hand by the Association Cotonnière coloniale, Segu,
1907–1918 (in metric tons)

1907–1908	25
1908–1909	69
1909–1910	190
1910–1911	86
1911–1912	260
1912–1913	400
1913–1914[a]	220
1914–1915[b]	208
1915–1916[b]	224
1916–1917[b]	223
1917–1918[b]	496

Source: ANM, chef de service d'agriculture 1920.
[a]Drought year.
[b]The war witnessed a decline in textile imports and it encouraged an expansion of local handicraft production, which absorbed large quantities of local cotton.
8. ANS-AOF, Clozel 1908. It is possible that this large team was composed of the Bambara young men's association, which was already mobilized to provide labor within their
community. Their willingness to engage in work outside their community, however, sig-
nifies a departure from their traditional role within Bambara society. Several Maraka informants have said that they had hired such Bambara labor groups (interviews: Binke
Baba Kuma, 1977; Amadu Sanogo, 1977).
Certainly agricultural labor had been scarce, but it had existed prior to 1905. As late
as 1903, a Bamako report noted that "agricultural workers rarely consent to work the fields
of another. Only those natives whose own fields were destroyed by bad luck consent to
work for others. Hiring of this nature is short term, never more than one month; especially
young men who want to buy a boubou [Bambara: long gown] or other small object, work
three or four days" (ANM, notices 1903).

former slaves, especially from the eastern sahel, also gravitated to the Banamba region, where they added to the new labor force of the region. Despite the propensity of former slaves to establish themselves as independent farmers, the end of slavery brought a fundamental change to the labor market. Labor shortfalls could now be made up through hiring freedmen, young men who had escaped their households in search of independent income, and even former masters.

The end of slavery and the emergence of a wage-labor market had considerable effect on family and household composition, but more research needs to be conducted on it. In their study of a western sahelian community, Pollet and Winter note that the end of slavery weakened the hierarchical principle of both society and the family (Pollet and Winter 1972: 371, 394). The new opportunities for wage labor probably encouraged dissatisfied sons to desert their fathers and earn the capital to marry and start their own farms.[9] In a study commissioned by the Bureau d'Affaires indigènes, the administrator of Banamba in 1909 linked together the decline of patriarchal authority, the end of slavery, the imposition of taxes, new economic opportunities, and the new ideology of individual liberty:

Villages are not as closed to strangers as they were in the past. Freed slaves either stay or go into the country forming stranger communities. The higher taxes have increased the needs of everyone; in most families, young men leave their villages in order to trade or sell their products. In so doing, they acquire new knowledge, they see practices and customs different from their own. . . . A man separated from his family can now survive, develop independently and develop his intelligence. The authority of the head of the family and the chiefs of villages is not what it was in the past. (ANM, Robin 1909)

Banamba was not the only region to witness the linked set of transformations set in train by the end of slavery and French policies. Thoron de Laur, assistant district officer of Gumbu, waxed eloquently on the changes in the society and the economy which he was observing:

[The loss of slaves was] a just punishment for the race which considered their relatives [i.e., other Africans] as their slaves and who have pushed them to leave. But there are some significant difficulties created by their departure. Destruction of the family, abandonment of children, raping of children, litigenous questions

---

9. The effects of migrant labor on communities were uneven. Bambara communities managed the complex process of having their young males participate in migrant labor and yet attracted migrants home again at crucial times in the agricultural and social cycles (Lewis 1979, 1981).

[are] connected events. The movement [of slaves] appears to be diminishing and the exodus proceeds without incident. Nonetheless, it does cause profound changes in the customs of the land. . . . (ANM, de Laur 1909)

Although de Laur saw the social crisis of the slave-owners as a just retribution, his assessment smacks of a nostalgia for a social order firmly rooted in patriarchal authority. He also worried that former slaves were unrealistic — childish — about their new freedom.

Without doubt some slaves are happy to return to their homelands. But many are ignorant [of it]. . . . [Their] goal is to escape the presence of the Sarakolet [also called Soninke, Maraka] population and this is why many have left the land, abandoning ancestors. . . . The natives have an incontestable right to complete liberty, and it would be interesting to know why certain of them, much too young to have ever been in the land to which they want to return, persist in wanting to establish themselves [there]. . . . (ibid.)

De Laur and many other French administrators were also anxious to maintain the economic productivity of their districts and thus the continued flow of tax revenue. Massive population departures and abruptly changing labor regimes promised to cause unwelcome disruptions.

On the whole, however, the French soon decided that the end of slavery was working to their advantage. Governor-General Ponty, for instance, had been committed to the gradual course of ending slavery. But in 1907, when the liberation was a reality, he chided the Segu commandant for his fears of economic disaster following the massive departures of that year. "The positive factors," he wrote, "will be the definitive establishment of the principles of individual liberty. It forces owners to work for themselves and creates the need for free workers" (ANS-AOF, Ponty 1907). The very next year, Clozel identified the free worker as the reason for the continued prosperity of the Banamba region. "It is worth noting the appearance of a new social class, which will be called on to develop rapidly: the class of free paid agricultural workers" (ANS-AOF, Clozel 1908). The annual report of 1910 was most explicit about the triumph of the new economy. "The first economic result of this social transformation has been clearly encouraging. Everywhere, the free worker affirms his superiority and intelligence vis-à-vis the captive" (ANM, rapport politique d'ensemble 1910). The development of a labor market was one of the major consequences of the end of slavery.

The new economy of the French Soudan saw the fullest expression of the end of slavery in the emergence of free workers and in the erosion of ethnic monopolies over economic resources. This erosion allowed former slaves to move into all sectors of the economy. The erosion of ethnic monopolies over economic resources was probably one of the most revolutionary changes to have occurred during the early colonial period, but it is also among the most difficult to trace. Sometimes the changes were dramatic; mostly they were gradual. In all cases, they had profound long-term effects on economic and social history. Conflicts over access to economic resources predated the end of slavery, but the movement of freedmen into all sectors of the economy accelerated the change. The first visible signs of declining ethnic monopolies occurred in the early years of the new century, even before the end of slavery. By 1905, the Segu commandant wrote that "trade, agriculture, herding, monopolies long recognized [as belonging] to this or that race, are today contested by all, and make rapid progress" (ANM, rapport général 1905). The end of slavery accelerated the process as former slaves moved into occupations whose skills they had learned as slaves, including the textile industry, commerce, transportation, and herding. As the end of slavery gave freed slaves new opportunities to earn their livelihood, it also transformed established forms of capital accumulation. Since capital could no longer be invested in slaves, Africans invested capital in livestock and trade goods.

Conclusion

The French were inclined to take credit for the end of slavery, for the subsequent patterns of economic change, and for the development of a free wage-labor force. The annual report of Bamako stated self-righteously: "The year 1906 will remain a historic year for the Marka. . . . It was during the course of this year that an event [changed] that population and which would not have occurred except as an ineluctable consequence and logic of our *pénétration civilisatrice*" (ANM, rapport général 1906). The Bamako commandant was right to claim credit for the events which changed the political economy of the French Soudan, but he overestimated the role of the new ideology of state power. It was not ideas of individual liberty so central to the French bourgeois political economy which transformed social and economic organization. The gradual triumph of a new economy and the implantation of capitalist relations of production were only indirectly a consequence of French antislavery policy. The French, by withdrawing state support for slavery and by outlawing new enslavement and slave-dealing, created conditions which enabled the slaves to take the initiative and free themselves. Although French administrators had not wanted such a precipitous end to slavery, they quickly abandoned efforts to oppose it and to control it, and they let events take their course. To their surprise, they found that production in many areas actually increased. But the changes in the organization of production relations were most often determined by Africans, especially former slaves.

The end of slavery provides a glimpse into the struggles waged by slaves to liberate themselves, into the efforts of the colonial state to direct and control the processes of social change, and into the linked sets of transformations in social organization. But these remain glimpses. Only more detailed research on the postemancipation era will provide answers and certainly raise new questions about the nature of social change in colonial Africa and of the centrality of labor organization to these changes.

GLOSSARY

boubou long gown.
cercles French administrative units, districts.
rimaibe agricultural slaves of the FulBe.
zakkat tithe, tax; originally collected by Islamic authorities for social welfare.

REFERENCES

Oral sources

Taped originals and French translated versions of these interviews are available at the Institut de Sciences humaines, Bamako, Mali, and at the Green Library, Stanford University.
Amadu Sanogo, 8 January 1977, Sinsani.
Bamakan Kulubali, 26 February 1977, Segu.
Baye Fofana, 21 July 1981, Banamba.
Binke Baba Kuma, 19 December 1976 and 21 March 1977, Sinsani.
Binke Sukule, 21 March 1977, Sinsani.
Koke Jara, 25 January 1984, Gouni.
Mamuru Fomba et al., 22 July 1981, Sinzena.
Musa Kouyate, 26 January 1977, Segu.
Santa Kulubali, 21 March 1977, Sinsani.
Sidi Yaya Kone, 1 February 1977, Sinsani.

Archival sources

ANM: Archives Nationales du Mali.
 Bulletin agricole, Bamako, 1st quarter 1906. ANM 1 R 31.

Charnet, rapport général du Capitaine Charnet, commandant du cercle, Bamako, 1st quarter, 1899. ANM 1 E 18.

Chef de service d'agriculture, revue des grands produits et examen des principaux facteurs du dévélopement économique, pays du Segu et regions voisines, 1920. ANM 1 R 232.

de Laur, rapport sur la tournée de recensement, 5 May 1909. ANM 1 E 38.

Gaubert, rapport sur l'arrangement passé en Macina entre les Peuls et Rimaibes au sujet du remplacement de toutes redevances anciennes par la régime de la location des terres, Jenne, 24 December 1908. ANM 1 E 192.

Grodet, lettre au commandant de Bamako, 27 July 1894. ANM 1 E 169.

Logeau, notice sur les questions des eaux et puits dans le cercle de Sokolo, 1913. ANM 1 D 57#3.

Notices historiques et géographique du cercle de Bamako, 1880–1900, 1903. ANM 1 D 33#1.

Ponty, lettre au commandant de Segu, 18 April 1907. ANM 1 E 177.

Rapport général sur la situation politique du cercle de Bamako pendant l'année 1906, Bamako. ANM 1 E 19.

Rapport général sur la situation politique du cercle de Segu, 15 October 1895, Segu. ANM 1 E 71.

Rapport général sur la politique du cercle pendant l'année 1905, Segu. ANM 1 E 77.

Rapports politiques, Bamako, May and June 1905. ANM 1 E 19.

Rapport politique, Bamako, June 1906. ANM 1 E 19.

Rapport politique, Bamako, May 1907. ANM 1 E 19.

Rapports politiques, Bouguni, October, November, and December 1906. ANM 1 E 28.

Rapports politiques, Bouguni, May, June, and October 1907. ANM 1 E 28.

Rapports politiques, Gumbu, 1908 through 1909. ANM 1 E 38.

Rapports politiques, Gumbu, 1910 through 1911. ANM 1 E 39.

Rapport politique, Segu, January 1898. ANM 1 E 71.

Rapport politique, Segu, June 1907. ANM 1 E 72.

Rapports politiques, Sokolo, June and November 1910. ANM 1 E 76.

Rapport politique d'ensemble du Soudan, 1910. ANM 1 E 12.

Rapport politique d'ensemble du Soudan, 2d quarter 1912. ANM 1 E 12.

Rapport politique et militaire, Bamako, January 1895. ANM 1 E 18.

Rapport sur la captivité, Segu, 1904. ANM 1 E 156.

Rapport sur la politique du cercle en 1907, Bamako. ANM 1 E 19.

Rapport sur la répression de la traite des captives, 1 July 1895, Bamako. ANM 1 E 156.

Rapport sur les coutumes et institutions juridiques, Segu, 1909. ANM 1 D 206.

Robin, réponse au questionnaire sur les coutumes indigènes, cercle de Bamako, residence de Banamba, 1909. ANM 1 D 186.

Roume, telegramme [to Fawtier], 28 May 1905. ANM 1 E 118.

Rougier, enquête sur l'Islam, Banamba, 1914. ANM 1 D 33#3.

Saillard, rapport sur la tournée de recensement, 20 December 1907. ANM 1 E 28.

Trentinian, lettre, 22 July 1895. ANM 1 E 183.

ANS-AOF: Archives Nationales du Sénégal, Gouvernement de l'Afrique Occidentale Française, Dakar.

Brevié, rapport sur l'esclavage, Bamako, 1904. ANS-AOF K 19.

Clozel, rapport politique, Haut-Sénégal–Niger, 1st quarter 1908. ANS-AOF 2 G 8-1.

Clozel, rapport politique, Haut-Sénégal–Niger, 2d quarter 1912. ANS-AOF 2 G 12-12.

Deherme, l'esclavage en Afrique occidentale française, 1906. ANS-AOF K 25.

Etude sur la captivité, Segu, 1894. ANS-AOF K 14.

Fawtier, telegramme, 29 May 1905, Kayes. ANS-AOF 15 G 170.

Governor-general, lettre au consul général d'Angleterre, 22 February 1911. ANS-AOF K 26.

Governor-General Roume, lettre au ministre de colonies, Dakar, 11 July 1905. ANS-AOF 15 G 170.

Instructions accompanying decree of 10 November 1903. ANS-AOF K 16.

Ponty, lettre au commandant de Segu, Kayes, 25 May 1907. ANS-AOF 2 G 7.

Ponty, rapport politique, Haut-Sénégal–Niger, February 1901. ANS-AOF 2 G 1-14.

Ponty, rapport politique, Haut-Sénégal–Niger, May 1906. ANS-AOF 2 G 6-6.

Ponty, rapport politique, Haut-Sénégal–Niger, 3d quarter 1907. ANS-AOF 2 G 7-3.

Rapport politique, Haut-Sénégal–Niger, 2d quarter 1906. ANS-AOF 2 G 6-2.

Rapport politique, Haut-Sénégal–Niger, 1st quarter 1908. ANS-AOF 2 G 8-1.

Rapport politique, Haut-Sénégal–Niger, 2d quarter 1909. ANS-AOF 2 G 9-12.

Roume, telegramme au [lieutenant] gouverneur à Kayes, 26 May 1905, Gorée. ANS-AOF 15 G 170.

Trentinian, circulaire aux administrateurs, 22 July 1895. ANS-AOF K 19.

ANF-OM: Archives Nationales de France, Dépôt d'Outre-Mer, Aix-en-Province.

Governor-general, lettre au ministre de colonies, 22 June 1908, Dakar. ANF-OM Soudan I 11.

Other sources

Bouche, D. 1968. *Les villages de liberté en Afrique noire française, 1887–1910*. Paris: Mouton.

Cooper, F. 1977. *Plantation slavery on the east coast of Africa*. New Haven: Yale University Press.

Cooper, F. 1980. *From slaves to squatters: plantation labor and agriculture in Zanzibar and coastal Kenya, 1890–1925*. New Haven: Yale University Press.

Deherme, G. 1908. *L'Afrique occidentale française: action politique, action économique, action sociale*. Paris: Bloud.

Echenberg, M. 1975. Paying the blood tax: military conscription in French West Africa, 1914–29. *Canadian Journal of African Studies* 9(2): 171–92.

Foner, E. 1983. *Nothing but freedom: emancipation and its legacy*. Baton Rouge: Louisiana State University Press.

Holmes, L. 1978. Tieba Traore, Fama of Kenedougou: two decades of political development, 1873–1893. Ph.D. dissertation, University of California, Berkeley.

Kanya-Forstner, A. S. 1969. *The conquest of the Western Sudan: a study in French military imperialism*. Cambridge: Cambridge University Press.

Kersaint-Gilly. 1924. Essai sur l'evolution de l'esclavage en AOF: son dernier stade au Soudan français. *Bulletin du comité d'études historiques et scientifique de l'AOF* 3.

Klein, M. 1983. Slavery, forced labour and French colonial rule in colonial Guinea. Paper presented at the American Historical Association, San Francisco.

Klein, M. 1986. Slavery and emancipation in French West Africa. Paper presented at Woodrow Wilson International Center, Washington, D.C.

Klein, M. 1987. The demography of slavery in the Western Soudan during the late 19th century. In *African population and capitalism: historical perspectives*, ed. D. Cordell and J. Gregory, 50–61. Boulder: Westview.

Klein, M., and P. Lovejoy. 1979. Slavery in West Africa. In *The uncommon market: studies in the economic history of the Atlantic slave trade*, ed. H. Gemery and J. Hogendorn, 181–212. New York: Academic Press.

Lennihan, L. 1982. Rights in men and rights in land: slavery, wage labor, and smallholder agriculture in Northern Nigeria. *Slavery and Abolition* 3(2): 111–39.

Lewis, J. V. D. 1979. Descendants and crops: two poles of production in a Mailan peasant village. Ph.D. dissertation, Yale University.

Lewis, J. V. D. 1981. Domestic labor intensity and the incorporation of Malian peasant farmers into localized descent groups. *American Ethnologist* 8(2): 53–73.

Lovejoy, P. 1979. The characteristics of plantations in the nineteenth century Sokoto Caliphate (Islamic West Africa). *American Historical Review* 84(5): 1267–92.

Lovejoy, P. 1986. Fugitive slaves: resistance to slavery in the Sokoto Caliphate. *In resistance: studies in African, Caribbean, and Afro-American history*, ed. G. Okihiro, 71–95. Boston: University of Massachusetts Press.

Meillassoux, C. 1975. L'esclavage à Gumbu. In *Esclavage en Afrique precoloniale*, ed. C. Meillassoux, 221–51. Paris: Maspero.

Person, Y. 1968–1975. *Samori: une revolution Dyula*, 3 vols. Dakar: IFAN.

Pollet, E., and G. Winter. 1972. *Société Soninke (Dyanhunu, Mali)*. Bruxulles: Editions de l'institut de sociologie.

Renault, F. 1972. *L'abolition de l'esclavage en Sénégal: l'attitude d'administration française, 1848–1905*. Paris: Société française d'Outre-Mer.

Roberts, R. 1980. The emergence of a grain market in Bamako, 1883–1908. *Canadian Journal of African Studies* 14(1): 37–54.

Roberts, R. 1981. Ideology, slavery, and social formation: the evolution of Maraka slavery in the middle Niger Valley. In *Ideology of slavery in Africa*, ed. P. Lovejoy, 171–99. Beverly Hills: Sage.

Roberts, R. 1987. *Warriors, merchants, and slaves: the state and the economy of the Middle Niger Valley, c. 1700–1914.* Stanford: Stanford University Press.

Roberts, R., and M. Klein. 1980. Banamba slave exodus of 1905 and the decline of slavery in the Western Sudan. *Journal of African History* 21(3): 375–94.

Schoelcher, V. 1880. *L'esclavage au Sénégal en 1880.* Paris: Libraire centrale des publications populaires.

Schoelcher, V. 1886. *Polemique coloniale.* Paris: E. Dentu.

Shenton, R. 1986. *Development of capitalism in Northern Nigeria.* Toronto: University of Toronto Press.

Wiener, J. 1978. *Social origins of the New South: Alabama, 1860–1885.* Baton Rouge: Louisiana State University Press.

10 *Lee V. Cassanelli*

The Ending of Slavery in Italian Somalia:[1] Liberty and the Control of Labor, 1890–1935

The history of Italian colonialism in Somalia falls into two distinct phases, divided by the advent of Fascist administration in 1923. While the abolition of slavery was effectively achieved in the two decades before 1923, the most important attempts by the state to control the labor of the ex-slaves occurred only in the succeeding 15 years. This chapter outlines the major developments that affected slaveholders and slaves in each period, and concludes in 1935 when Somalia became part of the larger Italian East African Empire. The discussion is limited to the towns of the Benadir coast — Mogadishu, Merka, and Brava — and the agricultural regions of southern Somalia along the Juba and Shabelle rivers, where most of the slaves in Somalia were concentrated.

Colonial Policies to 1923: A Brief Chronology

The cession of the Benadir coast to Italy by the sultan of Zanzibar in 1892 inaugurated a 13-year period of private and chartered company rule

---

1. Although the British referred to the former Italian colony as Italian Somaliland, the colony's official name was Somalia Italiana. The name Somalia was popularly used in Italian, Somali, and Arabic in colonial times as it is today. In this article, "Somaliland" is used interchangeably with "Somalia" to refer to the former Italian colony.

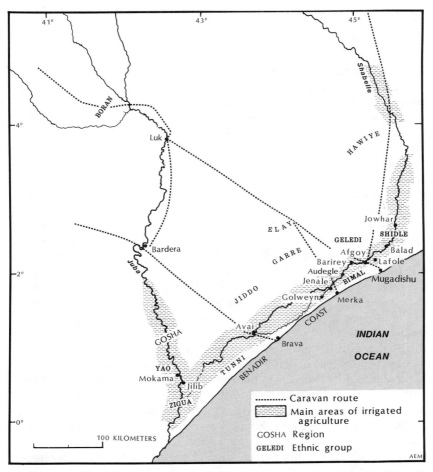

Map 10. Southern Somalia

in southern Somalia, during which the Italian presence was limited to a few garrisons along the coast and in the commercial towns of Luk and Bardera on the upper Juba River. Beginning in 1873, the sultans of Zanzibar had issued a series of decrees ending the slave trade and suppressing the institution of slavery along the Somali coast, but their representatives and the first Italian company officials in the Benadir lacked the manpower and authority to enforce them. As late as 1903, Governor Dulio could claim that he knew nothing about the decrees and that no one had given him any directives on enforcing them (Chiesi and Travelli 1904:

232). This candid revelation came in the midst of a series of journalistic exposés charging Benadir Company employees with tolerating and even collaborating with local slave-dealers. The resulting scandal prompted an official investigation resulting in the publication of a 384-page report, which is one of the major sources for this study (Chiesi and Travelli 1904). As a result of the inquiry the Italian government issued three new ordinances in 1903–1904 outlawing the slave trade and providing for the immediate emancipation of all slaves born after 1890 (Perricone-Viola 1936; Hess 1966: 64–84).

Although the Italian government took direct control of the colony in January 1906, the military occupation of the fertile Shabelle River valley did not begin until September 1908. Thus, the major slaveholding clans of the interior remained outside the direct control of the state for several years. Somali opposition to the new regime took the form of occasional raids against towns and attacks on trading caravans headed for the coast. The militant Bimal clan also blockaded the town of Merka in 1904. Only relief supplies brought overland from Mogadishu under armed escort saved the town from starvation (Cassanelli 1982: 201ff.). Continued rural resistance to the freeing of slaves coupled with Muslim Somali opposition to the presence of infidels on the coast finally forced the government to despatch troops and set up fortified outposts in the farming towns along the Shabelle in the autumn of 1908.

This belated use of force to suppress slavery left the early initiative to the slaveholders and slaves themselves, and severely circumscribed the ability of colonial authorities in subsequent years to direct freed slaves into forms of labor that the state preferred. Ex-slaves began to find viable alternatives to conscription for work on colonial plantations even before the effective European occupation of the countryside.

After 1908, as the frontier of colonial pacification gradually pushed beyond the Shabelle Valley to the more distant interior, government officials grappled with the question of how best to develop their new domains. From the beginning, they looked to expatriate commercial farming as the foundation for the colony's future prosperity, even though pastoralism was the dominant form of Somali economic activity everywhere except along the lower Juba and Shabelle rivers. The Italians had no doubt been impressed by the plantation economy that had flourished briefly along the Shabelle in the second half of the nineteenth century and had produced grain, cotton, sesame, and organic dyes for export to Zanzibar and Arabia. This had rested almost exclusively on the labor of slaves imported from other parts of East Africa. The Italians believed that all farming in Somalia was done by slaves or long-resident servile cultivators descended from slaves, and that the majority of Somalia's pastoralists regarded farming as an undignified pursuit. The colonial authorities therefore concluded that ending slavery would liberate the one population group that could help them build a new agricultural economy.

Early on the decision was made to promote the development of private European concessions on irrigable land along the rivers in districts where the land seemed underutilized but where ex-slaves and other settled populations were available as labor. From 1907 to 1909, the government leased 46,800 hectares of irrigable land along the Juba and Shabelle valleys to 15 private (chiefly Italian) concessionaires. The 60-year leases provided them with a generous timetable for putting the land under crops (cotton, tobacco, and rice were the earliest attempted), and with tax and loan incentives. These expatriate pioneers had scant success; only four were still operating their concessions in October 1910. Most failed because of inadequate capitalization and inability to attract workers (Hess 1966: 111–12).

In 1911, the activist Governor Giacomo De Martino declared all uncultivated riverine land the property of the state, extended concessions to 99 years, and launched an experimental farm at Jenale in the Shabelle Valley, just inland from Merka (Guadagni 1981: 146–47). Between 1910 and 1916, the government conscripted local Somalis for construction and road work through the agency of clan leaders and stipended officials; but it left the concessionaires to recruit their own labor. The idea of importing Indian, Chinese, Arab, and even Ethiopian farmers as an initial work force was discussed and dismissed as impracticable. Dr. Romolo Onor, an energetic young agronomist, spent seven years in Italian Somaliland investigating the local agricultural economy. He concluded on the basis of detailed research into household production that small European concessions would never succeed in the colony, unless the state was prepared to confiscate all Somali farmlands, use forced labor, or provide huge wage subsidies to attract cultivators away from their own farms. He urged instead the promotion of indigenous peasant production, with a few well-subsidized expatriate or state farms as models to show Somalis the benefits of agricultural modernization (Onor 1925). Despite Onor's recommendations, however, the government continued its policy of development through foreign agricultural concessions (Guadagni 1981: 180–81). The scarcity of rural labor remained a major obstacle to colonial agricultural development, until the Fascist regime (1923–1935) marshalled the resources and coercive power to mobilize it.

The End of Slavery in the Coastal Towns

Cerrina-Ferroni, governor of Italian Somaliland in 1906–1907, estimated that there were 25,000–30,000 slaves in the colony (cited in Hess 1966: 100). Only a few thousand of these resided in the Benadir coastal towns, but they played an important role in the urban economy. A household census in the spring of 1903 revealed that nearly one-third of Mogadishu's 6,700 inhabitants were slaves. In Brava there were some 830 in a town population of 3,000, and Merka had 720 slaves among its 5,000 residents (Robecchi-Brichetti 1904: 68–72, 90, 179–203; Chiesi and Travelli 1904: 248). Most town slaves belonged to wealthy Arab and Somali merchants and worked as weavers in the large local textile industry, as operators of the seed presses that produced sesame oil, or as porters, dock workers, or domestic servants.

The coming of Italian company administration to the coast in 1893 did not at first bring any dramatic change for these slaves. Company officials claimed that, in general, urban household slaves were well treated and were cared for in sickness and old age by masters in whose service they had spent their entire lives. Administrative records and legal documents prepared by the *qadis* (Islamic legal experts) of Mogadishu and Brava, however, show that slaves were frequently transferred from one owner to another as collateral for loans or payment for commercial debts (Chiesi and Travelli 1904: passim; and see below, page 317). These transactions may have increased in the years immediately preceding abolition owing to the growing economic uncertainty of the early colonial period. The emancipation of individual slaves as acts of Islamic piety also probably increased as abolition efforts intensified (see, e.g., Robecchi-Brichetti 1904: 80–85).

The Benadir Company used part of its government-subsidized budget to reimburse urban slave-owners for the slaves it freed, and directed the freed slaves to pay a small daily tribute to their former masters for continuing to lodge and feed them. This kept the administration on good terms with the leading local families of the town and kept the ex-slaves off the streets. The authorities were not eager for newly emancipated slaves to abandon their former masters. Very little salaried work was available except on government-sponsored public works.[2] And the authorities claimed that increased prostitution, crime, and poverty accompanied the influx into the towns of runaway slaves from the country, who had no owners to take them in (Gasparini 1912: 48–49; Carletti 1912: 192–93). Visitors to the Somali coast in the first few years after emancipation noted that, for the towns at least, there was some truth in the local saying "To

2. Robecchi-Brichetti (1904) reported that during his visit the company administration provided the only paid employment in the town of Mogadishu. Male porters, manual laborers, and domestic servants received between 12 and 25 *besa* (one-tenth to one-fifth Maria Theresia thaler [U.S. 5–10¢]) per day, women approximately half that amount. Many recently emancipated slaves continued to pay a daily tribute of four besa to their former masters, perhaps a form of rent.

free a slave is to make him a pauper." Later, the same fear of creating a class of unproductive and impoverished ex-slaves was to lead to a policy of gradual abolition in the countryside. In the towns, on the whole, the ending of slavery meant a gradual transition for most slaves into domestic service with former masters or into poorly paid employment as porters, sweepers, waiters, or house servants.

Rural Slavery and Clientship before Emancipation

The transition from slavery in the coastal towns is well-documented in comparison with its suppression in the interior. Few eyewitness accounts of agricultural slavery are available for the period before 1910, though we can infer a good deal from colonial district reports dating from that year and from the earlier testimonies of escaped slaves and government informers recorded at the coast. In order to understand the impact of the abolition decrees on rural society, however, it is necessary to review certain aspects of plantation slavery during the second half of the nineteenth century, when the Benadir hinterland began to export considerable quantities of grain, sesame, cotton, and orchella (a lichen used in making dyes for textiles). The rise of this agricultural-export economy was the result of the establishment of a slave system of production along the lower Shabelle River (Cassanelli 1982: 161–82).

The absorption of sizable numbers of slaves into the riverine areas of southern Somalia — probably some 50,000 over the period of 1800–1890 — accompanied the growing importance of the Benadir coastal towns as transit points in the Zanzibar–Middle East slave trade. The slaves who were landed in the Somali ports or brought overland from the Kenya coast came from many parts of East Africa. Testimonies of freed slaves and the presence of surviving linguistic communities of runaway slaves along the lower Juba River in the early twentieth century indicate that Zigua, Yao, Nyasa, Makua, Ngindo, Nyika, Nyamwezi, Kikuyu, and Swahili captives were all brought to Somaliland (Grottanelli 1953; Cassanelli 1987). Slaves sold to Somali farmers were used to clear, irrigate, and cultivate fields along the Shabelle, to transport cotton and grain to the coast for export, and to tend livestock and build houses. While quantitative evidence on this slave system of production is not available, we can infer something of its scale from twentieth-century documents and oral traditions. Few rural Somalis, it seems, had more than 15 or 20 slaves, and many owned only 1 or 2. The limited evidence suggests that the size of individual farms worked by the slaves was small by Zanzibar or Pemba standards. In Afgoy, one of the centers of nineteenth-century slaveholding, even wealthy landholders rarely had farms of more than 40 hectares

— the average was more like 5 or 10. Calculating that one farm worker could manage at most 1.0–1.5 hectares of the heavy alluvial soil found along the Shabelle, a ten-hectare farm would have required from five to eight slaves. The composite picture which emerges from oral and ethnographic evidence is of small groups of slaves living as families on the land of their Somali owners and working the fields under their masters' supervision (Luling 1971: 99–106, 119–20; Cassanelli 1982: 170–74; ASMAI, Casali 1910).

Complicating the picture in the Shabelle Valley, however, was the existence even before the large influx of slaves in the nineteenth century of a substantial population of dependent farmers whom we might most appropriately call client-cultivators. These were known by a variety of generic local names which referred either to their negroid physical features or to their presumed servile origins (Colucci 1924: 213–14; Luling 1971: 45–47). Early Italian colonial writers called them *liberti* ("freedmen"), but it is unlikely that all of them were formerly slaves in the strict sense. Many were probably descendants of early Bantu-speaking settlers whose numbers had been augmented over time through intermarriage with agricultural Somalis and who had been assimilated linguistically and genealogically into the local Somali population (see, e.g., Cerulli 1959: 115–21).

Most client-cultivators formed lineage groups owing political allegiance to and identified with local Somali clans. Their relationship with these so-called noble clans was corporate rather than individual; that is, the clients were entitled to a certain portion of blood compensation and shared in both the responsibilities and the rewards of the work and warfare of their pastoral overlords. The client-cultivators also typically enjoyed uncontested rights to the land they worked, rights sustained both by their specialization as farmers in an essentially pastoral society and by their acknowledged ritual powers, which included control over the behavior of river crocodiles. However, they could not easily renounce their "client" status, since it rested on a position of perceived social as well as political inferiority. They were represented in clan councils by the elders of the noble lineages to which they were allied, and they rarely intermarried with the nobles. For the most part, the client groups cultivated while their pastoral patrons managed livestock and engaged in raiding, trading, and politics (Cucinotta 1921: 493ff.; Luling 1971: 45–48, 150–52).

The labor of the client-cultivators was thus controlled indirectly through social and political mechanisms which made them an integral but subordinate component of an agropastoral system of production. This division of labor was reinforced by an ideology of social superiority/inferiority and sanctioned by the language of corporate kinship. The nature of this system of corporate clientship provides an interesting contrast to the system of slave production that emerged in the second half of the nineteenth century. By purchasing slaves, Somali overlords obtained a class of dependent laborers whose deployment was not constrained by custom as in the case of the client-cultivators. Slaves had neither legal nor political rights. If a slave were killed, the owner had the right to claim as compensation the prevailing market value of the slave, not the standard bloodwealth. Slaves could be freed only by the individual owner's decree. Most significant, slave labor could be controlled directly. Slaves could be consigned to plantation work without either threatening subsistence production or disrupting the social relations that bound patron clans to their client-cultivators. The acquisition of slaves in the nineteenth century thus provided owners with the means to produce an agricultural surplus and to respond to foreign demands for cash crops.

There is little question that the importation of foreign slaves to Somalia permitted an unprecedented expansion of agricultural production along the Shabelle River, to the point where the quantity of surplus grain exported to Arabia impressed several nineteenth-century travellers (Cassanelli 1982: 166–67). With the suppression of the slave trade after 1890, however, the boom came to an end. As the import of new slaves rapidly diminished and the price of slaves rose,[3] plantation production declined. Runaway slaves could not easily be replaced, so that in some areas supervision of slave labor intensified and treatment grew harsher (see below, page 317). Commercial transactions involving the transfer of slaves between merchants and landowners had increasingly to use the existing pool of servile workers, so that the movement of slaves within the country itself probably became more common.

Another process that seems to have intensified as slave imports declined was the absorption of longer-resident slaves into the client-cultivator population. This process was aided by the fact that slaves and client farmers performed similar work and often intermarried,[4] and individual owners periodically emancipated their most trusted slaves as acts of piety. Upon emancipation, it was customary in some Somali clans for owners to give their ex-slaves a small parcel of land (ASMAI, Casali 1910; Colucci 1924: 213; Luling 1971: 123), and this, coupled with the slaves' conversion to Islam, sped the process of assimilation of ex-slaves into client groups.

One of the earliest colonial reports from the river district noted the

---

3. Casali (ASMAI, 1910) noted that young healthy slaves occasionally sold in inland markets for between 200 and 300 MT thalers (U.S. $120–180), up from 75–100 MT thalers in the last days of the slave trade (see also Cassanelli 1982: 191–92).

4. Somali patrons sometimes gave young female slaves as gifts to their client-cultivators.

existence of two categories of slaves: those recently imported, whom the author labelled *jaja* (Somali: *ooji*), and those he called *del-mascio* (Somali: *habash*) (ASMAI, Casali 1910: 3; cf. Colucci 1924: 213–14; Luling 1971: 95–96). Of the latter, the report noted:

they know the language of the country and many are close to the families to whom they belong and to the land on which they are born; living from childhood alongside the children of the free-born, they build up a bond which naturally lasts into adulthood. (ASMAI, Casali 1910: 3)

This describes perfectly the status and conditon of the client-cultivator population identified above, and in fact the term *habash* was uniformly applied by "noble" Somalis to clients and ex-slaves alike as late as the 1960s. The assimilation of slaves into the client-cultivator population was certainly well advanced by the time colonial forces occupied the Shabelle Valley, which helps explain why early colonial observers found it difficult to distinguish between the two groups, calling them all liberti.

Initial Responses to Emancipation: Slaves, Slaveholders, and Administrators

If the cessation of the slave trade accelerated the "clientization" of former slaves, the abolition of slavery by the ordinances of 1903–1904 produced a new set of responses. It must be emphasized that official emancipation was not accompanied by immediate forceful intervention on the part of the colonial authorities; thus, slaveholders and slaves had time to deal in their own way with the threat, or promise, of emancipation. In the riverine regions of Italian Somaliland, they held the initiative for some five years and for longer beyond the frontier of colonial pacification. The Italian ordinances abolishing slavery, which before 1908 could be enforced *directly* only at the coast, nonetheless increased the incidence of desertion by plantation slaves along the Shabelle. Growing numbers of runaways arrived at the coast in early fall 1903 (Chiesi and Travelli 1904: 244), when word had spread quickly to the plantations along the river that the new ordinances were being enforced more rigorously than in the past and that the likelihood of Italian authorities restoring fugitives to their masters was diminishing. Runaway slaves interrogated by the resident of Mogadishu in November 1903 reported that the entire riverine population was in agitation over rumors of abolition: "people talk of nothing else" (ibid.: 351).

The testimony of an escaped slave recorded earlier that year is typical. One Salemi, native of Quelimane, had been captured on the Mrima coast some 20 years earlier and transported with about 40 companions by Arab traders of Sur to the Somali port of Merka. There he was sold to and kept by one Sherif Omar, who treated him well, until about 1896 when he was sent as payment of a debt to Barirey, an agricultural village along the Shabelle River. His new master, Abiker bin Mire, put him in leg irons and made him work in the fields alongside other longer-resident slaves who were not chained. By the time of Salemi's escape, Abiker bin Mire's slaves had been reduced by desertion from 20 to 8 (Camera dei Deputati 1905).

Salemi fled to the coast in the company of Kabiro, an Oromo (Galla) whose story is equally revealing. He had been taken from his village by Abyssinian soldiers on the pretext of hiring him as a porter. Instead, he was sent in a caravan through Konsoland into Boran country, where he was sold to a trader. The latter sold him to some Hawiye Somali merchants, who in turn sold him to Abiker bin Mire at Barirey, where he worked for a little more than two months before escaping (ibid.).

These testimonies and others like them suggest that, while recently arrived slaves may have been more likely to flee the plantations, the atmosphere of uncertainty in the months around emancipation prompted even long-resident slaves to desert. One reason may have been a worsening of the conditions of slave life on the plantations. As prospects of desertion increased, masters became more vigilant in supervising their slaves and harsher in punishing those who tried to escape. Two slaves appeared in Mogadishu after an all-night flight from Lafole with their hoes still in hand, suggesting an escape directly from the fields. Another group of five men and women, their filed leg-irons still around their ankles, reported that "now nearly all slaves in the interior are chained by their legs, so that desertion is becoming rarer" (Chiesi and Travelli 1904: 351). During this period, a few slaveholding clans acquired a reputation among slaves for particularly harsh treatment; ex-slaves reportedly had been terrified of being sold in the districts around the towns of Balad and Audegle (ibid., 256–57). It is difficult to ascertain the facts in this case, except to note that both were areas where there were large concentrations of newly imported slaves, whose attachment to the land was recent and thus whose propensity to desert was presumably greater.

The weight of the evidence suggests that the conditions of life for recently imported and unassimilated slaves did indeed deteriorate in the years just before effective abolition. We can probably assume that the phenomenon repeated itself as the frontier of colonial occupation moved steadily inland after 1908. While some slaves escaped to the newly pacified areas, those who remained just beyond the reach of colonial sanctuary may have found their subjugation more severe. This in turn almost certainly conditioned relations between former slaves and masters in the immediate postemancipation period, the freed slaves being more reluctant to stay on in a dependent relationship with their recent oppressors. There is also some evidence to suggest that slaveholders confronted with imminent abolition sometimes tried to sell their slaves to buyers farther from the centers of colonial authority (ASMAI, Casali 1910: 18), taking advantage of slave prices that briefly rose to 200 MT thalers (ca. U.S. $120) or more from a preabolition level of 70–100 MT thalers (ca. $40–60).

In the tumultuous period between formal and effective emancipation, the slaveholders sought to defend their cause, playing upon the fears of Italian officials that the abrupt end of slavery would provoke widespread Somali resistance and destroy the local economy. In their letters, usually dictated in Arabic to qadis or literate sheikhs, clan leaders complained that the desertion of slaves was ruining their prosperity, creating disloyalty to the new government, and pushing disgruntled landholders towards armed rebellion. The following letter, incorporated into the report of the Italian Commission of Inquiry of 1903, is typical:

After we lived for years with our custom [of slavery] the government of Zanzibar came to our land and prohibited the import and export of slaves by sea; but in the towns and in the country they could not prevent the trade. The [Filonardi] Company which governed for three years [1893–1896] restored our fugitive slaves. So did [Governor] Dulio, who passed seven tranquil years among us. In 1903, a ship of war reached Mogadishu to impede slavery. From this time, we received only money and no longer the restitution of the slaves [who had escaped to the coast]. We have awaited the government's deliberations on this question.

The inhabitants of the interior are in great agitation. Part of them, the weak and the poor, pray for the coming of Sheikh Muhammad bin Abdullah and invoke his name day and night. Others think of emigrating to other places. And all this is prompted by the strong sentiment regarding our slaves. (Chiesi and Travelli 1904: 272–73)

A delegation of Somali elders from the Geledi clan of Afgoy complained to the resident of Mogadishu:

We have protected the trade routes and remained faithful for fourteen rainy seasons. Now our slaves no longer get returned to us. Ill will grows among our people, especially among the poor who, having only a few slaves, when these flee, lose all means of earning a living and don't know whether to leave or stay. (ibid.: 353)

Even allowing for some exaggeration, these protests indicate that slaveholders were disturbed by the scale of changes being wrought in their economy and society with the impending abolition of slavery. They also confirm that the early company administrators returned many runaways to their masters, especially if they belonged to clans deemed friendly to the government, and paid compensation for those not restored. From 1904, the policy of redeeming slaves through payment to the former masters was ended at the coast, though it was applied again after 1908 in the interior during the early years of colonial administration there.

The refusal to return runaway slaves and the cessation of payments to slaveholders were undoubtedly factors in the armed resistance against Italian rule raised by riverine clans like the Bimal after 1904. As the preceding letters show, Somali clan leaders were quick to raise the specter of an alliance of their disgruntled countrymen with Muhammad Abdullah Hassan, the Islamic teacher and dervish leader whose armed resistance to the authorities in British Somaliland threatened to spill over into the Italian colony. In fact, opposition to colonial rule in Italian Somaliland was assisted from 1905 by guns and inspiration from Muhammad Abdullah Hassan (Cassanelli 1982: 240–51), and opposition to the abolition of slavery merged there for a time with the wider currents of Islamic resistance to colonialism.

The threats by disaffected slaveholders helped reinforce what was already a widespread conviction in colonial circles that gradual suppression of slavery was the wisest course in the interior, and would avoid the increase of theft, prostitution, and pauperism which had accompanied liberation in the towns. The first resident of Afgoy spoke for most Italian officials when he claimed that virtually all crimes in the district were the work of slaves freed by the government (ASMAI, Casali 1910: 17). He wrote:

The slaves liberated by us have formed a new class entirely independent of all authority. . . . While slaves previously freed by the Somalis [the liberti of colonial writings] form with the free population a community united with respect to customary law, those newly freed by the government have no ties whatsoever. Calling themselves servants of the government, they believe themselves and are regarded by the Somalis as completely independent. They roam freely about the colony, settling where they wish; work when it pleases them; break their labor contracts; and worst of all are responsible only to themselves for the acts they commit, having no tribe or clan to whom they are accountable. I foresee the danger that in time they will contribute to the destruction of that principle of collective responsibility which now prevails and which permits us to govern with limited resources, and to maintain public order undisturbed by the actions of capricious individuals.

Thus, officials in the rural districts applied the emancipation decrees cautiously. Slaves with obvious signs of maltreatment were freed, but others were sent before a judicial tribunal and urged to work out some type of accommodation with their former masters (Gasparini 1912: 50ff.).

The reluctance of colonial authorities to give slaves their immediate and unconditional freedom had an economic as well as a social and political rationale. They argued that it would take time for the idea of salaried labor to root itself in rural society, and that

to free all the slaves at once would force the free Somalis, unaccustomed to working their own fields, to abandon them and resume the pastoral way of life . . . and for reasons of public security as well as for commercial ones, it is preferable that the nomadic tribes become sedentary rather than the reverse. (ASMAI, Casali 1910: 13–14)

With these arguments, the colonial government in the years before 1920 clearly aligned itself with the former slaveholders, aiming to keep ex-slaves on the land of their former owners and subject to the discipline of the "traditional" corporate group. This policy ran counter to the objectives of the expatriate concessionary farmers, who from the start needed a local source of agricultural labor. Nevertheless, the contradiction between the desire for law and order and the need for a free-labor market was resolved by the early colonial state in favor of the former, and this may go a long way in explaining why most of the early European plantations failed. It also points up the relative weakness of the pre-Fascist regime in Italian Somaliland. With the bulk of Italian military and economic expenditures directed towards their colonial enterprises in Libya and Eritrea, authorities in Somalia were left to find the most inexpensive ways of keeping the peace.

Responses to Emancipation: The Freed Slaves

Although rural slaveholders found some support from the government in their attempts to retain control over the labor of their former slaves, they never recovered their earlier economic position. Italian Somaliland's agricultural output never reached the levels attained in the second half of the nineteenth century under a slave system of production. One reason was the government's unwillingness to support Somali landowners through loans and technical assistance. Another was its commitment to ending all overt forms of slavery. However equivocal the early policy of "gradualism" was, most colonial administrators were ultimately responsive, if not to ex-slaves' complaints of ill-treatment at the hands of former masters, then to pressures emanating from the metropolitan government. While they preferred freed slaves to remain attached to the families of their former masters, they nevertheless authorized many to resettle in villages under the control of their own headmen or of lineages of client-cultivators. The major reason for the decline of Somali plantation agriculture after 1900, however, was that the ex-slaves themselves found other alternatives to staying on as direct dependents of their former masters.

One such alternative was to join one of the several communities of client-cultivators settled along the Shabelle Valley from Jowhar to Golweyn. These communities appear to have consisted of two types: lineages of client-cultivators living in distinct villages but continuing to work on the land of Somali patron clans for daily wages, and independent communities of freedmen who cultivated their own farms (Gasparini 1912: 51; Maino 1959: 75–117). Both enjoyed the protection of membership in a corporate lineage, even though their social status as despised farmers changed very little. The biggest disadvantage of joining a community of liberti, however, was the constant threat of conscription into government work projects. Though all Somali subjects were in theory equally subject to the corvée, local custom and the prejudices of colonial officials conspired to ensure that client-cultivators and ex-slaves were the first to be taken.

For this reason, many freed slaves chose to settle in the more distant villages founded by runaway slaves during the heyday of plantation slavery in the nineteenth century. The best known of these sanctuaries was in Gosha, a region of dense brush and forest along the lower Juba River. Here some 60 villages ranging in size from 30 to 500 or 600 inhabitants were in existence by the first decade of the twentieth century (Cassanelli 1987). The earliest settlements appear to date from the mid-nineteenth century. The first villages were occupied by runaway slaves of like ethnic origin—for instance, there were villages made up exclusively of Zigua or Yao families. This suggests that the founders had not been in slavery long enough to be assimilated into Somali client communities. By the turn of the century, however, many villages were ethnically heterogeneous, and in some the inhabitants identified themselves as ex-slaves of particular Somali clans: thus, Jilib was founded by escaped Jiddo slaves, whereas Mokama was known as a village of former Tunni slaves.

By the 1890s, most of the Gosha settlements had come under the control of Nassib Bunda, a freed slave whose reputation for sorcery and political intrigue is legendary in the lower Juba area. He styled himself "sultan" of Gosha and was feared as much by the nearby Somali pastoralists (who generally avoided the tsetse-infested bush country along the river) as by his own subjects. Following his death in 1906, the Italian authorities recognized and provided government stipends to several dozen village headmen in the Gosha District.

In 1891, a British naval officer who navigated the lower course of the Juba estimated the population of Gosha at 30,000–40,000. Later estimates put the figures at 20,000–30,000, still a substantial number when one realizes that nearly the entire population of this region consisted of former slaves. These runaway-slave villages were well established before the official suppression of slavery and continued to attract ex-slaves through the early and uncertain years following emancipation.

Another small cluster of runaway-slave villages grew up in the swampy lands at Avai, downstream from the lower Shabelle River town of Golweyn. Some 3,000 escaped slaves from Bimal, Garre, and other adjacent Somali clans found refuge at Avai from as early as the 1840s. As in the case of the Gosha communities, oral traditions recorded by early colonial officials tell of leadership struggles within the emerging freed-slave settlements and of battles against neighboring Somali clans seeking to recapture the fugitives (Cassanelli 1987).

On the eve of the Italian occupation of Somalia, both Avai and the Gosha villages were agriculturally self-sufficient and actually supplied small surpluses of grain to coastal markets and to Zanzibar traders who brought their dhows to the mouth of the Juba. They had also struck pragmatic accords with their nearest Somali neighbors, who agreed to respect the liberty of the established villagers in exchange for their returning further fugitives; in addition, agricultural products were exchanged for pastoral ones. The formation of these alliances between independent ex-slave villages and their militarily dominant neighbors reminds one of the similar arrangements that were struck between the maroon communities of runaway slaves and their former plantation owners in the Caribbean and South America (Price 1979). In Somalia, the process of political accommodation was reinforced by the exchange of foodstuffs and craft goods in a pattern that was typical of transactions across the agricultural/pastoral divide throughout the Horn of Africa.

From the larger perspective, we can regard these runaway-slave communities as the nearest thing to a free peasantry that existed in early colonial Somalia. At the same time, a look at the internal workings of these refugee communities reveals that land and labor tasks were allocated in accordance with seniority; that is, the founders and earliest settlers controlled both the distribution of new farm lands and the major political offices, and newcomers could expect to find themselves in a subordinate position, much as they would have if seeking membership in a client-cultivator lineage. The disadvantages suffered by latecomers may explain the proliferation of small villages in the refuge districts, as each new group of runaway slaves sought to establish its own autonomous community.

Yet another option open to freed slaves in the early days of emancipation — and one which has received remarkably little notice in the literature on Somalia — was to join one of numerous Islamic religious settlements that had begun to spring up throughout the Somalilands in the late nineteenth and early twentieth centuries. Virtually all of these settlements were affiliated with one of three major Islamic religious orders, or *tariqāt* — Ahmediya, Salihiya, or Qadiriya. While the religious influence of these orders was noted by early colonial authorities and by subsequent observers, their role in agricultural and social change has received scant attention. Our knowledge of the internal structure of the Islamic settlements is limited; thus, we can only suggest some possible lines of inquiry as they relate to the question of the ex-slaves.

A few religious settlements were founded by tariqa sheikhs in the middle years of the nineteenth century, but they really emerged as a significant institutional force in the first two decades of the colonial period: 93 were reported in the colony in 1920 (Cerulli 1964: 171), most of them in cultivable zones along the two rivers or in the rain-fed plains between the rivers. The head sheikh sometimes received a tract of land from one of the clan heads in the area, perhaps some farmland that had been abandoned following the flight or emancipation of slaves. In other instances, the sheikhs obtained grants of land for mediating disputes between neighboring clans, the religious settlement then serving as a buffer between the disputants. The sheikh and his followers then settled down to farm and pray. Typically each member or family of the religious community cultivated their own plot. While most of the settlements consisted of members of one clan, a few of the larger ones drew adherents from several clans and thus represented a new form of multiclan territorial organization.

The rapid diffusion of the Islamic settlements was not unique to Somalia — similar developments could be found in many parts of Islamic Africa in the later nineteenth century. However, conditions in Somalia were particularly conducive to their growth. The tariqa settlements tended to absorb many recently uprooted or marginal elements of Somali rural society — "individuals without kin, small groups forced out of their clans, slaves without masters and clients without protectors" (Colucci 1924: 82) — and others who had suffered losses following the drought, warfare, and livestock epidemics of the late nineteenth century. Some of the founders themselves were reputedly men of servile origins — ex-slaves or client-cultivators (Cerulli 1957: 181–89) — and hence most likely of farming background. The adepts, whatever their social backgrounds, enjoyed the protection of Islamic law and a voice in decision-making within the community.

If social dislocation and the need for security in turbulent times help to explain the attraction of the religious settlements, their proliferation also owed a great deal to colonial policy, which initially favored and even promoted their diffusion. The reasons for this were more political than economic. Faced with growing opposition from the slaveholding clans of the interriver area and with hostility from forces sympathetic to the dervish movement of Muhammad Abdullah Hassan, the Italian government saw in the religious farming communities potential allies in the pacification process and a counterforce to hostile clan leaders. To enlist their support, the government gave stipends to the settlement sheikhs and frequently sided with them in the inevitable disputes that arose over land rights and jurisdiction over individuals who fled from clan law to seek refuge in the Islamic communities (Cerulli 1957: 200–204; Cerulli 1964: 169–74; Colucci 1924: 262–71). Members of the tariqa settlements were also exempt from corvée labor (Cerulli 1957: 203), partly because they promoted sedentarization and productive agriculture and partly because Italian policy sought to avoid stirring up religious sentiments.

There is very little information on economic activities within the religious settlements. The largest, located at Bardera on the Juba River, had an estimated membership of 8,000 according to a census in the early 1950s (ASL, Castagno papers, n.d.). Most were considerably smaller, however, with memberships of 50–500. Some large settlements had as much as 500 hectares of land, though most of it was pastureland. Four to 15 hectares of cultivated land were more typical. Productivity was sufficient to meet the subsistence needs of the adepts and their families and to enable them to pay a tithe in grain (one-tenth of the harvest in most cases) or in a monthly cash payment to the head sheikh. Though this obligation was couched in terms of Islamic custom, called *sekko* (Arabic: *zakaat*), it clearly represented an appropriation of surplus by the community leaders. In fact, it seems clear from records of litigation that the settlement leaders competed with clan leaders for the loyalty and labor of local farmers (Cerulli 1964: 169; Colucci 1924: 83; Guadagni 1981: 57–58).

The religious settlements thus provided another alternative for ex-slaves and farmers who sought to escape dependency on pastoral overlords, corvée requirements (which were typically organized through the offices of stipended clan heads), and wage work on European-owned farms. Though the figures are very speculative, we might estimate that the religious settlements took in somewhere between 15,000 and 30,000 farmers through the first four decades of the century. They, together with the runaway-slave villages along the Juba, where another 20,000 ex-slaves resided, absorbed perhaps a third of the entire agricultural population of Somalia during this period, the remainder being client-cultivators or part-time herders.

Given the range of alternatives available to freed slaves in the early postemancipation period, it is scarcely surprising that private European concessionaires found it difficult to secure a steady supply of farm hands. The planters along the Juba had to compete with the well-established tradition of freed-slave farming, while those on the Shabelle vied with Somali patrons and settlement sheikhs for labor. As we have seen, the state did not intervene extensively on behalf of the concessionaires and often had difficulty securing enough labor for its own needs.

To be sure, during times of drought and meager local harvests, Somali migrants turned up seeking work on the irrigated farms along the Juba and Shabelle rivers. Most of these casual workers, however, came from dry-land districts between the two rivers, where in normal years they could combine pastoralism with rain-fed farming. The onset of drought almost invariably propelled poorer families to send some of their members in search of work on the plantations. But as soon as the rains returned with the promise of good planting, the migrants just as quickly returned to their own land. Throughout the colonial period, the concessions drew most of their voluntary labor from clans living in marginal agricultural zones, not from the stable farming populations of the riverine areas. This latter group, which included most of the ex-slaves, found it preferable to farm in client-cultivating, freed-slave, or religious-settlement communities.

Epilogue to Emancipation: The Fascist Regime and Forced Labor

The advent of Fascism in Italy in 1922 had important repercussions on labor policy in the colonies which affected not only the ex-slaves but the entire agricultural population of Italian Somaliland. In fact, by this time the problem of labor in the Somali colony had become general; and administrative policy after 1920 no longer distinguished between recently freed slaves and riverine farmers as a whole. This itself is evidence that freed slaves had come to be placed in the general category of low-status cultivators. To the noble Somalis, they were habash (clients of slave ancestry) or jerir (lit., people with "curly hair"); to the Italian authorities, they were all liberti. However, since colonial labor conscription after 1923 fell most heavily on these groups, whether ex-slave or not, it is worth outlining the major developments of the period.

The first Fascist governor of Somalia, C. M. De Vecchi (1923–1928), attacked the question of agricultural development and the rural labor shortage head on. For the first time the state assumed a leading role in marshalling labor for private as well as public enterprises. It did this by imposing the first direct tax on the Somali population (in the form of an annual hut tax), by extending the corvée system, by energetically seeking capital for new agricultural ventures, and by building an infrastructure that extended economic control to the inland borders of the colony (and, as it turned out, beyond them into Ethiopia!) (Hess 1966: 149ff.).

In 1920, only four agricultural concessions were actively operating in the colony. By June 1933, the government had granted 115 new concessions, which brought nearly 30,000 hectares under cultivation. The most successful agricultural enterprise was that launched by the Società agricola italo-somala (SAIS) with an initial capital investment of 24 million lire (ca. U.S. $5 million). It obtained some 25,000 hectares of land in the middle Shabelle Valley near Jowhar, and by 1926, 10,000 were being farmed. More than 420 miles of irrigation channels watered fields of cotton, sugar cane, maize, coconut palms, and bananas. The government played its part in SAIS's development by subsidizing capital equipment purchases and low-interest loans, as well as a railway line to Jowhar from Mogadishu (Maino 1959: 81–104; Scassellati-Sforzolini 1926; Hess 1966: 163–65).

The SAIS experiment drew considerable attention for its innovative approach to obtaining land and labor. The company negotiated directly with elders of the local clans on whose land the irrigation works and processing plants were to be situated, in effect leasing it directly from them. Local farmers living in the district were encouraged to settle on the estate: each family received a hectare of land, half of which was given over to commercial crops (initially cotton) and the other half to whatever food crops the family chose. The cotton harvested was sold to SAIS at a price fixed annually by a board made up of local headmen and community leaders; the produce of the remaining half hectare was at the farmer's disposal. The company also provided its workers with housing, tools, well water, seeds, and medical care.

Most of the early work force at Jowhar were members of the Shidle, a sizable community of former client-cultivators which had absorbed an indeterminate number of freed slaves during the preceding two decades (Gasparini 1912: 53; Maino 1959: 77). Their working and living arrangements on the SAIS concession were carefully managed and monitored; councils were set up under locally appointed headmen; and time off for marriages and burials was written into their contracts. The scale of the SAIS operation and its careful attention to relations between employer and employees made it something of a model project. One could say that of all the labor-control systems introduced by the Italians, SAIS's most closely resembled the traditional client-cultivator one: a paternalistic system which managed workers by guaranteeing security of tenure, regulating social behavior, and recognizing the reciprocal rights and obligations of both supervisors and workers. The SAIS regime seemed compatible both with the corporate statist ideals of the Fascist administrators and with older Somali patterns of patron-client relations.

Other concessions set up in the Fascist era did not fare as well as the regime hoped; the main reasons once again stemmed from the scarcity of manual labor. Even SAIS did not escape this chronic problem, especially as its operation expanded to include sugar production. As early as 1924, when the combination of an epidemic of plague at SAIS and the flooding of the Shabelle above Jowhar drove Somali workers off the estate to plant their own fields, the company was forced to seek the intervention of the state. Declaring SAIS's work to be a vital "public service," the government directed each nearby village along the river to furnish a certain number of workers for employment at SAIS—a form of paid corvée (Maino 1959: 99–100, 122–23).

To meet the continued labor problems at SAIS and on the other concessions along the lower Shabelle, the colonial authorities instituted two new forms of "contract" labor. One involved a rotating system of service, each village providing workers for a six-month "turn" (Somalis recall this as the "*teen*"). The second resulted in the forced recruitment of workers to serve as "colonists" on the concessions for a renewable four-year period. The colonists had to sign contracts which stipulated in great detail their work obligations; in places like Jenale, these included the excavation of extensive canals and the construction of dikes and dams (ibid.: 124–29). As late as 1970, many old Somalis still recalled vividly this period of the *colonya* (colonial contracts) as a time when families were broken up, workers suffered fatal accidents at canal sites, and coercion was regularly employed by the authorities (interviews: informants in Afgoy, Jenale, and Merka, March–September 1971). These oral recollections also make it clear that the jerir (referring to the negroid farmers) bore the brunt of conscription to the teen and colonya. Among those groups were almost certainly numerous ex-slaves, but it is impossible to know if they were victimized any more severely than other low-status farmers.

One final development of the Fascist era that doubtless affected the former-slave populations was the government's decision to recruit workers from the religious settlements. From the beginning of Italian rule, as we have seen, it had been government policy to curry favor with the Islamic tariqa leaders and to exempt their adepts from the corvée. Though I could find in the records no explicit formulation of the shift in policy, it seems that the state began to refuse potential workers the right of sanctuary in the religious settlements soon after the teen and col-

onya were introduced. I am nearly certain that at least two uprisings led by
Somali religious leaders in 1924 and 1925 — those of Sheikh Ahmed Nur "El
Haji" and of Sheikh Fareg — were linked to the new labor policies. Colonial records portray both of these tariqa leaders as religious fanatics; but in
the case of Ahmed Nur, the official history acknowledges that his "seditious
ideas" found response among the local manual laborers on the agricultural concessions at Jenale (Ufficio Storico 1960: 177–78). And Sheikh
Fareg acquired a sizable following among the Jiddo (Cerulli 1964: 166–68),
a clan that also provided numerous workers for the Jenale plantations.

The evidence is compelling that the increased use of coercion by the
state was a factor in these uprisings of the mid-1920s. While colonial
records of the Fascist years are (not surprisingly) nearly silent about the
excesses of their policies of forced labor, one can learn much about the
quality of life and work for rural laborers by reading the testimonies of
Somalis interviewed by the Four Power Commission, set up after the Second World War to decide the disposition of the ex-Italian colonies (Council of Foreign Ministers 1948). These interviews reveal that forced labor
was the one abuse most frequently associated with Italian rule in the
Fascist era, and that it was a bitter memory even for those witnesses who
told the commission that they preferred the return of the Italians to the
trusteeship of the British or another power.

Conclusion

While the defeat of the Italian forces in the Horn of Africa in 1941 brought
an end to forced labor and inaugurated a period of liberal government,
first under the British and then under Italian trusteeship, the legacy of
slavery and its suppression in Somalia left their institutional marks. For
the former slave-owners, the end of slavery had meant the end of their
full participation in the agricultural export economy, though not the end
of their influence over clients. As late as the 1960s one could still find
individuals and lineage groups in the interriver area who received public displays of deference from the descendants of their former slaves and
client-cultivators, and for whom the latter provided occasional services
like house repair or preparation of a large meal on an Islamic feast day.

For the slaves, official abolition accelerated the process of their incorporation into a variety of local farming communities. Some were assimilated into client-cultivating lineages, which assured them certain rights
in land and the protection of corporate customary law. However, when
the colonial regime began conscripting labor from clan leaders along the
Shabelle, the socially despised clients and ex-slaves were the first to go.
Thus, the options of fleeing to the runaway-slave villages or to the sanc-

tuary of the Islamic settlements became more attractive to the freed slaves even as colonial administration was extended to the interior.

All the alternatives open to ex-slaves involved putting their labor at the disposal of someone else. The selective allocation of land and work by the founders of the runaway-slave villages and the exaction of a portion of the harvest by the tariqa-settlement heads were ways of appropriating labor's surplus value for their benefit. There were in fact multiple forms of labor control that emerged in the early colonial period. This variety of labor systems, all with a strong corporate-communal character, probably retarded the emergence of a free-labor market in Italian Somaliland. Not until the rapid mobilization of Somali subjects for the Italian war effort against Ethiopia and the later growth of towns after the Second World War did a substantial wage-labor force appear on the Somali scene.

I have argued that the colonial government in Italian Somaliland was slow both in formulating a consistent labor policy and in implementing it, which explains why it lost out to other "recruiters" of labor in the years before 1920. Only with the Fascist regime do we find the state resorting to the classical colonial techniques of creating a labor pool: the alienation of native land, a hut tax, and — these failing — a resort to coercive measures, however veiled in the language of labor "contracts."

Because ex-slaves formed a substantial part of the farm-labor pool, these forms of state coercion fell heavily on them. Though they had been absorbed into an earlier population of client-cultivators, they could not escape the low status that the latter groups also bore. In the Fascist era, the burdens of menial and dangerous work fell to the same population that had performed them in the precolonial period. Until quite recently, in fact, the farming population of southern Somalia continued to be stigmatized as the group most suited for tasks of clearing, tilling, constructing, carrying, and serving. Bearing this legacy perhaps was made easier for the ex-slaves by their belonging to corporate communities like the lineages of client-cultivators, the villages of runaway slaves, or the settlements of sheikhs. Even in a society which prescribed their economic subordination, they clearly found some forms of labor dependence more acceptable than others.

GLOSSARY

colonya (Somali)   from the Italian *colonia*, a form of labor tenancy used to encourage Somalis to settle on colonial plantations.

habash (Somali)	term used by Somalis to designate people of low status and presumed servile origin; slave or client-cultivator.
jerir (Somali)	lit. "curly-haired"; a term used to designate people of Negroid origin.
liberti (Italian)	freed men and women.
ooji (Somali)	slave.
qadi (Arabic)	Islamic legal specialist.
sekko (Somali)	from the Arabic *zakaat*, tithe; a portion of earnings paid to the head of the religious community.
tariqa (pl. *tariqat*) (Arabic)	religious order.
teen (Somali)	from the Italian *torno*, a rotating system of labor; corvée.

REFERENCES

Archival sources

ASMAI: Archivio storico dell'ex-Ministero dell'Africa italiana. Ministero degli Affari Esteri, Rome.
    Casali, G. Schiavitu, 1910. Box no. 85/2, folder 117.
ASL: African Studies Library, Boston University, Boston.
    Castagno, A. Private notes and papers, n.d.

Other sources

Camera dei Deputati. 1905. *Documenti diplomatici presentati al Parlamento italiano dal Ministero degli Affari esteri: Somalia italiana (1899–1905)*. Rome: Tipographia della Camera dei Deputati.
Carletti, T. 1912. *I problemi del Benadir*. Viterbo: Agnesotti.
Cassanelli, L. V. 1982. *The shaping of Somali society*. Philadelphia: University of Pennsylvania Press.
Cassanelli, L. V. 1987. Social construction on the Somali frontier: Bantu ex-slave communities in the nineteenth century. In *The African frontier*, ed. I. Kopytoff, 216–38. Bloomington: Indiana University Press.
Cerulli, E. 1957, 1959, 1964. *Somalia. Scritti vari editi ed inediti*. 3 vols. Rome: Istituto Poligrafico dello Stato.
Chiesi, G., and E. Travelli. 1904. *Le questioni del Benadir: Atti e relazione della commissione d'inchiesta della Società del Benádir*. Milan: Bellini.
Colucci, M. 1924. *Principi di diritto consuetudinario della Somalia italiana meridionale*. Florence: La Voce.
Council of Foreign Ministers. 1948. *Four Power Commission of Investigation for the former Italian colonies*. Vol. 2. *Report on Somaliland*. Unpublished report; cyclostyled.

Cucinotta, E. 1921. La costituzione sociale somala. *Rivista coloniale* 16: 389–405, 442–56, 493–502.

Gasparini, J. 1912. Sulla liberazione degli schiavi e servi domestici e sui metodi di assistenza e di tutela nel primo periodo della liberazione. *Agricoltura e Colonizzazione. Monografie e Rapporti No. 1.* Rome: Ministero degli Affari esteri.

Grottanelli, V. 1953. I Bantu del Giuba nelle tradizioni dei Wazegua. *Geographica Helvetica* 8: 249–60.

Guadagni, M. 1981. *Xeerka Beeraha. Diritto fondiario somalo.* Milan: Dott. A. Giuffrè.

Hess, R. L. 1966. *Italian colonialism in Somalia.* Chicago: University of Chicago Press.

Luling, V. 1971. The social structure of southern Somali tribes. Ph.D. dissertation, University of London.

Maino, C. 1959. *La Somalia e l'opera del Duca degli Abruzzi.* Rome: Istituto Italiano per l'Africa.

Onor, R. 1925. *La Somalia italiana: Esame critico dei problemi di economia rurale e di politica economica della colonia.* Turin: Fratelli Bocca.

Perricone-Viola, A. 1936. La liberazione degli schiavi nel vecchio Benadir. *Rivista delle colonie* 10: 882–86.

Price, R. 1979. Introduction. In *Maroon societies*, ed. R. Price, 1–30. Baltimore: Johns Hopkins University Press.

Robecchi-Brichetti, L. 1904. *Lettere dal Benadir.* Milan: La Poligrafica.

Scassellati-Sforzolini, G. 1926. *La Società Agricola Italo-Somala in Somalia.* Florence: Istituto agricolo coloniale italiano.

Ufficio Storico. 1960. *Somalia. Vol. 2. Dal 1914 al 1934.* Rome: Stato Maggiore Esercito.

11 *James McCann*

"Children of the House": Slavery and Its Suppression in Lasta, Northern Ethiopia, 1916–1935

The first third of the twentieth century has been widely described as critical to the maturation of the colonial state in Africa and to the transformation of relations of production in African societies through the growth of new institutions of labor and property (Coquery-Vidrovitch 1976; Berman and Lonsdale 1979). The suppression of slavery and the slave trade provided a direct link between policies of the metropole and production relations at ground level in Africa. Ethiopia's economy and social institutions evolved outside of the formal colonial system, yet the Ethiopian imperial state between 1923 and 1935 launched its own program to suppress slavery and the slave trade.

The purpose of this chapter is to examine the circumstances in which the Ethopian state took action against slavery, the effectiveness of government policies, and their effects at the grassroots level in the Lasta region

This chapter is based on data gathered over a period of 21 months in Ethiopia, Sudan, Britain, and Italy under funding from the Social Science Research Council, the Fulbright-Hays Doctoral Dissertation Abroad Program, and the National Endowment for the Humanities. Research included eight months of interviews carried out in Lasta migrant communities in and around Addis Ababa. A later period of study in northern Shawa was part of the evaluation of an Oxfam America rehabilitation project. I am grateful to Donald Crummey, Dennis Hickey, Martin Klein, Charles McClellan, Richard Roberts, and Suzanne Miers for their comments on earlier drafts.

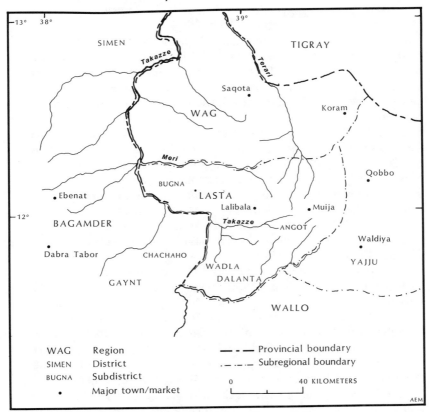

Map 11. Northern Ethiopia

of northeastern Ethiopia. A prime concern also is to describe the social and economic context in which slavery declined, by providing a comprehensive view of the institution in the early twentieth century. While modern Ethiopia's complex social formation contained a wide range of slavery types, this study focusses on the institution as it existed on the northeastern highlands, its relationship to the modern Ethiopian political economy, and the relative roles of internal factors versus external pressure in its suppression. This examination of the suppression of slavery in Ethiopia thus provides an important "control" study which helps separate for colonial Africa the specific effects of the colonial state from more generalized effects of the world economy.

Slaves have long played an important role in the social and economic fabric of the Ethiopian region. The highly stratified state systems which have existed in the Ethiopian highlands participated in the trade in and extraction of unfree laborers from the periphery since well before the Indian Ocean trade revived in the early nineteenth century. From early in the first millennium A.D., Axum and its successor states shipped frontier captives down the Nile and through the Red Sea to markets in the Mediterranean and Hejaz (Kobischanov 1979: 150–59, 172, 177; Pankhurst 1977: 1, 6). Control of the revenues from this trade probably contributed to state formation and the continued exploitation of the highland periphery. Slaves in the distant past, like those more recently, were a product of wars of expansion and frontier relations of tribute as well as a part of a self-reproducing slave stratum. Captives were both a primary item of foreign trade and participants in the production of the local surplus, both of which sustained the elaborate religious and administrative bureaucracy of the Ethiopian highland state systems (Kobischanov 1979: 150–59; Taddesse 1972: 85–88).

The policy of the highland imperial state in Ethiopia towards slavery had long been ambivalent despite slavery's important position in both long-distance trade and local production. Emperors Tewodros, Yohannes IV, and Menilek II had each expressed their disdain for the trade in slaves, though often not for the institution of slavery itself, and issued proclamations for its curtailment (Pankhurst 1968: 93, 98–99, 104–5). The violence of nineteenth-century state expansion and imperial consolidation nevertheless generated large numbers of captives, who were quickly absorbed by the Red Sea trade or used locally at regional courts or in the homes and fields of conquering soldiers, farmers, or aristocrats. The use of slaves as laborers and members of rural households was widespread up to and including the reign of Haile Selassie, and any description of labor and property relations in Ethiopia must include slavery, although few studies have done so.

By the early twentieth century, at least two general types of slave systems existed in Ethiopia: the first was on the southern and western frontiers, where highland armies or smaller client states raided small-scale societies on the empire's periphery. There soldiers or officials took captives as booty for their personal retinue or sent them into major markets — Jimma, Gindabaret, Enarea — which passed them along well-established trade routes. By his death in 1913, Menilek's expansion to the south, west, and east had created a broad and fluid frontier zone which had already extracted ivory, gold, and slaves in prodigious amounts. By the accession of Ras Tafari Makonnan as head of government in 1916, these frontier areas still fueled the growth of the central state, but increasingly by providing coffee, hides, and formal tribute rather the products of a more violent process (McClellan 1978a; Marsae Hazan 1942: 104–7).

A second locus for slavery, and the area to be considered in this chapter, was in the northern plow-based rural economy. There, slaves formed part of the labor force which worked in the smallholder subsistence production of cereals, pulses, and small-scale livestock holdings. In contrast to the burgeoning commodity production on alientated lands in the south, northern agriculture took place on small, fragmented plots worked by peasant households, and rested on an elaborate set of social and political traditions which moderated conflict between classes and gave peasant smallholders rights to land.

Slavery and Production in the North: The Case of Lasta

Slavery in Lasta, and in most of northern Ethiopia, differed considerably from slavery in the southern and frontier zones of Ethiopia. Lasta's production centered on the cultivation of cereals and pulses in a rural economy increasingly deficient in capital. A survey of ecological history from the mid-nineteenth century to the present reveals intensifying patterns of famine and production shortfalls resulting from discernible climatic and demographic trends. Population pressure on land led to a gradual movement of cultivation up steep mountain slopes to the frost line at 4,000 meters and a similar movement down into easily flooded and malarial lowland valleys. Overall, by the early twentieth century, pressure to open up new land to cultivation had reduced fallow periods, limited the size of plots, and severely constrained the amount of pasturage for draft animals. Deforestation and the effects of rainfall fluctuations in northeastern Ethiopia simultaneously promoted erosion and consistent patterns of drought.

These conditions, by the early twentieth century, had substantially altered Lasta's production equation from earlier patterns. Far more than land—which was still available to the vast majority of Lastans—the breeding, borrowing, and maintaining of rural capital determined household strategies of land and labor allocation. The area could now no longer consistently reproduce its own supply of plow oxen, and depended on a steady flow of cattle and oxen to come from more salubrious climes to the south and west. Locally, those who did not control oxen, labor, and land grew increasingly dependent on those who did. These conditions of decreasing productivity and competition for scarce resources contributed to the formation of a rural society in which the annual survival of household units was a real issue (McCann 1984: 21–58).

In the production system of rural Lasta and most of northern Ethiopia, peasant households were the primary unit of production and consumption. The nature of property and labor within these units was critical in determining the position of slaves and slavery in the rural north.

The linchpin of property relations in Lasta was the *rist* system of ambilineal descent, which allowed individual Lastans to claim land and
property through either the male or female line, regardless of order of
birth or gender. Household claims on land or property were not commonly held rights of the unit, but a collection of individual rights. Each
individual, therefore, maintained the right to secede from the whole.

In theory and in practice, the Lasta household was a political and economic unit which reflected the composite interests of its members; kinship as a unifying factor was secondary. Moreover, a clear linguistic and
cultural distinction existed between the economic unit of the household
and the notion of family and kin. The Amharic word for household, *beta
seb*, translates not as "family" or "kin," but as "members of a house."
Household members usually consisted of a nuclear family and an auxil-
iary labor force made up of distant relatives, slaves, and others offering
their labor in exchange for membership. These units remained together
as long as they proved able to activate land claims, control capital (oxen
and seed), and mobilize a labor force sufficient to work their landholdings.

Lasta households were fragile, single-generation units which did not
survive the death of their heads. No transgenerational family estate existed, and household members divided property according to the principle of equal shares to all who could claim ambilineal descent. No single
offspring in the unit had claim on all the household land or capital holdings. Reproduction of the production unit, therefore, required each individual to muster sufficient factors of production to set up and maintain
a new household unit capable of operating within the material and social demands of a highly stratified rural society (Bauer 1977: 15; Hoben
1975; McCann 1984: 68–102). In these circumstances, slaves had an important economic role as part of both the household's property and its
labor force.

Households also participated in a range of rural institutions which
linked producing households to the state, the Ethiopian Orthodox church,
and local administrative elites through taxes, labor obligations, and a legal
apparatus which adjudicated disputes in the property system. Lastans
owed taxes, ritual obeisance, and labor obligations to a largely hereditary class of military and ecclesiastical elite who held political or church
offices or who held special rights of collection over goods in kind and labor
(McCann 1984: 68–102). Both political offices and churches in Lasta also
maintained special lands called *hudad*, cultivated by corvée labor from
resident households. Special access to land and labor, plus the resultant
ability to attract and maintain new members, differentiated elite households from their peasant counterparts.

Slaves were an important part of the Lasta and northern Ethiopian

MCCANN: *Northern Ethiopia* 337

society and production system from at least the first millennium A.D., although their points of origin shifted with the changing frontiers of the central state. Very early on, Lasta's slave population came from the ethnic frontiers of the post-Axumite state in southwestern Eritrea and from Bagamder's western marches through the Nile Valley (Pankhurst 1977: 2, 7; Wylde 1901: 332, 328). This pattern of supply continued into at least the mid-nineteenth century. This evidence suggests that Lasta, and its key market at Saqota in particular, linked the slave-trade routes through Gallabat, on the Sudanese border, to the Red Sea coast at Massawa and tied it to northern Ethiopia's middle and long-distance routes, which generally ran southwest to northeast. By the late nineteenth century patterns of supply had shifted farther south and into Ethiopia's southwestern border with the Sudan to reflect the expansion of the Shawan state under Emperor Menilek. Slaves in Lasta and elsewhere in northeastern Ethiopia in this period were products of the same southern wars of expansion which supplied captive labor to southern garrison towns, Addis Ababa, and virtually all of Ethiopia.[1]

Lasta soldiers who joined Emperor Menilek's armies in the south, if they did not choose to remain on conquered land there, returned home with easily transported human booty. This process in the southwest and west continued well after 1916, when Ras Tafari's regency began. One Lasta informant who had ventured south as a young man in 1930 after the major conquests described how soldiers and officials in the southwest obtained slaves:

At that time they [slaves] were bought cheaply. Didn't we go there to govern? We were going to Gama Gofa, Kulo, Wollamo, Gimira, Shanqilla, to where they were available. We went to border regions to govern. When we went there we bought them cheaply from the local governor of the region. A landlord in the border regions could have 15 or 20, the price was small.

When they [the local population] did not have money to pay the tax they used to give a young slave instead. If they could not get money they would give a young

1. For a detailed description of the use of slaves in gold mining in western Ethiopia, see FO, Barton, 3 August 1931. The process of southern expansion is best described in McClellan 1978a. Reports of slave-raiding and slaveholding on the southern and western frontiers of Ethiopia are replete in the Foreign Office correspondence with the Maji, Gore, and Gambela British consulates (FO, 371 file), in the Intelligence files of the Central Records Office in Khartoum, and in the personal memoirs of British agents in the area. While foreign-language materials must be carefully corroborated, Amharic-language sources and my own interviews with participants confirm the importance of the slave trade and of slaves in agricultural production on the frontier (see Marsae Hazan 1942: 104–7). Chakola Lamma, one of my informants who participated in slave raids in the southwest, described in great detail the movement of slaves to northern markets.

slave and it would cover the yearly tax. Also, when asked another time he would give another. The others would do the same and this would bring the number to 50, 40, 30. Then he [the soldier or official] would collect them and add some by buying and leave for another place.[2]

Still other slaves arrived in Lasta through the slave-trading network which channelled southern captives northward through markets of Dangla, Boru, and Gindabaret, in Gojjam, Walo, and northern Shawa, respectively. Slaves brought to Lasta joined an already existing population of second- and third-generation slaves who were the household servants, tenants, and retainers of wealthy peasants and of the rural administrative class (Annaratone 1914: 41; Grottanelli 1939: 114–18).[3] They made up one of several landless castes which coexisted with Christian Amhara peasants in the northern highlands.

Slaveholding patterns in Lasta appear to have not necessarily favored the hereditary elite class. There were no class or occupational barriers to ownership.[4] Most captives entered Lasta society as the property of soldiers, either the hereditary military elite or farmer-soldiers who went south to accompany the imperial armies. Once in the rural economy, slaves could then be brought and exchanged. Notwithstanding reports that Christians were prohibited from purchasing slaves, anyone with the economic means could hold or purchase a slave.[5] According to my informants, re-

2. The quote derives from an interview with Chakola Lamma (6 May 1982), the aforementioned native of northern Lasta who had travelled south in 1930 and participated in the tail end of the slaving activities in the southwest. His general description is corroborated in Marsae Hazan 1942: 110. After one 1904 expedition, Lij Iyasu's retinue returned to the capital with 1,785 slaves. Lastans who joined expeditions of this type often returned home with several slaves apiece. For a further description of this process, see Annaratone 1914: 41.

3. Chakola Lamma (interview: 10 March 1982) also offered the best description of the markets which fed slaves into the north. The most prominent of these was Gindabaret, northwest of Addis Ababa. Although oral data cannot confirm the ratio of new slaves to second- and third-generation ones, for the 1920s Montandon (1932: 15) noted that 75 percent of slaves in the north were born of slave parents, 15 percent were purchased, and 10 percent had been captured in raids. Figures for earlier periods would presumably have had a higher ratio of new slaves to second- and third-generation ones.

4. Patterns of procurement and ownership became clear during most of my interviews on the topic of slavery. The fairly open nature of slaveholding contrasts with restrictions between classes in food and drink consumption, clothing, and status at ritual occasions. Grottanelli (1939: 114–15) observed that even artisan caste groups in the Lake Tana region held slaves.

5. The idea that Ethiopian Christians were prohibited from engaging in the slave trade or from holding slaves seems to derive from Abir 1968: 53–69 and accounts from the courts of nineteenth-century emperors. This notion is not corroborated in any of my oral sources or twentieth-century accounts.

gional governors held 40–50 as a part of their extended households; local soldiers and military officials might have 5 or 6, and successful farmers might accumulate 4 or 5. Unless they obtained them directly as booty on a military expedition, however, the lower economic rung of farmers probably did not have the means to buy or keep slaves, especially given the rapidly increasing prices in the 1920s and the declining state of Lasta's rural economy.

A few examples may serve to illustrate patterns of slaveholding as they evolved in the 1920s and 1930s. Alamu Warqnah was born in 1896 and reached his majority in 1915 or so. He was the son of a soldier with some local influence but no recognized military rank. While Alamu was a youth growing up his father had had two slaves, probably the product of an expedition to the south in his own youth. Alamu himself rose in the ranks as a result of his service with Italian forces in Libya and supported his family by buying oxen and bribing officials to activate his claims on his rist lands. Despite this influence and position, he did not acquire slaves, nor did he inherit those of his father. In another case, Chakola Lamma was the son of a peasant farmer whose brothers had successfully risen in the ranks of the regional army. Each of Chakola's uncles had five or six slaves who served as part of their retinue. Chakola's father, however, did not own slaves, nor did Chakola, even though he participated as a youth in raiding activities in the southwest. When he returned to northern Lasta to take up agriculture he did so without the help of slaves. Although the sample is obviously small, the experience of my informants would suggest that the incidence of slave-owning dwindled rapidly among the generation which reached its majority after 1916. The reasons would appear to be economic: slaves had simply become too expensive to purchase and opportunities to obtain them directly dwindled with the establishment of a strong administrative presence in the 1920s and 1930s (Hickey 1984; Edwards 1982; interviews, passim).

Lastans do not seem to have adhered to a hard and fast religious or ethical dogma regarding the treatment, economic role, or legal status of their slave population. Except for those who belonged to the well-differentiated households of the rural elite, my informants could point out no major differences between the work performed by slaves and that undertaken by free members of the household or in the conditions in which they lived. Slaves engaged in all types of labor, lived alongside their fellow household members in the same dwellings, and ate similar food. Sexual relations between male masters and female slaves were common and openly acknowledged. The only exception to the close social relations between the owner, the family, and the household slaves was in the rather more elaborate elite household, where slaves lived as a part of a socially differentiated workforce in separate quarters surrounding the household's reception halls, granaries, and sleeping quarters (McCann 1984: 89–90; Grottanelli 1939: 118).

In rural farming households female slaves did household chores, ground grain and spices, and participated in weeding and harvesting. Males worked in the fields, plowing, sowing, and harvesting along with other male members of the household. However, these were tasks for the culturally adapted. One of my informants argued that slaves newly introduced to Lasta work roles were "clumsy" and needed training in the skills of cereal cultivation. Until they learned, they did arduous but simple tasks around the homestead (McCann 1984: 89–90; Grottanelli 1939: 117). The closeness in which slaves and free householders lived spawned close social interaction, and most slaves quickly adapted to the cultural milieu, especially expected deference behavior. Such assimilation took place more quickly than in those African societies where slaves regularly occupied separate quarters and villages.

Nevertheless, slaves were often subject to hard work, deprivation, and physical abuse. In times of food shortages or strenuous household workloads, slaves were probably the first to receive short rations or tedious tasks, since freeborn members of households retained the right to leave. Elite households were, perhaps, more dependent on slave labor. The following letter from a certain Grazmach Tafari[6] to a Sudanese border official reflects the elites' attitude towards slaves and their economic role:

May God show you justice. The government is the protector of the poor and their properties. The issue is that all slaves of the Qabtia territory have run away towards Gedaref. Accordingly, we your poor men, have become oppressed because it is difficult for us to continue living without slaves. On account of this I am sending you my son in order that you may help in this matter. I offer you my thanks times ten.

Demographic data on the slave population in northern Ethiopia do not exist beyong the oral sources or the estimates of travellers. The Italian political agent Dr. Carlo Annaratone estimated in 1914 that one-fourth of the population of northeastern Ethiopia were slaves. His estimates for areas farther to the south were considerably higher (Annaratone 1914: 42).[7] In general, female slaves fetched a higher price and were probably

6. See FO, Grazmach Tafari 1924. Abba Getu Endasaw (interview: 1 June 1982) described his cousin's beating of a slave.
7. Allan Hoben has told me that he believes these figures would have been much too high for the Damot region of Gojjam. Annaratone, who otherwise has proved to be an accurate rapporteur, may have been referring to areas along major trade routes. Grotta-

marginally in more demand. Informants did not, however, indicate a clear preference based on sex. Because households often owned single slaves as domestic or agricultural workers, it would seem likely that the overall fertility rate for slave women would have been lower than in the free population, although, as previously stated, sexual liaisons between masters and female slaves were not uncommon. This may not have been the case in elite households, however, where a number of male and female slaves occupied separate quarters away from the main homestead. Although marriage practice in Lasta and the north did not require either brideprice or a dowry, formal marriage between a slave woman and a free man was less likely than between free individuals. Marriages and the new households established from them relied on both sets of parents to "capitalize" the new unit (Hoben 1963: 112–20). Since slaves could bring neither property nor land rights to the union, they made poor choices as formal marriage partners. Moreover, marriage or liaisons between slaves of separate households were often discouraged by the master of the male slave, since the progeny always belonged to the mother's master. According to the widespread Amharic expression, "the calf belongs to the owner of the cow, not the owner of the bull."

Slaves' access to freedom either through the law or assimilation was linked to a large degree to the society's partible, ambilineal property system as a whole. Slaves were always the property of a particular member of the household, not of the collective whole. For this reason, the death of the owner, usually the household head or his wife, brought on a set of possibilities for slaves ranging from manumission to being considered inheritable property for transfer to offspring of the deceased master. The exact dispensation in each case, according to my informants, depended on the desires expressed in the owner's will, the degree of the slave's assimilation, and the interpretation of property law by local officials. The presence of second- and third-generation slaves in Lasta and elsewhere in the north in the 1930s suggests that, at least in the late nineteenth and early twentieth centuries, slaves were passed as property of offspring setting up new household units after the death of the household head.

Lastans most commonly manumitted slaves on the death of the master by means of a will read and sworn before witnesses of the community and the church. Other slaves managed to gain *de jure* freedom during the lifetimes of their masters, and in rare cases laid claim to a share of household property equal to that of the natural children. In any case, manumission was probably a largely symbolic act, since manumitted

nelli (1939: 197–98) had reported large numbers approaching Annaratone's in the Lake Tana region of Gojjam and Bagamder in the mid-1930s.

slaves almost always remained within the household of a master compassionate enough to free them. The children of a master and a female slave were free, usually with full rights of inheritance. Children of a slave who were fathered by a free man other than their mother's master could be freed in a court of law, providing the father or another free person chose to raise the issue before a judge.[8]

The nature of the rural production equation in northern Ethiopia raises a basic question about the efficiency of slavery as a form of labor. Given the availability of family and free labor, why were slaves such a ubiquitous facet of rural production in Lasta? This question is all the more vexing when one considers the fairly high opportunity costs of obtaining slaves either through warfare or the marketplace. An adult male slave cost around 150 thalers (ca. U.S. $75.00) in the mid-1920s, more than twice the price of a pair of oxen in the capital-poor north.[9] These costs were especially high given the universal availability of kin and free labor willing to attach itself to a promising household. A good rifle might be as prudent a purchase for enhancing personal prestige as a slave, and less costly.

The key to the slave's attraction as a form of labor for the rural household was in the slave's "marginality" to Lasta society. Slaves belonged to the specialized social category of *yabet lij* (lit., "child of the house"), which defined them as outsiders both in terms of their actual point of origin and their restricted access to those symbolic elements which defined other individuals as *yasaw lij* (lit., "child of a person") (McCann 1984: 90; Tsehai 1980: 42). Kinlessness perhaps best describes the condition of yabet lij. As in most African societies and legal systems, rights to property, social rank, and the means of production stem from membership in a particular matriline or patriline. The inability to call upon either living kin or ancestors cast one as an outsider dependent on others to define one's role in society. This was especially true in light of the competitive inheritance system based on individual claims to property and land. When asked about slaves' rights in Lasta, one informant laughed and responded, "Barya men zamad allaw?" ("What kin does a slave have?"). Lastans also used other, more tangible prejudices to define and differentiate the unfree yabet lij from the free laborer. My informants

8. My sources on these customary legal practices sometimes contradict one another. See interviews, passim; Annaratone 1914: 40–42; RHL, De Halpert Papers: 103–6; ASMAI, Notiziario politico 1931.

9. This figure came from Alamu Warqnah, an ex-soldier and tax assessor whose family had held slaves. The prices for slaves in the north varied over time, but generally corroborate Alamu's statements. See, for example, ASMAI, Pollera 1929; UKL, Sudan Intelligence Report 1925; and FO, Zaphiro report 1925.

most often claimed hair texture and skin color to be the characteristics most likely to differentiate the two. The relatively darker skin of the captives preferred by Lastans set these slaves apart and marked them as outsiders.

The designation yasaw lij carried the connotation of "citizen" or one with access to rights in society by virtue of his or her birth. Freeborn Lastans belonged to an ambilineal-descent corporation which shared rights to land and to a genealogy traceable back to an area's founding father. Men and women born into Lasta society and to a particular descent corporation had the right to claim land by virtue of their ability to trace their ancestry through male and female lines to the original founder. The most important feature of the slave's marginality, therefore, was the inability to claim land. Outsiders from other Amhara areas might not be able to claim land through descent in a particular area, but their right to do so elsewhere qualified them as yasaw lij. Slaves were those people clearly drawn from outside of Lasta's social world. Not even the Cushitic-speaking Oromo of the lowlands of eastern Lasta could be enslaved.[10] Being Christian was a sign of assimilation, but the required baptism of newly acquired slaves did not entitle them to freedom.[11]

It was precisely this continued marginality to the land system which made slaves a desirable, if expensive, form of labor. The relatively abundant "free" labor of family members, distant kin, or labor entrepreneurs had always proved unreliable, since young members of a household, whether male or female, ultimately wished to activate their own land claims and establish an independent household. The land tenure system encouraged them to do so. The "stem" family consisting of a young married couple living on their parents' land estate was a fairly common, but highly unstable, form of household-labor unit. Young people making their own land claims left their parents' homesteads and parishes to activate claims in other areas. Rather than risk the loss of "free" labor, rural households that could afford slaves kept them as a hedge against a future labor shortage.

10. The term *Galla* in documents and interviews should be handled carefully, since it sometimes refers to all non–yasaw lij and not necessarily to speakers of the Oromo language (see Appendix A). Information from Lastans themselves on whether neighboring Oromo might have been enslaved contrasts with the information provided to the British Embassy in 1930 by their agent Phillip Zaphiro (see FO, Barton 1930). The question of defining precisely who belonged to the category of yasaw lij no doubt changed over time. For a description of the Amhara land system and the dynamics of descent, see Hoben 1973. For Lasta variations in the 1900–1935 period see McCann 1984: Ch. 3.

11. The relationship between Christianity and manumission has been misunderstood, with many observers in the nineteenth century holding that conversion of slaves also brought automatic freedom (see Edwards 1982).

Like oxen, the presence of slaves, far more than unpredictable kin or free persons, in a farming household increased its opportunity to mobilize or maintain its land claims and increase the security of its production over time. As Gavin Wright has argued for the American South, a key feature of slavery was that it provided an elastic supply of labor to a farming household, offering assurance of meeting seasonal labor needs and an expanded capacity to cultivate more land even if returns to scale were constant (Wright 1978: 55). Before supplies became scarce and prices exorbitant in the late 1920s and 1930s, slaves provided much more security in such an expansion, since family labor tended to be a temporary and finite source. Even if slaves within a household did not work directly in agriculture, their presence increased the household's status-honor and therefore increased its chances of success in land litigation.

Why did not the high prices of slaves in the Red Sea trade and in distant clearinghouse markets pull slaves out of the rural Lasta economy? There are a number of reasons why areas like Lasta retained a resident slave population. Certainly a slave's "salability" decreased as acculturation took place; manumission of slaves meant that they remained as household servants and not as chattel. Most slaves by the 1920s were therefore not subject to market conditions unless kidnapped by bandits or unscrupulous merchant caravans. A primary reason for their continued presence, however, was related to the "moral economy" of the rural society and the importance of minimizing risk to household reproduction. Lasta peasants valued the physical and social reproduction of their household and community more than crude profit maximization.

Even if capital was the scarcest factor of production in the rural Lasta economy, slave labor nevertheless had important attractions to rural producers as well. Over time, however, slaves came to be an extremely expensive form of labor for new householders when the purchase price rose and the opportunity to obtain them through raids waned.

Sources of Slavery's Demise in Lasta and Northern Ethiopia

The ending of slavery in Lasta and throughout northern Ethiopia in general was a slow process only partly affected by the formal attempts at suppression advertised in Geneva and Addis Ababa. Neither the imperial decrees of 1923 and 1931 nor pressure from the League of Nations had much effect by themselves on the institution in Lasta. Rather it was the Ethiopian Empire's changing political economy which gradually diminished slavery's role. Over time, two processes reduced the strength of the institution in the north. The first was a rapid decline in the supply of new slaves from Ethiopia's southern and western frontiers as a result of the growth of commodity production, the results of the imperial government's efforts to suppress raiding and the open operation of the slave trade, and the effective defensive strategies employed by the southern populations at risk (Hickey 1984; Edwards 1982). The second was the response of the local household economy to economic and social change on the national level. The end result in the north was the creation of a landless stratum of ex-slaves which merged after the Italian occupation with a new impoverished agricultural work force.

Between 1916 and the Italian war the imperial government issued three major proclamations regarding slavery and the slave trade. On 15 September 1923 Ras Tafari and Empress Zawditu issued a proclamation which outlawed the slave trade on pain of death, placed the responsibility for its prosecution on local officials, and stated that slaves taken from their home were entitled to freedom. Two weeks later Tafari signed the League of Nations' covenant with its antislavery clause. Six months later on 31 March 1924 he issued a decree which made the first provisions for slave emancipation and established the Bureau for the Liberation of Slaves. On 15 July 1931 the newly crowned Emperor Haile Selassie issued a strong edict which called for the liberation of all slaves on the death of their masters, placed further restrictions on the trade, and was followed by the establishment of a new antislavery bureau under the direction of a Briton, Frank De Halpert (RHL, De Halpert Papers). Some observers at the time noted that the 1931 regulations if enforced would end slavery within one generation.

Seen in the context of the growth of the central state's power, the campaign against slavery in the empire as a whole was part of a much larger program of state transformation led by the young Ras Tafari, later Haile Selassie I. During the 1920s Tafari's aggressive policies of centralization and modernization hardened political alignments between those who stood to benefit from reform and those who preferred the political and economic norms of Menilek's expansionist state. Attitudes towards slavery and its abolition were symbolic of the struggle between new and old oligarchies. The fundamental differences between conservative and progressive elements in the central government derived from their economic base and from visions they had of Ethiopia's future. Three basic groups emerged: neoconservatives, who pursued Menilek's vision of a federated oligarchic but centralized state; conservatives — primarily northern elite families — who sought to maintain greater regional autonomy; and a "progressive" party led by Ras Tafari, which hoped to build a centralized fiscal and political structure dominated by decisions made in Addis Ababa. Neoconservatives at court tended to rely on the tribute and strength of regional governors engaged in extractive activities in the south and west like slave-raiding, ivory-hunting, and the rapacious collection of tribute from the population of frontier zones. Their aggressive soldiery, usually first- and second-generation migrants from Shawa and farther north, was a military entrepreneurial class which had grown wealthy on the booty and land available in the wake of Menilek's conquest of his southern frontier.[12]

In the north, the conservative faction relied on the rural military and ecclesiastical classes, which wished to retain their direct control over local customs and their rights of collection over peasant producers. The power of northern conservatives derived from their ability to retain their collected wealth within their governates by minimizing their tribute transfers to the central government. Money and payments in kind were redistributed locally to build grassroots constituencies. Slaves formed an important part of the rural work force and of the retinues of the rural elite. In elite households slaves did household chores, tilled state lands, performed as specialized musicians, and attended household guests. In the far northwest some slaves lived in separate villages and produced durra for export to Eritrea.[13]

Tafari and his cadre of "young Ethiopians" were a clear threat to both of the above groups, since the former aimed to build central-state power by supporting an expanded state and a provincial bureaucracy maintained by salaries, central-state control over customs and courts, and a national economy based on the shift to cash cropping, commodity production, and the free labor of a rural proletariat (Marcus 1979: 559–68; McClellan 1980). As Tafari's power increased in the 1920s he maneuvered regional appointments to favor his loyalists and reduce the incidence of raiding in frontier zones.[14] This action and the announcement of policies

12. The lines of division among these groups were rather fluid, but I believe that the general categories hold. There is some debate about the use of the term *progressive* to describe Tafari's party. Here I refer more to method of administration than to ultimate goals. An excellent account of the career of Dajach Balcha, a neoconservative southern governor, can be found in McClellan 1978a. For Ras Tafari's own retrospective views on the struggle for power, see *The Autobiography of Haile Selassie I: My Life and Ethiopia's Progress 1892–1937* (Ullendorff 1976: 62–171). A good insider's view can also be found in Marsae Hazan 1942: passim.

13. See CRO, "Report on the Kafta Caravan" 1907. The use of slave villages for the production of food crops for sale to the Eritrean market seems to have been confined to the northwestern region of Nuqara and possibly some areas of Tigray. Slave labor in the north could also be used to cultivate hudad, or state lands, which were one of the perquisites of office in the north. The evidence from interviews, however, would suggest that this was not a widespread practice in Lasta or the north in general, where peasants usually worked hudad lands, since the social and political symbolism of the corvée obligation may have been as important as the labor itself.

14. See FO, 371 files; and CRO, INTEL. for negotiations on southwestern border re-

against slavery and the slave trade were pointed directly at weakening the economic base of his political rivals. In 1932 his extension of the anti-slavery courts throughout the south probably reflected the growth of his central government's power more than its ability to end slavery immediately. Nevertheless, he also helped to reduce the market for agricultural slaves in the south by shifting the soldier-settler relations (*neftenya-gabbar*) of Menilek's period of expansion to a more centralized — and profitable — landlord-tenant relationship which relied on the labor of a landless proletariat.[15] In the north the prosecution of slavery emerged along different lines.

The Fight against Slavery in the North

Although a part of the northern political and economic system, Lasta, and the northeast in general, was not a major focus for the slave trade, nor was it a major force in the national economy. This was partly because Lasta was relatively small, did not produce goods directly marketable in the world economy, and was under the control of Ras Kassa Haylu, a Shawan loyalist and Tafari's cousin, who ruled the area as an absentee governor from 1917 to 1935. Kassa generally supported Tafari's programs of fiscal and judicial reforms. He had, in fact, been a key figure in Tafari's 1928 appointment as *negus* (king) of Ethiopia (Marsae Hazan 1942: 432). Although a committed reformer in the areas of judicial administration and tax collection, Kassa nevertheless chose to rule conservative Lasta through local relatives and appointees who had little contact with the political and economic issues which were fostering changes in the capital and in commodity-producing areas to the south. Although Kassa took an active role in instituting reforms in rural administration in Lasta and personally opposed slavery, he seems not to have actively prosecuted slavery there. None of my informants living in Lasta at the time recalled the 1923–1924 proclamations or any effects from them.[16]

---

gions and prosecutions of raiding. Notes on frontier raiding for slaves and animal trophies can be found on a continuing basis in the Sudan Intelligence Report (UKL, Sudan Collection) from 1898 through 1935, although the appointment of Ethiopian border governors loyal to the central administration lessened its frequency over time.

15. The best account of the shift to landlord-tenant relations is McClellan 1978b: 439. Although cash cropping began under the military neftenya-gabbar system, the measuring of land and its allocation by the imperial government was a major watershed in the process of proletarianization in the south. Balata Darasa, a governor on the southern side of the Blue Nile, supposedly released the slaves working his fields and mines and allowed them to stay on as wage laborers (see FO, Cheesman memorandum, 4 July 1932). Harold Marcus has pointed out to me that Ras Tafari did the same on his fruit plantation at Erer, near Harar.

16. In a comprehensive file of over 400 of Ras Kassa's administration decrees, only one

Much better remembered was the antislavery proclamation made in 1931 by Emperor Haile Selassie. Its greater impact was a direct result of the increased presence of the central government in national politics after 1930, when Tafari's forces defeated the most bothersome of his northern rivals and cowed the rest into submission. Unlike the 1923 proclamation, Haile Selassie's 1931 decree on slavery involved specific administrative action. By 1932 the emperor had already set up 67 slave courts to enforce antislavery regulations. Forty-eight of these courts were under the aegis of the Ministry of the Interior, 14 were directly dependent on regional governors, and 5 had been established directly by the Central Slavery Department and were financially supported by it (RHL, De Halpert Papers: 17).

Of the 67 slave courts, only a handful existed in northern Ethiopia, none in Tigray and in the northern districts controlled by Ras Kassa. Kassa nevertheless sought to comply in general terms with the central government's antislavery program.[17] Shortly after the 1931 proclamation, he established a slave court at his regional capital of Dabra Tabor, adjacent to southwestern Lasta. Kassa appointed a local official, Qagnazmach Gassasa, as chief judge of the court. Gassasa was directly responsible to Kassa's son Wandbawassan, who governed Kassa's northern regions of Lasta and Bagamder.[18]

The antislavery effort in northeastern Ethiopia centered on the compound of this antislavery court at Dabra Tabor. The compound itself was a converted banquet hall, surrounded "like a prison" by a thorn fence patrolled by an armed guard.[19] The facility could house about 100 people. When news of the emperor's proclamation first filtered into the

deals with slavery or its prosecution (see McCann, Tesema, and Dagnachew 1984: Document #144, which is also presented herein as Appendix A).

17. See RHL, De Halpert Papers: 84–85. Tigray and Ras Kassa's territories were specifically excluded from the jurisdiction of the Central Slavery Department. This agency placed its courts at strategic locations near the capital designed to choke off the movement of slaves northward through Shawa. In his home district of Salale, north of the capital, Ras Kassa granted freedom to escaped slaves and established a written contract to be signed between masters and slaves who chose to remain. For a discussion of the international political climate which produced the imperial government's anti-slave-trade edicts, see Miers forthcoming.

18. Interviews, passim. Italian records report another individual, a certain Qagnamach Emru, who occupied the post in 1931 (see ASMAI, notiziario politico 1931). In Gojjam after 1932 the government relied on its appointed governor, Dajach Mesfin, to release slaves held by the area's deposed governor, Ras Haylu Takla Haymanot (see FO, Cheesman, 28 June 1932).

19. I obtained this information in an interview with Abba Getu Endasaw (1 June 1982), who had served as a soldier in Dabra Tabor at that time and whose relatives had employed slaves released from the antislavery compound there. According to Abba Getu, the con-

countryside of Lasta and Bagamder, slaves fled from compounds all over the region and came to Dabra Tabor.[20] As the slaves presented their cases before the judge he issued freedom orders and placed the newly freed men and women in the protected holding compound, where the government provided for their food and care, in theory, until they could secure work in the town or with households in adjacent agricultural zones. Government granaries supplied food to the compound sufficient for one meal a day. Unfortunately, the initial optimism shown by the slaves and a few reform-minded officials could not and did not alter the basic economic and social conditions which persisted in the north.

The court compound's 100-person capacity quickly filled beyond its limits. Provisions ran short and living conditions within the compound deteriorated rapidly. According to one resident of Dabra Tabor, slaveowners gradually began to arrive at Dabra Tabor, and the slave judges allowed them to claim their property. Many slaves saw how few options they had and agreed to return. Judges in outlying areas had already begun returning slaves to their masters after the payment of a fee. Dajach Wandbawasan, the governor, seemingly took little interest in the proceedings and allowed former masters to claim their slaves. Most slaves remained in the compound no more than a month or two and then passed into contract labor, returned to their former masters, or agreed to join the households of nearby peasants, who at least offered them a livelihood.[21]

The initial effect of the antislavery policy in the north was an interesting shift in the distribution of unfree labor in the region which eventually produced a new category of labor in the rural economy. The slaves who had passed through the Dabra Tabor court or who had been liber-

---

tract offered to ex-slaves was similar to the one designed by Ras Kassa in Salale (see Appendix A).

20. There were similar movements of ex-slaves to the west into Sudan and north into Eritrea. Obviously the percentage of slaves able or willing to make the long journey to Sudan was low, perhaps less than 5 percent. As late as the mid-1930s, large numbers of Ethiopian slaves made their way to Sudan to claim freedom papers and reside in special camps set up by Anglo-Egyptian authorities. For a month-by-month tally of these migrations, see UKL, Sudan Monthly Record, 1929–1936.

21. Besides the formal courts of Addis Ababa, the only place ex-slaves could obtain freedom papers was in Sudan. In none of my interviews, including one with Kassa's personal secretary, could informants recall seeing legal documents regarding emancipation. Border officials in Sudan were authorized to issue the certificates and to place ex-slaves in temporary holding camps similar to those used for refugees during the Italian occupation. See the description of the flow of refugee slaves and camps set up for them in FO, Maffey 1927; CRO, report 1936; and CRO, INTEL, Kassala Province files, 1935–1937: passim.

ated by local judges from the small clandestine trade formed a new category of labor called *ya sar barya* (lit., "grass slaves"). These ex-slaves opted to join the households of the government officials who had "freed" them or farming households in the area which had agreed to maintain them in exchange for agricultural or domestic labor. In fact, the "grass slaves" had little choice. Those who tried to make their way to Addis Ababa or even to Dabra Tabor risked being captured again as slaves and perhaps being offered into the Red Sea export market. The freedom they had gained from the new imperial law was tenuous. Very few freed slaves were given formal freedom papers. Moreover, their chances of setting up an independent rural household were almost nonexistent. Lacking capital (oxen and seed) and access to land, ex-slaves could only attach themselves to an Amhara household which accepted their work in exchange for food and clothing—a condition not very different from slavery. Once the initial excitement of the news of the emperor's proclamation had subsided, few slaves chose to leave the security of their masters' households. Only a trickle of slaves were able to make their way across the Sudanese border into camps set up by the British for escaped slaves. A few also fled northward to Eritrea or sought opportunities for wage labor in Addis Ababa (McCann 1984: 254–58). Lasta's slave population was far-removed from any of these options. While no statistics are available, it would seem that most of them—like their counterparts all over the north—remained within the rural economy as unpaid domestic and agricultural labor, that is, as slaves.

It would be incorrect to argue, however, that slavery was not profoundly affected by imperial policy and the changing political economy of the south. Even before 1931 the effects of imperial policy in the north had already become evident. The slave trade had moved off the main caravan routes and onto minor ones. Lastans who returned from participating in the last of the southern slave raids with captives to add to their own households had to move carefully and avoid the regions of Wallo and Shawa, which were controlled by officials who supported Ras Tafari's anti-slave-trade policy.[22] While the movement of slaves into regions like Lasta, Tigray, and Bagamder continued, it was on a sharply reduced basis. Moreover, changes in the political economy of the south had placed large portions of the indigenous population beyond the pale of slaving activities by incorporating them into the neftenya-gabbar sys-

22. Chakola Lamma (interview: 10 March 1982) noted several places which those bringing slaves north had to avoid. These may well have been the sites of the Central Slavery Department stations (also, interview: Asras Walda Gabrael, 21 April 1982). I am grateful to Dennis Hickey for sharing his research on the effects of southwestern peoples' obtaining firearms and their defense strategies.

tem under the control of transplanted northern military officials. Those populations which remained outside of this labor system had become better armed or had fled out of range across the Sudanese or Kenyan borders. In 1929 the veteran Italian agent Alberto Pollera, then consul at Gondar, east of Lasta, observed:

> Provisions of the central government for the repression of slavery are not strictly observed, but they have influenced a limitation of trade. A slave judge for the treatment of slave cases has been instituted near every important chief. In Gojjam, I am assured, the customs posts and chiefs have the strictest orders to impede this traffic. It reaches Gondar from Beni Shangul [on the Sudanese border] via Alefa [in Gojjam]. Vigilance of the customs posts is relative. Agents make a tax of transit [for slaves] under another name. The tax is 3 Maria Teresa talers [U.S. $1.50] per head and contacts are clandestine, taking place at Gondar, Ifag, and Ebennat [all in Bagamder] and usually in Christian rather than Muslim caravans. (ASMAI, Pollera 1929)

That same year, Pollera noted that the reduction in the traffic had brought about a price rise and a recrudescence of the kidnapping of slaves along trade routes. He also believed that, although some border peoples continued to pay tribute in slaves, slavery was gradually diminishing, and the emperor's decrees would in the future have more impact (ibid.).

Pollera's observations notwithstanding, the direct effects of the emperor's anti-slavery-trade policy never penetrated the countryside of Lasta very effectively and few prosecutions took place. Although most local officials stopped exchanging slaves and forced Lasta's few slave markets underground, they did not relinquish their own slaves. The *wagshum*, governor of the Wag region north of Lasta, for instance, periodically harangued the public against slavery, but made no effort to dispose of his own contingent of 40–50 slaves. According to one informant, merchants or farmers caught selling slaves were fined lightly (about 40 thalers — one-quarter the price of a good slave) (interview: Abba Getu Endasaw, 1 June 1982).

Nor did the institution of slavery dissolve much faster in the rest of the north. In Gojjam in 1932, when the government formally freed Ras Haylu's slaves, the vast majority of them joined the households of local officials. As late as 1934 in the town of Gondar, the new mayor's attempts to actively prosecute the secret slave trade resulted in friction with the community and his eventual removal.[23] Success in curtailing the slave

---

23. ASMAI, Di Lauro 1934; interviews, passim. On 29 August 1932 after Ras Haylu of Gojjam had been deposed by the emperor, the imperial government ordered all of Haylu's slaves to be freed and given the means to earn their livelihood. Children under 10 years

trade was limited, therefore, by local forces of opposition circumventing the regulations and officials' losing interest. Thus, ex-slaves, like the slaves who remained with their masters, continued to live and work in a rural society and economy which denied them access to the means of production.

The redistribution of labor brought on by the creation of a class of ex-slaves and ya sar barya contributed to a new process of stratification in the rural society of northern Ethiopia. The expansion of the imperial state between 1916 and 1930 had already added a new bureaucratic class on top of the traditional military and ecclesiastical elite, which drew support from farming households' tax, tribute, and labor (McCann 1984: 211–32). After 1930 many slaves took advantage of the increased state presence in rural society to claim their right to leave households where they were ill-treated or where they had little chance for mobility. Even if they still lacked the right to claim land or property, they did exercise the right to offer their labor. The most attractive choices usually proved to be with the households of officials who could offer better living conditions, political protection from the claims of their masters, and a measure of status-honor. Similarly, many ex-slaves also chose to attach themselves to the households of wealthy peasants, who were less likely to require agricultural laborers than a poorer household with fewer labor resources. In these circumstances labor flowed out of the stratum of farming households and into the households of the administrative class.

The shift of many slaves to a new stratum of landless laborers changed patterns of labor distribution in the rural economy and exacerbated class differences. Peasant households living close to the margins of subsistence often lost the reliable source of labor which their slaves had offered. Together with the demographic effects of population increase — fragmentation of plots, reduced fallowing, and the clearing and cultivation of less productive soils — and an increasing shortage of draft animals, the shift of ex-slaves to the wealthier class reduced labor available to peasant households (McCann 1984: 239–40). Greater access to the labor of ya sar barya gave officials and local elite the ability to increase their control over land, since the ability to claim land in the social system in northern Ethiopia meant little without the capital and labor to put it under cultivation.

In 1935, in an attempt to win sympathy from world public opinion,

---

were to be educated in the church schools, while the elderly were to receive an allocation of grain from government granaries. Despite the government's best intentions, it appears that most slaves entered the service of local officials as ya sar barya. See FO, Cheesman quarterly report, 10 November 1932.

the Italian government announced a policy of the ending of slavery in all those territories taken by its advancing troops (see FO, League of Nations document 1936; and FO, Drummond 1937). The reality proved somewhat different from the legal ideal; most of my informants reported that the Italian administrators in Lasta and throughout the north actively prosecuted slavery. Slaves who arrived in the Italian administrative centers of Lalibala and Saqota obtained their freedom immediately, were free to leave their masters' compounds, and enjoyed the full protection of the colonial law codes within areas under Italian control, a somewhat limited sphere in northern Ethiopia.

After 1937, however, the Italian administration in the north abandoned its early attempts at fiscal and social reform in the rural areas and was content merely to collect tribute and to maintain security in the larger market towns.[24] Freed slaves again became ya sar barya when they sought out the Italian enclaves, which offered them wage employment and protection from their former owners. Many ex-slaves joined the ranks of the *banda*, the Eritrean militia. Others served as paid laborers in Italian military camps; female ex-slaves became concubines of Italian soldiers and Eritrean banda stationed in Lasta and nearby. Some slaves chose to leave Lasta entirely and took up tenancy in surrounding regions or moved to wage labor in Italian-controlled market towns, in Addis Ababa, or in Eritrea (Grottanelli 1939: 118–20; McCann 1984: 55–58). Although good data are still lacking, it would seem reasonable to assume that many ex-slaves provided labor for the ambitious Italian road-building projects in Lasta and throughout the country.

Other informants argued that poor security conditions during the Italian war and occupation brought about a resurgence of slavery and the slave trade in those areas which fell outside of Italian control. Many ex-slaves were captured and sold again to rich peasants, while some free Lastans were shanghaied and offered into the Red Sea trade. These isolated situations notwithstanding, my informants were unanimous in agreeing that the Italian occupation and ban on slavery seems to have effectively ended the legal status of slavery in Lasta and elsewhere in northern Ethiopia.

A Rural Proletariat

By 1941, when the imperial government returned to Ethiopia, the majority of the population of ex-slaves in Lasta, legally free since 1935, did

24. Interviews, passim; also see decree of governor-general of 27 September 1937, which restored "traditional tribute revenues" to all Italian-occupied areas (governo dell'Amara 1937: 423–26).

not enjoy a status substantially different from the one before the occupation; nothing had happened in Lasta's social or economic fabric to change the basic factor of slaves' marginality—their status as yabet lij, which deprived them of the right to hold land, except under the difficult terms of tenancy. Nor had the Italian occupation affected social patterns or land tenure practice in the north. Slaves' legal freedom in Ethiopian law, gained through a 1942 imperial government edict, had not lessened their basic marginality or patterns of endogamy, which maintained social distance between ex-slaves and freeborn in Lasta society. Moreover, ex-slaves still had little or no access to capital, which was the single most important factor determining the ability of a household to set itself up as a viable production unit.

With few opportunities to change their economic or social role, Lasta's ex-slave population remained tied to their former status of dependence. Most domestic ex-slaves remained with their former owners, although they now had the technical right to leave and seek a similar position in another household. Former agricultural slaves remained close by their former masters and engaged in *siso bala* (lit., "he ate one-third"), a type of tenancy where a landless farmer used the capital and land of the landlord and retained two-thirds of the produce in return for his labor.[25] This system allowed wealthy peasants and the rural administrative class to expand their control over land in a way not common before 1920.

Despite the inertia of rural conservatism, the composition of Lasta's ex-slave population had changed and would continue to do so over time. The fact that no new captives arrived in Lasta from the mid-1930s on meant that some aspects of ex-slaves' marginality had been reduced. Many in the ex-slave population were now culturally assimilated, first-generation or even second- and third-generation residents of the region. Those slaves who were not already native speakers of Amharic or Tigrenya were now fluent in these languages and understood the nonverbal signifiers of rank and deference essential in northern Ethiopia. Virtually all had converted to Orthodox Christianity (McCann 1984: 90). Moreover, many ex-slaves had now outlived their masters and obtained a recognized status within their community. Thus, even though ex-slaves generally were marginal to the essential factors of production in the rural economy, they could no longer be sold or transferred. In effect, they now had the same rights of movement between households that the freeborn had always enjoyed. The significant difference was that the young freeborn identified as yasaw lij held hopes of activating land claims and establishing

25. Interviews, passim, especially Segaye Setegn interview of 17 May 1982. Also see Cohen and Weintraub 1975: 28–42.

an independent household, while the ex-slaves' chances of achieving this culturally and economically valued goal continued to be minimal.

The general state of agricultural production in Lasta also reduced opportunities for ex-slaves; production conditions in the rural economy over the first four decades of this century had deteriorated perceptibly. Population pressure on land, reduced pasturage, and lowered agricultural productivity on eroded land had made both land and capital scarce relative to labor. Poor peasant families who did not control oxen or seed lacked the means to survive as a producing and consuming unit without supplementing their income through selling their labor. Rich households, especially those of the hereditary elite, who controlled oxen, had managed over the course of a few decades to increase their control over resources by loaning their capital resources to poor landholders in return for the lion's share of the produce (as much as three-fourths) (Grottanelli 1939: 120).

In these circumstances, a new class of rural proletariat had emerged which consisted of those households that lacked access to the means of production. Because of their historical status as yabet lij and their lack of access to land, Lasta's large population of ex-slaves formed a part of this class. Thus, as this stratum of ex-slaves joined the freeborn work force in the postwar years, they merged with this historically new class of dependent yasaw lij, who theoretically had access to land but lacked the capital resources to activate their claims. Whereas a century before, Lasta society had boasted a population of households which produced by means of their own labor, land, and capital, by 1945 Lasta's marketplaces included a specialized section of day-laborers offering their labor in exchange for payment in kind or in wages to be used for their own households' basic survival. Even if these households held some land it was often below the 1.48 hectares necessary to maintain the average farm unit, and members had to take up outside labor or engage in petty trade to survive. The growth of this class of rural workers was largely a result of Lasta's weakened ecological base and the maldistribution of economic resources in the rural economy. But, it was also a product of the ending of the legal status of slavery in the face of a rural property system which excluded "newcomers" from participation in the distribution of land and capital.

The size of the rural proletariat in Lasta and in northern Ethiopia in general was small when compared with the landless class in the areas in southern and western Ethiopia conquered by Emperor Menilek's troops in the late nineteenth century. Yet, in terms of the historical norms of production in Lasta, the shift was significant and was partly a product of the changes in the Ethiopian social formation which had generated the campaign against slavery. By the beginning of the postwar period, the imperial state had effectively broken the economic power of the regional elite and succeeded in placing its own officials in key positions in the rural administrative and economic structure. The campaign against slavery had been a part of this program, since it reduced the local influence of the traditional elite in the north and also created a new class of laborers whose low urban wages and subsistence production of food crops subsidized the growth of an urban "feudal bourgeosie," capitalist agricultural schemes, and a fledgling industrial sector (Addis Hiwet 1975).

Epilogue

The situation of the rural proletariat, including ex-slaves, in northern Ethiopia changed dramatically in 1975 with the Land Reform Proclamation issued by the Provisional Military Government of Revolutionary Ethiopia. The proclamation was the culmination of long-standing student demands for "land to the tiller," which had been current throughout the 1960s and abolished all tenancy as well as granting access to land to all who wished to claim it. The biggest changes in rural relations of production took place in the south and west, where tenants took control of the land they had been cultivating and ended oppressive relations with absentee landlords. In Lasta and the northern highlands many observers considered the effects to be minimal because most peasants had previously held the right to claim land. For the class of landless ex-slaves, however, it altered the basic factor which had kept them socially marginal in rural society. In effect, it raised their status to a point equivalent with their new compatriots in the rural poor.[26]

Tasfaye Walda Kidan, a farmer in the Tegulet Subdistrict of northern Shawa, offers a useful illustration of the economic status of former slaves in the northern rural economy. A 40-year-old son of former slaves, Tasfaye made his living as a weaver and part-time tenant farmer, paying one-third of his harvest to the legal landholder, an aristocrat living in Addis Ababa, for use of the land and oxen. With land reform in 1975 Tasfaye obtained direct access to his land. Without oxen, however, he continued to be dependent on wealthier neighbors who lent him a pair of oxen in

26. The best available study of the effect of the land reform in northern Ethiopia is Alula Abate and Tesfaye Teklu 1980. The effect of land reform on ex-slaves and landless castes, as Allan Hoben has reminded me, was often disastrous in areas without a strong government presence. Threatened by the end of the rist system, powerful landholders in the north killed or drove away landless tenants rather than allow them to press a claim for redistributed land. This happened in several places in the north, although it is unclear how widespread the phenomenon was.

exchange for two days of work for every day of oxen use. This arrangement continued for 10 years until a famine relief agency provided Tasfaye with an ox. Without that external intervention Tasfaye would have remained a typical example of an undercapitalized farmer whose poverty, in this case, derived from the residual effects of slave status.[27]

APPENDIX A

The following document is a translation of an original manuscript dictated by Ras Kassa to one of his court scribes and issued as a legal proclamation in the summer of 1924 (McCann, Tesema, and Dagnachew 1984: Document #144). It was an attempt to regulate the transition from slave to servant for those slaves held within his dominions. There is little evidence about how effectively it was carried out, although Kassa was known to have opposed slavery personally. While its primary application may have been the northern Shawan district of Salale, it may have been invoked in some cases in Lasta as well. Note the calculation of annual upkeep for a slave. Use of the term *Galla* in this context refers not to speakers of the Oromo language, but to outsiders.

Document #144   Subject: Contract Regulations between an Ignorant Galla and a Master

The master unequivocally agrees to the following terms:

1. I [the master] will provide him [the slave] with food and clothing; he, the Galla servant will not create trouble over this issue;
2. I will provide him with a church education to save his soul;
3. I will also educate him as much as I can to serve his bodily needs;
4. If the Galla servant wants to join another master or wants to go away I will calculate the cost of my provisions in educating him and taking care of him to be sure that he repays the cost or the cost is included in the selling price before he is allowed to leave. In case he runs away or escapes, I will not claim him as my slave;
5. I will not lend him as a commodity to another master; I will also refrain from overworking him or forcing him to work beyond his capacity;
6. I will refrain from selling or abusing him, or exploiting his ignorance;
7. I will keep his property and his body from enemies. If any harm is done to him or his property by others, I will avenge him.

If I do not carry out the above mentioned regulations may God burn my soul and I shall lose all my property.

To be sure that these regulations are carried out I as a master will provide

---

27. I gathered the case study of Tasfaye Walda Kidan and others of slave descent in the course of my work on the social impact of oxen distribution in the northern Shawa subdistricts of Tegulet and Ankober in 1985 and 1986.

a guarantor. Both the servant and the master shall sign this contract and the whole agreement shall be recorded in the government's register. [dated Hamle 15 1924]

The cost of providing food and clothing over a year is (six *qunna* of grain per month) 1 *dawla* of grain costing three-and-one-half birr; for salt, one birr; clothing, three birr. Altogether the total cost in cash is seven-and-one-half birr. The workday for the servant will be eight hours.

GLOSSARY

barya	Amharic general term for slave.
beta seb	lit., "those in one house"; the Amharic term for family or household.
hudad	land held by the local governor and worked by local peasants and slaves as obligations to the state.
neftenya-gabbar	a system of serfdom between a landlord, *neftenya* (lit., "one with a rifle"), and tenant, *gabbar* (lit., "farmer/taxpayer"), found in southern Ethiopia after Menilek's conquest.
rist	ambilineal land tenure system associated with northern highlands.
siso bala	lit., "he ate one-third"; a share cropping arrangement where the landlord takes one-third of the crop in exchange for use of the land and, in some cases, oxen.
yabet lij	lit., "child of the house"; a term used to describe slaves' kinlessness.
yasaw lij	lit., "child of a person"; a term used to describe a free person as opposed to a slave.
wagshum	the appointee of Wag; title given to hereditary ruler of Wag, the district north of Lasta.

REFERENCES

Oral sources

All oral material was collected in interviews in Ethiopia between January and September 1982 and in June 1985. Tapes and notes of the 1982 testimonies are in my possession and also on deposit with the Institute of Ethiopian Studies, Addis Ababa University. Interview notes from 1985 are in my possession.

Abba Getu Endasaw, interviews on 25 May, 1 June, 3 June, 8 June 1982.
Abba Gabra Masqal Tesfaye, interviews, 26 March, 28 March, 29 March, 31 March, 3 April, 5 April, 10 April, 21 April, 3 May, 2 July, 6 July 1982.
Alamu Warqnah, interviews on 22 April, 14 May, 24 May, 10 June 1982.

Asras Walda Gabrael, interviews of 14 April, 21 April, 30 April 1982.
Chakola Lamma, interviews on 10 March, 17 March, 6 May, 1 August 1982.
Lasta elders, group interview on 8 June 1982.
Nabiyaleul Takla Sadeq, interviews on 1 April, 9 June 1982, 10 July 1982, 17 July 1982, 23 August 1982.
Segaye Setegn, interviews on 13 April, 26 April, 28 April, 17 May, 28 May, June 1982.
Tasfaye Walda Kidan, interview on 18 June 1985.

Archival sources

ASMAI: Archivo Storico delle Ministerio Africana Italiana.
    Di Lauro to Ministero Affari Esteri, 3 September 1934. 54/9.
    Notiziario politico, 31 September 1931. 54/10.
    Pollera to Addis Ababa, 31 December 1929. 54/26.
CRO: Central Records Office, Khartoum, Sudan.
    INTEL, Kassala Province files, 1935–1937.
    "Report on the Kafta Caravan," May 1907. CAIRINT 3/1/9.
    Report on slave settlements in Sudan, 5 December 1936. CIVSEC 60/5/15.
FO: Foreign Office Correspondence, Public Records Office, Kew Gardens.
    Barton to Foreign Office, 8 July 1930. F.O. 371/14589.
    Barton to Henderson, 3 August 1931. F.O. 371/15385.
    Cheesman to Barton, encl. in Barton to Simon, 28 June 1932. F.O. 371/1259.
    Cheesman memorandum, encl. in Barton to Simon, 4 July 1932. F.O. 371/16096.
    Cheesman quarterly report, encl. in Barton to Simon, 10 November 1932. F.O. 371/1259.
    Drummond to Eden, 20 April 1937. F.O. 371/20927.
    Grazmach Tafari, Amharic letter, 8 June 1924, encl. in Maffey to Henderson, 5 November 1927. F.O. 371/12346.
    League of Nations document, encl. in despatch of 14 April 1936. F.O. 371/20209.
    Maffey to Henderson, 8 November 1927. F.O. 371/12346.
    Zaphiro report, encl. in Bentinck to Chamberlain, 28 September 1925. F.O. 371/10873.
RHL: Rhodes House Library, Oxford University.
    De Halpert, F. Papers.
UKL: University of Khartoum Library, Khartoum, Sudan. Sudan Collection.
    Sudan Intelligence Report, 1898–1935.
    Sudan Monthly Record, 1929–1936.

Other sources

Alula Abate and Tesfaye Teklu. 1980. Land reform and peasant associations in Ethiopia — case studies of two widely differing regions. *Northeast African Studies* 2: 1–52.

Abir, M. 1968. *Era of the princes*. New York: Praeger.

Addis Hiwet. 1975. *Ethiopia: from autocracy to revolution*. London: Review of African Political Economy Occasional Publication no. 1.

Annaratone, C. 1914. *In Abissinia*. Rome: n.p.

Bauer, D. F. 1975. For want of an ox: land, capital, and social stratification in Tigre. In *Proceedings of the First United States Conference on Ethiopian studies*, ed. Harold G. Marcus, 235–48. East Lansing: Michigan State University African Studies Center.

Bauer, D. F. 1977. *Household and society in Ethiopia*. East Lansing: Michigan State University African Studies Center.

Berman, B., and J. Lonsdale. 1979. Coping with the contradictions: the development of the colonial state in Kenya. *Journal of African History* 20: 487–506.

Cohen, J., and D. Weintraub. 1975. *Land and peasants in imperial Ethiopia: the social background of a revolution*. Assen: Van Gorcum.

Coquery-Vidrovitch, C. 1976. La mise en dépendence de l'Afrique noire: essai de périodization, 1800–1970. *Cahiers d'etudes africaines* 16: 8–57.

Edwards, J. R. 1982. Slavery, the slave trade, and the economic reorganization of Ethiopia 1916–35. *African Economic History* 11: 1–14.

Governo dell'Amara. 1937. *Bolletino officiale* (September–October).

Griaule, M. 1931. Labor in Ethiopia. *International Labour Review* 23: 181–202.

Griaule, M. 1934. *L'esclavage en Abyssinie. Etudes de sociologie et de ethnologie juridiques*. Paris: Institut de Droit Comparé de l'Université.

Grottanelli, V. 1939. *Richerche geografiche ed economiche sulle populazione. Missione de Studio al Lago Tana*. Vol. 2. Rome: Reale Accademia d'Italia.

Hickey, D. 1984. Ethiopia and Great Britain: political conflict in the southern borderlands, 1916–1935. Ph.D. dissertation, Northwestern University, Evanston, Illinois.

Hoben, A. 1963. The role of ambilineal descent groups in Gojjam Amhara social organization. Ph.D. dissertation, University of California, Berkeley.

Hoben, A. 1975. Family, land, and class in northwest Europe and northern highland Ethiopia. In *Proceedings of the First United States Conference on Ethiopian studies*, ed. Harold G. Marcus, 157–70. East Lansing: Michigan State University African Studies Center.

Hoben, A. 1973. *Land tenure among the Amhara of Ethiopia*. Berkeley: University of California Press.

Kobischanov, Y. 1979. *Axum*. University Park: Pennsylvania State University Press.

McCann, J. 1984. Households, peasants, and rural history in Lasta, Northern Ethiopia 1900–35. Ph.D. dissertation, Michigan State University, East Lansing.

McCann, J., Tesema Ta'a, and Dagnachew Tefera, eds. and trans. 1984. Ya Ras Kassa Astadadar Damb. Unpublished Amharic manuscript deposited in the Institute of Ethiopian Studies, Addis Ababa University (also a copy in Mc-Cann's possession).

McClellan, C. 1978a. Ethiopian expansionism: the case of Darasa 1895–1935. Ph.D. dissertation, Michigan State University, East Lansing.

McClellan, C. 1978b. Perspectives on the neftenya-gabbar system: the Darasa of Ethiopia. *Africa* 33: 426–40.

McClellan, C. 1980. Land, labor, and coffee: the South's role in Ethiopian self-reliance 1889–1935. *African Economic History* 9: 69–83.

Marcus, H. G. 1979. The infrastructure of the Italo-Ethiopian crisis: Haile Sellassie, the Solomonic Empire, and the world economy, 1916–36. In *Proceedings of the Fifth International Conference on Ethiopian studies*, 559–68. Chicago: University of Illinois at Chicago Circle Press.

Marsae Hazan Walda Qirqos. 1942. Ba Dagmawi Menilek zaman kayahut na kasamahut. Unpublished typescript, School of Oriental and African Studies, University of London.

Miers, S. Forthcoming. Britain and the suppression of slavery in Ethiopia. In *Proceedings of the Eighth International Conference on Ethiopia studies*. Addis Ababa: Addis Ababa University Press.

Montandon, G. 1932. *L'esclavage en Abyssinie*. Geneva: n.p.

Pankhurst, R. 1968. *Economic history of Ethiopia*. Addis Ababa: Addis Ababa University Press.

Pankhurst, R. 1977. The history of the Bareya, Shanqella, and other Ethiopian slaves from the borderlands of the Sudan. *Sudan Notes and Records* 63: 1–48.

Taddesse Tamrat. 1972. *Church and state in Ethiopia*. Oxford: Clarendon Press.

Tsehai Berhane Sellasie. 1980. The political and military tradition of the Ethiopian peasantry (1800–1941). Ph.D. dissertation, St. Anne's College, Oxford University.

Ullendorff, E., ed. and trans. 1976. *The autobiography of Haile Selassie I: my life and Ethiopia's progress 1892–1937*. London: Oxford University Press.

Wright, G. 1978. *The political economy of the cotton South: households, markets, and wealth in the nineteenth century*. New York.

Wylde, A. 1901. *Modern Abyssinia*. London.

12 E. Ann McDougall

A Topsy-Turvy World: Slaves and Freed Slaves in the Mauritanian Adrar, 1910–1950

> This world is topsy-turvy but the world to come is sure.
> Lineage is mixed, and this [present state of things] is
>   something between, neither one thing nor the other.
> Oh be more bountiful to us!
> The *Zwaya taleb*, and the warrior, are both of them poor in
>   this world's wealth;
> While the meager tributary now is fat and filled, and the
>   *hartani* — have no doubt — is proud and groomed.
> The slave is owner of two flowing shifts, while the slave
>   girl keeps her weight through drinking milk.
> He who is learned in the faith has since forsaken it. Thus it
>   remains, confused and in a tumult.
> This world is topsy-turvy but the world to come is sure.[1]

After half a century of French rule, a United Nations committee investigation in 1949–1950 found significant numbers of "servile peoples" in Mauritania (now the Islamic Republic of Mauritania), many of whom were unquestionably slaves. The explanations given by the French governor echoed those heard at one time or another almost everywhere slavery

I would like to thank the Social Sciences and Humanities Research Council of Canada for a two-year postdoctoral fellowship (1983–1985) which made possible research in Mauritania and Senegal; the Institut mauritanien de recherche scientifique of Nouakchott, RIM, which assisted me during my fieldwork; and the Department of History, University of Toronto, which financed my presentation of a draft of this chapter at the African Studies Association meeting in New Orleans, November 1985. My thanks to Dennis Cordell, Martin Klein, Gerry McSheffrey, Richard Roberts, and Suzanne Miers for comments on this chapter as presented at the Canadian Association of African Studies meeting in Montreal, May 1985.

1. Translated from *hassaniya* (Arabic dialect spoken in Mauritania) in Norris 1968: 30. The poet is described as "contemporary"; the poem probably dates to the 1950s or 1960s. The clerics (*zwaya*) and warriors (*hassani*) constituted the "nobility" of Mauritanian society. Zenagha (tributaries), *haratin* (freed slaves and their descendants), and '*abid* (slaves) — were found in lower echelons. (The term *haratin* has also been applied to the few people believed descended from the original black [Soninke?] inhabitants of the desert.)

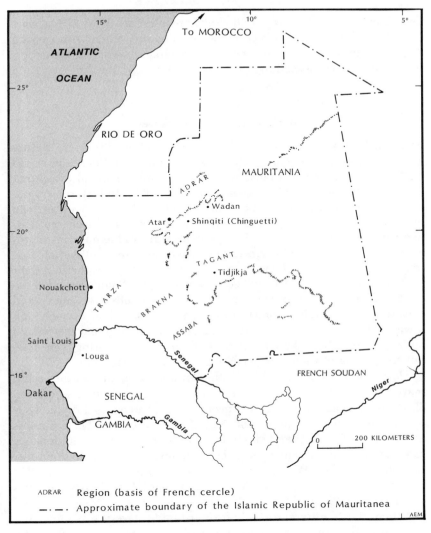

Map 12. Mauritania

was an issue: The colony was not yet ready for "mass liberation." There were no resources for the newly freed, who "would have nothing to do but turn to theft and vagabondage. . . . The end result would be the ruin of the economy," and everyone would end up a French responsibility (ARIM, gouverneur de la Mauritanie 1937; ANS, gouverneur de la Mauritanie 1950). The difference is that elsewhere in French West Africa, slavery reform had been addressed many years before, albeit with varying degrees of success. The governor's seeming helplessness in the face of persisting slavery was something of an anachronism by the mid-twentieth century.

The Condition Called Slavery

From the beginning, French administrators maintained that the "nature and law of slavery [were] different" in Mauritania, that liberation would be "revolutionary," and that it would cause much political discontent and social distress (ARIM, résident de Brakna 1905). In fact, slavery per se was much the same as in other Muslim regions along the West African sahel–southern Sahara.[2] "Slaves" were people recently purchased, kidnapped, captured, or born of slave parents. Male and female slaves provided labor for date-palm groves and whatever cereal cultivation that irrigation and seasonal flooding could support. They also herded their "noble" masters' herds of sheep, goats, and camels. Women supplied domestic labor in the camps and the towns, and were often wet nurses and concubines. Concubines sometimes became wives to their masters, and it was customary (though in Mauritania, not automatic) that they would be freed if they bore their masters' children. Their offspring were free, but the stigma of their slave origin usually remained.

Slaves had few choices in life. With their masters' approval, they could marry, but the children of the union belonged to the woman's master. Slaves were, legally speaking, "nonpeople." They had no legal rights. They could neither own property nor control their progeny. Their masters accepted — in fact, demanded — full responsibility for their maintenance as well as for the consequences of their actions. As notables in the Adrar explained in 1934, "We want to treat our slaves like our own children; we want to keep them and we want them to work for us" (AATAR, conseil de *jema'a* 1934).[3]

Where the "nature and law" of Mauritanian slavery was somewhat unusual in the West African context was in the importance of *haratin* (sing. *hartani*; fem. sing. *hartania*). These were "freed slaves," legally "persons" with the corresponding rights to own property, enter into contracts,

---

2. The most sensitive account of Mauritania's complex social structure, often erroneously referred to as a caste system, is Miské 1970: 93–113. For colonial perspectives see especially: ANS, "L'esclavage en Mauritanie" 1950; Fondacci 1946; and Hornac 1953.

3. In effect, slaves were treated as perpetual minors, with the ironic contradiction, as Suzanne Miers (pers. comm.) has pointed out, that had they really been minors, they would have been "people" with the corresponding rights allocated a "person."

and bequeath possessions to their children. Nevertheless, they were not the social equals of the nobles and remained tied in various ways to the families of their old masters. Their responsibilities varied depending upon whether they continued to live as part of those families, or established themselves as independent herders or cultivators. They owed "hospitality" to former masters and members of their masters' families, and usually gave them annual payments or presents in kind. Haratin participated as freeborn in the clan's collective obligations, including paying taxes and crime compensation. As a freedman who could take a wife, control his own children, and accumulate his own wealth, a hartani had considerable incentive to work. Given that all of his descendants continued to occupy the same status within the clan, the hartani had potentially far greater value to both the short-term and long-term fortunes of his master's family than the male slave.[4] Masters thus had an incentive to free male slaves. The same was not true of female slaves. Once a woman became a hartania her labor and reproductive capacity passed from her former master to the hartani or freeman she married. Masters' reluctance to free female slaves meant that a hartania was more likely to be born than "created." This was central to the difference between the male and the female slave experience in Mauritanian society.[5] It was also the source of much real misunderstanding on the part of local French residents trying to comprehend social relations among the peoples they purported to rule.

In spite of the fact that colonization brought only a minimum of infrastructure and investment, even the few scattered French military posts and administrative centers were of immense importance to Mauritania's sparse and largely mobile population. The military, commercial, and agricultural activities they generated enlarged both the amount and the scope of work to be done. Local people were presented with new opportunities to work for wages, as well as with the burden of requisitioned labor. Given that all work was customarily performed by servile groups, colonial labor requirements had a social impact on Mauritanians which far outweighed its broader economic significance. The categories "master," "slave," and "hartani" remained unchanged, but the experience of being a master, a slave, or a hartani did not.

Generally speaking, conditions during the first half of this century reduced the scope of masters' control over slaves and haratin, allowing

---

4. Given that we know both slaves and haratin continued to exist, the interesting question becomes when and under what circumstances was this potential likely to be realized and a slave actually freed?

5. Interviews: Saika wuld Messoud, 19 and 20 August; Mohamed Salem wuld Sehrool; ARIM, rapport de Monsieur Poulet 1949.

the latter greater leverage in negotiating work obligations and personal rights. However, within the servile experience itself, there are some notable distinctions to be made. On the one hand, it would seem that at least some of the improved quality of life enjoyed by haratin was achieved at the expense of slaves, as the better off among them began to exploit slave labor themselves and identify even more closely with the "noble" families with whom they were associated. And on the other, it is clear that life for a female slave was very different from life for a male. In fact, the very conditions which encouraged the already popular practice of freeing male slaves to create dependent haratin, coupled with the increasing difficulty of acquiring new slaves from pacified French zones in the south, may well have led to tighter control by masters over their female slaves. As becomes apparent when we begin to study the servile experience as distinct from servile institutions, class and gender cut across slavery just as they did freedom.

Policy and Practice: The Early Years

The French military conquest of the interior of Mauritania, the Tagant and the Adrar, took place between 1905 and 1910. The tribes who one by one surrendered included nomadic pastoralists, sedentary merchants and cultivators, clerics, and warriors. Submission was usually in exchange for guarantees of security, freedom to trade, or access to pasture. In all cases, Mauritanian chiefs and nobles were promised that their "customs, values, property and religion" would be respected (ARIM, résident de Brackna, 1905).[6] When Atar, the capital of the Adrar, surrendered on 9 January 1909, local notables made clear immediately which of these customs, values, and property were most important. "[They] specified that their only wealth was composed of sheep, donkeys and products of the soil, and that without their slave workers, their principal resource, their harvests would disappear" (ARIM, commissaire du gouvernement général en Mauritanie 1918). As a French administrator later explained, in the interests of preserving both social and economic stability in the Adrar, "It was well understood that their slaves would [be permitted] to stay with them" (ibid.).

But concern to disrupt the status quo as little as possible was common to all French West African colonies; Mauritania's exceptional status stemmed from an additional political concern. For centuries, the people

---

6. Désiré-Vuillemin (1962) and the Centre de Recherches et d'Etudes sur les Sociétés méditerranéennes (1979) provide an overview of Mauritanian colonial history; on the conquest of the Adrar specifically, see the account by the leader of the column Gouraud (1945).

of the Adrar had looked north. They had close familial, religious, and commercial relations with powerful, often bellicose, tribes inhabiting the Spanish Sahara and Morocco. Even after 1935, by which time most of them had been forced into formal submission, French control over their activities was minimal. The Awlad Bou Sba, Tekna, and Regueibat, especially, were skillful raiders, traders, and camel herders who flaunted their ability to penetrate the colony's so-called boundaries with disturbing impunity. When actively engaged in challenging French claims to control, they liked to steal and exact tribute from the Adrar tribes who had submitted and were co-operating with the new administration. More often than not, French military resources proved woefully inadequate, both in preventing these forays and in recovering stolen property.[7] The need for appeasement over slavery, therefore, stemmed not only from the concern to maintain internal coherence in a colony generally regarded as anarchical and of dubious loyalty, but to provide protection for it with an army which needed increasingly to rely upon the local population for its men, mounts, and provisions.

The situation was further complicated by the nature of "northern interests" in the Adrar. These *"grands nomades,"* who covered hundreds of kilometers annually in search of pasture, were both the major purveyors of slaves for the French Soudan, the Adrar, and southern Morocco, and important slaveholders themselves.[8] Most notable in this respect were the Regueibat, who on several occasions gained special concessions from French authorities regarding their domestic slaves.[9] As the governor of Mauritania readily admitted in the early 1930s, "Given the presence in our territory of Grands Nomades . . . in whose life we do not interfere," the possibility of completely abolishing the slave trade and reforming domestic slavery within the Adrar region remained "very much limited" (ARIM, réponse, gouverneur de la Mauritanie 1933).

Initially, there were really only two policies implemented regarding slavery: runaway slaves mistreated by their masters were freed, and all "trafficking" in slaves was prohibited (ARIM, résident de Brakna 1905).

7. See ANS, rapports politiques et économiques. Reports from the 1920s, 1930s, and 1940s include frequent accounts of the activities of these troublesome northern tribes.
8. Though French concern was primarily with slaves moved northward by these grands nomades, cases discussed in archival reports indicate that there was also a more erratic movement of slaves acquired by various means in the north (southern Morocco and the Spanish Sahara) towards central and southern Mauritania.
9. See in particular ARIM, instructions, commandant du cercle de l'Adrar 1929; ARIM, correspondance, résident à Chinguetti 1918; ARIM, correspondance, commandant du cercle de l'Adrar 1919; ARIM, correspondance, résident de Timbedra, 6 April 1920; ARIM, lettre, Capitaine Prudhomme 1919; ARIM, commandant du cercle de l'Assaba 1931; AATAR, conseil de *jema'a* 1933.

The former seems to have been a relatively minor issue in the Adrar, at least as far as the archival records indicate. But the question of trafficking, the buying and selling of slaves, raised considerable difficulties for all concerned. In 1918, the commander of the Adrar was actually accused by another administrator of allowing a local trade in slaves to flourish. In the inquiry which ensued, the resident in the Adrar subdivision of Shinqiti explained that he had indeed "closed his eyes" to it when the buyer and seller belonged to the subdivision and the sale was conducted "officially" in front of the local Muslim judge (*qadi*). The commander, however, denied authorizing any such transactions unless the aim was to free the slave. He had taken firm measures to prohibit the regular slave trade by the northern Regueibat, to the relief of the notables of Atar, who did not want to see the disappearance northward of the only source of manual labor they had to maintain their date-palm groves and fields. These differing perceptions of what constituted an "act of trafficking," not to mention repeated requests by merchants, especially Regueibat merchants, to export slaves, produced the first real policy guideline on the matter issued by Governor Gaden in 1918:

In effect all the agreements we have made with the Moors show that we will respect their social structure, property, customs and religion. We have therefore recognized a situation of fact: The slaves stay in the family of their owner for whom they constitute the labor force. . . . Having recognized this state of affairs, we do not want to say that we will authorize trade, that is the sale of an individual to strangers. This traffic, in addition to being reprehensible, *is also contrary to the interests of owners who lose a worker they are not able to replace, since the peace which we have brought to Mauritania no longer permits them to bring slaves from the South* [emphasis added]. . . . It can happen that in certain contracts between Moors, for the constitution of a bride price for example, it is specified that a slave be given by the spouse. This is not, in my opinion, an act of slave trading—a slave whose condition we have already recognized, remains in the family and does not leave the country. *This is not a loss for the masters. These are the only transactions to which we can close our eyes* [emphasis added]; but all those which result in departure from the Adrar, a purchase by a stranger no matter what, even a tirailleur, or European ought to be proscribed. (ARIM, correspondance, résident à Chinguetti 1918)

Thus, in 1918, the institution of domestic slavery, as distinct from the slave trade, remained virtually untouched by official policy. But the question of how to define and deal with an act of slave-trading continued to plague local administrators, as we see from a rather complicated affair in 1927. A female slave was kidnapped from the Trarza (southwestern) region by Regueibat merchants, then sold to an Adrar notable, who installed her as his concubine in the town of Wadan. There she was provided with property and, as the local resident argued when she was reclaimed, she probably wanted to remain. He recommended that she and her child be freed, and her original owner be reimbursed for his loss. The governor of Mauritania, however, decided this would be tantamount to condoning the slave trade. The woman, presumably, was returned, the ambiguities of official policy having overridden local-level concerns for the slave's welfare (ARIM, correspondance, résident à Chinguetti 1927).

Political Economy and Slavery

In effect, the new situation created by the colonial occupation had more immediate impact on the servile groups of the Adrar than did the antislavery policy. French posts needed supplies, many of which were carried from the south by camels and drivers requisitioned from local chiefs. They also needed cooks, "boys," interpreters, guards, and shepherds. Most of this labor was recruited from the ranks of local haratin. Though for many life did not radically improve while in the employ of the French, for some it provided the opportunity for considerable material advancement. Samba Diop, for example, was a hartani from Atar who first became a domestic with the French, then some years later was promoted to a guard and transferred to the Tagant. He married a slave woman, received what appears to have been some sort of "loan" to purchase her freedom, and eventually paid for the freedom of his slave mother (ARIM, correspondance, gouverneur de la Mauritanie 1926; ARIM, correspondance, commandant du cercle de l'Adrar 1918–1919). Another hartani, Hemmou wuld Mohamed, whose father had been an interpreter, was hired as a "boy" in the Trarza. In 1933 he moved to Senegal, where he engaged in commerce and eventually became a major trader, known as Hemmou Fall (AATAR, commandant du cercle de Trarza 1947).[10]

The appetites of administrators and *tirailleurs* (low-ranking soldiers, usually from Senegal or the Soudan, often Wolof- or Bambara-speaking) also expanded the local market for milk, meat, and butter. Enterprising entrepreneurs, among whom were numerous haratin, quickly exploited the new opportunities, especially the particularly lucrative ones for supplying fresh meat. In 1918, the commandant at Atar was already complaining that a group of haratin, the Azazir, was monopolizing the importation of sheep, thereby "raising the cost of living in Atar" (ARIM,

10. It would be interesting to know if the practice of changing one's name was common as a means of more easily integrating with another ethnic group or, as in this case, of reaffirming useful ethnic "roots" for commercial reasons.

rapport politique, Adrar, 1918). Generally speaking, then, haratin rapidly penetrated the "new world of work" and took advantage of opportunities to accumulate wages, negotiate small loans, acquire credit, and participate in petty trade.

Employment opportunities for women, slaves and haratin alike, were little more than an extension of the customary roles women played as domestic laborers and mothers.[11] The growing numbers of wage-earning haratin increased marriage possibilities for female slaves living in or around the towns of Atar, Shinqiti, and Wadan. But most important in this respect were the tirailleurs, most of whom were in Atar. In 1918, the commandant wrote that local slave women were always "hanging around the camp looking for the tirailleurs . . . [who are] mostly of the same race, and hoping for handouts. As these slaves are badly fed, they offer to give a hand to pound millet or draw water in exchange for food. When the season to cultivate comes, the masters come to reclaim their slaves. It is not without resistance that they return" (ARIM, commandant du cercle de l'Adrar 1918).

While it is true that women were willing to work as cooks and laundresses, they really wanted to be wives, for a relationship with a tirailleur frequently led to his purchasing her freedom. In Atar, an old Bambara sorceress reportedly counselled slave women to solicit such attention.[12] But this particular route to freedom was not always as direct or as sure as it appeared. In response to several requests by tirailleurs that local slave women be liberated so that they could marry them, Governor Gaden warned the local commander: "Never has a Bambara thought about the liberation of a slave in the sense we understand. What he wants is to take her home where she is 'foreign' and becomes his slave the moment he enters his village" (ARIM, commissaire du gouvernment général en Mauritanie 1918). How widespread this was is unclear, but in 1918 it was sufficiently serious to necessitate careful regulation of unions between Mauritanian women and tirailleurs. Among other things, no slave woman was to be taken in marriage unless she had been freed and a formal (if token) brideprice paid for her;[13] and should the man leave,

11. There is evidence, however, that some female haratin profitted much like the men from expanded commercial opportunities if they were associated with the larger merchant groups (see the "Story of Hammody," below); unfortunately, I do not know how widespread this experience was.

12. ARIM, commandant du cercle de l'Adrar 1918; ARIM, correspondance, commandant du cercle de l'Adrar 1918. The role of sorcery among Mauritania's slaves, both as an element of "slave culture" and as a form of "slave resistance" needs to be explored. See ARIM, Lieutenant Busquet 1936.

13. Brideprice for a hartania was paid to her parents or, presumably, to her "patron"

both brideprice and children from the marriage were to remain with the woman. Women were not to be permitted to follow their husbands out of Mauritania (ibid.).

The consequences of these liaisons, however, were unpredictable. On the one hand, masters did not like to free female slaves, even when pressed by French officers trying to provide their soldiers and employees with wives. Owners contrived ways to avoid it, including spiriting slaves *en brousse* and out of reach. On the other hand, there was the problem of differing "interpretations" of the law among different levels of the French administration. The story of al-Fatra, a Shinqiti slave who married tirailleur Keita Bamba in 1910 for a brideprice of 30 francs (F) (ca. U.S. $6.00), is a case in point. Bamba was transferred several times, first to Atar, then to the French Cameroon, and finally, from 1916 to 1918, to France. During his absences he sent money for the maintenance of his family. But in 1917, his wife's former master successfully reclaimed her and her daughter.[14] A year later, with the local resident's assistance, al-Fatra arranged to buy her own freedom and that of her child on condition that they remain in the service of her master until Bamba's return to the Adrar. Should he fail to come back, they were to be freed on 1 July 1920.

Al-Fatra had used 100F (ca. U.S. $20.00) of the money sent to her by her husband to buy her freedom, and problems arose when Bamba returned not to Mauritania but to Senegal, and wanted his family. The woman did not want to leave and Prudhomme, the commander in Atar, felt she should not be forced to go as long as she repaid her brideprice and the 100F.[15] But Bamba wanted compensation for all the maintenance allowance he had sent, and he demanded his child. Prudhomme argued in accord with French "recommended practice," that the child should

---

if she was a freed slave still attached to her former master. The archives discuss few cases of marriage between tirailleurs and female haratin, possibly because these marriages seldom posed problems, possibly because the brideprice for a hartania was too high for poor soldiers, or possibly because the black tirailleurs were seen as being little better than slaves in the eyes of haratin.

14. Though the archives do not make clear how or why the former master was able to do this, it must be remembered that he had merely given al-Fatra to Keita Bamba as a wife—*he had not freed her.* Therefore, he retained his rights over her as a master. Perhaps he assumed that her husband was not likely to return (given his long absence), and that his claim would not be challenged.

15. No reference is made to the earlier recommendations not to permit Mauritanian wives to leave the country; it is unclear how firmly these were ever enforced or for how long (see the decision rendered, below). In this case it could also be argued that, as the marriage had taken place before the recommendations had come into effect, the request to have al-Fatra join her husband in Senegal should have been considered.

stay with the mother. For reasons that are not clear, however, the governor of Mauritania decided that, although this policy had been justified during the "early days" of occupation, now that "peace" was firmly established, "local custom" (the decision of the qadi), should prevail. The child was subsequently sent to her father. As for al-Fatra, having repaid Bamba the money she had pledged for her freedom, she had no recourse but to remain with her master, presumably still as a slave (ARIM, correspondance, gouverneur de la Mauritanie 1926).

As al-Fatra's history suggests, freedom for a woman was precarious. It was difficult to obtain and frequently illusionary, because masters would sometimes accept brideprice and give their slaves in marriage but would ultimately refuse to sell them (ibid.; interview: Soued Ahmed wuld Abidum). Rights over children produced in these ambiguous relationships were a constant and continuing source of conflict; women were frequently the losers. Such was the case of the slave wife of the above-mentioned hartani Samba Diop. After Diop had been promoted to guard and transferred to the Tagant, he requested that his wife, Fatma mint al-Ayd (originally of Atar), and her two children be allowed to join him. The French administrators approached her master, Mohamed Sejid wuld Rahman wuld Abeidun, offering him 300F (ca. U.S. $60.00) (presumably to be deducted from Diop's salary) to buy their freedom. Mohamed Sejid agreed, but soon afterwards reclaimed them, saying he had given his consent only because he feared punishment by the authorities. The local resident advised that the slave be returned to her master and that the children be left with their father, as had happened in the Bamba case. A later reference, however, indicates that she actually remained with Diop, but that one of her children, a son already 11 years old and born before the marriage, had been returned to service in her master's household in 1923. The case was not closed. In 1926, following Mohamed Sejid's death, his son officially reclaimed both the woman and her child by Diop.[16] Unfortunately, the archives have not yet yielded the verdict of this case, which so graphically illustrates the complications presented by the new social opportunities for masters, haratin, and slaves alike. But it does underscore the particular uncertainty of life for the slave woman seeking freedom through marriage: not only could it be short-lived, it could cost her her children.

The control the authorities could exercise, however, was limited. In the face of more general slave movements it appears to have been largely ineffective. In 1922, for example, notables of Shinqiti complained that

16. ARIM, correspondance, gouverneur de la Mauritanie 1926; ARIM, correspondance, commandant du cercle du l'Adrar 1918–1919.

their slave women were fleeing in large numbers to the attractions of Atar. They wanted it stopped. The administration expressed sympathy and orders were given to end this "urban migration," but there is no evidence that any effective measures were taken. Altercations between masters and slaves over this issue continued into the 1940s.[17] Male slaves were also running away. From the early 1920s, administrators reported concern over the date-palm groves and millet fields which were being deserted; agricultural production was seriously declining.[18] Slaves were seeking alternative employment in the Senegal Valley and the southern Assaba region in commerce and agriculture. The story of these migrations has yet to be written, but accounts from the Adrar indicate they were not the "freedom flights" the slaves anticipated. They took nothing with them, for they had nothing to take, and found that the free blacks of the south, the Soninke and the Peulh, were as wedded to the use of slave labor as their Saharan masters. Many of these runaways were therefore forced to work under conditions which were, reportedly, little different from those of slavery.[19]

There was considerable movement taking place among the haratin as well. The French pacification and rapidly growing presence in neighboring Senegal encouraged an expansion in commerce. Trade links were reestablished between Wadi Nun, in southern Morocco, and Senegal, with Atar as the midway market. A thriving intercolony trade in sheep from the Tagant and sheep and cattle from the south also flourished. And during the 1920s and 1930s, the expanding Senegalese groundnut industry stimulated the large-scale use of Mauritanian pack camels for transport (ANS, rapports politiques et économiques 1918–1945, especially 1938, 1939). The development of all these strains of commerce involved a significant growth in the use of hired labor, both in retail trade and in camel-caravan transport. The workers were usually haratin. Transporters often worked seasonally, returning home to cultivate cereals or to harvest dates. Haratin who began as hired workers often moved on to manage their own petty trade, sometimes capitalized by their former employers.[20] In-

17. AATAR, gouverneur de la Mauritanie 1923; AATAR, rapport politique annuel 1943; AATAR, conseil des notables 1944; ASHIN, disputes mises aux piéds des résidents de Chinguetti, 1938–1940.

18. AATAR, rapport agricole annuel 1926; AATAR, rapport politique annuel 1929; ARIM, correspondance, 6 April 1927.

19. ARIM, rapport sur le problème des haratine, ca. 1949; ANS, gouverneur de la Mauritanie 1950. While there are no details given in these reports of the conditions under which escaped slaves worked, it is pointed out that they were often badly treated and were no longer guaranteed the material security their former masters had provided.

20. Interviews: Mulaye Fkih; Mohamed wuld Lemine wuld Ely, 21 and 25 August; Mohamed Lemine wuld Souelim; Mafoud wuld Amara.

deed, the extension of credit both by Saharan and French merchants was central to this commercial expansion; hartani workers seem to have been among its agents and its beneficiaries. By the early 1930s, men like Hemmou "Fall" wuld Mohamed were operating all over Mauritania and even into Senegal.[21]

Drought and Depression, Poverty and Prostitution

Success stories were few, however, in this difficult era. The 1920s were particularly severe for the people of the Adrar, who suffered through several consecutive years of drought, exacerbating the agricultural decline underway and contributing to the flight of servile laborers (ANS, rapports politiques et économiques 1923–1929). Then came the economic crisis of 1930–1933. It hit first and hardest in Senegal, where suddenly markets like Louga and Dakar no longer wanted Mauritanian meat. Groundnut production and trade collapsed, and with them the need for Mauritanian pack camels. Atar merchants who had extended goods on credit were unable to collect (ANS, rapports politiques et économiques 1930–1934). In the southern Trarza, which had long been part of the Senegalese economy, the crisis forced some owners to get rid of slaves they could no longer afford to keep (ARIM, rapport de Monsieur Poulet 1949). Many were purchased by Adrar merchants either for their own use or for sale to northern merchants like the Regueibat.[22]

If these problems were less immediate in the Adrar, they were no less crippling in the long run. During the severe drought between 1930 and 1933, nomadic groups were forced out of the Adrar in search of pasture, leaving many of their slaves behind. Left largely to their own devices, these slaves joined the ranks of the unemployed drifting into Shinqiti and Atar. Most dramatically affected were the women. The earlier trickle of runaways which had characterized the 1920s surged between 1930 and 1933. Indeed, the periodic fluctuations in the incidence of urban prostitution was one of the most sensitive barometers of changes occurring among female slaves.[23]

As for the fate of nomadic haratin who remained in scattered, mobile

21. See also the "Story of Hammody," of Atar, below.

22. Several instances of slave-trading were noted in the Trarza in 1933–1934; the commander of the cercle explained that they merely reflected the economic difficulties experienced by slave masters and not a real resurgence of this prohibited traffic (ARIM, gouverneur de la Mauritanie 1937).

23. ANS, rapports politiques et économiques 1930–1934; ASHIN, disputes mises aux piéds des résidents de Chinguetti, 1939 (contains a reference to 1930); ARIM, gouverneur de la Mauritanie 1933; ARIM, rapport politique annuel 1935.

camps, we have little direct evidence. Generally both men and women were given their own animals to tend, and lived more or less independently of their patrons,[24] employing slaves to assist them. The animals were customarily theirs to keep; however, the patron retained a variety of ambiguously defined rights to haratin services and the animals' products. As times became more difficult for nomads and recourse to French protection became easier for clients, the ambiguity of this relationship produced increasing tensions. It is difficult to say whether the tendency to seek new patronage relations was more prevalent during this period than in the precolonial era, but circumstances certainly conspired to deepen the bitterness of conflicts over animal ownership, pasture and water, and labor and financial obligations, especially from the early 1930s (AATAR, conseil de *jema'a* 1928; ASHIN, disputes mises aux piéds des résidents de Chinguetti 1937–1940s).

For the haratin in the towns of Wadan, Shinqiti, and Atar, on the other hand, the 1930s were a mixed blessing. Though the depression affected everyone, especially those in commerce, haratin fared better than itinerant slaves in securing manual labor. Furthermore, there is no evidence that haratin were among the ranks of the troublesome prostitutes and unemployed domestics swelling Atar's population. But the most significant changes occurred as a result of production problems in the local date-palm groves, and it is here that the "fate" of the hartani (and by extension, hartania) began to diverge most decisively from that of the slave. French concern over declining agricultural activity, and the attendant costs and difficulties of importing foodstuffs, led to the implementation of new policies. Local clan heads were not only instructed to give better attention to existing groves but to plant new trees and put new lands into grain cultivation. The problem was labor. In spite of the growing numbers of itinerant folk gravitating to the Adrar oases, there simply were not enough experienced agricultural workers. And with slaves still "tending to emancipate themselves," by the mid-1930s skilled date-palm labor was rare. Nobles, hard-pressed to meet French demands enforced by fines and the threatened reallocation of their land, turned to hartani labor.[25]

Haratin were usually engaged to plant and tend a specified number

24. I am using the word *patron* to distinguish the relationship between haratin and their "noble" families from that of slaves and their "noble" owners or masters. Many haratin families had occupied that status within the context of a "noble" tribe for more than a single generation; the slave relationship had never been a reality for them or their immediate patrons.

25. ASHIN, journal des plaintes 1939; ARIM, gouverneur de la Mauritanie 1933; ARIM rapport politique annuel 1935; ARIM, gouverneur de la Mauritanie 1937.

of trees, half of which would become theirs with the first fruition some seven or eight years later. Similar arrangements governed the cultivation of cereals under the trees, which were intended to feed workers during the early years of their employ. There is reason to believe that the emphasis the administration placed on more fully exploiting Mauritania's agricultural potential during the 1930s resulted in the increased use of, and possibly changes in, this "customary contract" and that this, in turn, created an enlarged hartani class.[26] Two interconnected factors may have accelerated the rate at which male slaves were freed. One was the masters' concern to stem the slow but steady stream of runaway slaves by offering them a "better deal"; the second was the need to free these "non-persons" in order to enter into a contract with them or offer them property in payment for their services. For only haratin, and not slaves, were in a legal position to exploit fully the new economic opportunities being generated by colonial agricultural policies. Though it is unlikely many became wealthy, in time most acquired some form of property—a few trees, perhaps a sheep or two. And the possibilities for augmenting this with earnings from seasonal wage labor or petty trade increased commensurately with the expansion of the colonial economy.

Slave women and children, however, provided another side to this coin. Masters continued to attach great importance to the ownership and control of females, central to which was the question of inheritance. In 1929, the French had formally recognized the right of masters to include slaves in customary inheritance settlements. But two years later, objections were raised because decisions in these matters almost always involved allocating fractions of the poor slave—"one-third, one-quarter, one-sixth and so on"—to different beneficiaries. This happened "above all to women," who were frequently separated from young children in the process. One resident suggested that inheritance practices be modified so that the slave would go with only one person and that young children would remain with their mothers. The nobles' objections, which were respected, made clear the real dynamic of Mauritanian slavery: "To receive even one-quarter of a female slave," they explained, "gives a possible profit of one or several children tomorrow" (ARIM, commandant du cercle de l'Assaba 1931).

26. A preliminary analysis of some scattered population data from Shinqiti and Atar between 1910 and 1954 suggests that the percentage of the servile population composed of haratin rose from being no more than 1–2 percent in 1910 to closer to 50 percent by about 1950. Even allowing for considerable inaccuracies in the reporting of these statistics over four censuses and two subdivisions, the evidence indicates that some significant change had taken place. Other kinds of evidence suggest when and why they happened (ASHIN, recensements 1910, 1930, 1943–1944; AATAR, recensements 1948–1954).

If colonial administrators thus helped ensure the potential future of domestic slavery, it must be pointed out that Mauritanian free women contributed substantially to its realization. Under Islamic law they held rights to property and inheritance, and did not hesitate to press their claims, including claims over slaves. In 1932 Darjala mint Sidi Ahmed wuld Mogueya, a noblewoman from Shinqiti, inherited from her father a slave woman, Mereyima mint Moilatou, whom she first gave to her brother as a gift, then changed her mind. Her brother, al-Mamy, agreed to loan her the "use" of Mereyima, provided the slave was returned to him or his heirs after Darjala's death. She appealed the arrangement to the local resident, who ruled that Darjala no longer had any rights to Mereyima. The dispute continued for well over a decade, during which time the slave in question seems to have been shunted back and forth between brother and sister. Finally, in 1945, a new resident to Shinqiti ruled that Mereyima was to be "placed at the disposition of Darjala" but only for her own use. She was not "to rent her out or in any way whatsoever to benefit from her [services] commercially." Darjala was to feed and clothe her and not mistreat her. If she failed in these obligations, Mereyima was to "be free *to chose her own master*" [emphasis added]. The reports do not explain why, but Darjala rejected the arrangement. Through the intervention of the resident, therefore, the slave was once again returned to the service of al-Mamy. As late as 1949, Darjala was still attempting to reclaim "her" slave (ASHIN, journal des plaintes 1946).

Though the story is perhaps an unusual one, it is a rich portrayal of both the expectations about slavery still held by Adrar nobles (irrespective of gender), and their general acceptance by French officials.[27] Moreover, the admonitions about renting out the slave, benefitting from her commercial services, and mistreating her suggest that these practices were not uncommon. Mauritania's small but nonetheless growing colonial economy seems to have generated opportunities to exploit slave, as well as freed-slave, labor.[28]

The 1940s are remembered for the devastation of the Second World War, accompanied by the worst drought people can remember prior to

27. Slaves also continued to be transferred as gifts, as brideprice, and in payment of debts (ANS, gouverneur de la Mauritanie 1950).

28. Slaves, especially women slaves, may well have been "hired out" to the administration, to merchants, or simply to other nobles as domestics, cooks, nannies, and laundresses, their masters or mistresses claiming the wages paid. It is worth considering whether the increased difficulty experienced in acquiring new slaves as a consequence of French pacification in former slave-producing regions generated more or new "slave-sharing" practices among masters.

1968.[29] While some managed to protect camel herds by sending them out of the Adrar for pasture, the *petits nomades'* sheep and goats, whose transhumant movements were more restricted, were for the most part wiped out. Slaves and haratin who could no longer be supported by masters or support themselves on dwindling resources flooded into Atar in search of work. But there was little to be found. The war had closed off markets to the north and south; there was, almost literally, nothing to buy, nothing to eat, and nothing to wear. The era is most vividly remembered today as "the time of nakedness." The complete absence of cloth in the Adrar actually confined people to their homes, and sent desperate men rummaging through army rubbish bins for scraps which could be sewn together.[30] In the midst of such misery, haratin and slaves who could not be absorbed as manual laborers were "reduced to vagabondage and theft." Once again, as in the crisis of 1930–1933, slave-trading revived, particularly in 1946–1947, and women turned to prostitution. Local notables complained that they were enticing domestic slaves to join them, and the numbers became significant enough to warrant special health precautions.[31] There is no evidence that masters touched the earnings of slave prostitutes, though the references in Darjala's story to masters benefitting from the sale of their slaves' "commercial services" raises the suspicion (AATAR, conseil des notables 1944; ARIM, lettres concernant "Le comité d'honneur" 1958).

While it is difficult to say whether it was preferable for slave women to provide sexual or domestic "services" within the owning family or to negotiate them in the marketplace, it does appear that conditions at home were undergoing some change. Complaints by masters tell of women refusing to work, showing "disrespect," and attempting to exercise more control over their children — hiding them and trying to reclaim them in cases of separation (ASHIN, journal des plaintes 1937–1947). In the face of limited prospects for paid labor outside the family, and because abandoning the master was tantamount to abandoning one's children, female slaves, for the most part, chose not to leave. Even in the late 1940s, their best options were still the "traditional" ones: becoming a favored concubine, family wet nurse, or, in rare cases, the wife of a noble or a well-off hartani.[32]

29. Particularly valuable discussions of the impact of the war years on the Adrar can be found in Lafeuille (1945) and in "Les nomades et leur exode vers le sud-est" (AATAR, ca. 1945).

30. ARIM, rapport de Monsieur Poulet 1949; interviews: al Hadrami, 7, 8, and 27 August; Mohamed Salek wuld Faroui, 9 and 10 August; Saika wuld Messoud, 19 and 20 August; Safia mint Hammody.

31. AATAR, rapports politiques annuels 1943, 1944; ARIM, rapport de Lieutenant Schneider 1943; ASHIN, journal des plaintes 1940.

32. Haratin seldom took slave wives unless they could afford to buy the women's free-

If slaves still had no rights, they were in a better position to push their demands. Masters found it increasingly difficult to cope with the combined problems of slave runaways, French policies, economic upheavals, and climatic disasters. Thus, from the late 1930s, slave men as well as women, cultivators as well as herders, began simply taking for themselves what they considered to be "their share" of harvests and milk products. Masters were upset and sought the support of the administration to restrain these slaves, but it is not clear how often they got it. What we do know is that complaints about slaves who refused to work, took things without permission, and publicly humiliated masters continued throughout the 1940s (ASHIN, journal des plaintes 1937–1950). Slaves remained a part of Adrar society, but they no longer accepted difficulties and humiliations attached to their condition without complaint or, on occasion, resistance.

The Story of Hammody and the Hartani "Work Ethic"

In light of the fact that the fortunes of most of the population of the Adrar did not improve during the 1940s, the "good fortune" of the few who did manage to prosper is particularly striking. The restricted commerce of the war produced an inevitable clandestine trade (especially with grain markets to the north) and a local black market which yielded enormous profits. Among the beneficiaries were many haratin who later used their illicit gains to develop their own trading operations. These few who profitted did so in large part because many others were being forced to sell off animals, property, and date-palms merely to keep their families fed. Nobles in Atar had to use their date trees (or prospective harvests) as collateral for provisions, and then were unable to meet their payments. Between 1940 and 1945, the prices of animals, trees, and land plummeted. Some haratin began to acquire such property cheaply and, like their patrons, they invested in slaves for their households and businesses.[33] In 1943, the resident at Atar wrote that the old social classifications no longer reflected the real importance of tribes: "A new social hierarchy founded uniquely on wealth is being established. Politically it is difficult to predict the consequences of this evolution which consecrates the importance of work and which destroys the ancient seigneurs" (AATAR,

---

dom, because they would otherwise have no control over the children of the marriage. Those who had the means, on the other hand, like Hammody (below), could purchase slaves in the market who had no "familial" relations to make claims on offspring.

33. AATAR, rapports politiques annuels 1943, 1944, 1947; interviews: al Hadrami, 27 August; Mohamed Salek wuld Faroui, 9 and 10 August; Mulaye Fkih; Mohamed wuld Aly Abdi.

rapport politique annuel, "Notes," 1943).[34] The hartani was the epitome of this new ethic being encouraged by the French, and in the 1940s there was no better "proof" of its success than the often recounted tale of Hammody of Atar, the hartani who "made it." His story provides an important corollary to the changes that occurred right across Mauritania's social hierarchy, and shows how these groups interacted and shaped each others' lives. Hammody's success was not typical, but the way in which he achieved it exposes dramatically the dynamics which underlay colonial social and economic change.

For a hartani, Hammody began life well.[35] His mother had been a slave of the Awlad Bou Sba (one of the powerful grand nomade tribes) who had been freed after giving birth to a son by her master. She later married Hammody's father, a hartani of the Yezid Mulay Ely fraction of the equally prominent Tekna tribe. The family first established itself in Shinqiti where Hammody's mother and sister became traders. They remained attached to the wealthy Tekna merchant Yezid and probably moved with him to Atar following the implantation of the French. Hammody's first employment was as a commercial representative for a hartani in the Trarza; but by 1915 he had squandered his earnings and was 4,000F (ca. U.S. $800) in debt. He returned home where his sister borrowed enough money from Yezid to pay off his debts. Once back in Atar, he borrowed from cousins to begin work as a butcher, selling meat to the French as well as on the local market. He derived additional profits from the tanned skins he sold to a French commercial house in Senegal. This company soon extended him credit, which he used to diversify his import business. In the early 1920s, he was extending loans of his own to people, some as important as the emir's mother,[36] and had acquired enough influence to exert pressure on them to repay him. By 1927, he had a house, a wife, and a slave. He was, as they say, well on his way.

His relations with the French were excellent, and on occasion he even passed on to them information gained in the course of commercial dealings with the Regueibat and others. When the authorities sought some-

---

34. As is suggested in this chapter's conclusions, the French tended to be too "optimistic" about the ability of redistributed wealth to destroy the "ancient" social system and with it the *seigneurs*.

35. The story of Hammody has been reconstructed from information scattered in Mauritanian archives (ARIM, AATAR, ASHIN) as well as ANS, series 2G. Interviews were with Safia mint Hammody, Hammody's eldest sister; Mulaye Fkih, an old employee who worked in commerce with Hammody; Mohamed Yehdih wuld Yezid wuld Mulay Ely, the son of Hammody's former "patron" Yezid; and al Hadrami, a knowledgeable Atar notable.

36. The emir was the political leader of the Adrar, drawn from an honored warrior family.

one to assure deliveries of meat to the Atar post, Hammody was a logical choice for the contract. Yezid financed the project, giving Hammody 3,000F (ca. U.S. $600) to buy sheep.[37] He undoubtedly took advantage of the generally disastrous drought years by purchasing animals and hiring shepherds cheaply. By the mid-1930s, his business was flourishing. Hammody advanced goods to herders to ensure they would sell him their animals the next season. Although the French purported to disapprove of this circumvention of the "free market," they still supported Hammody's claim in 1935 against a Tagant herder who had failed to honor his obligation. Hammody also rented camels to the administration for their annual convoys and used them for his own caravans, which some years numbered up to 300 animals.[38]

In 1937, Hammody saw his wealth transformed into real status, at least vis-à-vis the administration. After some discussion (after all, Hammody was still a hartani), he was officially recognized as chief of the Awlad Bou Sba in order to deal with the authorities in Atar.[39] Moreover, Yezid's Tekna fraction was to be joined with Hammody's for administrative purposes, apparently at the latter's request; perhaps this was because Hammody had just underwritten a loan for Yezid to the tune of 42,000F (ca. U.S. $8,400)![40] In brief, during the 1930s, Hammody expanded his interests and became the undisputed chief "host" and creditor in Atar. He invested in animals, hired herders, and opened boutiques. He developed long-distance commerce from Morocco to Senegal and hired drivers and agents to handle it. He used credit from his Tekna patron, Yezid, and from the French to extend credit to others. He also invested money loaned him by Yezid, returning the original capital and sharing equally in the profits. As his wealth multiplied, his reputation grew and his sources of credit expanded. He was able to extend limitless generosity — money, food, animals, clothing, whatever was needed. By 1938, he had

37. There is disagreement as to how the contract with the French was obtained. Mohamed Yehdih says it was Yezid who was responsible, while Safia credits the intervention of a particularly well-regarded interpreter.

38. ARIM, commandant du cercle de l'Adrar 1935; interviews: Mohamed Yehdih wuld Yezid wuld Mulay Ely; Mulaye Fkih; Safia mint Hammody.

39. Other instances of haratin being recognized as heads of clans and "chiefs" of towns (thereby responsible for collecting taxes and organizing requisitions) are to be found in the Adrar and Tagant. Most of these cases come to light in the archives because of problems over "abuse of power," a situation not restricted to haratin!

40. AATAR, correspondance, commandant du cercle de l'Adrar 1937; AATAR, commandant du cercle de l'Adrar 1937. The governor had second thoughts about this arrangement, but he was informed that "to go back on their word" would undermine confidence in French authority (correspondence also in ARIM, correspondance, gouverneur de la Mauritanie, 1937–1938).

well earned the reputation of being an "intelligent, rich and generous chief."[41]

The 1940s saw the emergence of Hammody the land baron. As nobles in need of food and clothing were forced to part with houses, date-palms, and land, Hammody rapidly acquired property. In 1942, he was described as having a great fortune, which continued to grow from one day to the next (AATAR, rapport politique annuel 1942). By the end of the war, he controlled most of the property in Atar, and few transactions did not pass through his hands. He sold some properties for a sizable profit (several to the administration), while others were rented to whoever had the labor to exploit them. Rent came in with the harvest, usually set at half the crop of dates or cereals. During the difficult war years, Hammody was one of the few who had sufficient resources to provide for those flocking into town looking for food and work.[42]

Over the years, Hammody also invested in slaves. At first he bought males to work in his businesses, then females to mate with them and assist in his household. Later slaves of both sexes were used in his fields and date-palm groves. He bought only "slaves of quality." In 1955, he married one of them, a woman from Mali who had served as housekeeper and concubine. She bore him a son. Hammody died in 1961, leaving some 200 slaves and a large portion of Atar's rich date-palm groves to his children, seven daughters and six sons. He also left quite a mark on the history of Atar. In all, this was a considerable achievement for someone who liked to refer to himself as a humble slave of the Awlad Bou Sba.[43]

Conclusions: A Topsy-Turvy World

By 1950, French policy and the colonial economy had effectively reduced the dependency of haratin on their masters, and encouraged their movement into salaried, contract labor. But it was also true that the success of some haratin, Hammody being the most blatant example, was rooted in the continuing subservience of others, notably slaves. The sources of much of the commercial development from which Adrar haratin profitted were the slave-holding, slave-trading grands nomades—the Awlad Bou Sba, Tekna, and Regueibat.[44] The nobles who owned and exploited

41. AATAR, correspondance, commandant du cercle de l'Adrar 1937; AATAR, rapport politique annuel 1942; ARIM, rapport politique annuel 1938.
42. Interviews: Mohamed Salek wuld Faroui, 9 and 10 August; Safia mint Hammody; Mohamed wuld Aly Abdi.
43. Interviews: Mohamed Salek wuld Faroui, 9 and 10 August; Safia mint Hammody; Mohamed wuld Aly Abdi.
44. It should be noted that many slaves moved back and forth across the Senegal River,

date-palm groves and cereal cultivation continued to employ slave labor and, most important, to depend upon the female slave element for the reproduction of their households.[45]

Haratin themselves bought slaves to help them herd, trade, cultivate, and raise families. If anything, their "rising expectations" from the 1930s contributed to a growing consciousness of being hartani as distinct from "slave." To own a slave or slaves was not only an achievement, it was a concrete realization of the difference between the "slave" and the "freed-slave" condition.

But there was another perspective to be considered. What was already clear in the 1930s was that the material improvement of haratin had not greatly impressed their "noble" former masters. Success in the market or the administration was fully recognized only in the work-conscious world of the French. As the commander of the Adrar wrote in 1937, re-assuring the governor-general about Hammody's appointment as "chief" of the Atar Awlad Bou Sba, "[Hammody's] situation as hartani will al-ways oblige him, no matter what his wealth, to have the greatest re-spect [for us]" (AATAR, commandant du cercle de l'Adrar 1937). In 1938, officials noted that "he tries to have his moderate origin forgotten through his public largess and bounty" (ARIM, rapport politique annuel 1938); but it is clear he never fully succeeded. As late as 1951, when a consid-erable piece of property he had just purchased was contested by several Atar notables, the qadi explained that the previous owner, "a man of rank," had had no problems in 20 years of proprietorship. "It comes down to social status," he went on. "You need only look at the social and re-ligious rank of the plaintiffs to understand" (AATAR, attestation, Had-ramy wuld Abeid, 1958–1959).

In contrast to slaves, whose position remained relatively well defined, haratin who "made it" found themselves in increasingly ambiguous po-sitions. Their economic status, which made them important in the eyes of the colonial administration, was incompatible with their customary social role. That ambiguity continues to plague independent Mauritania, where the noble elite retains control over most resources, especially land, and holds political power. It underlies many of the social tensions be-

---

usually the victims of kidnapping. Women and children figured largely in this trade. Many of these were absorbed in the southern regions, especially the Trarza, though some were probably among those sold by the Regueibat or Awlad Bou Sba in the Adrar region.

45. The role of slave women and children in the reproduction of Mauritanian society was clearly an important one. Some French sources suggest that slave women were more fertile and produced more children than "white," noble Mauritanians (ARIM, comman-dant du cercle de l'Assaba 1931; ARIM, gouverneur de la Mauritanie 1933; ARIM, Odette du Puigadeau 1945).

tween noble and servile, black and white, and, most important, black and black—haratin and slaves. Haratin, many of whom can trace familial links with a particular "white" nobility back several generations, are reluctant to reject the system which gives them identity. They continue to respect a social order in which they can hope to gain materially rather than to join with the lowest classes of that order, namely slaves and recently freed slaves, to change it. The act abolishing slavery, passed by the Mauritanian government in 1980, is not likely to be much more effective than French colonial policy in actually eliminating the conditions of slavery if it is not recognized that the so-called freed slave, hartani, remains a critical component both of the problem and of its perpetuation. Hammody was far from typical, but he and his family vividly illustrate the values and aspirations of his class, as well as the values and reactions of their former masters. Today, Hammody's family is still designated as haratin, even though one of its members served as the country's ambassador to the United Nations. And Hammody's "slave wife" and son still live apart from the rest of his children with whom relations are very strained. Although both mother and son are technically haratin, among those who know the family, and within the family itself, they will always be slaves.

GLOSSARY

abid	slaves.
grands nomades	tribes whose herds are composed principally of camels, necessitating annual transhumant movements of up to several hundred miles (e.g., the Regueibat and Tekna).
hartani (masc.)/ *hartania* (fem.) (pl. *haratin*)	a freed slave who retains defined "ties" with the family of the former owner; a hereditary social position.
jema'a	council of elders.
mint	daughter of.
petits nomades	tribes whose herds include some camels but are based principally on sheep and goats; transhumant movements tend to be more restricted in scope than those of the *grands nomades*.
qadi	judge.
wuld	son of.
zwiya taleb (pl. *zwaya*)	a cleric; student of Islam.

REFERENCES

Oral sources

interviews were recorded (except where noted) in Hassaniya in 1984 with the assistance of Sidi Mohamed wuld Cheikh and were translated into French by Abdullahi wuld Mohamed Lemine. Copies are deposited with the Institut Mauritanien de Recherche Scientifique, Nouakchott. The interviewee's tribal affiliation is shown in parentheses in each reference.

al Hadrami (Smassid), interviews on 7, 8, and 27 August, Atar.
Mafoud wuld Amara (Laghlal), interview on 19 August, Shinqiti.
Mohamed Lemine wuld Souelim (Tekna), interview on 22 August, Shinqiti.
Mohamed Salem wuld Sehrool (Laghlal), interview on 19 August, Shinqiti.
Mohamed Salek wuld Faroui (Ideishelli), interviews on 9 and 10 August, Atar.
Mohamed wuld Aly Abdi (Smassid), interview on 12 August, Atar (not recorded).
Mohamed wuld Lemine wuld Ely (Awlad Bou Sba), interviews on 21 and 25 August, Shinqiti.
Mohamed Yehdih wuld Yezid wuld Mulay Ely (Tekna), interview on 12 August, Atar.
Mulaye Fkih (Awlad Bou Sba), interview on 28 August, Atar.
Safia mint Hammody (Awlad Bou Sba), interview on 11 August, Atar (not recorded).
Saika wuld Messoud (Ida Ali), interviews on 19 and 20 August, Shinqiti.
Soued Ahmed wuld Abidum (Kunta), interview on 25 September, Tidjikja.

Archival sources

AATAR: Archives Régionales, Atar (Adrar).
Attestation, Hadramy wuld Abeid, Atar, 1958–1959.
Commandant du cercle de l'Adrar à monsieur le gouverneur de la Mauritanie, 30 November 1937.
Commandant du cercle de Trarza à commandant du cercle de l'Adrar, 26 July 1947.
Conseil de *jema'a*, 20 July 1928.
Conseil de *jema'a*, 5 October 1933.
Conseil de *jema'a*, 1934 (?).
Conseil des notables, 1944.
Correspondance, commandant du cercle de l'Adrar et le gouverneur de la Mauritanie, January-November 1937.
Gouverneur de la Mauritanie à monsieur le commandant, cercle de l'Adrar, 8 January 1923.
"Les nomades et leur exode vers le sud-est," Subdivision d'Atar, ca. 1945, E2 116.

Rapport agricole annuel, Chinguetti, 1926.
Rapport politiques annuels, 1929, 1942, 1943, 1944, 1947.
Rapport politique annuel, annexe 5, 1943.
Rapport politique annuel, "Notes sur les tributaires," 1943.
Recensements, subdivision d'Atar et de Chinguetti, 1948–1954.
ANS: Archives Nationales du Sénégal, Afrique Occidentale Français (AOF), Dakar.
"L'esclavage en Mauritanie," rapport des Nations Unies sur l'esclavage, 1950. 2K15 174 MAURITANIE.
Gouverneur de la Mauritanie à monsieur le gouverneur-général de l'AOF, 10 May 1950. 2K15 174 MAURITANIE.
Rapports politiques et économiques, 1905–1945. 2G5-2G45.
ARIM: Archives Nationales, République Islamique de Mauritanie, Nouakchott.
Administrateur assistant de Mederdra à monsieur le commandant du cercle de Trarza, May 1930. E1 18.
Commandant du cercle de l'Adrar à le commissaire du gouvernement général en Mauritanie, 27 October 1918. E1 33-1.
Commandant du cercle de l'Adrar à monsieur le gouverneur-général de l'AOF, 26 September 1935. B70.
Commandant du cercle de l'Assaba, 9 November 1931, faire suivi à monsieur le gouverneur-général de l'AOF, December 1931. E1 18.
Commissaire du gouvernement général en Mauritanie à monsieur le commandant du cercle de l'Adrar, 25 November 1918. E1 28.
Correspondance, 6 April 1927. B1.
Correspondance, commandant du cercle de l'Adrar, le gouverneur-général de l'AOF, February 1918. E1 28.
Correspondance, commandant du cercle de l'Adrar, le gouverneur-général de l'AOF, December 1918–November 1919. E1 28.
Correspondance, commandant du cercle de l'Adrar, le gouverneur-général de l'AOF, 3 May 1919. E1 28.
Correspondance, le commissaire du gouvernement général en Mauritanie et le gouverneur-général de l'AOF, October 1918. E1 33-1.
Correspondance, gouverneur de la Mauritanie et le commandant du cercle de l'Adrar, February-April 1926. E1 72.
Correspondance, gouverneur de la Mauritanie et le commandant du cercle de l'Adrar, 1937–1938. B76.
Correspondance, résident à Chinguetti, commandant du cercle de l'Adrar et le commissaire du gouvernement général en Mauritanie, October-November 1918. E1 28.
Correspondance, résident à Chinguetti et le gouverneur de la Mauritanie, March 1927. E1 72.
Correspondance, résident de Timbedra, le lieutenant-gouverneur général, Haut-Sénégal–Niger, le gouverneur général de l'AOF, April 1920–January 1921. E1 28.
Gouverneur de la Mauritanie à monsieur le commandant du cercle de l'Adrar, 23 April 1923. E1 28.

Gouverneur de la Mauritanie à monsieur le commandant du cercle de l'Adrar, 18 October 1938. B78.
Gouverneur de la Mauritanie à monsieur le gouverneur-général de l'AOF, 10 August 1933. E1 18.
Gouverneur de la Mauritanie à monsieur le gouverneur-général de l'AOF, 11 December 1937. B1.
Instructions, commandant du cercle de l'Adrar aux commandants des Goums Nomades, 13 December 1929. E1 18.
Lettre, Capitaine Prudhomme, 20 August 1919. E1 103.
Lettres concernant "Le comité d'honneur de l'Union française contre le traffique des femmes [et les problèmes des prostitués], Atar," 1958. E2 237.
Lieutenant Busquet, "Note sur la sorcellerie, Adrar," July 1936. E2 118.
Odette du Puigadeau, "L'évolution d'esclave noir en Mauritanie," ca. 1945. E2 223.
Rapport agricole annuel, Chinguetti, 1926.
Rapport de Lieutenant Schneider, 1943. B70.
Rapport de Monsieur Poulet, "Sur la question des serviteurs en Mauritanie," 17 May 1949. B1.
Rapport politique, Adrar, November 1918. E1 103.
Rapport politique annuel, 1935. E2 118.
Rapport politique annuel, 1938. E2 116.
Rapport sur le problème des haratine, n.a., n.d. (ca. 1949). B1.
Rapport de tournée, 1935. B70.
Rapport de tournée, 1936.
Réponse du commandant du cercle de l'Adrar au "Questionnaire des Nations Unies relatif à l'esclavage et à la servitude," 1949–1950. B1.
Réponse, gouverneur de la Mauritanie, 1933, au communication de Louis Hunkarin, 1 February 1932. E1 18.
Résident de Brakna à monsieur le commissaire du gouvernement général en Mauritanie, 25 December 1905. E1 61.
ASHIN: Archives Régionales, Shinqiti (Adrar).
Disputes mises aux piéds des résidents de Chinguetti, 1937–1940s.
Journal des plaintes, Chinguetti, 1937–1950 (most years).
Recensements, subdivision de Chinguetti, 1910, 1930, 1943–1944.
Rapport du résident, subdivision de Chinguetti, 6 February 1946.

Other sources

Centre de Recherches et d'Etudes sur les Sociétés Méditerranéennes. 1979. *Introduction à la Mauritanie*. Paris: CNRS.
Désiré-Vuillemin, G. 1962. *Contribution à la Mauritanie, 1900–1934*. Dakar: Editions Clairafrique.
Fondacci, P. 1946. Maures et serviteurs noirs au pays nomades d'Afrique (Mauritanie, Soudan). Monograph #811. Paris: Centre des Haute Etudes d'Administration Musulmane.

Gouraud, Gen. 1945. *Mauritanie Adrar.* Paris: Librairie Plon.

Hornac, J. 1953. Le problème des serviteurs en Mauritanie. Monograph #2,202. Paris: Centre des Haute Etudes d'Administration Musulmane.

Lafeuille, R. 1945. La crise économique chez les nomades de Mauritanie de 1940 à 1944. Monograph #756. Paris: Centre des Haute Etudes d'Administration Musulmane.

Miské, A-B. 1970. *Al Wasīt: tableau de la Mauritanie au début du XXᵉ siècle.* Paris: Librairie C. Klincksieck.

Norris, H. T. 1968. *Shinqiti folk literature and song.* London: Oxford.

V

NEW ECONOMIES AND NEW FORMS OF LABOR CONTROL

13 *J. S. Hogendorn and Paul E. Lovejoy*

The Reform of Slavery in Early Colonial Northern Nigeria

Between 1897 and 1903, the British, French, and Germans systematically defeated the separate emirates of the Sokoto Caliphate. The colonial conquest ushered in a period that saw three major changes: the effective elimination of enslavement, the sharp curtailment and ultimate demise of slave-trading, and a period of widespread flight by fugitives from slavery with the eventual transformation of slavery into milder forms of labor organization and an improvement in the social status of slaves. These changes, which created an entirely new situation for present and former slaves and slave-owners, were caused by legal and political reforms, by alterations in the precolonial land tenure and tax systems, and by the ultimate success of a campaign to construct a new railway line. The latter eventually led to rapid growth in the export of cash crops — both cotton, which had been expected, and groundnuts, which had not. The elimination of new supplies of slaves and the creation of a different economic and social base eroded the incentives that had for long provided the motivation for the northern Nigerian slave system, and that system began a gradual decline, until the enactment of Ordinance No.

This chapter is part of an ongoing study by the authors of the economic and social impact of early colonial rule in Northern Nigeria.

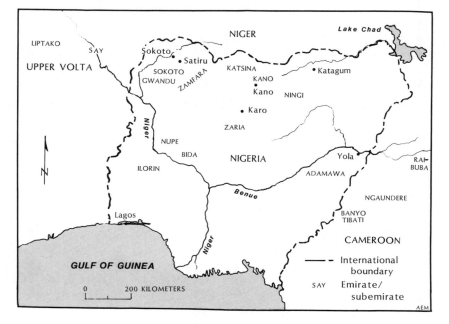

Map 13. Northern Nigeria

19 of 1936, whereby it was illegal to hold slaves in the northern provinces of Nigeria (NNA, Pembleton 1936).

France moved on the caliphate from the west, taking Liptako, Say, and other emirates, subsequently incorporating them into Haute Volta and Niger. Germany pushed northward from the Gulf of Guinea into southern Adamawa, and eventually severed the large subemirates of Tibati, Banyo, Ngaundere, Rai-Buba, and Lay from the overlordship of Yola to make part of German Cameroon. The British struck into the heart of the caliphate from a base on the Niger River, taking Ilorin and Nupe between 1897 and 1900, continuing northward into Zaria, Kano, and Sokoto, and conquering these emirates by 1903. As in much of the scramble for Africa, the British seized the largest and the best territory (Adeleye 1971). This study of slavery and its transformation under colonialism will be confined to changes in British Northern Nigeria.

The antislavery movement provided an ideological justification for the colonial conquest, not just of the Sokoto Caliphate but also of many other parts of Africa as well (Lovejoy 1983: 264–68; Miers 1975). Sir George Taubman-Goldie, director of the Royal Niger Company (RNC), which assumed quasi-governmental functions in the first phases of the conquest, and Sir Frederick (later Lord) Lugard, first high commissioner of Northern Nigeria, both believed that Britain's civilizing mission required the eventual destruction of slavery as a key institution in the emirates. But for practical reasons they attacked it very gradually. Thus, while officially the Royal Niger Company and then the British Government of Northern Nigeria, which replaced the RNC, were hostile to slavery, in practice only enslavement and slave-trading were seriously attacked. The colonial state was in effect determined to circumvent its public stance, but as quietly as possible for fear of arousing the suspicion of the anti-slavery lobby in Britain. The campaign against enslavement and slave-trading was publicized, but the status of those already in slavery was conveniently ignored. Lugard had acquired his knowledge of slavery and had formulated a strategy for dealing with it while in East and Central Africa. He knew well the conditions of slaves, both in Islamic and non-Muslim settings. When he planned the administration of Northern Nigeria, he had already decided that slavery was to be reformed, not abolished. He had the skill (and the considerable polemical support of the British press, through the efforts of his talented wife, Flora Shaw) to keep his policies out of the public eye (Lennihan 1982; Hill 1976).

Lugard's Reforms

In his subordinates, Lugard found a group of men who were fully committed to his policies towards slavery. They suppressed the slave trade while reporting secretly on the condition of slaves. Lugard's understanding of the economic and social importance of slavery was confirmed through his personal observation and the information that came in from his officers (Lugard 1970: 220–21; Hill 1976: 410). As early as 1901, Lugard made it clear that "it was not the intention of the Government to interfere with the institution of slavery *vi et armis* but gradually [to] substitute a better form of labor contract" (*Annual Report, Northern Nigeria* 1901). Information on slavery was assembled into a series of memoranda in 1905, at which time the official attitude towards slavery was fully enunciated. Lugard (1906: 136) argued that

to prematurely abolish the almost universal form of labor contract, before a better system had been developed to take its place, would not only be an act of administrative folly, but would be an injustice to the masters, since Domestic Slavery is an institution sanctioned by the law of Islam, and property in slaves was as real as any other form of property among the Mohammedan population at the time that the British assumed the Government, a nullification of which would amount to nothing less than wholesale confiscation.

Lugard feared that emancipation of slaves on a large scale would result in "a state of anarchy and chaos, and the whole social system of the Mohammedan States would be dislocated" (ibid.). Consequently, he and his administration developed policies that resulted in the reform of slavery rather than its abolition.

These reforms hinged on a reinterpretation of Islamic law as practiced in the emirates of the Sokoto Caliphate. They involved a redefinition of *murgu*, the practice of allowing slaves to purchase their own freedom, and of the legal rights of slaves in the Islamic courts (Lovejoy 1986a, b). Murgu had been a means by which masters could benefit from the labor of their slaves by allowing them to work for a number of years on their own account, in return for which slaves paid their masters a regular and agreed-upon amount of money. It was the right of the master to establish a murgu relationship, and it could also be terminated at the will of the master. Under the Lugardian regime, it became the legal right of the slave to have a purchase price set, whether the master agreed or not, and the ultimate decree establishing the freedom of the slave was issued by the courts (Lovejoy 1986a). In practice the law was often not implemented, but British intentions clearly encouraged the establishment of more murgu relationships (Ubah 1973: 369).

Lugard hoped that the termination of slave-raiding and -trading and the gradual emancipation of slaves through this reformed system of self-purchase would result in a steady decrease in the number of slaves in society. The demography of caliphate slavery was such that slaves did not sustain their numbers through natural increase. For one thing, many female slaves became concubines, and their children, being legally free, did not swell the number of slaves. For another, the rural slave population often suffered during periods of famine, and it is likely that their birth rates were lower and mortality rates higher than those of the population as a whole. Caliphate society depended upon annual slave raids for a steady flow of new captives, who were moved throughout the caliphate as items of trade and tribute (Hogendorn 1980). The elimination of the slave-supply mechanism (enslavement and trade) invariably had the effect of reducing the numbers of slaves in society. Lugard addressed the issue of a natural increase in numbers through birth into slavery by declaring all children born of slave parents after 31 March 1901 to be free. Since such children obviously did not leave their parents, they were brought up under conditions that modified slavery but did not end the institution. With the attack on the supply mechanism and the alteration in the legal status of children born after 1901, Lugard did indeed deal a major blow to slavery. The reformed institution of murgu was the essential corollary to these changes, because it allowed many slaves to terminate their servile status through means that were acceptable to local Islamic law and to the sensibilities of slave masters.[1]

These reforms succeeded to a great extent. The British could claim that they successfully altered the structure of society without causing serious social dislocation. Between 1897 and 1917, at least 55,000 slaves acquired their official freedom through the courts by murgu arrangements, ransoming by third parties, and legal intervention to protect slaves from ill treatment (Lugard 1970: 222). Not all these slaves achieved actual freedom, because at least a quarter of these court cases involved the transfer of female slaves, usually a thinly disguised method of obtaining concubines (Christelow 1985; Lovejoy 1988). Resident Orr, who actively promoted the use of courts to free slaves in Zaria, still had to admit that "the majority availing themselves of this facility [were] women whose freedom was purchased by intending husbands."[2] Other slaves gained their freedom without reference to the courts, however. Many slaves became effectively free through death-bed grants of emancipation and other pious acts that went unrecorded. It is likely, furthermore, that thousands of slaves were actively working towards their freedom under murgu arrangements in cases that were also unrecorded (Lugard 1970: 222). Despite the incomplete data, it seems safe to conclude that the incidence of murgu and emancipation greatly increased from the 1890s through the first decade of colonial rule. Benevolence towards slaves, as perceived by the masters, had always been an essential ingredient of this paternalistic slave system. Now colonial reforms reinforced such benevolence, so that the ideal of slavery under the caliphate came close to being the reality of slavery under colonialism.

Despite this shift in the opportunities open to slaves under the reformed slavery code, many slaves took a hostile attitude towards their masters, especially in the first few years of colonial rule. The transition of the early colonial period was more difficult than the British wanted and than they publicly admitted to the antislavery lobby in the United Kingdom. Many slaves simply fled from their masters in these early years; a good

1. The best discussion of Lugard's policy is his 1906 memoranda on slavery (Lugard 1906). Also see *Annual Report, Northern Nigeria* 1905–1906: 362–63, where Lugard observed that the sultan of Sokoto had assisted in these reforms: "A slave thus has an absolute right to redeem himself even against the will of the master, with the result that slaves, instead of running away and becoming vagrants, can now appeal to the native court." It seems, however, that slaves often had difficulty asserting this "right." See, for example, the statement of Walter Miller, as cited in Lennihan 1982: 135 fn.

2. *Annual Report, Northern Nigeria* 1905–1906: 387. Also see Annual Report, Kano Province, SNP 10/1 134/1913; Register of Freed Slaves 1905, SNP 15/1 Acc 90; Register of Freed Slaves 1906, SNP 15/1 Acc 121; SNP 10/6 179p/1918, all cited in Ubah 1973: 371.

estimate probably can never be made, but at least many tens of thousands
fled, and the total could easily have reached a hundred thousand or more.
The best available information indicates that the size of this exodus was
less than that during the massive slave crisis of the French Soudan between 1895 and 1905 (Roberts and Klein 1981: 375–94). Still, the scale
was enormous, especially in Nupe, Yola, and Sokoto. Slaves left the farms
and plantations of their masters, sometimes fleeing in relatively large
groups. They journeyed southward, back to the areas from which they
had been seized. Unlike those born into slavery, these slaves who had
been captured were the ones least likely to have accommodated themselves fully to caliphate society. In Bida Emirate, for example, fugitives
came from villages which had been settled only in the previous decade
or two. They fled across the Niger River back to their home country,
which had been largely devastated and stripped of its population but
which could be resettled now with the imposition of the *Pax Britannica*
(Lovejoy, 1986a).

Lugard's assessment of the fugitive crisis in Northern Nigeria stands
as convincing proof of the scale of the movement and makes it clear that
the colonial reform of slavery was not the success that he had hoped. By
1917, 21,711 slaves had achieved freedom through the courts in Sokoto, "figures [which] represent only a fraction of the number who have
acquired their freedom in this Province since 1903, for they do not include the large number who in the earlier days left their masters and
asserted their freedom without registration" (Lugard 1970: 222). Lugard
had no way of knowing the number of fugitives who left the Sokoto area,
but it is revealing that he considered the number of slaves emancipated
through the courts to be only a fraction of the total number of slaves
who achieved their freedom by whatever means. Understandably, estimates of the number of escaped slaves are few and unreliable. In Nupe,
where the exodus was of major proportions between 1897 and 1901, even
before the conquest of the northern emirates, it was thought that 30,000
slaves fled, mainly across the Niger River to the homelands where they
had been seized in the previous decades.[3] In the Sokoto region, many
fugitives congregated in Satiru, only 20 kilometers from the city of So-

3. Acting high commissioner to Colonial Office, 7 November 1901, as cited in Mason
1970: 401 fn. Also see *Annual Report, Northern Nigeria* 1902: 103, 133, where Lugard observed that the February expedition against Kontagora resulted in the flight of thousands
of slaves. Lugard estimated that 20,000 people had followed Emir Ibrahim, and that "large
numbers of these who were recently captured slaves fled into the bush and found their
way back to their villages." And in the *Annual Report, Northern Nigeria* 1903: 173, 177,
Lugard reported that during the march on Kano "the slaves of the Fulani deserted them
in large numbers." For Bauchi, see *Annual Report, Northern Nigeria* 1905–1906: 390, where

koto, where they joined a Mahdist community that had been established there in the mid-1890s. By 1906, when the Satiru community rebelled against British colonial rule and the Sokoto aristocracy, the community had an estimated population of 10,000, most of whom were fugitive slaves (Mohammed 1983: 164–83). While both the estimates for the exodus and the number of slaves at Satiru must be treated with caution, the scale of the fugitive crisis is well established by the available documentation. Slaves left in considerable numbers, and the concern of the British officials and caliphate slave-owners alike was that the crisis be contained. The efforts to reform murgu, the abolition decree of 31 March 1901, the eventual alterations in land tenure and tax policies, and the increasing attractiveness of the local economy for those who had made up the slave population, all combined to slow the exodus.

Farm slaves were most common among the early fugitives, and they may well have formed the vast majority of deserters. Slaves constituted a major source of labor in the agricultural sector. The plantations that ringed the various towns of the central provinces of the caliphate depended upon slave labor (Lovejoy 1978: 341–68; Hogendorn 1977). These plantations, which varied in size from large farms with a few score slaves to large villages with as many as a thousand slaves, supported the aristocracy and elite slave officials of the emirate capitals and formed the backbone of merchant households. Although the divisions between various categories of slaves were often blurred, officials, slave and free, could draw upon their rural slaves for soldiers and retainers. These rural slaves were, from all available evidence, a majority of the slave population. Hence fugitives from this group, not surprisingly, were more common than from slaves in domestic service, from palace retainers, or from the slaves of peasants. Furthermore, agricultural slaves were often most removed from the supervision of their masters and frequently entrusted to the overlordship of slave overseers, who sometimes were themselves under the authority of senior slave officials, such as the *shamaki* of Kano, a court slave and close advisor of the Kano emir (Yunusa 1976: 55–64). As a result of the distance separating masters and slaves in these situations, slaves could well develop closer relations with their fellow slaves than with their masters or the representatives of their masters. Certainly masters were aware of the dangers of the situation, but for slaves ac-

---

it is noted that the "entire Angass [Ngas] tribe . . . deserted their masters and returned . . . [to] the Angass Hills" at the time of the British conquest. Similar reports are scattered throughout the archival documents. See, for example, Lugard's comment in 1906 that returns of freed slaves "do not profess to be a complete record, more especially in the earlier years [when] large numbers were liberated by various military expeditions, of which no record was kept" (ibid.: 408).

quired just before the conquest there had not been sufficient time for masters to take measures to counteract their hostility. Neither slave discipline nor the attractions of acculturation had been brought to bear to break the resistance of slaves, and consequently many slaves deserted.

The early desire to escape from exploitation extended far beyond the rural slave population. Perhaps most striking, and certainly the most revealing of slave dissatisfaction, was the extent to which concubines availed themselves of the opportunities for escape that were presented by the colonial conquest (Lovejoy 1986a, 1988). Concubines, who should have been content with their lot, according to the British mythology about Muslim slavery, left in a steady stream, often fleeing to hill retreats and former homes where they were welcomed with angry relief. Efforts to round up these fugitives were met with armed resistance, despite active colonial intervention on behalf of slave-owners. These concubines demonstrated with their feet that Lugard's picture of an assimilationist, benign slavery was an illusion. Colonial officials had great difficulty understanding their plight; official views held that concubines were similar to — if not identical with — wives and had no right to desert their "husbands." The women thought otherwise, and their exodus dealt one more blow to slavery and forced colonial officials and slave masters alike to reappraise their position on slavery as an institution or to reappraise marital relations. It is perhaps no coincidence that the incidence of purdah increased from this time.

The period of widespread escapes, both among the rural population and concubines, reinforced and gave urgency to the efforts at reform. Murgu presented farm slaves with the possibility of staying in the vicinity of their masters and benefitting from the proximity to commercial centers. They had every reason to expect that they would improve their position as the colonial regime instituted its longer-term plans for economic development. Concubines could not gain from murgu, however reformed, but they could improve their status in the household under the colonial interpretation that concubines and wives were identical. Although their children were free, concubines chafed because they as slaves performed most of the labor around the household. It may be that the spread of female seclusion tended to equalize the relationships among women with respect to their men, just as the possibilities of murgu reduced the distance between rural slaves and free peasants; concubines did not become wives, but some colonial officials were sufficiently impressed to suggest that they did.

Many slaves stayed put, presumably because they did not have any place to go or because they were relatively content with their lot. Nonetheless, most slaves who did not leave soon realized that they could change the terms of their relationships with masters. In an effort to improve their position and status, they struggled to reduce work loads, to increase their share of output, and to secure more autonomy in the social sphere. As Lugard (1906: 149) himself noted in 1905, "It has become a common practice in some districts for slaves to refuse to do any work, and to threaten to run away, unless bribed by presents from their masters, who complain that they have no longer any discipline over their slaves." Lugard's bias is evident in these remarks, but equally clear is the fact that slaves were renegotiating the terms of their servility. The results were that many slaves reduced their labor obligation from five or six days per week to three or four. They also received "presents"— new clothes, more food, kola nuts, tobacco, salt — in connection with weddings, naming ceremonies for children, funerals, and the major Islamic festivals. While the basis of reciprocity shifted in favor of slaves during this period, it was not transformed into a monetary payment for services rendered. Slaves were not becoming wage earners; a large wage-earning class was still many years in the future. Rather, a new form of dependency and servility was in the making, one that ultimately swelled the size of the peasantry and undermined the position of the former slave-owning class.

Equalization with the peasantry invariably lowered the wealth and status of the masters. According to Baba of Karo, the daughter of a plantation owner on the border between Zaria and Kano emirates, the masters had to work their own fields for the first time, although they still had those slaves who had not fled. Owners now found themselves using the short-handled hoes to break the ground like common peasants (Smith 1954). Gone were the days of the master class—those aristocrats, merchants, wealthy farmers, and craftsmen who had owned dozens, even hundreds, of slaves. Slavery continued, but the scale of slaveholding declined dramatically. Baba's family, to use one example, lost many of its slaves at this time. Thereafter, master-slave relations were much better than they had been, no doubt because of the smaller number of slaves, their closer contact, and the greater need to appease slave sentiments.

The Economic Impetus to the End of Slavery

The 15 years after the initial British conquests heralded longer-term attempts by the colonial authorities to alter the relations between slaves and masters, mainly through the major reforms in taxation, land tenure, and currency introduced during this period. These changes largely preceded the opening of the Lagos-Kano railway in 1912 and the boom in peanut exports, at which time the colonial economy of Northern Nigeria became firmly established. By 1912 a vigorous and productive peasantry was in a position to exploit the commercial opportunities presented by the railroad. The railroad allowed the possibility of cheap transport for peanuts, cotton, and whatever other crops could be produced at a price competitive on world markets. In effect, world demand for cash crops reached in via better transport to raise the returns to rural labor (Hogendorn 1978). In Kano Emirate, peanuts were the crop that offered the farmers the advantage; eventually cotton filled a similar role, although on a somewhat reduced scale. In the interim, Zaria cotton supplied the local textile industry, which experienced a temporary boom in response to greater purchasing power earned from peanut sales (Watts 1983: 173–74; Hogendorn 1978: 106).

Neither at the time nor subsequently was any formal analysis undertaken of all these effects of colonial economic policy, working usually through the mechanism of the market, on the institution of slavery. The absence of adequate data, then and now, makes such analysis difficult. But in the longer term, the effects of the various government policies were significant, even crucial, and it is clear that they contributed substantially to the eventual emancipation of slaves.

Taxation and the Slave System

The most significant of the government policies involved developments within the colonial tax system. Indeed tax reform was a major component of the policy to reform slavery, a point fully recognized by Lugard (1906: 86):

Direct taxation . . . , as being the State recognition of the rights and responsibilities of the individual, is the moral charter of independence of a people. Communities, however, who have only recently emerged from such a state of servitude, are not, at first, wholly fit to appreciate those rights and to assume those duties, and they take some time to acquire the sense of responsibility and its obligations.

Lugard showed a clear understanding of the potential effects of tax reform when he noted that "direct taxation is unsuitable to a people who are held in a state of slavery or serfdom, for the responsibility of the individual is then assumed by the slave-owner" (ibid.). In other words, under the caliphate, slaves themselves were exempt from paying most taxes directly. To the extent that taxes were due the state, their masters were responsible. In fact most large slave-owners were fully or partly exempt from taxes, and therefore the burden of state taxation did not fall on the slaves even indirectly. However, large slave-owners were more visible targets for irregular exactions related to defense, famine, and other state emergencies. Under British rule slaves were eventually made subject to taxes; such a drastic change in the basis of tax assessment forced masters to reconsider their relationship with slaves. Masters had to be responsible for these taxes, or they had to allow their slaves the wherewithal to pay them. By levying tax on slaves as well as freemen, Lugard was doing more than providing a "moral charter of independence"; he was increasing the tax base for the colonial state and forcing masters to renegotiate the terms of dependency with their slaves. To avoid a substantial share of tax liability, masters were implicitly encouraged to reduce their slaveholdings, but they could retain income acquired through murgu payments, which were not taxed. Any owner who maintained a large, rural slave establishment on the precolonial pattern, therefore, faced a much steeper tax bill than those who began to emancipate their slaves or who lost slaves through flight.

Tax policy in Northern Nigeria was the product of several divergent processes: the desire to retain precolonial institutions as part of the general policy of indirect rule; efforts by British officials to "reform" and rationalize these precolonial institutions; and attempts by the British government to tinker with the social, economic, and political institutions to obtain more favorable results. The consequences were a complex and layered system of taxation, which fed the precolonial officeholders and financed the new colonial administration. Only when these layers are disaggregated can we observe how changes in policy affected the institution of slavery.

The precolonial tax system of the Sokoto Caliphate was certainly not a unified one; complex differences in types of tax and their incidence existed from emirate to emirate.[4] The complexity of the tax system has, to this day, impeded an understanding of how the colonial changes worked to eliminate plantation slavery, for there was a major explanatory link among all the different early taxes. The precolonial tax regimen, unlike the colonial one, bore lightly on slave establishments. The shift in incentives against holding large numbers of slaves can be traced in each of three major tax levies—the grain tax, the land tax (both of these sometimes collected as a capitation levy), and the special crop taxes, which are considered below in sequence.

4. The best discussion of taxation is the excellent thesis of Garba (1986), which to a great extent corrects the observation of Hill (1977: 50) that "much less was known about variations in pre-colonial taxation systems . . . than Lugard supposed." In addition to Garba, also see Okediji 1972: Ch. 3; Tukur 1979: Ch. 8; Fika 1978: Ch. 5; Hill 1972: 323–25; Hogendorn 1978: Ch. 4; Bello 1982: 32–34; Mahadi, 1982: 456–73. Also see Orr 1911: Ch. 4, "Taxation Problems in 1903–1904": and PP, Memorandum on the taxation of natives 1907; NNA, report, Kano Emirate, 1908; NNA, Palmer 1910.

Zakka (also spelled *zakah, zakat*), a tithe on grain only, was directly rooted in Koranic principles of taxation. Collected on guinea corn (sorghum) and millet, it was paid in kind.[5] In Kano, for example, officials attempted to assess the tax as a percentage of production. In most areas, however, it came to be levied as a fixed sum per village (Lugard 1906: 90; PRO CO, Girouard 1908). Zakka was continued in the early years of colonial rule as a proportional tax on grain, paid in kind. A slave-owner could substantially reduce his own tax payment when murgu payments in cash from slaves ransoming themselves could be substituted for grain.

The land tax, *kudin* (or *kurdin) kasa,* had a variety of forms before the colonial officials made serious attempts to reconstruct it shortly preceding the First World War. Lugard (1906: 90) believed kudin kasa was a levy on the assessed value of arable land, generally from six pence to one shilling per acre. Polly Hill (1977: 50) has noted how misleading this statement is, since there was little indigenous attempt to measure area accurately, and application of this tax varied substantially (Hogendorn 1978: 63). "The usual practice," according to Adamu Fika (1978: 39), was for kudin kasa "to be levied as a poll tax on household heads, probably to avoid a tedious enumeration of all farmsteads."[6] Significantly for our case, fief-holders and titled officials were exempt from paying kudin kasa (Tukur 1979: 200; Okediji 1972: 107; Bello 1982: 104 fn.; Mahadi 1982: 464). Their slave estates were thus for the most part not touched by this levy. Many nonnoble plantation owners also held their estates under a system of tenure that exempted them from paying kudin kasa. This tax was not even collected in Sokoto and Gwandu emirates, the twin capitals of the caliphate, which relied on zakka and tributary payments from their subordinate emirates before the British arrival. It is only with colonial rule that this tax was extended to these emirates and to all land of fief-holders, titled officials, and prosperous commoners that had previously been exempted (Tukur 1979: 532–33, 562–639).

With colonial rule, kudin kasa became an important element in the decision-making by slave-owners. The flat-rate aspect of this tax in the late precolonial period (4,000 cowries per farm in some places) gave way to some variability in the early colonial years, with landowners paying different amounts according to the size and productivity of their holdings (Hill 1977: 50). The result was that both large landholdings and large

---

5. Hill 1977: 51–52; Watts 1983: 257–58; Hogendorn 1978: 63, 65; Fika 1978: 39; Lugard 1906: 89. Slaves using their "free time" to grow grain for their own personal use were responsible for tax payments, at least in Kano (see Lugard 1906: 300).

6. Also see Tukur 1979: 552, citing C. L. Temple.

slave establishments were increasingly caught in the taxman's net (Fika 1978: 200–201).

The British administration changed the land tax policy after 1906. Where kudin kasa continued to be collected (alternatives were imposed in some areas — see below), it increasingly became a tax on assessed value of landholdings and household size. This trend was strong between 1906 and 1911, after which kudin kasa tended to revert to a type of poll tax (Tukur 1979: 564–69). Though in theory it could have been charged on each adult male, "in practice," according to Tukur (1979: 573–74), "it was only the householder that was held responsible for payment by his slaves." Females were not originally subject to kudin kasa, but by 1910 they too were being assessed, at least in some emirates (ibid.: 575; also see NNA, Palmer, Land Tenure).

These developments were important, because it is generally believed that, of the main types of taxation in the Sokoto Caliphate, kudin kasa yielded the greatest amount of revenue. In a detailed accounting of Kano's revenue in 1908–1909 (the only early year for which this is available), Resident C. L. Temple calculated that, excluding the tax on cattle (*jangali*), about 44 percent of revenue came from kudin kasa, 28 percent from the zakka tithe, and 26 percent from the special crop taxes, to be considered below (Hogendorn 1978: 63). Rates were raised very generally and sometimes sharply in the first years of the colonial period (six pence per adult male was a common initial figure; by 1907 rates were as high as three shillings in some emirates) (Tukur 1979: 569; also see NNA, Gepp 1910). With personal income very low, these rates could represent a very significant proportion of total earnings; in Katsina, for example, kudin kasa "frequently amounted to 20% or more of net returns" (Watts 1983: 261).

The overall implication of the land tax for an owner of slaves was clear enough: income from those working the land would be taxed, while income from manumission payments such as murgu would not.

The last of the main taxes to affect rural slavery were the special crop taxes, *kudin shuka* and *kudin rafi*. Both stemmed from the idea of zakka, the tithe on grain, but were applied to crops more easily assessed in the field than after harvest (Fika 1978: 39). Kudin rafi was the name applied to the tax on crops grown in irrigated (*fadama*) plots; the name kudin shuka was used when the crops were not irrigated. The two were levied in Zaria on sugar cane, onions, cassava, and tobacco; in Kano on these plus rice, wheat, indigo (according to Lugard and Okediji but denied by Hill), yams and cocoyams, sweet potatoes, peanuts, and beans. Sometimes the levy was by plot, sometimes by furrow length (Watts 1983: 258). The slave-owner whose slaves produced these crops was of course taxed proportionately to the number of plots or furrows. Special crop taxes were of considerable importance in Kano and Zaria emirates, but generated fewer revenues in other areas (Okediji 1972: 94; Hill 1977: 50–51; Hogendorn 1978: 63, 65; Lugard 1906: 91).

One colonial reform, if fully adopted, did have the potential to capture a portion of cash income and would have led to taxation of murgu payments. Under Lugard, the Land Revenue Proclamation of 1904 and the native Revenue Proclamation of 1906 attempted to institute a "lumpsum" system. The 1904 plan was to replace all agricultural taxes with a single levy, a general tax of 10 percent of the annual value of production, derived or derivable according to the average standard of land use in the neighborhood (Lugard 1906: 110–11; Hogendorn 1978: 63–64; Okediji 1972: 96). The 1906 amendment widened the tax base to include nonfarm revenues (also to be taxed at 10 percent). The provincial residents were to do the assessing on a village basis, with village heads responsible for apportioning the exact amount of tax among the local residents on the basis of ability to pay. Manpower was so limited that assessment of this rough form of income tax virtually failed in Kano and Zaria.[7] Though the general tax was largely unsuccessful, it should be noted that by 1904 slave-owners were already on notice that their tax liability might in the future rise very sharply, since income from slaves—both direct and indirect—would be subject to the lump-sum assessment. Lugard himself fully appreciated that a direct tax of this sort would have the effect of reducing the profitability of slaveholding (Swindell 1984: 15; Lugard 1906: 86).

Sir Percy Girouard, who succeeded Lugard as high commissioner in 1907, tried to change the system (which by then had been consolidated as a tax on the produce of land) to a land rent to be assessed on individuals (Okediji 1972: 101).[8] Girouard's reform proved very difficult to implement, however, because limited manpower made it impossible to survey and map the taxable lands and assess them adequately (Okediji 1972: 104; Shenton 1981: 100–101; Tukur 1979: 663–64). Nonetheless, the effect on slavery was similar to that of Lugard's tax policies. Since a land tax could not capture cash income any more than a produce tax could, colonial tax policy continued to hit large estates but not cash payments from murgu.[9]

7. The income tax aspect is clearly noticed by Swindell (1984: 13). Also see Hill 1972: 324; Fika 1978: 118; Hogendorn 1978: 64; Okediji 1972: 97–100; Shenton 1981: 78.

8. See Shenton 1981: Ch. 3 for the unlikely Burmese antecedent. Girouard's reforms, inspired by the American economist Henry George, were said to resemble the tax policy concurrently employed in parts of Burma.

9. This was stated vividly in testimony by C. L. Temple before the Northern Nigeria

The confusing quality of colonial tax policy was never more apparent than in this effort to introduce a single land tax. For the most part, it had to be scaled back to a simple attempt to measure roughly the size of individual farms and plots. This, called *taki* assessment (after taki, meaning "pacing"), was introduced from 1909 in parts of Kano and Katsina and from 1913 in Sokoto and Gwandu (Hill 1977: 49, 53; Hill 1972: 312; Hogendorn 1978: 65).

Where the new land tax was adopted, zakka and kudin kasa were scrapped, and it was hoped that the innovation could be transferred rapidly to all other emirates. This proved a slow and difficult process, however (Hill 1977: 53).[10] Taki assessment seems very generally to have raised the level of taxes, especially in low-tax Sokoto and Gwandu, but also in high-tax Katsina and Kano.[11] The measure thereby increased the incentive to earn income in nontaxed forms, and further undermined the large landholdings which were central to the slave economy (Okediji 1972: 107). It also had the incidental effect of institutionalizing a flat-rate system, so that increments to farm production accrued to the farmer and not to the tax collector. From the standpoint of slaves, income for murgu payments could still be acquired; there was no disincentive to participate as the colonial economy developed.

All these reforms were slowly and unevenly implemented, causing considerable fiscal confusion but with an underlying common result for slavery. A visitor to Northern Nigeria just before the First World War would have found some lump-sum assessment of villages and farms, some flat-rate assessment, some taki assessment based on land area, and considerable survival of the old traditional taxes (Hill 1972: 324–25; Shenton and Freund 1978: 14). In general, however, the incidence of all these taxes was heavy on land and virtually nil on rural cash income unassociated with production. The statements of colonial officials that their tax reforms would serve to break up the slave estates were therefore correct.

Lands Committee in June 1908: Mr. Wedgewood asked, "On that point, would it not rather tend to be the collection of rent under the name of a tax, and be simply no income tax whatever. . . ?" Answer: "—Yes." (PP, Northern Nigeria Lands Committee 1910).

10. Once adopted, taki assessment lasted longer than the older policies. It remained the basis of taxation in Kano until 1926 (Fika 1978: 183).

11. Swindell 1984: 14; Tibenderana 1974; Watts 1983: 260, 279–80; Hogendorn 1978: 65–66. Any concept of "low tax" does not take into account the unknown degree of corruption and extortionary ad hoc collections by the *jakada* (fief-holders' agents) and other indigenous officials in charge of the precolonial and early colonial collections. Nor, more important, does it consider that a system of slave labor is of course tantamount to a confiscatory tax by the the owners of the slaves. Girouard (PRO CO, 1908: 2) recognized this when he wrote that the "original taxes of a primitive nation are those of service and slavery."

From tax payments in cowries and in kind, there was a rapid transition to taxes paid in colonial coin. The authorities very early applied pressure to have all taxes paid in silver coin, a major reason being that the need to acquire the coins would lead farmers to produce crops for export. By 1911, actually much sooner than the authorities expected, the colonial government's share of all taxes in Kano was indeed being paid in coin (Hogendorn 1978: 66; also see Hogendorn and Johnson 1986: Ch. 10). There being as yet no railway on which to ship export crops, the coins at this time were coming to Northern Nigeria through long-distance trade with more southerly areas and through the large government payroll. The coins could be acquired for goods and cowries from the currency sellers at village and town markets.

A year later, on 1 April 1912, the new railway to the south was opened for traffic, and within a few months the improved transport plus favorable European prices brought about a thoroughly unexpected "peanut revolution" in areas within economic reach of the rail line. To a lesser extent, there was an increase in cotton shipments (which had been the main economic reason behind British support for the rail link) from the cotton areas, especially in Zaria Emirate (Hogendorn 1978: Ch. 6). From October 1912, a minimum of £70,000 (ca. U.S. $350,000), all in silver (from sales of over 10,000 tons of nuts), was injected into the Northern Nigerian economy by the first year's proceeds from peanuts alone. Though this may seem "peanuts" to modern ears, consider that even in relatively well-off Kano Emirate enough food for a person's daily subsistence could be purchased in the market for less than one-half penny (Hogendorn 1978: 97–100).[12] There were, of course, multiplier effects as this new income generated additional spending — most obvious in the cotton areas, where the increased demand for locally produced cotton garments undermined the export of raw fiber, to the discomfiture of the British Cotton Growing Association that had lobbied hard and long for the railway. There was also increased demand for grain from areas beyond the reach of rail transport to feed the peanut and cotton regions.

The economic boom had several effects on slavery. With taxes now payable in coin, cash-crop exporting was an easy way to acquire the wherewithal;[13] the new opportunities for earning cash, due in the first instance to the exports but also to the resulting multiplier effects, made it more feasible for slaves to ransom themselves; taxes rapidly increased

12. There may have been as many as 2 million people in Kano Province (Hogendorn 1978: 5).

13. According to Shenton and Lennihan (1981), the requirement of tax payments in coin in turn "limited the avenues of production through which the tax could be met."

as a result of the boom, adding to the pressure to break up the slave estates. The tax increase in the Kano region, where the boom was centered, was particularly sharp; close to the city, per-acre rates rose on some farms from about one shilling and seven pence to four shillings between 1913 and 1914 (Hogendorn 1978: 107).

The degree to which slaves ransoming themselves participated in the cash-crop boom is largely unknown; though most modern authorities believe it to have been considerable, the evidence is mostly circumstantial.[14] But where slaves under self-ransom did not benefit directly in the boom, they could do so indirectly, even in areas far removed from actual peanut and cotton production. A slave-labor force is largely immobilized, whereas laborers paying murgu could take advantage of new opportunities for employment in trade, transport, and dry-season irrigated farming, all of which were stimulated by the boom. Dry-season migrant labor increasingly became a way of earning murgu: *cin rani* ("eating up the dry season") migration included many former slaves, especially in Sokoto (Swindell 1984: 11, 12, 16). To the extent that peanuts and cotton were produced at the expense of foodstuffs, there was also an increased demand for grain, which allowed farmers who did not produce for export to share in the boom. Expanded opportunities for market trade in goods of all kinds were another alternative.

Land Tenure and the Slave System

British policies towards land tenure also affected the fate of slaves. The British claimed ownership of land on the basis of the conquest, just as, it has been argued, the caliphate aristocracy had done during the *jihad*. Existing practices of tenure were often ignored in theory, although not in fact. Before the British conquest, land was held under a variety of tenures.[15] Some land was attached to offices, whether slave or free, and changed hands when new officials were appointed. These lands could not be bought or sold. Other land was granted to individuals, including aristocrats, merchants, craftsmen, livestock herders, or other freemen with skills and a substantial nonagricultural income, upon application to the emir. These lands could be bought and sold and were usually ex-

14. Fika (1978: 210) states, "It is likely that they [freed slaves] played a large role in the expansion of groundnut cultivation."
15. This summary does not include common lands, including cattle trails, and religious lands (*waaf*). A full examination of precolonial land tenure cannot be attempted here, but see Bello 1982: 27–29; Mahadi 1982: 456–63; NNA, Palmer, Land Tenure; NNA, Stanley 1908; NNA, Dupigny 1909; NNA, Gepp 1911; PRO CO, Girouard 1908; PP, Northern Nigeria Lands Committee 1910.

empt from taxation or paid reduced rates, at least in Kano, except for the grain tithe. The land of non-Muslim, protected peoples, such as the Maguzawa, fell into a third category. Ownership was communal, dependent upon payment of a special tax (*jizya*). This land could not be alienated. Finally, individual smallholders received usufructuary rights to land upon application to the headmen of villages where they wanted to farm, and upon payment of a fee they were given access to any land that was not being used or not otherwise claimed. These lands were subject to the several taxes that have been described above. The most common holding was relatively small. Individuals often had more than one farm, sometimes located in different areas or villages. Technically, these lands belonged to the fief-holders as representatives of the emir, but they were inherited and could be bought and sold. The kudin kasa tax was a rent, a portion of which was kept by the fief-holder or his agents (jakada).

Colonial policies towards land tenure encouraged, to some degree, land acquisition by former slaves and slaves who were acquiring their freedom through murgu, even though fugitives were restrained from gaining access to land. Those slaves and former slaves who chose to stay close to their masters established new relationships of dependency, which included access to land, usually without title to that land. In contrast, before the colonial period, slaves had worked their masters' land, and on plantations they had their own plots (*gayauna*) to which they had usufructuary rights. Under colonialism, slaves acquired more land, first on the plantations themselves and then from village headmen, often in the same vicinity. Thus, slaves obtained land and participated directly in agricultural expansion, because slave-owners, anxious to reduce their tax liability, had an incentive to make land available to ex-slaves and to those slaves buying their freedom. Land-tenure policy tended to reinforce the effects of tax reform and the peanut boom on the expansion of the peasantry.

The land question was much studied by the Northern Nigeria Lands Committee, which made its recommendations in 1910.[16] The committee decided to recognize usufruct only, with the ownership of all land vested in the colonial state. Private property, particularly the estates of the merchants and aristocracy, were thereby ignored, which provided further incentive for large slaveholders to enter into murgu arrangements with their slaves. Often grants of land to slaves were accompanied by annual

16. See the discussion of CD. 5102 (*Reports of Committees*), Cd. 5103 (*Minutes of Evidence*), and the consequences of the Lands Committee in Lennihan 1983; Shenton 1981; and Watts 1983.

gifts that amounted to a rent or mortgage payment, and incidentally provided further nontaxable income and consolidated relationships of dependency. The large landholder had several incentives to acquiesce in these developments. What was he to do otherwise with the slave-labor force declining in numbers through flight, self-purchase, and the closure of the slave market? He found it impossible to work the land himself, even given a large family, and the market for wage labor in the all-important wet season was as yet poorly developed. Selling off plots, if not impossible, was discouraged by the Lands Committee ordinances. The incentives pointed to some accommodation with the existing slaves; murgu payments and gifts yielded an income, while usufruct of land fell easily and naturally to the former slaves.

By assuming title to land the administration discouraged slaves from fleeing the estates. Lugard (1906: 142–43) instructed residents in 1906

not [to] permit . . . fugitive farm slaves to occupy land to which they have no title, nor to build new villages at will. . . . Residents will, therefore, inform each other either of slaves fugitive from their own, or arriving from a neighboring, Province; and if, after investigation . . . it transpires that there was no sufficient cause for their running away, and that they have not redeemed themselves, the Resident of the Province in which they desire to take up land may decline to grant permission. It will, moreover, be made known that everyone who takes up new land, without having first obtained the consent of the Resident, will be liable to eviction, and that Chiefs giving land to fugitive slaves will lay themselves open to censure. The latter should, therefore, report all cases of arrival of fugitive slaves to the Resident.

Many slaves or serfs will, unknown to Residents, attach themselves to existing villages, but such cases will be dealt with in the same way as new communities, and Chiefs will be forbidden to accept these immigrants, and to grant them land to farm, without the assent of the Resident.

It is not possible to know exactly how often slaves managed to evade these official restrictions. Certainly there was unused land available, even in areas suitable for peanuts and in reach of the railway. Where population pressure was light, land was kept fallow longer than necessary to restore fertility, and was conceivably available to newcomers. Between Katsina and Kano even tracts of uncultivated bush land remained, partly because of warfare and raids in the late nineteenth century (Hogendorn 1978: 105). As early as 1908, people were moving into these areas, as Girouard noted in his annual report: immigrants came from French territory, while other people moved from Kano into southern Katsina, took up land between Katsina and Zamfara, pushed southeastward towards

Ningi, or established new settlements in Katagum.[17] Lugard imposed restrictions to stop slaves from entering unused areas, but there was no legal bar against a stranger from one part of an emirate taking up unused land in some other village if he could support himself until the harvest came in.[18] Fugitives did not usually have such resources, but slaves paying murgu did. Furthermore, slaves who were buying their freedom were known to local officials and therefore had patrons — usually their masters — to speak on their behalf if necessary.

But any such mass movement faced serious impediments. The newcomer had to obtain the consent of the village head and elders (just as a local villager would). Lugard's instructions make patently obvious the official disapproval of making land available to fugitive slaves. He went further, decreeing that the residents or provincial courts, and not the native courts, were to deal with cases involving fugitive slaves taking up wasteland. He went further yet in stating that the "right of disposing of waste lands is one which, in practice, the Government only rarely exercises, as in the case of denying permission to settle to Freed Slaves" (Lugard 1906: 188, 252). The nuance of this last statement is possibly that even slaves making murgu payments might find a hostile reception in attempting to carve out a new farm far away from their old villages, but short-distance migration was probably encouraged.

There is, however, little doubt that hostility greeted fugitives. In a discussion of the plight of the runaway, Walter Miller, head of the Church Missionary Society at Zaria, wrote in 1908:

in no province would anyone give him any land or a farm. . . . Moreover in this province as you know, according to the by-law of Captain Orr's no man is allowed, under heavy penalties, to let runaway slaves stay in his house, give him food or in any way help him, so that it would be impossible for this man anywhere to get even lodging, much less a farm in this province.[19]

The general impression is that the administration made it as difficult as possible for fugitive slaves to acquire suitable land for farming, and slaves engaged in self-ransom were encouraged to farm their masters' land. It was much more practicable to continue farming where one al-

17. *Annual Report, Northern Nigeria* 1907–1908: 613, 625. Also see NNA, Dupigny 1909.

18. Lennihan (1982: 136 fn.) states that the colonial regime did not impose measures against "vagrants." Though Lennihan's claim is technically correct the restrictions aimed at fugitives by the native courts and approved by the British authorities were strong enough to be tantamount to much the same thing.

19. Quoted by Lennihan (1983: 85) and discussed by her (1982: 134).

ready was, making arrangements with the erstwhile slave-owner, who in any case had great difficulty in working all his land himself. Thus, tenure problems discouraged running away but did not involve serious restraints for slaves willing to arrive at some local accommodation with owners.

By 1914 slavery had changed dramatically in the Hausa emirates of Northern Nigeria. Colonial policies on taxation, land, and transportation, all promoted the consolidation of a peasantry engaged in export production. The pressures brought to bear by the slaves themselves — either through flight or negotiation over the terms of dependence — reinforced this trend. Consequently the slave regime of the Sokoto Caliphate was dismantled piecemeal without the general emancipation of slaves. The serious drought of 1913–1914 that temporarily interrupted the boom in the peanut trade further undermined the old relationships. Famine conditions demonstrated tragically to masters and slaves alike that old obligations no longer mattered, so that when prosperous times returned and peanut exports rose to astronomical heights, small-scale production was the order of the day. Slavery continued in modified form; relations of dependency that derived from slavery governed the interactions of large sections of the rural population. Emancipation through the courts continued to be common for another decade, and concubinage remained a viable institution, although its scale was greatly reduced. These aspects of the old order would remain for many decades to come, but the economic basis of a society that had once depended upon slave labor had changed for good.

REFERENCES

Archival sources

NNA: Nigerian National Archives, Kaduna.
Dupigny, assessing report on Sarkin Dawaki Tsakkar Gidda's district, Kano Province, 1909. SNP 7/10 5570/1909.
Gepp, N. M. report on Dan Makoyo's subdistrict. Encl. in H. R. Palmer, report for Kano Province for the year ending 31 December 1910. SNP 15/1 Acc. 167.
Gepp, N. M., assessing report on Dan Isa's subdistrict, Kano Province, 1911. SNP 7/12 1035/1911.
Palmer, H. R., Land Tenure in the Hausa States. SNP 15/1 Acc. 369.
Palmer, H. R., report for Kano Province for the year ending 31 December 1910. SNP 15/1 Acc. 167.
Pembleton, E. S., secretary, northern provinces, "Slavery — Report of the

Advisory Committee, League of Nations," 17 October 1936, Sokprof 3/1 C.33.

Report, Kano Emirate, 1908. SNP 6/4 C.111/1908.

Stanley, report #36 on Sokoto Province for the half year ending 30 June 1908. Sokprof 2/9 985/1908.

PRO CO: Colonial Office Confidential Print, Public Record Office, London.

Girouard, E. P. C., Land Tenure and Land Revenue Assessment, Memo. No. 25, 1908. C.O. African (W) Confidential Print 906.

Other sources

Adeleye, R. A. 1971. *Power and diplomacy in Northern Nigeria, 1804–1906. The Sokoto Caliphate and its enemies.* New York: Humanities Press.

Annual Reports, Northern Nigeria, 1901; 1902; 1903; 1905–1906; 1907–1908.

Bello, S. 1982. State and economy in Kano, 1894–1960. Ph.D. thesis, Ahmadu Bello University, Zaria.

Christelow, A. 1985. Slavery in Kano. *African Economic History* 14: 57–74.

Cole, C. W. 1949. *Report on land tenure, Zaria Province.* Kaduna: Government Printer.

Fika, A. M. 1978. *The Kano civil war and British over-rule.* Ibadan: Oxford University Press.

Garba, T. 1986. Taxation in some Hausa emirates, C. 1860–1939. Ph.D. thesis, University of Birmingham.

Hill, P. 1972. *Rural Hausa: a village and a setting.* Cambridge: Cambridge University Press.

Hill, P. 1976. From slavery to freedom: the case of farm-slavery in Nigerian Hausaland. *Comparative Studies in Society and History* 18 (3): 395–426.

Hill, P. 1977. *Population, prosperity and poverty: rural Kano 1900 and 1970.* Cambridge: Cambridge University Press.

Hogendorn, J. S. 1977. The economics of slave use on two "plantations" in the Zaria Emirate of the Sokoto Caliphate. *International Journal of African Historical Studies* 10 (3): 369–83.

Hogendorn, J. S. 1978. *Nigerian groundnut exports. Origins and early development.* Zaria: Ahmadu Bello University Press, and Ibadan, Nigeria: Oxford University Press.

Hogendorn, J. S. 1980. Slave acquisition and delivery in precolonial Hausaland. In *West African culture dynamics: archaeological and historical perspectives,* ed. R. Dumett and B. K. Schwartz, 477–93. The Hague: Mouton.

Hogendorn, J. S., and M. Johnson. 1986. *The shell money of the slave trade.* Cambridge: Cambridge University Press.

Lennihan, L. 1982. Rights in men and rights in land: slavery, labor and smallholder agriculture in Northern Nigeria. *Slavery and Abolition* 3 (2): 111–39.

Lennihan, L. 1983. The origins and development of agricultural wage labor in Northern Nigeria: 1886–1980. Ph.D. dissertation, Columbia University, New York.

Lovejoy, P. E. 1978. Plantations in the economy of the Sokoto Caliphate. *Journal of African History* 19 (3): 341–68.

Lovejoy, P. E. 1983. *Transformations in slavery. A history of slavery in Africa.* Cambridge: Cambridge University Press.

Lovejoy, P. E. 1986a. Fugitive slaves: resistance to slavery in the Sokoto Caliphate. In *"In resistance": studies in African, Afro-American and Caribbean history*, ed. G. Okihiro, 71–95. Amherst: University of Massachusetts Press.

Lovejoy, P. E. 1986b. Problems of slave control in the Sokoto Caliphate. In *Africans in bondage, Studies in slavery and the slave trade*, ed. P. E. Lovejoy. Madison: African Studies Program.

Lovejoy, P. E. 1988. Concubinage and the status of women slaves in early colonial Northern Nigeria. *Journal of African History*.

Lugard, F. 1906. *Instructions to political and other officers, on subjects chiefly political and administrative.* London: Waterlow.

Lugard, F. 1970. *Political memoranda: revisions of instructions to political officers on subjects chiefly political and administrative.* Ed. A. H. M. Kirk-Greene. 3d ed. London: Cass.

Mahadi, A. 1982. The state and the economy: the Sarauta system and its roles in shaping the society and economy of Kano with particular reference to the eighteenth and nineteenth centuries. Ph.D. thesis, Ahmadu Bello University, Zaria.

Mason, M. 1970. The Nupe Kingdom in the nineteenth century: a political history. Ph.D. thesis, University of Birmingham.

Miers, S. 1975. *Britain and the ending of the slave trade.* New York: Africana.

Mohammed, A. S. 1983. A social interpretation of the Satiru revolt of c. 1894–1906 in Sokoto Province. M.S. thesis, Ahmadu Bello University, Zaria.

Okediji, F. 1972. An economic history of Hausa-Fulani Emirates of Northern Nigeria: 1900–1939. Ph.D. dissertation, Indiana University, Bloomington.

Orr, C. 1911. *The making of Northern Nigeria.* London.

PP: *Parliamentary Papers*, Great Britain.
Memorandum on the taxation of natives in Northern Nigeria, 1907. [Cd. 3309].
Northern Nigeria Lands Committee, 1910. *Minutes of Evidence*, (1910), [Cd. 5103], 78.

Roberts, R., and M. Klein. 1981. The Banamba slave exodus of 1905 and the decline of slavery in the western Sudan. *Journal of African History* 21 (3): 375–94.

Rowling, C. W. 1949. *Report on land tenure, Kano Province*, Kaduna: Government Printer.

Shenton, R. W. 1981. Studies in the development of capitalism in Northern Nigeria. Ph.D. thesis, University of Toronto.

Shenton, R. W., and B. Freund. 1978. The incorporation of Northern Nigeria into the world capitalist economy. *Review of African Political Economy* 13: 8–20.

Shenton, R. W., and L. Lennihan. 1981. Capital and class: peasant differentiation in Northern Nigeria. *Journal of Peasant Studies* 9 (1): 47–70.

Smith, M., ed. 1954. *Baba of Karo. A woman of the Moslem Hausa.* London: Faber and Faber.

Swindell, K. 1984. Farmers, traders, and laborers: dry season migration from north-west Nigeria, 1900–33. *Africa* 54 (1): 3–19.

Tibenderana, P. 1974. The administration of Sokoto, Gwandu, and Argungu emirates under British rule, 1900–1946. Ph.D. thesis, University of Ibadan.

Tukur, M. M. 1979. The imposition of British colonial domination on the Sokoto Caliphate, Borno and neighbouring states, 1897–1914. Ph.D. thesis, Ahmadu Bello University, Zaria.

Ubah, C. N. 1973. Administration of Kano Emirate under the British, 1900–1930. Ph.D. thesis, University of Ibadan.

Watts, M. 1983. *Silent violence. Food, famine and peasantry in Northern Nigeria.* Berkeley: University of California Press.

Yunusa, Y. 1976. Slavery in 19th century Kano. B.A. thesis, Department of History, Ahmadu Bello University, Zaria.

14 *Linda M. Heywood*

Slavery and Forced Labor in the Changing Political Economy of Central Angola, 1850–1949

This chapter deals with slavery and its transformation in the central highlands of Angola from the 1850s to the 1940s. It explores the connections between African slavery and related institutions of dependency in the highlands and Portuguese forced-labor policies.[1] At the beginning of this period, slavery and pawnship among the Ovimbundu, the principal inhabitants of the central highlands, were commonplace and expanding along with Ovimbundu commercial enterprise. The demand for labor on the Portuguese islands of São Tomé and Príncipe and the economic reorientation in the interior kept up the demand for a steady supply of slaves. The demand continued after the Portuguese conquest of the highlands, which began in 1890. In the early colonial period, indigenous slavery dovetailed with and supported Portuguese forced-labor recruitment, designed to supply the expanding European economy in Angola and on the islands at the expense of the indigenous economy. By the 1940s, the Portuguese, by the imposition of high taxes, compulsory wage labor, and price regulation, had gained virtually complete control over labor. Slavery and pawnship were still practiced in the villages and continued to

1. There has been much debate about the distinction between slavery and forced labor. Many of the authors writing in the late nineteenth and early twentieth centuries did not make a clear distinction between the two systems; and this has carried over into more

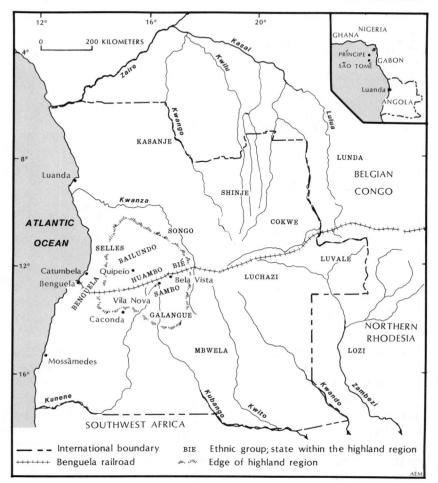

Map 14. Central Angola

support the Portuguese system, but master and slave alike were subject
to forced labor. The Ovimbundu as a whole had become impoverished
workers in the Portuguese sector of the economy.

---

modern academic studies of the issue (see, for instance, Duffy 1959, 1967) and into the
radical critiques of colonialism in general and Portuguese colonialism in particular during
the 1960s and early 1970s (see, for instance, Davidson 1955, 1972).

Slavery in Central Angola: Nineteenth Century

Commerce between the Ovimbundu of the central highlands and the Portuguese began in the early sixteenth century, and intensified after the founding of Portuguese ports and colonies at Luanda and Benguela in the later part of that century. Until the late eighteenth century the Portuguese colony and the highland states both raided each other and traded with each other regularly. However, by the beginning of the nineteenth century the relationship was based mainly on the acquisition and sale of slaves.

The gradual abolition of the south Atlantic slave trade began in 1810 and for the most part was completed by 1852 (Duffy 1967: 6–39). Up to this period the Ovimbundu had been the main agents in long-distance trade, and had provided the bulk of the slaves from southern Angola (Miller 1983: 151–59). The Ovimbundu states of Bailundo (in Umbundu: Mbailundu) and Bié (Viye) hosted *feiras* ("markets") to which Portuguese merchants or their agents from the coast came mainly to purchase slaves. This slave trade provided luxury goods for the Ovimbundu dominant groups (rulers and their immediate dependents) who offered their slaves in these feiras. Ovimbundu rulers organized their own slave caravans (*macas*), destined for both the coastal and interior markets. Caravans provided employment and entrepreneurial opportunities for many Ovimbundu, since they were often composed of as many as 5,000 people. By the 1830s, the highland economy relied on the imports bought in exchange for slaves: imported cloth was not only the main item of dress but also the principal currency (Heywood 1984: 75). Thus, closing of the feira of Bié was so resented that in 1843 some Ovimbundu physically attacked the Portuguese merchants and their families resident in the feira. The ruler of Bié explained to a Portuguese diplomat that this violence was occasioned by the anticipated and actual loss of revenue from the ending of the Atlantic slave trade (Graça 1890: 397–98).

The end of the overseas trade created conditions for the proliferation of slavery, which was already widespread, in the highlands. Reports from the 1850s noted the predominance of slaves in the Ovimbundu population (Magyar 1859: 287–90). By the 1870s even ordinary Ovimbundu owned slaves. The Ovimbundu largely monopolized the new commodity trade in gum copal, ivory, wax, and later rubber, which sprang up between the coastal ports of Benguela and Catumbela and in the interior markets beyond the central highlands as the Atlantic slave trade declined. Thus, they had money to buy the slaves that the contraction of the export market made more readily and cheaply available on the internal market.

Ovimbundu slave caravans, actively operating in Lunda, Luba, and Lozi country as well as in southeastern Angola, supplied slaves to these new buyers in the highlands and to peoples in other parts of central Africa. Many of these caravans were operated by ordinary Ovimbundu, who established close economic ties with rulers beyond the highlands. This expanded slave-trading initiated new commercial links between the highlands and the coast, and the trade in these new commodities gave many Ovimbundu caravans the opportunity to capture and buy slaves from the areas beyond the highlands.

The Ovimbundu also occasionally acquired fellow Ovimbundu as slaves by kidnapping, purchase, or raids — practices which had existed prior to the abolition of the Atlantic slave trade (ABC, W. E. Fay 1886). Many were also acquired as a result of debts.[2] Reports detail numerous instances of indebtedness which were settled by the payment of a slave or by pawning wives, nephews, or nieces (ABC, A. E. Fay 1889). Theoretically, pawns were transferred to creditors only until the debt was repaid, but in practice, the distinction between slavery and pawnship hardly mattered, for pawns were often sold as ordinary slaves. In addition, slaves were always available through judicial proceedings, which often resulted in the assessment of fines, payable in slaves, especially in cases of witchcraft (Magyar 1859: 286–87, 291–92; Silva Porto 1942: 95–96). Despite the occasional enslavement of Ovimbundu, most slaves were foreign born, and they were generally despised and treated worse than Ovimbundu slaves.

Most slaves worked the land and provided domestic services including drawing water, collecting firewood, and the like (CCFMS, Currie 1896: 3). If the master was a trader, slaves accompanied him on caravan trips and were often sent out on their own to trade on his behalf (Heywood 1984: 145–89). Individuals with large slaveholdings established villages of their slave dependents, and converted the wealth acquired from commerce into titles, thus gaining a permanent place in the political structure of their respective states.

Portuguese and foreign merchants in the highlands also had large slaveholdings. Silva Porto and Lázló Magyar, for example, possessed several slave villages, and they regularly equipped caravans, made up almost totally of slaves, which were sent into the interior to trade (ibid.: 120–22). In 1852 Magyar travelled with his own caravans, which included slave elephant hunters (Kun 1960–1964). In the 1870s and early 1880s

2. The 1920s oral testimony collected by the black American missionary C. McDowell recalled a variety of terms referring to indebtedness and the insecurity of the times which resulted in enslavement (ABC, MacDowell 1925). Similar evidence was recorded in the 1940s and 1950s supporting the notion that there was widespread slavery (Childs 1969: 30, 42, 131).

Silva Porto sent caravans under Ovimbundu management to trade in slaves; he sometimes accompanied them as far away as Lunda (Silva Porto 1885).

In 1869 the Portuguese abolished slavery in the coastal towns under their control. There, slaves became *libertos* ("freedmen") subject to certain restrictions until 1878, when they were completely freed and called *pretos livres* ("free blacks"). Whatever the significance of these new terms and legal changes, many of those acquired as slaves by the Ovimbundu and Portuguese in the areas outside Portuguese control were taken to the Portuguese coastal market towns of Benguela and Catumbela, where there was a demand for their labor. As late as 1883, the American consul general noted: "At the southern ports of Benguela and Catumbella . . . large caravans of two and three thousand negroes are constantly arriving from the interior. . . . [They] always find a ready market with brisk competition" (NAUS, consul general 1883). Some were used as domestic servants in the towns, but the majority of them were sent on as theoretically free "contract laborers" (*contractados*) to the islands of São Tomé and Príncipe, even though the method of their recruitment was in no way voluntary.

These two offshore islands were emerging as major producers of cocoa (financed by British capital) and increasingly needed labor to work the estates of the local landowners, who pressed the Portuguese government to provide them with cheap labor. This could be supplied only by impressing the contract workers recruited from the slaves and former slaves (now libertos or pretos livres) available in the coastal markets of Angola. Thus, although Africans were no longer being transported to the Americas as slaves, they were still subject to a more-or-less involuntary migration to the islands in the Gulf of Guinea (Duffy 1967: 27–39).

Portuguese Conquest and the Transformation of Slavery, 1890–1910

The Portuguese had no direct political authority over the highland states before 1890, but they did have a fairly long tradition of indirect influence through the system of "vassalage," which had been applied since the late sixteenth century in various regions bordering areas under their direct control (Heintze 1980). The vassalage system, designed largely to control Portuguese commerce, was introduced in the highlands during the late eighteenth century as a result of some military campaigns. A feira for Portuguese merchants was established in each vassal state under an official (*capitão mor*) nominated by the Portuguese government and drawn from the resident Portuguese community. Although this official had no power to influence the political affairs of the African rulers of the principal Ovimbundu states, Bailundo and Bié, he did have an indirect impact on their economic policies. However, this weak influence was greatly enhanced between 1890 and 1910, when the Portuguese conquered central Angola and established direct Portuguese administrative control. Indigenous rulers now lost most of their political power and authority, and surrendered a substantial portion of their economic autonomy (Heywood 1984: 279–82).

During the course of this conquest a major source of friction between Portuguese and Ovimbundu authorities was the issue of control over labor. Various interests pressed the colonial administration for preference in obtaining cheap labor. In addition to the continuing demands for labor from the offshore islands, the colonial state also required labor for various public works projects, including the building of railroads, roads, and ports. Portuguese settlers developing fishing on the coast or engaged in large- or small-scale farming also pressed the government to supply them with laborers. Labor recruiters from the Congo Free State also looked to Angola to meet their labor needs. The high population densities of the central highlands made this newly conquered region the logical choice for large-scale recruiting.

The government exercised its control over labor by forcing the rulers of the Ovimbundu states to be the state's suppliers. The rulers, in turn, used their own domestic authority to call up workers. However, as a result of the Portuguese conquest and the explosion of long-distance trade, the authority of the traditional rulers had been eroded, and most freemen could not be compelled to work. Moreover, their own commerce was so lucrative that they were uninterested in contract labor on the terms the government offered (Heywood 1984: Ch. 8).

As a result, many of the contract laborers were recruited from slaves in the highlands or other slaves arriving in the country from lands farther east. The general unavailability of free labor created strong competition for the limited supplies of slaves, resulting in a rise in their prices. In 1891 the price of a slave in Benguela was U.S. $43–76, and he could be sold in the Congo Free State for as much as U.S. $163. Not surprisingly, Portuguese recruiters went into the highlands, bought slaves and pawns cheaply, and sold them to dealers in the Congo Free State (NAUS, Chatelain 1891). In 1893 a young boy of 9 or 10 years, who formerly would have been left on the road to die, fetched U.S. $15 on the Benguela market (CCFMS, Currie 1893).

To meet this scarcity Ovimbundu sold their own slaves and pawns, even as they continued to obtain slaves in the interior. Many Ovimbundu who accompanied caravans as porters bought slaves along the Kwanza and sold them to Portuguese in the interior and on the coast. In 1893 an Ocimbundu could purchase two slaves in the interior for a Martini-Henry rifle (NAZ, Fisher Diary: 60, and 26 March 1891: 398–99). In 1900 a Martini-Henry, worth U.S. $30, bought eight "fair-sized slaves." At the coast each slave could bring between $100 and $150 (CCFMS, Currie 1900).

The Ovimbundu especially benefitted from these high prices because of their ready access to the Luvale area on the border between Northern Rhodesia and Angola, where unstable conditions and the absence of external control led to the enslavement of large numbers of people. Caravans continued to bring slaves from this area into Bié well into the early 1900s. Even though no accurate statistics exist for the number of slaves involved in this forced migration, a military report of 1909 estimated that 50,000 persons a year — a significant number of whom were undoubtedly slaves — passed the Portuguese posts bordering the Ovimbundu highlands and the Nganguelas (CDIH, commander, Cuima, 1909). This same region was also the center for the production of wild rubber — its marketing largely in the hands of Ovimbundu merchants — which became the greatest revenue earner for Angola between 1890 and 1914 (Heywood 1984: 373–74). Thus, the Ovimbundu provided the Portuguese economy of Angola with both an exportable commodity and supplies of cheap labor.

The bulk of these laborers, now officially called *serviçães* (sing. *serviçal*), or "servants," were channelled towards fulfilling the demand for laborers in São Tomé and Príncipe. Many commercial houses on the coast paid the high sum of 60,000 reis, or 60 milreis (ca. U.S. $63), for each serviçal, thus encouraging this slave trade (CDIH, monthly report 1903). Over 50,000 serviçães were shipped to São Tomé and Príncipe between 1870 and 1900 (Duffy 1967: 98), and 1,066 were transported in 1909 (AHU, Angola estatística, 1909–1913).

While this labor was flowing out of the highlands, some Portuguese settled there in the wake of the Portuguese conquest. Most established trading houses or worked in a short-lived but vigorous rum-manufacturing industry, which made use of local potatoes and tapped local sources of labor. These settlers used mainly female and younger male slaves, whom they had to buy because free, adult Ovimbundu, male labor was unavailable (Heywood 1984). Ovimbundu also used their slaves in commercial and agricultural ventures. Thus, both Portuguese and Africans benefitted from the continuation of slavery under the early Portuguese administration.

Official Portuguese attempts to draw income from the colony and build up the prosperity of Portuguese settlers in Angola encouraged this barely disguised slave trade and set the conditions for direct links among the slave trade, slavery, pawnship, and forced labor. In 1906 the government imposed a hut tax on Africans which required each African male to pay 600 milreis (ca U.S. 63¢) on each hut he owned. Payable at first in agricultural and collected forest products, by 1912 the tax on each African dwelling was payable only in cash (Heywood 1984: 383–85). In order to pay it, some Ovimbundu borrowed money from Portuguese merchants, promising rubber in return, which the Ovimbundu then obtained from the interior. When the supply of rubber was not sufficient, Ovimbundu debtors transferred slaves or pawns to their Portuguese creditors. In 1910, the British consul noted that an Ocimbundu who owed a Portuguese 40 kilos of rubber settled his debt with the transfer of a slave and received as balance "80 yards of cloth, three bottles of rum and a hat" (PRO, British consul 1910). The same year one Joaquim da Silva Garcia was accused of selling two serviçães — one for a blanket and the other for an ox — both of whom had earlier been taken from their African owner when he failed to pay his debts (CDIH, questões gentílicos). As late as 1915–1916, individuals identified themselves as slaves of Portuguese merchants to whom they had been sold by African owners (CDIH, chefe do posto, Huambo, 1915; CDIH, chefe do posto, Quipeio, 1916: 1).

Portuguese Antislavery Policy, 1890–1918

Slaving and slave-dealing under the guise of voluntary labor and the transfer of slaves from the African- to the Portuguese-controlled sector of the economy in Angola and on the islands brought international pressure to bear on the Portuguese government. A key point in the international efforts to end slavery was reached in the conference at Brussels in 1889–1890, which resulted in the Brussels Act of 1890, binding signatories to suppress the slave trade but not slavery itself. At this conference the Portuguese emphasized their long tradition of antislavery legislation; they denied that slavery was practiced in Angola, arguing that it was long dead, even though they admitted that in remote corners of the colony some Portuguese might still be involved in the slave trade (Duffy 1967: 126–29). In fact, the Portuguese were reluctant to attack slavery directly because they realized the economic importance of the institution as a source of labor, particularly because most of the Portuguese immigrants to the colony relied heavily on existing methods of recruiting, which largely depended on slavery and the slave trade. A careful study of the treaties of vassalage drawn up between the victorious Portuguese armies and their African opponents during the period of conquest provides no evidence that they sought to abolish slavery.[3]

3. I have studied approximately 30 such treaties as they are published in the official

The British, anxious about public opinion at home and possibly fearing that the drain of labor from British Northern Rhodesia through Angola might damage their interests there, condemned Portugal in international circles. International criticism of Portuguese labor policies was especially strong in 1899 and 1902–1903. George Cadbury threatened to appeal to British cocoa interests to buy their cocoa elsewhere when rumors began to circulate that the plantations which supplied his company were using slaves, because the laborers had never been repatriated (Duffy 1967: 182–98).

Consequently, the Portuguese government passed legislation requiring that all laborers contracted for the islands offer their services freely, sign contracts, receive remuneration, and be guaranteed repatriation when their contracts expired (ibid.: 169–82). Between 1905 and 1909, the Portuguese press denounced the persistence of slavery in the colonies (*Jornal das colonias*, 29 April 1904: 3). Consequently, the new Portuguese Republic abolished all forms of slavery in its colonies in 1910 (Duffy 1967: 198–219). As a result of this law, African domestic slavery, as it was practiced in the highlands, was officially abolished. The Portuguese believed that passing such a law would satisfy their critics by eliminating the legal status of slavery throughout their colonies, especially if the laws concerning repatriation and remuneration were also enforced.

Indeed, Robert Smallbones, the British consul general in Luanda, wrote in 1913 that he believed the new laws were resulting in the gradual emancipation of "an unfree people," even though the original contracts had been "a sham" and merely disguised slavery (ibid.: 222). However, the long-standing place of slave labor in the Ovimbundu and Portuguese economies of the highlands made this legislation meaningless. Although the returning contract laborers were indeed free in the legal sense, their freedom was limited by the situation in the highlands.

In the central highlands, there were no clear definitions of a slave and of the forms of coerced labor that constituted slavery. Moreover, there was a divergence of views between Portuguese and Ovimbundu over what constituted freedom. For the government, a free laborer was an individual who possessed a contract stipulating that he would be paid for his services, work for a definite period of time, and be returned to the area of recruitment at the end of his service. This contractual arrangement was the crucial factor which distinguished the contract laborer from the slave.

----

journal *Boletim oficial do governo geral da colonia de Angola* over the years 1890–1910. The only treaties requiring that slavery or the slave trade be abolished were those with smaller states nearest the coast, where the suppression of slavery and slave-raiding was part of a larger program of defending trade routes from raiding and ensuring that slaves captured by such brigandage were to be freed.

Once a person had a contract, the Portuguese authorities did not deem it necessary to inquire further into how it had been obtained. As far as Portuguese law was concerned, a laborer was legally free if he had been guaranteed repatriation at the end of the contract.

The decree of 1910 extended this definition by calling for the repatriation of slaves held by Africans if the slaves desired it. On the other hand, those persons who had been held as slaves might remain in the village and be "treated as the children" of their former masters (CCFMS, Woodside 1912: 4–5). For the Ovimbundu, however, a slave was defined as one who had no right to be considered part of the kin group, and there was no mechanism allowing the full incorporation of former slaves into the kin group, as children or otherwise. Slaves could be accepted into a kin group only on a different basis from those born into it (Hastings 1933: 88).

Thus, since no government decree could force the integration of slaves into kin groups on equal terms, former slaves could never be truly free if they remained within their masters' communities. Consequently, slaves who had been recruited and were repatriated, as well as slaves who were freed by the decree of 1910 and elected to remain in the central highlands, simply continued to be regarded and treated as slaves. Those who wished to leave also faced difficulties. Many slaves, especially those who had been captured as young children, had nowhere to go because they did not know from whence they had come (CCFMS, Woodside 1912: 6). Therefore, the decree of 1910 had no real effect in changing the status of slaves under local law or of making freedom, as understood by the Portuguese or the international community, realizable.

This was a matter of concern to Protestant missionaries who knew the situation in the highlands well from their position as first-hand observers. But these missionaries were also relatively powerless to change established practices. Until 1910 Protestant missionaries had condoned the holding of slaves by African converts. With the legal abolition of slavery in 1910, the Protestants formally decided that "buying, selling or owning slaves is incompatible with church membership" (ibid.). Although a few leading converts emancipated some of their slaves (one *seculo* freed more than 100), the majority of Ovimbundu could not free slaves individually. Most slave-owners were bound to family and other members of their kin group by a tangle of common interests and were not free to dispose of the slaves without consent of the other interested parties, who might not have been Christian (ibid.; CCFMS, Chattel 1916; Childs 1969: 20).

In fact, slavery actually increased between 1911 and 1915, because a drought left many people destitute. Victims responded through the familiar route of enslaving themselves or family members in exchange for food and support. This was especially true in the eastern and southeastern areas of the highlands, which were the most seriously affected. Many of these people enslaved themselves or their children to the residents of the northern and western areas; Ovimbundu from the west even travelled eastward beyond the highlands to acquire these slaves (ABC, Woodside 1911). Women and children were especially liable to be sold. Indeed, in 1915 one gang of slave-dealers who sold "boys and girls for a bushel of corn" was arrested by Portuguese authorities (CCFMS, Kamundongo report 1927).

While the drought threw additional people on the market, economic reorientation provided more opportunities for their use and for the exchange of pawns and slaves by both the Ovimbundu and the Portuguese. Developments associated with the arrival of the Benguela railway in the agriculturally rich central highlands as well as the increase in the settler population in the 1920s and 1930s kept the demand for labor high (Heywood 1984: 374–76). Many settlers were merchants who came, not to farm, but to capitalize on the new vigor of the regional economy.

The Colonial Economy and the Struggle to Control Labor, 1918–1949

This new economic vigor was not so much the result of settler enterprise as of the decision by the Ovimbundu to redirect their economic activities from trade to agriculture. Ovimbundu men, who had formerly gone to the hinterlands as traders or porters along with their wives and slaves, now turned their attention to growing cash crops — corn, beans, wheat, and, to a lesser extent, rice (Heywood 1984: 375–81).

As the Ovimbundu turned increasingly to cash crops, the government adopted a dual economic and fiscal strategy. On the one hand, it required African labor for state as well as private enterprise. On the other, it also taxed African production. This guaranteed revenue collection, since both African laborers and producers had to pay taxes to meet administrative expenses and to leave a surplus for transfer to Portugal. The government further ensured its revenues by making women as well as men liable for taxation from 1918. The forced-labor policy eventually led to the establishment of a permanent pool of readily available labor, most of which would be recruited from the central highlands, whose population of approximately 1 million was the largest in Angola (ibid.: 405–12).

In 1919, local white settlers began to push for legislation requiring each African male between the ages of 14 and 45 years to work for a white man for no less than three months a year with heavy penalties for noncompliance (CCFMS, Sanders 1919). In response, the government enacted legislation giving local Portuguese officials the authority to intervene directly in recruiting labor for both government public works and private enterprise (Heywood 1984: 382–83). Such labor could be obtained by offering contracts, but it might also include unpaid labor for public works (and occasionally other activities). This new policy did not distinguish between slaves and free persons, since Portuguese law considered all Africans free. Thus, free Ovimbundu became subject to unpaid government labor or contract labor along with those whom they regarded as slaves.

In actual practice, neither the new labor laws nor increased taxation directly affected free Ovimbundu, because most were either growing maize to sell in the market or using their slaves to grow it. Traditional rulers (the ones most likely to own slaves) continued to retain control over their labor. Those who owned slaves sent them to meet the government demands for labor, and moreover, the authorities paid the rulers a percentage of the recruiting fee for fulfilling government quotas. This policy increased slave-dealing. A report for 1917 noted that Ovimbundu rulers, required to send men to the government post to work, would buy slaves from the interior and send them as though they were Ovimbundu freemen (ABC, Ennis 1917: 3). When these workers were repatriated to the highlands after their contracts ended, as the law required, they returned to their owners, who still regarded them as slaves (CDIH, administrator, Bailundo 1917).

Despite this available labor, complaints about the shortage of labor became commonplace, not only from large businesses such as the diamond consortium (NAUS, vice-consul 1917; TANKS, Africa report 1917), but from the growing number of fisheries on the coast, some of whom offered to pay transport for workers' wives as an incentive (CDIH, administrator, Huambo, 1917). In response to these demands the government acted vigorously to ensure that sufficient labor was available by requiring that all Africans who were unable to pay taxes offer themselves as contract labor.

By the 1920s, therefore, increasing numbers of Ovimbundu were subject to taxation and called out for forced and contract labor. The effects of these policies were so dramatic, they caused one observer to conclude that "forced labor is being pushed with vigor and unpaid government labor to the point of murder. People are being put into slavery in a way that surpasses previous records" (CCFMS, Hollenbeck 1921). At times the efforts of men to avoid forced labor by hiding only spread the burden to women, who were taken instead of the men. In one case some women were forced to work in a brick kiln "at the closest remove from stark nakedness" (CCFMS, 1920).

The laws required that employers using contract laborers deduct their taxes from their wages. This meant that the majority of workers received no pay at the end of their contract. Cases were reported where male contract laborers worked six months or more and received only a tax receipt (ABC, Minto 1925). One notorious case reported to the British Anti-Slavery and Aborigines Protection Society concerned a laborer who had worked 15 months on a sugar plantation in one of the larger concerns on the coast and returned to the highlands having received as wages only "a cheap cotton suit" (ibid.), and he was still liable for taxes the next year.

This situation increased the incidence of pawning. As one report notes, "Men pawn their children into what amounts to slavery to obtain money to pay their taxes and sometimes later find it necessary to pawn another instead of releasing the first" (ibid.). These pawns thus passed into slavery and undoubtedly were the first ones offered up as contract laborers when requests for labor were made to the village heads. Wealthier Ovimbundu, however, almost certainly had slaves in their households who produced cash crops, thus earning money to pay their masters' taxes.

The dual Portuguese policies of requiring Africans to pay taxes and perform government labor, or to work for a contract if they could not pay taxes, were mutually reinforcing. The Estado Novo (New State), established in 1927 with the advent of António Salazar, continued and elaborated this tradition. The most dramatic changes resulted from the introduction of a new currency, the angolar, into the colony in such a way that the existing currency was automatically devalued by 20 percent. It was estimated that this added an additional month, now four instead of three, to the time it took Africans to obtain wages to pay the hut tax. In addition they were liable for corvée labor on the roads and for other unpaid services (PRO, Smallbones 1928). Since the minimum wage and the price paid to maize producers remained the same as before the devaluation, more Ovimbundu found themselves unable to avoid contract labor through local wage work or independent farming.

Free Ovimbundu males did all they could to avoid contract labor, because they regarded this type of work as being akin to slave labor. They increasingly resorted to the local system of pawning wives and nieces whenever money for taxes was due and the returns from their cash crops were not adequate. Pawning became even more pronounced in the late 1920s when a drought caused a drop in income. Many formerly prosperous Ovimbundu were ruined, while others were on the brink of starvation. Observers reported that in some of the hard-hit areas, significant numbers of children were exchanged "for a bushel of corn and beans" (CCFMS, Hollenbeck 1927). In other cases they were exchanged for money to pay taxes. Portuguese officials, without adopting relief measures, continued to make demands for laborers and at times sent soldiers to force starving Ovimbundu to enter into contracts (ibid.).

The reason that the Ovimbundu dreaded contract labor and considered it nothing other than slavery was that working conditions, remuneration, treatment, and the lack of freedom to move about, change masters, and return home were no different from (but indeed worse than) the conditions common in Ovimbundu slavery. This led observers to note that "the people came to consider themselves as more slaves [of the Europeans]" (NAUS, U.S. consul 1922). Some Ovimbundu noted that in former times slaves were no worse off than many free Ovimbundu were now under the Portuguese (ABC, Miller 1925: 5).

At this time, critics of the system provided information on incidents of enslavement and abuse of the contract-labor system to the local Angolan press and the metropolitan press and to international organizations such as the League of Nations, often through the Antislavery Society. Thus, when in 1925 the American sociologist Edward Ross published his celebrated accusation that Portuguese policies were contributing to slavery in Africa, it received international attention. Ross, who visited the central highlands and interviewed Ovimbundu spokesmen, accused the Portuguese of supporting a system of servile labor and of subjecting increasingly large numbers of Ovimbundu to it. According to Ross, many Ovimbundu, formerly exempt from contract labor, were being forced into taking contracts by the colonial state. As Ross (1925: 37) noted: "The old contract system was slavery in every sense of the word, but only slaves and some unfortunate half-wits and incorrigibles were subject to it. Under the present system anyone is liable." He also interviewed some Ovimbundu and recorded their reactions to their new situation. In one such interview, an Ovimbundu was reported to have said: "Twelve years ago when there was slavery the slaves faced the hardship while the free Negroes were not badly off. Now we are all slaves. The slaves were better fed than we forced laborers are, for we are not property" (ibid.: 20).

The Portuguese reacted to this barrage of international criticism by requiring district governors to collect statistics detailing requests for labor. They regarded better record-keeping as a first step towards preventing unauthorized recruiting. Even though publicly denying the complicity of Portuguese settlers and the government in this type of slavery, the colonial officials were privately aware of the practice of using slaves and pawns as contract laborers in the central highlands and elsewhere. In 1925, a confidential letter from the governor of Bié to a local official warned that he had been informed that

in this part of Angola domestic slavery is practiced, that the buying and selling of persons increases dramatically at the time of tax collection and because of this, a majority of the workers requisitioned by the authorities are slaves, they being the ones exclusively who are subject to support the hard labor of opening up of roads. (CDIH, governor, Bié, 1925)

Many of these individuals were likely to be minors under 18 years of age, as in the case of the 212 partly clothed and malnourished children who arrived in Mossâmedes in 1924 as contract laborers (CDIH, governor, Benguela, 1924). Other cases were reported involving minors under 18 years old who were often apprenticed to local commercial houses for terms of up to five years (CDIH, 1923).

No attempt, however, was made to dismantle the system of forced labor and high taxes — the two conditions which directly contributed to making this new form of slavery the dominant form of labor relations in the highlands. In Bailundo, where Ross undertook his short investigation, the local administration stopped the practice of using women in road service and stipulated that children should not be pawned to pay taxes — even returning the tax money in one instance where children had been sold (ABC, Minto 1926: 6). However, there was no general overhauling of the labor-recruiting or taxation policies; thus, the conditions for continuing slavery remained.

New State policies also provided a significant watershed for the further institutionalization of the contract-labor system and thus an increase in the incidence of enslavement and pawnship. Assured that the state would provide sufficient African labor, large and small Portuguese operations expanded. Increased pressure on labor resources put at risk Ovimbundu agriculture and led to more forced recruitment of contract labor. In 1927, for example, the authorities forcibly recruited 5,464 men for plantations in São Tomé in return for a loan from the planters needed to avoid the collapse of the Angolan economy (PRO, Smallbones, 25 July 1928).

The American vice-consul, suspicious that the Portuguese were still recruiting laborers under conditions akin to slavery, noted in frustration: "The districts from which these natives were recruited are distant and difficult of access and no information is available as to the methods pursued. . . . It appears very doubtful if this number of natives could have been recruited entirely of their own free will" (NAUS, American vice-consul 1927). Commenting on 145 male laborers who were on their way to Mossâmedes, another observer wrote, "Where do they come from and why must they go against their will to this far off region from which it is certain they will never return?" (ABC, Minto 1926). Ovimbundu spokesmen believed that the Portuguese were still not repatriating their laborers contracted for work outside the highlands.

In the 1930s even more drastic measures were taken to promote contract labor. Laws limited opportunities for independent, African economic activities, and in 1933 the colonial state made all Africans farming less than 10 acres of land liable to contract labor and taxation (PRO, Consul Bullock 1933). Moreover, this period witnessed the establishment of marketing boards in cereals which regulated the price to be paid for wheat and maize grown by Africans, and which required that all of these crops be sold to the board. These prices were far below those the Africans would have received on an open market (Heywood 1984: Ch. 9). The ability of the Ovimbundu to acquire money from activities other than the restricted set of economic options set by the state and settlers was severely limited by the abolition of markets frequented by Africans and the elimination of porterage and trading (*Boletim oficial* 9, 5 March 1927: 114; *Boletim oficial* 34, 23 August 1941: 383).

For all this, however, the government continued collecting taxes; taxes paid by Africans provided 20 percent of the colony's budget and represented the single largest source of revenue (PRO, Portuguese possessions 1930). Most of this income came from the taxes the employers deducted directly from the wages of contracted laborers, not from income earned by Africans in independent economic activity. Despite the fact that the use of forced labor by private individuals was in contravention of the Slavery Convention of 1926, the colonial state directly intervened in contracting labor on their behalf. The Angolan economy had reached the point where forced contract labor was regarded as a necessity. As the British consul general noted in reference to the central highlands in 1930, "Unless the administrative authorities used their influence with chiefs or natives themselves and caused them to enter into contracts the farming and prosperity of the colony would suffer unjustifiable injury" (PRO, British consul general, 26 September 1930).

Private firms continued to be supplied with Africans recruited against their will, as slaves had been, and forced to work under a system akin to slavery. Reports from contractors of the Benguela railway in 1933 noted the ease with which such workers were obtained. In July: "The chefe of the Posto of Quingenge . . . is a very good man and very helpful to me, he arranged for 120 contract boys for me for nothing"; and in November the former secretary of Ganda (an administrative post) arranged "200 boys" for the company's sisal plantations (TANKS, Hermanns 10 July and 3 November 1933). The system also encouraged the famous private recruiters, or "slave catchers" as they were known, some of whom lived in relative luxury, like Armando Guedes Rufino of Bailundo, who dispensed large quantities of presents to the local population from the profits of his activities as a way of enticing them into contracts (CDIH, administrator, Bailundo, 1934). Unfortunately, specifics about such people only occasionally appear in the reports and documentation of the time.

A drought and locust invasion, which destroyed corn and wheat harvests in 1934, worsened an already critical situation. Without any resources and with the knowledge that taxes had to be paid to avoid forced labor, enslavement increased. In one report on the Nganguelas area, it was noted that only Africans nearest the rail line were able to sell their corn at a price sufficient to allow them to pay the taxes of 80 angolares (U.S. $3.80). Less fortunate Africans sold their children to the more fortunate in order to obtain money for taxes to avoid imprisonment or contract labor. Young girls were sold to the highest bidder (CDIH, Keiling 1934). In 1936, perhaps because of the Great Depression, other cases of sales of girls were also noted. This affected other aspects of life; for instance, in the administrative post of Quipeio, receipts fell to 40 percent of those of the previous year, and Africans resorted to "selling all their livestock and valuables which constitute their small daily capital fund and selling clandestinely women and children" (CDIH, chefe do posto, Quipeio, 1936).

The actions of Portuguese settlers themselves did much to prolong slavery. During the 1930s many Ovimbundu became indebted to Portuguese merchants through a system of credit commonly known as *fuca*. In some cases merchants sent their African agents into villages to encourage the residents to obtain credit for foodstuffs and money to pay taxes. Inability to repay the debts and the interest, which often amounted to 400 percent of the loan, resulted in the seizure of entire families. Thus, merchants obtained laborers for their own businesses or for subcontract to larger concerns (CDIH, administrator, Bailundo, 1939; *Jornal de Benguela*, 5 February 1941: 3).

International criticism of Portugal's complicity in slavery in Angola continued throughout the 1930s, especially as a result of activities associated with the emerging International Labor Organization. In 1930, when British Consul General Smallbones accused the Angolan government of condoning slavery through its recruitment policies, the governor-general maintained that the policy of requiring African chiefs to supply contract labor could not be regarded as promoting slavery (PRO, report of consul 1930). He was supported by the minister of the colonies, who denied that wages in Angola were too low to attract voluntary labor — as some of Portugal's critics had charged (PRO, British ambassador, Lisbon, 1930).

International critics had recognized that the Portuguese responded to neither moral nor humanitarian appeals. One American organization, interested in ending these abuses, felt that the only way to force the Portuguese to change the system was to get banks to withhold loans pending changes in labor-recruiting policies and the ending of slavery (NYPL/S, Bunker 1932).

By the 1940s the state's system of forced labor had been fully institutionalized despite international concern. Within the local village economy, slavery and pawnship were still practiced, especially to meet short-term crises. In the settler and state economy, all Ovimbundu were subject to forced labor. Those who cultivated the land had to sell their products at controlled prices which left them barely enough to pay the taxes. For the rest, forced labor on large enterprises outside the highlands or on smaller concerns within the area, as well as working for Portuguese traders, was now the norm. Not surprisingly, the British consul general, referring to conditions in the central highlands, wrote in 1941, "From an agricultural point of view, the producer has become the government's serf" (PRO, British consul general 1941).

Government policies which directed labor into state enterprises, larger businesses such as the Benguela Railway Company, and migration outside the highlands were often at odds with the interests of local settlers, who wished to see Ovimbundu agriculture prosper so that their marketing business would continue. Many Portuguese settlers gained a livelihood by buying maize products from the Ovimbundu and then reselling them to the government at the higher prices set for white producers. The contradictory nature of this development is illustrated by an incident in 1944. In that year a group of these small-scale Portuguese traders in the highlands "held up a train carrying forced laborers to the coast on the grounds that such emigration was excessive and injurious to their trade" (PRO, report, February 1944). The Ovimbundu had become the mainstay in a colonial system which rested on the maintenance of domestic slavery and pawnship, high taxation of peasant producers, forced labor for the state and white private enterprises, and private settler exploitation of producers through a system of forced credit and uncompetitive prices for their products.

The system of forced labor prevalent in the mid-1940s is well demonstrated in a memorandum from the governor-general to the Department of Native Affairs. The governor-general stated that Angola should send to São Tomé not only "individuals subject to punishment imposed by the administration" but also those who were unemployed and did not complete their obligations to work (CDIH, governor-general 1945).

By this time also the labor pool increasingly incorporated younger age categories, because some adults openly defied government orders and refused to be contracted. In 1949, officials at administrative posts in Vila Nova and Bela Vista were asked to "send urgently 50 boys between the ages of 14 to 16 to do contract work for 90 days with the Benguela Railway Company." Among the 21 boys sent only 7 were between 14 and 16;

the others were all under 13, and 4 of these were only 6 years old (CDIH, Pereira de Figueiredo 1949).

These forced-labor policies clarified the now subordinate relationship of the Ovimbundu to the colonial state and settlers. The Ovimbundu became an impoverished laboring group. An investigation of demographic structures shows that by the mid-1940s the Ovimbundu were much worse off than they had been when they were first brought under Portuguese rule, with lower life expectancies and greatly disrupted family lives (Heywood and Thornton 1987). In addition, some of their best land had been alienated. Moreover, a major dislocation of the Ovimbundu population was occurring. The British consul noted this trend as early as 1942 when he observed that approximately 20,000 Angolans had crossed the border from Angola to the Congo and Rhodesia in the first three years of the Second World War (PRO, Kitts 1942). Most of these were attracted by the prospect of the high wages as well as the higher living standards which the Congo and Rhodesia offered or by the better pay obtainable in mine work in South Africa.

Conclusion

This chapter has argued that slavery and other forms of dependency existed among the Ovimbundu in central Angola during the period of the Atlantic slave trade. These institutions did not decline but expanded in the period from 1836 to 1890. Portuguese military conquest caused the integration of these institutions into the colonial economy, because the demand for laborers was met by the use of slaves. Although the Portuguese officially abolished slavery in 1910, taxation requirements, labor demands, and restrictions on Ovimbundu economic activity perpetuated many of the features of slavery. Finally, the policies of the New State in Portugal in 1926–1927 led to an expansion of forced labor and undermined Ovimbundu economic independence, which essentially prevented the growth of a free-labor market and established the state as the major controller and beneficiary of the system.

As this chapter has demonstrated, studies of the economic features of slave labor can go a long way in bringing about an understanding of the modern history of Angola. African slavery also had political dimensions, particularly under the constraints of the colonial state. Political domination of Angola promoted the maintenance of labor practices associated with slavery in the economy and facilitated the forced-labor systems which characterized Portuguese colonial policies in the postwar years. Ultimately, it was the latent reaction of Angolans to these policies

434 V. NEW ECONOMIES AND LABOR CONTROL

which fuelled the uprisings from 1961 and the demise of Portuguese colonial rule in 1975.

REFERENCES

Archival sources

ABC: American Board of Commissioners for Foreign Lands, Houghton Library, Harvard University, Cambridge.

Ennis to Barton, 31 August 1917. Vol. 19, doc. 214.
Fay, A. E., to friends, 6 June 1889. Vol. 23a.
Fay, W. E., 7 December 1886. Vol. 23a.
MacDowell, C., 1925. Vol. 24, doc. 133.
Miller, J., 1925, Vol. 2, doc. 389.
Minto, 1925. Vol. 23, doc. 388.
Minto to Folks, 1 May 1926. Vol. 23, doc. 390.
Woodside to Barton, 11 April 1911. Vol. 19, doc. 300.
AHU: Arquivo histórico ultramarino, Lisbon.
Angola estatística, 1909–1913. DGC.
CCFMS: Canadian Council of Foreign Missionary Societies, University of Toronto.

All documents are from the section Angola Mission, General Correspondence.

Chattel, C. C., 1916. File 45.
Currie to Hill, 29 November 1893.
Currie report, 1896. File 8.
Currie to Massey, 1900. File 11.
Hollenbeck to Moore, 11 March 1921. File 52.
Hollenbeck, 1927. File 28, box 3.
Kamundongo report, 18 August 1927. File 25.
Sanders to Tucker, 23 November 1919. File 45.
Sanders to Tucker, 1 January 1920. File 47.
Woodside to Barton, 28 August 1912. File 28.
CDIH: Centro de Documentação e Investigação Histórica, Luanda.

References are provisional, reflecting organization of the archive in 1979–1980.

Administrator, Bailundo, 1917. Shelf 103, box 3.
Administrator, Bailundo, 11 October 1934. Shelf 24, box 7, doc. 16.
Administrator, Bailundo, 20 July 1939. Shelf 24, box 28, doc. 2.
Administrator, Huambo, 17 September 1917. Shelf 33, Huambo, box 10.
Chefe do posto, Huambo, 18 September 1915. Shelf 78, box 2, Huambo.
Chefe do posto, Quipeio, 1916. Shelf 67, box 1, Huambo, doc. 7.
Chefe do posto, Quipeio, 24 April 1936. Shelf 24, box 16.
Commander, Cuima, to commander, Huambo, 1909. Shelf 69, box 3, Huambo.

Governor of Benguela to governor of Huíla, 24 February 1924. Shelf 11, box 23.

Governor of Bíe to local official, 23 September 1925. Shelf 40, box 89.

Governor-general, memorandum to Department of Native Affairs, 1 September 1945. Shelf 40, box 93.

Keiling to intendent, Huambo, 1934. Shelf 24, box 16, doc. 18.

Monthly report, 1903 (identifying month torn from document). Bailundo.

Pereira de Figueiredo, Matias, to intendent, Huambo, 22 February 1949. Shelf 25, box 31, doc. 24.

Questões gentílicos. Shelf 24, Huambo, box 2. 1923. Shelf 33, box 55, doc. 18.

NAUS: National Archives of the United States, Washington, D.C.

American vice-consul, 19 March 1927. RG 28.

Chatelain, H., 31 December 1891. 5T430.

Consul general, 18 March 1883. 5T430.

U.S. consul, confidential memo to secretary of state, 4 August 1922. RG 28.

Vice-consul to secretary of state, 17 July 1917. General correspondence 1921–1928. C 42.8.

NAZ: National Archives of Zambia, Lusaka.

Documents are from the Bruce Miller Papers (HM 8).

Fisher Diary. F.I. 2/3/2, fol. 60. F.I. 2/1/1, 26 March 1891, fol. 398–99.

NYPL/S: New York Public Library—Schomburg Collection, New York City.

Bunker to Jones, 28 October 1932. Stokes files, Portuguese Africa, 1932–1936.

PRO: Public Record Office, London.

British ambassador, Lisbon, to Foreign Office, 26 September 1930. F.O. 241, W10146/26.

British consul, 22 February 1910. F.O. 367, 10 Africa.

British consul general, 10 September 1941. F.O. 371, Portugal 26846/3284/36.

Consul Bullock's translation of Legislative Diploma no. 439 with comments, 5 April 1933. F.O. 371, 1933 Political, Western Europe 17418/1073-1629, W3757/1315/36.

Kitts to Lawson, 28 August 1942. F.O. 371, 68721/38/36.

Portuguese possessions, confidential report, 1930. F.O. 371, 2533/42/36.

Report, February 1944. F.O. 371, C48879/39/36.

Report of consul, 30 August 1930. F.O. 371, W11384/9695/36.

Smallbones to Foreign Office, 25 July 1928. F.O. 371, A5725/58/52.

Smallbones, 28 July 1928. F.O. 371, A5743/58/52.

TANKS: Tanganyika Concessions, Ltd., Archives, London.

All documents are from the sections Benguela Railway Company (BRC) and Benguela Estates (BE).

Africa report, 1917. BRC.

Hermanns to Greenwood, 10 July 1933. BE.

Hermanns to Greenwood, 3 November 1933. BE.

Other sources

Boletim oficial do governo geral da colonia de Angola (Luanda). Various issues.

Brásio, A. 1969. *Angolana. Spiritana monumenta historica.* 5 vols. Pittsburgh: Duquesne University Press.

Childs, G. M. 1969. *Kinship and character of the Ovimbundu.* London: International African Institute.

Clarence-Smith, W. G. 1985. *The third Portuguese Empire.* London: Heineman.

Davidson, B. 1955. *An African awakening.* London: Cape.

Davidson, B. 1972. *In the eye of the storm: Angola's people.* Garden City, N.Y.: Anchor.

Duffy, J. 1967. *A question of slavery.* Cambridge: Harvard University Press.

Graça, J. R. 1890. Expedição ao Muatayanvua. *Boletim da Sociedade de Geographia e de História de Lisboa* 9: 365–468.

Hastings, D. A., 1933. Ovimbundu customs and practices as centered around the principles of kinship and psychic power. Ph.D. dissertation, Hartford Seminary, Connecticut.

Heintze, B. 1980. The Angolan vassal tributes of the 17th century. *Revista de História económica e social* 6: 57–78.

Heywood, L. M. 1984. Production, trade and power: the political economy of Central Angola, 1850–1930. Ph.D. dissertation, Columbia University, New York.

Heywood, L. M., and J. Thornton. 1987. Demography, production and labor: Central Angola, 1890–1950. In *African demography and capitalist development,* ed. J. Gregory and D. Cordell, 241–54. Boulder and London: Westview Press.

Jaspert, W. n.d. [1928?]. *Through unknown Africa.* London: Jarrolds.

Jornal de Benguela. 5 February 1941.

Jornal das colonias. (Lisbon). 29 April 1904.

Kun, N. de. 1960–1964. La vie et voyage de Ladislaus Magyar dans l'interieur du Congo en 1850–52. *Bulletin de l'Academie royal des Sciences d'outre mer* 6.

Magyar, L. 1859. *Reisen in Sud-Afrika, 1849–57.* Trans. T. Hunfalvy. Pest, Hungary: Lauper and Stolp; reprint, New York: Kraus, 1974).

Miller, J. C. 1983. The paradoxes of impoverishment in the Atlantic zone. In *History of Central Africa,* ed. D. Birmingham and P. Martin, Vol. 1, 118–59. London and New York: Longmans.

Portugal em Africa (Lisbon). Various issues.

Ross, E. 1925. *Report on employment of native labor in Portuguese Africa.* New York: Abbot Press.

Silva Porto, A. F. da 1885. Ultima viagem. *Boletim da Sociedade de Geographia e de História de Lisboa* 5.

Silva Porto, A. F. da. 1942. *Viagens e apontamentos de um Portuense em Africa. Excerptos do "Diario" de António Francisco da Silva Porto.* Ed. José de Miranda and António Brochado. Lisbon: Agência Geral das Colonias.

15 *Don Ohadike*

The Decline of Slavery among the Igbo People

Slavery among the Igbo People before 1850

The Igbo-speaking people, numbering over 14 million, rank as one of the three major ethnic groups of Nigeria and occupy more than half the total area of its southeast as well as a small portion of its southwest. Despite the size of their population, the Igbo were organized on strict kinship lines. Their social and political organization was fragmented. Both political and judicial powers rested with the elders, even though the various age groups and title associations played some part in political processes. Although some communities like Nri, Onitsha, Aboh, Isele-Ukwu, and Agbor had head chiefs, called *eze* or *obi*, their authority was limited and confined to the towns, villages or clans. There was no central Igbo political authority.

Most Igbo towns and villages, including those that had head chiefs, also had titled chiefs, especially the class known in recent times as red-cap chiefs because of the red caps that were a part of their regalia. Like head chiefs, so too were most titled chiefs called eze or obi. Whereas a head chief earned his position either by divination (as in Nri) or by inheritance (as in Agbor), most titled chiefs in Igboland earned theirs by purchase. In times of prosperity their numbers could rise astronomically, because men invested their surplus wealth in titles. This was the case dur-

437

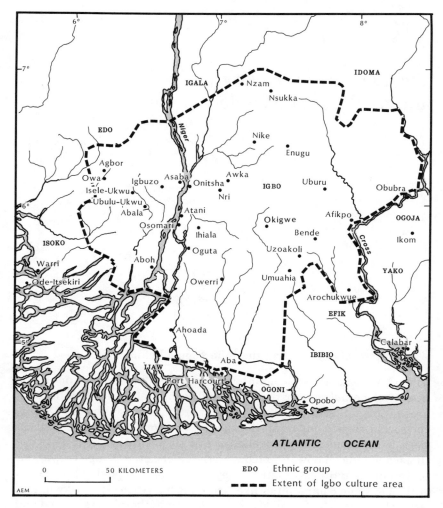

Map 15. Southeastern Nigeria

ing the second half of the nineteenth century when the temporary palm-
oil boom enriched many Igbo. For instance, in 1888, Asaba, with an estimated population of 5,000, had between 300 and 500 titled chiefs (CMS,
Rev. Johnson 1888).

One important cultural trait that ran through Igboland was the rigid
distinction between freeborn and slaves or strangers. The freeborn (*amadi*
or *nwamadu*) claimed origin from the founding fathers of the clan,

whereas slaves and strangers (*ohu* and *obia*, respectively) were outsiders or insiders whose status had been debased. Although the Igbo word *ohu* refers to bought slaves, the Igbo have used the term loosely to include cult slaves (*osu*) as well.

Three broad classes of unfree persons have been identified in Igboland. These were the cult slaves (osu), pawns (*nvunvu ego*), and chattel slaves (ohu). Like *ohu*, the term *osu* has also at times been loosely applied to any slave, but strictly speaking it refers only to persons dedicated to the service of a deity. In Onitsha Province the expression *osu alusi* was used to distinguish the cult slave from the bought slave. Among the Nzam, who speak a mixture of Igbo and Igala languages, the cult slave was called *adu ebo*, an expression probably derived from Igala (NAE, senior district officer, Onitsha, 1935). Certainly, osu were not slaves in the ordinary sense of the word because, once dedicated to a deity, they could neither be bought nor sold and could move about freely. The main restrictions which they suffered were that they could marry only other osu, they could not belong to the clubs of the freeborn, and when they died their corpses could be buried only by other cult slaves in places reserved for them. But despite this apparent freedom, some Igbo believe osu were inferior to or-dinary slaves (i.e., ohu) because an osu could never hope to attain the status of a freeborn.

There were two forms of osu, the voluntary and the involuntary. In the Nsukka and Owerri areas youths were sometimes dedicated to cer-tain deities without their consent when a priest, believing that the deity he served needed some glorification, demanded a slave from the village. Money would be collected and a slave purchased and dedicated to the deity (NAE, district officer, Owerri, 23 November 1936). The victim was thus an involuntary osu — a chattel dedicated to a deity. Voluntary osu willingly dedicated themselves to the services of a god. Thus, a freeborn man, fearing attack by his enemies, or a woman unwilling to marry a man chosen by her parents might run to a *juju* (oracle) and place himself or herself under its protection. Osu were neither ill-treated nor made to perform any servile duties. They were well fed, being given free access to the yams, fowl, and other food items brought as offerings to their dei-ties. It was the responsibility of the chief priest of their cult to look after their welfare, enabling them to secure farmland and other necessities. Because they served a deity, the osu were feared and despised by the free-born (Basden 1966: 249; Isichei 1976: 47–48).

Pawns belonged to quite a different class of unfree persons. These were debtors, or their representatives, pledged to work for their creditors until the debt was discharged. Their work was the customary substitute for interest. Pawns did not have to live in the homes of their creditors and, unlike the ohu and osu, they lived like other members of the community, except for the compulsory labor they performed, which was terminated promptly upon repayment of the debt.

On the other hand, some involuntary pawns ended up as slaves. In most parts of Igboland it was customary for a man who borrowed money to pawn his son or daughter. Such a child lived in the home of the creditor and worked for him until the loan was fully repaid. Although the creditor was not allowed to part with the child, the latter could remain in indefinite bondage if his father failed to repay the debt. Sometimes the creditor ran into a serious financial difficulty (or pretended to have done so) and sold the child. In 1936, 9 out of 10 female children who had been pawned ended up marrying the creditors upon reaching marriageable age (NAE, district officer, Owerri, 23 November 1936).

The most common unfree persons in Igboland were chattel slaves. The true slave, ohu, was an outsider acquired by purchase or by some other means and treated as a stranger, obia, because he had no place in the kinship organization. Sometimes he was reckoned as of no more value than his resale price. Thus, if the intention was to resell him or use him for sacrifice, he remained in his marginal state until the hour of his disposal. However, if the intention was to retain him, custom demanded that he undergo a prescribed process of acculturation and assimilation.

Despite ritual sacrifice and other occasional harsh treatment, the majority of slaves were fairly well treated. It was in the best interest of the masters to treat them kindly, and custom demanded it. In Ubulu-Ukwu, for instance, it was an offense to sell one's slave in public (interview: Henry Abili Mordi, 1982). In Atani and Osomari a successful female trader could, with the permission of her husband, purchase a male slave to accompany her during her trading tours up and down the Niger River. The slave paddled her trading canoe and helped her dispose of her merchandise. He was well treated, but when his owner died he was buried alive with her in the same grave (Ojiakor 1982: 75).

The Igbo people acquired outsiders partly for prestige and partly for economic or even strategic reasons. The Aro, the great interregional traders, retained as servants, porters, and colonists some of the slaves passing through their hands. The Aboh, who traded extensively on the Niger River, kept some to serve as trading assistants, canoe men, and farmers. The people of Nike planted large numbers of slaves in satellite villages in distant farmlands to give their villages early warning of attack (W. R. C. Horton 1954; Uchendu 1977: 130–31).

Before 1830, these various categories of slaves constituted a small proportion of the total number of Igbo people, largely because most captives were destined for the overseas markets. Although slave populations were large in some isolated centers, they were never so large as to generate any serious crisis for their host communities. It was not until the mid-nineteenth century, when the overseas outlet for West African slaves finally declined, that domestic slavery generated its first major crisis for the Igbo people.

The Expansion of Domestic Slavery after 1850

The slave-producing regions of Nigeria continued to supply increasing numbers of slaves even after the ending of the transatlantic slave trade in the late 1860s. This was the result of the Islamic reform movements which generated wars and raids yielding thousands of captives. Neither the northern markets and the trans-Saharan trade routes nor the southern bulking and redistributing centers could now cope with the superfluity of captives. The market was glutted.

The vast majority of slaves acquired by the Igbo in the nineteenth century were victims of these Islamic jihads. They came from Ilorin, Kabba, Nassarawa, Wukari, Idoma, Igala, Gwari, Nupe, and beyond. Poor peasants and their families were pillaged and sold into slavery. Entire ethnic groups sometimes fled their homelands to escape the Nupe-Fulani onslaught. Until its conquest in 1897 by the forces of the British Royal Niger Company, Nupe remained the center of a great Islamic upheaval in which the warring aristocratic families carried out raids over a wide area, depopulating the middle belt.

Even in Igbo heartland, slaving continued after the end of the Atlantic slave trade. Intergroup conflicts, kidnapping, judicial incrimination, and the demands of the various Igbo oracles continued to generate slaves. The Aro expanded their activities and their trading network flourished. Thus, between 1850 and 1900 the supply of slaves to the Igbo communities matched and sometimes outstripped the demand. Although every freeborn adult was free to purchase slaves, the vast majority of the Igbo slaves were owned by the head chiefs and titled chiefs. Some had 100 or more. Nor was slave-ownership restricted to men. In 1831, Macgregor Laird visited "a jolly good-tempered dame" at Aboh who was mistress of more than 200 slaves, whom she employed in collecting palm oil and cultivating yams (Laird and Oldfield 1971: 100).

Among the Igbo, slave-ownership was a mark of social and economic advancement, and in the more affluent communities, slaves outnumbered free citizens. For instance in the 1890s Osomari and its surrounding farms were estimated to have a population of 20,000, of whom only 6,000–8,000

were freeborn (Isichei 1973: 63). At Oguta, where there was a rapid proliferation and expansion of slave camps, known as *ihe*,[1] "noble" families
kept an average of about 20 slaves each, and by the end of the century
nearly half the population were slaves (interview: A. Agorua, 1984).

This increase in slavery among the Igbo was stimulated by the sudden
expansion of the export trade in palm produce. In the era of the Atlantic
slave trade only small amounts of palm oil were taken by ships' captains
to feed African slaves during the Atlantic voyage (Northrup 1978: 29).
Large quantities of palm fruit rotted away in the bush as the palm trees
remained virtually unattended.[2] During the last years of the eighteenth
century and the first decades of the nineteenth, however, the export trade
was stimulated by European demand for lubricants, candles, soap, and
later margarine, and by the second half of the nineteenth century several
thousand tons of palm oil and kernels were being shipped to Europe each
year.

Despite its already dense population, southeastern Nigeria, including
the eastern and western deltas, could never have emerged as the world's
greatest palm oil-producing region without the labor of captives. In fact
the most famous palm oil-producing and -trading areas such as Calabar,
Opobo, Oguta, Aboh, and Ode-Itsekiri, were all important slaveholding
communities. What Emmanuel Terray (1974) has described as a slave
mode of production was thus emerging in southeastern Nigeria during
the second half of the nineteenth century, when the economic strength
of many communities lay in the production of palm oil, whose extraction depended on slave labor. Although the palm trees grew wild and
belonged to the communities at large, only men and women who could
mobilize labor on a large scale to harvest and process oil and kernels
were in a position to profit from the business. The wealth of the local

1. Slave villages at Asaba and Igbuzo were called *ugwule*. At Oguta, Asaba, Igbuzo,
and other places each parent quarter or lineage owned a separate slave camp (or village)
where most of its slaves were kept. Igbuzo, for instance, had 10 quarters and therefore
had 10 slave camps. Only trusted slaves were allowed to live in their masters' compounds.
The slaves who lived in the slave villages received harsher treatment. As Elizabeth Isichei
(1976: 100–101) has shown, when a titled chief died and the drum (*akaja*) sent out the
dreadful message "choga ugwule, choga ugwule," meaning "go for slaves, go for slaves,"
the young men pursued them in the slave villages and captured the number required to
accompany the dead chief into the land of the ancestors. Because of this custom the people
of Asaba have the saying, "obeli na Asaba, obeli na ugwule," meaning "when the freeborn
of Asaba mourn their dead, the slaves in the camps mourn theirs too."
2. In 1831, Macgregor Laird observed that the quantity of palm oil being produced
on the banks of the Nun River (west of Aboh) was not one-twentieth of the natural production. He claimed to have seen "the palm oil nuts of that season lying on the ground ne-
glected as an article too plentiful to be valuable . . ." (Laird and Oldfield 1971: 108).

chiefs and principal merchants was in reality accumulated from the surplus labor they extracted from slaves. Thus, as long as the palm-oil trade remained profitable, and as long as the chiefs and merchants continued to extract surplus labor from servile classes, any attempt by the Europeans to abolish slavery was hotly contested.

The Suppression of Slavery in Igboland — First Attempts

The gradual ending of the overseas slave trade and the rise of the palm-oil trade generated a major crisis among the various ethnic groups of southeastern Nigeria. Among the Efik, for instance, they led to slave revolts, political tension, and witchcraft accusations (Latham 1972, 1973). In the Niger Delta, they generated unprecedented expansion of the canoe houses,[3] intense rivalry between the city states, and the tightening of laws regulating the acculturation of slaves (Dike 1956; Jones 1963). In Igboland these changes brought about class differentation and introduced major contradictions between the ideology and practice of slavery. Igbo society became visibly polarized. The slaves became more alienated from their host communities, and because of their large numbers, masters adopted more coercive methods of social control.[4] Human sacrifice became more frequent. "What harm is there in sacrificing slaves?" asked some Igbuzo men of Father Carlo Zappa of the Society of African Missions. "Because slaves are men like you and me," he replied. "Oh no," they protested, "not at all, not at all, slaves are not men" (SMA, Annals of the Propagation of Faith 1902).

The assault on slavery in Igboland was pioneered by the Christian missionaries. Initially, however, their main concern was not the immediate eradication of slavery but the amelioration of the treatment of slaves. In fact, some missionaries actually purchased slaves to use as domestic ser-

3. In the central and eastern delta of the Niger River the basic political unit was the lineage, or *wari*, literally known as a house. Largely because of the overseas trade this political unit underwent some transformations. The head of the wari became a trading chief, and the other leading members of the wari bought slaves to enlarge the numerical strength of the lineage. The war or trading canoes were vital to the survival of the Ijaw (Ezon) houses, on account of which European traders described them as canoe houses. By the eighteenth and nineteenth centuries a canoe house was no longer a lineage in the ordinary sense of the word but a corporate trading unit, admitting people of diverse origins. Any successful trader could break off from the house to which he belonged and form a new one. Even a slave, like Jaja of Opobo, was able to lead a canoe house. For further information about canoe houses see Dike 1956; Jones 1963; R. Horton 1969; and Alagoa 1972.

4. Martin Klein and Paul Lovejoy (1979: 186–87) recognize that the treatment of slaves was determined not only by the customs of the acquirers' society but also by the relative number of slaves in the society.

vants or to train as missionaries or interpreters. In 1886, for instance, Roman Catholic missionaries bought 48 young slaves at Lokoja (Hilliard 1963: 15). Other missionaries, like the future bishop Samuel Crowther of the Church Missionary Society (CMS), refused to be involved in any transaction that could be termed slave-dealing (Crowther and Taylor 1968: 33). However, missionaries of all denominations were united in their opposition to the harsh treatment of slaves. Such opposition can be considered part of their attack on established African religion and society, which they held in great contempt. "I will tell you without fear," Father Zappa told Obi Egbuna, the head chief of Isele-Ukwu, "that we do not approve of what you do. You spill the blood of your slaves in front of your idols. This is evil. I must tell you that the lives of these slaves do not belong to you, and that the slaves, like you, are the children of the Great God" (SMA, *Les Missions catholiques* 1903: 586). Like Father Zappa, Bishop Crowther confronted the traditionalists of the lower Niger in the belief that theirs was a conflict between "light and darkness" (Mackenzie 1976: 15).

One of the central issues was human sacrifice. The taking of titles demanded elaborate feasts and the payment of exorbitant initiation fees, which only the affluent could afford. These lavish ceremonies were accompanied by sacrifices, both animal and human. At Asaba, as in Onitsha, and other places, missionaries exposed and denounced human sacrifice and other aspects of traditional religious practices, sending back to Europe exaggerated "eye-witness" reports of "African barbarism," which were published in their periodicals. In 1879, for instance, an Asaba-based missionary wrote:

The power of life and death over slaves is in the hands of the masters, as allowed by the custom of the country; the number of slaves destroyed annually in sacrifices to the gods, to ratify the investiture of a new office, or to accompany any dead of importance as servants into the world of spirits, is really appalling. (*Church Missionary Intelligencer* 1879: 239)

Missionaries also incited the slaves to rebel by openly preaching against human sacrifice. Finally, they persuaded the agents of the Royal Niger Company, which had secured a charter to rule the area from the British government, to take military action. In April 1888, Asaba was attacked and half of it destroyed (PRO, MacDonald 1889). Having subjugated the local chiefs, the company issued a decree prohibiting human sacrifice in the town.

The slaves of Asaba rejoiced over this decree, demonstrating their gratitude by gathering at the mission stations to enroll in baptism classes.

"The slaves now realise their freedom," wrote Rev. Johnson. "The joy depicted on their faces as you move about amongst them is sufficient to convince you that each one knows that the former days are gone, and that a new dispensation has dawned." Some slaves became very bold, violating local customs "in the name of Christianity" and spying for the missionaries, exposing what went on in town (Onianwa 1980: 45). Hence, the people of Asaba nicknamed all Christians *ndi na kanyi uka* or *ndi uka*, meaning "those who backbite us."

All over Igboland, slaves were the first people to enroll at the mission schools. They were invariably the first Christian converts. The people of Asaba called the CMS church *uka ugwule* ("the assemblies of slave") because each Sunday it was jammed with slaves. Since it was undignified for the freeborn to be found among large crowds of slaves, the majority of the free severed all contact with the Christian missionaries.

While the freeborn of Asaba lamented the curtailment of their rights over their slaves, the slaves themselves hoped that the decree against human sacrifice would be followed by another declaring the complete eradication of slavery. When their expectations were not realized immediately, many began slowly to withdraw from the Christian missions. In 1891, Rev. Spencer expressed disappointment that

nearly the whole of the slaves who began to attend church at that time, did so merely to please the *Oyibos* (civilized men) who delivered them from death: for up to the present moment, very few have shown the slightest signs of determination to give up themselves to the Lord. (CMS, Rev. Spencer 1891)

He went from one slave village to another, exhorting them to abandon their old customs and give themselves entirely to the service of God, but without success. Thus, while the missionaries denounced the backsliding of the slaves, the slaves continued to hope and pray for complete freedom. Contrary to their expectations and despite reports that slave-dealing was everywhere common, neither the agents of the British government in southern Nigeria nor the agents of the Royal Niger Company made any sustained effort to fight internal slavery in Igboland. It was only after 1899, when the charter of the Royal Niger Company was withdrawn and the British government assumed direct responsibility for the administration of all Nigeria that the slavery issue was seriously taken up.

Continued Suppression of Slavery, the Use of Forced Labor, and the Establishment of a Free-Labor Market in Igboland

The measures leading to the effective suppression of internal slavery in Igboland actually began in 1900 with the adoption of a policy which

British Colonial Office officials described as the suppression of slavery and the establishment of a free-labor market in the colonies (PRO, Moor 1902). In pursuance of this policy the government of Southern Nigeria issued a proclamation forbidding all transactions in human beings and at the same time setting free all slaves (PRO, Proclamation No. 5, 1901). But fearing this might lead to serious social unrest, the administration immediately issued another proclamation — the Native House Rule Proclamation No. 26 of 1901 — forbidding slaves to leave their masters. Then, fearing this might not produce the desired objective, a third law was enacted — the Master and Servant Proclamation No. 12 of 1903. Former slaves were now to be called apprentices, and both they and their masters were to be bound by contract laying down terms of service. Children were to be apprenticed for up to 12 years.

Officials argued that these measures were meant to guarantee a constant supply of labor for chiefs no longer able to recruit it by purchase. The British commissioner Sir Ralph Moor had explained that chiefs had to be able to procure apprentices to instruct them in native industries or employ them as domestic servants (PRO, Moor 1902). Although Moor further explained that the restriction placed on the movement of freed slaves was necessary "to preserve the masters' authority over the energies and movement of their slaves," the fact is that the government was afraid of being saddled with a large population of fugitive slaves. For the Brussels Act of 1890 had bound signatories to repatriate or rehabilitate freed slaves in suitable locations near European stations. Adult slaves were to be encouraged to enlist in the forces of the nations which liberated them, and children were to be educated (Miers 1975: 252).

The foregoing clearly illustrates the ambivalence of colonial administrators theoretically committed to the abolition of slavery but unwilling to end social control over labor. Proclamation No. 12 of 1903 also provided for the arrest of "any person wandering abroad or having no apparent means of subsistence." If such a person was escaping from the house to which he belonged, he could be sent to prison. Thus, under British law, freed slaves dissatisfied with their treatment could not even leave. Most officials strongly felt that it was premature at the time to make a determined attempt to establish a free-labor force in Southern Nigeria. It was soon revealed during an inquiry instituted to investigate reports of labor abuse in Nigeria that officials who had hoped to bridge "the gulf between slavery and free labour . . . with minimum interference with existing customs and traditions" actually legalized a system similar to African slavery (Miers 1975: 302). Under this system of labor control, officials were empowered to call on chiefs or heads of houses to provide forced labor.

It should be pointed out that the Native House Rule Proclamation was originally intended for the Niger Delta communities, where corporate canoe houses were a principal feature of social and economic organization. As British influence spread into the hinterland, the law was extended to the Igbo-speaking areas because of the wrong belief that in Southern Nigeria all "natives" belonged to some houses. As the Igbo society was not organized like the Niger Delta city states, the principle enunciated in the House Rule Proclamation could not function properly. In due course, the final say in matters relating to slavery and labor generally was left in the hands of warrant chiefs, district officers, and native courts.

British officials were well aware that slavery in Igboland could not be suppressed by proclamations, particularly because the vast majority of the Igbo people had not even recognized British rule. Military subjugation was inevitable because, without complete control, the economic aims of the British could not be realized. The Aro, who dominated trade east of the Niger, posed the greatest threat to effective British rule. As the palm-oil trade expanded in the nineteenth century, the Aro entered it but did not give up slave-dealing. This disturbed the British less than the power and influence the Aro exercised, particularly through their oracle the Long Juju (*ibinokpabi*), which served as a court of appeals for many of the people of southeastern Nigeria. Not only was such a court incompatible with British control, but the Aro had forged a system of alliances with many Igbo and non-Igbo groups calculated to frustrate British penetration of the interior. They also armed Abam mercenaries, whom they sent against their enemies. In 1901, officials finally decided to embark on a massive invasion of Igboland in order, as they explained,

to abolish the slave trade which is actively carried out throughout the entire territories. . . . To abolish the fetish of the Aros known as "Long Juju." . . . while this Juju exists it is impossible to establish effective Government in the territories. . . . To introduce a currency in lieu of slaves, brass rods and other forms of native currency that exist in the territories. . . . Finally to introduce a labour market to take the place of slavery. (PRO, memorandum on Aro expedition 1901)

The British, like the other imperialists of western Europe, used the slave-trade issue to justify their invasion and appropriation of "native" lands. Joseph Chamberlain, the British colonial secretary from 1895 to 1903, stated in connection with Nigeria:

Sooner or later we shall have to fight some of the slave dealing tribes and we cannot have a better casus belli. . . . public opinion here requires that we shall justify control of these savage countries by some serious effort to put down slave dealing. (as quoted in Miers 1975: 24)

It is thus clear that the suppression of the slave trade and slavery was inextricably bound up with British political and economic objectives.

The Aro expedition ended with the destruction of the Long Juju and many Igbo settlements, but it did not completely subjugate the Igbo. Annual punitive expeditions had to be sent into the area for the next 15 years. Nevertheless, with the Aro subdued in 1902 and impressive victories scored over the Ekumeku society in western Ibgoland in 1902 and 1904, the government felt able to recruit labor for the colonial exploitation of southeastern Nigeria. Proclamation No. 15 of 1903 — the Roads and Creeks Proclamation — empowered officials to "regulate the compulsory labor existing under the tribal system" and to exact labor from local communities with or without pay. The proclamation stated:

Every chief may require all able-bodied men between the ages of 15 and 50, and all able-bodied women between the ages of 15 and 40 residing within his jurisdiction . . . to work in accordance with his direction on any river, creek, or road. . . . (PRO, Proclamation No. 15, 1903)

Anyone who refused to comply was to be punished by fine, imprisonment, or flogging.

To tighten up the process by which labor might be appropriated, colonial administrators appointed warrant chiefs to regulate local affairs. Most of these were "upstarts." They were the instrument with which the colonial government centralized the fragmented political institutions of the Igbo. Against all Igbo traditions, the warrant chiefs overrode the decisions of the local community, rounded up labor for public work, and collected taxes (Afigbo 1972).

These policies had a great levelling effect on Igbo society. Both freeborn and slaves were made to work side by side on government projects. A district officer would suddenly descend upon the warrant chiefs and order them to assemble their people for road construction. The chiefs and other leading members of the community would then organize their people into work teams. A work team in this instance was synonymous with an age-grade or a communal labor force known as *iyi ohu* in Agbor or *otu olu* in Asaba, Onitsha, and Owerri. Each team was expected to work on the road for a specified number of days. Initially the various communities sent their slaves, but the warrant chiefs, familiar with government feelings about slavery, made no distinction between freeborn and slave when sending conscripts to construction sites.

The Asaba-Benin road was constructed with forced labor. In 1906, the district commissioner in Agbor reported that it was not uncommon to find 2,000 "natives" at work on this road for a considerable period

(PRO, Watt 1906). Pressure was put upon chiefs to supply such labor. Conscripts were often away from their homes for five or more days at a time, causing their farmlands to suffer from lack of care. As a road progressed farther and farther away from a settlement, recruits might have had to walk up to 18 miles to construction sites. Heads of families had to provide their own food during such tours, as well as provide for the families they left behind. In 1906 when some clans in the Agbor District protested against the incessant use of forced labor, several hundreds of them were shot by colonial troops (PRO, memorandum on operations in Agbor District 1906). Even domestic slaves must have been baffled by the new forms of slavery introduced by the white man.

Throughout Southern Nigeria, youths, tired of endless work on government projects, began to absent themselves and were severely flogged. Because of the harshness of recruiting methods, the mere rumor that a white man was coming or the appearance of a policeman or a court messenger sent entire villagers fleeing into the bush. At Ikom several people drowned trying to escape (Tamuno 1972: 320). One provincial commissioner noted that such widespread flight was an effective system of "passive resistance" and that the chiefs either could not suppress it or, more likely, were themselves involved in it (NAE, annual report, Ikom Division, 1917). Certainly, such widespread flights and withdrawal of labor from agriculture and craft manufacture could not but have far-reaching consequences on the domestic economy, especially on food supply.[5]

Appalled by reports of this forced labor and the flogging and shooting of protesters, the secretary of the British Anti-Slavery and Aborigines Protection Society, a humanitarian organization, complained to the British government, pointing out that this "employment of forced labor, lending itself to grave abuse in the hands of injudicious administrators, is in the nature of slavery" (PRO, secretary, Anti-Slavery and Aborigines Protection Society, 1906).

This protest and unfavorable comments in the press led the Colonial Office to rebuke the government of Southern Nigeria, which was not only flogging chiefs but was demanding "unnecessary and even useless work." The high commissioner of Southern Nigeria admitted in 1906 that

it has always been customary to fine towns and villages for rising against the Government . . . and in lieu of the exaction of fines, chiefs have been required to provide labour for road construction or for clearing of sites and the erection of buildings or new stations. (PRO, Egerton 1906)

5. The origins of food scarcity in southeastern Nigeria can be traced to this period. The food crisis was worsened by the influenza epidemic which broke out at the end of the First World War. See Ohadike 1981.

Stern warnings from the Colonial Office against the use of forced labor were not heeded, and the Colonial Office itself sometimes ordered the practice stepped up, notably during the First and Second World Wars. Only after 1945, perhaps as part of the policy of planned decolonization, did the British dismantle the more obvious forms of colonial labor abuse.

Wage Labor and the Decline of Slavery

From the outset it was recognized that the recruitment of labor by force was inefficient and expensive, since it ultimately involved violence, close supervision, and waste. As early as 1906, the Southern Nigerian Road Construction Department had recognized that unpaid labor was "unsatisfactory," partly because of its fluctuating nature and partly because the laborers had to be changed too often, each batch of new recruits requiring fresh instruction (PRO, Egerton 1906). Moreover, not all forms of labor could be recruited or made to perform by force. Thus, even during the early colonial period a certain amount of free wage labor slowly emerged in Igboland. The mercantile houses and the civil administration needed clerks, messengers, domestic servants, policemen, soldiers, miners, and railway and dock workers. The mission schools wanted teachers, and the plantations required farm laborers. As these job opportunities widened, many slaves left their masters for distant commercial, administrative, and mining centers within and outside Igboland. They went to the sea ports and to plantations and timber concessions. As time went on, the freeborn followed the slaves. Although job opportunities were limited, the prospect of securing a job was a powerful incentive for slaves to leave their masters. It is therefore accurate to say that the rise of wage labor in Nigeria played a major role in accelerating the decline of slavery in Igboland.

Other factors also contributed to the decline of slavery in Igboland. The British conquest of the jihadist states of Northern Nigeria and of the Aro cut off the main supply of slaves. The presence of British colonial forces, especially the police, discouraged kidnapping. The palm-oil trade began to decline after 1896, and this compelled producers to reconsider the economic logic of holding large stocks of slaves. The British dealt the house system a final blow with the Native House Rule Ordinance of 1912. This did not abolish the system, but the authority of heads of houses over their members was no longer recognized by the courts, and the police could no longer recapture those who left (NAE, governor's deputy 1939). In 1916, the legal status of slavery was finally abolished throughout Nigeria (NAE, Cameron 1933).

When slaves became aware of these decisions, the greater majority of them asserted their freedom. Many simply wandered off, either singly or in little groups, and perhaps were not heard of anymore. Some left in large bodies and founded new settlements elsewhere. For instance, a large body of slaves left Abala and founded a new settlement a few miles away (NAI, William and Miller 1930–1931). Also at Osomari, thousands of slaves left their masters and established autonomous settlements in the nearby farms (NAE, district officer, Onitsha, 1928). Partly because of their superior numbers and partly because of British military presence, their masters could not recover them even if they so wished. For many decades thereafter, both "host" and "stranger" communities remained antagonistic to one another. But despite this, these ex-slaves organized their settlements like those of their former masters, with their own head chiefs, titled chiefs, councils of elders, and age-grade associations.

It was not always possible for ex-slaves to leave, however. Some remained behind and, in due course, redefined their relationships with their former masters. Some ex-slaves melted into the free society, while a number of former slave villages merged with the parent villages. Rather than merge with the parent villages, a few former slave villages established themselves as semiautonomous settlements within the communities in which they found themselves, with their own titled chiefs (not head chiefs), councils of elders, and age-grade associations.

On the other hand, female ex-slaves fared better than their male counterparts. For even though many Igbo still frowned at intermarriage between the freeborn and the descendants of slaves, once women were married to freeborn men, they sooner or later lost the stigma usually attached to slave origin. Also, children born of freed slaves and freeborn men were equally regarded as free.

The Persistence of Slave-Dealing and "Voluntary" Servitude

In view of these important changes, slavery and other forms of social discrimination in Igboland might have been expected to die a natural death very quickly. However, they lingered on because of developments that had been in train over the previous four centuries. A class of people had come to depend on slave-dealing for a livelihood, and as long as they could find a market they continued to deal in slaves. Thus, for over 40 years after the British invaded the Aro homelands, slave-dealing continued, albeit on a reduced scale. As late as 1924 the government of Southern Nigeria declared that slavery had not been "automatically and completely suppressed" but was gradually dying out (NAE, chief secretary 1924).

The most persistent type of slave-dealing was in small children, who were usually kidnapped and sold at recognized centers. In 1913, the most notorious markets were at Uzoakoli and Uburu in the Bende and Afikpo districts, respectively. They were connected to Okigwe, Awka, and other major centers, and sometimes captives came from as far away as Lokoja (NAE, provincial commissioner, Calabar, 1913). Most transactions were carried out at night in the homes of the slave-dealers. Buyers included the childless, elderly women, and retired prostitutes in the Ikom and Obubra divisions of Ogoja Province (NAE, resident, Ogoja, 1935). Men also purchased little boys to use as laborers when they grew up. However, most of these children were not necessarily treated like slaves but like adopted children, hence, the system has been described as "adoption of children by purchase" (NAE, Williams 1939). Some of the girls ended up as the wives of their male purchasers. Others were made to work as prostitutes for their female purchasers, especially when these owners had been prostitutes themselves. In Owerri Province, women were sometimes kidnapped and given out as wives by persons who were not entitled to receive the dowry (NAE, district officer, Degema, 1936). Not all the children were obtained by kidnapping, however. In some provinces some parents sold their children for economic or other reasons (NAE, Williams 1939).

Throughout the early colonial period, the police sometimes recovered stolen children and returned them to their parents if they could be traced, or placed them in foster homes. An interesting example was the recovery in 1918 of three girls between the ages of four and six, one of whom had been found being carried at night, tied to the back of an unidentified man, who upon being questioned, dropped the child and ran (NAE, Coupland-Crawford 1918). Hausa traders who travelled widely in Nigeria were also sometimes found with purchased or kidnapped children.

Equally disturbing to the administration was the persistence of "voluntary" servitude. By the 1930s all "slaves" in Nigeria were fully aware that they could not be forced to remain with their former masters and that if they left no court could compel them to return. Despite this, some remained and suffered from social discrimination and economic exploitation. The League of Nations Advisory Committee of Experts on Slavery asked the British government to explain this, suggesting that either the abolition enactments were not operative or that circumstances were so extraordinary that the life of a slave was preferable to that of a free person (NAE, League of Nations Report 1936). In reply all British officials in Igboland declared that there were no more slaves in their areas, but certain people still lived in conditions of incomplete freedom. The district officer of Okigwe stated that if the *Concise Oxford Dictionary* definition of a slave is "a person who is legal property of another or others and is bound to absolute obedience, human chattel," then there were no slaves in his district (NAE, district officer, Okigwe, 1936). The district officer of Aba declared that if slavery was considered to be an economic institution, no man in his district was entirely dependent for his physical livelihood on another. The descendants of former slaves now possessed land of their own, worked as laborers, and were as completely independent as they could be. The prohibition upon their actions, he explained, was not sanctioned by law but by custom backed by public opinion, and no court of law could alter this. For instance, no court could compel a freeborn woman to marry the descendant of a slave against her will (NAE, district officer, Aba, 1936).

Most district officers also recognized that pawning approximated voluntary servitude. It was not slavery because, apart from the actual labor which the debtor rendered to the creditor, the pawn was free to lead his or her own life and could at any time terminate the agreement and pay interest in lieu of work (NAE, district officer, Bende, 29 November 1936). Nor were osu slaves in the strict sense of the word, although religious taboos made their position in society inferior to that of the freeborn (NAE, district officer, Owerri, 23 November 1936).

Throughout Igboland some ex-slaves continued to live with the families who had originally acquired them. Their labor was sometimes exploited, and they suffered under a social stigma. That they were content to remain in voluntary servitude was shown when the district officer of Ogoja in 1936 visited a village in the Kumba Division of Cameroon Province, where ex-slaves said they rendered annual service to their "masters." "This," he wrote, "was told to me as a fact not by way of complaint." He offered to try to arrange for their repatriation but was laughed at. "Not one of the slaves wished to take advantage of my offer," he lamented (NAE, resident, Ogoja, 1936).

Another government official explained the reasons for this. Some ex-slaves were tied to their ex-masters by bonds of life-long affection, and "it was unthinkable to either of them that they should part" (NAE, officer administering the government of Nigeria 1936). Elderly ex-slaves often did not want to risk having to seek a less sheltered life elsewhere. Some stayed because they enjoyed the protection and patronage of their former masters. Others did not remember their villages of origin, or if they did, they did not want to start life again among strangers. As late as 1936, in the midst of the depression, a district officer declared that domestic security counted far more in the minds of some classes of Africans than personal freedom (NAE, district officer, Calabar, 1936).

Although we shall never know the exact number of people who lived in this quasi slavery in southeastern Nigeria, a district officer furnished rough estimates. In 1936, Calabar Province, with a population of 900,000, had an estimated 10,000 ex-slaves who had "never formally been emancipated" or were "persons of slave descent who voluntarily endured certain restrictions." Out of a population of 1,108,000 in Onitsha Province, some 20,000 still lived in quasi servitude. In Ogoja Province, there were about 14,000 persons who were ex-slaves or their children. In Warri Province only about 1 percent of the 444,000 population were still tagged with the stigma of servitude, the rest having melted into the free population. (NAE, Whitely 1936).

Colonial Office officials in London, uneasy with the situation, informed the governor of Nigeria that "the continuance of any form of servitude, even if described as 'voluntary' cannot be acquiesced indefinitely" (NAE, Colonial Office 1936). However, in the 1930s there was nothing the government could do for those who were legally free to leave the communities that kept them in "bondage" but who, in practice, could not or would not do so. As has been seen, no court of law could free them from their servitude or elevate them to higher levels on the social ladder or even make them enjoy all the rights and privileges of other sections of society. Thus, the post–Second World War problem of slavery in Igboland was not one of emancipation but rather of incomplete assimilation. Some communities continued to regard ex-slaves and their descendants as social inferiors, denying them certain rights and privileges. Marriage between them and the freeborn was still considered an abomination. Sometimes they were not allowed to officiate at ritual ceremonies or to purchase important titles.

Increasing Numbers of Osu

Also, despite British laws, the dedication of people to juju — osu slavery — continued unabated. In 1939, two cases were tried in Nsukka District, but the accused were acquitted as there was no evidence that the girls concerned had been held as slaves against their will. They had been given to the priests of the juju, who intended to marry them when they came of age. They were not ill-treated and in theory could leave, but in practice they could not do so, since they knew their parents would not have them back (NAE, acting secretary 1939). Paradoxically, while the other classes of unfree persons gained their freedom in the later colonial period, the members of osu multiplied dramatically, largely because they could marry only each other, so all their offspring were osu. Moreover, whereas many ex-slaves abandoned their former masters, the osu remained bound to the deities to which they or their forebears had been dedicated, even if they never set eyes upon the shrines of these deities.

The Persistence of Pawning

Pawning of children remained common throughout Igboland, although the British outlawed it as a form of servitude. In the Ihiala area, men unable to settle a big debt sometimes gave their daughters away in marriage to the creditor, "the cancellation of the debt forming all or part of the dowry" (NAE, district officer, Onitsha, 1931). In the Ahoada area, adults and children sometimes worked for a creditor instead of paying interest. The British imposition of taxes led to a new form of pawning in some parts of Igboland. A bridegroom would be required to pay the annual taxes for the bride's parents instead of paying the traditional bride-price. If he failed to complete his payments, the parents could recover their daughter without refunding the amount he had already paid (interview: Obi Nwobi, 1982). The pawning of children to pay poll taxes were so widespread that in 1931 the government was asked in the Legislative Council of Nigeria whether they were aware of it. Predictably, many district officers denied any knowledge of the practice because no one had complained about it (NAE, secretary, Southern Nigeria, 1931). However, as the assistant commissioner of police pointed out, this was no excuse, since in all forms of pawning the relatives of the pawn were parties to the transaction, and therefore, no one was likely to lodge a complaint (NAE, assistant commissioner of police 1931). Not only was pawning difficult to detect but the few accused, who were tried, were acquitted for lack of evidence.

Conclusion: The Emergence of New Classes

In spite of the continuance of social discrimination, British antislavery measures, together with the economic and political changes in the twentieth century, widened the horizons of former slaves and their descendants by providing them for the first time with the choice of remaining in their host communities or going elsewhere. Those who chose to stay suffered social disabilities, but their labor was freed from arbitrary exploitation by their masters. Those who left often suffered initial inconveniences, such as difficulty in locating their natal homes or in adjusting to new communities, and, most important, in acquiring land or securing wage labor. Nevertheless, once these problems had been overcome, they and their descendants lived as free members of their new communities. They were no longer slaves as defined by the International Slavery Convention of 1926, since no one exercised "any or all of the powers attaching to the right of ownership" over them.

A large number of freed slaves sold their labor power in return for wages, while others took to petty trading, farming, and the professions. Many of them, especially the youths, bent their energy to the pursuit of Western education and soon surpassed their masters in book learning and wealth. Ex-slaves were quick to recognize the importance, in the new colonial situation, of Western education as an avenue to wealth — itself a prerequisite for economic independence. They were, thus, the first Igbo to enroll in schools. Only a generation later did the freeborn seem to recognize that education was a powerful weapon in colonial society and begin to embrace Christianity. This delay by the freeborn enabled the ex-slaves to emerge as the first educated elements in Igbo society, as well as the first to accept wage labor and to take advantage of the other openings that came with British rule. This was not just an Igbo phenomenon. In 1936, the chief secretary of Southern Nigeria informed the governor that "it is a popular superstition in Ijebu that ex-slaves had luck with them, and it is a fact that the more prosperous members of the country today are the children of ex-slaves, though they would naturally resent any reference to their descent" (NAE, chief secretary 1936).

Today, despite the lingering social stigma, many descendants of slaves have taken advantage of their superior wealth and education to purchase higher titles. Some of them have been elected to important political offices. Many have married into the families of the freeborn, and a good number have assumed lineage and political leadership. In fact, it is said that many Igbo who today parade as amadi do not know that their parents were ohu unless a dispute arises over land, titles, or political leadership during which slave descent is revealed. In a recent newspaper article a prominent Igbo political leader expressed great concern at the tendency of the osu and ohu to rule the Igbo people (*Sunday Concord*, 12 June 1983).

For the class of slave masters, the suppression of slavery resulted in great loss of wealth and prestige. Most slaves had been purchased, and their emancipation without compensation meant the destruction of their masters' accumulated capital. The land made available to freed slaves represented a net loss to the host communities in general and to the slave-owners in particular. Colonial administration forbade the eviction of former slaves from farmlands and dwellings (NAE, district officer, Bende, 29 November 1936). Sometimes owners solved the problem by asking their freed slaves to pay a small rent. These rents were in recognition of the ex-master's ownership of the land, but in time the descendants of the slaves gained permanent possession of such lands (NAE, chief secretary

1924). However, if they voluntarily vacated the property or produced no male heirs, the land reverted to the family of the former master (NAE, district officer, Agwu Division, 10 December 1936). In some areas such as western Igboland, masters, apparently frightened by continued British military presence, voluntarily gave out land to former slaves.

Perhaps the most painful consequence of emancipation was the loss of prestige and authority suffered by the class of titled chiefs. The ending of slavery robbed them of the opportunity to "give outward expression to their wealth and position" (ibid.). Stripped of their slaves and therefore their wealth, many Igbo chiefs became as poor as the ordinary members of the society. Emancipation thus played a part in levelling Igbo society. British labor and judicial policies also played a part by further undermining the institution of kingship. First, in a sense, the whole society became the white man's slaves. Second, traditional chiefs were relegated to positions of insignificance, while "upstarts" without local standing were elevated to the rank of warrant chiefs and given executive and judicial powers unprecedented both in degree and in territorial scope (Afigbo 1972: 67). Even titles lost their significance. In 1936, a district officer at Asaba declared, "Since the government of Nigeria imposes the sanctions of law equally and without favour upon all, the corporate titles have now little function beyond the decorative" (NAI, Vaux 1936).

The ending of slavery in Igboland thus witnessed the dissolution of the old classes and signified the emergence of new ones. Most Igbo titles and offices are purchasable. Although in theory only the amadi may purchase them, in practice it is now difficult to prevent any man from doing so. Since wealth is virtually the only qualification for office and titleholding in twentieth-century Igboland, and since the descendants of the ohu are today relatively more affluent than the amadi, the ohu are rapidly emerging as members of the upper classes and the amadi are being relegated to the lower classes.

GLOSSARY

Note: Except where otherwise noted, these words are used both for singular and plural forms.

adu ebo	cult slave.
akaja	wooden drum in Asaba.
amadi	freeborn.
eze	king, head chief, titled chief, red-cap chief.
ibinokpabi	an oracle of the Aro.
ihe	slave camp or slave village at Oguta.

iyi ohu	a work team in Agbor.
juju	deity; fetish; masquerade; oracle; talisman.
nwamadu	freeborn.
nvunvu ego	debtor-slave, pawn.
obi	king, head chief, titled chief, red-cap chief.
obia	stranger.
ohu	slave.
otu olu	work team in Asaba, Onitsha, and Owerri.
osu	cult slave.
oyibo (pl. *oyibos*)	white man; "civilized" man; educated man.
ugwule	slave camp or slave village, sometimes used for a slave as well.
wari	lineage, canoe house among the Ijaw (Ezon) of the Niger Delta.

REFERENCES

Oral sources

A. Agorua, interview on 12 June 1984.
Henry N. Abili Mordi, interview on 10 December 1982.
Obi Nwobi, interview on 8 December 1982.

Archival sources

CMS: Church Missionary Society Archives, London
    Rev. Johnson to Lang, 5 July 1888. 93/A3/1888/77.
    Rev. Spencer reporting from Asaba, December 1891. G3/A3/1892/52.
NAE: National Archives, Enugu
    Acting secretary, Southern Provinces, to the secretary for the government, Lagos, 13 December 1939. CSE 1/85/2924, EP 5279, Vol. 1.
    Annual report, 1915, by Resident Fremantle, Muri Province. RIVPROF 1/2/2, C31/16.
    Annual report, 1917, Ikom Division. ONPROF 7/9/36, OP427/22.
    Assistant commissioner of police to inspector general of police, Lagos, 13 April 1931. CSE 1/85/4181, EP 7684.
    Cameron to Colonial Office, correspondence relating to International Slavery Convention, 4 May 1933. CSE 1/85/2924, EP 5279, Vol. 2.
    Chief secretary for the government, 5 February 1924. CSE 1/85/2924, EP 5279, Vol. 1.
    Chief secretary to secretary of state for the colonies, 15 August 1936. CSE/1/85/2924, EP 5279, Vol. 3.
    Colonial Office to Bourdillon, 4 May 1936. CSE/1/85/2924, EP 5279.
    Coupland-Crawford to Divisional Office, Abakiliki, 4 April 1918. CSE 1/85/4188, B 322/18.

District officer, Aba, to resident, Owerri Province, 24 October 1936. RIVPROF 2/1/42, C219.

District officer, Agwu Division, to resident, 5 December 1936. CSE/1/85/2925, EP 5279, Vol. 2.

District officer, Agwu Division, to provincial officer, 10 December 1936. CSE/1/95/2925, EP 5279, Vol. 2.

District officer, Bende, to resident, Owerri Province, 24 October 1936. RIVPROF 2/1/42, C219.

District officer, Bende, to resident, Owerri Province, 29 November 1936, RIVPROF 2/1/42, C219.

District officer, Calabar, to the officer administering the government of Nigeria, 16 December 1936. CSE 1/85/2925, EP 5279, Vol. 2.

District officer, Degema, to resident, Owerri Province, 9 November 1936. RIVPROF 2/1/42, C219.

District officer, Okigwe, to resident, Owerri Province, 24 October 1936. RIVPROF 2/1/42, C219.

District officer, Onitsha, to resident, Onitsha, 6 March 1931. CSE 1/85/4181, EP 7684.

District officer, Onitsha, to resident, Onitsha Province, 2 January 1936. ONDIST 12/1/873, OP1322.

District officer, Onitsha, to senior resident, Onitsha Province, 17 January 1928. ONDIST 12/1/1987, OP 2893.

District officer, Owerri, to resident, Owerri Province, 24 October 1936. RIVPROF 2/1/42, C219.

District officer, Owerri, to resident, Owerri Province, 23 November 1936, 2925, EP 5279, Vol. 2.

Governor's deputy to secretary of state for the colonies, 20 December 1939. CSE/1/85/2926, EP 5279, Vol. 3.

League of Nations Report and discussion on slavery, 24 October 1936. RIVPROF 2/1/42, C219.

Officer administering the government of Nigeria to secretary of state to the colonies, 16 December 1936. CSE 1/85/2925, EP 5279, Vol. 2.

Provincial commissioner, Eastern Provinces, Calabar, to secretary, Southern Nigerian Government, 22 October 1913. CALPROF 13/6/103, E 115/13.

Resident, Ogoja, to secretary, Southern Provinces, Enugu, 2 January 1935. CSE 1/85/5518, EP 1/206.

Secretary, Southern Nigeria, to provincial officers, 31 July 1931. CSE 1/85/4181, EP 7684.

Senior district officer, Onitsha, to resident, 7 May 1935. ONDIST 12/1/873, OP1322.

Whitely to secretary of state for the colonies, 16 December 1936. CSE/1/2925, EP 5279.

Williams, acting secretary, Southern Provinces, to governor, 13 December 1939. CSE 1/85/2924, EP 5279, Vol. 1.

NAI: National Archives, Ibadan.

Vaux, H., Intelligence Report on the Asaba Clan, 1936. CSO26/4, 30927.

William and Miller, Intelligence Report on Aboh-Benin Clans, 1930–1931. CS026/10, 26769.
PRO: Public Record Office, London.
Colonial Office to the government of Southern Nigeria, 15 March 1907. CO52/38.
Colonial Office comments on Moor's proposals, 20 April 1902. CO520/13/83.
Egerton, W. high commissioner, Southern Nigeria, to Colonial Office, 7 October 1906. CO520/37.
MacDonald, Major C. M., report, 1889, enclosed in Chapter 9. FO84/2109.
Memorandum on instructions with regard to the Aro expedition, 12 November 1901. CO520/10.
Memorandum on operations in the Agbor District, Southern Nigeria, June–August 1906. CO520/54.
Moor, R., to Colonial Office, 26 February 1902. CO52/13/83.
Proclamations:

	Number	Year
Slave Dealing	5	1901
The Native House Rule	26	1901
The Master and Servant	12	1903
The Roads and Creeks	15	1903

Note: For proclamations 1894–1906, see CO588/1.
Secretary, British Anti-Slavery and Aborigines Protection Society, to Elgin, secretary of state for the colonies, 19 September 1906. CO520/39.
Watt, J., to acting provincial commissioner, Central Province, 8 September 1906. CO520/37.
SMA: Society of African Missions Archives, Rome.
Annals of the Propagation of Faith, 1902, from the letters of Father Zappa.
Les Missions catholiques, No. 1279, 8 December 1893, p. 586.

Other sources

Afigbo, A. E. 1972. The warrant chiefs: indirect rule in Southern Nigeria, 1891–1928. Ibadan: University of Ibadan.
Alagoa, E. J. 1972. A history of the Niger Delta. Ibadan: University of Ibadan.
Basden, G. T. 1966. Niger Ibos: a description of the primitive life, customs and animistic beliefs and. . . . London: Frank Cass.
Crowther, S. A., and J. C. Taylor. 1968. Gospel on the banks of the Niger. Journal and notices of the native missionaries accompanying the Niger Expedition of 1857–1859. London: Dawson (originally published in 1859).
Church Missionary Intelligencer. 1879 (a yearly periodical produced by the CMS; now located in the CMS Archives, London).
Dike, K. O. 1956. Trade and politics in the Niger Delta, 1830–1885. Oxford: Clarendon.
Henderson, R. N. 1972. The king in every man: evolutionary trends in Onitsha Ibo society and culture. New Haven: Yale University Press.
Hilliard, J. J. 1963. Father Zappa and his mission. Exitt 3: 13–15.

Horton, R. 1969. From fishing village to city-state: a social history of New Calabar. In *Man in Africa*, ed. M. Douglas and P. M. Kaberry, 37–58. London: Tavistock.

Horton, W. R. G. 1954. The Ohu system of slavery in a northern Igbo village-group. *Africa* 24: 311–36.

Isichei, E. 1973. *The Ibo people and the Europeans*. London: Faber and Faber.

Isichei, E. 1976. *A history of the Igbo people*. New York: Macmillan.

Jones, G. I. 1963. *The trading states of the oil rivers, a study of political development in eastern Nigeria*. London: OUP.

Klein, M., and P. Lovejoy. 1979. Slavery in West Africa. In *The uncommon market: essays in the economic history of the Atlantic slave trade*, ed. H. A. Gemery and J. S. Hogendorn, 181–212. London: Academic.

Laird, M., and R. A. K. Oldfield. 1971. *Narrative of an expedition into the interior of Africa*. London: Frank Cass.

Latham, A. J. H. 1972. Witchcraft accusations and economic tension in precolonial Old Calabar. *Journal of African History* 13: 249–60.

Latham, A. J. H. 1973. *Old Calabar 1600–1891: the impact of the international economy upon a traditional society*. Oxford: Clarendon.

Mackenzie, R. P. 1976. *Inter-religious encounters in West Africa, Samuel Ajayi Crowther's attitude to African traditional religion and Islam*. Leicester: University of Leicester.

Miers, S. 1975. *Britain and the ending of the slave trade*. London: Longmans.

Northrup, D. 1978. *Trade without rulers, pre-colonial economic development in southeastern Nigeria*. Oxford: Clarendon.

Ohadike, D. C. 1981. The influenza pandemic of 1918–19 and the spread of cassava cultivation on the Lower Niger: a study in historical linkages. *Journal of African History* 22: 379–91.

Ojiakor, N. E. 1982. A cultural history of Ogbaru community of the lower Niger. B.A. thesis, University of Jos.

Onianwa, C. N. 1980. The coming of Christianity to Asaba. B.A. thesis, University of Jos.

Sunday Concord. 12 June 1983. MA 1, 5, xi (weekly newspaper; Ikeja, Nigeria: Concord Press).

Tamuno, T. N. 1972. *The evolution of the Nigerian state*. Ibadan: University of Ibadan.

Terray, E. 1974. Long-distance exchange and the state: the case of the Abron Kingdom of Gyamen. *Economy and Society* 3: 315–41.

Uchendu, V. C. 1977. Slaves and slavery in Igboland, Nigeria. In *Slavery in Africa*, ed. S. Miers and I. Kopytoff, 121–32. Madison: University of Wisconsin Press.

16 *David Northrup*

The Ending of Slavery in the Eastern Belgian Congo

From September 1876, when King Leopold II of Belgium hosted the Geographical Conference of Brussels to explore ways to bring "civilization" to central Africa, his public campaign for abolition of the slave trade was linked to his more covert plans to carve out a colonial empire there. The latter bore fruit in 1885 when he gained international recognition for his Congo Free State and measures were taken against slave-trading and slavery in its territories. Yet from the beginning there was serious conflict between Leopold's abolitionist and imperialist ambitions. To control the eastern third of the colony, he had to appoint as governor the Zanzibari slave-trader Tippu Tip. To come up with enough labor to make the colony profitable, the Free State employed "redeemed" slaves under slave-like conditions and created a vast and brutal system of forced labor, whose scandalous revelation brought down Leopold's personal rule in 1908.

In part the failure to bring a swift and satisfactory end to slavery oc-

This research was made possible by grants from the National Endowment for the Humanities, the Fulbright-Hays Commission, the Social Science Research Council, and by funds made available to Boston College from the Mellon Foundation. An earlier version of this chapter was presented at the annual meeting of the Canadian Association for African Studies in 1983. I gratefully acknowledge the helpful criticisms received there and those received more recently from Professor Tshimanga wa Tshibangu of the University of Kisangani. All translations are my own.

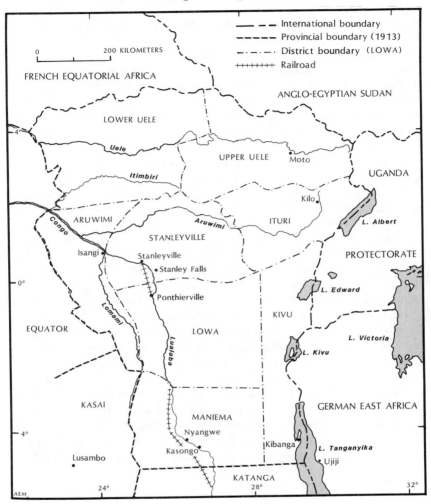

Map 16. The eastern Belgian Congo

curred because Leopold's commitment as a reformer was often subordinated to other ends (see Emerson 1979: 241), but the Free State's failure in this was also related to more complex issues that were widespread in early colonial Africa. First, what social status could emancipated men and women have? "Freedom" was an elusive and ambiguous concept, as the introduction to this book stresses (see also Kopytoff and Miers 1977), whether ex-slaves remained in traditional African milieux or were employed by the colonial government. Second, when slave labor was abolished, what form of labor would replace it? "Free" wage labor also has its ambiguities, since labor is rarely performed without some form of compulsion, but in general it refers to a system in which the economic constraints of the market are more important than direct political or social compulsion. While colonial rule in the Congo was no worse than elsewhere in providing slaves with personal freedom, the Free State's failure to create anything like a free-labor system led contemporaries to charge it with perpetuating slavery.

This chapter examines the problems associated with instituting alternatives to slavery in the Congo. Because of its importance in the history of the Congo, the link between slave labor and forced labor receives particular attention. In focusing on the continuities between slavery and what followed, this chapter does not join in the effort to distinguish slavery precisely from other forms of dependency. Though that remains a vital and difficult task, it is equally important not to lose sight of the fact that the practical difference to the individuals involved was often slight. In that regard the broad and ambiguous usage of the word *slavery* by contemporaries reflected the real-life ambiguities they observed.

Geographically this study is confined to the Congo's giant Eastern Province, which corresponds to the present Kivu and Haut-Zaïre provinces of modern Zaire. The eastern Congo, thus defined, has received little attention, though it was a very important area, which by the end of the Free State era was supplying two-fifths of the colony's ivory and rubber exports. It can be argued that an evaluation of Free State and Belgian antislavery policies may be suitably based on this area because of its importance and because the colonial government was the largest employer of African labor there until the 1920s, unlike the areas controlled by giant concessionary companies that were the scene of the Free State's most notorious abuses.

Precolonial Slavery

Nearly 1,000 miles from either ocean, eastern Zaire was among the most isolated spots in mid-nineteenth-century Africa. Population densities were low; economic development was limited. Labor mobilization and social stratification were effected largely through institutions defined by kinship, marriage, age, and political subordination. The most significant concentration of slaves existed in the Mangbetu, Babwa, and Azande kingdoms in the northern savannahs, where unredeemed captives obtained in recent conquests became slaves for life. A majority of these slaves, among the Mangbetu at least, were women, who were acquired by commoner lineages to build up their numbers and by royal lineages to produce the food used in royal largesse. Rulers also distributed slave wives as a way of attracting followers, a practice particularly important among the Azande. Slavery was not hereditary, but the children of slaves retained an inferior social status (De Bauw 1901: 73–74; Lagae 1926: 46–53; Lloyd 1978: 254–74; Keim 1983: 144–59).

The purchase or capture of women as wives was also widespread in the southern part of the region, although it is not clear how much their status differed from wives acquired by the payment of bridewealth. In 1869, while travelling through Maniema in the southeastern portion of the region, David Livingstone (1875: 305, 310) found local people interested in purchasing only female slaves intended as wives; male slaves were considered more vexatious than valuable, being generally criminals, troublemakers, and sorcerers sold by their own people. Likewise in the conflicts between the petty states throughout most of Kivu Province, male prisoners of war were generally killed or ransomed and the women were incorporated as wives (Birhakaheka 1978, 1: 142–43; Kabemba 1979: 45). Even allowing for the sparseness of the historical record, slavery appears to have been rare in most parts of the region before the arrival of ivory traders from Zanzibar.

In effect, this low incidence of slavery was linked to the relatively low level of economic and political development in the region, which, in turn, reflected its low population density and isolation. In most of the region the small size of political units limited the degree of social differentiation that might be present: the distance between a chief and his lowest subject was not great. Economically the low level of exchange meant that there existed neither a way of marketing war captives and other potential slaves far enough from their homelands to impede their return nor a demand for labor that might serve larger economic ends.[1] All of this was about to change.

The Growth of Slave Labor under Zanzibari Rule

The penetration of eastern Zaire in the 1860s by Arabs, Swahili, and other peoples from East Africa in the service of the sultan of Zanzibar was a major watershed in the history of the region and in the incidence of slav-

---

1. It is possible that the Wagenia, a fisherfolk on the upper Congo, may have been exceptional in their use of slaves, like their confreres the Bobangi on the Middle Niger (Harms 1981). A Wagenia chief whom V. L. Cameron met at Nyangwe in 1874 was willing to sell the explorer canoes only in exchange for slaves, arguing that "cowries would be lying idle and bringing him nothing till he managed to buy slaves with them, whereas if he received slaves in payment he could set them at work at once to paddle canoes between the markets,

ery. Initially these Zanzibari traders and their Nyamwezi servants had allied themselves with locally powerful chiefs to attack neighboring rivals. Gaining power, the Zanzibari eliminated their erstwhile allies, replacing them with ambitious younger persons whose loyalties were entirely to the Zanzibari and not to the local lineages. By the 1880s Zanzibari, under Tippu Tip, were firmly established around Stanley Falls (Kisangani), rival groups dominated the upper river, and bands of Zanzibari auxiliaries were spreading "like an oil slick" through the northern river valleys as well as in the southeast (Senga 1978; Van Eetvelde 1895: 108ff.).

Ivory was the driving force behind the Zanzibari expansion, but slaves were a useful by-product. The razzias they launched resulted in the slaughter of many local people and in captivity for many others, especially women and children. Some of these captives were ransomed by their relatives with ivory. The remaining women were either "distributed among the soldiers" (Coquilhat 1888: 427) or became concubines of the major Zanzibari chiefs.[2] The latter were not required to work (MRAC, Chaltin, n.d.: 20).

The male captives were used to meet the growing labor demands of commerce, conquest, and cultivation, demands which would escalate under Free State and Belgian rule. Captive youths were transformed into loyal servants for their new masters. In 1876, for example, Tippu Tip had about 50 whom he was training "as gun-bearers, house servants, scouts, cooks, carpenters, house-builders, blacksmiths, and leaders of trading parties" (Stanley 1878, 2: 129–30). Many such captives became soldiers, head men, and outpost commanders. Detached from their roots and cultural restraints, these new recruits were often guilty of the most brutal pillage of the countryside (MRAC, Chaltin, n.d.: 20; AA. Dhanis 1893?; see Senga 1978: 32–34).

The growing trade, in ivory especially, demanded more and more porters. While the Zanzibari might have preferred hired porters (such as the Nyamwezi they employed east of Lake Tanganyika and during their earliest years in Maniema), such free labor was unavailable in eastern Zaire. Instead, captives had to be employed to carry the tusks to the

to catch fish, to make pottery, or to cultivate his fields; in fact, he did not want his capital to lie idle" (Cameron 1885: 290). On the other hand, Hinde (1897: 157–58) reported that the Wagenia at Nyangwe were "all free men" and had no slaves.

2. By the mid-1870s Muini Dugumbi (alias Molemba-Lemba), one of the first Zanzibari to settle the region (in 1868), had 100–300 harem slaves. His chief henchman, Mtagamayo, had 60; his rival Abed bin Salim (alias Tanganyika) had a more modest 30. Tippu Tip and his entourage had 50 slave women in 1876 (Cameron 1885: 285; Stanley and Neame 1961: 7 November 1876; Stanley 1878, 2: 117–20, 130).

markets east of the lake. V. L. Cameron (1885: 305) reported that Tippu Tip and other traders "asserted that they would be glad to find other means of transport for their goods instead of trusting it to slaves: but . . . they availed themselves of the means at their disposal." Of course, such labor was also cheap, as Tippu explained to Henry M. Stanley: "Slaves cost nothing; they only require to be gathered" (Stanley and Neame 1961: 7 November 1876). A major drawback of slaves was their tendency to run away. Cameron (1885: 256) reported that half of those impressed into porterage escaped before a caravan reached Lake Tanganyika,[3] but most of those who completed the trek to Ujiji or Uyanyembe then hired out as "free porters." Whether this means that they were then entirely free from obligations to their former owners is unclear. In any event, sending such valuable labor out of the region soon came to an end. "For some time," Tippu Tip told a Free State agent in 1885, one team of "domestic slaves" had conveyed the ivory from Stanley Falls to Nyangwe, from where another relay of slaves took it to Ujiji, and so on to the coast, each team of porters returning to their homes (Coquilhat 1888: 415–16).

There were uses besides conquest and porterage to which the Zanzibari put their new subjects. The major permanent Zanzibari settlements in the region, such as Kasongo, Nyangwe, and Stanley Falls, were distinguished by well-built dwellings and surrounded by well-laid-out, flourishing plantations featuring many crops new to the region, such as rice, citrus fruits, and sesame. These impressive estates required considerable labor, which was supplied through levies on local inhabitants, whose own farms suffered in consequence, and through the use of slaves captured in campaigns. There is no way to estimate the quantity of these plantation slaves, but regular replenishment of their numbers was necessary, for, like those at Ujiji and other Arab settlements, most died within a year of overwork and undernourishment.[4]

Redeeming Slaves and Recruiting Labor in King Leopold's Congo

During the last decade of the century the incidence of slavery and forced labor underwent considerable change as the region came under the control of Belgium's King Leopold and became the Congo Free State. As an adherent to the general acts of the Berlin and Brussels conferences, the state was officially committed to ending the slave trade. When the

3. See C. S. Forester's (1948) moving tale of just such an escapee.
4. AA, Tobback 1887–1892b: 18; MRAC, Chaltin, n.d.: 20, 34; Le Clement de St.-Maroq 1890: 42; Senga 1978: 34.

Zanzibari leader Tippu Tip was appointed governor of the eastern Congo in 1887, part of the agreement was that he was to suppress slave-trading. It is significant that the first Free State antislavery legislation on record, the decree of 8 November 1888, concerned regulating labor contracts to prevent their degenerating into slavery (Van Eetvelde 1889).

Yet the Free State government faced a desperate labor shortage throughout the colony because few local Africans were willing to hire out their labor. Men to serve in the Free State army and build the lower Congo railroad had to be recruited from Liberia and British West Africa, from northeastern Africa and Zanzibar. Efforts were made to bring in labor from Portuguese Africa, Indonesia, India, and even from China (Stengers 1953: 827–30). Foreign recruitment was expensive and was unable to supply an adequate labor force. Moreover, it raised opposition from other colonial powers fearful of labor shortages in their own colonies and from critics who saw much of this recruitment as a thinly disguised continuation of the slave trade.

Greater internal recruitment of labor was thus essential, and the existing slave population of the eastern Congo constituted a potential resource. As an inducement to tap it, Free State recruiters were given funds sufficient to redeem men, women (for cleaning and farming), and adolescents for the colonial militia, or Force Publique, and to allow a cut for themselves. At Stanley Falls the state's agents had begun redeeming slaves of the Zanzibari for money and goods in 1886. During his five years there Captain Nicholas Tobback bought and freed a total of 2,000 slaves, though he refused to profit personally from these transactions (Ceulemans 1959: 225; AA, Tobback 1887–1892b: 20). In 1890 an accord was made with the Zanzibari chief Djuma-Dina to supply 500 able-bodied young men from Maniema to serve nine-year contracts. In December 1891 and March 1892 contracts were signed with Tippu Tip (then in Zanzibar) to furnish 3,800 free men and 800 free women as railroad laborers and soldiers.

These laborers, most of whom would probably have been redeemed slaves, were to be delivered to Bena-Kamba on the Lomami by the end of 1892, but the outbreak of hostilities between the state and the Zanzibari that year prevented the completion of the contracts (Ceulemans 1959: 224–30). However, the military campaigns against the rebellious Zanzibari and their African ally Ngongo Lutete produced large numbers of captives, who were then declared liberated. In the three years of the campaigns more than 5,000 of these arrived at the Lusambo military camp in Kasai, which served the eastern Congo. In a manner strongly reminiscent of the fate of the captives of Zanzibari razzias, many of these were retained locally as soldiers and laborers, while the surplus was parcelled out among local chiefs and even given to individual soldiers (ibid.: 233–34). The Tanganyika commander had 175–200 freedmen serving as soldiers in February 1895, plus "two villages of former Arab slaves who belong to the State" engaged in agriculture, including "about 150 youths suitable to be soldiers in two to three years and that I have not given to the missions, because they form the reserve of the Force Publique in Tanganyika" (AA, Descamps 1895). Many other former slaves and dependents of the Zanzibari were settled along main roads to raise food and supply porters to the government.

Catholic missionaries were also active in redeeming bodies, as well as souls, starting long before the Free State had an effective presence. The White Fathers' orphanage at Kibanga on Lake Tanganyika redeemed 76 boys, 10 girls, and 21 young women during 1886. Their 1,450th redemption came in November 1891 at a time when the Zanzibari leader Rumaliza was establishing control over the northern part of the lake and churning up considerable numbers of captives. The White Fathers' redemptions passed 1,500 early in 1892, but the supply of redeemable slaves fell sharply once the Free State established its control (APB, Chronique 1887: 463, 614; APB Chronique 1892: 413, 417). These redeemed slaves worked for the mission — mostly as farmers — until they married, or longer if they remained on mission grounds. For the most part those redeemed at Kibanga seem to have stayed willingly, but elsewhere ex-slaves were driven to desert their mission masters. The White Fathers' boys' orphanage at Old Kasongo began suffering from large-scale desertions by orphans "considering themselves slaves and wishing a more complete freedom," and had to be closed down in 1913 (APB, rapport annuel 1912–1913: 578; APB, rapport annuel 1913–1914: 314). Many of these "graduates" of the mission stations joined the labor market.

As the Free State became better established, it began to fulfill its labor needs more directly, but in ways that still closely paralleled those used by their Zanzibari predecessors. This continuity, quite evident to the Africans involved, was recorded by the head of the Catholic mission at Kasongo, Tippu Tip's old headquarters, in 1906:

. . . in the past when an Arab set himself up in a region, one of his first moves was to demand some children from the local chief as a pledge of their alliance or of their submission: these children, having become the property of the Arab, were then installed either among the soldiers or the servants of this slave trade. From that moment on they could not dream of returning to their relatives or their homes.

Now there is apprehension of a similar system on our part . . . : thus a certain near-by chief has been seen to collect some twenty boys in his village, mostly orphans and vagabonds, and to send them to us, saying: "Here are the children

you want, take full charge of these who live with you; henceforth they are yours."
(APB, rapport annuel 1907: 403)

The conscription of Congolese militiamen for the Force Publique, which
began in July 1891, followed the same lines. In theory the recruits were
chosen by lot by their African chiefs, but in practice the chiefs filled their
quotas from among the weak and friendless under their control, including substantial numbers of their slaves and prisoners of war.

Thus, to the numbers of freedmen serving a sort of apprenticeship in
the military were added substantial numbers of other ex-slaves. The line
between them was further blurred in September 1892 when the term
freedman (*libéré*) was officially suppressed, *militiaman* being used for both
the freedmen and the new recruits. Recruits from the eastern Congo were
especially valued, notably those from Upper Uele, Aruwimi, and Maniema (Conseil Colonial 1913–1914: 758–59; Cattier 1898: 261; AA, Wahis
1892b). Male slaves too young to be employed at the time of their emancipation were sent to "school camps" (*colonies scolaires*), where they were
trained to become militiamen or laborers. In 1892 Governor-General
Wahis encouraged "unceasing efforts" to round up enough of these youth
to keep these camps producing future state employees (AA, Wahis 1892a).

Labor for large government projects, such as the lower Congo railroad from 1890 and the Stanleyville-Ponthierville railroad from 1902, was
also obtained through conscription. The process began unofficially with
conscripts for the Force Publique being directed to other tasks, at times
with the promise of becoming regular soldiers later. These "soldier-
laborers" were joined by others conscripted through the chiefs to work
on these projects. Several victims of these practices were interviewed by
the Commission of Inquiry of 1904–1905 (AA, Commission d'Enquête,
Nos. 338 and 345), which concluded that few of the 3,000 workers on
the Stanleyville-Ponthierville railroad had been informed of the terms
of their employment or were in possession of the contracts required by
the law of 1888. The commissioners noted: "It is rare that a free man
signs up with the State of his own initiative. . . . Very often then, to obtain laborers, there has been recourse to compulsion and the chiefs are
obliged to furnish laborers as they furnish soldiers" (Commission d'Enquête 1905: 257–59). In furnishing these soldiers and laborers for the state,
the chiefs drew first upon the slaves, former slaves, and other weaker persons under their control.[5]

Chiefs met the government's demands for labor at the local level in
similar fashion. Some powerful chiefs reduced their weaker neighbors

5. Two members of the Colonial Council, the Reverend A. De Clercq, former provin-

to slavery to provide all or part of this labor. This was done by the Yalu-suna in Isangi Territory of Aruwimi District, for example, to meet their quotas of rubber, and by the Mangbetu chiefs in Uele (AA, Rapport Yamfira, n.d.; Keim 1983: 154–55). Some made use of surplus captives from the "Arab wars" who had been put in their custody. What became of those distributed from the military camp at Lusambo is unclear, but testimony before the Commission of Inquiry in 1904–1905 revealed how little freedom other ex-slaves had experienced even a decade after their emancipation. One witness, the chief of a village of laborers near Stanley-ville (whose non-African name, Apache, suggests how thoroughly he was a creature of the administration), complained that a Catholic mission-ary was telling his men that they were free to leave, either to sign labor contracts with the state or to return to their homes. Apache said he had been given these men by Lieutenant Lothaire at the end of the "Arab wars" in 1894, and he used them and their descendants to work his coffee and rice plantations and to provide the porters requisitioned by the state. Since these men had not signed the written contracts required for hired laborers, it is likely that they were not aware that they were no longer slaves, only that they had changed masters (AA, Commission d'Enquête, No. 346).

This was not an isolated instance of the meager difference which legal emancipation made in the position of slaves. According to the British vice-consul, chiefs all along the road leading eastward from Stanleyville were obliged to furnish porters to carry the loads of travellers. The vice-consul reported:

In some instances these porters are literally slaves, and are considered so both by their masters and themselves. They formerly belonged to Bangwana [Islami-cized, former Zanzibari slaves] raiders. When the slaves were emancipated they were supposed to leave their masters, though hardly any did so, and they im-mediately returned. The State then made the masters "Chiefs," and when por-ters are wanted these Chiefs are called upon to supply them. They naturally send these former slaves, who cannot refuse to go. (PP, Michell, 18 September 1906)

In 1909 another British vice-consul found former Zanzibari dependents still furnishing rice and porterage along the eastern part of the main road from Stanleyville to Lake Albert (PRO, Campbell 1909: 60).

---

cial of the Scheut missionaries in the Congo Free State, and Captain R. Dubreucq, a Free State administrator, indicated that slaves were important in providing a labor force in the Kasai and Equator provinces, but suggested that the practice was more general (Conseil Colonial 1908–1909: 165–67). For the Aruwimi District of the eastern Congo, see PP, Mi-chell, 27 November 1906.

It is clear from these examples that one feature of the Free State period was the continuation of forced labor for official purposes by substantial numbers of persons who had been enslaved by the Zanzibari. To them the terms and conditions of "liberation" by the Free State must have seemed more like a continuation of slavery.

Another feature of this period was the growth of a compulsory labor system so arduous and time-consuming that it seemed a new form of slavery to the large number of Africans affected. Some forms of compulsory labor had existed since the beginning of the Free State period, but the exaction of goods and labor services was broadened tremendously by the decree of 6 December 1892, which authorized the collection of special impositions in the eastern Congo to pay for the "Arab wars." These taxes were to be paid in porterage, ivory (one tusk of each elephant killed), and wild rubber. In theory the labor was to be remunerated, but only the labor, since the wild rubber and elephants were considered state property already. In practice remuneration was erratic, as was noted by a former Free State employee who passed through Maniema in 1894–1895:

The State conducts its pacification of the country after the fashion of the Arabs, so the natives are not gainers at all. The Arabs in the employ of the state are compelled to bring in ivory and rubber, and are permitted to employ any measures considered necessary to obtain this result. They employ the same means as in the days gone by, when Tippu Tib was one of the masters of the situation. They raid villages, take slaves, and give them back for ivory. The state has not suppressed slavery, but established a monopoly by driving out the Arabs and Wangwana competitors. (Glave 1897: 705–6)

In the river valleys and forests of the eastern Congo exactions in wild rubber became progressively larger and more onerous around the turn of the century. The requirement of the Congolese to spend more and more of their time deep in the forest at the unpleasant task of collecting latex provoked several open revolts, which brought on government reprisals. By the reform decree of 18 November 1903, labor exactions were not supposed to exceed 40 hours a month per adult male, but local officials, under great pressure to increase the annual production of their districts, tended to exaggerate the quantity of rubber that could be collected in 40 hours (PP, Grey 1908). As the burden on Africans mounted, colonial officials resorted to increasingly severe measures to enforce the collections in the Uele and Aruwimi valleys of the northeast (Commission d'Enquête 1905: 167–71, 192–96, 234–35). Rubber collection from the eastern Congo peaked at nearly 2,000 metric tons in 1906. New efforts at reform that year reduced the quotas of rubber demanded to more realistic levels, but by that time reports of scandalous abuses elsewhere in the Congo were undermining the Free State's international mandate.

Slavery and Forced Labor under Belgian Rule

An international campaign against the abuses of the rubber-collection system of forced labor led to the transfer of the administration of the Congo in 1908 from the absolute control of King Leopold to his much more circumscribed control as constitutional monarch of Belgium. Although the Belgian takeover produced no abrupt changes in policy and few in personnel (Gann and Duignan 1979), administrative reforms, already begun in the last years of the Free State rule, were stepped up as Belgium tried to prove itself no worse a colonial ruler than its more experienced European critics.

The British, who withheld official recognition of Belgian sovereignty until 1913, kept several consular officials on nearly constant tours, checking on the progress of the promised reforms, furnishing invaluable information on this period. Consul Jack P. Armstrong, for example, wrote the scathing "Report on the Condition of the Natives in the Uele District" in 1910, charging that in this vast northern territory slavery and the trade in slaves were rife, that slaves were forced to collect a chiefdom's quota of latex, which the free Africans brought to market and collected payment on. He charged that Belgian officials were either ignorant of this situation or chose to ignore it (PRO, Armstrong 1910). Differing with Armstrong's assumption of bad faith on the part of the Belgian government, Britain's ambassador to Belgium, Sir Arthur Hardinge, argued that the minister of colonies, Jules Renkin, was eager to correct existing abuses but needed time to solve the practical problems involved (PRO, Hardinge 1911).

The problems of emancipating the slave population of Uele were substantial, and the Belgian administration, which made slavery illegal there in 1910, moved with caution in enforcing the order. In 1913 the Government General of the Congo sought the reaction of the head of the Lower Uele District in 1913 to this policy statement: "Even though all the efforts of the Administration ought to tend toward the suppression of their traditional institution of domestic slavery, it seems inopportune for the moment to campaign against it by any *active* measures." The reasons he gave for this inexpediency were: slavery was already rapidly diminishing because of the ending of slave-trading and -raiding and the introduction of conscription and other measures separating many slaves from their masters; the condition of slaves was improving as "barbarous customs" were suppressed; and a general suppression would cause great disruption of political, social, and economic life. The vice-governor added that naturally slaves claiming their freedom should be given it (MRAC, vice-gouverneur-général 1913). The head of the Lower Uele District concurred with this passive approach, noting that slavery was uncommon there, existing slaves were being assimilated, and the institution would die a natural death (AA, Bertrand 1914).

However, as recent research by Curtis Keim (1983: 154–57) has made clear, female slaves in the Upper Uele District were still numerous and had been largely untouched by emancipation. There, female slaves served as a sort of high prestige currency essential to bridewealth payments, and such transactions constituted most of the slave trade that Armstrong had reported. Few female slaves had any practical chance of escaping to their original homes or of laying claim to legal emancipation, since the local courts were in the hands of the principal slave-owners. Most stayed where they were and experienced little change in their legal status and less in their social situation. Keim (1983: 156) cites meeting a former slave still serving a Mangbetu king in 1972 as evidence of the persistence of this servile relationship. The experience of female slaves among the Mangbetu does not appear to have been unique. A midcentury study of slavery in the Congo states that the condition of female slaves had not changed since the beginning of Belgian rule (De Jonghe 1949: 15–16).

For male slaves Belgian rule offered somewhat greater possibilities of meaningful emancipation. Men were better able to escape from their masters and to find security as employees and dependents of the colonial state, just as they had been doing since the beginning of European control of the area. Until the military expedition into East Africa in 1916 made that route to freedom unpopular, service in the Force Publique continued to offer a new start to slaves who could meet its physical requirements. In the colony's report on that year the governor-general regretfully reported, "The slave in earlier times would perceive a serious amelioration in his lot under the flag; it is no longer so today" (RACB 1916: 90). The problem, he explained, was that there were no longer so many male slaves in the colony and that other forms of employment were now more attractive to those who fled from their masters. Evidence that the Force Publique and other forms of direct government employment had been seen by slaves as routes to gradual emancipation is also found in the pronounced tendency of veterans of such service not to return to their villages but to settle near government posts or mission stations where paid employment was available and where they would be free from the impositions of chiefs.

For many other male slaves emancipation produced less noticeable changes. The enforcement of abolition decrees was far from vigorous, since, as the minister of colonies explained to the sympathetic British ambassador, to do so risked producing serious dislocations in the labor market (PRO, Hardinge 1911). His meaning was that actual emancipation would seriously disrupt the labor forces under the control of African chiefs, on which the government depended heavily to perform local corvées and to provide recruits for government projects. Not all of this labor was performed by former slaves, but in many places chiefs used, and were made to use, the expanded coercive authority with which the government had endowed them to reduce their free subjects to a more servile status. Among the Mangbetu the line between free and slave became so fine that when word of emancipation spread there in 1910 Belgian officials were hard pressed to make clear to Mangbetu commoners that the law did not free them but only the "domestic" slaves (Keim 1983: 155).

This was not an isolated example. Increasingly administrators as well as Africans found it hard to distinguish the conditions of "free" labor from slavery. Nor could the process of recruiting free labor be easily distinguished from slave-trading. As one official Belgian investigator put it: "The slave traders did the task themselves, we make use of the native chiefs we have invested. The procedure of the former was simply somewhat less hypocritical, somewhat less diplomatic than ours" (AA, Maertens 1917: 28–29). A decade later a local administrator voiced what he felt was a common complaint against being forced to spend his time in "recruiting, recruiting, always recruiting," causing villages to empty ahead of him just as they had before the slave-traders of bygone times. "If the Arabs formerly deported slaves for the eastern coast," he continued, "we do the same thing ourselves, *in the eyes of the natives*, by recruiting 'by way of authority,' or, in other words, by force, laborers for regions very far from their homes" (as quoted in Buell 1928, 2: 542).

Despite such complaints, the new Belgian administration was reluctant to abandon the forced conscription of laborers for public works projects enormous distances from their homes and for private employers. Indeed, one of the first acts of the new government was to extend the authority to recruit 2,500 laborers by force from all parts of the colony for railroad construction in Katanga (now Shaba) Province, although this policy was reversed a year later in January 1910 as a result of Belgian and foreign opposition (Conseil Colonial 1908–1909: 55–56, 211–17, 382; Conseil Colonial 1910, 1: 9). Forced recruitment of railroad laborers and porters was reinstated during the First World War, then strongly repudiated at its end (Northrup 1982). It almost came back in 1926 when the Ministry of Colonies approved using forced labor to complete the reconstruction of the lower Congo (Matadi to Ango-Ango) railroad, but the measure was never enacted, despite the vehement protests of the governor-general of the Congo, M. J. Rutten, because of fear of a public outcry (Conseil Colonial 1926: 392–403; AA, Rutten 1926).

While metropolitan policy thus turned against forced recruitment for public works projects, the use of force in meeting the growing labor demands of both public and private employers remained a notable feature of Belgian rule until 1928. The gold-mining company of Kilo-Moto, one of the largest single employers in the eastern Congo, may serve as a useful example of such intervention. Because the gold mines were in a mountainous area of low population density, labor recruiting had been extremely difficult from the beginning, as was obtaining adequate supplies of food for the mining camps (Bakonzi 1982: 131–42). The government wavered between authorizing forced recruitment (for "public utility") and shutting its eyes to unauthorized forced recruitment. The British vice-consul at Stanleyville, who spent five months investigating, concluded that in the last three years of Free State rule the labor sent to Kilo had consisted of "criminals, cannibals, 'revoltés' and 'recrutés' . . . , including some riffraff which had been made to work on the Ponthierville Railway, but had proved too unruly." The Belgian takeover had brought about an improvement which heartened the vice-consul, but it turned out to be short-lived (PRO, Campbell 1909: 73–75). By 1913 various Belgian officials were reporting that for the mines "the laws on the recruitment of labor existed only on paper." In 1914–1915 another official report found the engagement of mine laborers "anything but voluntary." The chiefs were asked to "procure" a certain number, whom they chose from among those "they liked the least and feared the most." These were sent to the local administrator and then to the mines, tied together around the neck like slaves. In 1917 seven-eighths of the mine workers were recruited through coercion and, as a consequence, desertions were running at 25 percent a year (AA, Maertens 1917: 1–35). Official government participation in the recruitment of labor for Kilo-Moto and other private employers ended at the beginning of 1928, but new shortages and abuses led to the recurrence of the old problems. An investigating commission in 1930 concluded that labor in the Kilo-Moto region was still obtained by requiring chiefs to supply a given number of "recruits" (Bertrand 1931: 190–91). This is not to say that the situation had not improved greatly over the years, but, while the severity of the abuses had indeed diminished, the number of Africans affected by them had increased substantially. The mines employed 800 men in 1908, 8,500 in 1916, nearly 21,000 in 1930 (RACB 1909: 253; RACB 1916: 74; RACB 1930: 135).

Nor had the abuses in rubber collection and other forms of taxation in kind been corrected by the Belgian takeover of 1908. Reports by a British vice-consul in 1912 and 1913 on several areas of the eastern Congo charged that the labor tax still made Africans "purely and simply a machine for the convenience and enrichment of the State, and trading companies" (PRO, Purdon 1912; PRO, Purdon 1913). In 1911 a British consul found the demands imposed by rubber collection were producing, in the words of Baptist missionaries, "a deplorable state of things in the Aruwimi district," though without the actual atrocities of the past (PRO, Mackie 1911: 140). Abuses on company-owned concessions also persisted into the Belgian period, as in the case of the 3.7-million-acre concession of the Société Forestière et Minière (Forminière) in Uele, the 9-million-acre concession of the Compagnie du Chemin de Fer du Congo Supérieur aux Grands Lacs Africains (CFL), and the Compagnie du Lomami (MRAC, Verbist 1912; PRO, Purdon 1913: 3–5). The introduction of tax in coin in 1910–1912, the reduction in the level of taxation, and the enforcement of new laws eventually removed the grossest abuses from the tax system, but in many a locality supplies for government outposts, and even for missions and private companies, continued to be collected through various forms of force and at below-market prices. As the 1930 Labor Commission concluded, with few exceptions "the markets are provisioned by what one could only call a requisition, at least in bananas, cassava, and grain" (Bertrand 1931: 20).

This forced provisioning of posts affected relatively few Africans compared with the nearly universal compulsion to grow certain crops, which was introduced in 1917, regulated and extended in the 1920s, and, although reduced after 1942–1943, remained in effect until the end of Belgian rule (Peemans 1975: 176–77). The Belgian Congo's director general of agriculture argued that compulsory cultivation was not prohibited by the forced-labor provisions of the League of Nations Slavery Convention of 1926, because, by ensuring regular food supplies, export growth, and general economic progress of the masses, it was in the public interest (Leplae 1929: 449–77). When the International Labor Organization addressed itself to this issue in a 1930 convention which rejected forced labor for the production of export crops, Belgium delayed ratification until 1944, and even then made reservations concerning "compulsory and educational cultivation" (Heyse 1957: 530). The defense of the practice of compulsory cultivation by the Belgian representative to the Economic and Social Council of the United Nations in 1953 is revealing of how long a questionable rationale could remain official policy: "Belgium is responsible for primitive peoples that do not have a taste for agricultural labor and it is thus indispensable to have recourse to compulsory cultivation in order to provide agricultural training for these peoples" (quoted in

Heyse 1957: 531). This rationale is the same one offered for introducing compulsory cultivation in 1917, a policy that was declared a success by the director of agriculture in 1933 (Leplae 1933: 647–48). As Jewsiewicki (1972: 225) has shown, the system operated to keep Africans in tutelage to a paternalistic system, "prisoners of the ideas, good or bad," of those in power, a paternalism removed in time but not in spirit from that of the rubber extractions.

Conclusion

The legal abolition of slavery in the eastern Congo did little to change the social and economic circumstances of those it supposedly freed. Many of those freed, especially female slaves, had no choice but to remain with the same masters and to perform the same duties. Others were able to change masters but remained tied to a system of labor exploitation that resembled slavery in its severity.

One reason slavery had increased in eastern Zaire in the nineteenth century is that it was a means of mobilizing labor. The European colonial regimes could proclaim an end to slavery, but they had to recruit even greater numbers of laborers. This was done by transforming slaves through monetary redemption or capture into state militiamen and laborers and by forcibly recruiting labor either directly or indirectly through African chiefs. At their worst the Free State's impositions condemned enormous numbers of Africans to a continuous servitude. A series of reforms beginning before the end of the Free State rule reduced the severity of this forced labor, but expanding demands for labor brought many more people under some sort of coerced-labor system. Thus for the affected Africans, slavery had changed its form more than its character.

Although many of the details are different, much of wage labor in Europe was also closer to the coerciveness of slavery than to the ideal of free-market labor, as was well recognized by contemporary critics across the political spectrum. In a pamphlet published in 1890 opposing a government loan to the Congo Free State, the Belgian Socialist leader Louis Bertrand raised some provocative issues about the connections between slavery and wage labor:

Does [slavery] exist only in Africa? Doesn't Belgium also have its slaves, economically and socially speaking? . . . Are our miners who spend 12 to 14 hours underground so happy that there's no room for bettering their lot? Are our factory workers any less to be pitied, having to work long hours in unhealthy factories for a few francs a week? (Norton 1965: 23)

Bertrand, of course, was echoing the *Communist Manifesto*, which had termed the industrial laborers of Europe slaves of the bourgeois class and of their machines. A similar judgment would be rendered the year after Bertrand's outcry in Pope Leo XIII's encyclical *Rerum Novarum*, which charged that industrial capitalists had laid "a yoke almost of slavery on the unnumbered masses of non-owning workers." Like Marx, Engels, and Pope Leo, Bertrand believed that slavery had an economic and social aspect as well as a legal aspect, that many persons who were not slaves in a legal sense were held in servitude by the harshness of their working conditions and the meagerness of their remuneration. The ending of slavery in Africa had many unique features, but it is necessary to bear in mind that it was also part of a much larger struggle against political and economic exploitation.

REFERENCES

Archival sources

AA: Archives Africaines, Brussels.
> Bertrand, A., au gouverneur-général, Bondo, 19 March 1914. D(778)A.I.
> Commission d'Enquête de 1904–1905. Dispositions. AE(349-350)528.
> Descamps, Capitaine, au gouverneur-général, Mtowa, 8 February 1895. AE(200)4.
> Dhanis, B.F., à G. Five, 1893? D(387)4.
> Rapport Yamfira, Rapport d'enquête, chefferie de Yamfira, territoire d'-Isangi, district d'Aruwimi. n.d. D(385).
> Maertens, Du recrutement, 1917. MOI(3548)33.
> Rutten, J., au ministre des colonies, no. 339, Boma, 3 August 1926. MOI(3600)141.
> Tobback, I., 1887–1892. a. Lettres. b. Journal. BMC(46)11.
> Wahis, T., 1892. Letter to commissaires de district, Boma. a. 28 March. b. 1 September. D(387)2.
APB: Archives de la Société des Missionnaires d'Afrique (Pères Blancs), Rome.
> Chronique trimestrielle de la Société des Missionnaires de N.-D. des Missions d'Afrique. Alger. 1879–1909 (pro manuscripto, ad usum internum).
> Rapports annuels. 1905ff. (pro manuscripto, ad usum internum).
MRAC: Musée Royale de l'Afrique Centrale, Section Historique, Tervuren.
> Chaltin, L. N., Notes redigées sur la question arabe. n.d. R.G. 1078, carnet 1.
> Verbist, Dossier, 1912. 50.30.314.
> Vice-gouverneur-général au commissaire du district, Bas Uele, Boma, 28 October 1913. 50.30.316.

480   V. NEW ECONOMIES AND LABOR CONTROL

PRO: Public Record Office, Kew Gardens, Foreign Office Correspondence (FO).
Armstrong, J. P., Report on the Condition of the Natives in the Uele District, 1910. FO 403/425, no. 16, pp. 13–32.
Campbell, G., Report on a Tour in the Aruwimi and Haut Ituri Districts of the Congo State, 1909. FO 403/410, no. 43, pp. 59–91.
Hardinge to Grey, Brussels, 8 March 1911. FO 403/425, no. 59, pp. 84–90.
Mackie, Consul, Report, 1911. FO 403/425, no. 85.
Purdon, R. J., Report on a Tour of the Districts of Stanleyville, Lowa, Maniema, and a portion of Aruwimi, 1912. FO 403/443, no. 6, pp. 26–42.
Purdon, R. J., Report . . . on the Political and Commercial Situation of Stanleyville, 1913. FO 403/444, no. 43, pp. 2–13.

Other sources

Bakonzi Agayo. 1982. The gold mines of Kilo-Moto in northeastern Zaire, 1905–1960. Ph.D. dissertation, University of Wisconsin–Madison.
Bertrand, A. 1931. *Le problème de la main-d'oeuvre au Congo belge. Rapport de la commission de la main-d'oeuvre indigène 1930–1931. Province orientale.* Brussels: A. Lesigne.
Birhakaheka Njiga. 1978. La principauté de Nyangezi: essai d'histoire socio-économique (1850–1960). 2 vols. Mémoire de Licence en Histoire, Institut Supérieur Pédagogique, Université Nationale du Zaïre, Bukavu.
Buell, R. L. 1928. *The native problem in Africa.* 2 vols. New York: Macmillan.
Cameron, V. L. 1885. *Across Africa.* London: George Philip.
Cattier, F. 1898. *Droit et administration de l'état indépendant du Congo.* Brussels: Larcier.
Ceulemans, P. 1959. *La question arabe et le Congo (1883–1892).* Brussels: Academie royale des Sciences coloniales.
Commission d'Enquête. 1905. Rapport. *Bulletin officiel. Etat indépendant du Congo:* 135–285.
Conseil Colonial. 1908ff. *Compte rendu analytique des séances.* Brussels: A. Lesigne.
Coquilhat, C. 1888. *Sur le Haut-Congo.* Paris: J. Lebègue.
De Bauw, G. 1901. La zone Uere-Bomu. *Belgique coloniale* 7: 63–67, 73–75, 88–91.
De Jonghe, E. 1949. *Les formes d'asservissement dans les sociétés indigènes du Congo belge.* Brussels: IRCB.
Emerson, B. 1979. *Leopold II of the Belgians: king of colonialism.* New York: St. Martin's Press.
Forester, C. S. 1948. *The sky and the forest.* Boston.
Gann, L., and P. Duignan. 1979. *The rulers of Belgian Africa, 1870–1914.* Princeton, N.J.: Princeton University Press.
Glave, E. J. 1897. Cruelty in the Congo Free State. *Century* 54: 699–715.
Harms, R. W. 1981. *River of wealth, river of sorrow: the central Zaire basin in the era of the slave and ivory trade, 1500–1891.* New Haven: Yale University Press.
Hinde, S. L. 1897. *The fall of the Congo Arabs.* London: Thomas Whittaker.

Heyse, T. 1957. *Congo belge et Ruanda-Urundi. Notes de droit public et commentaire de la charte coloniale.* Vol. 2. Brussels: G. Van Campenhout.

Jewsiewicki, B. 1972. Notes sur l'histoire socio-économique du Congo (1880–1960). *Etudes d'histoire africaine* 3: 209–41.

Kabemba Assan. 1979. Les rapports entre Arabes et Manyema dans l'histoire du xixe siècle. *Cahiers du CERUKI,* série C2, 1: 31–51.

Keim, C. A. 1983. Women in slavery among the Mangbetu c. 1800–1910. In *Women and slavery in Africa,* ed. C. Robertson and M. Klein. Madison: University of Wisconsin Press.

Kopytoff, I., and S. Miers. 1977. African 'slavery' as an institution of marginality. In *Slavery in Africa,* ed. S. Miers and I. Kopytoff. Madison: University of Wisconsin Press.

Lagae, C.-R. 1926. *Les Azande ou Niam-Niam. L'organisation zande. Croyances religieuses et magiques. Coutumes familiales.* Brussels: Vromant.

Le Clement de St.-Marcq, Lieut. 1890. Untitled article. *Mouvement géographique,* No. 11, 25 May.

Leplae, E. 1929. Les cultures obligatoires dans les pays d'agriculture arriérée. *Bulletin agricole du Congo belge* 20: 449–78.

Leplae, E. 1933. Histoire et développement des cultures obligatoires de coton et de riz au Congo belge de 1917 à 1933. *Congo* 1: 645–753.

Livingstone, D. 1875. *The last journals.* Ed. H. Waller. New York: Harper.

Lloyd, D. T. 1978. The precolonial economic history of the Avongara-Azande c. 1750–1916. Ph.D. dissertation, University of California, Los Angeles.

Northrup, D. 1982. Porterage in eastern Zaire, 1885–1930: labor use and abuse in war and peace. Paper presented at the 25th Annual Meeting of the African Studies Association, Washington, D.C.

Norton, W. B. 1965. *A Belgian socialist critic of colonialism: Louis Bertrand (1856–1943).* Brussels: ARSOM.

Peemans, J.-P. 1975. Capital accumulation in the Congo under colonialism: the role of the state. In *Colonialism in Africa,* Vol. 4, *The economics of colonialism,* ed. P. Duignan and L. Gann, 165–212. Cambridge: Cambridge University Press.

PP: *Parliamentary Papers.* Great Britain.
   1907a. Michell to Nightingale, Bafwesendi, 18 September 1906. *Africa,* no. 1; no. 23, 48.
   1907b. Michell to Nightingale, Stanleyville, 27 November 1906. *Africa,* no. 1; no. 29, 59.
   1908. Grey, E., to A. Hardinge, 27 March 1908, *Africa,* no. 3, 10–11.

RACB. 1909ff. *Rapport annuel du Congo belge.* Brussels/London.

Senga Ongala. 1978. Les arabisés Kusu et la création et l'évolution du poste de Walikale (1901–1954). Travail de fin d'étude en histoire, Institut Supérieur Pédagogique, Université Nationale du Zaïre, Bukavu.

Stanley, H. M. 1878. *Through the dark continent.* 2 vols. London: Harper.

Stanley, R., and A. Neame, eds. 1961. *The exploration diaries of H. M. Stanley.* London: William Kimber.

Stengers, J. 1953. Correspondance Leopold II–du Cuvelier. *Bulletin de l'Institut royal colonial belge* 24: 824–37.

Van Eetvelde, E. 1889. Rapport au Roi-Souverain sur la législation de l'Etat indépendent du Congo au point de vue de la suppression de l'esclavage et de la protection des noirs. *Bulletin officiel. Etat indépendent du Congo:* 200.

Van Eetvelde, E. 1895. Rapport sur les mesures prises par l'Etat indépendent du Congo en exécution de l'acte de Bruxelles. *Bulletin officiel. Etat indépendent du Congo:* 100–119.

VI

REFLECTIONS

17 *Igor Kopytoff*

The Cultural Context of African Abolition

To an anthropologist, for whom historical events serve both to construct and to illustrate general patterns, the studies in this book raise, collectively, a set of related questions: Why did the European colonial officials almost universally predict serious dislocations to follow from the abolition of internal African slavery? Why did these expectations fail to materialize? What was there in the European image of African slavery that led to this failure of prediction? What was the pattern of the actual processes of abolition? And what may account for this pattern?

Predictions about and the Reality of Abolition

Like modern scholars, early European colonial officials held certain ideas about the nature of African slavery. These ideas led nearly all of them to see dire, even catastrophic, consequences in emancipation, and they pursued cautious policies accordingly. They expected emancipation to bring about massive and inevitable desertions by the slaves of their masters; and this, in turn, was to lead to economic crises, especially in production, and to crises in the social and political order. On the whole, their predictions turned out (rather to their relief) to be off the mark, showing that their understanding of African slavery was in some way flawed. The desertions turned out to be variable and selective and to in-

485

volve a minority of the slave population, and the social and political orders adjusted remarkably well to these changes. Yet, here were societies in which institutions of slavery appeared to be deeply embedded, with the proportion of slaves in the population often being as high as half. The relative smoothness with which emancipation proceeded might therefore appear startling—to them no less than to modern scholars. What, then, did in fact happen?

Guesses by officials about the numbers of desertions were inevitably refracted through their preconceptions, and they could underestimate or overestimate them in any given region. The authors of the studies are therefore often forced to make qualitative judgments: some are inclined to see rather massive desertions (and sometimes to take them as proof of the essential harshness of African slavery) and others are not. But the exact quantitative basis for these judgments is often difficult to grasp. Much of the time we are perforce caught between an archival anecdote ("in November, twenty-eight recalcitrant slaves . . .") and an unquantifiable quantitative statement ("a great number of slaves . . ."), and we are nagged by an uneasiness about the meaning of whatever meager figures can be had. Nevertheless, even a rough overall picture can suggest some of the main issues with which a sociology of emancipation in Africa must deal.

We may begin with cases which, it is generally agreed, represent the highest desertion rates—those in the French Soudan and Guinea. Here, the consensus among scholars is that the overall proportion of "slaves" (a category whose precise boundaries are usually unclear to all concerned) was somewhere between 25 and 40 percent in a population that, at the time of abolition early in this century, was between 5 and 6 million (the ranges of these figures are cogently supported by Klein's [1986] estimates). If we take, then, the higher figures (say, 40 percent of 6 million), the total number of "slaves" in the French Soudan and Guinea may be put as high as 2½ million. If we go for the lower figures (say, 25 percent of 5 million), the total is about 1¼ million.

The figures, to be sure, encompass some serious systemic problems. Dumett and Johnson's discussion of Akan categories illustrates very well the issue for Africa as a whole: scarcely ever is there, among the several overlapping African social categories of dependency, one that corresponds exactly to the Western category of "slave." To this should be added the notorious difficulties that even contemporary anthropological fieldworkers experience in placing specific individual Africans in these categories. Consequently, the guesses of turn-of-the-century colonial officials about the percentages of "slaves" in the population must be taken with a fistful of salt. On the whole, official figures would be apt to underestimate the numbers of "slaves" *qua* acquired dependents. The reasons lie in the Western tendency to make an association between "slavery" and palpable deprivation (which, in Africa, need not occur) and in the African tendency to hide from any outsider the number of dependents under one's control (as indeed is also true of children, lineage members, and, in general, all human and material resources). Finally, Klein (1986) adduces other reasons for taking the higher rather than the lower figures. A figure of 2 million, then, give or take a few hundred thousand, seems probable.

Of these 2 million "slaves," how many deserted their host groups when abolition came? Writers who are inclined to see a massive exodus (e.g., Roberts and Klein 1980: 393) quote official estimates of a half a million and suggest that about a third of the "slaves" left their masters over approximately a decade. At the level of precision possible here, the various numbers do tie together reasonably well to produce something like a 25–35 percent desertion rate in the first decade, which is when desertions overwhelmingly took place.

What of other areas? For Northern Nigeria, Hogendorn and Lovejoy tell us in Chapter 13 that the best possible estimate is that "many tens of thousands fled" their masters, 55,000 alone acquiring their autonomy through the courts over a 20-year period. The relevant area here seems to be the old Sokoto Caliphate, whose population at the time may have approached 8 million (1911 census, in Meek 1925, 2: 177). Sociologically, the societies involved are of the type that have a rather high proportion of "slaves" in the population. Even the conservative figure of 25 percent would give 2 million "slaves." If we take "many tens of thousands" of deserting slaves to mean as much as 200,000, we get a desertion rate of some 10 percent over two decades. And indeed, Hogendorn and Lovejoy state that the scale of desertions in Sokoto was less than in the French Soudan. But if we narrow down on Nupe within Sokoto—with a population of about 350,000 (ibid.), of which we may assume a third to have been "slaves," an exodus of 30,000 reported by Hogendorn and Lovejoy would represent a desertion rate of some 25 percent.

These rough calculations do suggest a relatively normal desertion rate of 10–25 percent, and in some cases one as high as 35 percent. This in societies where slavery was sufficiently pervasive and exploitative to lead some writers to see them as dependent on a "slave mode of production." To put these figures another way, we must confront the fact that in these African societies at least two-thirds and sometimes as many as nine-tenths of the "slaves" stayed within the sociological and physical ambit of their masters' districts after the imposition of abolition. It is not surprising, then, that the colonial officials' worst fears of disaster quickly disappear soon after abolition.

Western Notions of Slavery and the Scenario of Abolition

Why was the official scenario of abolition so exaggeratedly pessimistic in the first place? The officials constructed it, perforce, out of their culturally given ideas of "slavery" on the universal presumption that other societies can be understood through the cultural assumptions, the categories, and the vocabulary of one's own. When African reality challenged these ideas, the officials preferred (as one usually does) to retain them and question the recalcitrant reality rather than the relevance of their conceptions. In brief, their view of "slavery" was commonsensical and, as all common sense, profoundly ethnocentric (see Geertz 1975).

According to this Western commonsensical view, "slavery" is a discrete institution. The status of "slave" is unproblematic, an all-or-none thing, marked by precise and unfailing indicators, such as the purchase of the "slave." The relationship of the master to the "slave" is that of an "owner" to an "object" or "property"—in the uncomplicated sense that nineteenth-century thought found natural and that modern anthropology finds utterly cultural, since "ownership" involves quite different rights in different cultures and "objects" are themselves culturally constructed entities (see Appadurai 1986). In the commonsensical view, the relationship between "owner" and human "objects" is absolute and unitary and structurally narrow in compass because it is bereft of formal variations. The only room left for variation is in the informal aspects, summed up by the blanket term *treatment*. This sentimental reductionism leads, in turn, to the temptation (one could say the obsession) to see treatment as the principal dimension for examining and comparing slave systems, to use treatment as the major influence on the slave's behavior, and to create bipolar typologies of slavery in terms of "harshness" and "benignity."

In this view of slavery, the logical opposite of "slavery" (and its overwhelming existential unhappiness) is "freedom" (to pursue happiness). To move meaningfully out of "slavery" one must move towards "freedom" and not towards some other form of dependency. "Freedom" means autonomy and detachment from binding social relations; any lingering of social obligations is suspect as a sub-rosa continuation of slavery. Finally, the essence of the slave's role resides in labor (and occasionally in sex), and the fundamental reason for acquiring or holding on to a slave is to derive benefit from his or her labor. This makes slavery an essentially "economic" institution and the master-slave relationship an essentially "economic" one. This model of slavery—shared by nineteenth-century colonial officials and many contemporary *marxisant* interpreters of African slavery—is clearly a Whiggish amalgam of Enlightenment political philosophy and nineteenth-century bourgeois economism.

The model imposes upon its holders implicit predictions about the "slave's" behavior—predictions that most colonial officials promoted and feared. The model reduces the slave to a Political Economic Man who maximizes the utilities of liberty and happiness and yearns for detachment from his social position. Given the chance, the slave will naturally choose to leave the master. Only two factors may affect this decision: "treatment" so exceptionally good as to overcome the drive for autonomy, and conditions of autonomy so exceptionally bad as to make it unpalatable. But these factors are interferences with the natural thrust towards social autonomy. Nonautonomy is denied any possible attractions in and of itself. Given all this, the behavior of the slaves under abolition becomes inevitable: massive, nearly universal desertions of masters following a maximum rejection by the slaves of their social identity. And this, in turn, inevitably leads to a labor crisis.

These predictions were, to be sure, quite likely to come true in those places where the Western model of slavery formed an applied theory, so to speak, that shaped the workings of the institution. Such was the case in much of the New World. And elsewhere, the outcome of abolition might also at least approach the model's predictions to the extent that notions of slavery were similar—as, for example, on Arab plantations on the East African coast. The lessons of abolition in the West Indies, with its economic dislocations, could not but be on the minds of colonial officials as they contemplated abolition in their African territories. And because the demands for abolition by various metropolitan interests were framed within a moralizing discourse, the officials justified their caution by resorting to the morally loaded argument of "treatment"—namely, that African systems of slavery were benign by the standards of the Western model. There is a paradox in this: fearing results predicted by their Western image of slavery, the colonial officials argued against hasty abolition by pointing out that African realities were different—a fact that might have tempered their fearful predictions in the first place. They seem to have known enough to see that they were dealing with a different kind of slavery but not enough to see the difference as fundamental.

Unlike colonial officials who used the implications of the Western model predictively, the modern scholar who clings to such a model may use it as an after-the-fact template for interpreting incomplete historical records. Instances of desertion, for example, may be seen to indicate harshness of treatment and even as an ideological rejection by the slave of the institution of slavery. Lack of desertion in other instances may be taken to show that the natural drive to autonomy was offset by the harsh uncertainties of striking out on one's own. Thus, the behavior of the slave comes to be interpreted in terms of a circular and self-validating utilitarian calculus whose assumptions about human motivations are much closer to eighteenth-century political philosophy than to contemporary psychology and anthropology. If we are to achieve an African "history from the bottom"—of slavery as of anything else—then we should, it seems to me, construct a less aprioristic and a more culturally realistic model of the African "actor" to be used to give flesh, bone, and mind to the figures of which the dry documents in the colonial archives speak.

African Cultural Notions of "Slavery"

What, then, is the complex of indigenous African notions relevant to the issues we are discussing here? We have used the terms *slave* and *slavery*, yet one hardly need dwell on the fact that their meanings, shaped in one cultural-historical setting, cannot be expected to disentangle very well the institutions of another time and place. At best, the term *slavery* can serve as a "pointer" towards certain kinds of phenomena. But once these phenomena have been identified, it is they that must thereafter frame the analysis.

The term *slavery* points our attention to the fact that in traditional African societies people were captured or bought and thereby came under the complete control of the captor or buyer. In principle, as also in ethnographic reality, this fact predicts very little about the uses to which the acquired persons are put, the social identities to which they are assigned, or the social networks into which they are inserted. To the host society, an acquired person is initially a nonperson in the social and legal sense, lacking any fixed position within it. But unless he or she is to be resold or killed, this total marginality to the host society must be reduced and the physical individual socialized. This reduction in marginality may be very extensive or, as in the case of a "chattel slave," minimal. But in all cases, the acquired person's new role is shaped by cultural norms, the cultural imagination, existing social arrangements, and the pragmatic limits of what is possible economically, socially, politically, and technologically in the society at hand. In African societies, where the dominant social and legal unit was the kin group, the rights over the acquired person were in various ways vested in the acquisitor's kin group, and demarginalization involved various degrees of belongingness in and to that or another kin group. This was the basis for the conceptual interdigitation in Africa between "slavery" and kinship.

Several points need be stressed here, if only because they have sometimes been misunderstood in the recent literature on African "slavery." For example, to insist on the close conceptual relationship between African acquired persons and their positions in the acquisitors' kin groups does not mean (as Cooper [1980: 11] and Klein and Lovejoy [1979: 182, 184] claim it must) that African "slavery" must therefore be seen as "kinship based," or as "conceived of primarily in terms of kinship structures," or as "assimilationist." What it does mean is that when and if demarginalization progresses (which it need not), it does so through the establishment of kinship and kinshiplike relations and by way of kinship metaphors (see, on this issue, Kopytoff and Miers 1977: 22–24; Kopytoff 1979). This is clearly unlike the path that demarginalization took in Western systems of slavery. Nor does this connection with kinship mean that the system must therefore be "benign." For benignity is not a necessary feature of kinship relations. In most African societies, a "blood member" may be sold or eliminated when the interests of the corporate kin group demand it. Hence, even a complete assimilation of a "slave" into the kin group does not alter his or her position in this respect.

The stress in our analysis on the ethnographic fact of the relationship between kinship and "slavery" in Africa has sometimes been seen an an "idealization" of African slavery (e.g., Wright 1983: 247). But we must beware of adopting the perspective of the modern Western middle class with its notion that kinship relations are naturally benign and that kinship metaphors necessarily convey goodwill and nurture and not, as they constantly do in Africa, authority and obligation (see Kopytoff and Miers 1977: 55–61). Kinship does not in itself preclude harshness or economic exploitation within the African compound or plantation any more than it did in European royal families and peasant households. The analytical danger, then, is that of sentimentalizing the social context in which African "slavery" operated — a context in which social relations (including those of kinship) were authority-ridden and predominantly nonvoluntaristic, in which relatives could legitimately be sold, but where, by the same token, those who had been captured or bought could become relatives with whom one's relationships carried the same intimacy and closeness with which modern Westerners endow kin relationships.

In sharp contrast to highly specialized and unusual New World plantation societies but in common with many other systems, the uses of acquired persons and their sociological descendants in African societies range very widely, reflecting greatly varying degrees of reduction in their marginality. Some of these uses are conceptually assimilated into other dependency relationships (such as those of adoptees or retainers), and all of them are usually subsumed under conceptual umbrellas that indicate dependency or the dependents' fundamental sociological outsidedness. Examples are the Akan *akoa-awura* ("subject-master") relationship, that encompasses "slavery" as well as numberless other relationships of dependency, and, in Buganda, the similar classification as "servants" of a whole range of different types of dependents. This is in contrast to the Western assumption about the natural discreteness of the "slave" status.

The cognitive boundaries implied by this structure of categories carry with them some analytical pitfalls. One must beware of extending arguments relevant only to one portion of the range — say, the African chattel "slave" who resembles the Western slave — to the entire range of acquired persons, which includes retainers, quasi kinsmen, and kinsmen. Whatever lessons one draws from chattel "slaves" deserting their masters in large numbers do not apply to African "slavery" as a whole. It was this kind of semantic confusion that led colonial officials to expect mass desertions of all African "slaves" because they saw the chattel part of it as naturally paradigmatic of the whole system.

The issue, then, is more than merely terminological. For one thing, it bears on the meaning of our statistical evidence. Large-scale African societies tended to have a large proportion of acquired persons and their sociological descendants and also to distribute these persons over a wide range of roles and degrees of marginality (a range that small-scale societies obviously lacked). As pointed out above, contemporaneous Western observers tended to miss the less marginal "slaves," underestimate the overall proportion of "slaves," and hence also to underestimate the numbers of "slaves" who did not leave. To gauge the sociological significance of desertion more than superficially, we need some indication of the relative proportions of "slaves" and dependents of different categories and separate desertion figures for each of these categories. Alas, the archives are not likely ever to yield such data.

The lack of correspondence between Western slave (essentially chattel slave) and African acquired person not only misled Western observers. It also led Africans to misinterpret the meaning of emancipation and to make their own faulty projection of its consequences. Colonial officials' and their edicts' talk of the removal of "slaves" from their present status meant to Africans the removal of a whole range of dependents, adoptees, and retainers (as Northrup, Cassanelli, and Dumett and Johnson point out in this book). No wonder Africans, too, panicked at the idea of emancipation, spoke darkly of the profound disintegration that it would bring to their societies, and thereby seemed to confirm what colonial officials had assumed from their own side of the cultural divide.

It should be stressed that we are concerned at this point with specifically African notions of "slavery" and dependency. That is, we are concerned with cultural meanings and not with social systems. The distinction is important, for a system involving African slaves was not always shaped by African notions. Obvious examples were the slave systems of the New World, overwhelmingly shaped by the masters' ideas about slavery, in which the role of African ideas was extremely subtle (and still awaits analysis). Examples closer to Africa itself were the European-owned plantations in such places as Fernando Po, the Seychelles, or Reunion, and, by the same token, the Arab plantations on Zanzibar and the East African coast — and, somewhat more problematically and to an extent yet to be determined, kindred coastal Swahili plantations (both examined as a single "African" type by Cooper 1977, 1980). These systems obviously cannot be simply thrown, without further analytical ado, into a single sample of "African systems of slavery" containing other systems in which masters and slaves belonged to the same cultural universe. Nor can they be treated in the same sociological category as the plantation systems in Dahomey or Ashanti merely because their regimes were often also harsh and exploitative — as if variations in "treatment" exhausted all the issues of their comparative sociology.

Slavery and emancipation in heavily Islamicized African societies demand a special look. What has been the interpenetration in them of indigenous African and imported Islamic notions of slavery? and with what consequences? Some features of their sociology may indeed arise from their amalgamated cultural tradition rather than, as has usually been assumed, from their being complex, or large-scale, or socially dense societies. This may partly account for the difference between the processes of abolition in the French Soudan (described by Roberts in Chapter 9 and Klein in Chapter 6) and in Ashanti (described by Dumett and Johnson in Chapter 2). Both areas, after all, contained equally complex societies. But in Ashanti (as in most of Africa) the sociology of slavery was one in which "master" and "slave" shared fundamental cultural assumptions; in the Soudan the situation is less clear and probably varied among societies. If so, we need a culturally aware sorting of the different societies of the Soudan when looking at the statistics on "slavery" and its abolition.

This is not to say that such duocultural systems of slavery *in* Africa — as opposed to African systems of "slavery" — are not relevant to the study of African slavery, for they do point to interesting issues of cultural contrasts in the conception of "slavery." We can, for example, see in the case of the Bantu slaves of the Somali, presented in Chapter 10, how the racial and cultural concepts of the Somali masters made it impossible for Bantu captives to merge into Somali clans and how the characteristic African patterns of assimilation could work themselves out only in relation to the clans of African cultivators. And in an environment more favorable to the "slaves," we see in Chapter 7 the Chikunda of Mozambique acting out their African self-definitions in ways utterly different from what their self-styled Portuguese masters vainly expected of them.

The Anthropology of Emancipation

In terms of the Western model of slavery, emancipation means a complete reversal of the slave's legal position from total unfreedom to freedom. The reality, of course, is far less straightforward. Sociologically, emancipation represents a remarginalization of the slave, who is removed from an established niche in the host society without being clearly placed elsewhere. As at the time of initial acquisition, the acquired person becomes a nonperson — one that belongs nowhere, although this time he or she also belongs to no one (abolition in the American South was an extreme example of the conundrum that this could entail). Yet, in terms of Western folk sociology, this total social alienation represents the ultimate state of freedom. African folk sociology sees it differently.

Western thought focusses on the total appropriation of the slave by the master. African thought focusses instead on the initial alienness, outsidedness, and social nonbelongingness of the "slave," and on the partial undermining of that alienness (and to that extent, of the "slave" status) by the incorporation of the "slave" into the acquisitor's group. This is the sense of the oft-repeated statements in the literature that the quintessential "slave" in Africa is a "kinless person"— one lacking the benefits of true kin ties with established kin groups. By the same token, the mark of being a full person is to have true kin. Hence the metaphorical use of the term *slave* for someone who, in a quarrel, withdraws from one's kin group or community. And hence also the reason why a lineage segment, when it breaks off from a parent lineage, retains some (ritually marked) tie with the parent lineage; for total autonomy would imply the kind of rootlessness, nonbelongingness, and kinlessness that characterizes "slavery." A final break is acceptable only when one has developed, constructed, or invented connections elsewhere, to some other social entity. The value, in brief, is social dependence — not maximum autonomy with its alienation.

Kinlessness here has existential implications. Thus, after the 1986 disaster at Lake Nyos in western Cameroon, where an eruption of poison gas from a crater lake killed many people and herds of cattle, the official in charge of the disposal of bodies was talking cultural sense when he said that the human dead were being buried first, whereas "the cows have no relatives, so their burials will be last" (Friedman 1986: A6). The line between humans and animals was being drawn in terms of the possession or the absence of kinship; what makes animals animals is their nonrecognition of kinship (most notably expressed by the absence among them of incest taboos).

The existential predicament in which an African "slave" is caught arises from the tension between his being simultaneously a "slave"—a nonperson—through his nonbelongingness and a non-"slave" through his belongingness to the host group. Emancipation therefore touched upon some central issues of social identity; being a form of alienation, emancipation threatened to enhance precisely that which is characteristic of the "slave" identity.

There are, in every society, certain kinds of social identities and relationships that are culturally regarded as existential rather than situational, defined by immanent rather than circumstantial qualities. Such identities rest on notions of what people "are" in some fundamental sense rather than what they "do." Western folk sociology has traditionally seen in this light ethnic, gender, and often religious identities, as well as kinship identities and relationships among them.

To clarify the issue, let us look at Western kinship relations in this perspective. For Westerners (or at least the less deculturated among them), there exists a universe of existential relationships of which "kinship" is the immanent quality. Within this universe, great variations exist in the content of the relationships. Some are equal and others not, some imply greater dependency than others, and some carry greater and more onerous obligations than others. Some have no obligatory content at all, yet they continue to "exist" within the universe of kinship; to expel them from it requires a positive act of denying or renouncing them. This universe, moreover, is not frozen; the behavioral content of these relationships is subject to reshuffling. When, for example, kinsmen move away or suddenly acquire a fortune, or when young kinsmen come of age or old kinsmen become indigent or infirm, relatives alter ("renegotiate," if you will) their relationships: they may repudiate their duties or expand their obligations, increase or diminish their material exchanges, tinker with their social distance, and so on. But no matter how radical the specific changes may be, the existential relationship of kinship per se continues—unless it is formally broken and the relationship with the person involved is pushed out into another universe.

In Africa, the incorporation of an acquired person (that accompanies his or her induction into the host group) confers upon the "slave" a new existential identity as a social being. Hence, the induction is accompanied by some kind of ritual, similar in its logic to other rituals of social transformation, as in coming-of-age, adoption, or initiation into office. Becoming a "slave" (of whatever kind) thus involves the acquisition of a fundamental and unconditional relationship of dependency with the acquisitor's kin group, significantly analogous to the "naturalization" of new citizens by modern states. Similarly, legal "emancipation"—involving a break in the existing relationship—is necessarily an existential transformation: one relinquishes one's established social identity and one's entire relationship to the acquisitor's social group and the society to which one is linked through it. To return to the analogy, to be "emancipated" is like being "denaturalized" and rendered "stateless."

This identity loss might be repaired by the construction of another social identity, which in Africa means belonging to some other group. One might do this by attaching oneself to another kin group (as a dependent stranger and, hence, a "slave") or to the one to which one originally belonged (among the Kongo, for example, one still became a "slave" of one's own natal group when one rejoined it [MacGaffey 1977: 244]). Finally, if one were brave or the circumstances exceptionally favorable, one might set out on the difficult task of constructing one's own quasi-kin or quasi-ethnic group and rooting it historically. Thus we find, in Chapter 8, the formation of such a new ethnic identity, the WaMisheni, in coastal Kenya, rooted in a past common allegiance as liberated slaves to the Christian "mishen." Similarly, the Chikunda of Mozambique built a quasi-ethnic identity on the basis of their having been slaves of the Portuguese. By the same cultural logic, escaped Bantu slaves in Somaliland formed quasi-kin groups on the basis of their having belonged to the same Somali clans (Cassanelli 1987). And in Surinam and other places in the New World, African escaped slaves forged new kinds of kin and community ties in the interior on the basis of the shared existential experiences of having crossed the Atlantic on the same slave ship or of having belonged to the same plantation master (Mintz and Price 1976: 22–26). These examples vividly show that emancipation called for decisions about the acquisition, retention, or abandonment of identity as an issue in and of itself, quite apart from the issue of "treatment" that is so central to the decision model implicit in Western notions of emancipation.

Such was the framework within which African "slaves" had to decide on a course of action when they were faced with the new opportunities offered by a colonial power's abolition of slavery. The most fundamental decision to be made was whether to break one's existential relationship to (in effect, one's belongingness in) one's present ("master's") kin group. The existential gravity of the decision was of the same order as is, in the West, the decision about whether to break or not with one's position in the existing network of relatives. To choose emancipation was to abandon not the structurally narrow identity of a Western slave but the widely inclusive identity of a dependent, with all the wide range of potential variations that it accommodated.

The implications of the two kinds of break are quite different. Having broken the discrete slave relationship, the Western slave could then establish a new discrete relationship with the former master, such as that of client. The African "slave" could not do this, for by opting for emancipation he would have necessarily rejected the entire dependency relationship in the full range of its possible manifestations as "slave," client, retainer, quasi relative, etc. If he wished to become a client, he had to refuse emancipation in order to be able to negotiate a new content within the continuing dependency relationship. To use the analogy with Western kinship, when a son renounces his relationship to his father, he thereby breaks the kinship relationship as such. He cannot thereafter expect to renegotiate with his father some lighter and more egalitarian kinship arrangement like that, say, between cousins. This helps explain the consistent failure of government-sponsored attempts at establishing new dependency relationships between former "masters" and their officially emancipated "slaves" (relationships conceived by Western officials only in economic terms!). And it also explains the consistent success of dependency renegotiations by the Africans themselves. This success was possible because of the retention of the dependency, achieved by shielding it from the colonial authorities' intrusion. As in the case of a full lineage member wishing to negotiate greater autonomy for his segment, so here too the last thing a dependent wishing to renegotiate his position would do is take the case to a court or an administrator. One does that when one breaks relationships, not when one alters them.

In the calculus of choice that the possibility of emancipation evoked, one of the main considerations was the comparison between one's present existential identity and other identities — not fundamentally dissimilar — that could be established elsewhere. This was the complex and subtle choice that official abolition imposed — and not the simple theatrical choice between "slavery" and "freedom" that the Western model of slavery implies. In each case, the decision concerned a package of social, political, ritual, and economic considerations (as do such existential decisions in the West as marriage, conversion, or change of occupation). The package, to be sure, contained the issue of "control over one's labor"— or, to put it in terms more appropriate to Africa, the issue of which kin group should control the fruits of one's labor — and it also included the issue of "treatment." But these were by-products of one's position in a given structure of social relationships — the social and the material dimensions of relationships being essentially fused (see LeVine 1976) — and it was within this structure that the choices had to be made.

Abolition opened choices to "slaves," each choice carrying with it comparable rigors and implying some kind of dependency in a cultural ambience in which dependency was regarded not as onerous or dishonorable but as necessary and desirable. The first decision was whether to retain or abandon one's present identity as a dependent in the host group, and if abandonment were the choice, whether to make this an irrevocable break by taking the issue to the colonial administration or courts. This issue resolved, the second decision was about where one would reside. To retain one's present identity was to retain one's residential affiliation with the "masters," whatever one's actual residence might be. That is, as with "blood" members of the kin group, to move away physically in search of better opportunities — no matter how protracted the absence — was not to discontinue one's sociological residence in one's home base. To renounce one's present identity — that is, to opt for emancipation — was to renounce one's sociological home base as well; one might then leave the area or still remain in the community or the district. Out of these decisions there could result three kinds of actions of which only some parts were noticeable to colonial officials: (1) the "slaves" could retain their affiliations with the kin group and thus retain their home base, though physically they might stay or leave; (2) they could break the affiliation with the host group, officially or unofficially, but remain in the area; and (3) they could break with the host group, officially or unofficially, and move away.

The colonial officials' observations, statistics, and estimates of "desertions" would, in various ways, conflate cases from all these categories of action. Nevertheless, the data from Banamba throw some light on the patterning of these choices. In Chapter 9, Roberts states that of those who officially declared their wish to break with their "masters," 80 percent actually left the district. Assuming a one-third total desertion rate, this means that of those "slaves" that remained in the district, over 90 percent retained their affiliation with their host groups. The pattern makes cultural sense in a way that transcends the specific situation of Banamba. If one changed one's existential identity at all, one usually left the district, for a break with one's host group entailed a fundamental change in one's relations to the entire local social network, since these were mediated through the host group. If one stayed, only rarely were there possibilities for a successful local restructuring of one's fundamental relations. This was sometimes possible by attaching oneself as a dependent to some other local kin group, but it became politically unfeasible if it disturbed the local political balance. Or, with more difficulty, one could try locally to construct a new viable independent kin group; but failure in this brought about precisely the kind of social isolation ("kinlessness"), with its attendant political weakness, that was culturally defined as the quintessence of "slavery." One way out of this weakness was to band together with other "slave" grouplets and form a quasi-kin or quasi-ethnic group — what to administrators looked like independent communities of ex-slaves; however, such communities were unlikely to be spared the culturally standard politics of domination, subordination, and clientage.

Thus, the sociology of choice we have outlined makes it understandable that, in the great majority of cases, the decision was to stay, retain one's affiliation with the host group, and, if possible, try to redefine its terms in a more favorable direction. As Dumett and Johnson point out for the Akan, this redefinition took place against the backdrop of emancipation ordinances: the existence of the option of emancipation could usually play in the "slave's" favor as long as the option was not formally exercised. Within these constraints, the redefinition could range from minimal to radical. For example, Nadel (1942: 196) has pointed out that among the Nupe many of the former "slaves" had ceased to pay any tribute to their host kin group; yet, they retained the dependent relationship as such and continued to visit and "salute" them — actions that the Western model of slavery cannot account for. Before one dismisses them as being merely token or symbolic, one must ask what is it that they symbolize. For such "saluting" visits in Africa maintain the essence of a relationship in the same way that, in the West, seemingly trivial gestures signal recognition of someone as a "relative." The preservation of the relationship, even in its most attenuated form, is also a kind of insurance — it allows one to renegotiate it in future into some other form. Emancipation precludes such a possibility.

On the whole, then, the most frequent result of abolition was a reshuffling in the statistical frequency of the various degrees of marginality *within* the continuing broad relationship of dependence. This raises the larger question: what was the effect of these reshufflings on the "structure" of these societies; that is, did abolition bring about a fundamental change in these societies or did it not? To answer this question requires a brief conceptual side-trip.

There is, in the social sciences, a tradition of distinguishing between what might be called the surface phenomenal reality and the underlying principles that give rise to that reality. In linguistics, this is the classic Saussurean distinction between *langue* (the structure of a given language as expressed in its rules) and *parole* (the actual utterances in the language). In anthropology, Firth (1954) has suggested an analogous distinction between "social structure" (the principles governing social relations in a given society) and "social organization" (the actual and transient configuration of social relations that exist in the society at any given moment). And in a similar vein, Gearing (1958) has proposed the term *structural pose* to indicate the specific transient posture that a given social structure takes at a particular time. Such a distinction may be usefully applied in the matter here at hand. The question is this: In a given case, do the changes that emancipation brought about represent primarily changes in the "social organization" of various dependencies rather than in the "social structure" of dependency? That is, are we dealing primarily with changes of social structure or changes of structural pose?

The central structural principle of a continuum of dependencies, organized around kin groups, remained stable. This is most clearly seen in this book in the three "backwater" cases (northern Ethiopia, Bechuanaland, and Ubangi-Shari), which provide a kind of test for the effects of emancipation per se, because the processes in them were largely unconfounded by such analytically extraneous factors as economic expansion promoted by colonial rule. Where, on the other hand, emancipation coincided with such changes, one must take care to differentiate analytically between the spheres of "slavery" and other social spheres, precisely because the processes in them are often conflated in reality. For example, when the colonial system created new jobs and entrepreneurial opportunities, many Africans—both "free" and "slave"—are known to have moved to take them up. In such cases, it is scarcely valid to concentrate only on the movement of the "slaves" and mechanically interpret it as proof of their fundamental rejection of their position, without taking the "free" as a control group in the analysis. Similarly, when one sees, with the coming of abolition, a number of "slave" concubines desert their husbands, one cannot simply conclude that they are escaping from and thereby giving recognition to the fundamental harshness of "African slavery." Since African divorce rates are generally high and since concubines in Africa are notoriously quick at changing partners, we may be witnessing here the enactment of patterns unrelated to "slavery" as such, patterns which "slave" concubines were prevented from expressing before abolition.

The latter case illustrates the fact that, within the continuing stability of fundamental structure, abolition did bring about significant changes — significant in ways that mattered to the Africans involved. Emancipation made abandoning the "master" possible as an open act. Dependents of extreme marginality—true chattel slaves—disappeared; they either left or established a less marginal relationship to the host group as clients, retainers, or tenants. The previously unavailable possibility of open desertion enlarged the whole range of choices open to the "slaves" and expanded their social "bargaining" powers. What "slaves" could flock to was not "freedom" (for which neither the concept nor the possibility existed) but the judicious exercise of broader and more varied choice. It is significant that the drive to leave the "masters" followed almost explosively upon the first appearance of the possibility of desertion, exhausting itself after a few years. This suggests that abolition allowed the social organization of dependency to purge itself, so to speak, of the accumulated dissatisfactions within it. The purge lost to the "master" kin groups their most marginal affiliates—the chattel "slaves"—and brought about a retrenchment around their more integrated members, dependents, and "slaves." After this cleansing, the process within the groups became largely invisible to the official eye as the "masters" and the remaining "slaves" became engaged in the gradual, unofficial, and subtle redefinition of their relations of dependency. What is paradoxical in all this—paradoxical, that is, not to African realities but to Western renditions of it—is that the cleansing of the dependency system must have reinforced it in most cases: the new social organization gave greater stability to the continuing social structure of dependency.

To be sure, the cleansing was not without its costs. We learn that King Ata in the Gold Coast lost most of his slaves and perhaps went broke, that the power of many Igbo elders was diminished, and that some rich Hausa farmers had to go back to work in the fields. How significant are these cases in the perspective of the social systems as such? They are the functional equivalents of individual bankruptcies in Western crises. Sometimes, they are not even that: the Ganda elite that suffered losses, we are told, was small and its position as an elite does not seem to have been altered any more than the position of the hundred or so people among the Bangwato who had Basarwa "slaves." In other cases, as in northern Ethiopia, the reshuffle in fact strengthened the elite at the expense of the middle stratum. But in all cases, the political structure has either remained unaltered or been altered by forces other than abolition. Partly, this is because these are societies in which political power creates economic power rather than the reverse. Whatever the losses at abolition, the political position of the elite permits them to recoup their losses as they turn to newly emerging opportunities. And partly it is because these are economically segmented societies: economic losses are largely confined to the immediate losers and do not ramify through the whole system. The bankruptcies, that is, do not systemically proliferate into more bankruptcies. Rather, the lowering of one kin group makes room for the rise of another.

But the fundamental reason that these societies exhibit such a remarkable structural continuity through the period of abolition lies in the long-term adaptiveness of African sociopolitical systems to the kinds of changes that abolition brought with it. Successive changes in the fortunes of individual kin groups have always been part of the normal workings of these systems—and it was, after all, not the elites but the innumerable small kin groups that, taken together, held the overwhelming majority of acquired persons. For such a kin group, shrinkage through the loss of several dependents and redefinition of control over human beings were scarcely unprecedented or deeply wrenching structural events. There have always been wars and raids in which "masters" became "slaves"; famines and epidemics in which kin groups suddenly lost large numbers of their members; dissensions in which kin-group segments hived off, leaving the parent groups decimated; and the perpetual competitive struggles among kin groups, with their endless permutations of winners and losers. The problems that abolition brought with it were not new, and the ways of dealing with these problems were a well-established part of the cultural repertoire. Indeed, there is an argument to be made (Kopytoff 1987) that such disruptive events were both systemic features of African societies and an integral part of the repetitive process that insured, historically, the social structural continuity and homogeneity of sub-Saharan Africa. The significance of abolition cannot be assessed unless one compares its impact with the impact of normal and routine social processes.

What Dumett and Johnson say in Chapter 2 about Akan appears applicable to most of the rest of Africa: if the end of slavery is to be called a revolution, then it "must be one of the quieter social revolutions of the late nineteenth and early twentieth centuries." The paradox of the smoothness of the abolition of a profoundly ingrained institution lies not in the African reality but in faulty conceptual renditions of it. It lies in a misplacement of institutional boundaries. For what was deeply ingrained was not the narrow "slavery" of Western conception but the wide institutional complex of interrelated and interchangeable dependencies, containing within it numerous functional alternatives. The abolition of one of these dependencies — slavery as the West defines it — could not undermine the larger complex on which so much of the structural continuity of African societies rested.

REFERENCES

Appadurai, A., ed. 1986. *The social life of things: commodities in cultural perspective.* New York: Cambridge University Press.

Cassanelli, L. V. 1987. Social construction on the Somali frontier: Bantu former slave communities in the nineteenth century. In *The African frontier: the reproduction of traditional African societies,* ed. I. Kopytoff, 216–38. Bloomington: Indiana University Press.

Cooper, F. 1977. *Plantation slavery on the east coast of Africa.* New Haven: Yale University Press.

Cooper, F. 1980. *From slaves to squatters: plantation labor and agriculture in Zanzibar and coastal Kenya, 1890–1925.* New Haven: Yale University Press.

Firth, R. 1954. Social organization and social change. *Journal of the Royal Anthropological Institute* 84: 1–20.

Friedman, T. L. 1986. In Cameroon, scenes of a valley of death. *New York Times* Vol. 135, No. 46,879, August 27: A1, A6.

Gearing, F. 1958. The structural poses of 18th century Cherokee villages. *American Anthropologist* 60: 1148–57.

Geertz, C. 1975. Common sense as a cultural system. *Antioch Review* 35: 5–26.

Klein, M. A. 1986. Slavery and emancipation in French West Africa. Colloquium paper, History, Culture, and Society Program, Woodrow Wilson International Center for Scholars. Washington, D.C. Mimeo.

Klein, M., and P. Lovejoy. 1979. Slavery in West Africa. In *The uncommon market: essays in the economic history of the Atlantic slave trade*, ed. H. A. Gemery and J. S. Hogendorn, 181–212. New York: Academic Press.

Kopytoff, I. 1979. Commentary one. In *Roots and branches: current directions in slave studies*, ed. M. Craton, 62–77. Toronto: Pergamon.

Kopytoff, I. 1987. The internal African frontier: the making of African political culture. In *The African frontier: the reproduction of traditional African societies*, ed. I. Kopytoff, 3–84. Bloomington: Indiana University Press.

Kopytoff, I., and S. Miers. 1977. African slavery as an institution of marginality. In *Slavery in Africa*, ed. S. Miers and I. Kopytoff, 3–81. Madison: University of Wisconsin Press.

LeVine, R. A. 1976. Patterns of personality in Africa. In *Response to change: society, culture, and personality*, ed. G. A. DeVos, 112–36. New York: Van Nostrand.

MacGaffey, W. 1977. Economic and social dimensions of Kongo slavery (Zaire). In *Slavery in Africa*, ed. S. Miers and I. Kopytoff, 235–57. Madison: University of Wisconsin Press.

Meek, C. K. 1925. *The northern tribes of Nigeria*. 2 vols. London: Oxford University Press.

Mintz, S. W., and R. Price. 1976. *An anthropological approach to the Afro-American past: a Caribbean perspective*. ISHI Occasional Papers in Social Change, No. 2. Philadelphia: Institute for the Study of Human Issues.

Nadel, S. F. 1942. *A black Byzantium: the kingdom of Nupe in Nigeria*. London: Oxford University Press.

Roberts, R., and M. A. Klein. 1980. The Banamba slave exodus of 1905 and the decline of slavery in the Western Sudan. *Journal of African History* 21: 375–94.

Wright, M. 1983. Bwanikwa: consciousness and protest among slave women in Central Africa, 1886–1911. In *Women and slavery in Africa*, ed. C. Robertson and M. Klein, 246–67. Madison: University of Wisconsin Press.

Index

Index

507

Agbor (town in Southern Nigeria), 437
agriculture, 259–60, 263–64, 269, 273–
74, 276, 299n, 310–11, 325–26, 364,
373–75, 382, 467, 469, 477–78. *See
also* colonial economic development;
farmers; plantations; slaves, uses and
treatment
Ahmed bin Fumo Luti (warlord in
Kenya), 257
Ahmed Nur "El Haji," Sheikh (leader of
religious uprising in Somalia), 328
Ahoada (town in Southern Nigeria), 455
Akan (cultural area in Gold Coast), 72,
75, 76, 78, 85–87, 95, 106, 108, 486
akaporo ("slaves" in Mozambique), 227
akoa ("subjects" in Gold Coast), 75–76
Akyem Abuakaw (missionary station in
Gold Coast), 87, 88, 91, 96, 107, 108
Al-Sanusi, Muhammad (sultan of Ubangi-
Shari), 158ff
Al-Zubayr (ruler of Dar Fur), 157
Albert, Lake (Congo), 471
Algeria, 41
amambo (land chief in Mozambique),
227
ambilineal descent (in Ethiopia), 343
Americo-Liberians. *See* Liberia
Amharic Empire of Ethiopia, 19. *See
also* Ethiopian Imperial State
Anglo-Egyptian Sudan. *See* Sudan
Anglo-Mazrui War (1895, Kenya), 274
Angoche (plantation zone in Mozam-
bique), 235
Angola, 26, 43, 44, 240, 242
Antilles. *See* Caribbean
antislavery, antislave trade policies, 7,
14–15, 19, 28, 82, 100–104, 127–33,
177, 178, 196, 228–29, 286, 468–73.
See also abolition of slavery
Antislavery Society, British, 178, 190,
194, 196
Antislavery and Aborigines Protection So-
ciety. *See* British Antislavery and Abo-
rigines Protection Society
Apankwa (ex-slaves' town in Gold
Coast), 89
Arab-Swahili (people in Kenya, Zanzi-
bar), 22, 233, 257, 274. *See also*
Swahili
ARabai (people in Kenya), 259–76

Arabs, 275, 465, 469, 472. *See also* Arab-
Swahili; Zanzibar
Arden-Clarke, Charles (official in Bechu-
analand), 193
Armitage, Commissioner (official in Gold
Coast), 97–99
Armstrong, Jack P. (British consular offi-
cial in Congo), 473–74
Aro (people in Southern Nigeria), 440–
41, 447–48, 451
Aruwimi district (in Belgian Congo),
470, 471, 472, 477
Asaba (town in Southern Nigeria), 438,
444–45
Asante. *See* Ashanti
Asante, David (missionary in Gold
Coast), 87, 88
Asantehene (chief of Ashanti), 96
Ashanti (people in Gold Coast), 12, 73,
76, 81, 82, 89, 91, 98, 105, 493
Ashe, Robert (missionary in Buganda),
123, 128
Asia, 55
Atani (town in Southern Nigeria), 440
Athlone, Earl (high commissioner and
governor-general of South Africa), 181,
182, 184, 185, 186; Athlone Declara-
tion (1926), 182–83, 184, 186, 196
Atlantic slave trade, 73, 205, 415, 417.
See antislavery; antislave trade policies
Audegle (town in Somalia), 317
Awka (town in Southern Nigeria), 452
Awlad Bou Sba (people in Mauritania),
367, 383–84
Axum (state in Northeastern Africa), 334
Azande (kingdom in North Central Af-
rica), 464
Azazir (people in Mauritania), 369

Babemba (chief of Sikasso), 282, 286, 292
Babwa (kingdom in North Central Af-
rica), 464
Bafoulabe (district in French Soudan),
289
Bagirmi (state in North Central Africa),
156, 158
Bahr al-Ghazal (state in North Central
Africa), 162, 165
Bailundo (state in Angola), 417, 420, 429,
430

520

Index

Roume, Governor-general (French West Africa), 288, 290
Royal Niger Company, 392–93, 441, 444–45
Ruanda-Urundi (German, then Belgian colony), 47
rubber, 25, 44, 152, 159, 160, 163, 164, 167, 206, 207, 422, 472–73, 477
Ruffino, Armando Guedes (enslaver, labor recruiter in Angola), 430

Sa da Bandeira (prime minister, Portugal), 228
Sabaki River (Kenya), 257, 273
sachikunda (military leader in Mozambique), 224, 225
Sahara, 151
sahel, 34, 151–52, 296, 300
St. Domingue (island in Caribbean), 14
St. Helena (island in Atlantic), 12
Saint Louis (town in Senegal), 14, 284
Salaga (town in Ashanti, Gold Coast), 101, 105
Salazar, Antonio (dictator of Portugal), 427
salt, 159, 165
Samori. *See* Touré, Samori
San. *See* Basarwa
São Tomé (island in Gulf of Guinea), 15, 43, 55n, 415, 419, 421, 429
Sara (people in North Central Africa), 154
Satiru (town and fugitive slave community in Northern Nigeria), 396
Say (subemirate in Upper Volta), 392
Schmoll (official in Ubangi-Shari), 166
Schrank, Elia (missionary in Gold Coast), 78
Schweinfurth, Georg (traveler in North Central Africa), 153
Second World War, 21, 45, 108, 164, 377–79, 382, 433
Segu (town and district in French Soudan), 285–86, 189, 291, 292, 294
Sekgoma II (Batswana king), 182
Sena (district in Mozambique), 227, 230, 231, 232, 237, 238, 239
Senegal, Senegambia, 14, 35, 42, 167, 242, 369, 371, 373–74, 380–81, 382n

sepais (soldiers in Mozambique), 235, 237–45
Serowe (town in Bechuanaland), 182, 191, 192, 193, 194
servicaes, 421. *See also* contract labor
Sese islands (Uganda), 126
Setswana (people in Bechuanaland), 172, 195
Shabelle River (Somalia), 35, 310, 313, 314, 315, 317, 326
Shamaki (slave official in Northern Nigeria), 397
sharecroppers, squatters, tenants, 33, 57, 213–14, 283, 290–91
Shashi River (Bechuanaland), 191
Shehu Amadu (ruler of Umarian state), 285
Shidle clan (Somalia), 326
Shimba Hills (Kenya), 257
Shinqiti (region in Mauritania), 368, 370–75, 377, 380
Shire (district in Malawi), 235
Shona (people in Southern Rhodesia), 234
Sierra Leone, 27, 29, 37, 38n, 52, 73, 206, 208, 215, 258
Sikasso (town and district in French Soudan), 285, 289, 291
Sikh soldiers (in Uganda), 137
Silva Porto, Antonia (merchant in Angola), 417
Silva Garcia, Joaquim de (merchant in Angola), 422
Sinsani (town in French Soudan), 294
slave cult, 122, 439, 453–55
slave mode of production, 81, 153, 155
slave owners, 41, 162, 312, 314–20, 328, 369, 380–83, 395; chiefs, 77, 103, 121–22, 224, 226, 464–65, 470–71; Eurafrican, 204–5; lineage, 464–65, 490; missionaries, 124, 127, 156, 469
slave supply, enslavement: caravans, 101, 104, 418; judicial forms, 123–24, 394, 418; kidnapping, 18, 26, 40, 41, 176–77, 185–86, 188ff, 368, 382n, 418, 440ff, 451–52; linked with slavery, pawnship, forced labor, 422–23; markets, 101, 105, 122, 132, 256–57, 337; persistence of, 157, 166, 421, 431; prices of slaves, 342; raiding, 101, 105,

Tanzania, 119

Tati District (Bechuanaland), 186, 191

Tawara (people in Mozambique), 229, 232, 243

taxes, colonial tax policy, 152, 163, 164, 167, 213, 400–408, 415, 422, 425–27, 430; in Ethiopia, 336, 351–57; obligations in Ethiopia, 336, on slaves, 351; as support for new bureaucracy, 352

tea, 159

Tekna (people in Mauritania), 367, 380–82

Temporary Slavery Commission. *See* League of Nations

Ternan, Tevor (official in Uganda), 131–32

Teso (district in Uganda), 122

Tete (district in Mozambique), 224, 227, 230–35, 237–39, 240, 241, 245, 246

Tewodros II (Emperor of Ethiopia), 334

Tibati (subemirate in Northern Nigeria), 392

Tieba (king of Sikasso), 285, 292

Tinker, Hugh, 138

Tippu Tip (slave trader, warlord in Congo), 462, 466–68, 472

Tirailleurs Sénégalais, 244, 284, 288, 368, 370–71. *See also* recruitment of slaves and freed slaves into police and military

Tisserant (official in Ubangi-Shari), 156, 157

Tobback, Nicholas (official in Congo), 468

Togoland, 20

Tonga (people in Central Africa), 52

Toro kingdom (Uganda), 122, 141

Touba (town in French Soudan), 286

Touré, Samori (ruler of Wasulu), 83, 102, 282, 285–86, 292

transition from slave to free:

— evidence for a disruptive transition, 90–93, 131, 136–38, 287–94, 300–303, 378–79, 382–84, 399

— evidence for a smooth transition, 50, 90, 91, 105, 256, 265–66, 273, 275–76, 410–11, 486, 500–502

— impact of the end of slavery (causes): international economy, 25, 58, 164; regional changes in the economy, 18, 20,

23; Western ideas of individuals, 54

— impact of the end of slavery (consequences): on children, 33, 40–41, 145, 194, 213, 270*ff*, 295, 364–65, 370–72, 376, 378, 384, 394, 431; on economy, 81, 90, 100, 104, 194–95, 216, 267–74, 300–302, 366, 368–70, 373–77, 379–82, 399, 400, 406–7, 411, 501; on households, 41, 42, 54, 90–91, 295, 296, 297, 300, 398–99; on lineages, 31, 32, 501–2; on marriages, 31, 40, 42, 108, 139–41, 265–67, 270, 297, 370–72, 378–79, 500; on men, 473–74; on population distribution, 274, 294–99, 500; on property rights, 255–56, 263–64, 269–72, 274, 300, 407–10; on political power, 103, 107, 139, 195, 294, 300, 475–76, 501; on relations of production, 163; on slave owners, 41–42, 189, 191, 213, 415, 433; on women, 40, 42, 52, 130, 131, 133, 140, 213, 268, 295, 378–79, 426, 431, 473–74, 500

— masters' responses: efforts to retain slaves, 94, 95, 134–35, 209, 258, 286, 316–19, 399, 409–10, 471; owners flee, 163; threaten to leave area, 212; tried to force slaves to stay, 213

— slaves' choices: compromise with former masters, 212; establish new communities, 161, 163, 215, 440–42, 445, 451; exodus, 6, 21, 26, 80, 105, 141, 226, 229, 283, 287–93, 372, 375–76, 379, 395–98, 450–51, 486–90; ex-slaves' choices, 6, 33–42, 85, 88–89, 92–93, 105, 108, 189, 190, 194–95, 229–45, 263–65, 275, 293–98, 369–76, 379–82, 395–99, 474, 496–500; find free land, 167, 212–13; flight, 166, 210, 254, 257–58, 273, 275, 367, 373–76, 379; meaning of freedom, 6, 27, 32, 50, 188, 190, 193–95; opt for autonomy, 256, 293–94, 396–97, 488; opt for greater integration, 193–94, 294–95, 296, 354, 382–84, 491–502; refuse to work, 203, 209, 210; remained with owners, 6; resistance, 205, 226, 286, 378–79; return to former homes, 34, 39, 162, 167, 215

Trarza (region in Mauritania), 374, 380, 382*n*, 396

Treillard (official in Guinea), 212